Buckley

The
Right
Word

Buckley:
The Right Word

ABOUT THE USES AND ABUSES
OF LANGUAGE, AND ABOUT
VOCABULARY; ABOUT USAGE,
STYLE & SPEAKING; FICTION,
DICTION, DICTIONARIES; WITH
REVIEWS AND INTERVIEWS;
A LEXICON; ON LATIN &
LETTERS, ELOQUENCE &
JOURNALISM; AND MORE,
ALL DRAWN FROM THE
WORKS OF

William F. Buckley, Jr.,

HIS CORRESPONDENTS, HIS
CRITICS, FRIENDS, AND OTHERS

SELECTED, ASSEMBLED, AND EDITED BY

Samuel S. Vaughan
WITH AN INTRODUCTION & SUNDRY
COMMENTARIES

A HARVEST BOOK
HARCOURT BRACE & COMPANY
SAN DIEGO   NEW YORK   LONDON

Requests for permission to make copies of any part of the work should
be mailed to: Permissions Department, Harcourt Brace & Company,
6277 Sea Harbor Drive, Orlando, Florida 32887-6777.

Published by arrangement with Random House, Inc.

ISBN 0-15-600569-7 (pbk.)

Printed in the United States of America
First Harvest edition 1998
   C E D B

This book is for Jo Vaughan.

(This dedication is the joint idea of author, WFB, Jr., and editor, SSV, who arrived at the same thought independently.)

Editor's Acknowledgments

My gratitude is great for the limitless help, and loyal but not uncritical commentary of Mr. Buckley's peerless assistant Frances Bronson, who still finds music in his writing; to Liz Altham, who made the first gathering of WFB's words on words, and for other important contributions; to Chaucy Bennetts, copy editor extraordinaire, who has come out of retirement more times than Sinatra to work on WFB's manuscripts; to Joseph Isola; and to the hard-pressed production, art, and design talents at Random House, who took a manuscript that looked as if it had been through a Cuisinart and baked a good-looking book.

And of course to the maestro himself, for proving me right once more.

Contents

What's It Like to Edit William F. Buckley, Jr.?

This is a book Bill Buckley didn't realize he had written. Or at least was unwilling to believe he had. For years, as editor of his books, I had urged him to do a book on language—that is, a book that could be drawn from his letters, columns, essays, fiction, and lectures.

He would reply, "I haven't written enough to make up a book."

Finally he agreed to let me explore the possibilities. I had saved many copies of pieces he had written. He engaged Liz Altham, a lively, enthusiastic researcher, to gather material. Though retired as an active editor to become an active mother, she turned to the task with a will and imagination, and in due course delivered a box twelve inches high, fat with Xeroxes, here and there annotated. This book, reduced by some inches, is the result.

He needs no introduction but, as with after-dinner introducers, will get one anyhow. The voice you will hear most often in the pages following is that of Mr. Buckley, who nonetheless insists that this is "my" book.

To be clear about that point: Though the great majority of the words are his, or those of his correspondents, critics, friends, enemies, and fellow word mavens, it is my book in that I initiated the idea and I chose what to include or not. I organized and made notes on the contents. As he wrote while we were discussing the possibilities: "The liberating perspective, in

my judgment, is the relationship between the project and its executioner . . . [Suddenly I saw myself in a black hood, ax in hand. Ed.] We are
talking about a book you conceived, gathered, even lassoed, and it is vital
to know whose eye is at work here . . . The task then becomes entirely
your own, also the responsibility." Thus, following his wishes, it is fair to
say that this is not a book about words that Bill himself might have gathered; his would be far different—and shorter. It is my book of his words
about words and related matters.

In it you will find largely the apolitical, although hardly neutered,
Buckley. The point is to show not his politics but his language in action.
Much of it has appeared in print, but a considerable portion has never
been in book form.

What is it like to edit William F. Buckley, Jr.? Some might think it daunt-
ing, even terrifying. After all, he is a famous debater, an enthusiastic opponent, quick to beat plowshares back into swords; he is remarkably fluid,
fluent, formidable; respected and/or feared; well educated, well traveled,
worldly. Before I came to the vocation as Buckley's editor, he was already
the author of hundreds of thousands of published words, including at
least a dozen books. The first, *God and Man at Yale*, made him a national
figure before the ink was dry on his diploma.

Accordingly, I set about editing his first novel cautiously. Editing him,
I would soon find out, is more terrific (or, as he would say, "Turrr-ific!")
than terrifying. For one thing, he is a pro. You never get an uninteresting
manuscript. There are stimulating ideas in the air, constant surprises, a
narrative rush, and a voice entirely his own. Some of his books are more
serious than salable, such as *Gratitude*, his short 1990 book about patriotism and national service, or *In Search of Anti-Semitism* (1992). But in
general, the success rate with the public is high and has been sustained for
decades.

Bill is among the most appreciative of authors. He welcomes editing
and copyediting, in part because they require first of all an attentive reading. He has informal advisers—family members and trusted friends and
colleagues. They serve as a sort of Greek chorus of coeditors, contributing
usefully to early drafts. Buckley writes quickly (see "What's So Bad About
Writing Fast?," page 185. He is open but hardly docile about just any suggestion, let alone one that proposes he rewrite the entire manuscript. This
is because he abominates ennui much more than he shrinks from work.
The First Great Commandment for Buckley is: Thou Shalt Not Bore, and
he obeys it faithfully. He cuts his own stuff with the joy of a surgeon. Hap-

pily his drafts do not require organic rearrangement, and he accepts a multiplicity of ideas for revision. The fact that he is an editor himself is life-saving. He is demanding of his editors only as he is demanding of himself. Writing speedily, he feels the need to be read quickly, and wants reactions promptly (almost universal among authors). His routine for years has been to produce, while on "holiday" for six weeks in winter, a draft of a book, ready to deliver to me. He does not undertake revisions until three months later when, in early summer, his demanding schedule permits. Meanwhile the manuscript has cooled.

He is ever so grateful (that phrase is his; I fall into the locutions of authors I like) for useful editorial suggestions, responsive to reactions on word, sentence, paragraph, punctuation, chapter changes, to thoughts about characters, plot, length. He is at all times considerate, a man of manners, rather than mannered.

Editing Buckley is akin to reaping the pleasures of his friendship: he is fun to be with, and to correspond with; full of enthusiasm, humor, insight, opinion. You become a part of his informal extended family, which brings the great good fortune of getting to know those who really are family, starting with the remarkable Pat Buckley, his wife, who speaks *entirely* in italics, followed by a splendidly smoky laugh; their son, the phenomenal Christopher Buckley, himself a prodigious author and editor; and on and on through sisters, brothers, friends and colleagues.

Why does Buckley write so much?* First, because duty calls: the deadlines of his syndicate, his magazine, and the newspapers and magazines that commission his work; deadlines for his TV and lecture dates; and, over-archingly, a sense of duty to his ideas and ideals. Second, to earn a living (though lecture fees go to support *National Review*). But then also to keep from being . . . yes, bored. And therefore to amuse, entertain, educate, instruct, illuminate and seek to influence events; and, at times, to infuriate or simply provoke.

Bill Buckley said somewhere, sometime, that he cannot "think" without a pen or a keyboard at hand. He writes in a sort of parallelism to the much quoted *Cogito, ergo sum*—I think, therefore I am. He claims to be not at all introspective, yet clearly he is always thinking. Which would then give us a case of *Scribo, ergo sum*—I write, therefore I am. His writing is one with his identity and sense of self.

* These are my speculations. WFB speculates, much more authoritatively, in the chapter on columnists, page 189.

Though not intended as such, this became in part a book on the subject of Buckley himself. For all his celebrity, not enough is really known about him. The man seen for so long on television, leaning away from his discussants, pen by jowl, at the ready, sighting down his nose at the target, eyes occasionally glittering, smile intermittently flashing—none of this reveals much about the "whole" man. His astonishing generosity to all sorts of individuals, more than a few of whom do not share his politics, religion, or "lifestyle"; his capacity to be instructed as much as to instruct; his deep-dyed loyalties—such qualities are not readily apparent in the pixels of the omnipresent living-room box that supposedly brings us the news.

And he discovers writers. Working for him early were—in addition to those noted by Charlie Rose in the book's interview chapter—Joan Didion, George Will, Arlene Croce . . .

To show William F. Buckley, Jr., fully engaged at work is to display language itself in full deployment. (I had called him an Equal Opportunity employer of words but Bill winced, understandably, preferring the sentence that follows.) The man is a comprehensive employer of words, spoken by himself, through his characters in fiction, in his paradigmatic political and philosophical fancies. The reader will find many and varied examples of thought and writing by him and by others: curious, amused and amusing, witty and barbed, sometimes pugnacious, smug, slashing. He is infinitely resourceful in his own defense, yet in style usually responsive and gracious, even to those who would score points off his own hide. There are examples in what follows of language too snappish for my taste. But most often he writes to attract interest, to inform, to heal, and, sometimes, to serve as a lingering last kiss or salute. (See "On Saying Good-bye.")

Buckley can, in my own judgment, be wrong, or overload a sentence, but it is the brio that one notices, rather than any bravado. He antagonizes but does not wrong; more often he is wronged. There are in these pages samples of Early Buckley, Middle Period Buckley, and Late Buckley. (No Blue Period: Buckley represses depression, as well as most profanity.)

To show his words in action and his consideration of others' concern for words is to document that to be intricately, intimately involved with language is more than merely a transient affair; it is a lifelong marriage. He gives himself up to his belief in the power of words, by which we live or die. Auden wrote, "Poetry makes nothing happen." What is under the surface here is the assumption that you might just change minds, even change the world, with words—words thoughtfully, lovingly assembled.

Buckley is one writer whose words have stimulated curiosity, scorn, legal action, reaction, reform, and affection. They have helped to educate and elect Presidents. His language continues to generate exasperation and admiration for the man behind them.

"My" book? This book may show what it is like to be a person, perhaps like the reader, who loves words, lives by and stands by them.

—Sam Vaughan

Samuel S. Vaughan was president, publisher, and editor in chief of Doubleday & Co. for many years, and later senior vice president at Random House, Inc., for which company he is currently editor at large. He has edited most of William F. Buckley's books since Saving the Queen *(1976).*

Buckley

The
Right
Word

Chapter 1

Usage I:
"Notes & Asides"

Some of WFB's time and a considerable portion of his correspondence is taken up with word usage—his own and that of others. Correspondents curious, combative, or admiring may disagree on who/whom and such, but most write out of a conviction that words, as the expression has it, can make a difference; that words can affect the way we perceive, think and act.

This continuing concern for just the right word is not common in our age.

Most of Buckley's correspondence is disposed of in the *National Review* column "Notes & Asides," which, although not wholly devoted to questions of language, is one of the longest-running features in journalism to give usage such attention.

Buckley relies for answers not only on his own knowledge but on friends and correspondents. They act as resources and also as antagonists. These masters have included the august critic Hugh Kenner, the newspaperman James J. Kilpatrick, and the late author and editor William F. Rickenbacker, as well as experts on his own staff, the longtime *NR* managing editor (his sister) Priscilla Buckley, Linda Bridges, his editors and writers, and others.

Samples from "Notes & Asides" (the format of which has changed over the years) introduce us to his resourceful concern for the language and continue throughout the book, showing the stimulation he provides his readers—and vice versa.

———

Dear Mr. Buckley:

What, pray tell, is a quantum jump?

This phrase has annoyed me for years, and I was most displeased to see it appear in my favorite journal. I am well aware that the expression is commonly used to indicate an upward change in the order of magnitude of whatever phenomenon interests the user, but this is not the meaning of quantum. A portion jump? A jump of a portion? A jump of the element unit of energy? An elemental unit of energy jump? The physicists would be aghast.

> *Quantum sufficit.*
> TERRENCE J. MCGHEE
> LAWRENCE, KAN.

Dear Mr. McGhee:

Webster recognizes the use of "quantum" meaning "large quantity." The OED does not. We suggest reader McGhee exorcise his rhetorical demons with Robbie Burns's song:

> *I waive the quantum o' the sin,*
> *The hazard of concealing;*
> *But och, it hardens a' within,*
> *And petrifies the feeling!*

> Cordially,
> —WFB   AUGUST 8, 1967

Dear Mr. Buckley:

Please, please elucidate. If you are too busy writing on world problems, perhaps some fellow reader of *National Review* will solve my problem, not shared by a single one of my friends.

What bothers me is the phrase "by and large," used constantly by both the literate and the illiterate. What do people think they are saying, with a preposition and an adjective connected by a conjunction? Take "by." By what? Now take "large." What is it that is large?

For over a year I have waited for a break in terrible world events to bend your ear about this. Now, although a born optimist, I've been forced to conclude that I'd better wait no longer.

Sincerely,

HELEN W. SANBORN

EL CERRITO, CALIF.

Dear Mrs. Sanborn: Well now, you might have reason to be dismayed at its use, but not surprised. See, e.g., *A Dictionary of American Usage,* Bergen Evans, Random House: "**by and large.** In the sense of 'generally speaking, in every aspect': *by and large (By and large, the worries of summer residents concerning snakes are far out of proportion to the dangers that exist)* is standard in American usage, though not very often used in England. Apparently it is becoming more common there, for Sir Ernest Gowers states that this 'current usage . . . exasperates the sailor' who knows the true meaning of the phrase—'alternately close to the wind and with the wind abeam or aft.' An even stronger reason for avoiding the phrase than the fear of exasperating sailors is that it is often meaningless, used simply as conversational filler." You will be happy to learn that *NR* never uses the phrase in the last, condemned, sense. Cordially,

—WFB   NOVEMBER 15, 1985

Dear Billic:

Silly Question #1: Is there a difference between Democratic and democratic?

Silly Question #2: Is there a difference between Democrat and democrat?

Then why?

An ic before the big D I could tolerate.

Sincerely,

ANDREI KOVEN

SUPREME EXAULTED PRESIDENT

PTUI FAD

(PEOPLE TOGETHER TO UNSTICK IC

FROM AFTER DEMOCRAT)

BETHEL, CONN.

Dear Mr. Koven: As far as we're concerned, it's the Democratic Party, the alternative sounding phony-baloney.

—WFB   SEPTEMBER 17, 1976

Dear Mr. Buckley:

Almost as "removed from matters of the day" as Nelson Algren, I was going through last May's *Times* this weekend and was stopped cold by the enclosed piece of your writing. The context is of course much too momentous for such a trivial point to cause Reader Arrest, but you are getting a reputation as a Word Man and hence have a certain potential for influence, for good or ill, upon the few and precious literate young. Besides, I happen to have heard you commit the same mistake recently on the air. The word in question may just possibly be on the way to being a favorite with you.

Authorities you surely respect as I do insist upon a distinction between *restive* and *restless*—the first meaning "stubbornly standing still . . . resisting control, intractable, refractory," conservative to the point of rebellion, as it were. Quotations in the OED include examples where the refractoriness is coupled with violent action: "His lordship's horse became restive and attempted to throw its rider." But resistance in the face of real or imminent compulsion is surely an implication that respect for the language would have us preserve in the use of this word. I enclose a couple of other clippings: you and Anthony Burgess seem to me to be abusers; Michener seems O.K.

Sincerely,

CLEM C. WILLIAMS, JR. (YALE '42)

(Enclosed: "Can the present-day cinema audience watch without restiveness a film in which a couple fall deeply in love without taking off their clothes?"—A. Burgess, *N.Y. Times,* July 1, 1973. "Many felt him to be unqualified to lead the nation, and when, that summer, meat prices rose, the nation grew restive."—J. Michener, *N.Y. Times,* July 1, 1973.)

Dear Mr. Williams: "Restive" also means "balky." So that it can be used halfway between restless and mutinous.

—WFB (YALE '50)   FEBRUARY 15, 1974

Dear Mr. Buckley:

Tch-tch . . . you'll never learn.

I don't really mind your dipping into your pathetic little treasury of Shakespeare quotes . . . the effect is nice and you don't overdo it. But, please . . . get them right.

On page 622 of *NR* [June 8], you reply to a letter from reader S. Manning with the most threadbare of your quotes stock thus: "Dear Mrs. Manning: That would be gilding the lily. Yrs. Cordially, etc.," and that rumbling sound you've been hearing ever since is ol' Bill Shakespeare spinning like a top. Ol' Bill *never* said anything about gilding the lily, and were you playing hooky during the term they taught *King John*?

Act IV, Scene 2, Earl of Salisbury in reply to Earl of Pembroke:

> *"Therefore, to be possessed with double*
> *pomp,*
> *To guard a title that was rich before,*
> *To gild refined gold, to paint the lily,*
> *To throw a perfume on the violet,*
> *To smooth the ice, or add another hue*
> *Unto the rainbow, or with taper light*
> *To seek the beauteous eye of heaven to garnish,*
> *Is wasteful and ridiculous excess."*

Did you get any other letters on this? Or am I the only Shakespearean hawkeye among your readers?

Cordially,

SAUL GLEMBY

NEW YORK, N.Y.

Dear Mr. Glemby: (1) To call to the attention of anyone over fourteen that Shakespeare didn't say gilding the lily is like calling to the attention of anyone over ten that Voltaire didn't say the one about how he would fight to the death for your right to say it. Come to think of it, I doubt very much that Voltaire would fight to the death for the right of anyone to remind anyone that Shakespeare didn't himself use the phrase gild the lily. (2) The phrase gild the lily, and a number of other phrases, can be used even though Shakespeare did not originate them. (3) When we use a cliché around these parts, boy we mean to use a cliché, understand, Glemby? (4) Of the four editors of *National Review,* one used to teach Shakespeare, one still does, and, when I retire, I intend to.

Cordially,

—WFB   JULY 20, 1973

Dear Mr. Buckley:

Your three columns on the *Titanic* were extremely moving and splendidly written. I have one acidulous comment to make and here goes: Why, oh why, do you assume that when a ship dies *she* loses *her* gender? Time and again, you refer to the corpse of a majestic, devastated lady as "it"! I'd consider you, therefore, guilty of an unmitigated solecism, all the more horrendous in coming from you, a seasoned salt.

Sincerely,

CONSUELO IVES, M.D.

NEW YORK, N.Y.

Dear Dr. Ives: It was unconscious. But not uninteresting, Freudian-slipwise. Maybe a fallen lady isn't any longer a lady??? Cordially,

—WFB   DECEMBER 18, 1987

Dear Mr. Buckley:

In the editorial "Cruelest Month" [May 8, 1987], *NR* has it *"shoures soote."* Has Chaucer been revised since the 1929 edition of *The Student's Chaucer* (The Clarendon Press, Oxford), which has it *"shoures sote,"* or has someone been guilty of carelessness?

Cordially,

ROBERT E. KOHLER

KOHLER, WIS.

Dear Mr. Kohler: It is an old rivalry (Oxford *v.* Cambridge). The Chaucer we use around here (at *National Review* we always speak in Middle English until noon) we get from the New Cambridge Edition, ed. F. N. Robinson (Houghton Mifflin), a fine book in which all *shoures* are *soote*. Cordially,

—WFB   SEPTEMBER 11, 1987

Dear Mr. Buckley:

No! No! No! No!

I will not be "convinced" to do anything by your ad for *Firing Line* video cassettes [March 27]. The word is *persuade*.

Respectfully yours,

HUGH M. FITZPATRICK

CHEVY CHASE, MD.

Dear Mr. Fitzpatrick: Quite right. Moreover, your conviction is persuasive. Cordially,

—WFB

Dear Mr. Buckley:

John Roche's contrast between a trustful Ronald Reagan and a mistrustful Lyndon Johnson ["Taming the NSC," March 27] points up the virtues of an underrated human quality that is often confused with *distrust*. Despite the fact that so much of our Constitution was founded upon healthy mistrust, there is a part of us all that yearns to trust, freely and completely, in accordance with Henry L. Stimson's maxim that "the only way to make a man trustworthy is to trust him." But for an executive, the problem arises when trust is so all-encompassing that it leaves no room for in-house review and oversight. In the best of trusting relationships, critical review is viewed not as an intrusion but as a welcome antidote to human fallibility. Indeed, it is the keen awareness of one's own fallibility that seems to spawn the quality of mistrust in the first place. Quite simply, to be mistrustful is to be intellectually honest. Bill, as someone who counts so many bright people among his acquaintances, would you say mistrust, of themselves and others, is a common denominator?

Sincerely,

WILLIAM E. COOPER, PH.D.

PROFESSOR OF PSYCHOLOGY

UNIVERSITY OF IOWA

IOWA CITY, IOWA

Dear Professor Cooper: The difficulty is semantic. I would not use the word "mistrust" to do the work you assign it. So far as I know, the word that reaches out for your inflection does not exist. You would need to make a verb out of "blind trust." The English language, as Clifton Fadiman once wrote, is wonderfully versatile, but there are some things you simply can't do with it. Cordially,

—WFB   MAY 8, 1987

Dear Mr. Buckley:

I take exception to your sentence in "Full Circle" [June 2] that ends the episode of the incorrect baggage tally, i.e., too many bags aboard the plane. "Whose they were, we never knew; and, being a genial lot [of bags or people?], there has been no public speculation over the question." I think your participle dangles.

WARREN SNYDER

CHICAGO, ILL.

Dear Mr. Snyder: You are quite right. Introducing the word "we" before "being" would have fixed it up grammatically, though there is, you will concede, a little euphonic damage left over. Cordially,

—WFB   AUGUST 18, 1989

Dear Mr. Buckley:

Admittedly, you are articulate and fluent to the point that any attempt at criticism has to descend to mere nit-picking.

Accordingly, in my opinion, you could be more precise in your positioning of limiting adverbs, e.g., "The government can *only* do something for the people, in proportion as it can do something to the people" ["State-loving in the GOP," Dec. 18, 1987] might have been better were you to have said: The government can do something for the people, *only* in proportion etc. . . . *D'accord?*

JOHN A. HEINLEIN, M.D.

GREAT NECK, N.Y.

Dear Dr. Heinlein: You're right, but remember I was quoting Jefferson, though granted it was Jefferson who spoke of making a "more perfect" union. On the general point, see Richard Weaver's *The Ethics of Rhetoric* for the flexibility of adverb placement. Only John is sick. John only is sick. John is, only, sick. John is sick, only. All can be used accurately to communicate that only John is sick, but there are kind and less kind ways of treating the ear. Cordially,

—WFB   MARCH 18, 1988

Dear Mr. Buckley:

Don't start a sentence with "and." In the last paragraph of your column I see this, and apparently the *Star-Ledger* proofreader did not. (She sleeps a lot.)

I am beginning to wonder just how good (or bad) your high school was, and how good (or bad) a student you were.

Very truly yours,

DAVID DEARBORN, JR.

ELIZABETH, N.J.

Dear Mr. Dearborn: Verses 2–26 and 28–31, Chapter I, Genesis, all begin with "And." The King James scholars went to pretty good high schools. Cordially,

—WFB   JUNE 10, 1991

Dear Mr. Buckley:

Please be assured that there is not now, nor has there ever been, a rule against beginning a sentence with *and*, although there have been a good many admonitions to that effect by soi-disant arbiters of usage. Most of this nonsense originated among the late Victorians and their turn-of-the-century successors (but not including the brothers Fowler).

This silliness survives in some high schools, apparently, but not, I should think, in the better ones. Surely, one of the characteristics of a good high school is that it teaches its students to pay attention to what they read. Anyone who believes that there is a "rule" against beginning a sentence with *and*—or with any other coordinating conjunction—simply isn't paying attention.

To convince yourself that I'm telling the truth, all you need do is grab the first half-dozen books at hand and begin turning pages at random. You'll quickly find examples in good plenty of sentences beginning with *and.*

> Sincerely yours,
> DOUGLAS CRENSHAW
> ANTIOCH, TENN.

P.S. To save you some trouble, I herewith append some examples culled from the books nearest my own hand. In the event that these fellows aren't sufficiently authoritative for Mr. Sidorsky to acknowledge your "high scholarly right to begin a sentence with an 'and' " ["Notes & Asides," July 29], I also append examples from a longer list I keep for another purpose (including sentences from the prose of Wordsworth, Coleridge, Shelley, Lamb, Hazlitt, De Quincey, Carlyle, Mill, Dickens, George Eliot, Arnold, Newman, Ruskin, T. H. Huxley, Pater, Wilde, Shaw, Conrad, Yeats, Joyce, Lawrence, T. S. Eliot, Beckett, Forster, Woolf, Lessing, Hulme, Richards, and Empson). After all, high scholars shouldn't be denied rights everybody else has.

1. And then the fog rose from the ground and from the very leaves and through the fog I saw the body.

—William Goyen, "In the Icebound Hothouse"

2. And the strategy worked.

—Paul Johnson, *Intellectuals*

3. And would you write "The worst tennis player around here is I" or "The worst tennis player around here is me"? The first is good grammar, the second is good judgment—although the *me* might not do in all contexts.

—Strunk & White, *Elements of Style*

4. And, for a good fisherman, the object was not to bring home a mess of fish.

—Franklin Burroughs, *Billy Watson's Croker Sack*

5. And although it is arguable that a faction might insinuate itself into the control of a legislature, this will be the less likely in proportion to the greater size of the area represented.

—Max Beloff, introduction, *The Federalist*

6. And a further reason for caution, in this respect, might be drawn from the reflection, that we are not always sure that those who advocate the truth are actuated by purer principles than their antagonists.

—*The Federalist* (#I Hamilton)

7. And what inspired guesses there have been!

—Malcolm Muggeridge, *Confessions of a Twentieth-Century Pilgrim*

8. And wearily, but not *simply* wearily, he returned that look.

—John Barth, *The Last Voyage of Somebody the Sailor*

Dear Mr. Crenshaw: Crenshaw! Stop! I can't stand any more, and you have sent along sixty-two! Massive retaliation was repealed at the Summit last week. Cordially,

—WFB   AUGUST 26, 1991

Dear Mr. Buckley:

As a nine- or ten-year-old reading Dear Abby, Charlie Brown, and the Royals' scores, I found your columns incomprehensible. In high school I discovered you were simply boring.

Early in my college days at Kansas State University in the journalism department and political-science classrooms I learned to admire your style but could not understand how you could be so wrong on so many issues. As a cub reporter for the *Topeka Capital-Journal* I frequently found myself agreeing with your positions but resented your patronizing tone and use of big words and foreign phrases. You abuse the reader, I thought.

Now, as a twenty-eight-year-old homeowner; underpaid, overworked director of communications for the Kansas Republican Party—concerned about over-taxation, over-spending, and under-presence in the world—and newly wed, I find we share opinions on most critical issues and that I enjoy your writing savoir-faire.

Boy, Bill, have you changed!

Yours,

ROGER AESCHLIMAN

TOPEKA, KAN.

P.S. Please, please, let's do something about the non-word "factoid." An item of information is either a fact, or it is fiction. It can not be "like a fact," even if it is trivial. It is either a trivial fact or trivial fiction, but not a "factoid." HELP!

Dear Mr. Aeschliman: We don't use "factoid" here at *NR*, but I promise to *slay* the first person I hear using it, now that I'm confident you will find my action mature. Cordially,

—WFB   AUGUST 18, 1989

The preceding letter from Mr. Aeschliman, which is reminiscent of the discovery of how one's parents get wiser as one gets older, did not end the healthy discussion of "factoids" (which sounds like a disease—and is). A subsequent correspondent suggested that the word, and perhaps the practice, originated with Norman Mailer, while another disputed Aeschliman's charge that factoid is a nonword (as it more than suggests a nontruth) because it is in The Random House Dictionary of the English Language, and proposed a "factoid" contest. Such exchanges can go on and on. And that's a fact.

Dear Mr. Buckley:

What is a fell swoop, and why is there always one fell swoop? Do fell swoops ever come more than one at a time? For example, can democracy be established in South Africa in two or three fell swoops (see "First Step to Democracy," *NR,* Nov. 25)?

> Sincerely,
> RICHARD PICKRELL
> BERKELEY, CALIF.

Dear Mr. Pickrell: Interesting question. I haven't asked Bill Safire, but my intuitive feeling is that a swoop can't be fell unless it is consummated, even as one can't, oh, vault a pole in two or three stages. Besides, don't you get the feeling that there is an onomatopoeic imperative at work here—that the word "swoop" suggests a beginning, and requires an end? Let's think about it. Cordially,

> —WFB   FEBRUARY 24, 1989

Dear Mr. Buckley:

Tell me it isn't so. Tell me the typesetter goofed. Tell me a ghostwriter improvised. Tell me anything except that you really wrote about "hot air rising *upward.*" I don't believe it. I can't believe it. I *won't* believe it.

> Hopefully,
> ELLEN D. PARKER
> NORFOLK, VA.

Dear Mrs. Parker: Even reactionaries don't believe that hot air descends downward!

> —WFB   APRIL 18, 1980

Dear Mr. Buckley:

Shame on you! See page 1113 of *NR*, Oct. 13, for the following words attributed to you in a letter to JKG [John Kenneth Galbraith] the Harvard Prof:

"It raises implicitly two points, the one, *Ought anyone* to sue for libel; the second, Is the Vidal suit, assuming the answer is yes, *to be one of them?*" [Emphasis supplied.]

I ask: One of *what*? The only plausible antecedent to "them" is "anyone," and a person (even if unspecified) can hardly *be* a libel suit, although he may perhaps initiate one. Have I caught you with your antecedents down? Or, perhaps, this Mr. Anyone will shortly sue *you* for libel (in that you asserted he *was*, or ought to be, a *libel suit* against Gore Vidal—fighting words beyond a doubt).

Have you anything to say for yourself?

Chidingly,
BILL WINGO
BIRMINGHAM, ALA.

No, nothing. Chidedly,

—WFB   JANUARY 19, 1973

Dear Mr. Buckley:

There is an irritating mannerism of speech, an affectation of style, used all too frequently these days—so pernicious that it has even found its way into the "On the Right" pages of *National Review*. I have always admired your elegant and expressive use of English, and now that I find even you to be slipping into this style I feel the time has come to launch a protest.

In "The Irreverent Dr. Graham" [*NR*, June 11] you say: ". . . one might excuse a Chamberlain's making flattering references to Adolf Hitler, or a Nixon's praising Mao Tse-tung." *A* Chamberlain? *A* Nixon? How many Chamberlains and Nixons have there been? And of these, how many made flattering references, etc.? (And why not "a Hitler," or "a Mao Tse-tung"?)

I really am surprised to see this from the pen of a William F. Buckley, although if it could be shown that the device was ever used by a Chesterfield or a Chesterton, a Samuel Johnson or a Samuel Clemens, a Wolfe, a Woolf, a Wylie, or a Wilde, a Beerbohm, a Benchley, a Mencken, a Maugham, a Lardner, a Lippmann, an A. P. Herbert, or an F. P. Adams, I would consider retracting my criticism.

Meantime, do you know if this maddening mannerism has a name? Indefinitization, perhaps?

Sincerely,
JILL CLISBY
SANTA MONICA, CALIF.

Dear Mrs. Clisby: "A Chamberlain" is here used, obviously, to convey: "someone situated as Chamberlain was situated." It's not called indefinitization. It is called antonomasia. Cordially,

—WFB   AUGUST 20, 1982

———

Buckley contributes a Foreword to Kilpatrick's book *The Writer's Art*, published by Andrews, McMeel & Parker, Inc., 1984, and even there gets involved in a spot of disagreement. But he does not shrink from an uninhibited admiration for some of his contemporaries, and "Kilpo" is one of them.

———

WELCOME: THE WRITER'S CRAFT

. . . Those of us disinclined to biological curiosity experience no temptation to look at pictures of livers, upper intestines, or tonsils, let alone the real thing. And we all know about those many who having experienced grammar at school, and been made to parse sentences, and to distinguish between dependent and independent clauses, subjunctive and indicative moods, have no more curiosity about the morphology of English than most of us have about the innards of a diesel engine. But now listen.

Spring is coming to Scrabble, Virginia. There is the profusion of flowers. Among them "the trillium, loveliest of them all, which kneels as modestly as a spring bride, all in white, beside the altar of an old oak stump. If you're not familiar with the trillium, imagine the flower that would come from a flute if a flute could make a flower. That is the trillium, a work of God from a theme by Mozart."

I shouldn't really need, in order to make my point that prejudices about anatomical structures are not always warranted, to do much more than to say that the man who brought off those lovely sentences—casual commentary on a natural cycle in an earlier book—has up and written an engrossing and majestic treatise on the English language. He calls it *The Writer's Art*. It is not only the best book of its kind I have ever experienced (the incomparable Fowler wrote a different kind of a book), it is the most compelling reading about writing I have ever seen. If such a book were written about human biology, I would be tempted to become a doctor. But never mind if you have a vocation: James Jackson Kilpatrick's book will be read for the sheer pleasure of the experience; read by people who intend to make no special effort to improve their writing, let alone harbor any ambition to write belletristically. But I warn that Mr. Kilpatrick's book is so seductive that the temptation to improve is not easily resisted.

It requires a chastity belt on the spirit to read and not experience temptation in the voluptuous delights of language.

It requires only a reading of a few paragraphs of the book to know that you are embarked on an important trip, under the direction of a guide who (most important) has labored intensively to understand what it is that works in English, what it is that does not work in English; moreover, a writer whose aptitude (indispensable) for words, and for the composition of sentences, is so marked that the distinctions he makes convince us in part because they hit with revelatory force, in part because we have come to trust him deeply. Kilpatrick engages at first attention; then respect; finally devotion. This last is done, I think, because he insinuates his own veneration for the proper sentence and, sensing now what it is that we may have been missing, we are grateful to the man (person?—see Chapter 4) who helped open our eyes.

Notice that JJK has named his book *The Writer's Art.* It is art he speaks of in two senses. The first is that fine writing—he speaks of Rebecca West, for instance; Lawrence Durrell, Hemingway, and Twain—is not something we can master in the sense that, say, we can master a word processor. But it is also true, where art is the object of our scrutiny, that differing judgments can be made. It required many centuries before the aesthetic consensus crystallized that Notre Dame de Chartres was possibly the most beautiful thirteenth-century cathedral in Europe and that Westminster Abbey was possibly the ugliest thirteenth-century cathedral in Europe. Some questions about English are unresolved ("It's I" or "It's me"?). And then, too, there is the matter of usage. Although the overwhelming majority of technicians may agree that a particular usage is offensive and should be quarantined, manacled, deported—maybe even executed, if only the Supreme Court will go along—that use will at some point overwhelm us, like old age. JJK is sensitive to the autonomous inertia of words and for that reason accepts the likes of "access" as a transitive verb. But his ear is so good, his good sense so gratifyingly reliable, that we find ourselves volunteers in the good usage army, disposed to spend blood, sweat, and tears.

Over the years I have been much interested, and frequently amused, by the author's Hundred Years' War against Unusual Words. Interested because he makes his case so well; amused because he is not particularly constrained by it. He tells several amusing stories in this volume, one of them about stumbling into the word *limicolous,* which is to say, "living in mud."

He found himself using the word, and woke the next day with a most dreadful hangover. "No advice is more elementary, and no advice is more difficult to accept: When we feel an impulse to use a marvelously exotic word, let us lie down until the impulse goes away. . . . My brother pundit, Bill Buckley, falls into sin even more easily than I. He has had affairs with *decoctable, anfractuosity,* and *endogamous.* He has taken to bed with *chiliastic, phlogistonic, sciolism, incondite,* and *osmotically.* He has fallen for *hubristic, otiose, repristinate, adumbrated,* and *synecdoche.*" Two sentences later, the author uses in a dense little cluster, *arcane, syntactically,* and *bibulousness.* And this notwithstanding that there are those who believe that *arcane* is an arcane word, that *syntactically* can be made to sound like the malapropism of someone far gone in bibulousness.

I have a private theory about unusual words so simple it is embarrassing, in such august auspices, to disclose. It is as simple as that, say, we tend to conclude that people who use words with which we happen not to be familiar are using unfamiliar words. If John knows 8,000 words and Susan knows 8,000 words, inevitably John will know 250 words that Susan does not, and Susan will know 250 words that John does not, and John will think Susan exhibitionistic, and Susan will think John affected. I like to cite the waiter of a restaurant in Garden City who approached me twenty-five years ago to complain that he had subscribed to *National Review* and was absolutely certain that its circulation would greatly increase if only it stopped tolerating such unfamiliar words. Exactly two years later I was at the same restaurant, same table, same waiter, who greeted me joyfully, congratulating me on having taken his advice.

There are reasons for using words even when they are unfamiliar, a term which has to mean unfamiliar to those unfamiliar with them, a description whose geographical coordinates I would hate to have to specify. It can be a matter of rhythm, it can be a matter of the exact fit—and it can be something by way of obeisance to the people whose honed verbal appetites created the need for such a word, which therefore came into being. Call it supply-side linguistics; but whatever you call it, pray be thankful that someone invented the word *velleity* and that a few refuse to permit it to die, even as others would die to preserve the lousewort. Kilpo tells us that "as writers, we ought to take advantage of all the glorious riches of the English tongue, and to use them as best we can, but always taking into account one thing: the audience we are writing for." I would not dispute the relevance of this injunction directed at those terrible people who write those inscrutable instruction manuals (the computer-folk now call this "documentation"), but I think that writers also have an obligation to keep the frontiers of language open, else the weeds grow, the tall trees out there atrophy, and our patrimony is eroded.

I would not have thought it possible for someone other than a professional bibliographer to gather so many pointed examples of the kind of thing that is awfully wrong, that is less than quite right, that is okay, that is quite beautiful. In one section, JJK gives us Version One of a paragraph he wrote, lets us see its weaknesses even as he slowly descries them; lets us trace his corrections, on into drafts four and five. This is truly exciting stuff, like seeing a documentary on Picasso painting a canvas. And listen to the titles of the subchapters in Chapter 4, which are: "The Things We Ought Not to Do." They are: 1. "We ought not to use clichés." 2. "We ought never to fall into gobbledygook." 3. "We ought not to mangle our sentences." 4. "As a general rule, we ought not to use euphemisms." 5. "We ought not to pile up our nouns as adjectives." 6. "We ought not to coin words wantonly." 7. "We must not break the rules of grammar." 8. "We ought not to write dialect or slang unless we are certain of both our ear and our audience." 9. "We ought not to be redundant." 10. "We ought not to use words that have double meanings." 11. "We ought not to write portmanteau sentences." 12. "We ought not unintentionally to give offense by sexist words or phrases, but we ought not to be intimidated either." 13. "We ought not to make mistakes in spelling."

Right there we have the plainspokenness that characterizes Kilpatrick together with evidence of the ear that exactly catches what it is he wants to say, and, I guess I should add, a whiff of the imperial manner. If you feel strongly about words, it is downright offensive when someone says "hopefully," unless he is referring to a whaler's wife, looking hopefully out over the horizon from her widow's walk. Kilpatrick, while understanding and flexible to the point of acknowledging the dynamic imperative, is a firm custodian. I would trust the family treasure with him, you bet. There will be no attrition of the language at the gravesite of the collected works of James Jackson Kilpatrick.

He confesses that this is in some ways a personal book. I would guess that most proficient word-users would agree with somewhere between 90 and 95 percent of what he pronounces upon. But some things aggrieve him more than others, and that is both to be expected and, in a sense, welcomed, because once again it reminds us of the factor of art. He provides a huge chapter devoted to at least a hundred personal crotchets, of which the initial dozen are "A" AND "AN"; A.M. IN THE MORNING; ABSOLUTE WORDS; ABSTRACT/ABSTRACTION; ACCESS (v); AD HOC; AD NAUSEAM; ADAGES, OLD; ADAPT/ADOPT; ADVERSE/AVERSE; AFFECT/EFFECT; and AFFI-

DAVIT. Under ABSOLUTE WORDS we read, "My own modest list of words that cannot be qualified by 'very' or 'rather' or 'a little bit' includes *unique, imperative, universal, final, fatal, complete, virgin, dead, equal, eternal, total, unanimous, essential,* and *indispensable.*"

I dunno. Wouldn't the idiomatic ring of "altogether unique" strike you as okay? Or how about, "It was, so to speak, rather a final gesture when Dominguin dedicated the bull to his loyal public and proceeded to get killed." But . . . we are taking advice from a man whose ear is a Stradivarius, and there is reason to give him the benefit of the doubt, always allowing for the supremacy of one's own conscience. And again, everyone has his own crotchets. While I was reading Kilpo's manuscript aboard an airliner, the captain's voice rang in, "We will land at La Guardia in approximately fifty-nine minutes." *Approximately?* What's approximately for, if not imperatively conjoined to one hour, or forty-five minutes; or, at most, fifty-five minutes?

But this kind of thing can go on and on. For instance, we can agree that the "h" is not pronounced, requiring therefore "an" as the indefinite article. But then doesn't a difference come in precisely in the emphasis the individual elocutionist gives to the "h" sound? *I* would say, "a historical novel" because it happens that when I pronounce the adjective, the aitch is definitely present and accounted for. Again, mightn't a historian, even one so sure of tone that he would never think heedlessly of an "old cliché," find himself so situated as desiring to distinguish between a new and an old cliché? ("The arsenal of democracy, that very old cliché, has given way to a new cliché, namely the military-industrial complex.")

If you wish to pursue the game, the list of demurrals grows (I said I agreed with 95 percent, and 5 percent is, really, a whole lot). Consider the author's dislike for such locutions as "with deference to the learned opinion of my able and distinguished friend." But, don't you see, there is a rhetorical point to be served in occasional tushery. You are reminding the reader—and your distinctly unlearned and undistinguished colleague— that you are aware of the boundaries of diplomatic exchange, and willing to observe them, even as Winston Churchill would have addressed a communication to his German counterpart, "Dear Mr. Hitler."

While I am at it, Mr. Kilpatrick uses the exclamation *aargh!* to communicate disgust: wrongly, I think, influenced as I was when thirty years ago, reading the letters of Swinburne, I came upon him using it to express orgasmic delight in one of his vapulatory fantasies. (Mr. Kilpatrick is reaching for ugh!) Again, do we proper word-users need to stay away from the "long day" on the martinet's grounds that a day cannot have more than a fixed number of hours, and didn't Galileo or somebody go to jail to prove Kilpo's point?

On the matter of *expertise* I get deadly serious. It happens that I learned the word from a scholar bilingual in French, and that I was present when he and a renowned philosopher discussed ruefully the deterioration in the use of the word, whose corruption has been depriving us of a marvelously useful resource. Invited formally to define the word, they came up with: "*Expertise* is the body of operative knowledge" (that attaches to the subject under discussion). So that, for instance, you can say, "There is expertise in politics up to a point, after which it becomes an art." There is no way of saying this if you attach to *expertise* the vulgar meaning Mr. Kilpatrick correctly advises us would justify throwing the word away altogether. Throw out the bad word, struggle to reclaim the good one.

And then, as lagniappe, I am amused by the author's insistence that *remains to be seen* is tolerable only when you are talking about a corpse awaiting inspection in a funeral parlor. I see (and use) the phrase intending to inject doubt. Man-from-Missouri-wise-kind-of-thing. "It remains to be seen whether Harry Truman's bid for the farm vote is going to pay off." Remember that by authorizing one usage you are not committed to preferring it. "I am not so sure that Harry Truman's bid for the farm vote is going to work" would satisfy whatever doubt I desire to invest in the observation.

But what a barrel of fun. The author wrote to me that this would be his "last book." Then we find, under Number 10 above ("Avoid Words That Have Double Meanings"), "Another word that occasionally gives trouble is *last*. Its first meaning, unmistakably understood, is *final, terminal, ultimate*. But *last* also can mean 'most recent.' If we fall into a sentence involving *the last few months* or *his last book,* we may cause a flicker. By contrast, *past* admits of no confusion in a context of time: the *past few* months. Instead of *his last book,* I would suggest *his latest book.*"

Just so. It may be that James Jackson Kilpatrick will never write another book at once so charming, instructive, resourceful, and useful. But something will gestate in his mind, you watch. You know what? Something like the coming of spring we began with. This is a spring that

> . . . tiptoes in. It pauses, overcome by shyness, like a grandchild at the door, peeping in, ducking out of sight, giggling in the hallway. "Heather!" I want to cry, "I know you're out there. Come in!" And April slips into our arms. The maples do not come forth in green; they are flowering red, soft as slippers, in tassels like a jester's scepter. The flowering almond is pink, absurdly pink, little-girl pink, as pink as peppermint and cream. The apples display their milliner's scraps of ivory silk, rose-tinged. All the sleeping things wake

up—primrose, baby iris, candytuft, blue phlox, the Scotch heather that had seemed dead beyond resurrection. The earth warms—you can smell it, feel it, crumble April in your hands.

Kilpatrick was writing about the coming of spring, but as much could be written about the materialization of another book in the mind of a man who cannot stop making poetry, whether he is writing about the spring, the Supreme Court, or the English language.

Chapter 2

On Vocabulary

Speaking of the right word, let's get right to it. The word for today is on the blackboard: *vocabulary*. WFB's Introduction to the Kilpatrick book in the preceding chapter is the first of several comprehensive essays on the subject. These are needed because more people know William F. Buckley, Jr., for his vocabulary than know the details of his politics. Some are amused by it, some bemused, some attempt to equal or exceed his abilities (few succeed) while others are annoyed and a number are outright hostile. Some are simply bothered by his use of a word that the "ordinary" reader might not know and others are apt to confuse or conflate their opposition to his political views with opposition to his vocabulary.

Over the decades, Buckley has had to defend his use of what he considers the right word. There are those who have come to his defense. Some of these defenses—or, given the American theory of sports that a good offense is the best possible defense, some of his most offensive pieces—are grouped here. They are largely but not always in chronological order, as will be obvious.

Quite apart from the merits of the say-it-plainly, say-it-simply school versus the use-the-word-you-need faction, there are some splendid words involved in the never-ending debate. Many correspondents simply ask questions; others suspect Buckley of having misused or perhaps having invented a word. Whichever, there are words contained in this running debate to admire, puzzle over, or cause that delightful shock of definition. Here is an early example, a newspaper column from the early sixties.

―――――

THE HYSTERIA ABOUT WORDS

Have you noticed that the use of an unusual word sometimes irritates the reader to such a point that he will accuse the user of affectation, than which there is no more heinous crime in the American republic? The distinguished political and social philosopher and columnist Mr. Russell Kirk used the word "energumen" to describe in his Introduction to my book *Rumbles Left and Right* who it is I agitate against, and one reviewer fairly exploded with annoyance. Now the word in question means "someone possessed by an evil spirit," and fanatically addicted to a particular idea. Can you think of a better word to describe certain kinds of people who seek to reorder public affairs according to their hypnotic visions? Should one refuse to use a venerable word for which there is no obvious synonym, simply because it is a word that does not regularly appear in the diet of the average reader?

I raise the problem because I am often accused of an inordinate reliance on unusual words, and desire—as would you in my shoes, I think—to defend myself against the insinuation that I write as I do simply to prove that I have returned recently from the bowels of a dictionary with a fish in my mouth, establishing my etymological dauntlessness. Surely one must distinguish between those who plunder old tomes to find words which, in someone's phrase, should never be let out . . . and such others as Russell Kirk, who use words because (a) the words signify just exactly what the user means, and because (b) the user deems it right and proper to preserve in currency words which in the course of history were coined as the result of a felt need.

There is a sort of phony democratic bias against the use of unusual words. Recently I heard a young movie actress being interviewed on a radio station. She was asked by her interrogator what it meant to be an actress, and replied that an actor's life is "multifaceted."

"What are you trying to pull on me?" demands the radio announcer.

She ran panicked from the argument—what else, in the democratic age, when it is deemed an effrontery on the democratic ideal to use a word that is not used twice a week by Little Orphan Annie? "I'm sorry I used such a fancy word—I guess I don't really know what it means—I should have said, there are lots of aspects to being an actress." Democracy won the day, and the show droned on.

A while ago I was on Jack Paar's television program, and he asked me a number of questions having to do with this and that, which I tried vainly to answer, as best I knew how. I wrote about that experience . . . and described the ensuing tantrum of Mr. Paar and his associates, who steamed on and on about my ideological vices, expressing special outrage at my unintelligibility.

It is a curious thing, this universal assumption by a number of prominently situated opinion- or rather mood-makers, that the American people are either unaware of the unusual word or undisposed to hear it and find out what it means, thus broadening not merely their vocabulary—that isn't the important thing—but their conceptual and descriptive powers. Those who say that the average American is incapable of appreciating the meaning of the word "energumen" are, in my humble judgment, nuts. The average American is, in Franklin P. Adams's phrase, a bit above average, and his intelligence is not tied umbilically to Jack Paar's anti-intellectualist muse.

It is curious, too, that a man who is offended by the use of the word "multifaceted" or "energumen" is perfectly capable of expressing a sentence of death-defying mechanical complexity. I am unfortunately innocent in the world of science and I wish I knew what in the world the TV hawker is talking about when he reels off something having to do with a "double action injector system in the valve mechanism" but it does not occur to me to suggest that he is putting on airs; it occurs to me to rue my patently inadequate knowledge of the mechanical a b c's.

The point about unusual words is that they are as necessary to philosophy, economics, aesthetics, and political science as they are necessary in the world of higher mechanics, in which so many people displaying the natural American genius are so much at home. It is possible, I suppose, to describe the refinements of an Astrojet fan injection through-ventilated engine in words understandable to me, but the exercise is not often resorted to because the manufacturers assume a level of mechanical literacy, even as they assume that those who do not have it ought not to set the standards for those who do have it. So it is in other fields, which is why, in my judgment, when Mr. Russell Kirk uses the word "energumen," he should be allowed to use it, and the thing for book reviewers to do when they come upon it, if they are unfamiliar with it, is not to pout, but to open a dictionary and see if the word is one whose meaning they wish to learn. They must guard against going about like anti-literate energumens.

—WFB   JUNE 15, 1963

. . . What the blazes is the meaning of the "bloviations" indulged in by Attorney William Kunstler?

The Random House Dictionary gives *blouse, blouson, blousy, blow.* The New Imperial Reference Dictionary gives *blot, blotch, blouse, blow.* And a 1928 edition of the Concise Oxford Dictionary gives *blotch, blottesque* (well done, Oxford!), *blouse* and *blow.* But I'm blowed if I could find *bloviation* anywhere.

I believe you made the word up and it is nothing more than a lot of blatant blather.

Bless you.

R.N. USHER-WILSON

BRONXVILLE, N.Y.

Yes, we did make it up—and don't think it was easy!

—ED. (WFB)   OCTOBER 22, 1968

R. N. Usher-Wilson's letter raises my eyebrow, but the response of "Ed." my hackles. The good dominie (for Usher-Wilson, in modesty, forbore to flaunt his cloth) has simply consorted with the lower class of dictionary. Had he consulted a good workmanlike Funk & Wagnalls (e.g., New Standard Dictionary of the English Language, 1913 edition as revised in 1938), he would have found, much to his delight, the following exquisite gem of unbloviated lexicography: "*blo'via'tion . . . n. Loud, defiant, boastful talk; blowing.* Literary Digest *Oct. 23, '09, p. 666.*" The word was particularly popular as an elegant variation in the United States during the second half of the nineteenth century. I believe Mark Twain indulged a certain fondness for it.

Now I pass to the more heinous lapse, the editor's claim to having invented this fulsome lip-shaping word. Many things, among them not a few both noble and sightly, the "Ed." and his merry crew may rightly lay claim to having introduced into civil discourse—but bloviation never. Bloviation belongs exclusively to publishers.

WILLIAM F. RICKENBACKER

BRIARCLIFF MANOR, N.Y.

. . . Judging from the tone of your editorials, which I enjoy very much, I'm sure that you are indeed capable of making up the word, especially if you discover at a critical moment that none of the other several hundred thousand English ones don't seem to fit the occasion. I admire your zeal.

I wonder, however, whether in this instance you may have overlooked the fact that one of our Presidents, the late and hardly lamented Warren G. Harding, is reputed to have used the word "bloviate" to describe some of his own utterances.

Mr. Harding's chief qualification for public office was considered by many to have been a something more than modest talent in chuffing wind into the small end of a bass horn, a "tin grunt," or a "helicon," to some of the older devotees. This process was accomplished by pressing down one or more of the valve buttons installed partway along such cumbrous but useful plumbing. By dint of years of devoted practice of this art Mr. Harding found that he could attract much attention by this use of his personal wind, especially if he pressed the right valves down.

After assuming high office, in the parlance of other days, Mr. Harding achieved some notoriety as a "blow-hard," i.e., a strenuous exuder of flatulence accompanied by speech. Turning such a questionable compliment to happier use, he used to say that he would "bloviate" a little bit for various assemblages. Thus came into some modest usage the term which you have turned into a sort of noun when originally it was a verb.

Although I can't cite chapter, book, verse, page, or line, I believe you will find corroboration of this essay's central theme if you will refer to Mr. Harding's usually unflattering biographies.

I hope this doesn't break your rice bowl, or spoil your day.

Yours for more neologisms and some new adaptations of the old words to tell things as they are.

ROBERT J. DEMER
HARRISBURG, PA.

As the drumfire—dumbfire?—increased, suggesting strongly that Buckley dumb down his language, he fired back, via another author of impressive vocabulary and returning again to his friend Kilpatrick's book, in a column this time, making a few new points.

THE STUDENTS, WHAT IS THEIR PROBLEM?

I spotted the scholarly and irrepressible Anthony Burgess, the English novelist essayist fantasist (author of *A Clockwork Orange,* among other things) giving advice publicly to his students (he is visiting America, teaching at the City College of New York). And what he said to the students, among other things, was: "I would ask you only to expand your vocabularies, develop a minimal grace of style, think harder, and learn who Helen of Troy and Nausicaa were. And for God's sake, stop talking about relevance. All we have is the past."

Mr. Burgess was musing about the college student he comes in contact with, at a university that practices an open admissions policy. Mr. Burgess was tactful about the whole thing, but he gave away his meaning, which is that the adulteration of education results in phony education. And when that happens, what you develop is new universities. When egalitarian ideology overtakes these, then "super universities will be built"; and after that, "super super universities . . . This can go on forever. Ultimately, the gods of learning are not mocked. The term 'university' may be rich in noble connotations, but it means only what we want it to mean."

Professor Burgess gave an example of a student essay on *Macbeth* "to which soon I must give a pass mark: 'Lady Mackbet says she had a kid not in so many words but she says she remembers what it was like when a kid sucked her nipple so I reckon she was a mother some time and the kid must have died but we dont hear no more about it which is really careless of Shakesper because the real reason why Macbeth and his wife are kind of restless and ambitious is because they did not have a baby that lived and perhaps this is all they really want and S. says notin about it.' "

Mr. Burgess provokes us by juxtaposing against that passage one from another student, presumably in the same class, whose grade—one assumes—is going to be indistinguishable from that of the young man who penetrated to the heart of Mr. and Mrs. Macbeth's difficulty. The other student wrote: "The weakly placed negatives in Dr. Faustus's penultimate line—'Ugly hell, gape not, come not, Lucifer'—may conceivably be taken as expressive of a desire, not implausible in a Renaissance scholar, to dare even the ultimate horrors for the sake of adding to his store of knowledge."

Now hang on to the point for a minute please, and reflect on one of the recommendations of Mr. Burgess. He believes that "the division between a scientific discipline and a humanistic one is already manifesting itself in undergraduate life-styles. The banner-waving students who hold protest meetings are merely indulged. They will, regrettably perhaps, never rule America; America will be controlled by the hard-eyed technicians who have no time for protest."

We should shrug off those intimations that fuel the superstition that we are being managed by a military-industrial complex. (It would appear plain that this is not the case.) But one hears plaintively the call of Mr. Burgess to his students to "expand" their vocabulary. I note among the Christmas advertisements lying around, one for a new radio receiver: "There's 150 watts IHF power, a loudness compensating switch, power output/heat sinks, IF/FM/multiplex decoder, FM muting, FM Stereo."

Now, the advertising agency that wrote those words is not putting on the dawg. The ad was, as they say, "communicating." Communicating, one supposes, not only to the "hard-eyed technicians" who are getting educated in the colleges, but to students in general. It is not afraid to use words and terms which are demanding—I, for instance, deficient in the appropriate education, do not have the least idea what the manufacturer is talking about: "power output/heat sinks" indeed! Lady Macbeth was never so inscrutable.

The moral is that the resistance to a rich vocabulary is inconsistently exercised. When the talk is of scientific or mechanical things, the public is altogether acquiescent to strange and minutely differentiated terms. Is this what Mr. Burgess is saying?—that the difficulty in making distinctions in human and social affairs leads people to Tarzan-talk in the classroom? The same people who can talk to the hi-fi people with maximum scientific sophistication? Worth musing, between the holidays.

—WFB   DECEMBER 28, 1972

THE WRITER'S CRAFT: PART TWO

Someone recently sent along an editorial from a newspaper in Wisconsin denouncing me and all my works, or I suppose more accurately denouncing all my works, on the grounds that they are strewn with unusual words. And I am glad the whole subject came up because I have been looking for a peg to celebrate the publication of a book that is useful, exciting, and beautiful, namely James Jackson Kilpatrick's *The Writer's Art*.

The protocols of full disclosure require that I instantly communicate that I wrote the Introduction to that book, but also quickly to add that I was not paid for it and have no financial stake in the book's success. But we all have a huge cultural stake in the book's success if we care about the dearest part of our patrimony, which is our language.

But first, on the matter of the unusual word. "My brother pundit, Bill Buckley, falls into sin even more easily than I. . . ."

I quarreled with him in my Introduction. . . . I said that I have a private theory, a theory so simple, so rudimentary, that it almost embarrasses me to trot it out. But think it over. It is that we tend to believe that a word is unfamiliar because it is unfamiliar to us . . .

Concede, of course, that there are words neither you nor I know. Should those words be quarantined? I wrote in my Introduction: "There are reasons for using words even when they are unfamiliar. It can be a matter of rhythm, it can be a matter of the exact fit—and it can be something by way of obeisance to the people whose honed verbal appetites created the need for such a word, which therefore came into being. Call it supply-side linguistics." . . . How is that for a defiant gesture?

But the whole business amuses. Kilpatrick knows the names of more flowers and trees and shrubs than I know names appropriate to describe Soviet policy. Are we supposed to admire the cook whose menu is unchanged?

I have recently pursued the whole question in another connection, and found myself wondering whether it is sufficiently recognized that writing is, as Mr. Kilpatrick's book title advises us, an art. We do not expect the amateur to try to play the Grieg Concerto in A Minor for Piano and Orchestra, but should we be resentful that some can do it?

John Updike is what one ought safely to be able to call a "performing writer," at whose hands the taxing demands of language are confidently met. Whereas most people don't paint canvases or play a musical instrument, everyone writes. The mistake is to suppose that one should discourage the profusion of verbal forms.

What Kilpatrick does in his book is useful to anyone with any interest either in self-expression or in the evaluation of others' expression. He lists common errors, discourses wittily on clichés and word traps, lists common solecisms. One huge chapter is devoted to one hundred personal "crotchets," he calls them: the kind of thing he often spots in print, which violates his verbal code. No adventure story is brighter, more intriguing, more heavily charged with suspense, leading to greater delights.

The Writer's Art is in my judgment the most readable book on the English language I have ever come upon, and you should get it, read it, give it to your children to read—give it to your tailor and candlestick maker. As I say, we all have a stake in it. You will shimmer with gratitude to the author, and to our forefathers, who gave us this blessed tongue.

—WFB   MAY 15, 1984

Dear Mr. Buckley:

I am enclosing an article written by one of our local columnists for the *Maries County Gazette,* which I think you will find amusing.

Sincerely,

GAIL MALONE

VIENNA, MO.

From the Front Seat
By Henry Evans

THE OBFUSCATOR

A few years ago someone in Washington had the bright idea of asking all the government bureaus and departments there to write all their papers and memos in everyday English which everyone could understand instead of their usual "federalese" which no one but the writer could understand. When that news story came over the wire a newspaper editor decided to have a little fun with it so the heading he wrote for the story said Eschew Obfuscation, or, avoid lack of clearness.

Today I would like to nominate a new Champion of Obfuscation who is not a government bureaucrat at all but, rather, a syndicated newspaper columnist and magazine publisher and editor who ought to know better and who probably does but is being perverse. He is William F. Buckley, Jr., whose column appears in several hundred newspapers and whose magazine, *National Review,* is one of the major voices of the conservative side of the political spectrum.

To put it bluntly, Buckley is worse than a bureaucratic obfuscator; he is a lexicographical snob, to use a kind of phrase he might use himself. He is a show-off who uses words no one but himself knows the meaning of and by sending his readers to the dictionary with every other paragraph he writes he thinks he is demonstrating his superiority over us lesser mortals. For my part, I think he belongs in jail; I do not believe the freedom of speech or of the press was meant for the likes of him.

Now, we have to be a little careful here. In a book of his I read last week, *Execution Eve,* which is a collection of his columns and essays as well as some correspondence, I encountered six unfamiliar words in a matter of forty pages, pages 419 through 459. I went to the dictionary for every one of them and got madder and madder with each one of them. I started hoping I would not find them in the dictionary so I could accuse him of making them up, but I found them all. Now, he can claim he should not be blamed for using properly any word found in the dictionary, but let's be reasonable about it: I have spent all these years using the English language to earn a living and I have a reasonably good, maybe not great, but reasonably good vocabulary and when I have to go to the dictionary six times within forty pages, I can only assume I am reading the words of a lexicographical snob.

First he gives us SYNECDOCHE, a figure of speech in which the whole is used for the part or the part for the whole. Then ADUMBRATED, to darken or conceal partly, to overshadow; this was followed by VELLEITY, a mere wish with no effort to obtain it. From there he takes us to MAIEUTIC, the Socratic mode of inquiry, bringing out ideas latent in the mind. Then on to PROVENANCE, the location of a beginning such as where a painting was painted or a book written. Finally, he unloads PASQUINADE on us, a publicly posted lampoon or satire or ridicule.

At this point in the book I stopped running to the dictionary at every one of his show-off words. I just skipped them. In this same book he says that among the things he likes best is good English prose. It's too bad he did not learn to write it at Yale, which along with other Ivy League institutions specializes in making snobs out of otherwise normal people.

He did not use the words in some kind of an article discussing seldom-used words. He used them in his normal writing on a variety of subjects, for which I still think he belongs in jail. Lacking that, I still have one recourse: I am going to eschew Buckley, and that is not mere velleity; I'm actually going to do it.

Dear Miss Malone: Mr. Evans is wrong. It's not so. It's *not* the company I keep. Some of my best friends don't know the meaning of the word "provenance." But he failed to note the lexicographical snobs who created the need for the words he listed. They came into being because there was what the economists call a "felt need." (Come on, Evans, you've obviously experienced a velleity at some point in your life, but what would you say if someone asked what it was you were experiencing? See? You *can't* eschew Buckley. It's bad for you.) Cordially,

—WFB   AUGUST 4, 1989

Dear Mr. Buckley:

In the August 4 "Notes & Asides," a column by journalist Henry Evans is reprinted scolding you for using words "no one but [yourself] knows the meaning of and . . . sending [your] readers to the dictionary." He complains that he had to go to the dictionary six times within forty pages, then roundly condemns you as a "lexicographical snob." Mr. Evans seems to be the sort of columnist who keeps his dictionary—indeed, all hard-bound books—out of arm's reach and his one point of view always at his fingertips.

I can readily imagine the smile turned to despair on Mr. Evans's face were he ever to encounter (in *Dear Bertrand Russell . . .* , 1969) Bertrand Russell's "twenty favorite words": wind, alabaster, incarnadine, heath, chrysoprase, sublunary, golden, astrolabe, chorasmean, begrime, apocalyptic, alembic, pilgrim, ineluctable, fulminate, quagmire, terraqueous, ecstasy, diapason, inspissated.

And I have found in a collection of brief book reviews (*Urgent Copy*, 1969) by the novelist Anthony Burgess, in rather less than forty pages, these wonderful literary chord progressions: collocation, demotic, antinomies, polymathy, diaspora, eponym, rarefaction, gamboge, variorum (which Bernard Shaw would have said no Englishman can pronounce), etiolations, fictile, numen, neologism, repine (E. Waugh's favorite), gulosity, carious, tragoid, tabascoid, statify, anabasis, exophthalmic, "fiery laconicism" (Keats), sempiternal, bandersnatch, palindromic, tumid, interstices, and panjandrum.

Mr. Evans's column caught me at high tide and high surf astride J.I.M. Stewart's *Eight Modern Writers* (Oxford University Press, 1963), where barely through the third author, in about two hundred pages, one hears distinctly Oxford harmonies, many requiring looking up for pronunciation: subfusc, nescience, divagation, finically, thaumaturge, hortatory, recusant, conflation, viscidity, sanative, esemplatic power, prosopopoeia, facture, concatenate, deliquesces, plangently, desuetude, homothetic, mythopoeic, chthonic . . . and proem! This from a teacher.

But there is a darker side to the Evans *v.* Buckley encounter. It is expressed nicely by the American author David Leavitt in his novel *The Lost Language of Cranes* (1986), where he writes a fine paragraph on a copy editor's addiction to crossword puzzles, "the meshing of meanings, the knitting of one set of words into another," and their creators ("the vultures of the thinking world"). Leavitt concludes . . . : "And Rose was learning that such carrion was better than alcohol. This benign activity literally tied up the brain; it blocked grief, anxiety, panic. In a burst of bitter energy, Rose thrust Thomas Mann and Timon of Athens into the fray. She fired out synonyms like bullets. But in the end, her head ached horribly . . ."

Yours,

THOMAS GOLDTHWAITE

HILO, HAWAII

Dear Mr. Buckley:

I am a nineteen-year-old who knows five of the six words cited by the querulous Henry Evans as cause to nominate you "Champion of Obfuscation" [Aug. 4]. While it is true I am currently an Ivy League student (with clenched teeth I will have to look down my nose upon Mr. Evans due to the snobbery he alleges I and my fellow students have), I learned those words at my public high school in Ohio.

ADAM R. STAUFFER

BROWN UNIVERSITY

PROVIDENCE, R.I.

Dear Mr. Stauffer: Perhaps Mr. Evans will forgive you if you manage to forget those words before you are his age. Cordially,

—WFB   SEPTEMBER 15, 1989

This time, WFB takes the fight to a higher court, answering a one-two challenge: first by the respected Meg Greenfield of *The Washington Post,* and then (an edged query) by a good editor, Ed Williams, of the *Charlotte Observer,* in the pages of *The New York Times Book Review.* Even so, he starts off by setting the record straight on the matter of titles.

Newspaper and magazine editors usually arrogate to themselves the right to write titles for pieces they get from authors, a nicety not known to many unsuspecting readers. A piece the editor Harry Evans once commissioned me to write for *The Sunday Times* (London), which I called "The Londonization of New York," for that was the theme, appeared under the heading "A Tale of Two Cities."

I could have sworn another writer got there first.

––––––––

Editor
The New York Times Book Review
Dear Sir:

For the record, I had nothing to do with the choice of the two headlines ("Joy of Sesquipedality" and "I Am Lapidary but Not Eristic When I Use Big Words") imposed on my essay on the use of long words and foreign phrases (*TNYTBR,* Nov. 30, 1986).

Yours faithfully,
WM. F. BUCKLEY, JR.

A DEFENSE OF THE USE OF UNUSUAL WORDS AND FOREIGN WORDS

One day in May I found on my desk my column, clipped from that morning's *Washington Post,* a red arrow—courtesy of my secretary—pointing to an editorial underneath it. It read, "ERISTIC: (i ris/tik) *adj* [Gr. *eristikos,* d. *erizein,* to strive, dispute d. *eris,* strife] of or provoking controversy, or given to sophistical argument and specious reasoning." I looked up to the corresponding asterisk in the text and there saw my sentence, "The action by Judge Robert Carter [in fining the National Conference of Catholic Bishops for contempt] has brought out a lot of smiles in judicial political circles (as a rule, you don't step up and fine the Catholic or the Protestant churches—or the Jewish synagogues) for failure to comply with eristic complaints." (The Abortion Rights Mobilization was suing to deny the bishops their tax deductibility, to which end it had persuaded the judge to subpoena the bishops' internal memos on abortion.) *Washington Post* editor Meg Greenfield was rapping me on the knuckles, a quite unusual public reproach: I couldn't remember when last she had thought to help the readers of the *Post* to understand unusual words, however much time she needs to spend explaining unusual editorial positions. Dear Meg, I thought. The instincts of the Jewish Mother just took her over this time.

And then, a week or two later, another clipping on my desk, red arrow, footnote, only this time it was the *Charlotte Observer,* explaining to its readers the meaning of "lapidary." (Their footnote: "Lapidary. Having the elegance and precision associated with inscriptions on monumental stones.") Presently there appeared a letter of explanation from Mr. Ed Williams, Associate Editor of the *Charlotte Observer,* and the challenge was now, well, lapidary. Mr. Williams wrote me:

"I oversee the *Observer*'s daily Viewpoint page, and in that capacity am in charge of preparing syndicated columns for publication in this newspaper. Sometimes I insert aids to the reader, such as the definition of 'lapidary' in your recent column, enclosed. A fellow editor asked why I didn't also define *à outrance.* I replied that I thought you use foreign words and phrases in your columns because 1) you like to show off, and 2) you take delight in irritating people. Far be it from me, I said, to deny you those pleasures. Then I realized I shouldn't presume to answer for you. So let me ask. Why do you use, in your column, foreign words and phrases, and unfamiliar English words, that are unlikely to be understood by the average reader, or at least the average editor? Surrounded by dictionaries, I await your reply."

The point here raised—When is it okay to use an unfamiliar word? When is it not okay?—is endlessly argued, yet even so, fresh insights and original formulations continue to be coined. One of these, I think, was Dwight Macdonald's distinction, made in his marvelous survey of Webster III for *The New Yorker* (March 10, 1962), in which he distinguished between unusual words (okay) and words that "belong in the zoo sections of the dictionary" (not okay). I should think most people would agree, for instance, that "arachibutyrophobia" would be an example of the latter (the word is said to define the fear of peanut butter's sticking to the roof of your mouth). James Jackson Kilpatrick . . . takes a position on the dogmatic side against the use of unfamiliar words and cites me, however kindly, as a prodigious offender (as it happened, the Lord delivered Kilpatrick into my hands, because his proscriptive passage against long and unusual words contained four long and unusual words). Kilpatrick likes to quote Westbrook Pegler, who denounced the use of what he called "out-of-town words."

The question, under the proximate prodding of Mr. Williams, is worth revisiting. And an easy way to begin is to examine the two words singled out for attention: the first one the word Mr. Williams thought that courtesy required him to translate for the benefit of his readers; the second, the French, which he let pass as arrant and provocative exhibitionism.

What happens when Mr. A. and Ms. B. flatly disagree about whether a word is "unusual"? Well, there is a problem of an obvious order, namely that some words are unusual but widely recognized, while others are unusual and widely unrecognized. Returning to the general theme a few weeks ago, Mr. Kilpatrick wrote in his column that he had recently published the sentence "The *Miami Herald* carried a 72-point four-column head, DADELAND IS DOYEN OF AREA MALLS." Whereafter he received a letter from a Floridian who wanted to know "How many people know what 'doyen' means?" Observed K.: "The more pertinent question: How many of the *Herald*'s 450,000 readers know what doyen means? Ten percent? 20 percent? 80 percent?" Kilpatrick is a man of troubled conscience. He goes right on to say that here he himself has just finished making reference to "72-point" type. That is workaday prose of the Dick and Jane order for anyone who has ever engaged in editorial enterprises—but what about those 450,000 readers? Might they not have preferred, K. tortures himself, "inch-high type"?

Nobody is going to pay Mr. Gallup a lot of money to find out how many people in Florida know what the word "doyen" means. And not many people would be willing to come up with a threshold percentage: *More than X know doyen?—Okay to use. Less than X, verboten* (forbidden). That's on the order of defining the line where obscenity begins.

All of which brings me to say that I do not think of "lapidary" as a word so unrecognizable as to interrupt the reading flow of the average college graduate. But in saying this it is important to reiterate one of the points I made in the public argument I had with Kilpatrick. . . . It is quite simply this, that people with vocabularies of the same size are by no means people who know the same words. A while ago I reviewed a book by John Updike (*The Coup*), discovering over twenty words the meaning of which I didn't know. Knocking these words around at an editors' session in my office one afternoon, I would find that, cumulatively, my five colleagues knew them all. Sam Johnson's apothegm, "In lapidary inscriptions a man is not upon oath," if it is not in the anthologies that circle Mr. Williams's desk, it ought to be.

But then let's take the tougher one. Here is what I wrote in a column on Professor Paul Weiss, the philosopher whose eighty-fifth birthday was something of a national event. "At Yale [Professor Weiss] was the political liberal *à outrance,* but his orderly mind made it hard for him to defend some of liberalism's zanier forms."

This, now, is concession time. How many people are familiar with *à outrance*? It is, no question about it, an out-of-town word, though Pegler certainly ran into it when he was out of town covering the war in France in 1918, where the Germans faced the French, British, and Americans, fighting their trench warfare *à outrance.* But the French word is given in Webster, an English dictionary. First, the inquirer gets plain "outrance," in

English ("the last extremity"), and then is invited to look at *à outrance,* a separate entry, that gives: "to the death, unsparingly." The OED also lists it in French, and cites uses of it by Tobias Smollett and Walter Scott. . . .

But why should a syndicated columnist use the word? I can hear Mr. Williams re-asking. Well, not really, just to show off—one doesn't "show off" one's workaday equipment. You see, that word, and a hundred or so others, are a part of my *working* vocabulary, even as a C augmented eleventh chord with a raised ninth can be said to be an operative resource of the performing jazz pianist.

Are we now closing in on the question, by using the exclusivist word "performing"?

Yes, in a way we are, I suppose. Because just as the discriminating ear greets gladly the C augmented eleventh, when just the right harmonic moment has come for it, so the fastidious eye encounters happily the word that says exactly what the writer wished not only said but conveyed, here defined as a performing writer sensitive to cadence, variety, marksmanship, accent, nuance, and drama.

What of the reader who misses the refinement? Well, what of the listener deaf to the special reach of the C augmented eleventh? That reader has the usual choices: he can ignore the word; attempt, from the context, to divine its meaning precisely or roughly (not hard, in the narrative above, on Professor Weiss's liberal politics); or he can look it up. Are these alternatives an imposition? Yes, if the newspaper's columnist that day is giving instructions on how to treat a rattlesnake bite. You would not instruct the reader to fight the poison *à outrance.*

But newspapers, in particular in one-paper cities, tend to acknowledge an obligation beyond merely reporting the news. The very idea of a "feature," whether designed to advise (Ann Landers), amuse (Art Buchwald), satirize (G. R. Trudeau), or opine (the syndicated columnist), presupposes that the performer should use the full range of his relevant skills, even if the percentage of readers who turn to that feature is reduced. Surely there is a corner, in spacy papers that carry five pages on sports, for Addison and Steele? It required a Pulitzer Prize to alert some editors to the very existence of Murray Kempton, the most entertaining analytical belletrist in town, and now we read him, hungrily, in the *Stamford Advocate.* Readers have diverse interests, resources, skills, appetites. The Latin Mass Committee in London petitioned for the resumption of a single mass to be said in Latin after the postconciliar ban of 1965, and was turned down—on the grounds that Latin was only "for the educated few." Evelyn Waugh said it all in a letter to the *Times:* "Surely," he wrote, "in all her charity, Mother Church can make a little room, even for the educated few?"

—WFB   NOVEMBER 30, 1986

Dear Mr. Buckley:

As a longtime reader of *NR,* I've enjoyed your ongoing flirtation with abstruse English words.

After learning the meaning of "deipnosophist" the other day, I realized that I had not seen it in *NR.* One would expect it to pop up all over the place.

How do you explain this lapse?

Puzzled,
HAL MUNN
ALHAMBRA, CALIF.

Dear Mr. Munn: The word defines someone "skilled at table talk." It is used rarely for the obvious reasons. Cordially,

—WFB

Dear Mr. Buckley:

". . . savoring the highbrow's *dysphemism* for the relatively inoffensive 'stupid.' " ("The Assault on Whittaker Chambers"—WFB, Jr., Dec. 15.)

No one minds recondite words, provided they *are* words, like calling Liberals "puberulent lotophagi"—but "dysphemism"! Come now, you wouldn't josh a guy!

T. RIEDER
TORONTO, ONT.

Actually, we would. But the word exists. See Merriam-Webster III, p. 712.

—WFB   JANUARY 12, 1965

Dear Mr. Buckley:

Pray tell us readers the difference between "certain inalienable rights," as I read in my copy of The Declaration, and "certain unalienable rights," as printed on page 554 of *National Review.*

Sincerely,
COLONEL FRED W. MILLER
SCOTTSDALE, ARIZONA

P.S.: My dictionary says that "inalienable" and "unalienable" are synonymous.

Dear Colonel: "Unalienable" is the word Jefferson used. "Inalienable" is what is nowadays used. "Alienable" is what describes the rights we fought for.

Cordially,
—WFB   JUNE 25, 1976

And still the requests come in, asking WFB to explain and also defend his use of words that seem to some eyes, as his diction seems to some ears, affected. This latest (1996) was written at the request of *Sky* magazine, Delta's in-flight publication. This invitation must have appeared to Buckley, who virtually invented frequent flying, a chance to arm himself against the guy in the next seat who begins a conversation fortified by three little bottles of vodka.

He also manages to make, even now, new explanations and elaborations, elaborating on "zoo" words, getting the same advice over and over about his magazine's style, etc.

WORDS

The editor, Mr. Duncan Christy, having bombarded the readers of this magazine for eleven months with words judged "unusual" taken from my opera (Dear Sir: What does he mean, "opera"? As in *Madame Butterfly?* CURIOUS. Dear Curious: He means "works." The word is the plural of opus—a creative work. Best, Ed. Dear Sir: Well, why didn't he *say* "taken from my 'works?' " CURIOUS AND ANNOYED. Dear C & A.: He was asked to write an essay about *words,* so you shouldn't be surprised if he starts out by using an unusual word. Let's hear him out, okay? Ed.), has now decided to end the regular sessions and invites me to write in general about words. "I hope such an essay would be an encomium to words, alloyed with some direct observations about why we should not let words like 'encomium' and 'belletristic' and 'valedictory' go." Well, sure, so let me get a few things off my chest, since the question of me and words has come up before.

1. Two people of the same approximate age and education won't have identical vocabularies. She will know the meaning of maybe one hundred words that he doesn't know. But he will know an equivalent number of words—or more—that puzzle her, when and if he runs into them.

2. The reader's attitude toward an unusual word often depends on the context in which it is used. Two stories hang on this point. Years ago a classmate took me delicately to one side and said, "Bill, *National Review* would have a much larger circulation if you would just forbid the use of so many arcane words." I told him it was his imagination that so many such words congested my magazine, and I made him a bet. Sight unseen, I said, here's ten dollars that the next issue of *Time* magazine will have

more words you judge unfamiliar than you can target in any back issue, take your pick, of *National Review*.

Well, you can guess I would not be telling you this story if I had lost the bet. I won it. Question, Why was my friend under an illusion that cost him ten bucks?

Explanation. If a sentence or paragraph of prose is analytical in nature, any unusual word springs out at you. If the identical word appears in a passage in which the writer is describing something, or telling a story, the eye leaps over a word otherwise arresting. Since *National Review* is a journal of opinion, most of its articles and features are, as one would expect, analytical and critical—which means that an unusual word, in a verbally demanding environment, comes at you more aggressively.

An example:

She was a ravishing beauty, from sunlit hair to the limpid eyes to the full lips, sparkling teeth, and curious, tectonic smile. What kind of smile? The reader doesn't know, exactly, and isn't going to ask, not unless whatever the writer goes on to say about the beautiful lady can't be understood without knowing what makes up a "tectonic" smile, whatever the hell that is.

In that plane the practiced eye can discern the tectonic disruptions of an early geological age. The word tectonic (*Relating to, causing, or resulting from structural deformation of the earth's crust*) reaches out at you, and you see in its eyes the candid stricture: Buddy, unless you know what a tectonic disruption means, you can't swing with me on this one. Go read something else; or if you want to, stick around and see if you can follow what comes next.

The context often establishes whether the unusual word can coast by without interrupting the reader's thought.

3. The law of the flexed muscle. The following episode is my all-time favorite. After a lecture, at dinner . . . , one man of about fifty was visibly excited by my presence. At the end of the meal he drew me to one side to disclose the reason. He belonged, it turned out, to a militant labor union to which he was required to pay dues. Every month the union newsletter featured proudly its most recent political activities on behalf of its membership. "They are *terribly* Democratic," he complained, "and I am a *Goldwater* Republican. So when I saw you come in I really cheered."

I thanked him, and then he leaned and whispered into my ear. "Let me tell you something, Mr. Buckley. I subscribed to *National Review* just a month ago. Now if you would do something about all those long words you will"—he stretched out his arms expansively—"double . . . no, *triple* your circulation.

"Do you agree with me, Mr. Buckley?"

"Yes, sure. We'll certainly try to do something about those words."

Flash forward, one year. Same man. Same dining room (different speech). He beams when he sees me. "You took my advice. It's made the magazine!"

I was carried away by the underlying meaning of it all and smiled back exultantly. I thanked him. "It was *very* good advice." (Like the waiter's, earlier.)

The moral here is really liberating. The unused muscle begins to work out. In January it hurts awfully, looking at all those unfamiliar words—like the first day of skiing, or tennis. In February, the incidence of such words is a little less, and you feel the relief. In March it still happens to you, but only now and again. By June?—yes. You feel no pain at all.

It isn't necessarily that your vocabulary has increased at a geometric rate. It is that the words you used to think of as alien and intimidating are less and less that, as they continue to crop up and your mind and imagination are gradually including them in your immediate-visibility range. If you are assigned the job of sportswriter (my sister was, age twenty-three, by United Press) you gradually get to feel at home with any number of words you simply could not have defined before. Exactly the same thing happens, or has happened, to the reader of the Sports Section. Or of the Financial Section. After a while you feel quite at home.

4. It's fair to distinguish between different categories of unusual words. (Again) as Dwight Macdonald wrote, . . . some words belong in the "zoo section" of a dictionary—i.e., the words do exist, but the need for them is so remote, you can—and should—keep them caged up in the zoo until absolutely necessary to take one out, which may be never.

On the other hand, it is important to remember that every word berthed in the dictionary is there because at some point one of three things happened. Either an objective thing or concept or abstraction came on the scene which hadn't been descried before and now just had to be given a name ("cyberspace"); or an artistic hand closed in on what had been a void and the new word survives the infidelity of the season, earning its way into the dictionary ("seakindly"); or an authoritative writer simply uses the word and such is his prestige that his mere enunciation of it validates its legitimacy ("tushery").

Leading to my conclusion, (5), which is that while we can be very firm in resisting people who spout zoo-words, one should be respectful and patient with those who exercise lovingly the wonderful opportunities of the language. I went downtown a dozen years ago to hear a black pianist about whom the word had trickled in that here was something really cool and ear-catching, besides which his name rolled about the tongue releasing intrigue and wry amusement, and so I heard Thelonious Monk. He struck some really, sure-enough *bizarre* chords, but you know, it would never have occurred to me to walk over and say, Thelonious, I am not familiar with that chord you just played. So cut it out please.

Chapter 3

The Interview

A good interview can be a good way to get acquainted. Never definitive, it can nonetheless open windows into a character, a style, ideas. The price is often a certain mangling of the language, especially if the transcript is presented verbatim. There are oral imprecisions as well as modulations in voice and body language that cannot be caught in transcriptions. But even with its limitations, in the world of modern "media," in congressional hearings, and in police stations, the interview is a ubiquitous and sometimes even useful way to get to know someone. William F. Buckley, Jr., has been interviewed innumerable times and has interviewed some of our most interesting and most consequential contemporary figures, although he makes the point that his long-lived (thirty years) television program, *Firing Line,* is not, strictly speaking, an interview show. It is, by charter, an "exchange of views." Alistair Cooke, in an admiring but not sycophantic introduction to a book of such exchanges, *On the Firing Line* (1989), refers to Buckley as "lover of the last word," while Buckley himself confesses to leaving the studio sometimes "with much on my mind, *en esprit d'escalier,* a wonderful French term describing what you wish you had said by way of devastating retort: typically a sunburst that hits you as you reach the bottom of the staircase."

An enjoyable and revealing interview was the exchange with Charlie Rose, the affable, courteous, intelligent, and handsome Carolinian, who came to public television via Bill Moyers. This generally positive opinion of Rose still holds despite the tendency of the charming interviewer to put words into other people's mouths, sometimes while they are speaking. (This interview has been edited.) The occasion was, as it often is, the publication of a new book, *Happy Days Were Here Again*.

Given the usual barter for banter with Buckley—we'll talk about your book, Mr. B., if we can also deal with your politics, controversial positions, and opinions on world affairs and world leaders—he was asked all sorts of questions, some even pertaining to the book. Notice how quickly the interview begins to turn on specific words and their meanings. Notice, too, the prescience of WFB in October 1993 on the likely return to popularity of communism in Russia and President Clinton in the United States, each much more apparent as this book is readied for publication in early 1996.

The interview also touches on a little-known contribution of Buckley's work as an editor and employer—his role as a discoverer of other writers, of varying political persuasions but undeniable gifts.

CHARLIE ROSE: Welcome to our broadcast. The columnist George Will once said about William F. Buckley, Jr., that, quote, all great biblical stories begin with Genesis. Before there was Ronald Reagan, there was Barry Goldwater. Before there was Barry Goldwater, there was the *National Review*. And before there was the *National Review*, there was Bill Buckley with a spark in his mind, and that spark in 1980 became a conflagration.

BUCKLEY: And before that there was Adam.

ROSE: [*Laughs*] . . . with a spark in his mind, too . . . Good to have you here. Lots to talk about, but let me just say why *Reflections of a Libertarian Journalist* [as a subtitle] rather than—I mean, because—are you closer to libertarian than you are conservative? With no respect for any order or any government?

BUCKLEY: The conservative movement is often thought of as composed of two parts. There are those conservatives who feel it's important not to deviate too quickly from the standing order because the implications of that can be revolutionary. And there are those others who want to hang on to what we have to the extent that it augments liberty. I'm one of the latter, rather than the former. Otherwise, you get things like conservatives in the Kremlin today threatening a return to Stalinism. So you get that misuse of the word conservative.

ROSE: That must drive conservatives crazy to know that the conservatives in the Kremlin are considered those people who want to return to Stalinism, since the battle cry for conservatives for a long time was anti-communism.

BUCKLEY: Of course, a lot of conservatives are crazy. [*Both laugh*]

ROSE: How about Republicans?

BUCKLEY: It's a nice distinction. *The New York Times* once had a real problem when they reported a news story as follows: Conservatives in the Kremlin are cracking down on books imported illegally from the West. Among the proscribed titles is *The Conscience of a Conservative* by Barry Goldwater. [*Both laugh*]

ROSE: [John Leonard] used to write for the *National Review.*

BUCKLEY: Oh, yes! I read an essay by him in 1956 in a magazine called *Ivy* in which I had an essay. I thought, "Gee, this guy can write." . . . So I called him up and said, "Mr. Leonard, would you like to work for *National Review* during the summer?" He said, "I'd like to work for it anytime since I've just been kicked out of Harvard." He was then nineteen years old, twenty years old. So he worked for us for a couple of years, and then he went to Berkeley and was radicalized.

ROSE: Garry Wills is another example of someone who came through *National Review* and then went on to seemingly reflect a very different philosophy than a Buckley libertarian philosophy or a conservative philosophy.

BUCKLEY: In the case of poor Garry, he traveled in the wrong direction. I think he wrote exclusively for us for about thirteen or fourteen years. I got a manuscript, you know . . . So I called him up and he said, well, he'd like to talk to me about it. I said, "Well, I'd love to talk to you about it." So he said, "You would have to send me the money for the ticket," so I did. He flew—it was his first flight in an airplane, first time across the Mississippi River—and he married the stewardess. And I was a proud member of the wedding party.

ROSE: And how long did he stay with you?

BUCKLEY: About ten, twelve years.

ROSE: He seems to have come to a very different place now than you are, politically. Or do you say, "I hire them for their writing ability, not for the ideology"?

BUCKLEY: Well, he happened to be a very committed conservative. He was a Catholic seminarian, and then he got a classics degree at Yale. But he was—When I knew him, he was the nearest thing I ever ran into to a sheer warmonger. He thought that the Soviet Union was a menace against which we had to consolidate and be very tough with. He was pro-McCarthy and all those good things. [*Both laugh*] Then he was radicalized at the funeral of Martin Luther King.

ROSE: By the eulogies for King, or the whole—

BUCKLEY: The whole episode. It just—

ROSE: —sense of going down the streets of Atlanta and—

BUCKLEY: It just converted him. The next thing we knew, he became sort of a flower child, grunting every time Henry Kissinger spoke. That's too bad. I don't think I have an essay on him here [in the book], do I?

ROSE: No, you don't. Do you miss not being there [at the *National Review*]? Do you miss the sense that you are no longer running the place even though you are, in the end, the ultimate, I guess, authority?

BUCKLEY: Well . . . I own it. No, I think that John O'Sullivan [the Editor] is doing a superb job.

ROSE: . . . the Clinton Administration. Give me your own assessment of this administration as it now goes forward with a number of things on its agenda: health care, reinventing government, and NAFTA—plus Bosnia on the foreign policy front.

BUCKLEY: Well, it would be difficult in a single generality to touch all four of those bases. But I think that one can say this with confidence, and that is that Mr. Clinton is a genuine statist, by which I mean he thinks of the state as the apparatus through which all reforms need to be made.

ROSE: Albeit that he wants a state that is reformed, that is more effective, that is more efficient, that is more productive—

BUCKLEY: So did Hitler. So did Stalin. [*Both laugh*] Everybody wants an efficient state. It's more fun. But the point is that he . . .

ROSE: So the state has no role for—

BUCKLEY: Well of course it has a role.

ROSE: —defense.

BUCKLEY: Adam Smith outlined its role, I think definitively, but there are people who are infatuated with the state because it becomes an instrument of their policy. And if I may say so, Charlie, this is something that tends to be distinctive to the liberal mentality because a liberal is a critic, a critic of that which is. And under the circumstances, he feels, well how can I, by simply moving my fingers, affect the shape of the clay that's spinning around there. John Kenneth Galbraith will get up in the morning and think, "How can society be bettered?" To begin with, it would be better by following his advice, but in order to exert that advice, the instrumentality of the state is indispensable. Otherwise, he has to suffer such indignities as you and I have to suffer when we do a program or write books, people can pick them up or tune in, or not. You can't decide whether to tune in on IRS. It tunes in on you.

ROSE: So Mr. Clinton is a statist and believes very much [in] using the government and believes that government should play a role in terms of bettering the citizenry, bettering the life and the quality of life and—

BUCKLEY: Yes, a critical role. Yes, he has a total appetite for using the force, the resources of government. And of course, the trouble with that is that every time one has an appetite to fix your problem through the instrumentality of the state, I am affecting his freedom because in order to do something for you, I necessarily have to use his money, or reduce his independence, or whatever. That is really the basic distinction between the libertarian and the statist.

ROSE: What do you think of him as a leader?

BUCKLEY: Well, I think more of him than the American people do. He has only a forty-one percent approval now. I think his leadership qualities are really pretty considerable. Now he's got problems. One of them is that he can't understand figures. . . . It reminds me some historian told me that Hitler was that way, that Hitler would say, "Since we came to power, the steel production used to be 54 million 490 tons. Now it's 100 million 612 tons." And in that sense, Clinton uses figures without any sense that he's on top of them, which is why there are so many contradictions and why so many people accuse him of being coy in his use of these figures. For instance, he will say, "We have effected a tax reduction in Social Security." That means he's paying, the government's paying us less. But that tax reduction—that reduction in expenditures—turns out to be an increase in tax that we have to pay. If Tricky Dick were to try that, they'd run him out of town with wet towels. So he has these problems, but those are problems which, in my judgment, he has the telegenic and theatrical resources to overcome.

ROSE: Is that the leadership quality you admire about him, the telegenic and theatrical, or is it something else that you see there that . . .

BUCKLEY: No, I'll put it this way . . . Nobody would have guessed at the equivalent period in Bush's tenure that he wouldn't be reelected. Nobody at this point believes that Clinton could be reelected. I think he might very easily be reelected because there could be a swing in national sentiment about him. It would be an act of autohypnosis by the American people, but it could happen.

ROSE: Well, let me read to you, Mr. Buckley. "President Clinton is surrounding himself with the most spectacular zoo in history. His economic advisers are the despair of the thinking world. His civil rights advisers are aberrants deserving taxonomic curiosity [*Laughs*]. He proposes to bring to the State Department someone whose views on the uses of American power perfectly reflect the utter confusion of our policies in Bosnia." That's not a ringing endorsement for reelection.

BUCKLEY: No, but I'm saying it could happen. He's very unpopular right now. I told you, he has forty-one percent, and he brings this on by this ambition to be like Noah's ark, you know: Find one of everything and stick them in the White House. So I don't withdraw that at all. Don Feder of the *Boston Herald* wrote a marvelous column in yesterday's *New York Post* in which he simply took sixteen of these characters and enumerated this sort of taxonomic curiosity. And [Clinton] does collect them. Now, whether he collects them because he has this comprehensive appetite to be surrounded by one of everything, or because he just has sort of an orientation, which is a part of his general compassion for people who have problems, it's hard to say. But it has not resulted, I think, in the creation of policies that have consolidated. Nobody will accuse anybody of having a foreign policy.

ROSE: You believe there is no foreign policy. But what was George Bush's foreign policy?

BUCKLEY: You've hit a very good point. It was not by any means something that had cohered. He kept talking about a new world order, but that new world order which one thought was to have sprung out of the seeds of the rejection of Iraq when it aggressed against Kuwait did not take hold in respect to Bosnia and Yugoslavia. There was the incursion to Somalia, which seems retrospectively to have been a bad idea.

ROSE: It sure does.

BUCKLEY: So the formulation of a new world order never happened. And I'm not sure it's at all easy to have happen.

ROSE: But do you know anybody that's articulating a new American doctrine in foreign policy . . . or who has been the architect of a new approach?

BUCKLEY: Not a new approach, no, but certainly Jeane Kirkpatrick and Henry Kissinger, for instance, and *National Review* keep insisting on, not the new, but the old.

ROSE: And the old is what? I thought the old was essentially anticommunist and support of . . .

BUCKLEY: Anti-communism was the immediate aspect of a policy that was directed towards the perpetuation of American freedom, and anti-communism necessarily superordinated over all alternatives because that was what we had to begin by doing. But the central division was the division between Woodrow Wilson and John Adams. Woodrow Wilson wanted to make the world safe for democracy, and John Adams said the American people are friends of liberty everywhere, but guardians only of their own. And JFK, of course, was very much on the Wilsonian side in his famous inaugural address, but he had to retreat from it, as did all liberals retreat from it, because Vietnam forced him to do so. So it became clear that we couldn't send the marines around everywhere, but we could at least do this: Never shrink from asserting the principles of American exceptionalism . . .

ROSE: American exceptionalism in terms of how America stands as a beacon for democracy, or how the American experience is unique in the world?

BUCKLEY: Both. Both. But the ideals of the Bill of Rights are universal; i.e., you can take the Bill of Rights and stick it anywhere in the world, and if you abide by it, you would improve the lot of the human being measured in terms of liberty.

ROSE: So . . .

BUCKLEY: So therefore, we mustn't ever, in retreating from Vietnam, come back and say, "Not only do we have no business there, who says that George Washington [was] any better than Ho Chi Minh?" But that's what they were saying in Chicago when Garry Wills was turned around; i.e., there was no difference between us and them.

ROSE: Where does that bring you on Bosnia?

BUCKLEY: Well, I think it's too late to do anything about Bosnia. I would have welcomed it if Mr. Bush had moved with lightning speed and attempted to do early what now cannot be done. However, I would have a great deal of difficulty in absolutely integrating that move in my general philosophy about the reserves, or the use of American manpower because it is not a clear, apparent—it is not a clear threat to

	American vital interests. But to a certain extent, I think foreign policy is an art.
ROSE:	And not a doctrine, and not sort of a rigid equation.
BUCKLEY:	I think it is a transcendent vision of conservatism that recognizes that sometimes government is an art. You do something because you think *noblesse oblige,* it's the thing to do. I felt that way about Somalia.
ROSE:	You thought it was the thing to do. And now, would you now acknowledge that—
BUCKLEY:	I didn't want to sit around and . . .
ROSE:	—it was fraught with more danger than you ever imagined at the time, and perhaps, having thought it was the thing to do, on—
BUCKLEY:	It didn't work.
ROSE:	—reflection, it wasn't the thing to do. Are we acknowledging mistakes here?
BUCKLEY:	I didn't want to be a member of a society with a stuffed granary and have two thousand people die every day. It is the rate at which they were dying.
ROSE:	But wouldn't the same argument apply for Bosnia? Early on?
BUCKLEY:	Yes. I would have voted in favor of a lightning strike. But Mrs. Thatcher was marvelously consistent during that entire period. All I'm saying is that it might have worked in Somalia if a particular bullet had been lucky enough to land in a particular place, but it didn't. So now we simply have another sick war.
ROSE:	If, in American politics, there is a contest—bear with me because this is hypothesis—there is a contest for the Republican nomination, knowing what you know about these two people at the height of their power, it is a contest for the Republican nomination for the presidency, and the contestants are Ronald Reagan and Margaret Thatcher. Who do you support?
BUCKLEY:	I'll tell you why I don't play games like that. Because it's like saying, "If you take the best symphony of Beethoven and the best cantata of Bach—"

ROSE: You'd go Bach.

BUCKLEY: "—which do you support?" Now, I'd say, "I can't do that. They say different things to me. I can tell you why I can prefer *King Lear* to *Macbeth*. . . . But I can't tell you whether I prefer *Macbeth* to John Milton's *Paradise Lost,* because they don't compete in my judgment. And in that sense . . . Margaret Thatcher had the whole legislative authority of the Parliament. Ronald Reagan didn't. Now what would Ronald Reagan have done if he had had the authority that Margaret Thatcher—

ROSE: Let me talk about some other personalities, too. Clinton . . . can you find yourself in agreement with what he wants to do in the health care area, and the way he wants to go about doing it?

BUCKLEY: Well, yes to the former, no to the latter. He doesn't want anything that you and I don't want.

ROSE: Health care of all Americans.

BUCKLEY: Sure. We all want that.

ROSE: As a conservative, you want that, but if it means government—I mean, can you do that without a kind of statist attitude about—this is one of those problems.

BUCKLEY: You have to look at the phenomenon and say, "Okay, on the basis of experience, what is the best way to go after the problem?" Now we're spending almost twice as much for individual health—or for individual Americans—as Great Britain is spending, and they have socialized medicine. So the answer is that we have too much medicine. The answer to "Why do we have too much medicine?" Because we overtreat ourselves. Why do we overtreat ourselves? Because there are no real attractions to the practice of medical husbandry. And the reason there aren't is that all of our bills are overwhelmingly paid for after a very minor deduction. . . . But Mr. Clinton wants to put all in one great big pot and have one great big national program. I don't think that's the way to go.

ROSE: How about NAFTA?

BUCKLEY: Well, I'm very enthusiastic about NAFTA, but there's something you've got to watch for, and that is there are some people using NAFTA as a vehicle on which to graft their favorite causes. The labor unions are trying this, to a certain extent, and the environmentalists are trying it. So that it can run, conceivably, the danger of being the terrific instrument to promote free trade, which also brings you guaranteed longevity for spotted owls, and a certain—

ROSE: No sympathy for the spotted owl?

BUCKLEY: Well, I like spotted owls, but I'm not prepared to organize my life around their longevity. [*Both laugh*]

ROSE: Around the species, even if they're endangered as a species?

BUCKLEY: An estimated ninety-nine million species are extinct, and here we are. . . .

ROSE: Ross Perot. What do you think of him? How do you explain his attraction to the American public?

BUCKLEY: I think that he is a conduit for American frustration.

ROSE: He's a vessel that everybody fills their own—

BUCKLEY: Sure. Perot is the "none of the above," the incarnation of "none of the above," and people are so dissatisfied by Congress and by the Executive and to a certain extent by the courts that they want to commit acts of *lèse majesté,* and the way to do that is to back Perot. I think he's utterly irresponsible.

ROSE: In what way?

BUCKLEY: Well, anybody who says that we're going to lose five million jobs the moment we sign NAFTA is irresponsible. He cannot prove it, can't come close to proving it. The highest estimate is two hundred thousand with however many other hundred thousand new jobs we create.

ROSE: Clinton says two hundred.

BUCKLEY: He arrives to meet the press, you know, after running for President for fourteen months, and they ask him how he would reduce the deficit, and he says, "I didn't know you were going to ask me that question. I would have brought my notes." Well, I say that I wouldn't expose myself to a session with *Meet the Press* or a session with you if I didn't have my notes in my head on a matter as critical as how would I reduce the cost of government, which he had been talking about for two years.

ROSE: Turning to the other side, the Republican Party as opposition, do you think there is a known alternative agenda coming from the Party that you belong to that is convincing? And why not?

BUCKLEY: It's in part because our government is not set up that way. In England, you have a shadow government, and that shadow government always comes in with A when you come in with B, or with Z when you come in with W. We don't do that. There isn't a, quote, leader of the Republican Party with the authority to do that. So it is a situation in which you synthesize and distill when you get closer to the nomination time for a new President. Whatever you have learned from primaries, from polls, from experiences. What the shape of the Republican platform will be in ninety-six is not yet, in my judgment, discernible.

ROSE: Do you think it ought to have most of the tenets that were reflected in the Republican convention in Houston in 1992?

BUCKLEY: [*Laughing*] I know what you're leading to. I don't think the Republican Party is going to say, "Forget about family values. Go ahead and have a happy abortion."

ROSE: I just sat on a panel with Mary Matalin, who ran the Bush campaign, who thinks that the Republican convention in Houston was a disaster for their candidate. Disaster may not be her choice of words, but . . . was not helpful.

BUCKLEY: That's an extremely interesting question, and especially interesting given the fact that one week after the convention began—

ROSE: I knew you were going to say that.

BUCKLEY: —the polls rose by fourteen points.

ROSE: That's the Pat Buchanan argument, too.

BUCKLEY: Well, it's the argument, isn't it? But what then happened [during the campaign] was that the Republicans took it on the chin, and they permitted people to say this was a declaration of civil war. Well, I don't really think it was anything of the sort. I think some of the language that was used was incautiously used, but I've never . . .

ROSE: The Buchanan speech being one prime example?

BUCKLEY: Yes.

ROSE: Just incautious language . . . ?

BUCKLEY: Well, put it this way. For anything indefensible spoken in Houston, I can give you ten indefensible statements spoken in New York.

ROSE: Like— Give me two.

BUCKLEY: Well, the notion that the whole of the decade of the eighties was designed to make people richer who were rich. That's an indefensible statement. It is not true. But if you took the whole of everything that Clinton said in the last three years . . . and tried to write an economic history based on it, you would find he was less accurate than Karl Marx.

ROSE: Do you find—having read Milton Friedman and promoted him—and he's a Nobel laureate now—but having listened to his articulation of the relation between government and economy and his economic views, when you look at the piling up of the deficit in the eighties, can you say that was good for the economic future of the country?

BUCKLEY: Of course not. But—

ROSE: I never hear you—

BUCKLEY: Well, read my book, and you will find a hundred references to it are there. The fact of the matter is that revenues under Reagan did not decrease, but expenses—

ROSE: And government . . .

BUCKLEY: —expenses increased. Now they increased actually at a lesser rate than under the three preceding Presidents. But they still continued to increase. And of course, it increases geometrically. If you compensate for inflation and do the entitlements thoroughly and have an aging population, you have that much more money [committed].

ROSE: Most economists now believe that unless you do something about entitlements, you will not deal with the deficit, and you buy that idea?

BUCKLEY: Absolutely. You can prove it mathematically. Rudman says that in the year 2004—

ROSE: Warren Rudman, the former senator.

BUCKLEY: Sorry. Only four percent of the budget at this rate will be something over which Congress has any vote.

ROSE: Everything else will be paying the interest on the debt and entitlements which are already in the law.

BUCKLEY: That's right. So something has to be done about it.

ROSE: Do you think there's a political will in the Congress, in the public today, to do it? Or what has to change to create that public will?

BUCKLEY: Well, what you run into is *force majeure*. . . . The overwhelming force is, simply, you run out of money. The only way we can ultimately get out of this debt, unless we control the rate of expenses, is through inflation. . . . There's a tricky and rather easy way to do it and that is simply capital confiscation of a percentage of what everybody owns. But if we have inflation of ten percent, we reduce our national debt by $160 billion. So that's a relatively painless way to do it, but you've mortgaged other things about your future, the kind of security that people making investments and putting up capital have to worry about.

ROSE: There's a real problem in America that we're not a saving society, that we do not save.

BUCKLEY: Yes. I disagree in the sense that the American people have been trained to believe that their pension funds, which are enormous—we're talking about three or four trillion dollars—are their savings, that plus their Social Security. So they are not encouraged to save in the sense that the Japanese are encouraged to save, who will have to look after their own needs primarily on their own. So that a lot of the squandermania that America's all about—

ROSE: There's not so much squandermania. Well, okay, we are— we consume too much and save too little, and therefore we have too little to invest in creating and making ourselves a more productive economy.

BUCKLEY: Yes, but . . . if you're a working man and you're contributing ten percent to your pension account and thirteen percent to Social Security, you might say to yourself, "Well, that's as much as I'm disposed to save." Although I'm only saving three percent [in the bank, etc.], it's three percent on top of twenty-three percent, and that's really a pretty healthy amount to save.

ROSE: I want to turn now to the book.

BUCKLEY: That's good. [*Rose laughs*]

ROSE: I knew you were waiting for that moment. You have never been to a baseball game.

BUCKLEY: That's not a major point I'm making.

ROSE: No, I know. [*Laughs*] I just want to play for a minute before we get serious.

Why not? I mean, it's part of the Ameri— You know the famous quote by Jacques Barzun: To know America, you have to know baseball.

BUCKLEY: I wasn't aware of that . . . I know Jacques Barzun . . . Well, the answer is he's obviously wrong.

ROSE: Don't you feel any . . . I mean . . . Have you ever watched a game on television?

BUCKLEY: Yes.

ROSE: Do you understand the game?

BUCKLEY: I used to play it as a boy, sure. You know, I had a debate with John Kenneth Galbraith at Harvard on Reagan. It was televised. So he called me up and he said, "You know, Buckley, you're such a dumb producer. Here you schedule this at the same time as the Super Bowl."

ROSE: And you said?

BUCKLEY: I said, "Well, you know, the truth is I had nothing to do with the scheduling. That's PBS." He said, "Nobody will see it." And so about three hours later I walked down the street and every third person, it seemed to me, said, "Gee that was interesting," or "That was terrible," or whatever. Well, the answer is there are ninety million people watching Super Bowl and ten million who don't.

ROSE: And so ten million is a pretty damn good audience! You have never had any desire to go to a game . . . I mean, does sports itself, other than skiing and sailing, have any interest to you?

BUCKLEY: I play a little tennis. Here's the thing . . . I respect baseball enough to feel this about it: that in order to enjoy it, you've got to really study it, become a fan of a club, know something about the players, and it's an enormous investment of time. So it isn't just exposure to a single game that transmutes you into a fan. It's getting into the whole ritual, and that takes a long time.

ROSE: We're now talking about a George Will kind of commitment.

BUCKLEY: That's right . . . exactly right. He would be a marvelous example, George Will, or Bart Giamatti, the late president of Yale. So I don't feel an impulse to give it that kind of time. In fact, take learning Russian. Some people say, "Well, you've got to learn Russian because you can't read Pushkin unless you make the investment."

ROSE: And you say?

BUCKLEY: Sorry, I'm going to have to read it in translation.

ROSE: When you began these wonderful sailing extravaganzas, you would take . . . for example, I think on the first long, cross-Atlantic cruise on a sailboat you took *Moby-Dick*.

BUCKLEY: You have a good memory.

ROSE: But you don't do that much anymore. You're doing other things, aren't you?

BUCKLEY: I don't get to read a lot of novels, but I am a novel reader. I get a great kick out of novels.

ROSE: How about movies? Do you go to movies?

BUCKLEY: No, I get tapes and watch them at home, which is much more comfortable, I think.

ROSE: How about writing for you, writing novels? I mean, it always amazed me that you were able to create [Blackford] Oakes and be successful at it. What does that say about— does it say that you, a former CIA operative, just had a capacity to tell a story and that's what made you successful as a spy novelist?

BUCKLEY: Well, I suppose it probably has to do also with an individual's threshold of boredom. I get bored very easily.

ROSE: So you want to move the pages along for your own—

BUCKLEY: That's right. So you're sitting there clacking away, and some people—that lovely Southern lady can write about the wisteria for seven pages . . .

ROSE: Eudora Welty?

BUCKLEY: Yes, and I love her for it, but I can't do that. I don't have those skills. So therefore, I've got to have action and words.

ROSE: Do you like John le Carré?

BUCKLEY: Yes, I do . . . I haven't read all of his novels, but I think he's a marvelous writer. But he and I have a very interesting quarrel.

ROSE: What's that?

BUCKLEY: Well, he is kind of an egalitarian. His Western spy and the Russian spy are pretty much the same.

ROSE: Same moral/ethical—

BUCKLEY: Yes. And our guy is [always] sort of a paunchy—he gets cuckolded all the time, and he drinks a lot of booze, whereas my guy is just a better human being.

ROSE: Your guy is closer to Tom Clancy's guy.

BUCKLEY: Yes. Or his guy's closer to mine.

ROSE: Since you started earlier.

BUCKLEY: That's right. So I see no reason for this kind of insistence that there isn't really basically any difference between Lyndon Johnson and Khrushchev. There's an enormous difference between them.

ROSE: He also reflects a sense that somehow there was something—even though he also was part of British intelligence, which he acknowledges now, without talking about what he did, as I guess you don't talk about whatever you did during— You acknowledge that you were—

BUCKLEY: I was blown. I didn't know it. I was—

ROSE: How were you blown?

BUCKLEY: By William Sloane Coffin, who . . .

ROSE: Who also was Yale, who went into the CIA. And he blew your cover?

BUCKLEY: Yup. I don't know how he found out about me because if I'd been captured and tortured and spilled everything I knew, I would have been able to identify one human being, who was my boss, Howard Hunt. That was the only person I knew the name of, so I don't know how Coffin found out about me. But he did. . . .

ROSE: What's interesting about this [book] is not only that this is a collection of columns . . . between the years, what, eighty-eight to ninety-two? But there is also an appreciation of some people, of Malcolm Forbes, for example. I mean—speak about Forbes. You still communicate?

BUCKLEY: Oh, sure.

ROSE: He's a good friend? A friend?

BUCKLEY: Yes, he is. Indeed. I went to that crazy party of his in Tunis.

ROSE: Morocco?

BUCKLEY: Yes. And he was given a very hard time. So I wrote a piece where I said this is a guy whose joy in life is very conspicuous consumption, but you can't fault—

ROSE: It's his money, so therefore . . . ?

BUCKLEY: Well, it's his money and there is such good nature in it. Imagine sending a plane over to bring Gorbachev in, an airplane called *Capitalist Tool*. . . . So there's kind of a joyous, utterly unashamed buoyancy about this guy that I thought very captivating.

ROSE: Speaking of Gorbachev, how will history treat him? You reflect on him in this book.

BUCKLEY: I think history will acknowledge with some gratitude that he didn't decide massively to resist change, but I don't think history will necessarily believe that he had the power to do so. . . .

ROSE: What do you think of Mr. Yeltsin?

BUCKLEY: I think Yeltsin's got a hell of a job, and he's doing on the whole well. It's nice to know that he has Gaidar back . . .

ROSE: Right. He brought him back into the government.

BUCKLEY: Yes. You know, very few people remember Gorbachev—I know this intimately because I just finished a novel about him.

ROSE: A spy novel?

BUCKLEY: Coming out in January. But he was a very bad boy for a couple of years. When he first came into power. He came to power in March 1985, and he was absolutely determined to win that war.

ROSE: In Afghanistan?

BUCKLEY: In Afghanistan. And he said about Sakharov that he was a traitor to the sacred cause of communism. Then of course later on he bailed Sakharov out. But I would say this: It's safe to say that half the people who were killed in Afghanistan were killed while he was the Premier of the Soviet Union.

ROSE: You thought Carter did the right thing in refusing, in not going to Russia for the Olympics because of the Afghanistan invasion?

BUCKLEY: Yes. I think that a country that's determined to express its opposition to something but not going to war should use whatever instruments it has that are not military. And the psychological instrument of a sports boycott is huge. South Africa, for instance, felt it enormously. So I was very much in favor of using that particular weapon. And Moscow was terrified by it. They had a great psychological stake in the success of their Moscow games.

ROSE: It would mark them as a member of the world community. And if in fact they were rejected, it would paint them in the world community as the, to use the expression of a friend of yours, "Evil Empire."

BUCKLEY: You're exactly correct. And of course, the invasion of Afghanistan was the great big rupture in the accepted notion that the expansionism of the Soviet Union was done. Arthur Schlesinger and all of our resident pundits had told us that we didn't have to worry about this anymore. [The Soviets] had expanded as far as they wanted to go.

ROSE: They'd lost their expansionist urge? There was no more imperialism in the Soviets?

BUCKLEY: The doctrine of containment had worked. But there we were now with a brand-new aggression, and the implications of it were enormous. I think almost certainly on account of it that we succeeded under Mr. Reagan in deploying those theater weapons in eighty-three and eighty-four.

ROSE: Other than your father, tell me the three or four people that you think have had profound influence, on you, on your own personal and intellectual development.

BUCKLEY: Well, Mark and Paul and Matthew. That's three.

ROSE: By the way, you're writing a new book on Catholicism, aren't you? Have you finished it?

BUCKLEY: No, I've started it.

ROSE: What is it to be? An affirmation? A sort of Malcolm Muggeridge type affirmation of Christianity and Catholicism?

BUCKLEY: Just a little book you can consult when you need to see how much of a sinner you are. When you need a quick reading. [*Both laugh*]

ROSE: What's the church meant to you? And when Pope John the Twenty-third talks about liberation theology, you're right there with him.

BUCKLEY: Oh, John Paul the Second. I'm not only with him, I've anticipated him.

ROSE: You mean he's been reading Buckley?

BUCKLEY: We talked about liberation theology before he got around to it. Liberation theology was an effort to transmute Marxism into a theologically acceptable formula, and as such its principal spokesman was Bishop Arns of Rio de Janeiro. Incidentally, one of the nicest people in the whole world. I had him on my program. He's so damned nice, and he said these absolutely preposterous things, but he says them with such a benign smile.

ROSE: Speaking of this, it reminds me. They just had a big meeting of the Christian Coalition. I think, you know, a lot of people are worried about their influence on American politics. Do you worry about that at all?

BUCKLEY: Charlie, if every single thing that the Christian Coalition wants were done tomorrow, I would not recognize any difference between the society I lived in and the society I grew up in. But I don't think of myself as having been manumitted by the Warren Court. When I was at school, I could do everything that I wanted to. So I wouldn't be able to buy whisky on Sundays or buy pornographic literature as easily. Beyond that, what is it that they want to do that should upset me so?

ROSE: Well, their views on abortion are similar to your views on abortion.

BUCKLEY: Abortion is probably the interesting exception, although as you know, illegal abortions reached up to six or seven hundred thousand per year pre–Roe *v.* Wade. Now they're doubled. So it's inconceivable that in my lifetime or probably in yours, people who want an abortion won't get one pretty easily. But beyond that, what's all the fuss about? *Hustler* magazine?

ROSE: Well, no, I think the fuss is probably the belief among a number of people that there's too much of an intrusion . . . the Christian Coalition . . . notion being intolerant of another group's beliefs and values—

BUCKLEY: But we should be.

ROSE: —and therefore want to impose their values on them.

BUCKLEY: You should.

ROSE: You should be intolerant of another group's values?

BUCKLEY: Absolutely. The principal progress we've made in . . . civil rights is to be intolerant towards people who don't respect other people's rights. So that if somebody is anti-Semitic or if somebody is anti-black to the extent of manifesting it, intolerance of behavior of that kind is the principal force for change. Thomas Jefferson said laws are much less important than opinion because laws merely codify opinion. So to be intolerant of people who have illegitimate children every ten months is something we're very much behind on.

ROSE: But suppose the intolerance is of people who don't have the same religious view you have. Not whether they're anti-Semitic, not whether they're anti-black . . .

BUCKLEY: Name me one . . .

ROSE: —or the same sense of tolerance for— You know where the argument goes.

BUCKLEY: Name me one human being I've heard of who would limit the right of anybody I know of to practice his religion except perhaps to the extent that it implied polygamy or human sacrifice.

ROSE: Okay then, speaking of that, your political hero Barry Goldwater, who you supported early, has been very outspoken in arguing for the right of gays in the military. Do you part company—

BUCKLEY: Now why are you shifting around? I asked you to talk about the subject that you raised, namely the threat to the practice of other people's religion.

ROSE: What I'm doing is going through the engagement of the tolerance of the rights of minorities and tolerance—

BUCKLEY: Well, do me the favor—

ROSE: —and tolerance for minorities.

BUCKLEY: Well, do me the favor of saying, Bill, I retreat on that question because you were right. There is no threat to any other religion posed in the activity of the Christian Coalition.

ROSE: Well, I don't want to say that specifically about the Coalition without knowing everything—I don't know enough about all the things that the Christian Coalition believe and don't believe . . .

BUCKLEY: Don't you think you would have heard about it if one of them said, "We want to close down all synagogues"?

ROSE: Well, of course they're not saying something like that.

BUCKLEY: Well, then what are you talking about?

ROSE: But the point I raised about the tolerance in terms of the tolerance of other people's political—other people's religious views if they're not—it's not part of the Judeo-Christian tradition, that kind of thing.

BUCKLEY: Well, I don't know anybody who proposes the persecution of another denomination. I know some people who think you will go to hell if you don't become a Unitarian or a Catholic or whatever, but as long as this is a private, theological conviction . . .

ROSE: Can I go on to Barry Goldwater? Do you differ with him with respect to gays in the military?

BUCKLEY: Yes. Here's the principal error that he made . . . The people who wanted things to be different in the military in respect of gays had reached an accommodation with people who didn't want it to be different. And that was a formula that says, "Okay, we won't ask them whether they're gay and persecute them if we find out that they are gay; however, if they practice gay activity which we think is inconsistent with the correct deportment of the military, then we will let them out. Honorable discharge, not dishonorable discharge." Now that had been agreed on when Barry came in, Senator Goldwater came in and said, "No. Let's go back and start from scratch." And so he resubmitted in effect the Clinton proposals and in doing so in my judgment polarized the forces. He was speaking at this point not as a diplomat or as a politician, but speaking as a fundamentalist moralist, and he should have made that statement in January, not in June after fourteen agonized weeks of trying to come to a conciliation. . . .

ROSE: Well, you know what I thought about it? I thought, regardless of the issue, I just liked seeing him out there being as outspoken and as frank as he was even when he was going against the grain of what might have been expected.

BUCKLEY: He's one of my favorite people.

ROSE: For that reason. I know.

BUCKLEY: Yes. He came to my concert in Phoenix two or three years ago.

ROSE: Harpsichord concert?

BUCKLEY: Yes. And a reporter stopped him and said, "What'd you think of it?" And he said, "Terrific. Terrific. Of course, this is the first time I've ever been to a concert." Only Barry Goldwater would have the guts to say that at age eighty-two. . . .

                                              —OCTOBER 12, 1993

————

One has to be careful when interviewing Buckley; if your questions are good enough, you could get hired. As did this young woman, whose interview ran on August 17, 1979, and not long after, she became a full-time assistant editor of *National Review.* She is now a syndicated columnist.

————

Mona Charen, a New Yorker, graduated this spring from Columbia University. While there, she conducted an interview for the yearbook, *The Columbian,* with WFB—from which the following are excerpts:

Q. Lionel Trilling has written in *The Liberal Imagination:* ". . . the conservative impulse and the reactionary impulse do not, with some isolated and some ecclesiastical exceptions, express themselves in ideas but only in action or in irritable mental gestures which seek to resemble ideas." As you survey your colleagues on the Right, how much truth do you find in this assertion?

A. Not much. Trilling is correct only in the sense that conservatives are guided substantially by prescriptive reactions. One can, for example, register a disapproval of the proliferation of pornography without experiencing the necessity to externalize one's thoughts in theoretical parades. The liberals, on the whole, would rather write than think; let alone act.

Q. But if conservatives do not "experience the necessity to externalize [their] thoughts in theoretical parades," a few explanations present themselves. Either conservatives are mostly inarticulate, conservatives are complacent, or conservatives are somehow incapable of abstract theorizing.

A. I think it is correct to say about conservatives as a class that they engage less in abstract theorizing than ideologues or schematizers . . .

Q. Conservatives are distinct from ideologues?

A. I think so. Those conservatives who are ideologues are not conservatives, they're abstractionists. Burke's mistrust of schematism was a conscious preference, a thought that was guided by an accumulation of experience, and a transcendent morality. Now, I don't think anybody would accuse Burke of being inarticulate. A conservative in my judgment is guided less by absolutes than by presumptions. That is to say, there is a presumption against state interference, not an absolute law.

Q. All things considered, do you now regret having introduced Henry Kissinger to Richard Nixon?

A. No. Kissinger was the best of Nixon's advisers. An adviser who would have counseled Nixon to do what I wish he had done would probably have got him impeached before Howard Hunt got out of bed.

Q. Taking into account your temperament, which you have acknowledged to be something other than conservative, if you were an influential pundit in 1776, would you have been a Tory or a rebel?

A. Hard to say. I am easily irritated, and would probably have found His Majesty's interventions intolerable. On the other hand, I'd have looked for organic solutions. I'd have found little in common with Sam Adams, much in common with John.

Q. It is widely believed that three of the thinkers who have most influenced the intellectual life of the twentieth century were Freud, Marx, and Darwin. If you were granted the power retroactively to silence anyone of your choosing, would the work of any of the above troublemakers survive?

A. I am not disturbed by anyone's work. Only by how it is received. The problem is not heresy, but invincible ignorance.

Q. Well, leaving Marx aside, in what sense are Freud and Darwin heretics? From what orthodoxy do they depart?

A. The principal trouble with Freud and Darwin is really the trouble with their exegetes. This is particularly true of Darwin—a little less so of Freud; that is to say, Freud went a long way in constructing theological absolutes centered on himself . . .

Q. Theological?

A. I call it theological in the sense that he really calls upon you to have a faith which is non-empirical. I think "theological" as a metaphor is perfectly suited to Freudians who insist that there is *a* Freudian answer to all those enigmas, even as Ayn Rand believes the same thing about herself. It would be a word which would upset both of them, since they don't consider themselves to be theological about anything.

Q. In what ways would your life have been different if you had been born female?

A. I'd have seduced John Kenneth Galbraith and spared the world much pain.

Q. Who is your most formidable debating opponent?

A. Well, I've been asked that a hundred times as you can imagine, and I can't answer it. Different people have different strengths, and some of the people who are most formidable are very poor debaters.

Q. But they are formidable; why?

A. Because they have a way of appealing to an audience. You know the injunction you should never fence with an amateur because he'll likely kill you? He doesn't know the rules.

Ramsey Clark is really very maladroit as a debater, but almost certainly he would win any debate with me. You know, he puts on that humble-pie business, "I really believe in free speech. I know you-all don't agree with me, but I really respect your right, and gosh, I'm not cocksure. Why I go to bed every night thinkin' maybe I just made a lot of wrong decisions . . ." And you see these Ph.D.s and college students cheering lustily. Nixon, by the way, pulled that at the Oxford Union. He had those people cheering after the most intellectually disreputable performance I've seen in a lifetime of watching people debate.

So all I ask is that people who vote against me in debate have a hangover the next morning.

Q. Nabokov once described the "pen-poised pause." Do you ever stop in midsentence when writing and tap your pen on the desk, searching for the right word?

A. Seldom. Although occasionally I'll have trouble thinking of a word I know exists and it drives me nuts. Just the other day I couldn't recall for the life of me the word "reincarnation."

———

One of the exceptions to the no-interview format of *Firing Line* was when Buckley met Borges. The result was impressive—WFB's restraint and unabashed admiration, Borges's quiet eloquence, accomplishments, and dignity. (This is from WFB's book *On the Firing Line: The Public Lives of Our Public Figures.*)

———

Borges and Buckley: A Conversation

And, finally, a gentle titan.

Jorge Luis Borges (1899–1986) was living in Buenos Aires. I had lunched with him a few years earlier in Boston while he was visiting professor at Harvard. . . . Borges was already blind. He did not mind it, he said, because now he could "live his dreams with less distraction."

He took early to his craft, translating at age six from English into Spanish Oscar Wilde's demanding *The Happy Prince.* That translation was thought to have been the work of his father, and was used as a school text. He began to publish in the twenties—poems, essays, short works of fiction. In the late thirties he got his first job, as a menial assistant in a library.

When General Perón, against whom Borges had signed a declaration, was ousted, Borges was made director of the National Library. He traveled and lectured extensively, and was for decades the writer who for some unknown reason had not been awarded the Nobel Prize.

We met in Buenos Aires, in 1977, during the reign of the military junta. He seemed astonishingly frail, but he spoke without hesitation.

I did not interrupt him. The following pages I think of as the fairest ever minted by *Firing Line*.

WFB: You have been compared to both Milton and Homer in terms of a highly illuminated internal vision. Is this a correct judgment, as far as you're concerned?

BORGES: Well, I do my best to think it a correct judgment. At least, I try to put up with blindness. Of course, when you are blind, time flows in a different way. It flows, let's say, on an easy slope. I have sometimes spent sleepless nights—night before last, for example—but I didn't really feel especially unhappy about it, because time was sliding down that— was flowing down that easy slope.

WFB: You mean, you'd have felt more *un*happy if you *had* been able to see?

BORGES: Oh yes, of course I would.

WFB: Why?

BORGES: I can't very well explain it. These are the thoughts of years. When I first went blind—I mean, for reading purposes—I felt very unhappy. But now I feel that being blind is, let's say, part of my world. I suppose that happens. One's heard about it. When one is in jail, one thinks of being in jail as part of one's world; when one is sick, also.

WFB: How do you refresh yourself, as someone who is blind?

BORGES: I'm reading all the time. I'm having books reread to me. I do very little contemporary reading. But I'm only going back to certain writers, and among those writers I would like to mention an American writer. I would like to mention Emerson. I think of Emerson not only as a great prose writer—everybody knows that—but a very fine intellectual poet, as the only intellectual poet who had any *ideas*. Emerson was brimming over with ideas.

WFB: Well, you did a great deal to reintroduce many Americans to many American writers, including Emerson, isn't that correct?

BORGES: Yes, yes. I've done my best. Emerson and also another writer I greatly love.

WFB: Hawthorne?

BORGES: Well, but in Hawthorne—what I dislike about Hawthorne is, he was always writing fables. In the case of Poe, well, you get tales; but there was no moral tagged on to them. But I think of Melville, one of the great writers of the world, no?

WFB: How do you account for the failure of Melville to achieve any recognition during his lifetime, any significant recognition?

BORGES: Because people thought of him as writing travel books. I have the 1911 edition of the Encyclopaedia Britannica. There's an article about Melville, and they speak of him much in the same way as they might speak about Captain [Frederick] Marryat, for example, or other writers. Melville wrote many travel books; people thought of him as writing in that way, so they couldn't see all that *Moby-Dick; or, The Whale*, meant.

WFB: Yes. Well now, you say that you spend most of your time reading the older writers. Is it because you reject the new writers, or because you choose to continue to be unfamiliar with them?

BORGES: I am afraid that I'd find the new writers more or less like myself.

WFB: You won't.

BORGES: I suppose I will. I suppose all contemporaries are more or less alike, no? Since I dislike what I write, I prefer going back to the nineteenth, to the eighteenth century, and then, of course, also going back to the Romans, since I have no Greek, but I had Latin. Of course, my Latin is very rusty. But still, as I once wrote, to have forgotten Latin is already, in itself, a gift. To have known Latin and to have forgotten it is something that sticks to you somehow. I have done most of my reading in English. I read very little in Spanish. I was educated practically in my father's library, and that comprised English books. So that when I think of the Bible, I think of the King James Bible. When I think of the *Arabian Nights,* I think of Lane's translation, or of Captain Burton's translation. When I think of Persian literature, I think in terms of Browne's *Literary History of Persia,* and of course of FitzGerald's. And, frankly, I remember the first book I read on the history of South America was Prescott's [*History of*] *the Conquest of Peru.*

WFB: Is that right?

BORGES: Yes, and then I fell back on Spanish writers, but I have done most of my reading in English. I find English a far finer language than Spanish.

WFB: Why?

BORGES: There are many reasons. Firstly, English is both a Germanic and a Latin language, those two registers. For any idea you take, you have two words. Those words do not mean exactly the same. For example, if I say "regal," it's not exactly the same thing as saying "kingly." Or if I say "fraternal," it's not saying the same as "brotherly"; [then there is] "dark" and "obscure." Those words are different. It would make all the difference—speaking, for example, of the Holy Spirit—it would make all the difference in the world in a poem if I wrote about the Holy Spirit or I wrote "the Holy Ghost," since "ghost" is a fine, dark Saxon word, while "spirit" is a light Latin word.

And then there is another reason. The reason is that I think that of all languages, English is the most *physical* of all languages. You can, for example, say "He loomed over." You can't very well say that in Spanish.

WFB: *Asomo?*

BORGES: No; they're not exactly the same. And then, in English you can do almost anything with verbs and prepositions. For example, to "laugh off," to "dream away." Those things can't be said in Spanish. To "live down" something, to "live up to" something. You can't say those things in Spanish. I suppose they can be said in German, although my German really isn't too good. I taught myself German for the sake of reading Schopenhauer in the [original] text. That was way back in 1916. I had read Schopenhauer in English; I was greatly attracted to Schopenhauer, and then I thought I would try to read him in the text and then I taught myself German. And at long last I read *Die Welt als Wille und Vorstellung* in the text, and *Parerga und Paralipomena* also.

WFB: Do you write your poetry in English or in Spanish?

BORGES: No, I respect English too much. I write it in Spanish.

WFB: . . . Do you personally pass on the translations, or do you simply entrust them to people like Kerrigan or di Giovanni?

BORGES: No, I have people like Alistair Reid, di Giovanni, and Kerrigan, who are greatly better than I am at my texts. And then of course in Spanish words are far too cumbersome. They're far too long. For example, if you take an English adverb, or two English adverbs—you say for instance "quickly," "slowly," and then the stress falls on the significant part of the word. *Quick*-ly. *Slow*-ly. But if you say it in Spanish, you say "lenta*mente*," "rapida*mente*." And then the stress falls on the *non*significant part. And all that makes a very cumbersome language. But still, Spanish is my destiny; it's my *fate,* and I have to do what I can with Spanish.

WFB: Well, does the fact that the Spanish language is less resourceful than the English language necessarily make it less complete as poetry?

BORGES: No. I think that when poetry is achieved, it can be achieved in *any* language. It's more than a fine Spanish verse that could hardly be translated to another language. It would turn to something else. But when *beauty* happens, well, there it is. No?

What Whistler said—people were discussing art in Paris. People spoke about, well, the influence of *heredity, tradition, environment,* and so on. And then Whistler said, in his lazy way, "Art happens." "Art *happens*," he said. And I think that's true. I should say that *beauty* happens.

Sometimes I think that beauty is not something rare. I think beauty is happening *all* the time. *Art* is happening all the time. At some conversation a man may say a very fine thing, not being aware of it. I am hearing fine sentences all the time from the man in the street, for example. From anybody.

WFB: So you consider yourself a transcriber, to a certain extent.

BORGES: Yes, in a sense I do, and I think that I have written some fine lines, of course. *Everybody* has written some fine lines. That's not *my* privilege. If you're a writer you're bound to write something fine, at least now and then, off and on.

WFB: Even Longfellow?

BORGES: Longfellow has some very beautiful lines. I'm very old-fashioned, but I *like* "This is the forest primeval. The murmuring pines and the hemlocks." That's a very fine line. I don't know why people look down on Longfellow.

WFB: Is it in your experience possible to stimulate a love of literature, or is it something that also just happens, or doesn't happen? Is it possible to take twenty people and make them love literature more?

BORGES: Of course. I was a professor of English and American literature during some twenty years, at the University of Buenos Aires.

WFB: That's why I asked you.

BORGES: And I tried to teach my students not literature—that can't be taught—but the *love* of literature. And I have sometimes succeeded, and failed many times over, of course. If the course has to be done in four months, I can do very little. But still I know there are many young men in Buenos Aires—maybe they're not so young now—young men and young women, who have their memories full of English verse. And I have been studying Old English and Old Norse for the last twenty years. And I have also taught many people the love of Old English.

WFB: And so there is a pedagogical art? It isn't simply a matter of—

BORGES: But I think literature is being taught in the wrong way all the time. It's being taught in terms of history and of sociology. And I wouldn't do that. I have seen many teachers who are always falling back on dates, on place names.

WFB: You don't do that?

BORGES: I do my best to avoid it.

WFB: On the grounds that it is distracting?

BORGES: Yes, of course. Yes, I feel that it's irrelevant. For example, if I give you a beautiful line of verse, that verse should be as beautiful today as it was centuries ago. Or had it been written today, it should be beautiful also.

WFB: Well, doesn't the context in which you read it attach a certain meaning to it?

BORGES: Yes, but I suppose if a line is beautiful, the context can be safely forgotten, no? If I say, for example, that "the moon is the mirror of time," that's a fine metaphor, don't you think?

WFB: Yes.

BORGES: A mirror as being something round; it can be easily broken; and yet somehow the moon is as old as time, or half as old as time. Now, were I to add that that comes from Persian poetry, it wouldn't really add to the beauty. Perhaps it might add in a certain way. But still, had that metaphor been invented this morning, it would be a fine metaphor, no? The moon, the mirror of time? It happens to be a Persian metaphor.

WFB: But certain things are accepted as beautiful in part depending on the prevailing style. The kind of enthusiasm, for instance, that was shown for Restoration comedy. Some of that stuff isn't very funny now. Some of the romantic excesses of the nineteenth century aren't—

BORGES: But I suppose all that's rather artificial, no? That's one of the reasons why I'm so fond of Old English poetry. Nobody knows anything whatever about the poets [other than] the century they wrote in, and yet I find something very stirring about Old English poetry.

WFB: It has to stand on its own two feet, you mean?

BORGES: It has to. Or maybe because I like the sound of it. "Maeg ic be me sylfum sothgied wrecan,/Sithas secgan"—now, those sounds have a *ring* to them.

WFB: What does that say? What does that mean in dollars?

BORGES: That would say—in dollars that would be: "I can utter a true song about myself. I can tell of my travels." That sounds like Walt Whitman, no? That was written in the ninth century in Northumberland. "Maeg ic be me sylfum sothgied wrecan,/Sithas secgan"—and Ezra Pound translated it as this (I think it's a rather uncouth translation): "May I for my own sake song's truth reckon, journey's jargon." Well, that's too much of a jargon to *me*, no? Of course, he's translating the sounds. "Maeg ic be me sylfum sothgied wrecan,/Sithas secgan"—"May I for my sake song's truth reckon,"—"sothgied wrecan." He's translating the sounds more than the sense. And then "Sithas secgan"—"tell of my travels"—he translates "journey's jargon," which is rather uncouth, at least to me.

WFB: Whose translation did you say?

BORGES: It's Ezra Pound's translation. From the Anglo-Saxon, yes.

WFB: How would you have translated . . .

BORGES: I would translate it literally. "I can utter, I can say a true song about myself. I can tell my travels." I think that should be enough.

English can receive no higher tribute than that it was so loved by such a man, who used it from time to time to tell of his travels, in the world, and in his mind.

—WFB

Chapter 4

Usage II:
The Great
Who/Whom Wars
& Other
Matters

Herewith, some salvos from ancient, continuing wars, not only on *who/whom* but on the dispensable *the;* on *was/were* and the fading subjunctive; plus a ukase from Editor Bill which produces more than the usual number of demurrers, comma comments, plus a volley on *that/which,* than which there can be no thornier ambush. A welcome note on verbosity ends this short engagement, just in time.

Dear Mr. Buckley:

Reverting to James Burnham's objection to the "whom" in the *National Review* poll, "Please list the five men whom—as of right now—you consider the *leaders* contending for the Republican Presidential nomination . . .": I take it that "to be the leaders" is what this would say, expanded. And may I remind Mr. Burnham that the subject of an infinitive is in the accusative case? So you are, as always, right and impeccable.

MARION H. SAMSON

ABILENE, TEX.   DECEMBER 12, 1967

Re The Great Who/Whom Controversy, the subject of an infinitive is indeed in the accusative case—*except* if the infinitive is copulative. So Mr. Burnham is right. It should be "who," because "to be" is implied.

NEIL MCCAFFREY

PELHAM MANOR, N.Y.

(DECEMBER 26, 1967)

Dear Mr. Buckley:

Re The Great Who/Whom Controversy and Neil McCaffrey's letter [Dec. 26], I doubt many authorities will consider he to be correct.

CHARLES M. BARRACK

BAKERSFIELD, CAL.

. . . Grammatically, Mr. B. is wrong and the editor, right. However, "whom" is fighting a losing battle, especially in spoken English; e.g., *Who* do you mean? *Who* did you speak to? *Who* did you say I should see? All grammatically incorrect but normal in spoken English. So, Mr. B. has spoken usage on his side.

J. P. EGAN

BROOKLYN, N.Y.   JANUARY 30, 1968

Dear Mr. Buckley:

The contributors to, and the editors of, *National Review* all write in a lively, natural, easy style. Why must they be so damn prissy about such trivialities as who *vs* whom? And you are not always impeccable: I remember that the list of contributors on your cover once ended with "and etc."

RICHARD D. MULLEN

TERRE HAUTE, IND.

Correspondence on this topic is now closed.

—ED. [WFB]

———

But, of course, it wasn't.
  —Ed. (of this book)

———

Dear Mr. Buckley:

Since you often seem to be the American Grammar Clearinghouse, I wanted to ask you about this sentence I recently saw. "Who are risking their lives?" This sounds awkward, but I can't figure out why. "Who are they?" and, "They are risking their lives," are both correct as far as I can tell, but combined they sound very bad. Is this a proper, simply unusual, construction, or is there something subtly wrong with it?

Humbly,

BRUCE L. HOLDER

BOULDER, COLO.

Dear Mr. Holder: Why not? "They are risking their lives for world revolution." "*Who* are risking their lives?" "The Marx Brothers." OK? Cordially,

—WFB   JULY 21, 1978

Dear Mr. Buckley:

It has bothered me for years to see or hear people, including real pros like you, using the relative pronoun "that" in place of the personal pronoun "who," when the pronoun is referring to a person as opposed to a thing. An example would be "Henry was the only person that wore black to the funeral." I guess it's perfectly good grammar but it still grates on me. Am I being a silly old perfectionist?

A Faithful Follower,

HARRY BIRCHARD, CPA (RTD.)

WEST CHESTER, PA.

Dear Mr. Birchard: Waal, it's not *that* easy. Herewith a fragment from Evans (Bergen and Cornelia), page 505: "During the seventeenth century *that* almost disappeared from literary English and *who* replaced *which* as a relative referring to persons. But by 1700 *that* was coming into favor again. At first many educated people considered it a vulgar innovation. The *Spectator* of May 30, 1711, published a 'Humble Petition of *Who* and *Which* against the upstart Jack Sprat *That*,' in which *Who* and *Which* say: 'We are descended of ancient Families, and kept up our Dignity and Honor many Years till the Jacksprat *That* supplanted us.' Actually, they were the intruders and eventually *that* regained its old position. In the Authorized Revision of the Bible (published in 1885) we find *Our Father that art in heaven,* the form that had been used in the Wycliffe translation of 1389. Today we make a distinction between *who* and *which,* and use *who* in speaking of persons and *which* in speaking of anything subhuman. *That* is generally preferred to *which* where both words are possible, but many people prefer *who* to *that* when the reference is to a person. Twentieth-century translations of the Bible are likely to read, *Our Father who art in heaven.*" It does go on, does it not? Cordially,

        —WFB   NOVEMBER 2, 1992

MEMO TO: C. H. Simonds [assistant editor of *NR*]
FROM: WFB
 Who had does not contract to "*who'd.*"
 He has does not contract to "*he's.*"

MEMO TO: WFB
FROM: C. H. Simonds
 Subject: Lines to the man who succeeded, after sixteen years of education had failed, in teaching me the difference (I forget it just now) between "which" and "that"; and who has just called yet another failing to my horrified attention . . .

> *What'd I do widout Buckley?*
> *He's wonderful—really, he's swell!*
> *If he wasn't here, who'd do that voodoo*
> *(Or voo'd who?) that he do so well?*
> *When I "who'd" where I'd ought to've "who had";*
> *When, seized by the sleazes, I "he's";*
> *A missive descends*
>   *(It never offends);*
>   *I never defend,*
>   *But promise to mend;*
>   *To avoid future howlers*
>   *I brush up on Fowler's—*
> *But way down deep I mourn Bill's actions:*
> *He lacks the courage of my contractions.*

            DECEMBER 31, 1971

Dear Sirs:
Re "Notes & Asides," Dec. 31:
 "*Who had* does not contract to '*who'd.*'"
 "*He has* does not contract to '*he's.*' "???
 If, as I suspect, "Good English" comprises, inter alia, widely accepted locutions that would not cause the linguistically sophisticated instinctively to recoil, and "Bad English" those that would (e.g., "he flaunted all the rules"; "he is one of those people who does . . ."; "Charles' book"; "the spitting image"; "he inferred in his letter that he would arrive next week"; "he said that, very soon, that he would make an announcement . . ."; "he

used to always and emphatically say that . . ."; etc.), then I think you are wrong about "he's" and "who'd."

"He has got the whole world in His hands"? No! "He's had too much to drink"—yes; "he has had too much to drink" is awkward and unnatural in conversation. "He's been here for a week"—sorry, I don't recoil. Unless "I've" (as in "I've had enough, thanks"), we've (as in "we've been looking all over for you"), and "you've" (as in "you've changed quite a bit") are not part of our language, then, surely and logically, "he's" is a proper contraction for "he has."

"Who'd ever heard of Pearl Harbor before December 7, 1941?" "He's the man who'd warned us of it long before it happened." OED to the contrary notwithstanding, my not-entirely-insensitive ear is not offended by these sentences.

My failure to cite dozens of additional examples of the proper use of "he's" for "he has" and "who'd" for "who had" should be regarded as merely aposiopetic.

With best regards,
ROBERT J. CAHN
NEW YORK, N.Y.

Dear Mr. Cahn: Correct. I should have said, "Does not *normally* contract to he's."

—WFB   MARCH 3, 1972

One little misuse of a word by Buckley can provoke hundreds of words by a word-sensitive correspondent. In the following instance, a casual *momentarily* produced reams of the letter writer's unfavorite things.

Dear Mr. Buckley:
Only one American in five hundred knows the correct meaning of the word "momentarily." I have learned with amazement that you are among the four hundred ninety-nine.

In one of your newspaper columns I have read the statement that "Congress will close momentarily." Well, there is only one way that Congress might close momentarily; its members would have to leave their legislative chambers for just a minute—and then come right back again!

At one time, sleazy blunders in word usage could spread only slowly and sometimes died out before they got very far. But with press, radio and television, such errors are disseminated with the same frightening celerity as the spreading of wheat-rust by the wind. Let a popular columnist or commentator deliver himself of a blooper in New York and the next day his colleagues are inflicting his error upon the multitudes in Chicago, Atlanta, Dallas and LA.

Here is a collection of ghastly locutions which have made me grind my teeth for years.

a) "Senators and congressmen." This absurdity is employed thousands of times a year in print and on the air.

b) "Border-states." When a foreign visitor sees a reference to the "border-states" in one of our papers, he assumes inevitably that it refers to those commonwealths which touch Canada or Mexico. But no, it pertains to a group of states in the *middle* of the country (Delaware, Maryland, West Virginia, Kentucky, Missouri). The bewildered foreigner is bound to ask: Border of *what?* Well, that's what I want to know. It's true, these states touched the Southern Confederacy. But the Confederacy lasted only four years and perished more than a century ago. Apparently to a lot of journalists and editors, American history came to a stop in 1865.

c) "Underprivileged." The origin of this preposterous barbarism is an etymological mystery of the first class. It must have been put together by a genius in a nut-house. In order to appreciate its inanity, try to think of a dialogue between yourself and a friend.

The friend says he feels sorry for slum-dwellers because they are "underprivileged." You reply: "Well, perhaps you'd like them to become 'overprivileged.'" Your friend thinks about it for a moment and says: "No, I don't expect that." You then remark: "Then perhaps you'd like them merely to be privileged." When the impact of that strikes him, he probably can see the absurdity of applying the word "privileged" in any form to slum-dwellers. It's as nonsensical and contradictory as the Marxian slogan "dictatorship of the proletariat." Or the statement that Stalin invented "the cult of personality," an expression which probably means something in Russian but certainly means nothing in English.

d) "Ethnic." This word is a perfectly good adjective which has been turned into a noun by politicians and their dim-witted journalistic attendants. Then to make things worse, this bastard-noun is applied (with patronizing disparagement) to those Americans who belong to cultural and racial minorities. This is another idiocy which must have come straight from an asylum.

e) "Lugshury." One of the most repulsive nuisances of our time is the broadcasting-pitchman who rhapsodizes over the "lugshury" of consuming this or that commodity. Any advertiser who says "lugshury" is a "lug" himself and ought to be met by a necktie-party as he leaves the studio.

I dream of a constitutional amendment which would require the courts to impose a heavy fine upon any politician or publicist who thinks that "momentarily" is a synonym for "soon." . . . Very truly yours,

PATRICK B. HENRICKSON

Aw, lay off, fellas.

—WFB   JANUARY 19, 1973

Dear Mr. Buckley:

On April 15, 1987, an article of yours appeared in the *Los Angeles Daily News,* "Moralist Rooney plays Solomon," in which is this clause: "We would be morally engaged in the question if it was a Tobacco Road situation." The context and your sentence following the clause above make it quite clear that the condition is contrary to fact. Why, then, did you use *was* instead of *were?*

I know of the gradual disappearance of the subjunctive mood but have had no reason to think that the contrary-to-fact condition has joined the demise. At last printings, both Follett and Crews held with *were,* Follett considering the usage to be a dividing line between educated and uneducated speakers.

In short, why did you use *was?*

Sincerely,

DAVID E. JONES

VAN NUYS, CALIF.

Dear Mr. Jones: I don't object to using the subjunctive when its use is both euphonious and realistic. I would say, "If it weren't for Mother, I wouldn't be." But I would say, "If Jane was there, she'd be guilty." To say, "If Jane *were* there, she'd be guilty" comes close to letting form dictate fact. The first clearly implies that you don't think Jane was there; the second, that you're not sure. . . . Subjunctives are dying out, and in part it's a good thing. (You wouldn't go around, Jones, confess it, saying, "If I be wrong, correct me"?) Cordially,

—WFB   SEPTEMBER 3, 1990

Dear Mr. Buckley:

Is it true that you gave orders to your editors that the American Party ticket was not to be mentioned throughout the campaign, in the pages of *National Review*? If so how much did it monetarily profit you personally?

ANON.

Dear Anon.: No, it isn't true. I have only given one order to the editors, see below.

MEMORANDUM

December 18, 1972

TO: Priscilla, JB, Jeff, Linda, Kevin, Alan, Joe, Pat, Carol, Chris, Barbara, and George Will
FROM: WFB

Two things. We are suffering at *NR* from an epidemic of exclamation-itis. Two issues ago, in the review of Garry Wills's book, I was quite certain that Will Herberg would succumb from it, before finishing the review. It is a dreadful way to go. In the current issue, Mrs. Nena Ossa concludes her interesting essay on Chile, "That would be the moment to pack and leave!" "That would be the moment to pack and leave" I submit is a much tenser way of suggesting that that would be the moment to pack and leave. A few pages later, Herr Erik von Kuehnelt-Leddihn, discussing the economic situation in Spain, remarks that "it is significant that workers who had gone abroad are now coming back in large numbers because wages (for the skilled!) have become quite attractive." Why !? (or, if you prefer, Why?!) The reader had nowhere been led to believe that Erik had constructed his argument in order to mock the superstition that unskilled wages were attractive in Spain. So why? I ASK YOU, WHY!

The other thing. A ukase. *Un*-negotiable. The only one I have issued in seventeen years. It goes: "John went to the store and bought some apples, oranges, and bananas." NOT: "John went to the store and bought some apples, oranges and bananas." I am told *National Review*'s Style Book stipulates the omission of the second comma. My comment: *National Review*'s Style Book *used* to stipulate the omission of the second comma. *National Review*'s Style Book, effective immediately, makes the omission of the second comma a capital offense!

MEMO TO: WFB
FROM: PLB
Dec. 20
Lest you think there is insubordination in the ranks when you see the current mag (Jan. 5) and the next (Jan. 19) your Stakhanovite cohorts in Editorial had already sent up the Books and Arts & Manners sections of the Jan. 19 magazine by the time they received the Memo on serial commas and, rather than raise the, sleeping, dragons, of, the, Finance, Committee, for unnecessary Author's Alterations, have suspended the decreed change until the issue of Feb. 2, which, will, look, roughly, like, this.

FEBRUARY 16, 1973

Dear Priscilla:

I have read with dismay WFB's ukase on the serial comma. I can't do it. No way. It's just plain ugly. WFB says this is *un*-negotiable. You're his sister . . . How serious is he? Can I arrange a dispensation?

Look . . . I'll compromise. There should be peace in the family. Instead of "John went to the store and bought some apples, oranges, and bananas . . ." How about if he just buys oranges and bananas? Or a head of non-union lettuce. You see what this sort of restriction leads to. And they ask me why fiction is dying. Erich Segal, I bet, uses the serial comma.

You may tell WFB that, from now on and as ordered, I salute the red and white. Sincerely,

D. KEITH MANO
BLOOMING GROVE, N.Y.

P.S. However, the first ukase on exclamationitis was long overdue. The exclamation point may be used only in dialogue and then only if the person speaking has recently been disemboweled.

Dear Priscilla:

In re the serial comma controversy in the current *NR,* on *this* issue, amusing, as, your, comments, are, I agree 100 per cent with Bill's ukase on this matter. "My coats are green, red, black and white" means something different from "My coats are green, red, black, and white," as a rather silly example. But in my book the serial comma is a *must.*

CORINNA MARSH
NEW YORK, N.Y.

Dear Mr. Buckley:

About your *un*-negotiable Style Book ukase: Fowler says the comma before the "and" is considered otiose (his word). Too many sections.

Seventeen years of silence, then the ukase labored and brought forth a comma, by caesuran section no doubt. That indeed is exclamationitis! Yours,

VOX DICTIONARIUS
c/o GEORGE FOSTER
LOS ANGELES, CALIF.

Dear Vox: Otiose blotiose. *He dreamed of conquering Guatemala, Panama, San Salvador and Nicaragua?* Without the comma, San Salvador and Nicaragua appear positively zygotic. Is that what you want, Vox? Well, count me out!

—WFB

Dear Mr. Buckley:

As a bemused admirer of your continuing love affair with the English language, I am delighted to welcome you to the side of the angels in the matter of serial commas.

Now, if you are still in a ukase-handing-down mood, you might set a few people straight (including yourself, I'm afraid) on the uses of *that* and *which*. Even good writers, in which your stable abounds, fail to recognize the difference. The feeling seems to be, as Fowler points out, that *that* is the colloquial and *which* the literary relative—a feeling that he further suggests results from misreading the evidence.

In the interests of lucid writing, the rule is that *that* should be the pronoun introducing defining clauses, and that *which* should be the pronoun introducing non-defining clauses. Or, putting it another way, if the clause is necessary to the sense of the sentence, *that* is the word; and if the clause can be omitted without destroying the sense of the sentence, then *which* is the word. Further, if the pronoun itself can be omitted, then *that* is the word. And only if the clause can be set off by commas without looking stupid is *which* the word.

The only real problem with following this rule out the window is that one occasionally (frequently?) collides with the related question of prepositions at the ends of sentences, *which* will be the subject of our next lecture.

These examples, I think, show that an insistence on knowing the difference between these two words is more than just pedagogic petulance. (Lord knows I ain't no pedagogue, just an unfortunate with a technical education and a gut feeling for the language.) Their proper use can make a hell of a difference in how the message gets across. On the other hand, if your intent is obfuscation, then you just go on that/whiching the way you've always done it.

I can't think which I approve more, your political economy or your mode of expression. Probably I wouldn't appreciate either one so much if I didn't appreciate the other. Sincerely yours,

GEORGE A. HEINEMANN

PALATINE, ILL.

Dear Mr. Heinemann: You are wrong that the rule is absolute. The preference is absolute. Fowler himself confesses to misgivings on the point, though he knows the rule, and you state it correctly. Remember, you can even get away with saying, Our Father, which art in heaven. Thanks. Cordially,

—WFB   MARCH 16, 1973

Dear Kilpo [James J. Kilpatrick]:

A splendid column on Cornell. However, I disagree that a letter cannot be both verbose and redundant. Verbosity need not be redundant. Correct?

But I would write more confidently if it were not that you are Number One, being addressed by your faithful servant,

—BILL

Dear Bill:

I venture no positive pronouncements on this difficult issue. My tentative feeling is that it is quite possible to be redundant without being verbose, but I would think it difficult to be verbose without being redundant.

To say, as so many of our friends in broadcasting so often say, that a meeting will be held "at 10 A.M. in the morning" is to fall headlong into redundancy. But this is not verbosity.

I encounter verbosity (or what strikes me as verbosity) whenever I travel to the Senate press gallery and spend an hour marveling at the butter and marmalade professions on the floor. "Permit me to yield, Mr. President, to my able and distinguished friend, the senior senator from thus-and-so, for whom I entertain the highest regard and the warmest admiration. Indeed, Mr. President, I must say that no member of this deliberative body is held in higher regard, or more justifiably so, than my brilliant and erudite colleague, to whom I deferentially yield such time as he may require." That is verbosity; it is also redundancy.

I am supported in these impressions by the lexicographers of *Webster's*. Under the heading of "redundant," they encourage us to seek amplification under "wordy." At "wordy," we are educated in the subtleties that distinguish *wordy, verbose, prolix, diffuse,* and *redundant.* From these first cousins we are led to a remarkable array of second cousins, great-uncles, step-sisters, and great-aunts once removed: *tedious, garrulous, repetitious, loquacious,* and so forth. From all this I conclude that there are times, alas, when I am both verbose and redundant, while you, my mentor, are merely richly detailed.

Deferentially,

JAMES J. KILPATRICK

Dear Kilpo: We ought to put our act on the road. Herewith a trial balloon. Cordially,

—BILL   NOVEMBER 25, 1977

Chapter 5

Sexist, Anti-Sexist, and Other Foreign Languages

Dear Mr. Buckley:

I have thought long and deep about the problem of HARASS (perh. from O.F.: to set a dog on). Is it har'ass or harass'? Since the word really fills a need in our litigious age (where is the jurist who dares say: *de minimis non curat praetor?*) could not you start a movement to clarify this point?

Sincerely,

G. J. WAGENINGEN

CHICAGO, ILL.

Dear Mr. Wageningen: Want to know our preferences? Accent the first syllable when the construction is passive ("Jane was HAR-assed by Tarzan"), the last syllable when the mood is active ("Tarzan ha-RASSED Jane"). Cordially,

—WFB

Buckley has been responding to the more tortured efforts to de-sex English, usually by torturing back. This seesaw battle has been going on since the 1970s at least, and therefore not as long as he has had to defend himself (and others) against charges of a fulsome or undemocratic vocabulary, but it shows promise for the future. One senses that the battle stays joined partly out of the joy of combat but also because WFB believes himself to be on the side of what he calls Right Reason. His opponents are worthy. The cause is just, even if some of the proposed solutions are singularly lacking in grace or euphony.

Death to Textbook Sexism

I had an encounter recently with Ms. Germaine Greer, the anti-sexist sex bomb who has wrangled with lots of people including Norman Mailer, about whom, incidentally, she wrote the most galvanizing polemic in the recent history of the art (*Esquire,* September 1971).

Ms. Greer is a brilliant woman who, however, in the course of making her case against "sexism" exploits the hell out of sex. The kind of attention devoted to her in *Playboy, Evergreen Review,* et al., is inconceivable except that she obligingly spices her remarks with lascivious sexual detail as reliably as the boilerplate pornographers. I think—I am not absolutely certain, but I *suspect* that she is capable of humor, though her use of it is certainly embryonic; and that she will be rescued by humor. Somebody has got to rescue us from the women's liberation movement, and if Ms. Greer gets over her fundamentalist iconoclasm, she might be just the person to do it.

To do what? Well, for instance, to cope with Scott, Foresman & Company. They are the big textbook publishers, and I have here a pamphlet issued by the company called "Guidelines for Improving the Image of Women in Textbooks." How do you define sexism? "Sexism refers to all those attitudes and actions which relegate women to a secondary and inferior status in society . . ." The editors warn against stereotypes. "For example, writers should take care that a joke about a woman who is a bad driver, a shrewish mother-in-law, financially inept, etc., does not present these qualities as typical of women as a group."

Mercifully, the editors do not supply examples, though one can use imagination. Bob Hope has a line that goes something like this: "I bumped into a car today." Straight Man: "Why?" "There was a woman driver and she stuck out her hand for a left turn." S.M.: "What happened?" "She turned left." In the Scott, Foresman Joke Book presumably the line would be added: "The way men sometimes do."

The editors give examples of sexist language, and, opposite, examples of how to correct the abuse.

For instance, "early man." That should be "early humans." "When man invented the wheel . . ." should become "When people invented the wheel . . ." Now of course this is something we might be able to get away with when discussing prehistorical inventions. But Scott, Foresman funk the historical problem, unless they are prepared to recommend: "When the Wright people invented the airplane," or "When the Ford human invented the car." Will no one tell the people at Scott, Foresman about the synecdoche?

"Businessmen" is out: "business people" is in. Presumably the singular is a "business person." What do you want to be when you grow up,

Johnny? A business person. What do you do with "repairmen"? Not even Scott, Foresman dared come up with "repairperson," so they offer: "someone to repair the . . ." which can be spotted as a syntactical cop-out in sexist and non-sexist societies.

The use of the pronoun "he" to do androgynous duty is out. For instance, you can't say, "The motorist should slow down if he is hailed by the police." You have to say: "The motorist should slow down if he or she is hailed by the police" (or policewoman?).

They are so carried away, over at Scott, Foresman, that they appear to have lost all sense of inflection. For instance, the sexist "The ancient Egyptians allowed women considerable control over property" has got to be changed to "Women in ancient Egypt had considerable control over property"—which is, very simply, a totally different statement from the first.

Will they ever make a concession? Yes. "In some cases, it is necessary to refer to a woman's sex, as in the sentence: 'The works of female authors are too often omitted from anthologies.' " I don't know how you could come up with a permissible way of saying: "The works of female authors are too often included in anthologies." I guess you just can't think that. "Galileo was the astronomer who discovered the moons of Jupiter. Marie Curie was the beautiful chemist who discovered radium." *Wrong.* Try: "Galileo was the handsome astronomer who discovered the moons of Jupiter. Marie Curie was the beautiful chemist who discovered radium." But what if Galileo was ugly? Or, heaven forfend, what if Galileo was really handsome and Marie Curie was really ugly (which I happen to know was the case)?

Ms. Greer had better hurry. Her movement is gravely imperiled by the boys at—I mean, the boys and girls at, Scott, Foresman & Company.

NOVEMBER 25, 1972

Can We Avoid Sexism?

Twice in as many days I have been reproached as a sexist, having intended no offense, and I fear that the line I had thought best left undefined needs now a little chiseling, lest things get out of hand. I mean, more out of hand.

I am reviewing a book for the *New York Times*. It is a fine book about the Antarctic, and includes engrossing chapters about the great expeditions of a half century ago. I conclude the review by observing (can any observation I have observed in the past ten years have been more innocent?) that the book would appeal not only to scientists and students of the Arctic but to "boys who love adventure stories."

Two pieces of mail already, the first especially indignant. "Just what makes you think that only boys love adventure stories? I read adventure stories throughout my childhood, and it is typical of male chauvinists to assume that only boys like to read adventure stories."

A day later, in the company of two distinguished journalists, I sought to examine a question going the rounds, namely: "Where are American leaders?" That last is the question explored in the current issue of *Time* magazine, at great and rather resourceful length. A lady panelist raised her hand to ask had we noticed that of the two hundred young potential leaders in America, listed by *Time,* only nineteen were women? "Approximately nine and one half percent," she said, exactly. We were all temporarily nonplussed, and it was then that I found myself saying that, really, the figure was not all that surprising, because it remains a fact that more men than women are attracted to those conspicuous professions from which leaders are taken. I felt a chill in the audience, as if I had said the kind of thing Professor Shockley specializes in saying.

Accordingly, I issue herewith a modest manifesto.

The movement for equality between the sexes will not, at my hands at any rate, issue in a death sentence for the synecdoche.

That there are grown people in the world who go around saying things like "chairperson" is testimony not to bisexual attempts to create equality, but to the tendency of transsexual resolutions to sound stupid. The phrase "will appeal to adventure-loving boys" is not an exclusionary phrase, because the word "boys" in this case means not only boys, but also girls. You cannot maintain the equilibrium of the English language by saying that "man's inhumanity to man" is measured in part by the sexism of that phrase. Is it seriously thought that man's inhumanity to man is to be distinguished from man's inhumanity toward women? Or that "he who laughs last laughs best" means that girls laugh best when they laugh first, whereas boys laugh best when they laugh last?

And as for the business of future leaders: Ten years ago, at the start of the women's lib movement, approximately ten percent of the students in law school were female, and now that figure has risen by approximately fourteen percent. This statistic has been cited in such tones of despair as would be appropriate in saying that over a ten-year period, death from starvation had diminished by only a few percentage points in America.

It is the uniformity of the standards that is wrong, a tiresome point but no less true for the making of it: the notion that the male lawyer is necessarily engaged in more productive or more humane work than the female non-lawyer. This morning's newspaper brings the news that our Secretary of Health, Education and Welfare, Mr. Caspar Weinberger, has solemnly announced that it is not a regulation of his office that boys and girls attend jointly school lectures on sexual hygiene. At the University of Arizona, it has been announced that unless exactly as much money is spent on girls' sports as on boys' sports, the entire federal subsidy will be withdrawn.

What kind of prehensile lengths are we going to? Germaine Greer recently debated with me on the general subject, and asked me to propose a formal resolution. I typed out, "Resolved, Give them an inch and they'll take a mile"—but prudently thought better of it, as one does not play mischievously with metaphors with Germaine Greer. But, you know, it's true.

—WFB   JULY 13, 1974

Dear Mr. Buckley:

The recent discussion in your pages of sexist language prompts me to the following observations.

Among the more egregious of the many verbal insults to sexual equality is the use of "he" to mean both sexes. *Vide* the well known passage from Proverbs:

> *He that is slow to anger is better than the mighty;*
> *And he that ruleth his spirit than he that taketh a city.*

The blatant male chauvinism of this passage would be eliminated by replacing the ubiquitous "he" with "she" alone, viz.:

> *She that is slow to anger is better than the mighty;*
> *And she that ruleth her spirit than she that taketh a city.*

Unfortunately, while this version would be poetic justice, it must be rejected as discrimination in reverse.

Another method would be to substitute for "he" the compound "he or she" (or, in the appropriate context, "his or her"):

> *He or she that is slow to anger is better than the mighty;*
> *And he or she that ruleth his or her spirit than he or she that taketh a city.*

Thus revised the passage is entirely free of sexism, but the gain is offset by the loss of clarity and conciseness.

An unobjectionable solution might lie in a fusion of "he" and "she," for example, "heshe" or "shehe." There is greater precision in these composite words, but regrettably both are phonetically repellent.

I think the most acceptable answer is a compromise:

I propose the words "shim," a composite of "she" and "him," and "shis," from the union of "she" and "his." Although a mixed bag grammatically, these synthetic terms are compact, unambiguous, and wholly without sexual signification. Moreover, "shim" has its analogue in the common English word meaning a thin piece of material wedged into a joint to take up wear or prevent squeaking. The quoted passage from Proverbs would then read:

> *Shim that is slow to anger is better than the mighty;*
> *And shim that ruleth shis spirit than shim that taketh a city.*

The slight loss of elegance in the revision is more than compensated by the passage's utter freedom from sexual invidiousness.

Extensions of the principle will doubtless occur to the thoughtful reader.

Yours very truly,

BERTRAM EDISES

ATTORNEY AT LAW

OAKLAND, CALIF.

Dear Mr. Edises: . . . What worries me, Edises, is the slurs on mightyism, not to say the implicit disparagement of the spirited. So how about:

> *Shim that is slow to anger is betterworse than the mighty;*
> *And shim that ruleth shis spirit than shim that taketh or loseth a city?*

Cordially,

—WFB   MARCH 28, 1975

Dear Bill:

In a recent column in which you recounted a chance meeting in a broadcasting studio with J. K. Galbraith you wrote, quite in passing, that while you and the economist were conversing a "*lady theologian*" was on the air.

Reading that "lady" bit I was instantly reminded of Archie Bunker.

All in the Family, as you know, is the Americanized version of a popular British TV show designed to caricature the Anglo-Saxon bigotries and class prejudices of the lower class Englishman who is the last ditch defender of middle class Victorian attitudes.

Archie, the dock-walloper, like his British counterpart, considers himself a member of the superior race and sex. Archie is especially faithful to the genteel nineteenth-century tradition that a gentleman is a man who refers to any woman who isn't obviously a trollop as a "lady," Archie speaks of "lady cabdrivers," "lady cops," "lady short-order cooks." His gentlemanly mark of respect for the "weaker" sex is, however, not altogether unmixed with disdain and resentment. Archie makes it quite plain—all in the family—that "ladies" who try to do any "man's job" are really "ama-toors" who have no business to be in the business.

Even Archie's next door neighbors, the "Eyetalian lady" and the "col-ored lady," cannot trifle with Archie's masculine sense of racial and sexual superiority without being instantly downgraded into "that female wop," or "that colored female," who are ruining the neighborhood. Archie sel-dom refers to a woman as a "woman." This is probably because he views women less as persons than as the reproductive and nurturing function of a man-made world, made for men. A "woman" is what goes to bed with a man, has his babies, and gets his food on the table. In Archie's sex lexicon the men are men, but women who are not "ladies" or "females" are "the girls" or "the wives."

Altogether, Archie is a crude but powerful master of what feminists today call "verbal sexism"—the patronizing putup or contemptuous put-down of women *just because they are women*. When Archie speaks of women in any social relation to men, he never puts them on man's level. For exam-ple, in Archie's world the women are sometimes permitted to bowl with the men. As Archie might tell it, "Us men give them female bowlers a good licking," or "Us fellers let the lady bowlers win a few offn us."

So permit me, dear Bill, as woman writer, former congresswoman, and former ambassador, to remind you that professional women today view the "lady" bit as a conscious or unconscious masculine putdown. And allow me further to suggest that my favorite man columnist (who is also a gentleman) should leave the use of "lady" as a sex classifier and/or gratu-itous social status indicator of professional persons to the Archie Bunkers of the writing profession.

Affectionately,

CLARE [BOOTHE LUCE]

HONOLULU

Dear Clare: Your point is clearly made, and magnificently advocated. Henceforward I shall confine my use of the word to such references as "lady wrestlers," where the oxymoronic imperative clearly prevails.

Love,

BILL   NOVEMBER 22, 1974

FEMINISM: UNSEX ME NOW

What do Mary McCarthy, Joyce Carol Oates, Muriel Spark, and Joan Didion have in common?

Ans. They are first-class writers. If you like, you can say they are "first-class women writers." But it must be somewhere along the line communicated that by that you mean that they are first-class writers who are women. Otherwise there is a patronizing residue, as in "he is a first-class junior skier." Ironically, one of the reasons these ladies (patronizing? All right, these women) are first-class writers is that they would shun like the plague such exhortations as are being urged on all writers by the National Council of Teachers of English (NCTE), in the name of eliminating sexism.

As a rather agreeable surprise, the latest bulletin from the anti-sexist league is itself literate. We are told: "The man who cannot cry and the woman who cannot command are equally victims of their socialization." The trouble is that by the time they are through with their recommendations, they make everybody cry who cares for the mother tongue.

Unhappily, there is no way in the English of Shakespeare, Milton, Pope, and Faulkner to get rid of the synecdoche "man," which, as in "mankind," means man and woman. One of the things you cannot do in English is to replace "man" in some situations. Consider the efforts of the NCTE.

The common man becomes *the average person,* or *ordinary people.* Try it out . . . "The century of the average person." No. Why? If you don't know, I can't tell you. Ditto for "The century of ordinary people." Here, at least, you can point out that ordinary has several meanings and that whereas common does too, the conjunction of *common man* instantly excludes all but the Henry Wallace use of the word common; whereas the conjunction of *ordinary man* does not exclude such a sniffy remark as, say, Lucius Beebe might have made about vulgar people. Clarity is one of the objectives of good writers, which is why Mary McCarthy would never write about "the century of ordinary people."

The bulletin offers you a typical sexist slur: *The average student is worried about his grades.* Suggested substitute: *The average student is worried about grades.* There again, you will note a difficulty. The two sentences do not mean exactly the same thing. In the first, the student is worried about his (or her) grades. In the second, the student is worried about grades as a generic concern. Perhaps he is worried about, say, the role that grades play or do not play in getting into graduate school. Anyway, there is a residual indistinction, and English teachers shouldn't be teaching people how to write imprecisely.

The bulletin notes that English does not have a generic singular common-sex pronoun, the convention being to use the male. This will be proscribed . . . *If the student was satisfied with his performance on the pre-test, he took the post-test.* This becomes, *A student who was satisfied with her or his performance on the pre-test took the post-test.* That is called killing two birds with one stone. You eliminate the generic male singular, and reverse the conventional sequence (her and his). The distortions ring in the ear.

At one point, the NCTE wants us to validate improper usage. Here we are asked to rewrite *Anyone who wants to go to the game should bring his money tomorrow* to *Anyone who wants to go to the game should bring their money tomorrow;* and I say anyone who does that kind of thing at this point should not be hired as a professional writer.

So mobilized are these folk that they do not stop at a war far from the cosmopolitan centers, designed to wipe out little pockets of vernacular resistance. *Gal Friday* has to become assistant. A *libber* must become a *feminist* (here I think they have dealt from the bottom of the deck: what's inherently sexist about libber?). A *man-sized job* becomes a *big* or *enormous* job. Question: How do you describe a job that requires physical exertion beyond the biological powers of wopersons?

It is comforting to know that this effort to correct the language will precisely not succeed because the genuine artists among women writers are more concerned for their craft than for fashionable sociological skirmishes. Nothing more persuades the general public of women's inferiority (which doctrine is of course preposterous) than efforts at equality achieved by indicting good prose.

—WFB   APRIL 29, 1976

Stop!

A colleague the other day was aghast at seeing in print, in a piece he had written for a small magazine, the word "chairperson," where my friend in his manuscript had written "chairman." He takes seriously his responsibility for language that appears over his name, and so telephoned to the editor and said in words less than entirely conciliatory, Where do you get off putting "chairperson" where I specified "chairman"? Well, she said, it's just this simple, you were talking about a woman. To which he replied that it was just this simple, namely that "chairman" refers, and has done so for hundreds of years, equally to men as to women, which is so also of the word "man," which in certain formulations ("Man is made in the image of God") is genderless. And anyway, he said to her, what right do you have to impose your preferred forms over mine, given that I am the author of the piece? To which she said, smiling sweetly, to the extent this can be ascertained in the voice of someone coming in over the telephone, that that was the style rule of that magazine. And style rules govern.

Now magazines and newspapers are entitled to have style rules that govern such matters as whether "theatre" can be spelled that way or must appear as "theater." That is plain house editorial privilege. But what happened to my friend, of course, is that he was being inducted into a movement—the feminist movement, as it calls itself, although it must be understood that the feminist movement is not necessarily a movement all good men, or women, should come to the aid of.

There is no end to the lengths to which such impositions can go. Or was the extreme reached by the National Union of Journalists in Great Britain? About a recent experience there, I must inform you.

Most men and women who want to work in journalism need to join the NUJ because most newspapers are closed shops in Great Britain. The story begins when a Mr. Terry Lovell, a newspaperman in Manchester, got into trouble with the NUJ for writing a story in which he passed along the theory that, to quote the paraphrase of the London *Times*'s Bernard Levin, "women tend to concentrate on and encourage the part of them they think the prettiest." For this offense against equality—i.e., he suggested that in some respects women comport themselves differently from men—he was officially rebuked. His colleagues thought this very funny, and decided to punish him, and amuse themselves, by designating him as the Manchester branch "Equality Officer"—charged with hearing complaints alleging bias.

So a few weeks go by, and a complaint is brought against a colleague of Mr. Lovell who, when interviewing a football manager and his lady friend, described the latter as "bra-less."

As far as the complainant was concerned, the case was open and closed. The writer had violated Clause 10 of Rule 18 of the union's disciplinary code, which forbids discrimination on grounds, among others, of gender. How? Because he had not described the man's underwear, even though he had referred to the lady's lack of it.

In his response, Mr. Hughes was an absolute model of docility. He told the NUJ jurors that the reason he had referred to the subject's being bra-less was that indeed she was not wearing a bra. Moreover, he promised— "you may rest assured," he solemnly spoke, that if the football manager *had* been wearing a bra, he'd have made it a point to mention this.

Well, that kind of thing makes very good reading, but humor—spelled humour in England, which is perfectly OK—doesn't work when trafficking with ideologues. All the defendant got for his pains was a portentous reply by the complainant: "I may have my own criticisms of aspects of equality policy, not least the severe problems in their implementation in the face of open contempt from some sections of the membership . . ." snore, snore—and the defendant was put on probation. The Equality Committee will keep its eyes on him, and if ever he should make reference to a woman who had served as "chairman," well, kaput. Exit that writer from the national scene.

Here is an appeal. I direct it to Clare Boothe Luce, because she has been an ardent champion of women's rights throughout her lifetime. But Mrs. Luce is also an artist of refined literary taste. And, add to all this, she knows how to manage causes. I desire her to head up a committee of illustrious women writers to protest the lengths a movement is being taken in their name. The Women's Committee to Protest the Vulgarization of the Women's Rights Movement, how is that for a title?

—WFB   APRIL 30, 1985

Chapter 6

On Latin &
Other Lively
Languages

Clarification
What in the world is "entrepreneurial ebullience?"

MARJORIE KADERLI
AUSTIN, TEXAS

Ardor negotiorum curatoris, natch.

—WFB   AUGUST 28, 1962

Buckley's use of foreign languages is not affectation. Given his particular, peculiarly belated introduction to English, explained elsewhere,* it is perhaps not surprising. He speaks Spanish fluently; it was his original language; in fact, he later taught it. His feeling for Latin is not defensive; it is a passionate advocacy.

Not surprisingly, then, his mailbag and his writings often are concerned with the use of foreign words and phrases and he enjoys reaching for the right example in French, say, as much as he does the arcane, unusual, or recherché in English.

One column in 1965 began . . .

Pas d'Ennemi à Gauche

The reason writers are given in certain circumstances to using phrases from foreign languages rather than their English translation is not merely that they sometimes have a special piquancy in the original (*vive la différence,* for example) but because they have a special incantatory sound, suggesting a special, sometimes extrarational meaning—an abracadabra-

---

* In chapter 8 on diction, etc.

special magical authority. Such a phrase is *"pas d'ennemi à gauche"* which literally translated means: no enemies on the left. Freely translated it means: any two-bit leftist individual or nation can do whatever he or it desires to an American or America and get away with it. By contrast, a right-winger, or a right-wing nation, is by definition hostile. . . .

Dear Mr. Buckley:
I was more than surprised to see that most offensive term "hocus-pocus" in your editorial, "A Sane Explosion" [February 27].

Says Tillotson (an accepted authority): "Those common juggling words of *hocus-pocus* are nothing else but a corruption of the *hoc est corpus* by way of ridiculous imitation of the priests of the Church of Rome in their trick of transubstantiation." Works, Vol. 1, Sermon 26.

M. J. HOGAN

PHILADELPHIA, PA.

Dear Mr. Hogan: Oxford English Dictionary; *Volume V, p. 320:* "Hocus pocus . . . *17th c . . . the appellation of a juggler (and, apparently, as the assumed name of a particular conjurer) derived from the sham Latin formula employed by him . . . The notion that* hocus pocus *was a parody of the Latin words used in the Eucharist rests merely on a conjecture thrown out by Tillotson . . .*

—WFB   MARCH 12, 1960

Dear Bill:
Can you hum the *Die Meistersinger?*
How about the *Il Trovatore?*
Do you dine at the El Morocco?
Does your column run in the *Le Monde?*
No. Then don't say that Galbraith's theory of redistribution was originally discovered by *the* hoi polloi ("On the Right," July 16, 1972). Even with duplicated articles, I like your articles. Keep up the good work.

Sincerely,

BOB HARDWICK

FT. PIERCE, FLA.

Dear Mr. Hardwick: Nice. Thanks. And now, if I may, from Fowler: "**hoi polloi**. These Greek words for the majority, ordinary people, the man in the street, the common herd etc., meaning literally 'the many,' are equally uncomfortable in English whether the (= hoi) is prefixed to them or not. The best solution is to eschew the phrase altogether." "**Pedantry** may be defined . . . as the saying of things in language so learned or so demonstratively accurate as to imply a slur upon the generality, who are not capable or not desirous of such displays. The term, then, is obviously a relative one; my pedantry is your scholarship, his reasonable accuracy, her irreducible minimum of education, and someone else's ignorance. It is therefore not very profitable to dogmatize . . . on the subject." Cordially,

—WFB   AUGUST 18, 1972

Dear Mr. Buckley:

Greetings! Your country has called upon you at this critical . . . Now that I have your attention, I again call upon you to rectify the grievous *faux pas* perpetrated upon the theopneustic pages of *National Review*. I must battologize: there is not, nor has there ever been, a language called "Mongolese" ["On the Right," March 1]. Please rectify this grave *lapis linguae* . . .

Unmitigatedly yours,
ERIC S. OLIN
MENDHAM, N.J.

Dear Mr. Olin: Hey. I like that "theopneustic" to describe *NR*, but getting "battologize" out of battologist is, well, a bit much; and it's *lapsus* (as in *calami*) not lapis (as in lazuli). Cordially,

—WFB   MAY 10, 1974

Dr. Mr. Buckley:

I am stranded here without my reference library for a couple of weeks, and have come across a sentence from Terence used as an epigraph of sorts, which I am unable to translate. Would you be so kind as to do so, and let me have it in the enclosed envelope? It is: "*Bono animo es: tu cum illa te intus oblecta interim et lectulos iube sterni nobis et parari cetera.*" Many thanks.

M. PATRICK GLENVILLE
SUN VALLEY, IDAHO

Dear Mr. Glenville: It defeats me, sorry, and also one or two of my colleagues. Normally, I would write to Garry Wills and ask him to translate it for me. However, I am so outraged by his recent stupid, preposterous column on the Shockley debate at Yale, I declared a ninety-day moratorium on any correspondence with him. There are still thirty-two days left. If you can hold out, I'll ask him then, and ship you out the translations to Sun Valley.

Yours cordially,
—WFB   AUGUST 2, 1974

Dear Sirs:

Since Mr. Buckley has placed me under Interdict [August 2] I must translate for Mr. Glenville through your mediation: ["*Bono animo es: tu cum illa te intus oblecta interim et lectulos iube sterni nobis et parari cetera*"] "Relax. Amuse yourself inside, for a while, with her. Order the banquet couches spread and the other things prepared . . . "

Best,

GARRY WILLS

BALTIMORE, MD.

P.S. Bill—I thought you promised to stop reading my column if I promised to stop sending it!

Best,

GARRY

Dear Mr. Buckley:

It just struck me, Mr. Buckley . . . that you might get a chuckle from my commentary, "Tuning Up a Datum." Here's a copy.

Best regards,

WEN SMITH

ASHLAND, ORE.

Tuning Up a Datum

My neighbor Phil is a grease-monkey by trade, but his ear is almost as sensitive to bad grammar as it is to an engine out of tune. Phil came by yesterday with a copy of *National Review.*

"Bill Buckley is one writer who knows his grammar," Phil said. "Who else knows the difference between *datum* and *data*?"

"I do," I said. "I just don't know the difference between a gear box and a transmission."

Phil gave me a pitying look. "They're the same thing," he said.

"So what's new with William F. Buckley, Jr.?" I said.

"It's the precise way he uses grammar," Phil said. He had the magazine open to a Buckley commentary. "Here he's talking about minorities and crime. He says 66 per cent of black children are born to unwed mothers." [*NR*, May 16.]

"That's not a crime," I said.

"Not my point," Phil said. "Buckley goes on to say, 'This is a datum none of the disputants deny.' "

"Well, he used *datum* correctly," I said. "It's the singular, and *data* is the plural."

"Exactly," Phil said. "I took beginning Latin when I was in high school. But these days I hardly ever hear anyone use the word *datum*. And mostly I hear *data* used as singular. You know, 'The data *is* incomplete.' "

"Well," I said. "Nobody speaks Latin any more, except the Pope—and Bill Buckley. What about his English? Read that line again."

Phil read again from Buckley's article. " 'This is a datum none of the disputants deny.' You see? *'Is a datum.'* Perfect grammar."

"Well," I said, "consistency is for little minds. You wouldn't want to hang Bill Buckley with that noose. Anyway, a lot of people use none as a plural today."

"Yeah," Phil said. "I guess none of us are perfect."

"Thanks for the tune-up," he added, and he went home to read the rest of *National Review.*

Dear Mr. Smith: Enjoyable column, nice try, but, alas, no cigar. See below. Cordially,

—WFB   AUGUST 15, 1994

From the New York Public Library Style Book, *1994:*
None

None can be used with either a singular verb or a plural verb, but most grammarians and style manuals prefer the plural. The old belief that none means "not one" is not true in most cases; a closer look will usually show that "not any" is the thought being expressed in almost every instance.

None of the reporters were able to interview the defendant.

Television is the chief way that most of us partake of the larger world, of the information age, and so none of us completely escape its influence.

(*The New Yorker,* March 9, 1992)

Dear Mr. Buckley:

A recent issue of *The Nation* was given over to a sustained polemic against Daniel Patrick Moynihan in which he was indicted for, *inter alia,* being (1) a demagogue, (2) a racist, and (3) an unscrupulous scholar. One article revealed that Moynihan received wide press coverage because of his use of the word "floccipaucinihilipilification."

Now, I consulted three unabridged dictionaries before discovering in the New Oxford Dictionary that this polysyllabic monstrosity means "the act of estimating as unworthy."

Questions: (1) Have you ever heard of this word? (2) Have you ever used it? (3) Why is Moynihan the *bête noire* of the Left? (4) How come you know *everything?*

Admiringly yours,

GORDON HANSON

SEATTLE, WASH.

Dear Mr. Hanson: (1) Yes, have known it for years; it used to be tossed about in the young teen-age set during the thirties as a can-you-match-this-one word. You have it slightly wrong, by the way. It's flocci-nauci-nihili-pilification, and as the Oxford advises you, it is a humorous agglutination of Latinisms from an Eton grammar. Though I can't find authority for it, we used to give out as its meaning, "full of sound and fury signifying nothing." (2) No. (3) Moynihan is a *bête noire* of the Left because he has their number and is brighter than they are. (4) I don't know everything, but I absolutely know why Moynihan is a *bête noire* of the Left. Cordially,

—WFB   JANUARY 25, 1980

Dear Mr. Buckley:

Your syndicated column "Musings of a Deposed Dictator" [printed in *NR* as "Okay, Okay, I'm Coming," Feb. 5] appears to be in the form of a dramatic monologue, though the identity of the speaker is never given direct enunciation. In the course of the text, the following passage occurs, "I have plenty of plata, nice 24-karat plata."

Not all newspaper stylebooks require the italicization of such unassimilated foreign words as *plata,* for which reason you are not held to account for what may be a copy-editor's lapse. SPELL [Society for the Preservation of English as a Literary Language] does not doubt the utility, sometimes the necessity, of introducing foreign terms into English discourse. We pick bones, not nits.

We do, however, require that such terms be employed with some clear apprehension of the word's lexical meaning, derivation, and common usage on its home turf. It is on these standards that you stand in the dock on a charge of egregious and pretentious solecism.

In Spanish *plata* means silver; *oro* means gold. In the Anglophone world, the purity of gold is expressed in karats, units per 24 parts of absolute purity. The relative purity of silver is sometimes expressed as "sterling" (92.5 per cent pure) or "coin" (90 per cent). In all other formulations the purity of silver is expressed domestically in parts per thousand, as is the purity of both silver and gold internationally.

I am certain that you would never entertain a defense grounded in your ignorance, nor does it seem likely that some editor or gremlin substituted "*plata*" for "*oro*" as your prose proceeded from your teeming brain to my breakfast table. I invite your attention to this matter, with an aim to contrition.

In the hope, not only of contrition, but of amendment, I am,

Sincerely,

JOHN K. METCALFE

FACTOTUM AND ENFORCER

SPELL

PITTSBURGH, PA.

Dear Mr. Metcalfe: The word "plata" is commonly used in Latin America to signify: money; dough; bread. As in, "*Desgraciadamente, estoy sin plata.*" Direct your energies elsewhere. Cordially,

—WFB

ASSISTANT INSTRUCTOR IN SPANISH,

YALE UNIVERSITY, 1947–51

APRIL 1, 1990

———

Bill Buckley's sadness or anger over the loss of Latin in the Catholic mass is mixed, in the several pieces that follow, with parallel sympathies for his cousins in the Anglican Communion. He sees their fall from linguistic grace as a loss, also.

It might be said that his conservative instincts in matters political find resonance in his attitudes toward matters religious. In neither case are his sentiments . . . well, sentimental.

———

The End of the Latin Mass

In January of this year my sister died, age forty-nine, eldest of ten children, and mother of ten children, the lot of us catapulted into a dumb grief whence we sought relief by many means, principal among them the conviction, now reified by desire, that our separation from her is impermanent. It was the moment to recall not merely the promises of Christ, but their magical cogency; the moment to remind ourselves as forcefully as we knew how of the depths of the Christian experience, of the Christian mystery, so that when one of us communicated with her priest, we asked if he would consent to a funeral mass in the manner of the days gone by, which request he gladly granted. And so, on January 18, in the subzero weather of a little town in northwestern Connecticut, in the ugly little church we all grew up in, the priest recited the mass of the dead, and the organist accompanied the soloist who sang the Gregorian dirge in words the mourners did not clearly discern, words which had we discerned them we would not have been able exactly to translate, and yet we experienced, not only her family but her friends, not alone the Catholics among us but also the Protestants and the Jews, something akin to that synesthesia which nowadays most spiritually restless folk find it necessary to discover in drugs or from a guru in mysterious India.

Six months later my sister's oldest daughter—the first of the grandchildren—was married. With some hesitation (one must not be overbearing) her father asked the same priest (of noble mien and great heart) whether this happy ritual might also be performed in the Latin. He replied with understanding and grace that that would not be possible, inasmuch as he would be performing on this occasion not in a remote corner of Connecticut, but in West Hartford, practically within earshot of the bishop. We felt very wicked at having attempted anything so audacious within the walls of the episcopacy, and so the wedding took place according to the current cant, with everybody popping up, and kneeling down, and responding, more or less, to the stream of objurgations that issued from the nervous and tone-deaf young commentator, all together now, Who Do We Appreciate? Jesus! Jesus! Jesus! Je-*zus*—it was awful. My beloved wife—to whom I have been beholden for seventeen years, and who has borne with me through countless weddings of my countless relations, who was with me and clutched my hand during the funeral a few months earlier, whom I had not invited to my church since the vulgarizations of 1964, so anxious was I that, as a member of the Anglican Communion, she should continue to remember our services as she had known them, in their inscrutable majesty—turned to me early in the ritual in utter incredulity, wondering whether something was especially awry. Hypersensitive, I rebuked her, muttering something to the effect that she had no right to be so ignorant of what had been going on for three years, and she withdrew in anger. She was right; I was utterly wrong. How could she, an innocent Protestant, begin to conceive of the liturgical disfigurations of the past few years? My own reaction was the protective reaction of the son whose father, the chronic drunkard, is first espied unsteady on his feet by someone from whom one has greatly cared to conceal the fact. Let it be objected that the essential fact of the matter is that the sacrament of matrimony was duly conferred, and what else is it that matters? My sensibilities, that's what.

They do not matter, of course, in any Benthamite reckoning of the success of the new liturgy. Concerning this point, I yield completely, or rather almost completely. It is absolutely right that the vernacular should displace the Latin if by doing so, the rituals of Catholic Christianity bring a greater satisfaction to the laity and a deeper comprehension of their religion. There oughtn't to be any argument on this point, and there certainly isn't any from me. Indeed, when a most learned and attractive young priest from my own parish asked me to serve as a lector in the new mass, I acquiesced, read all the relevant literature, and, to be sure warily, hoped that something was about to unfold before me which would vindicate the progressives.

I hung on doggedly for three years, until a month ago, when I wrote my pastor that I no longer thought it appropriate regularly to serve as lector. During those three years I observed the evolution of the new mass and the reaction to it of the congregation (the largest, by the way, in Connecticut). The church holds 1,000 people, and at first, four hymns were prescribed. They were subsequently reduced to three, even as, in the course of the experiment, the commentator absorbed the duties of the lector, or vice versa, depending on whether you are the ex-commentator or the ex-lector. At our church three years ago perhaps a dozen people out of 1,000 sang the hymn. Now perhaps three dozen out of 1,000 sing the hymn. (It is not much different with the prayers.) That is atypical, to be sure; the church is large and overawing to the uncertain group singer—*i.e.,* to most non-Protestant Americans. In other Catholic churches, I have noted, the congregations tend to join a little bit more firmly in the song. In none that I have been to is there anything like the joyous unison that the bards of the new liturgy thrummed about in the anticipatory literature, the only exception being the highly regimented school my son attends, at which the reverend headmaster has means to induce cooperation in whatever enterprise strikes his fancy. (I have noticed that my son does not join in the hymn singing when he is home, though the reason why is not necessarily indifference, is almost surely not recalcitrance, is most likely a realistic appreciation of his inability to contribute to the musical story line.)

I must, of course, judge primarily on the basis of my own experience; but it is conclusive at my own church, and I venture to say without fear of contradiction that the joint singing and prayers are a fiasco, which is all right, I suppose—the Christian martyrs endured worse exasperations and profited more from them than we endure from or are likely to benefit from the singing of the hymns at St. Mary's Church. What is troublesome is the difficulty one has in dogging one's own spiritual pursuits in the random cacophony. Really, the new liturgists should have offered training in yoga or whatever else Mother Church in her resourcefulness might baptize as a distinctively Catholic means by which we might tune off the Fascistic static of the contemporary mass, during which one is either attempting to sing, totally neglecting the prayers at the foot of the altar which suddenly we are told are irrelevant; or attempting to read the missal at one's own syncopated pace, which we must now do athwart the obtrusive rhythm of the priest or the commentator; or attempting to meditate on this or the other prayer or sentiment or analysis in the ordinary or in the proper of the mass, only to find that such meditation is sheer outlawry, which stands in the way of the liturgical calisthenics devised by the central coach, who apparently judges it an act of neglect if the churchgoer is permitted more than two minutes and forty-six seconds without being made to stand if he was kneeling, or kneel if he was standing, or sit—or sing—or chant—or *anything* if perchance he was praying, from which anarchism he must at all costs be rescued: "LET US NOW RECITE THE INTROIT PRAYER," says the commentator, to which exhortation I find myself aching to reply in that "loud and clear and reverential voice" the manual for lectors prescribes: "LET US NOT!" Must we say the introit prayer together? I have been reading the introit prayer since I was thirteen years old, and I continue unaware that I missed something—*e.g.,* at the Jesuit school in England when at daily mass we read the introit prayers all by our little selves, beginning it perhaps as much as five seconds before, or five seconds after, the priest, who, enjoying the privacy granted him at Trent, pursued his prayers, in his own way, at his own speed, ungoverned by the metronomic discipline of the parishioners or of the commentator.

Ah, but now the parish *understands* the introit prayer! But, my beloved friends, the parish does not understand. Neither does the commentator. Neither does the lector. Neither, if you want the truth of the matter, does the priest—in most cases. If clarity is the purpose of the liturgical reform—the reason for going into English, the reason for going into the vernacular—then the reforms of the liturgy are simply incomplete. If clarity is the desideratum, or however you say the word in English, then the thing to do is to jettison, just to begin with, most of St. Paul, whose epistles are in some respects inscrutable to some of the people some of the time and in most respects inscrutable to most of the people most of the time. The translation of them from archaic grandeur to John-Jane contemporese simply doesn't do the trick, particularly if one is expected to go in unison. Those prayers, which are not exacting or recondite—are even they more galvanizing when spoken in unison? LET US NOW RECITE THE INTROIT PRAYER. *Judge me, O God, and distinguish my cause from the nation that is not holy; deliver me from the unjust and deceitful man.* Judge-me-O-God/And-distinguish-my-cause-from-the-nation-that-is-not-holy/Deliver-me-from-the-unjust-and-deceitful-man/—Why? How come? Whose idea—that such words as these are better spoken, better understood, better appreciated, when rendered metrically in forced marches with the congregation? Who, thinking to read these holy and inspired words reverentially, would submit to the iron rhythm of a joint reading? It is one thing to chant together a refrain—Lord deliver us/Lord save us/Grant us peace.

But the extended prayer in unison is a metallic Procrusteanism which absolutely defies the rationale of the whole business, which is the communication of *meaning*. The rote saying of anything is the enemy of understanding. To reduce to unison prayers whose meaning is unfamiliar is virtually to guarantee that they will mean nothing to the sayer. *"Brethren: Everything that was written in times past was written for our instruction, that through the patience and encouragement afforded by the scriptures we might have hope. I say that Christ exercised his ministry to the circumsised to show God's fidelity in fulfilling his promises to the fathers, whereas the Gentiles glorify God for his mercy, as it is written: 'Therefore will I proclaim you among the nations, and I will sing praise to your name.'"* These were the words with which I first accosted my fellow parishioners from the lector's pulpit. I do not even now understand them well enough to explain them with any confidence. And yet, the instruction manual informs me, I am to communicate their meaning "clearly" and "confidently." And together the congregation will repeat such sentences in the gradual.

Our beloved Mother Church. How sadly, how innocently, how—sometimes—strangely she is sometimes directed by her devoted disciples! *Hail Mary, full of Grace, the Lord is with you . . .* The Lord is with who? *Thee to you, Buster,* I found myself thinking during the retreat when first I learned that it is a part of the current edification to strip the Lord, His Mother, and the saints of the honorific with which the simple Quakers even now address their children and their servants. And the translations! *"Happy the Humble—they shall inherit. . . ."* One cannot read on without the same sense of outrage one would feel on entering the Cathedral of Chartres and finding that the windows had been replaced with pop art figures of Christ sitting in against the slumlords of Milwaukee. One's heart is filled with such passions of resentment and odium as only Hilaire Belloc could adequately have voiced. O God O God O God, why hast thou forsaken us! My faith, I note on their taking from us even the canon of the mass in that mysterious universal which soothed and inspired the low and the mighty, a part of the mass—as Evelyn Waugh recalled—"for whose restoration the Elizabethan martyrs had gone to the scaffold [in which] St. Augustine, St. Thomas à Becket, St. Thomas More, Challoner and Newman would have been perfectly at their ease among us," is secure. I pray the sacrifice will yield a rich harvest of informed Christians. But to suppose that it will is the most difficult act of faith I have ever been called on to make, because it tears against the perceptions of all my senses. My faith is a congeries of dogmatical certitudes, one of which is that the new liturgy is the triumph, yea the resurrection, of the Philistines.

—WFB   NOVEMBER 10, 1967

ANGLICAN AGONY

As a Catholic, I have abandoned hope for the liturgy, which, in the typical American church, is as ugly and as maladroit as if it had been composed by Ralph Ingersoll and H. L. Mencken for the purpose of driving people away. Incidentally, the modern liturgists are doing a remarkably good job, attendance at Catholic mass on Sunday having dropped sharply in the ten years since a few well-meaning cretins got hold of the power to vernacularize the mass, and the money to scour the earth in search of the most unmusical men and women to preside over the translation.

The next liturgical ceremony conducted primarily for my benefit, since I have no plans to be beatified or remarried, will be my funeral; and it is a source of great consolation to me that, at that event, I shall be quite dead, and will not need to listen to the accepted replacement for the noble old Latin liturgy. Meanwhile, I am practicing yoga so that at church on Sundays I can develop the power to tune out everything I hear, while attempting, athwart the general calisthenics, to commune with my Maker, and ask Him first to forgive me my own sins, and implore him, second, not to forgive the people who ruined the mass.

Now the poor Anglicans are coming in for it. I am not familiar with their service, but I am with their Book of Common Prayer. To be unfamiliar with it is as though one were unfamiliar with *Hamlet,* or the *Iliad,* or the *Divine Comedy.* It has, of course, theological significance for Episcopalians and their fellow travelers. But it has a cultural significance for the entire English-speaking world. It was brought together, for the most part, about four hundred years ago, when for reasons no one has been able to explain, the little island of England produced the greatest literature in history. G. K. Chesterton wrote about it, "It is the one positive possession, and attraction . . . the masterpiece of Protestantism; the one magnet and talisman for people even outside the Anglican Church, as are the great Gothic cathedrals for people outside the Catholic Church."

What are they doing to it? Well, there is one of those commissions. It is sort of retranslating it. As it now stands, for instance, there are the lines, "We have erred, and strayed from thy ways like lost sheep. We have followed too much the devices and desires of our own hearts. We have offended against thy holy laws. We have left undone those things which we ought to have done; and we have done those things which we ought not to have done."

That kind of thing—noble, cadenced, pure as the psalmist's water—becomes, "We have not loved you [get that: *you,* not *thee.* Next time around, one supposes it will be "We haven't loved you, man"] with our whole heart, we have not loved our neighbors as ourselves." "Lead us not into temptation" becomes "Do not bring us to the test."

Well, if the good Lord intends not to bring his Anglican flock into the test, he will not test it on this kind of stuff. As it is, Anglicanism is a little shaky, having experienced about a hundred years earlier than Roman Catholicism some of the same kind of difficulties. I revere my Anglican friends and highly respect their religion, but it is true that it lends itself to such a pasquinade as Auberon Waugh's, who wrote recently, "In England we have a curious institution called the Church of England . . . Its strength has always lain in the fact that on any moral or political issue it can produce such a wide divergence of opinion that nobody—from the Pope to Mao Tse-tung—can say with any confidence that he is not an Anglican. Its weaknesses are that nobody pays much attention to it and very few people attend its functions."

And it is true that in a pathetic attempt to attract attention, the Anglicans, and indeed many other Protestants, and many Catholics, absorb themselves in secular matters. "The first Anglicans," Chesterton once wrote, "asked for peace and happiness, truth and justice; but nothing can stop the latest Anglicans, and many others, from the horrid habit of asking for improvement in international relations." International relations having taken a noticeable turn for the worse in the generation since Chesterton made this observation, one can only hope the Anglicans will reject any further attempt to vitiate their line of communication with our Maker.

—WFB   JULY 16, 1975

His New Prayer

Those outsiders (I am not an Anglican) who have been following the agony of that Christian communion oscillate between feelings of sorrow and anger. It is conceivably a part of the Lord's design to torture his institutional representatives on earth, and of course it is generally conceded that the special object of His displeasure in the past decade has been His old favorite, the Roman Catholic Church, which He has treated with stepfatherly neglect. But as if some providential version of equal treatment under the Law were guiding Him, it has been recently the season of torment for the Episcopal Church, which indeed is now riven in factions so resolutely opposed to one another that schism itself has set in.

This last was precipitated by the question whether to ordain women priests. There is an Anglican bishop in New York who is given to extreme formulations in any field whatsoever. About a year ago he was anathematizing businessmen who were driven from New York, having looked at their ledgers and decided that, on the whole, they and their flock would be better off in an area in which the tax overhead was less, as also the incidence of murder, rape, and mugging. Bishop [Paul] Moore would have lectured Moses himself on his lack of civic pride in departing Egypt in search of greener pastures. Well, the bishop not only came out for ordaining women, for which there is at least a coherent argument, he proceeded to ordain a self-professed lesbian, which struck many of his flock as less a gesture of compassion than of defiance.

The other morning, the Church of England issued its rewording of the Lord's Prayer. Now the head of the Church of England, at least titularly, is the Queen of England. One would think that sometime before the British Court worried about anachronisms in dealing with God, they would accost anachronisms in dealing with the Queen of England. But while she continues to be addressed with all the euphuistic pomposity of Plantagenet prose, they are modernizing the form of address appropriate to God. One continues to refer to the Queen as Your Majesty, and as "Ma'am"; but for God, "Thee" and "Thou" are—out. The Lord's head has been placed on the Jacobinical block.

It now goes not, "Our Father, who art in Heaven, hallowed be Thy name"—but "Our Father in Heaven, hallowed be Your Name." Granted, they have left the capital letter in "Your," which must have been done after grave debate in the relevant councils. But clearly it was felt that "Thy" was simply—too much. Who does He think He is? The Queen of England?

It goes on, "Your will be done on earth as in Heaven."

One wonders what has been gained by that formulation over the traditional formulation, which read "Thy will be done on earth as it is in Heaven." There is transparent here something on the order of a Parkinsonian imperative: A venerable passage will be reworded by a rewording commission insofar as a commission to reword possesses the authority to do so.

Is it suggested that more people will understand the phrase in the new formulation? In the first place, we are hip-deep in the aleatory mode when we say, "Thy will be done," since we all know that it is very seldom done; and, indeed, some of us would go so far as to say that it is most unlikely that it is being done by the Royal Committee on the Vulgarization of the Book of Common Prayer when they take such a sentence as "Thy will be done on earth as it is in Heaven" back from the alchemists who worked for the Lord and for King James, and beat it into the leaden substitute which they have now promulgated.

One wishes that were all; but there is no sin of omission for which we might be grateful. "Lead us not into temptation, but deliver us from evil" has been changed to "Do not bring us to the time of trial, but deliver us from evil." Why? For the sake of clarity? (That is the usual answer.) I know, because every sense in my body informs me, and every misinclination of my mind, what is temptation, from which we seek deliverance. But "*the time of trial?*" That sounds as if the Supreme Court is in session.

Perhaps it was ordained that the Episcopalians, like their brothers the Catholics, should suffer. It is a time for weeping, and a time for rage. Do not go kindly into the night. Rage, rage against the dying of the light. That would be the advice of this outsider to my brothers in the Anglican Church. They must rage against those who bring upon Christianity not only indifference, but contempt.

—WFB   NOVEMBER 17, 1977

Introduction to *Amo, Amas, Amat, and More,* by Eugene Ehrlich. Harper & Row, 1985.

It is not plain to me why I was asked to write the Introduction to this book. (There are true Latinists around. Not in abundance, but for instance one thinks of Garry Wills, or Ernest Van den Haag, just to mention two noisy, and brilliant, writers.) Nor is it obvious why I accepted the invitation (the little stipend is being forwarded to charity).

I suppose I am asked because the few Latin phrases I am comfortable with I tend to use without apology. For instance, for some reason I find it handier even in idiomatic exchanges to say "*per impossibile*" over against, say, "assuming that the impossible were actually to take place." Nor is the usefulness of *per impossibile* sui generis—if you see the kind of situation one is capable of falling into. And, of course, there are those Latin phrases that have a utilitarian function, as for instance the lawyers' "*nolle prosequi*," which has become so thoroughly transliterated as to have acquired English conjugational life: thus, "The case against Dr. Arbuthnot was nol-prossed"—the lawyer's vernacular for "The prosecutor decided not to prosecute the case against Dr. Arbuthnot."

So, there are those Latin phrases—and, really, there are not so many of them—that cling to life because they seem to perform useful duties without any challenger rising up to take their place in English. Sometimes these special exemptions from vernacularization in the mother tongue derive from the distinctive inflection that flows in from the Latin. There is no English substitute, really, for "He faced the problem *ad hoc,*" which is much easier than the cumbersome alternative in English ("He faced the problem with exclusive concern given to the circumstances that particularly surrounded it"). Other Latin phrases, the kind against which Fowler inveighed, have the sense of being dragged in. The reader, when he comes across them, will judge on the basis of circumstances whether he is on to a felicitous intonation communicated by the Latin and not by the English. The scholarly Mr. Ehrlich, for instance, includes in this collection *Ab asino lanam,* giving as the English meaning (which is different from the English translation), "blood from a stone." And further elucidating, "Anyone who tries to achieve the impossible is doomed to failure. Thus, an attempt to get *ab asino lanam,* literally, 'wool from an ass,' will inevitably fail." The above is for the scholar, not the practitioner of idiom.

But then why not? Mr. Ehrlich touches on the difficulty of assembling a list meagerly. Inevitably some readers would be dissatisfied. For all one knows, there is someone about who, day in and day out, denounces efforts to reason with the Soviets as ventures *ab asino lanam,* and it would ruin their life if a collection of Latin sayings were published that left out that expression. Better, then, to include *ab asino lanam,* and also the kitchen sink; which Mr. Ehrlich does, and I am very glad that he decided to do so.

Probably the principal Latin-killer this side of the Huns was Vatican II. The other day, sitting alongside a Jesuit college president, I mentioned, by way of indicating the distinctive training of English Jesuits, that my schoolmasters at Beaumont College when engaged in faculty discussions addressed each other in Latin. He replied matter-of-factly that so it had been with him and his classmates. "But now, after fifteen years, I would have a problem with relatively simple Latin."

No doubt about it, the generations of Catholic priests trained in Latin, and the seepage of Latin to parishioners, students, altar boys, will diminish, drying up the spring which for so many centuries watered a general knowledge of Latin and held out almost exclusively, after the virtual desertion of Latin from curricula in which it held, in e.g., English public schools, an absolutely patriarchal position. But it is not likely that the remaining bits and pieces will all be extirpated by the vernacular juggernaut. And even if that should be so, it would happen generations down the line. Meanwhile I know of no book to contend in usefulness with that of Mr. Ehrlich, who has given us a resourceful, voluminous, and appetizing smorgasbord.

—WFB

Memo to: WFB
From: McF [James McFadden, publisher of *National Review*]

Bill: Did you see the review in the *Albuquerque Journal* of Christo's book, *Thank You for Smoking,* by Steve Brewer? I'll pass it along, and will quote just one line from it here: "[Christopher] Buckley, son of William F. Buckley and already twice the writer his old man will ever be, previously wrote [*The White House Mess*] . . ."

Dear Jim: Yes, I did see that. Poor Brewer. Or did you hear? He committed suicide. Left a note, something about atoning for a life of misjudgments. Poor guy. Well, at least he got to read Christo's book before popping off.

Warmest,

BILL

Supplementary memo to: McF
From: WFB

Jim: Just as I wrote you the above, I received a translation program for my computer: English-French, French-English. To practice, I followed instructions to translate from the English to the French, and the computer ground out the following:

De: McF

Bill: Vous faisait voit la révision dans *l'Albuquerque Journal* du livre de Christo *Merci pour Fumage,* par Steve Brasseur? Je passerai il, et citera l'on juste ligne de lui ici: "[Christopher] Buckley, fils de William F. Buckley et déjà deux fois l'écrivain son vieil homme jamais soyez, a écrit précédemment [*Le Désordre de la Maison Blanc*]."

Jim: Oui, j'ai vu ce. Brasseur pauvre. Ou vous faisait entend? Il s'a se suicidé. Gauche une note, quelque chose environ expier pour une vie de [misjudgments]. Type pauvre. Eh bien, au moins il a pu lire le livre de Christo auparavant crever teint. Plus chaud, Bill

I then asked the computer to take the French, as given above, and retranslate it into English. The result is utterly captivating. Hotter, Bill . . .

Of: McF

Bill: Did you make see the revision in the *Albuquerque Newspaper* of delivers of Christo *Thank You for Smoking,* by Steve Brewer? I will pass he, and will mention him one right line of him here: "[Christopher] Buckley, son of William F. Buckley and already two times the writer sound old man is ever, has written previously [*The Disorder of the House White*]."

Jim: Yes, I saw this. Poor brewer. Or did you make hear? He has himself killed. Left a note, something about expiate for a life of [misjudgments]. Poor type. Eh well, to the minus him could read the book of Christo before croak complexion. Hotter, Bill

—WFB   SEPTEMBER 26, 1994

Dear Mr. Buckley:

I agree with conservatives who want to make English the official language of America. But while we're at it, how about making English the official language of *National Review?*

Maybe it was a bad fortnight, but in the December 31 issue, we see *perestroika* (p. 20); *ad nauseam* (p. 26); *vere dignum et justum est* (p. 29); *ad infinitum, cogito ergo sum, Märchen, sum ergo cogito* (all on p. 31); *credo quia absurdum est* and *anima* (p. 32); *nomenklatura* and *glasnost* (p. 40); *magnum opus* (p. 41); *soi-disant* (pp. 41, 42); *de haut en bas* (p. 42); *a fortiori* (p. 44); *Kraft durch Freude, Ordnung,* and *Achtung* (p. 46); *jeu d'esprit* (p. 49); *tour de force* (p. 50); and *billets-doux* (p. 53).

Now, I consider myself reasonably well educated in languages: I have a degree in Russian with minors in German and French, and am fluent in legalese and nineteenth-century American English. But I confess that some of these phrases are Greek to me.

I'm not advocating eliminating foreign words from the lexicon. But if you cannot persuade your erudite writers to use English, could you at least provide translations for your harried readers?

> Yours truly,
> JOHN BRADEN
> FREMONT, MICH.

Dear Mr. Braden: It is an old complaint, the use of foreign words. I would even quote to you from Fowler, except that I can't find anything under "foreign words" in my Fowler here and I am isolated in Switzerland at the moment. However, delicately used, they do bring little piquancies and with them—well, *aperçus* which, because they are extra-idiomatic, give you a fresh view of the subject. As if, in a gallery, you could rise—or descend—ten feet, and look at the picture from that fresh perspective. Don't you think? Or is mine a *fausse idée claire?* . . . By the way, knowing no German, Russian, or Greek, I often experience your frustration; but when I do, I bite my tongue on the grounds that somebody, out there, is getting pleasure. *Noblesse oblige.* Yours cordially,

> —WFB   APRIL 29, 1988

Dear Bill:

As one who writes regularly on geopolitical affairs, you may be interested in the attached essay of mine re what I call "semantic black holes" in our language of politics relating to the Soviet Union. The three examples of namelessness examined in this piece, which is pending publication in a major newspaper, are:

a) the absence in our language of a proper antonym for the seductive Russian word *glasnost;*

b) the absence, also, of a proper antonym for the powerful Russian word *perestroika;* and

c) the continued namelessness of the Soviets' SDI equivalent—their "Starsky Warsky," so to speak.

If you agree that these gaps in our language pose a significant problem, please consider ways in which your own excellent Op-Ed writing might help to get *skrytnost* (the Russian word for the closedness, hiddenness, and official silence of the Leninist system), *pokazukha* (the Russian word for what is superficial, temporary, and essentially meaningless), and Soviet Star Wars (SSW) into common usage.

Your insertion of any or all of these terms into your writing would undoubtedly prompt others in journalism and in academia to follow suit with appropriate words and actions of their own.

With continued good wishes, I remain,

Sincerely,

JIM GUIRARD, JR.

WASHINGTON, D.C.

Dear Jim: See your point, but to go around talking about *skrytnost* and *pokazukha* would terminate whatever reputation I have left for writing in English. Cordially,

—WFB   JUNE 2, 1989

Dear Mr. Buckley:

I have noticed that advertisements for your magazine are quite good except for one minor omission. You forget to tell your prospective readers that they must be at least bi-lingual, but preferably multi-lingual in order to read *National Review.*

I am just an average citizen with only the average public school language requirements and I become quite dismayed when I cannot read the poems, quips, endings of articles, beginnings of articles because of the language barrier. I hope to see the Latin, African, Spanish, French, and Sanskrit kept to a minimum, or better yet, perhaps you could put out a special all-English edition.

MRS. E. F. WAKEFIELD

BALBOA ISLAND, CALIF.

FEBRUARY 26, 1963

———

Mrs. Wakefield's short letter to *National Review* was followed by another, much more graphic. It appears here as it appeared in the magazine, after we located a compositor who was a font of wisdom.

———

I agree with Mrs. E. F. Wakefield who complained in "Lecteuse Clamat" [Feb. 26] that your writers use foreign languages too much. Even the *English* of writers like Buckley and Rickenbacker is obscure enough.

J. VALENTINE BARTON
CHICAGO, ILL.

Mrs. E. F. Wakefield

National Review

สมอารมณ์ปอง. ทั้งพวกพ้องปรีค์เปรมเกษมศรี ว่าอยู่เย็นเป็นสุขทุก
เดือนปี แม้นใขนถามโรคที่โศกกาย ว่าคงจะเขายางเหมือนอย่างว่า
หรือถามหาลูกหนพน้องหาย ว่าคงพยพักตร์เหมือนทักทาย หรือถาม
หมายหาลาภไม่หยายคำ ว่าช้าๆคงจะสมอารมณ์นึก. ได้ถ้องกัก
เหล่ากอเย็นชัชิ่า สามหาคู่นักเหมือนซักนำ ขอายคำไว้ทีเท่านั้นเอยๆ

—ED.

Puis-je vous éclaircir sur une faute dans le titre d'une lettre? Tandis que "chanteur" se transforme en "chanteuse" la plupart des noms qui terminent en -teur au masculin veulent le suffixe -trice au féminin. Il est de même en ce qui concerne le mot "lecteur." Donc on devrait lire "Lectrice Clamat." *

MAURICE LEIBOWITZ
NEW HAVEN, CONN.

Lectrice, ist das nicht das, was Consolidated Edison hervorbringt?

—WFB   MARCH 26, 1963

---

* May I point out an error in the title of a letter? While *chanteur* does become *chanteuse*, most nouns that end in *-teur* in the masculine take the suffix *-trice* in the feminine. It is the same situation with the word *lecteur*. Therefore it should read "Lectrice Clamat."—Ed.

Chapter 7

On Dirty, Bawdy, Profane, Vulgar, Scatological, Etc., Words: A Short Chapter

Dear Mr. Buckley:

If it be true that resorting to the use of foul language is the result of a poor vocabulary, what is your excuse?

Sincerely yours,

ELEVRA M. SCORPIO

JOHNSTON, R.I.

Dear Mrs. Scorpio: Knowing just which word to use.

Cordially,

—WFB

Bill Buckley (to keep it colloquial) seldom uses or resorts to profanity, much less vulgarity. His usual signoff—i.e., what used to be called the "complimentary closing," is, as we have seen, "Cordially." But now and then, out of fatigue or boredom or in simple impatience, he becomes a little less than cordial. Ending one exchange, he used the simple word "Crap," thereby producing a torrent of mail. One defender, not surprisingly, cited the well-known attribution to Sir Thomas Crapper, who was knighted, one hopes, for reasons beyond his invention of the flush toilet. After many months, Bill had to call a halt to the correspondence (not reproduced here).

One column of thirty years ago (see next page) Buckley now sees as poor prophecy. But was he so far off?

PORNOGRAPHY: SHOWDOWN AHEAD

The *New York Review of Books,* which is the thing to read nowadays among the high literati, and not without reason, features in the Letters section of the current issue a discussion among its readers over whether it should have published a commonplace obscenity in a recent number. The letters are so angled by the editors—how easy it is, *mea culpa,* for an editor to do this kind of thing—as to present in a more favorable light those who professed themselves as utterly undisturbed at seeing the forbidden word in print. The principal objector presents his views in a long, plodding epistle. It has the effect of satisfying the reader whose judgment on the issue is suspended that those who oppose the obscenity speak out from the depths of Philistia. The editors' own position is of course clear: after all, they published the obscenity in the first place.

It seems to me surprising that taste has become so dead a language. It is not by any means necessary that an avant-garde should be tasteless. But the avant-garde *is* tasteless—passages in Mary McCarthy, the perennial Miss Avant Garde, are a case in point. And taste is not only a natural inclination that flows from the finer nature of man. It is usually explainable in rational terms.

Take the use of the controversial word. Ten years ago Professor John P. Roche (since become head of the Americans for Democratic Action) wrote a telling review of the incumbent lubricity of Norman Mailer and pointed out that the excuse that Realism is only achieved by literal transcriptions of the way people talk is for artistic reasons untrue. In barracks talk, obscenity is so commonplace as to be altogether unremarkable, no more noticeable than the act of breathing. In literature, the convention being against certain obscenities, the appearance of them unbalances the situation the author means to describe. This criticism would, on reflection, appear to be so self-evident as to cause special concern that the editors of a highbrow journal, engaged after all in tastemaking, should appear to be if not ignorant of it, at least unconvinced by it. Moreover, in the disputed case they had not even the excuse of transcribing a colloquy that took place in the men's room. The reviewer simply chose to use the word for his own purpose: it came, explicitly, from his own mouth.

The episode suggests the collision course that has been charted between American society and its intellectual class. The old Comstockian code had to go—no literary convention is defensible that would exclude the circulation of the works of James Joyce. But the liberal intellectuals took their victory in the famous case of *Ulysses* and ran with it—with no idea whatever of any goal line. They are still running with it, having defended such indefensibles as *Candy* and lesser-known works of pornography. "The controversy over obscene literature," the *Wall Street Journal* now observes, "which has raged periodically in this country for about 100 years, seems to be getting hotter than ever." The *Journal* cites various problems that lie before the Supreme Court. The pity is that such problems should end up in the hands of courts of law. As one might expect, the Supreme Court has in effect thrown up its hands in helplessness. On the one hand it is pressured by free speech fundamentalists who maintain that the First Amendment gives a man the right to merchandise his obscenities even as Galileo should have had the right to merchandise his understanding of the order of the universe. On the other hand, practical sense recognizes that a society has the moral right and the intellectual resources to distinguish between the right of dissent and the right to pander to a low voluptuousness. The Supreme Court, besotted by ideology, tends to acquiesce to the former pressures. But the pressure on the other end is mounting for a general showdown. The licentious use of privilege, whether by the demagogue or by the editors of a highbrow magazine, undermines the glory of freedom, and strengthens the hand of those lurking opportunists who are always looking to strengthen the case against it.

—WFB   MARCH 13, 1965

Dear Mr. Buckley: How do you square your "goddams" with your Catholicism? Are you *really* blaspheming (which I tend to doubt), or is there some distinction between "goddam" (*NR*) and "God damn" with which I'm not familiar? If so, I'd be interested to know how one makes this distinction in the *spoken* word; also, to have your definition and understanding of "goddams," not in *my* dictionary.

ANN JONES
NEW YORK HILTON HOTEL

Dear Miss Jones: No, I am not really blaspheming, or in any case, do not mean to be blaspheming, blaspheming being one of those things I am against. "Goddam" is nowadays a simple expletive, an intensifier. It is that by cultural usage. In the most cloistered convent in Catholic Spain, you will hear from the venerable lips of an aged nun, "Jesus Mary and Joseph, I forgot my umbrella!" "I would pray hard to his Maker to save his soule notwithstanding all his God-damnes," a writer is quoted by the Oxford English Dictionary as saying in 1647, back when they were fighting religious wars. Three hundred years later, the American Heritage Dictionary of the English Language lists "God damn" and "goddam" as a profane [i.e., a-religious] oath, once a strong one involving God's curse, now a general exclamation . . . used as an intensive."

                                    —WFB   NOVEMBER 18, 1969

Dear Mr. Buckley: Regarding your polemics on profanity [Nov. 18] I am somewhat comforted to know that you "do not mean to be blaspheming" when you employ the "expletive" God-dam. Further comfort may be derived from Thayer's Greek-English lexicon of the New Testament which ascribes blasphemy to those who by contemptuous speech *intentionally* come short of the reverence due to God or sacred things. Here the comfort ends giving place to a godly concern. For the Word of God which I equate with the Scriptures of the Old and New Testament specifically commands: "Thou shalt not take the name of the Lord thy God in vain" (Ex. 20:7). In the Hebrew the words "in vain" mean "to no good purpose," thus, "thou shalt not take [use] the name of the Lord thy God to no good purpose," which leads me to believe that unless you are willing to argue that your calling upon God to damn an inanimate or animate object is purposive and conscionable, you are guilty of transgressing the law of God, which is no light thing. As one who professes the faith of Roman Catholicism, I would expect you to yield more readily to the "thus saith the Lord" of Exodus 20:7 than to the culturally conditioned value of the *American Heritage Dictionary of the English Language.*

                              Sincerely,
                              (REV.) GEORGE MILADIN
                              Reformed Presbyterian Church
                              WOODLAND HILLS, CALIFORNIA

Dear Dr. Miladin: The meaning of words is established by their usage, which would suggest that blasphemy is defined by that which is intended, rather than by that which is spoken, at least in such cases as permit of ambiguity. In such cases, one should invoke the transcendent virtue: Charity shall cover the multitude of sins. IPe. 4:8.

                                    —WFB

Despite the damage done to "some Italian guy" in the following letter from column reader Moran and to used-car salesmen in Attwood's letter preceding, the following exchange may be instructive despite the stereotypical slanders:

Dear Bill:

Here's an amusing letter I thought you might like to answer personally.

I didn't realize Nixon had kept those leftover JFK and LBJ fructs in the White House, but what can you expect from a guy who looks like a usucar salesman?

Yours,

WILLIAM ATTWOOD

Publisher, *Newsday*

enc.

Dear Mr. Buckley:

Now really what the hell kind of word is this to use in a column directed to the average person with the average vocabulary. ["He likes being President. He likes the power, the usufructs of the Presidency . . ." *NR*, March 1.] It annoys me to run across any such ludicrous words that I'm supposed to leave my easy chair and dig out the old Funk—to find out what you are about. I realize you know what it means and probably a couple of other people on this planet like the professors of English at Oxford and a fop like Truman Capote. But I'll tell you this, to the average American "usufructs" sounds like some Italian guy telling another guy what kind of loving he enjoys. Really what a stupid word usage—sometimes you are just too much. Regards anyway.

ROBERT MORAN

WANTAGH, NEW YORK

Dear Mr. Moran:

What then would you do to the nursery rhyme,

> *Could eternal life afford*
> *That tyranny should thus deduct*
> *From this fair land*
> *. . . A year of the sweet usufruct?*

—WFB   MARCH 29, 1974

Dear Mr. Buckley:

Could I ask your view on something that has been bothering me for several years?

Why were Clark Gable, Gary Cooper, John Wayne, Spencer Tracy, Jimmy Stewart, and all of my other movie idols able to make great classic films without once uttering the "F" word on screen?

Several weeks ago I attended a cinema and the "word" was repeated so many times that out at the refreshment stand I absentmindedly asked for a "f—— tub of popcorn, a f—— box of Milk Duds and a f—— medium Coke" and got thrown out of the theater by the manager.

Even cute little Macaulay Culkin gets to say the "word" in his new thriller, *The Good Son,* so what was wrong when I repeated it at the concession counter? Is it realism when an actor declaims it on screen, but a vulgarity when I ask the popcorn girl to "please hold the f—— butter"? Is there some sort of double standard here?

Sincerely,

JOHN BOLAND

GODFREY, ILL.

P.S. You know Charlton Heston and Tom Selleck, so, if by any chance you also know June Allyson, would you tell her I've loved her forever?

Dear Mr. Boland: Hollywood gets away with f—— murder. . . . Sorry, I don't know Miss Allyson, but I understand how you feel about her. Cordially,

—WFB

ON THE USE OF "DIRTY" WORDS

I guess I was seven when I first heard the maxim that only people with a small vocabulary use "dirty" words. I am forty-seven and have just received a communication from a reader delivering that maxim as though he had invented it. The trouble with the cliché is (a) it isn't true; (b) it doesn't take into account the need to use the resources of language; and (c) the kind of people who use it are almost always engaged in irredentist ventures calculated to make "dirty" words and expressions that no longer are, and even some that never were.

The first point is easily disposed of by asking ourselves the question, Did Shakespeare have a good vocabulary? Yes; and he also used, however sparingly, profane and obscene words.

The second point raises the question of whether a certain kind of emotion is readily communicable with the use of other than certain kinds of words. Let us assume the only thing it is safe to assume about the matter, namely, that every emotion is experienced by everyone, from the darkest sinner to the most uplifted saint. The sinner, having no care at all for people's feelings, let alone for propriety abstractly considered, lets loose a profanity not only on occasions when his emotions are acutely taxed, but even when they are mildly stirred. The saint—or so I take it from their published writings—manages to exclude the profane word from his vocabulary, and does not resort to it under any circumstances. It was for the saint that the tushery was invented. "Tush! tush!" the saint will say to his tormentors, as he is eased into the cauldron of boiling oil.

Non-saints, it is my thesis, have a difficult time adopting the manners of saints; and even if they succeed most of the time in suppressing obnoxious words, they will probably not succeed all of the time. Moreover, as suggested above, they are up against a community some of whose members are always seeking to repristinate the world of language back to the point where you could not even say, "Gosh, Babe Ruth was a good baseball player," because Gosh is quite clearly a sneaky way of saying God, the use of which the purists would hold to be impermissible under any circumstances—indeed they, plus the Supreme Court, reduce the permissible use of the word to the innermost tabernacles. . . .

I had reason to reach, a while back, for a word to comment upon a line of argument I considered insufferably sanctimonious. "Crap," I wrote: And the irredentist hordes descended upon me in all their fury. I have replied to them that the word in question is defined in a current dictionary in several ways. That among these are meaning 2: "nonsense; drivel: *Man, don't hand me that crap.* 3. a lie; an exaggeration: *Bah, you don't believe that crap, do you?*" Notwithstanding that the word has these clearly nonscatalogical uses, there is an Anglo-Saxon earthiness to it which performs for the writer a function altogether different from such a retort as, say, "Flapdoodle."

There are those of us who feel very strongly that the cheapest and most indefensible way to give offense is to direct obscenities wantonly, and within the earshot of those who seek protection from that kind of thing. There will always be a certain healthy tension between Billingsgate and the convent, but in the interest of the language, neither side should win the war completely. Better a stalemate, with a DMZ that changes its bed meanderingly, like the Mississippi River.

—WFB   APRIL 14, 1973

Professor (emeritus) Thomas Bergin
Department of Romance Languages
Yale University
New Haven, Conn.

Dear Tom:
The enclosed letter challenges my scholarship in a most sensitive way. Would you kindly read, and comment?

Dear Mr. Buckley:
Commenting on the shocking behavior of Dutch Catholics during the Pope's recent visit to the Low Countries, you tried to explain "a term unknown to most nice people," namely "the *fico.*"

Unfortunately, you did not succeed very well.

First, the term is not "*fico*" ("*il fico*" being the fig in Italian) but "*fica*" (Italian vulgar term for vulva), and second, it does not mean to "keep all your fingers lowered and raise the middle finger erect," but it consists in thrusting the thumb between two of the closed fingers.

Surely you remember that, in Canto XXV of *The Inferno*, Vanni Fucci "*le mani alzò con ambedue le fiche . . .*" (which in the Binyon translation reads, "Raising his hands with both figs on high . . ."). In addition, Villani reported that on a high tower in Carmignano, destroyed by the Florentines in 1228, there were two marmoreal arms making "*le fiche*" toward Florence. "*Le fiche*" is, of course, the plural of "*la fica*" and not of "*il fico.*"

It would appear that you are not very conversant with terms "unknown to most nice people." You must shape up. The times require it.

Sincerely yours,
PLINIO PRIORESCHI
OMAHA, NEB.

Dear Bill: Mr. Prioreschi has indeed got it right . . . However, I would not urge you to "shape up." Stay as sweet as you are . . .

> *A scholar I knew in Woonsocket*
> *Would for lunch put into his pocket*
> *Tubes of library paste—*
> *It's not everyone's taste,*
> *But till you have tried it don't knock it.*
> *Saluti affettuosi,*
> TOM

Dear Mr. Buckley:

Abolitionists are indeed "hoist by their own petard" ["Notes & Asides," Dec. 17] if the word is used in its seventeenth-century sense: being caught in a trap by a trick of their own contrivance. Applied originally to cheating at cards, or rolling loaded dice, the phrase found favor with dramatists of that era to account for all manner of impudicity. A pox on the French meaning of the term!

> Sincerely,
> KENNETH ROSS
> LOS ANGELES, CALIF.

Dear Mr. Buckley:

. . . The word [*petard*] does basically denote breaking wind in French. Note the similarity in sound to our own vulgarism. Because of this, however, it was also the slang term used by French siege engineers for an improvised black-powder charge, usually on wheels, that could be advanced up to a gate or door to blow it in. We all know how unstable the ignition of such demolitions can be, and not infrequently the sappers would still be messing with the device when it went off, thus being "hoist by their own petard."

It is the curiously apt double entendre that entertains us here. When a man was thus truly "hoist," the occasion could be likened to his drawing unwelcome attention to himself by the unexpected blast of his own exhaust gases—figuratively so, as in Shakespeare.

> Cordially,
> JEFF COOPER
> PAULDEN, ARIZ.

Dear Mr. Buckley:

If recollection from a military-history course thirty-plus years ago serves me well, wasn't a petard a bomb for breaching *mounted on the end of a pole,* which is what differentiated it from a grenade? The pole facilitated placement of the explosive against a wall above the foundation, or against the hinges or bolt of a gate. This all dates back to the seventeenth or eighteenth century and the days of primitive black powder and fuses lit with a tinder or match.

Webster notes the correct usage of "hoist by (or with) one's own petard" but perhaps should add sufficient detail to its definition of the term so that the expression makes sense. The means of hoisting has to be the pole. Being hoist by, with, or on the point of one's own petard would at the very least have an element of surprise, suspense, and contemplation that gives the expression its commonly understood meaning. One could not be hoist with one's own grenade absent some other mechanical agent (a rope and a tree limb?) and, probably, the meddling of a cumbersome judiciary, which is to suggest the procedure would take forever if it ever happened and may explain why we stick with petards in verbal jousts.

> Best regards,
> MARIO E. DE SOLENNI
> CRESCENT CITY, CALIF.

Dear Bill:
The expression "hoist with his own petard" is used by *NR* with sufficient frequency as to approach triteness. Why the hell "hoist," a perfectly useful verb never meant to connote injury?

> Sincerely,
> VICTOR R. MATOUS
> SEATTLE, WASH.

Dear Messrs. Ross, Cooper, and de Solenni: Many thanks for the clarification. I shall feel free, henceforward, to use the phrase with with, or with by.

> —WFB

Dear Vic: Aren't you confusing this with heist? And there is certainly an injury to the victim there, unless he was heisted by his own petard. Cordially,

> —WFB   —JULY 29, 1991

Chapter 8

The Spoken Word: Speech, Students, Diction, Politicians

Words. Many of us in this room [the occasion was *National Review*'s twenty-fifth anniversary] live off them, if not by them. They are useful, dangerous, salvific. "If any man offend not in word," St. James tells us, "the same is perfect man, and able also to bridle the whole body. Behold, we put bits in the horses' mouths, that they may obey us; and we turn about their whole body. Behold also the ships, which though they be so great, and are driven of fierce winds, yet are they turned about with a very small helm, whithersoever the governor listeth. Even so the tongue is a little member, and boasteth great things. Behold, how great a matter a little fire kindleth!"

—WFB   DECEMBER 31, 1980

William F. Buckley, Jr., gives many speeches and formal lectures every year. A lecture by Buckley is never a crowd-pleasing piece out of the old school of Hollow Oratory, attempting to conjure up emotion while causing reason to disappear, though he can on certain occasions be touching. He always pays the audience the ultimate tribute of a prepared talk of substance and style.

Those who think Buckley's distinctive accent an affectation are unaware that Buckley spoke no English until he was seven. Spanish was his first language and French his second. He was schooled in France and England before starting school in the United States. His father, whose business was in Mexico, was a stickler not only about written language but about elocution. (See the first essay in this chapter.)

Given the reasons why he came late to English, Bill could be thought of as a passionate convert to his mother tongue. Coincidences: I am struck by his deep feeling for the uses of English and with that his interest in

Conrad (also a sailor), Brodsky (also an anti-Communist), Nabokov (a friend), and Borges (an idol). The thought of these very different but precise writers could lead to a perspective suggesting that a late start—and/or English as a *second* language—can lead to a high regard for it and in some cases a virtuoso result.

———

What Did You Say?

I recently spent the better part of a day with a college student who had much on his mind to tell me. I in turn was much interested in what he had to say. But after an hour or so I gave up. It wasn't that his thinking was diffuse, or his sentences badly organized. It was simply that you couldn't understand the words. When they reached your ear they sounded as faint as though they had been forced through the wall of a soundproofed room, and as garbled as though they had been fed through one of those scrambling devices of the Signal Corps.

"Somi iggi prufes tometugo seem thaffernun."

"What was that?"

(*Trying hard*) "So mi IGgi prufes tometugo seem THAaf fernun."

"Sorry, I didn't quite get it."

(*Impatiently*): "So MY ENGLISH PROFESSOR TOLD ME TO GO SEE HIM THAT AFTERNOON." And on with the story. By which time, let us face it, the narrative had become a little constipated, and soon I gave up. My responses became feigned, and I was reduced to harmonizing the expression on my face with the inflection of his rhetoric. It had become not a dialogue but a soliloquy, and the conversation dribbled off.

I remarked on the event later to a friend who works regularly with boys and girls of college age. "Don't you understand?" he said. "*Nobody* at college today opens his mouth to speak. They all mumble. For one thing, they think it's chic. For another, they haven't got very much to say. That's the *real* reason why they are called the Silent Generation. Because nobody has the slightest idea what they are saying when they *do* speak, so they assume they are saying nothing."

It isn't a purely contemporary problem. Two generations ago Professor William Strunk, Jr., of Cornell was advising his student E. B. White to speak clearly—and to speak even more clearly if you did *not* know what you were saying. "He felt it was worse to be irresolute," White reminisces in his introduction to *The Elements of Style*, "than to be wrong. . . . Why compound ignorance with inaudibility?"

I remember when I was growing up, sitting around the dining room table with my brothers and sisters making those animal sounds which are understood only by children of the same age, who communicate primarily through onomatopoeia. One day my father announced after what must have been a singularly trying dinner that exactly four years had gone by since he had been able to understand a *single* word uttered by any one of his ten children, and that the indicated solution was to send us *all* to England—where they *respect* the English language and teach you to OPEN YOUR MOUTHS. We put this down as one of Father's periodic aberrations until six weeks later the entire younger half of the family found itself on an ocean liner headed for English boarding schools.

Mumbling was a lifelong complaint by my father, and he demanded of his children, but never got, unconditional surrender. He once wrote to the headmistress of the Ethel Walker School: "I have intended for some time to write or speak to you about Maureen's speech. She does not speak distinctly and has a tendency, in beginning a sentence, to utter any number of words almost simultaneously. Anything the school can do to improve this condition [the school did not do very much] would be greatly appreciated by us. I have always had a feeling [here Father was really laying it on, for the benefit of his children, all of whom got copies] that there was some physical obstruction that caused this, but doctors say there is not."

Frustrated by the advent of World War II and the necessity of recalling his children from England before they had learned to OPEN THEIR MOUTHS, my father hired an elocution teacher and scheduled two hours of classes every afternoon. She greeted her surly students at the beginning of the initial class with the announcement that her elocution was so precise, and her breathing technique so highly developed, that anyone sitting in the top row of the balcony at Carnegie Hall could easily hear her softest whisper uttered onstage. Like a trained chorus we replied—sitting a few feet away—"What did you say? Speak up!" WE DID NOT GET ON. But after a while, I guess we started to OPEN OUR MOUTHS. (There are those who say we have never since shut them.)

No doubt about it, it is a widespread malady—like a bad hand, only worse, because we cannot carry around with us a little machine that will do for our voices what a typewriter does for our penmanship. The malady is one part laziness, one part a perverted shyness. Perverted because its inarticulated premise is that it is less obtrusive socially to speak your thoughts so as to require the person whom you are addressing to ask you twice or three times what it was you said. A palpable irrationality. If you have to ask someone three times what he said and when you finally decipher it you learn he has just announced that the quality of mercy is not strained, or that he is suffering the slings and arrows of outrageous fortune, you have a glow of pleasure from the reward of a hardy investigation. So let the Shakespeares among us mumble, if they must. But if at the end of the mine shaft you are merely made privy to the intelligence that the English professor set up a meeting for that afternoon, you are entitled to resent that so humdrum a detail got buried in an elocutionary gobbledy-gook which required a pick and shovel to unearth.

I do not know what can be done about it, and don't intend to look for deep philosophical reasons why the problem is especially acute now. . . . I nevertheless suggest the problem be elevated to the status of a National Concern. Meanwhile, the kindergartens should revive the little round we used to sing—or, rather, mumble:

> *Whether you softly speak*
> [crescendo] *Or whether you loudly call.*
> *Distinctly! Distinctly speak*
> *Or do not speak at all.*

WORDWISE, ZILCH

The good news is that there are people around who are trying to discover why it is that American youth, year after year, are having greater and greater difficulty in expressing themselves. There are a lot of wisecracks readily available ("they have nothing to say"), but one tires quickly of them, and then genuine worry sets in.

Professor George Miller, the distinguished psychologist at Princeton University, is studying the problem with heroic resolution, and it occurred to him and a colleague that perhaps two or three professional writers might shed light on the subject, which is how it came that on a Tuesday evening in April I found myself at dinner in a private dining room of a splendid restaurant with Tom Wicker on my left and Tom Wolfe on my right, answering questions, or—better stated—trying to answer them.

Question: Why is it that "Sam"—let us call him—scores well enough on multiple-choice verbal tests to get into Harvard but, having arrived there, it soon transpires that Sam cannot write a lucid, straightforward sentence. More properly, why now, when a generation ago the problem was less than epidemic?

Tom Wicker recalled that the most exciting event of the week when he was a boy was the arrival of the *Saturday Evening Post,* which was read from cover to cover, after which he—and everybody he knew—would re-sume the reading of books. Although Professor Miller advises that no cor-relation can be found between illiteracy and time given over to watching television during one's youth, Wicker remains skeptical—and so do I. You can't simultaneously spend four hours watching television and four hours reading good prose. Correct? Correct: but that does not explain the high literacy of many young writers whose youths in fact were spent watching television instead of reading Sir Walter Scott.

Tom Wolfe tried out a couple of ideas. The first is that learning to write requires application—about twelve years, he reckons. So that if you don't begin to write until you go to college, it isn't likely that you will learn to write competently until some years after you have left college. This generality holds a little water, but not a lot of it, because, of course, it does not account for those classmates of Sam, however few in number, who are writing very competently in their freshman year, but whose background was similar to poor Sam's.

Tom Wolfe then thought it might be worth stressing the social point. Wolfe is too fastidious to use words like "peer pressure," but that is what he meant. What would happen, he wondered out loud, if freshmen were divided in some rather ostentatious way between those who were literate and those who were not? Let us suppose, just to suppose, that those who could write lucidly were given a special card that gave them access to—whatever it is college students tend to desire access to. Some sanctuary for the privileged. Might this cause those left behind to wish to catch up? He then set out to undermine his own thesis by recalling that not long ago he had heard a program during which Dick Cavett had asked taxing questions of such professional wordsmiths as John Simon, William Safire, and Edwin Newman, all of whom were greatly disconcerted at the end when Dick Cavett suddenly asked, "Why does it matter?" Tom Wolfe permitted himself to wonder whether in fact it does matter, so long as communication is actually effected. Everybody then recalled Ike, whose verbal instructions, exhortations, and rhetoric communicated unambiguously. But if you transcribed what he said, you wouldn't know whether he had told you to invade Normandy or Brittany. We chewed on that one a bit.

I wondered whether there was a reason for the deadening of the mimetic faculty. For instance: a generation ago it was widely supposed that before long there would be a deregionalization of speech differences. Everyone would sound like Walter Cronkite. That hasn't, of course, happened: in the Deep South they still speak pre-CBS English. Another thing: Why is it that Mexican illiterates never make grammatical mistakes? The chances in America of going through a whole day without having someone say to you, "Between you and I" are, when I last checked with Lloyd's of London, very small. But no Mexican would ever confuse the objective with the subjective pronoun. Americans are supposed to be a musical people, right? We buy recordings by the hectare—all that time listening to music, but failing to develop any sense of cadence for words. How can that be?

We resolved, at the end of the evening, to put the problem right back in George Miller's lap, but we remembered to thank him for the meal, in impeccable sentences.

—WFB   APRIL 26, 1980

Dear Mr. Buckley:

Several months ago on a Saturday morning I began introducing my (then) eighteen-month-old daughter to various public figures. Prior to that time she was able to identify by name only family and friends she had met. She quickly, and first, mastered your name. Now, whenever she watches *Firing Line,* she points to you and says, "Buckey." (Please excuse her difficulty with the letter "L.") You may be interested in the company you keep. She also identifies, with much zeal, Jesus and Moses; the latter name sometimes being given mistakenly to Robert Bork. Although she will sometimes identify "Kenney" (J. F. Kennedy) for my wife, who is more liberal than I, she does not have a clue as to the identity of Roseanne Barr, Geraldo Rivera, or Oprah Winfrey. I hope her experience with the programs of the aforementioned continues to match your own.

Grace to you and peace,
RICHARD W. BOHANNON
STORRS, CONN.

Dear Mr. Bohannon: Your daughter is doing very nicely. Best you don't let her grow any older. Cordially,

—WFB

If Buckley is a man of a thousand speeches, he is also, despite a cherished private life, a man invited to a thousand parties and thus, to an extent, a social creature. He has had to develop exacting standards for how much socializing may precede or follow a lecture. When trapped into a party, or on the less frequent moments when he has happily risen to an occasion, he nevertheless finds himself at times, sophisticated fellow that he is, in the standard party predicament: whom to speak to and about what, and how to escape if it's your own foot you have suddenly discovered, not standing on someone else's but in your own mouth.

The dilemma has led to a splendid instance of finding the right word, one suggested by a writer friend of Buckley's, and a foreign word at that— although we could wish that finding our own *querencia* weren't so foreign to our experience.

PARTY POOPER

. . . There is the special problem raised by the party at which you have a so-cial objective. There are difficulties here because it may be necessary, hav-ing spotted your mark, to move over to him or her, passing by eleven people with whom, in the normal course, you would feel obliged to dally, even if only for a moment. And then in the pursuit of your quarry you may find yourself guilty of behavior if not exactly boring, certainly boorish.

I have a memory of this. Along with my wife, I arrived at a boat party with Mrs. Dolly Schiff, whom I liked, who was among my employers (she published my syndicated column in the *New York Post,* the newspaper she then owned) and who was an important political presence in New York at a time when my brother James was its junior senator, preparing to run for reelection. Boarding the boat, Mrs. Schiff said to me, "Do you know, I have never even met your brother?" Well, said I, I shall certainly cure that tonight—I knew that my brother was among the invited guests.

Some time later, chatting with my brother on the crowded deck, I spot-ted at the extreme other end the imperious forehead of Dolly Schiff. I grabbed my brother and told him we must forthwith go to the other end of the deck, past the eighty-odd people sipping champagne, so that he could be introduced to Mrs. Schiff. Ignoring a dozen old friends, we reached her—at a moment when her head was slightly bent down, ex-changing conversation with a petite woman whose back was to us. I charged in, "Dolly, this is my brother Jim, whom you wanted to meet. Jim, Dolly Schiff." The little woman we had interrupted turned around slowly to us and smiled.

She was our hostess, the Queen of England, but it was too late to undo the damage, so I proceeded with the introduction to Mrs. Schiff (Jim had sat next to the queen at dinner and needed no introduction to her; the rest of us had been through the receiving line). Jim said he was sorry to inter-rupt Mrs. Schiff, who smiled down at Her Majesty. I thought I'd break the ice by suggesting that the entire company join me in pleading with Mrs. Schiff to give me a raise. The queen reacted with a half smile and excused herself to greet another of her guests. There can be casualties of a deter-mined mission at a party.

It is, of course, the objective of some guests to mingle with absolutely everybody at the party. I remember at the casual cocktail hour in Califor-nia talking quietly at the edge of a social congregation with the president-elect of Yale University. I told him that a year earlier the outgoing president, Kingman Brewster, had been at this same affair. "The difference between King and me," Bart Giamatti said, "is that when he walks into a social gathering, his eyes fix instinctively on the center of the densest social activity and he homes right in on it, the true social animal. My own instinct is to look to the farthermost edges of the gathering and head softly in that direction. Where I am standing right now," he said, smiling.

Yes, and that raises the question of one's *querencia,* a favorite word of mine, one that I learned many years ago from Barnaby Conrad and have tirelessly used. The word describes a tiny area in the bullring, maybe fifty square feet, within which the fighting bull fancies himself entirely safe. The difficulty lies in that each bull has his own idea exactly where his *querencia* is, and it is up to the matador to divine, from a ferociously concentrated study of the bull's movements as he charges into the ring, its location; because the matador must, at peril to life and limb, stay well clear of it when executing his critical passes. The bull who finds himself close to his *querencia* and is pained or perplexed will suddenly head for it, and in doing so jerk his horns in an unpredictable direction, at the same spot the matador's groin or abdomen might find itself.

We all have, in any social situation, an undefined querencia, and we instinctively seek it out immediately upon entering the crowded room. Most usually, it is where one's spouse is—but that is a difficult sanctuary to avail yourself of because it is deemed socially backward at a party to glue yourself to your spouse. So you look elsewhere for your querencia. Generally, it is one human being, someone with whom you feel entirely comfortable, whom you can trust to greet you as if your company were the highlight of his day. You have tons to tell him, and he has tons to tell you, all of it of mutual interest. Is he . . . she . . . there? You look around.

No.

Is there an alternative querencia anywhere about?

Well, yes. Somebody told you that Algernon MacNair was going to be there. Not quite the company you most looked forward to attaching yourself to, but quite good enough to avoid the high stilt of tonight's social affair, and there is a specific point of interest. Maybe his Op-Ed piece this morning, in which he took those peculiar positions about taxation. But no. He is not there, nor is anyone else who will fill the bill in the same way.

Ah, but then the querencia can be greatly elastic. You can develop a consuming interest in the appointments of the sumptuous apartment. Every picture deserves close attention, worth at least three minutes of your time, as you look first this way at it, then that way, then examine the artist's signature. And the books! You pick up one from the fourth shelf and open it with delight transfiguring your face. How is it that this neglected volume found its place into this library? How discriminating the taste of our hostess! By the time you have examined that book, perhaps two or three others and a dozen pictures and a score of family photographs—it is time for dinner!

With some apprehension you look down at your card and wonder who will be seated on your right, who on your left; and it is at such moments, as when in a foxhole, or on a sinking boat, that you rediscover God and the need to utter a silent prayer.

———

But enough of niceties. To politics, land of parties—the Grand Old one, the always threatened new Ones, to fund-raisers, and, worse, to hair-raisers, the political speech-makers, recidivist abusers of language. In this arena, more than seldom is heard a discouraging word, but very rare is the right word, the felicitous phrase, or the graceful expression of an idea, whether issuing from Right or from Left.

Buckley, with a jeweler's eye, has been examining these pearls for a long time, starting in this instance with the now-silent voice of Nelson Rockefeller, who liked to greet strangers with "Hi'ya fella!"

———

MYSTIFIER

It must be very discouraging to be a politician. Here is the governor of the most influential state of the union, running hard for the presidential nomination of his party, richer even than Bobby Kennedy, abetted by one of the two or three most expensive speechwriters in the English-speaking world, addressing the editors of just about every newspaper in America, delivering a much-heralded speech in which he managed to spend prospectively 150 billion American dollars—and you know what the headline is the next morning? In one of the nation's most liberal newspapers, devoting maybe second most linage in the country to national and world affairs? "Rockefeller Speech/Heard in Silence."

Surely Mr. Rockefeller envisioned other headlines? "Rockefeller Solves/Problems of City," might have been one. Or, "Rockefeller Magnetism/Wows Editors" would have been satisfactory. Or even, "Rockefeller Speech/Brings GOP Raves." But the reporter (David Broder, one of the nation's best) was as uninspired as the general audience, as uninterested in what Mr. Rockefeller ended up saying as the editors who heard him. A total of two sentences from the massive speech was reproduced in the morning paper—way off, toward the end of the first-page story which began: "Governor Nelson A. Rockefeller of New York made his long-heralded debut as a 'non-candidate' yesterday, delivering a thirty-minute speech on urban problems, uninterrupted by applause, to the luncheon meeting of the American Society of Newspaper Editors at the Shoreham Hotel."

What happened?

Well, to begin with, the speech was so heavy with rhetorical pomposity that it would have required a Saturn IV Booster to launch it. Would you like a taste?—"Our time of testing now follows—like a twin heritage of challenge—from both these earlier ages [Lincoln's and Roosevelt's]. The signs of peril—and the chances for leadership—rise as high on both fronts: from within—and from without—our nation. For we are not only struggling to build peace in the world. We are also striving to live at peace with ourselves."

If you believe that I selected the single worst passage, I give you the peroration which, I have a paralyzing suspicion, somebody at Rockefeller's shop actually thought was eloquent . . .

"I believe deeply in such a new government, such a new leadership, and such a new America.

"We as a people, have—right now—a choice to make.

"We must choose between new division or new dedication.

"We can live together as bullies—or as brothers.

"We can practice retribution or reconciliation.

"We can choose a life of the jungle, or a life of justice.

"We cannot have both.

"We cannot live for long with parts and pieces of both.

"We must choose."

We must cut the crap.

Really, we must. And it is an objective indication that such emptinesses are boring that they bored the audience, and bored the reporters, and permanently traumatized the muses. "The audience reaction," says the account in the *Washington Post*, "was noted with concern by some Rockefeller for President sponsors in the room. One of them said afterwards, 'I hope this convinces Emmet Hughes [the Rockefeller adviser and writer whose stylistic touches were evident in the text] that it will take more than the power of *his* words to nominate Rockefeller."

A pity, really. Because Mr. Rockefeller is a very able man. His delivery is first-rate. He has great facility for extempore talk and his ideas, if one excavates them from all that lard, are worth pondering. For instance, the recognition that the private sector is five times more resourceful than the public sector, and that if the cities are to be saved it will have to be largely by private enterprise. For instance, his observation that we are spending five times as much money subsidizing our rich farms as our poor cities. But it takes men of archaeological passion to find Mr. Rockefeller's ideas in Mr. Rockefeller's current prose. Next time he should furnish his audience with a trot.

—WFB   APRIL 23, 1968

THE SIGHTS AND THE SMELLS (OF A POLITICAL CONVENTION)

KANSAS CITY.—What kind of a show is it? A few observations:

After a couple of days, one got the impression that to be a member of the Mississippi delegation is a profession. It is one that requires political skills, high physical stamina, and a theological flair. "What did grand-daddy do, Mommy?" "He was a member of the Mississippi delegation" would be an appropriate response. . . .

The level of oratory has not been uniformly high. Howard Baker was very good, though he knoweth not the virtue of brevity. Speaking to that huge auditorium requires that the speaker do a good bit of what Mencken once called "plain hollering." The only way you can get a political convention actually to stop and listen to what you are saying is either to intimate in advance that you are going to do something very dramatic (say, defy the Mississippi delegation); that, or summon the eloquence of a very great speaker. This does not mean that you need to say anything—Barbara Jordan subdued Madison Square Garden as totally as Bob Dylan in concert ever did, and said even less.

Once you have the audience listening to you, your narrative must roll, and you must at all costs avoid telegraphing the huge expanses of wisdom you have left to deliver. Do not, after thirty-five minutes, say such a thing as: "We come now to the field of foreign policy . . ." Those who view these speeches over television should close their eyes if they mean to listen, because inevitably the television director will distract you—by flashing his camera on a ninety-seven-year-old lady with a Carmen Miranda Reagan hat, swigging from a bottle of hooch.

We must be grateful that Brutus delivered his oration away from the television cameras, otherwise at the moment the crowd was finally stirred to action, the cameraman would be showing an urchin scribbling on the wall, *Kilroy hic erat.*

John Connally made the mistake of overadvertising his oration. There is a danger that attaches to a press announcement along the lines of, "At 8:35 P.M., on all networks, the Honorable John Connally will deliver the Gettysburg Address." He is a very eloquent man, but makes the mistake of screwing up his face in a contortion of lapidary concern for the republic at moments that suit less the requirements of the text than the rhythms of the paragraph. He must not look equally gloomy in anticipation of a nuclear war and a rise of one penny in the price of a gallon of gasoline.

Nelson Rockefeller's enemies will no doubt conclude that his speech—which was really quite quite awful—was intended to subvert the ambitions of the Republican Party, now that [as retiring Vice-President] he will not have an official role within it. I don't really believe that, disinclined as

I am to the conspiracy view of history. But I have to confess I can't think of a plausible reason for someone to say about his own unsuccessful pursuit of the presidency that the reason for it was, "Somehow I could never get to the church on time . . ."

—WFB   AUGUST 21, 1976

Few occasions summon the full oratorical resources of William F. Buckley more than the anniversary dinners held to celebrate the continued existence of his magazine. Here is the conclusion of one such speech, as the festive, glittering evening wore down. . . .

. . . Still, the campfires continue to burn, and every now and then you hear the chorus singing—the old songs, free of the tormented, tormenting introspections of the new idiom; ignorant altogether of the litany of reasons why we should hate our own country; axiomatic in their demand for human freedom; and the heart stirs, and the blood begins to run, and each one of us in his own way continues the effort. Those who doubt that the spiritual resources are left have only to read a speech—almost any speech—by Patrick Moynihan in the United Nations. Those who doubt that the analytical resources are left need only read any issue of *National Review,* or of *The Public Interest.* Viewed from the right angle, we suddenly see that: Communism is theoretically and empirically discredited. That all over the world enslaved people continue to dream about freedom. That inroads against poverty are successful in almost exact correspondence to the vitality of the private sector. And—most significant—that there are no signs at all that God is dead; He appears to have survived even Vatican II. "I see it as one of the greatest ironies of this ironical time," Malcolm Muggeridge recently wrote, "that the Christian message should be withdrawn for consideration just when it is most desperately needed to save men's reason, if not their souls. It is as though a Salvation Army band, valiantly and patiently waiting through the long years for judgment day, should, when it comes at last, and the heavens do veritably begin to unfold like a scroll, throw away their instruments and flee in terror."

We have stood together for one-tenth of the life span of this Republic, and we must resolve to stand with it, and its ideals, forever.

DECEMBER 5, 1975

And what follows is part of the author's speech on the occasion of *National Review*'s thirty-fifth anniversary, given at a dinner at the Waldorf-

Astoria in New York on October 5, 1990, when he made a surprise announcement about his future with his beloved magazine.

———

There are too many men and women to whom I am indebted to make it feasible to enumerate them. So I won't even mention my sister Priscilla, nor pause to say that without her my thirty-five years at *National Review* would have been intolerable. . . .

I suppose that if there is a single occasion in which a professional will be indulged for speaking personally, it is the occasion when he retires. (If that isn't the case, then *National Review* will establish yet another precedent.) When my father first saw the offering circular with which in 1954 I traveled about the country attempting to induce American capitalists to invest in our prospective journal, my father spotted only one sentence that disturbed him. I wrote in the offering circular that I pledged to devote ten years of my life to *National Review.* My father, who was very . . . formal about personal commitments, told me he thought this exorbitant: "Ten years is simply too long," he said. "Suppose you decide you want to do something else with your life?"

Well, the warning became moot, because there never was anything else around seriously to tempt me. For the fun of it I divulge that in 1970 I was approached by a very small delegation of what one is trained to call "serious people" whose proposal was that I should run for governor of New York, that I should expect to win the election, and position myself to run for the presidency. I was nicely situated to say two things, the first that anyone who had run for mayor of New York getting only 13 percent of the vote shouldn't be too confident about winning an electoral majority in a general election. And I finally silenced my friends by adding that I didn't see how I could make the time to run for governor, given my obligations to *National Review.* My friends couldn't understand my priorities. But I was very content with these priorities.

Oh yes, I won't cavil on that point. The magazine has been everything the speakers tonight have so kindly said it was—is. It is preposterous to suppose that this is so because of my chancellorship. How gifted do you need to be to publish Whittaker Chambers and Russell Kirk, James Burnham and Keith Mano? But yes, the journal needed to function. Somehow the staff and the writers had to be paid—if an editorial note is reserved for me in the encyclopedias, it will appear under the heading ALCHEMY. But the deficits were met, mostly, by our readers; by you. And, yes, we did as much as anybody with the exception of—himself—to shepherd into the White House the man I am confident will emerge as the principal political figure of this century. And he will be cherished, in the nursery tales told in future generations to young children, as the American President who showed the same innocent audacity as the little boy who insisted that the emperor wasn't wearing any clothes at all, when Ronald Reagan said, at a critical moment in Western history, about the Union of Soviet Socialist Republics that it was an evil empire. It is my judgment that those words acted as a resolution to the three frantic volumes of Solzhenitsyn. *The Gulag Archipelago* told us everything we needed to know about the pathology of Soviet communism. We were missing only the galvanizing summation; and we got it, in the Mosaic code: and I think that the countdown for communism began then.

I owe you all an account of my exercise of my fiduciary authority in handling the journal you have sustained. I am, speaking now the language of corporate America, its owner: The stock of *National Review,* which commercially is about as valuable as Confederate bonds, is mine. My resignation as chief executive officer will give me the opportunity to receive the magazine in the mail, as you do, with no specific knowledge of what I'll encounter between its covers, save for my own continuing editorial contributions in my new role as editor-at-large. It is my plan, at some point in the future, to deed my stock to a successor. The highest tribute I can pay to Wick Allison and to John O'Sullivan is that I am turning over to their management a property to the health and hygiene of which I have devoted practically the whole of my adult lifetime. It is inconceivable to me, having watched them in operation for over a year, that I have made a mistake. Still, I elect not to risk being designated at some point in the future as another King Lear. While I am still intact, I'll be there to judge the continuing performance of *National Review,* conscious that I owe to all the readers who have sustained it an obligation that cannot be lightly discharged, and won't be.

Since you were so kind as to ask about my personal plans, I intend to continue to be active on other fronts. Early this week I performed a harpsichord concerto with the North Carolina Symphony, and resolved, with the full acquiescence, I am certain, of the orchestra and the audience, that I will not devote my remaining years to performing on the keyboard. One month from today I will set out, with my companions, on a small sailboat from Lisbon, headed toward Barbados via Madeira, the Canaries, and Cape Verde, forty-four hundred miles of decompression at sea, the cradle of God; needless to say, a book will come out of this. But on reaching the Caribbean, unlike the Flying Dutchman I will jump ship, to get on with other work. I have not scheduled the discontinuation of my column, or of *Firing Line,* or of public speaking, or of book writing. But these activities by their nature terminate whenever the Reaper moves his supernatural, or for that matter, democratic hand, whereas *National Review,* I like to think, will be here, enlivening right reason, for as long as there is anything left in America to celebrate.

And of course, it will always crowd my own memory. Two thousand seven hundred and fifty fortnightly issues of *National Review.* The hour is late, nearing five in the afternoon of press day, and the printer's messenger is already there waiting, so we move into the boardroom, the only room at *National Review* in which more than four people can fit, and Priscilla [Buckley] reads out the editorial lengths, and I mark them down on the paleolithic calculator I bought in Switzerland in 1955, and Linda [Bridges] checks to see that I have got the right count. We have 1,259 lines of editorial copy but space for only 718. We absolutely need to run something on the subject of Judge Souter's testimony, but I see we can't afford the 78-line editorial I processed earlier in the day. "Rick [Brookhiser], would you shorten this?"

"To what?" he asks, as a tailor might ask what the new waistline is to be.

The copy is spread about the room, occupying every level surface, and you walk about, counterclockwise, turning face down any editorial that can wait a fortnight to appear, and subtracting on your little calculator its line count from the rogue total. I need to cut 541 lines. First your eyes pass by the editorials and paragraphs that deal with domestic issues, Priscilla having grouped them together; then those that deal with foreign countries or foreign policy; then the offbeat material. You look down at the calculator, having made the complete circle of the room, returning to where you began: it shows 854 lines, and so you start the second counterclockwise circuit, the killer instinct necessarily aroused: You have *got* to cut another 136 lines. "Jeff, shrink this one by ten lines, okay?" . . . The editors always say okay when a deadline looms.

So it is done, down to line length. And then you ask yourself: *Which paragraph is just right for the lead?* The rule: It has to be funny, directly or obliquely topical, engaging. I remember one from years and years ago: "The attempted assassination of Sukarno last week had all the earmarks of a CIA operation. Everyone in the room was killed except Sukarno."

And, during the days when we feuded almost full-time, "Gerald Johnson of *The New Republic* wonders what a football would think about football if a football could think. Very interesting, but not as interesting as, What would a *New Republic* reader think of *The New Republic* if a *New Republic* reader could think?" Last week there wasn't anything absolutely, obviously preeminent, but ever since it came up on the dumbwaiter from Tim Wheeler's fortnightly package, this one about colors burrowed in the mind. . . . Time is very short now. Okay, we'll lead with this. It reads,

Iraq and the budget are as nothing compared to the firestorm following the retirement of maize, raw umber, lemon yellow, blue grey, violet blue, green blue, orange red, and orange yellow, and their replacement by vivid tangerine, wild strawberry, fuchsia, teal blue, cerulean, royal purple, jungle green, and dandelion, by the makers of Crayola crayons.

Nice, no? Orson Bean used to say that the most beautiful word combinations in the language were Yucca Flats and Fernando Lamas; though Whittaker Chambers, along with Gertrude Stein, preferred *Toasted Suzie is my ice cream.*

And then you need the bottom eye-catcher, the end paragraph, traditionally very offbeat, usually nonpolitical but not necessarily. You knew which would be the end paragraph the moment you laid eyes on it, early in the day, another by Tim, whose reserves of mischief are reliable, and now you find it and designate it as such. It reads:

This week's invention is a sort of miniaturized bug zapper, battery-powered, to be inserted in the cervix for contraception and, the inventor hopes, prophylaxis.
If you aren't shocked by this, you will be.

The editorials are now in order, and the line count is confirmed.

Another issue of *National Review* has gone to bed; and you acknowledge, the thought has ever so slowly distilled in your mind, that the time comes for us all to go to bed, and I judge that mine has come, and I leave owing to my staff, my colleagues—my successors—my friends, my muses, my God, an unrequitable debt for having given me so much, for so long. Good night, and thanks.

Perhaps no invitation summons up the best in any speaker more than one held in honor of, or in the spirit of, Winston Churchill. Bill's call from the International Churchill Society came, and he complied on October 27, 1995, with a speech that combines personal recall with an analysis of the precise meaning of certain Churchillian utterances, and no attempt to imitate the inimitable. His American eloquence is a fitting salute to a grand master.

Ladies and gentlemen:

When I was a boy I came upon the line, *Let us now praise famous men.* In succeeding decades I found myself running its implications through my mind. The evolution of my thinking is of possible interest to you under the auspices of this celebration.

Early on I found myself wondering why exactly it was thought appropriate, let alone necessary, to praise famous men. If such men as were to be praised were already famous, as the biblical injunction presupposes, then would they not disdain as either redundant, or immodest, the solicitation of more praise than they had already? It seemed, in that perspective, just a little *infra dig* to enjoin such praise.

Some time later I bumped into the melancholy conclusion of the historian who wrote that "great men are not often good men." That finding curdled in the memory. Does it require of a famous man to be praised, that he be praiseworthy? And if he is not a good man, merely a successful man who became famous by inventing the wheel or invading Russia or writing *War and Peace,* should not the praise be confined to bringing to the attention of those who are behind in the matter that which the person being praised actually did that merits more vociferous admiration? Or is that obvious? Jack the Ripper was famous, but our praise of him, if such it is to be called, does not focus on his attainments.

And then much later, much, much later, on reading recently a review of the life of Abraham Lincoln justified, or so it seemed, primarily by the author's diligence in bringing to light episodes in Lincoln's life and aspects of his character that serve to diminish the myth, I found myself wondering at what point is it in the interest of civilization to devise a line between research designed to satisfy the curiosity and research bent upon defacement, this last often an instinct of the egalitarian, who really thinks that all men should be equally famous, in the absence of which all men should be equally infamous. As in, If everybody can't be rich, then everybody should be poor. I am at this stage in the development of my thought on that passage from Ecclesiastes more and more inclined to believe that the point comes when it is prudent, unless one's profession is in historical clinics, to accept that which was legendary as legend; that which was mythogenic, as myth—fortifying myth, ennobling myth.

When I was a junior in college and editor of the student newspaper I received an invitation to attend the speech at the Massachusetts Institute of Technology to be given by Winston Churchill, commemorating a mid-century celebration. I drove with a fellow editor to Cambridge and awaited the appearance of the great man with high expectation, made higher by advance notice given by Mr. Churchill to the press, to the effect that the speech he would give at the M.I.T. celebration would be an important historical statement.

Mr. Churchill's preceding visit to the United States had been to Fulton, Missouri, and we wondered whether he would go further in characterizing the Soviet Union and its leader. We watched him with fascination come to the chair—he was shorter than I had envisioned, less rotund. He guided a cane with his right hand, but even so needed help to rise to the lectern. The hypnotizing voice boomed in, and our attention was at tiptoe.

I remember rushing back to New Haven with some trepidation, hoping that the story I would write might feature something Winston Churchill had said that was different from what the *New York Times* and the Associated Press and the United Press agreed was the major news story. In fact Mr. Churchill hadn't said anything different from what he had said before, which was that the discovery of the atom bomb, as we then called it, might prove to be the greatest humanitarian invention in history, making war so awful that wars would never again be fought. That hope did not prove prophetic, in that eighty million people have been killed in warfare since he gave it voice, but then it is true that most of them were killed in battles in which there was no general at hand with the atom bomb in his quiver.

But what mattered in 1949 was the *possession* of the bomb. When Mr. Churchill spoke it was exclusively ours, copyright Los Alamos, U.S.A.; but the pirate paid no attention and within months he would develop his own or, more exactly, succeed in transforming blueprints provided by U.S. and British spies into a nuclear bomb.

Of course the real nightmare had already come, by the time of the mid-century celebration of M.I.T., to Eastern Europe, and had only a year before spread to Czechoslovakia. Mr. Churchill was to some extent on a diplomatic rein that night, because he did not mention the name of Stalin, referring instead to "thirteen men" in the Kremlin. But the image of Stalin was clearly in his mind when he reminded his audience that the Mongol invasion of Europe, well underway seven hundred years earlier, had been interrupted by the death of Genghis Khan. His armies returned seven thousand miles to their base to await a successor, and they never returned. Might such a thing happen again? Churchill wondered.

Four years later, Stalin obliged us all by going, one hopes, to a world even worse than the one he created, assuming such exists; but it was not as when Genghis Khan left the world without a successor: Stalin's successors would keep intact the evil empire for almost forty years. The plight of the captive nations, the dismaying challenges that lay ahead, the struggles in Berlin and Korea and Vietnam, the hydrogen bomb, the Cuban crisis, all unfolded with terrible meaning for those whose statecraft had failed us.

In October of 1938, a despondent Churchill had spoken in Commons about the failed diplomacy of his colleague Neville Chamberlain. He said then, "When I think of the fair hopes of a long peace which still lay before Europe at the beginning of 1933 when Herr Hitler first obtained power, and of all the opportunities of arresting the growth of the Nazi power which have been thrown away; when I think of the immense combinations and resources which have been neglected or squandered, I cannot believe that a parallel exists in the whole course of history." Well, but of course a parallel would come again, in Mr. Churchill's lifetime, and in that parallel he was a major player, if not, alas, the critical player.

In the same speech after the Munich conference in 1938 Mr. Churchill had ruminated on British history. Only an Englishman, surely, is capable of the following commentary except in parody. "In my holiday," he said, "I thought it was a chance to study the reign of King Ethelred the Unready." (What did you study during *your* holiday, Mabel?) "The House"— Mr. Churchill was addressing Parliament—"will remember that that was a period of great misfortune, in which, from the strong position which we had gained under the descendants of King Alfred, we dove swiftly into chaos. It was the period of Danegeld and of foreign pressure. I must say that the rugged words of the Anglo-Saxon Chronicle, written a thousand years ago, seem to me apposite, at least as apposite as those quotations from Shakespeare with which we have been regaled by the last speaker from the Opposition Bench. Here is what the Anglo-Saxon Chronicle said, and I think the words apply very much to our treatment of Germany and our relations with her. 'All these calamities fell upon us because of evil counsel, because tribute was not offered to them at the right time nor yet were they resisted; but when they had done the most evil, then was peace made with them.'

"That," Mr. Churchill said, "is the wisdom of the past, for all wisdom is not new wisdom."

Seven years later, after England's and his finest hour began to tick when England denied to Herr Hitler the right to enslave Poland, Churchill prepared for the Yalta summit meeting in January 1945. He confided to his private secretary, "*All the Balkans except Greece are going to be Bolshevised. And there is nothing I can do to prevent it. There is nothing I can do for poor Poland either.*" To his cabinet, he reported that he was certain that he could trust Stalin. The same man whose death he so eagerly anticipated at M.I.T. five years later, in 1945 he spoke of as hoping he would live forever. "Poor Neville Chamberlain," he told Mr. Colville, "believed he could trust Hitler. He was wrong. But I don't think I'm wrong about Stalin."

His concluding experience with Stalin came just six months later, at Potsdam, at which Winston Churchill had come upon another historical force, for which he was, this time, substantially unprepared. The first week in June he had gone on BBC to alert the voters against a domestic catastrophe which he was quite certain would never overpower even a country exhausted by the exertions of so fine an hour. "My friends," he spoke, "I must tell you that a socialist policy is abhorrent in the British ideas of freedom. Although it is now put forward in the main by people who have a good grounding in the liberalism and radicalism of the early part of this century, there can be no doubt that socialism is inseparably interwoven with totalitarianism and the abject worship of the state. It is not alone that property, in all its forms, is struck at, but that liberty, in all its forms, is challenged by the fundamental concept of socialism."

But it was the fate of Winston Churchill to return to power in 1951 resolved *not* to fight the socialist encroachments of the postwar years. He, and England, were too tired, and, as with Eastern Europe and Poland, there was nothing to be done. There was no force in Europe that could move back the Soviet legions, no force in Great Britain that would reignite, until twenty-five years later, the vision Mr. Churchill displayed, speaking to the BBC microphones on June 5, 1945, since nobody else was listening.

Mr. Churchill had struggled to diminish totalitarian rule in Europe which, however, increased. He fought to save the empire, which dissolved. He fought socialism, which prevailed. He struggled to defeat Hitler, and he won. It is not, I think, the significance of that victory, mighty and glorious though it was, that causes the name of Churchill to make the blood run a little faster. He spoke diffidently about his role in the war, saying that the lion was the people of England, that he had served merely to provide the roar.

But it is the roar that we hear, when we pronounce his name. It is simply mistaken that battles are necessarily more important than the words that summon men to arms. The battle of Agincourt was long forgotten as a geopolitical event, but the words of Henry V, with Shakespeare to recall them, are imperishable in the mind, even as which side won the battle of Gettysburg will dim from the memory of men and women who will never forget the words spoken about that battle by Abraham Lincoln. The genius of Churchill was his union of affinities of the heart and of the mind. The total fusion of animal and spiritual energy:

"You ask what is our policy? I can say: It is to wage war, by sea, land and air, with all the might and with all the strength that God can give us.

"What is our aim? I can answer in one word: It is victory. It is victory, victory at all costs, victory in spite of all the terror, victory, however long and hard the road may be."

In other days, from other mouths, we would mock the suggestion that extremism in defense of liberty was no vice. Churchill collapsed the equivocators by his total subscription to his cause. "Let 'em have it," he shot back at a critic of area bombing. "Remember this. Never treat the enemy by halves." Looking back in his memoirs on the great presidential decision of August 1945, he wrote, "There was never *a moment's* discussion as to whether the atomic bomb should be used or not." That is decisiveness we correctly deplore when we have time to think about it, but he was telling his countrymen, and indirectly Americans, that any scruple, at that time of peril to the nation itself, was an indefensible and unbearable distraction. He was from time to time given to reductionism in other situations, and Churchill could express frustration in searing vernacular. Working his way through disputatious bureaucracy from separatists in New Delhi he exclaimed to his secretary, "I hate Indians." I don't doubt that the famous gleam came to his eyes when he said this, with mischievous glee—an offense, in modern convention, of genocidal magnitude.

But this was Churchill distracted from his purpose. The little warts Cromwell insisted be preserved; which warts, however, do not deface the memory of Churchill, because of the nobility of his cause and his sense of the British moment. "Hitler knows that he will have to break us in this Island or lose the war. If we can stand up to him, all Europe may be free and the life of the world may move forward into broad, sunlit uplands. But if we fail, then the whole world, including the United States, including all that we have known or cared for, will sink into the abyss of a new Dark Age made more sinister, and perhaps more protracted, by the lights of perverted science. Let us therefore brace ourselves to our duties and so bear ourselves that if the British Empire and its Commonwealth last for a thousand years, men will still say, 'This was their finest hour.' "

It is my proposition that Churchill's words were indispensable to the benediction of that hour, which we hail here tonight, as, gathered together to praise a famous man, we hail the memory of the man who spoke them.

Chapter 9

On Style & Eloquence, Dress and Address

Whatever else he may be taken for, Buckley is a man of style, not all of it a model. Correspondents reproach him, among other things, for his manner of dress. Admittedly, his style in clothing is as far from elegant as his expositions are eloquent. (Speaking of the limits of language—were we?—there seems to be no surplus of synonyms for "rumpled," although "disheveled" comes to mind.) No matter: the style we are considering here is more than a matter of matching socks and color-coded shirts and ties. Perhaps no one has summed up, or served up, a deconstruction of WFB's style better than James J. Kilpatrick in *National Review* ten years ago.

UTTER BUTTER

James J. Kilpatrick
Right Reason, by William F. Buckley, Jr. (Doubleday, 454 pp., $19.95)

Is it a chrestomathy? A collection? An anthology? Whatever it is, this latest volume from the genial gentleman who helms this magazine is Buckley at his stylish best.

The master of revels at *National Review* sailed past his sixtieth birthday on November 24. He matches the young Cleopatra. Age cannot wither him nor custom stale his infinite variety. In this omnium-gatherum, edited splendidly by Richard Brookhiser, Buckley looks at Mexico, at Poland, at Spain. He writes about Karl Marx, Pope Paul VI, and Henry Kissinger. He concludes that style in human relations is largely a matter of timing. He offers a paean to peanut butter, as follows:

> *I know that I shall never see*
> *A poem lovely as Skippy's peanut butter.*

This he grandly describes as "a couplet." If he had composed some such rhapsody as "I know that I shall never utter / Two words to rank with peanut butter," he would have had a respectable couplet, but no matter. When Buckley attacks the language, the language had better get the hell out of the way.

Let me turn around on this business of style. I have known and corresponded with the ineffable WFB for twenty-five years and have delighted in his company; I have read twenty of his books and hundreds of his columns, and except when he instructs me in navigation I have understood most of them. Long ago I concluded that style is half of what Buckley has going for him. I am not thinking of his neckties, dummy; everyone knows that Buckley's ties are thirty years old and that he wears the two of them on alternate days. I am thinking of style totally.

Right Reason opens with an essay Buckley wrote in response to critics who attacked his book *Overdrive*. Most readers will recall that *Overdrive,* like the earlier *Cruising Speed,* was a journal of one week in his life. The book stirred up an astonishing response—a response distilled from awe and envy, but mostly from envy. *Kirkus Reviews* called the work "tedious at best, sleekly loathsome at worst." The *San Francisco Chronicle* called it overdone, overwritten, and overblown. Nora Ephron, in the *New York Times,* found parts of it "appalling." Some really mean things also were said about it.

The reaction of these green-eyed critics, if I am not mistaken, was miles removed from the reaction of thousands of persons who bought the book and found it absorbing. Buckley was writing happily and engagingly about his own lifestyle, and in the world of arts and letters this is a lifestyle that few can enjoy with equal gusto. I delighted in the book, but, as Buckley says, the major reviews were terrible.

It is a pleasure to read his response to the critics, for this is pure Bill. If your purpose is to tick someone off, this is how it should be done—stylishly, with grace and civility and an unbuttoned foil. In this same way he disposes of Henry Fairlie: "To the great relief of Great Britain, he is an expatriate." He contemplates a welcoming address by Yale's president A. Bartlett Giamatti to the freshman class of 1981: "To be lectured against the perils of the

Moral Majority on entering Yale is on the order of being lectured on the danger of bedbugs on entering a brothel." He takes on the Reverend Jesse Jackson, a "man of transient fixations." But in the thirteen pieces that Brookhiser has grouped under the heading of "Assailing," you will never see the red eye of anger or hear the coarse voice of rage. This is style.

A second group of twenty-two writings, chosen almost entirely from Buckley's syndicated columns, deals mostly with foreign affairs. In a third section we find nine essays defined as "Commenting." . . . Every one of these hundred-plus passages of English prose is written with—style.

In that observation I am not thinking so much of grace, or manners, or civility, but this time of style in writing. If you were putting Bill's stuff to music, you would score it for harpsichord and cello, two good muscular instruments that sound best only when a virtuoso plays them. The criticism is made—I have made it unavailingly, myself—that my friend employs too many hard words, unfamiliar words. . . . Such objections leave him puzzled: The words, he says, are not unfamiliar to *him*. Let others look them up. It is the Marie Antoinette school of prose composition.

What's the other half? I said that style was half of what makes Buckley's work such a constant pleasure to read. The other half is substance. All of us in our racket, the syndicated-column racket, write thumb-suckers now and then. These are the pieces that wash thinly over a topic and leave no residue of thought behind. We had nothing to say that was worth saying in the first place. Bill writes very few of these. He nearly always has something thoughtful to say, and even his throwaway pieces—such as the column he wrote when he got mad at Varig, the Brazilian airline—are thumb-suckers of a different sort. Buckley reads, listens, experiences, thinks. They say his stuff is infuriating. I find it a joy.

JANUARY 31, 1986

––––

Questions of style inevitably take us from matters of dress to forms of address. In an age when not many people seem to know who William Jefferson Clinton is—the man competing with "Bob" Dole for the presidency—Buckley's "Just Call Me Bill" (1975) bears revisiting.

––––

JUST CALL ME BILL

Very soon I will be fifty, a datum I do not expect will . . . revive the fireworks industry. I reflect on it only because of a personal problem of general concern I had not solved twenty years ago, the nature of which keeps changing as you grow older. It is, of course, the first-name problem.

My inclinations on the matter have always been formal. In part this was a matter of inheritance.

I heard my father, days before his death at seventy-eight, refer to his best friend and associate of forty years as "Montgomery"; who, in deference to the ten-year difference in their ages, referred to him only as "Mr. Buckley."

I grew up "mistering" people, and discovered, after I was fully grown (if indeed that has really happened), that in continuing to do so I was bucking a trend of sorts: the obsessive egalitarian familiarity which approaches a raid on one's privacy.

So on reaching thirty, I made a determined effort to resist. Even now, on the television program *Firing Line*, I refer even to those guests I know intimately as "Mr. Burnham," or "Governor Reagan," or "Senator Goldwater." (This rule I simply had to break on introducing Senator Buckley, but even then the departure from the habit was stylistically troublesome.) The effort, I thought, was worthwhile—a small gesture against the convention that requires you to refer to Professor Mortimer Applegate as "Mort" five minutes after you have met. I suppose a talk show host would have called Socrates "Soc."

I came on two difficulties. The first was the public situation in which mistering somebody was plainly misunderstood. Or, if understood at all, taken as an act of social condescension. For a couple of years I would refer, on his program, to "Mr. Carson." In due course I discovered that the audience thought I was trying to put on an act: Mr. Carson does not exist in America. Only Johnny does.

The second problem, as you grow older, lies in the creeping suspicion of people a little older than you that your use of the surname is intended to accentuate an exiguous difference in age. If you are eighteen and the other man is twenty-eight, you can, for a while, call him Mr. Jones without giving offense. But if you are forty and he is fifty and you call him Mr. Jones, he is likely to think that you are rubbing in the fact of his relative senescence.

The complement of that problem, which I fear more than anything except rattlesnakes and détente, is trying to be One of the Boys. "Just call me Bill," to the roommate of your son at college, is in my judgment an odious effort to efface a chronological interval as palpable as the wrinkles on my face and the maturity of my judgments. On the other hand, one has to struggle to avoid stuffiness: so I arrived, for a while, at the understanding that I was Mister to everyone under the age of twenty-one or thereabouts, and only then, cautiously, Bill. It is a sub-problem, how to break the habit. Here I made a sub-rule: that I would invite younger people to call me "Bill" exactly one time. If thereafter they persisted in using the surname, well that was up to them: a second, redundant gesture on my part could be interpreted as pleading with them to accept me as a biological equal.

My bias, on the whole, continued in the direction of a tendency to formality, so in the last few years I made a determined effort to overcome it, wherein I came across my most recent humiliation. Mrs. Margaret Thatcher was my guest on *Firing Line*. Rather to my surprise, the English being more naturally formal than we are, halfway through the program she suddenly referred to me, once, as "Bill." I declined to break my *Firing Line* rule, and so persisted with "Mrs. Thatcher." However, the next day when we met again at a semi-social function, I braced myself on leaving and said, "Good-bye, Margaret." And a week later, writing her a note congratulating her on her performance, I addressed it: "Dear Margaret."

Today I have from her a most pleasant reply, about this and that. But it is addressed, in her own hand (as is the British habit: only the text is typed): "Dear Mr. Buckley." Shocked, I looked at the transcript of the show—only to discover that, on the program, she was talking about a "Bill" that lay before the House of Commons.

The trauma has set me back by years, and I may even find myself addressing "Mr. Carson" next time around. I suppose, though, that at fifty, the problem becomes easier in respect of the twenty-five-year-olds. At seventy it will be easier still. Well before then, I hope to be able to address Margaret, I mean Mrs. Thatcher, as Madam Prime Minister.

—WFB   OCTOBER 28, 1975

House of Commons
London SWI

Dear Bill,

Having just read your article in the *Washington Star* of 28th October, I have made my first New Year Resolution. From 1st January, 1976, Mr. Buckley shall be "Bill."

I shall assume the appropriate reciprocity.

Yours sincerely,
MARGARET THATCHER

———

Funny, how discussions of style can swing quickly from matters of dignity and privacy to the near-scatological.

———

Dear Bill:

I remember a column you wrote a while back in which you clucked about unseemly familiarity in modes of personal address. I agree with you. In fact, I'm rather standoffish myself; I've been at Dartmouth for over a month now, and I haven't even met Jeffrey Hart. Oh, I've *seen* him, but I haven't actually met him, and when I do I'll certainly call him Mr. Hart, at least to begin with.

But I presume to call you Bill. There are several reasons. I did actually meet you once, years and years ago—you were on the lecture circuit at St. Michael's College in Winooski, Vermont (and you spoke very well). Also, I got a nice little note from you several years back, in which you signed yourself "Bill." I had responded to your annual appeal for funds to keep *NR* afloat by saying that I wished I could kick in a hundred or two but I didn't have any money (I was writing my dissertation at the time and really didn't have any money—still don't). Your reply was a gracious gesture, and it made me feel as though I knew you a little better. In fact, as an almost-charter subscriber to *NR* and a regular viewer of *Firing Line* I feel that over the years I have grown to know the contours of your mind excruciatingly well.

Still, I don't think I would be calling you Bill even now if it weren't for the startling familiarity with which you greet me, through your subalterns, every other week when I rush to the mailbox to pick up my copy of *NR*. What do I see?

> M BRWNOOIR 010 7721 — 3 25 —
> ROBERT E BROWNE
> CLAREMONT ANUS
> 1 VALIANT WINTER ST
> CLAREMONT NH 03743

Never mind that this perfectly captures my feelings about Claremont, New Hampshire; do you think you could send future issues in a plain brown wrapper with the address on the inside? Or change it to "Arms"? Or talk to Mr. McFadden? Him I shall continue to address with decorous formality. Thanks, Bill.

Yours appreciatively,
ROBERT E. "BOB" BROWNE
ENGLISH DEPARTMENT
DARTMOUTH COLLEGE

Dear Bob: I checked with James McFadden, our Associate Publisher. He is awfully busy, and began by muttering something that sounded like "Up Claremont." But he was mollified, the correction will be made, and he says you can call him Jim.

Cordially,
BILL

In the two essays following, Buckley turns to the subject of eloquence, a style so rare as hardly to seem a subject any longer.

In the first, he speaks to a lament by James Reston, a newspaperman who had frequent brushes with eloquence, in the course of composing thousands of columns. That Mr. Reston seems to have been seeking examples of eloquence at the United Nations, a fabled house of talk but little of it memorable, troubles WFB. It involves the question not only of verbal felicities but of truth, and Buckley, himself a veteran of the United States Mission there, has seen both too often lacking.

In the second piece, he speaks to a little-noticed quality in those who have style, a finely tuned sense of timing,

Why No Eloquence?

James Reston, who is a very eloquent man, wonders what has happened to eloquence these days. His reference is to the performance thus far at the United Nations, where the mighty of the world have met to deplore the huge planetary budget for arms. It isn't that Reston expected that anything would come of it; nothing, really, ever does under U.N. sponsorship. But Reston bemoans the absent voices. Men like Roosevelt, and Churchill, and de Gaulle, he said, could by their eloquence affect events. Their successors—Carter, Giscard, Callaghan—speak, and all the birdies stay perched on the trees. Meanwhile the objective situation, as described, is quite awful. He recites the figures.

We are spending four hundred billion dollars per year on arms in the world, which is more than we are spending on education.

The figures rise notwithstanding the nuclear factor. One would think that with the invention of nuclear power, there would be less of a need for the conventional weapons. But of course it doesn't work that way because the success of nuclear technology has precisely the other effect: the weapon is so apocalyptic, it is necessary to rely on lesser weapons, so that the production of airplanes and tanks and machine guns and rifles continues unabated. And the poor nations are buying weapons valued at eight billion dollars per year. Symbolic of the emptiness of the big [U.N.] ritual in New York is that in the opening days, as much time was given over to discussing a border fracas in Zaire as to the problem of armaments.

One hesitates to instruct Mr. Reston, but one does so anyway. True eloquence is based on reality, even mythic reality. Prince Hal, delivering the most famous charge in the history of literature, exceeded even Knute Rockne's to the Notre Dame football team.

What would Shakespeare say about disarmament? He could make almost any cause beguiling, witty, ingenious; he could harness the language wonderfully to the uses of seduction, or ambition, or even treachery, these being great human passions. Indeed, viewed through contemporary prisms, King Harry was up to no good at Agincourt, coveting French territory on flimsy genealogical authority. Still, he stirred what then were accepted as honorable passions: to fight for king and country.

But the problem with attempting eloquence at the United Nations is that that which is affirmed by all the surrounding moral maxims is regularly and systematically flouted. The United Nations is about things like a covenant on human rights; about things like genocide; about self-rule; about the dignity of man. But [most of] the countries that dominate the United Nations have no use for these goals. This does not prevent them from praising them, which they do copiously. A speech by the ambassador from East Germany praising human liberty and democracy is as routine at the U.N. as a water fountain in Central Park.

But how then does a statesman go about appealing to such an assembly for world disarmament? Nations take up arms for reasons good and bad: to defend their liberties—and to wrest from others their liberties. We have not fought an imperialist war in the lifetime of all but American octogenarians. But it was only ten years ago that the Russians used their vast army to douse a flicker of liberalism in Czechoslovakia. The size of our hundred-billion-dollar-per-year budget is a function of the budget of the Soviet Union. If the communists disarmed, we could disarm; if the communists armed purely for the sake of self-protection, even then we could disarm. But the reality is that two great superpowers, the Chinese and the Russians, are bent on world revolution, and every state that opposes them, however tatterdemalion—Shaba Province is their most recent objective—is a nubile target. But how do we address them?

The trouble with the search for eloquence is that eloquence cannot issue except from telling the truth. And in the United Nations one is not permitted to tell the truth, because protocol is higher than the truth. The problem, then, is not so much the deterioration of the gift of eloquence as it is that constipation that must come when we are told to speak untruths, or to build our speeches on untruths. That is why the only great eloquence in the world today is that of Solzhenitsyn and his fellows—and they are not permitted to speak at the United Nations.

—WFB   JUNE 1, 1978

A MATTER OF STYLE

I feel the need to admit that I have not given much explicit thought to the definition of style, notwithstanding that I am said to possess it, by which a compliment is sometimes but not always intended ("style" is widely mis-read as affectation). But finding myself in the pressure cooker, it came to me after very little ratiocination that style is, really, timing. Let me tell you, by giving you a story, what I mean by this.

It is a story by one of the nineteenth-century Russians . . . Tolstoy, I think; in any event, the story I read sometime during my teens was about a very rich young prince who one evening engaged in a drinking bout of Brobdingnagian dimensions with his fellow bloods, which eventually peaked, as such affairs frequently did in that curious epoch of genius and debauchery, in a philosophical argument over the limits of human self-control. The question was specifically posed: Could someone succeed in voluntarily sequestering himself in a small suite of rooms for a period of twenty years, notwithstanding that he would always be free to open the door, letting himself out, or others in? In a spirit of high and exhibitionis-tic dogmatism, the prince pronounced such hypothetical discipline pre-posterous, and announced that he would give one million rubles to anyone who succeeded in proving him wrong.

You will have guessed that a young companion, noble but poor, and himself far gone in wine's litigious imperatives, accepted the challenge. And so with much fanfare, a few days later, the rules having been carefully set (he could ask for, and receive, anything except human company), Peter (we'll call him) was ushered into the little subterranean suite of rooms in the basement of the prince's house.

During the first years, he drank. During the next years, he stared at the ceiling. During the succeeding period, he read—ordering books, more books, and more books. Meanwhile the fortunes of the prince had taken a disastrous turn, and so he schemed actively to seduce Peter to leave his self-imposed confinement, dispatching letters below, describing evocatively the sensual delights Peter would experience by merely opening the door. In desperation, as the deadline neared, he even offered one half the premium.

The night before the twentieth year would finish at midnight, half the town and thousands from all over Russia were outside to celebrate and marvel over the endurance of Peter upon his emergence. One hour before midnight, the startled crowd saw the celebrated door below street level open prematurely. And Peter emerged.

He had, you see, become a philosopher; and in all literature I know of no more eloquent gesture of disdain for money. One hour more, and he'd have earned a million rubles. What *style,* you say; and I concur.

But what is it about that one hour that speaks so stylishly, in a sense that Peter's emergence one year before the deadline would not—lacking, as one year would, in drama; or, at the other end, one minute before midnight, one minute being overfreighted in melodrama?

It is style, surely.

Even so the speed of human responses which, indicating spontaneity, communicate integrity. "Is it all right if I bring Flo's sister and her husband along for the weekend?" demands *instant* assent; the *least* pause is, to the quick ear, lethal. When such a proposition is posed, the man of style will make one of two decisions, and he must here think with great speed. He will either veto the extra guests, going on to give whatever reason he finds most ingenious, or he will accept them *on the spot*. Absolutely nothing in between. In between are many other things defined as lacking in style.

It is so, I think, with language, and with that aspect of language on which its effectiveness so heavily relies, namely rhythm. It matters less what exactly you say at a moment of tension than that you say it at just the right moment. Great speed might be necessary, as above, or such delay as suggests painful meditation as required to ease, console, or inspirit the other person. Style is not a synonym for diplomacy. Style can be infinitely undiplomatic, as in the stylish means selected by John L. Lewis to separate his union from the CIO. "We disaffiliate," he wrote on an envelope, dispatching it to headquarters. It is sometimes stylish to draw attention to oneself, as Lewis was doing. Sometimes the man of style will be all but anonymous. Some men are congenitally incapable of exhibiting a stylish anonymity. Of Theodore Roosevelt it was said that whenever he attended a wedding, he confused himself with the bride. The Queen of England could not feign anonymity, neither could LBJ, or Mr. Micawber. But whichever is sought—being conspicuous or inconspicuous—timing is the principal element. Arrive very early at the funeral and you will be noticed, even as you will be noticed arriving at the very last minute. In between, you glide in, on cat-feet.

In language, rhythm is an act of timing. "Why did you use the word 'irenic' when you say it merely means 'peaceful'?" a talk show host once asked indignantly. To which the answer given was: "I desired the extra syllable." In all circumstances? *No, for God's sake.*

In the peculiar circumstances of the sentence uttered, and these circumstances were set by what had gone just before, what would probably come just after. A matter of style. A matter of timing.

—WFB   JANUARY, 1983

Chapter 10

Usage III:
W. H. Fowler
Lives

Even *National Review* columnists—perhaps especially *NR* columnists—write to Buckley, protesting certain interpretations put on words. Here, the formidable and unique Florence King...

———

Dear Mr. Buckley:

I am sitting here under a pile of letters from readers about my "Tender Hooks" column (*NR*, June 21). Most of them start out, "Imagine my despair . . ." Several people sent me Xeroxes of the dictionary page containing "tenterhooks," and one man wrote a disquisition on the textile industry, explaining that a "tenter" is the frame on which fabric is stretched to dry, and the "hook" is the nail driven into the frame to hold the fabric while it dries; the fabric is thus in a state of suspended tension, etc. etc.

As I plan to say in my address to Congress as soon as they invite me, the State of the Punnybone is not good. My use of "tender" hooks was deliberate, designed to take a poke at the tender-hearted people who worry constantly about the tender sensitivities of others.

Since you believe in public service, here is your chance. I enclose a flag, hand-sewn by me, containing a coiled snake and the motto, SHE SAID IT

ON PURPOSE. Please fly it from the roof of the *NR* building so I don't have to answer all these letters.

Yours sincerely,
FLORENCE KING
FREDERICKSBURG, VA.

P.S. Keep the flag. I'm sure you'll need it again. In the immortal words of Lizzie Borden: "I have a feeling somebody is going to do something."
P.P.S. Stet the "P" in Punnybone.

Dear Miss King: Your flag flutters even as I do, in addressing you. Cordially,
—WFB   JULY 19, 1993

Dear Mr. Buckley:

I feel somewhat like the parent who, as he raises the strap, says, "This is going to hurt me more than it hurts you," for I must assure you that I am a devoted but discreet admirer of yours—and I never thought that I could come to this point: I am about to criticize you for a fairly flagrant mistake in grammar contained at the front of *American Conservative Thought in the Twentieth Century*, headed Acknowledgments.

The offending sentence is, "I wish to record . . . my thanks to Professor Leonard W. Levy for his patience and for the excellence of his advice which, if he had given any more of it, this would have been a book about twenty-first-century American thought."

It can readily be seen that if one takes out the clause "if he had given any more of it," the word "which" is left dangling without a verb.

In view of the thousands of words that you turn out, my criticism may seem niggling so I would be obliged if you would regard it as a gentle reproach. Yours truly,

BARBARA LAMON
(MRS. R. LAMON)
LONDON, ONTARIO

Dear Mrs. Lamon: The grammatical error isn't *fairly* flagrant, it is *very* flagrant. Indeed, it was first called to my attention by Professor Levy himself. The verbal wrench is designed to superordinate the idiomatic over the grammatical, for rhetorical effect. The late Professor Willmoore Kendall, at the time a senior editor of *National Review*, once wrote an editorial paragraph the first sentence of which began, "The weekend conference at Arden House, which by the way why doesn't somebody burn it down, reached several conclusions . . . ." Reproached by the (then) managing editor Miss La Follette with a large dictionary in hand, Professor Kendall said, "Suzanne, don't you realize that when people get around to writing dictionaries, they come to people like me to find out what to put in them?" I don't mean that the way it sounds, which by the way isn't so good, is it? Anyway, you are right grammatically. Many thanks. Cordially,

—WFB   JULY 21, 1972

ERRATUM (of sorts): Our esteemed friend and colleague Professor Hugh Kenner writes in to correct a misreference to him in our last issue. An entire line—we say, in our defense—was inadvertently omitted at the printers, resulting in a mad but plausible confusion in giving the biography of Mr. Kenner. But we shall take our punishment like a man, and reproduce Mr. Kenner's letter, as follows: "March 23, 1960, Dear Sir: Reluctant though I am to interfere with the mixture of encomium and fantasy that animates your doubtless eyewitness description of me as 'critic, philosopher, yachtsman' (March 26), I must intervene on behalf of my alma mater when you ascribe to me an academic post at the University of Toronto. The English Department of which I am chairman is located far from native skies, at the University of California, Santa Barbara.

"I must also protest your statement that I recently authored a study of T. S. Eliot. I composed that book, sir, and I typed it, but author it I did not, and author, while a tatter of the English language remains mine to defend, I never shall, Yours faithfully, Hugh Kenner."

We refer Professor Kenner to the words of another Eliot (Sir J.) who wrote (in 1632) of "The divine blessing . . . which authors all the happiness we receive," and confess to digging Warner in his contention (1602) that "A good God may not author noysome things"—not even noisome verbs like author. And finally, appreciating as we do Mr. Kenner's epistles, we devoutly pray, sir, that yours of the 23rd instant will not prove (Chapman, 1596) "the last foul thing Thou ever author'dst." To us, that is.

—WFB   APRIL 9, 1960

Dear Mr. Buckley:

I have just read your thoroughly enjoyable *Marco Polo, If You Can*. As one who had more than a casual connection with the U-2 program, as a Buckley aficionado, and as one who loves the graceful use of the language, I was absorbed and delighted.

But with what dismay did I read the final (excluding epilogue) sentence: "The meeting between the three allies lasted another two hours"! How could the man who serves up such succulents as "adumbrated" and "brummagem" be so lax with "among" and "between"?

If, perish the thought! you are among the Safire-phobes who rebel against grammatical discipline—if this is the sort of pedantic nonsense up with which you will not put—consider that "between" stems from the O.E. roots of "two," an etymological heritage that simply cannot be ignored for the sake of freedom.

I beg you to restore my faith in you. Tell me you made a mistake.

With great respect,

JOHN A. WOLFE

BURLINGTON, MASS.

Dear Mr. Wolfe: Sorry, you lose. See Fowler: "between is a sadly ill-treated word . . . 1. *B.* and *among.* The OED gives a warning against the superstition that *b.* can be used only of the relationship between two things, and that if there are more *among* is the right preposition. 'In all senses *between* has been, from its earliest appearance, extended to more than two. . . . It is still the only word available to express the relation of a thing to many surrounding things severally and individually; *among* expresses a relation to them collectively and vaguely: we should not say *the space lying among the three points* or *a treaty among three Powers.*' " Cordially,

—WFB   MARCH 22, 1985

─────

A Simple Little In-house Memo in Which One William (Rickenbacker) Corrects Another William (Buckley), Forgiving Nothing.

─────

Wm—

It is now almost exactly thirty years since I sent you a copy of my long letter to *Modern Age,* in which I gave my comments on several dozen mistakes in the then current issue. *Modern Age* has for many years been produced with care, and I haven't had to crack the whip again in that direction. But, old shoe, what's happening on East 35th Street? I attach a discussion of the mechanical problems in the current issue [March 19] of dear old *NR* and hope you'll tie a bomb to it and place it on the appropriate desk. I couldn't refrain from talking about one or two points that are strictly stylistic; questions of style would have covered twenty pages more, and, besides, that's not my business any more. [Rickenbacker had resigned his position as a senior editor a year earlier.] But I do care very much about *NR* and about my mother tongue, which I need not defend myself for defending. I have in that regard what Ortega so nearly calls *una razón vital.*

Ever of thee (as AJN* liked to sign off),

WM

* Albert Jay Nock.—Ed.

Dear Wm: Your note is welcome and deserved. Much happened during the fortnight in question, not least the vacation of the managing editor, and in-house experiments of a recondite technological character. We have imposed a *frein vital* on all projected changes that make us vulnerable to your criticisms.

Ever,

WM

[Rickenbacker's] Notes on March 19 *National Review*

p. 12—Second paragraph: Here I find "apparatchiks." The "t" is correct (the noun is *apparat*). However, on p. 29 I find *"apparatchiki,"* the Russian plural transliterated correctly, and the word in italic as befits the foreigner. You offer still another variant on p. 31, where I find *apparatchiks,* i.e., the English plural while the word is in italic. Then on p. 33 I find the "t" missing in both *apparachiki* and *apparachiks.*

p. 13—"What better way," etc., should end with a question mark. What better way to show it's a question?

p. 17—Lefthand column, mid: A "quorum" can't be reduced to a "symbol." A quorum is a body competent to do business. A symbol need be no more than a flag. If we stationed only one soldier in Europe, he would stand as the symbol of our resolve to carry out our policy; but he would not constitute a quorum.

p. 17—Righthand column, top: "As Clemenceau might put it" would be all right if the old boy were still alive. "Might have put it" keeps us properly oriented in history.

p. 20—Middle column, uppish: "Already-existing" is a phrase that exhibits the needless hyphen. "Already" is a fully grown adverb and can modify any damned adjective it takes a shine to.

p. 20—Right, mid: "Because of his curious role the junk bond market." This would be good syntax in Hebrew, but we need a piece of connective tissue between "role" and "market." Probably "in" is the word everyone overlooked.

p. 22—Left, high: It's "Eastern Air Lines" (three words), unless Frank Lorenzo has started stealing capital letters from his unhappy subsidiary.

p. 23—Bottom left: We need a full stop after Tito's death in 1980. Hell, we needed a full stop to him forty years earlier.

p. 24—Left, top: "Drags" should be "drag." The subject is "the crisis . . . and inflation."

p. 24—Tense sequence, that forgotten art, causes trouble at the end of the next paragraph. "With Slovenia gone, . . . would deteriorate . . . , had been getting is diminishing." The idea should be clear, and I'll let you clean up this mess during your own business hours.

p. 24—Right, lowish: A real monster: *dejá vû.* That's a new one to me, certainly the furthest thing from *déjà vu.*

p. 25—Left, lowish: *Verboten* is not a noun and need not take the initial capital. Such gaffes around *NR* were at one time *streng verboten.*

p. 25—Left, bottom: "The only known example of the Germans actually *shortening* a word." The Germans are like all speakers of all languages: they use apocopations when they can. *Der Oberkommandant* becomes *Der Ober,* and so on, and why not?

p. 25—Last paragraph: L.A. is not "the City of Angels." It is La Ciudad de Nuestra Señora, Reina de los Angeles—the City of Our Lady, Queen of the Angels. The name is far too beautiful to be ignored.

p. 28—Lefthand, mid: I see the cheeky hyphen barging into German now. It's not *Mittel-Europaische,* but *Mitteleuropäische,* and don't forget the umlaut over the "a," or my armies move at dawn.

p. 28—Next para: Out, out, damned hyphen! All my life it has been ice floes, and now *NR* has discovered "ice-floes." What *is* it about your fulminating hyphenosis? Did you buy an oversupply of them and are you trying to work off the inventory? They're a drug on the market, I say. Take your losses, throw the bum stuff out, and start with a clean slate.

p. 30—Left, top: *Newshour* should be *NewsHour.* I know it's weird, but so are Jim and Robin sometimes.

p. 30—Five lines down, "doubtlessly" should be "[sic]ced," and sicced good and hard.

p. 31—Left, middle: Who's the worry wart who wrote, and allowed to stand, "an highly decentralized federation"? Must have been some escapee from an herb farm.

p. 31—Left, bottom: "Multicandidate" is much ugliness. Oh, Hyphen, where art thou when we need thee? The little busybody is so bemused by sticking his nose in other people's business that he has neglected his own rightful chores.

p. 32—Right, bottom: "A stem-winding speech." This is what linguists call a "back formation"; starting with a known term ("stem-winder"), someone proceeds by analogy to create its other formations. Trouble is, the ignorant make the wrong assumption. In this case, "stem-winder" is not "someone who stem-winds." In the old days men told time by sundials, water clocks, roosters, the moon. By and by they invented clocks, big ones. Then by and by they made smaller and smaller clocks until they had one so small they could carry it around. It was on its way to becoming a pocket-watch. But it was still wound up by inserting a key in the face, just like the old grandfather clock. Then some genius hit upon the novel idea of rearranging the gears so that the watch could be wound up by working the "stem" at the top (it was the knurled knob at 12 o'clock high). The English unimaginatively called this a keyless watch, but the delighted Yankees called it a stem-winder, and from that moment anything fine, anything first rate, anything that commanded attention and respect, was a real stem-winder. So, in American idiom, a fine speech can be a stem-winder. But you cannot give a stem-winding speech, nor can an audience be stem-wound by it. Sorry! And by the way—is the idiom, as distinguished from grammarbook talk, a dying form of speech?

p. 37—Left, near bottom: "Likely" is not an adverb, at least not yet, at least not in my book, at least not in my neck of the woods. And we don't need it. (There is one special locution in which it is acceptable, but I won't tell you about it; you might misunderstand.)

p. 38—Righthand: We have Smuzynski, and Sumzynski, and I say it's spinach. But his mother would like to have the name treated with some respeck.

p. 42—Middle, uppish: "Thankfully, the debtor nations have . . ." The debtor nations don't know the meaning of thankfulness. Somebody else must be thankful. I wonder who?

p. 56—Right, mid: FDR did not "serve four terms." He was elected four times, and dropped in his tracks shortly after the last election.

p. 59—Left, near bottom: "The *Grief* concerto." It's Grieg, need I say? and no italic is needed. It's not a title. The title is *Piano Concerto in A Minor.* Good "Grief," indeed!

p. 64—Middle, middle: What a nice surprise it would have been if you had had the courage to use an exclamation point after the sentence that starts, "What a nice surprise"! It is the one time, other than in the imperative or the interjection, when the use of the exclam is positively commanded. Seeking to avoid the monster because it has been abused by careless writers, one should not shrink from its ordained use. Hop to it! What a fine chance to hit 'em with a bang!

(WFB's columns not proofed by me.)

For which, thank the Lord!

—WFB   MAY 14, 1990

Chapter 11

A Journalist
on Journalism

It might surprise some that Buckley thinks of himself as a journalist. Not only a journalist, to be sure, but more than a journalist in spirit: a working one, with the curiosity, nose for news, talent for telling stories quickly, and empathy for other journalists that characterize the best of them. He responds promptly to queries from magazine writers and newspaper reporters, believing them to be doing their jobs, as he is doing his. To be sure, he is the owner and was the founder and longtime editor of a journal of opinion; an author, a lecturer, a television host-plus, and a political force in his own right, etc.; but part of his everyday basic work is his syndicated newspaper column, an obligation he takes as seriously as breathing—getting ideas, researching, meeting deadlines, even on occasion suggesting ways for a newspaper editor to shorten his columns. Journalism is part of the rhythm of his busy, peripatetic life. He is friends with journalists of many political colorations and convictions. In his comments on or quarrels with or admiration for other journals and journalists, we see a great deal of how his character expresses itself as well as his continuing passion for the meaning of words.

Oh, yes: and for a man who spent less than a year in the CIA, just out of college, Bill Buckley has had an awful lot of explaining to do for his first job *before* going into journalism.

ON LEVELING WITH THE READER

In recent weeks several correspondents, thoughtfully sending me copies, have triumphantly advised editors of newspapers in which this feature appears, that "Mr. Buckley was himself a member of the CIA," and that under the circumstances, that fact should be noted every time a newspaper publishes a comment by Mr. Buckley on the CIA.

Now the *Boston Phoenix,* which is that area's left-complement to the John Birch Society magazine, publishes an editorial on the subject that begins with the ominous sentence, "William F. Buckley, Jr.'s past is catching up with him. In the 50's he served as E. Howard Hunt's assistant in the Mexico City CIA station. . . ." Accordingly, the *Phoenix* has protested to the editor of the *Boston Globe,* and reports to its readers, "Ann Wyman, the new editor of the *Globe*'s editorial pages, is now considering whether to append Buckley's past CIA affiliation to his column, which appears regularly in the *Globe.* Wyman intends to consult with other *Globe* editors. . . . The *Globe* may finally be on to him."

If so, it would indeed have taken the *Globe* a very long time, since it began publishing me in 1962, and my CIA involvement, [and] twenty-five-year-old friendship with Howard Hunt, are, among newspaper readers, as well known as that Coca-Cola is the pause that refreshes. But one pauses to wonder what is the planted axiom in the position taken by the *Boston Phoenix?*

It is true that I was in the CIA. I joined in July 1951, and left in April 1952. Now the assumption, not always stated, is that obviously anybody who was ever a member of an organization defends that organization. But one wonders: Why should this be held to be true? The most prominent critics of the CIA are former members of it.

I attended Yale University for four years. Is it the position of the *Boston Phoenix* that, therefore, everything I write about Yale is presumptively suspect, because as a Yale graduate I am obviously pro-Yale? But it happens that shortly before entering the CIA I wrote a book that was very critical of Yale. And, as a matter of fact, I have in recent years written critically about Yale on a dozen occasions. So consistently, indeed, that Miss Wyman may feel impelled to identify me, at the end of every column I write about Yale, in some such way as: "Mr. Buckley, a graduate of Yale, is, as one would expect, a critic of that university."

I am a Roman Catholic, and have written, oh, twenty columns in the last ten years critical of developments within the Catholic Church. Should I be identified as a Roman Catholic?

I like, roughly, in the order described, (1) God, (2) my family, (3) my country, (4) J. S. Bach, (5) peanut butter, and (6) good English prose.

Should these biases be identified when I write about, say, Satan, divorce, Czechoslovakia, Chopin, marmalade, and *New York Times* editorials?

I wonder if Miss Wyman is being asked, implicitly, to label the religious or ethnic backgrounds of her columnists? "Mr. Joseph Kraft, who writes today on Israel, is a Jew." That would presumably please the editors of the *Boston Phoenix*. Or, "Mr. William Raspberry, who writes today about civil rights in the South, is black." Or how about: "Mr. John Roche, who writes today in favor of federal aid to education, receives a salary from Tufts whose income depends substantially on federal grants."

Pete Hamill, who laughed his head off a few years ago at the hallucinations of Robert Welch, asks in the *Village Voice*: "Is Bill Buckley still a member of CIA? Have any of Buckley's many foreign travels been paid for by CIA?" One columnist recently wrote that *National Review*'s defense of the CIA, and my own friendship with Howard Hunt, might suggest that the CIA had indeed put up money for *National Review* over the years, though he conceded that if that were the case, the CIA was indeed a stingy organization—Mr. Garry Wills knows, at first hand, something of the indigence of that journal. Unfortunately Mr. Wills is the exact complement of Mr. Revilo Oliver, who was booted out of the John Birch Society for excessive kookiness some time after he revealed that JFK's funeral had been carefully rehearsed. Both are classics professors by background. Perhaps one should identify anyone who writes about politics and is also a classics professor as such? The *Boston Phoenix* and Miss Wyman should ponder that one.

—WFB   MARCH II, 1975

THE CIA ON THE DEFENSIVE

The CIA investigation unfolds, mostly in the press—and there is no doubt that the Agency has become the major hobgoblin of the day. The height of the hysteria was voiced at Yale University. Mr. John Lindsay, briefly in residence there to be debriefed on his experiences in municipal affairs, attacked the composition of the Rockefeller panel ("not one of them [the members] has a record of civil liberties"), and added that he himself always knew that "the CIA would become a monster and smite us all." Presumably the CIA is to blame for the bankrupt condition of New York City after eight years of leadership by Mr. Lindsay. Come to think of it, there is no more plausible explanation for the mess in New York than that the enemies of Mr. Lindsay were secretly running the government.

There was seldom a situation in which journalistic semantics played so great a role. Thus, the newspaper sentence, "Mr. Angleton believes that anti-war efforts were backed by foreign agencies" is read by one and all to mean, "Mr. Angleton entertains the obviously absurd notion that anti-war efforts were backed by foreign agencies."

The spokesmen for CIA have not rushed forward to give detailed accounts of the Agency's activities, and that's wrong. Or, as it is usually put, the CIA has "refused to specify the basis of its allegations." But it is okay for Seymour Hersh of the *New York Times* to make unqualified statements on the basis of unspecified "well-placed sources." You will perhaps have observed the technique. One day Mr. Hersh alleges that the CIA has done thus-and-so. The next day he quotes his own report of the day before beginning with the phrase, "Yesterday the *New York Times* revealed . . ."

Then there is the subtle use of quotation marks. "Richard Helms told the Senate Foreign Relations Committee that he could not 'recall' whether the White House had urged the CIA to engage in domestic spying. The *New York Times,* quoting well-placed sources, said that the CIA had violated . . ." Why the quotes around Helms's "recall," where they do not belong? Why *not* quotes around "well-placed sources"—where, according to the rules of punctuation, they *do* belong? Consider, for a moment, how differently these two sentences would read if the placing of the quotation marks had been reversed.

The topsy-turviness progresses. Mr. Miles Copeland, the author who has had considerable experience with and within the CIA, wrote recently a letter to the *London Times* skewering a typical report on the williwaw. The *Times's* reporter had quoted President Ford aboard *U.S. One,* flying to Vail. "The President said he had been assured in a mid-flight telephone call from Mr. William Colby, the CIA Director, that such activities 'did not exist' now." Commented Mr. Copeland: "What Mr. Colby said was that such activities 'do not exist.' The 'now' in the *Times's* story was added by your reporter. 'I do not beat my wife now' conveys a meaning rather different from 'I do not beat my wife.' "

The only fresh air recently was the story in the *Washington Post* quoting the former liaison man between the CIA and the FBI who said that there are "gray areas" in the law, resulting in the CIA's crossing into domestic operations for legitimate reasons. Mr. Sam Papich blamed these murky areas on a statute that "goes from the vague to the ridiculous."

"For example, he said"—I quote the *Post* story—"a CIA training program for local police departments was widely thought to have been aimed at anti-war activists and therefore represented an incursion into the domestic field. In fact, its purpose was to share with local police several devices and methods the CIA had developed in its own work. One device, he said, is engaged in the apprehension of murderers by detecting whether a suspect has held a piece of metal in the last 24 hours."

The charter says that the CIA shall have "no police, subpoena, law enforcement powers, or internal security functions." But, Mr. Papich reminds us, it also says that the CIA Director is "responsible for protecting intelligence sources and methods from unauthorized disclosure."

"A Soviet spy in France out of the blue travels to the U.S.," he said. "You don't just pick up the telephone and tell Hoover. . . ."

Complexities are being lost to the ideological rigidities. One wonders whether the critics of the CIA would really demand that it reveal its files on connections between U.S. protests and foreign money. Or—conceivably—will a thorough investigation reveal that the CIA has not done enough? Does it make sense, in any case, to repeal the law of hot pursuit when the enemy is detected flying into your own territory?

—WFB   FEBRUARY 4, 1975

Well in advance of the Pentagon Papers, the Nixon tapes, Whitewater, Vincent Foster, etc., Buckley raised questions of the right to privacy, or confidentiality, of a public figure or a public official.

PUBLIC FIGURES AND THE PRESS

"An indignant Mayor Lindsay arrived at La Guardia Airport from Washington at 5:10 P.M. yesterday"—says the item in the newspaper—"and told waiting reporters he did not have to answer any of their questions. Besieged with queries about City Hall's asserted intrusion in police matters, John Lindsay did say: 'That's ridiculous.' When a radio reporter held a microphone close to his face, the mayor roughly shoved it away and said: 'I'm the mayor of the City of New York and you have an obligation to treat me with respect.' As he left the airport in a small sports car, Lindsay partingly told a reporter, 'I don't have to answer your questions, I don't have to talk to you—I'm the mayor.' "

Well, Mr. Lindsay certainly made *that* clear, i.e., there is no doubting that he *is* the mayor, although it isn't exactly clear what he means by requiring that he be treated with respect on that account. He cannot mean that a reporter must not ask Lindsay questions when he arrives at the airport—it is the duty of the reporter to attempt to appease the public curiosity. On the other hand, it is up to the public official to decide when he desires to speak, and under what auspices; and if he doesn't like to give running interviews while going to, or coming from, an airport, that is a decision for him to make; but Mr. Lindsay should recognize that you don't have to be mayor of New York in order to enjoy that privilege.

Everyone has an obligation to treat everyone else with respect, if by respect is meant a regard for that man's sovereignty over his own affairs. If anything, the public figure is, in this narrow respect, perhaps less entitled than others to respect for the simple reason that the press is indispensable to the achievement of his own ambitions and the press, under the circumstances, comes to expect reciprocal accommodations. When you become, say, President of the United States (I am no longer addressing Mr. Lindsay), all the rules are broken because you are such a hot property that you need grant no interviews, not even to Walter Lippmann, and still you have a hope of surviving. But for lesser public officials, the relationship with the press is a two-way thing.

Now the press can be very bumptious indeed. An airline stewardess told me a few days ago of having been on an airplane with Senator Goldwater and his family in the fall of 1963, en route to the funeral of Mrs. Goldwater's mother. The plane pulled in at Chicago, the door opened, and a reporter fell through it, grabbed Senator Goldwater and said: "President Kennedy has just been shot and killed. How do you figure that affects your chances to become President?" Goldwater turned white, sucked in his breath, brushed the reporter aside and walked quickly down the ramp. He might very easily have hit the reporter. But he would not have said to him, "I am a United States Senator. You have an obligation to treat me with respect."

I remember an occasion in 1952 when President Truman's presidential train stopped at Stamford, Connecticut—the President was making stops along the line from New Haven to New York, campaigning for Adlai Stevenson as his successor. He had a little five-minute speech prepared, half folksy, half don't-let-them-take-it-away anti-Republicanism; and a few minutes after he began, a soprano voice rang out from a boy perched on a tree branch above the tracks: "Tell us about the red herring, Harry!"—an allusion to Truman's unfortunate designation of the Hiss investigation as a red herring. The crowd laughed good-humoredly. Mr. Truman did not laugh. "Young man," he snapped, "have you no respect for the President of the United States?" It was like a sudden cold snap. And Truman knew it, and rushed through the rest of his little talk; the candidates were quickly introduced, and the train pulled out, leaving the crowd nervous, undemonstrative. It is not known how the little boy was handled by his parents, but if he said "Gee, isn't the President stuffy!" he merely echoed his elders' unverbalized reaction.

If a treaty between public officials and press were to be written I should think it would stress one point, namely that the press would agree not physically to obstruct a public official—i.e., to stand directly in his way to where he is going, or to thrust a microphone in his face in such a way as to require him to duck, if he would avoid it. So that a mayor of New York, arriving at an airport, could on the one hand hear the questions directed to him by the press and weigh the desirability of replying to them then and there; on the other hand, be left free, if that is his pleasure, to walk quietly and resolutely out the door, without having to stop to lecture anyone at all on the importance of himself and the unrequited respect owing to his great office.

—WFB   MARCH 15, 1966

Easy Does It

MADRID. They didn't give a very big play to the *Washington Post* hoax in Madrid, and this is relevant because evidence of United States degeneracy is on the whole lavishly memorialized. I suspect the reason for it is that, really, Miss Janet Cooke's dishonor* was something that fell in newsrooms considerably on this side of the Donation of Constantine or the Protocols of Zion, but it is being given treatment about that heavy.

Let us, first, attempt a distinction of some importance. Some years ago, I sought to make the point that the Pentagon Papers collected and released with such fanfare by Daniel Ellsberg were tendentious—i.e., that they collected idiocies that could only have been one part of the whole story, unless we were prepared to believe that the people who staffed the Pentagon during the early and mid-sixties were all morons. Accordingly, I assembled three or four artisans and together we sat down and in three days composed, even unto imitating the prose style of generals and admirals and assistant secretaries of defense, memoranda, the difference between our own and the real ones being that ours were intelligent analyses of the deteriorating Indo-Chinese situation under the subversive attrition of the North Vietnam–backed Vietcong.

The *Washington Post* assigned a small platoon of reporters to check out what we had labeled as the "Secret Pentagon Papers." The results were quite extraordinary. A reporter would call, e.g., retired Admiral Arthur Radford, over whose signature we had written several memoranda, and Admiral Radford would say over the telephone, "Gee, fellows, I don't actually remember those exact memoranda—but after all it was eight years ago. But it does sound like me, and it's certainly what I was thinking of saying at the time." Others (for instance Dean Rusk) reacted similarly. Accordingly, the *Washington Post* ran full accounts of the "Secret Pentagon

* Ms. Cooke was the *Washington Post* reporter who wrote an account of an eight-year-old heroin addict, won a Pulitzer Prize, and later admitted that the child she wrote about was a fiction, or a composite.—Ed.

Papers." Back in the office we were alarmed that the hoax hadn't been penetrated, and so called a press conference to explain that the documents were forgeries, and to give the motive for their fabrication. To say that the editors of the *Washington Post* (and others) were annoyed with us is on the order of saying that Medea was irritated with Jason or that King Lear fell into a pout.

The similarity is that just as the Pentagon Papers we fabricated probably did and do substantively exist, in other forms to be sure, so the story of an eight-year-old addicted to heroin is, in our wretched times, far from unlikely. In this world, routinely twelve-year-old girls get pregnant, girls even younger—and boys—engage in sex for hire, and get their kicks from drugs. We don't need Pulitzer-quality reporters to tell us what crawls under the stones of our culture, and not only in black Washington, but in white East Hampton.

So that Miss Cooke's dishonorable act was less heinous than what it might have been. She did not violate the commandment against bearing false witness. She was not the woman who took the stand at the murder trial intentionally misidentifying the defendant and then happily watching him swing on the gibbet while she collected the bounty. The distinction between a *malum in se* and a *malum prohibitum*—the distinction between that which is inherently evil and that which is forbidden—is not entirely out of place here. Miss Cooke acted badly, she exposed certain supervisory frailties in the system, the prize was taken from her and she was fired.

But my goodness, the wailing and gnashing of teeth! When a generation ago Professor Charles Van Doren was shown to have been apprised ahead of time of the information that permitted him to gain fame and riches as the omniscient scholar on the $64,000 quiz program, people wrote about how the entire American academy was forever disgraced. The American academy may be disgraced, but hardly because one of its members yielded to the temptation of cupidity.

Ellen Goodman, the columnist, writes as though Miss Cooke had diminished the entire profession of journalism, which is to suggest that the entire profession of journalism enjoys a level of esteem the National Opinion Research Center declines to validate (ninth out of thirteen in institutional esteem as of 1979). And Roger Wilkins, the prominent black journalist who writes for the *Washington Star,* has gone so far as to say that Miss Cooke has set back the entire cause of black journalism because her misrepresentations will cause editors to lower their esteem for black perceptiveness.

As one member of the white majority, I'd prefer the company of a black newspaperwoman who fabricated a story centered on a mythic but entirely plausible little victim of drugs, to the company of the relatively untroubled black (or white) drug pushers who ride around in their Cadillacs sowing their poison. If you wish to know who to get mad at, go back and read Claude Brown's *Manchild in the Promised Land.*

So I say: Forget it. Probably, net, it was a salubrious experience, since some members of the press have got rather bloated notions of their sanctity. Elmer Gantry was, on the whole, a good thing, reminding us of the endemic weakness of the flesh, restoring our perspective.

—WFB   APRIL 25, 1981

REVIVE THE NATIONAL NEWS COUNCIL

The attention given to the Sharon (General) versus *Time* (magazine) trial goes beyond American curiosity on whether the magazine libeled the general. The professionals were interested, of course, in the evolution of the libel law. But the public was interested in the drama.

Drama here is defined as the press at the bar.

The *New York Times*'s version of the verdict: "The jury found an absence of malice, but no shortage of arrogance."

And then the *Times* went on to deliver a lecture worth contemplating. It is time, said the editorial, "for journalists to stop muting their criticism of one another. The best protection of free speech is more free speech, not less. To deserve the extraordinary protections of American law, *Time* and all of journalism needs a stronger tradition of mutual and self-correction. The more influential the medium, the greater the duty to offer a place for rebuttal, complaint, correction and re-examination. Beating the arrogance rap is even more important than escaping one for libel."

Flash back now to the San Francisco Republican Convention in 1964. General Dwight Eisenhower is speaking. He says the usual things, hohum, and then suddenly he utters the following sentence: "Let us particularly scorn the divisive efforts of those outside our family, including sensation-seeking columnists and commentators..." The crowd rose spontaneously to its feet and cheered as if, single-handed, Dwight Eisenhower had just won the Super Bowl.

Flash forward to November 1969. Vice President Spiro Agnew, speaking in Des Moines, Iowa, denounces the bias of network television, charging that TV's immense power over public opinion was in the hands of "a small and unelected elite" of network producers, commentators and newsmen, "to a man" reflecting the "geographical and intellectual confines of Washington, D.C., or New York City." The result? Practically the whole country hoists Mr. Agnew on its shoulders, and for a brief period he is a popular hero. Something indeed was going on.

In 1973, the Twentieth Century Fund, without acknowledging the Agnew assault on media bias, let alone stressing it, made possible the founding of something called the National News Council. The council was set up as a fifteen-man board composed of responsible citizens, half of them members of the media, half of them so-called "public members." The council had a staff of a half dozen that operated under the presidency of a series of distinguished figures, among them Richard Salant, the eminent former director of news for CBS.

The procedure was as follows. If a person or an institution thought he or it had been wrongly treated by a newspaper, magazine or television station, he could file a complaint with the National News Council. But—listen to this—before the council would agree to look at the complaint, the plaintiff had to agree that whatever the council decided, he would waive a libel action. The council, in short, knew that it could not get the cooperation of the media at large if, in effect, the council was acting as a pre-trial discovery panel.

Members were given staff reports on the alleged unfairness, including—when available—the defense of the alleged tortfeasor. I say when available, because some, indeed a significant number, of media flatly declined to cooperate. And most conspicuous of these was: the *New York Times.*

So here we had an organization begun in 1973 . . . that, in 1982, just plain ran out of steam. It folded for lack of funds. But that lack of funds was the result of the indifference with which its findings were treated in the press. The press, in effect, denied the council the only sanction that could keep it alive: public respect for its findings.

The National News Council was a body that, if beefed up by institutional respect, might have acted as a satisfactory alternative to a jury trial. It could have received the complaint of General Sharon (alongside his promise not to bring legal action), heard the response of *Time* mag, conducted its investigation, and issued its finding. But of course these things don't work unless people pay them some heed. In the relevant case, *Time* would have bound itself to reporting the finding of the National News Council.

Well, the editors of the *New York Times* have aptly phrased what's troubling so many people. It is a pity that when presented the opportunity to do something about it, as recently as in 1973, they were out to lunch.

—WFB   JANUARY 31, 1985

(Excerpt from The New Yorker, *January 31, 1983,*
"A Journal—Overdrive—I" by William F. Buckley, Jr.)

The *Times* called to ask who had taken a photograph of Pat and me on the Orient Express that they will use in the travel section; they want to send the photographer a check (for $75). I tell Frances that the picture in question was taken with my own camera by a waiter, and it would not be feasible to find him. The spread will not be out until next Sunday, and I haven't seen it, but the galleys, corrected over the weekend, amused me, because I had privately gambled that one sentence I wrote would never see the light of day. On learning that the *Times* had, as represented, a strict limit of $500 for any travel piece . . . I had written that aboard the Orient Express "the consumption of [drinks from the bar] is encouraged, by the way, and they are cash-and-carry, and there is no nonsense about special rates. A gin-and-tonic is $4, a liqueur $6. These prices, weighed on the scales of the Old Testament, are not prohibitive, unless you are trying to make a living writing for the travel section of the *New York Times.*"

I won—the third sentence did not survive. It's a funny thing about the *Times:* I don't know anybody who works for it who *doesn't* have a sense of humor. (Big exception: John Oakes. But then he retired as editorial-page director several years ago, and is understandably melancholy about having to live in a world whose shape is substantially of his own making.) A. M. Rosenthal, the working head of the newspaper, is one of the funniest men living. Arthur Ochs Sulzberger, the publisher, is wonderfully amusing, and easily amused. And so on. But there is some corporate something that keeps the *Times* from smiling at itself: don't quite know what.

(Telegram addressed to WILLIAM F. BUCKLEY, JR. NATIONAL REVIEW NEW YORK, *February 2, 1983.)*

YOUR VICIOUS AND TOTALLY UNCALLED-FOR CHARGE THAT THE NEW YORK TIMES HAS NO SENSE OF HUMOR ABOUT ITSELF WAS SIMPLY ANOTHER EXAMPLE OF THE NATIONWIDE ATTACK AGAINST THE FIRST AMENDMENT. WE PLAN TO RESIST THIS CONSPIRACY DIRECTED AT THE FREE PRESS WITH ALL OUR MIGHT.

A. M. ROSENTHAL
EXECUTIVE EDITOR
THE NEW YORK TIMES

TED TURNER'S RUSSIA

If you want to lift your eyes for a tiny moment from events in the Democratic convention center in Atlanta, let them travel to another part of the city that is the headquarters of the Turner Broadcasting Co. This is the outfit that has given us the most innovative (and valuable) TV programming idea of the decade: round-the-clock news. That news is reported evenhandedly. But the strangest transformation since the discovery of the transsexual operation is what has happened to Ted Turner, the founder of CNN. He has become a Soviet apologist. In fact, his stuff is so red it would embarrass the *Daily Worker* to publish it.

But not the Encyclopaedia Britannica, and here lies the story. Last March, Turner Educational Services, which is an arm of the broadcasting company, aired a seven-hour program called "Portrait of the Soviet Union." The next thing we knew, Turner teamed up with the Encyclopaedia Britannica to take those seven hours and run them for the education of schoolchildren. And this notwithstanding the universal panning received when "Portrait" was broadcast on WTBS. The first sentence of *Washington Post* reviewer Tom Shales, who guards the liberal tablets in this world as Fafner guarded the Nibelungs' treasures, was, "Does Ted Turner have a few thousand acres in the Urals that he's trying to unload?" Shales was just warming up. "This is not a 'Letter from the U.S.S.R.' It's more like a postcard from Binky and Biff at Camp Whitewash."

Even so, the E.B. people undertook to make it a seminal instrument for the instruction of America's schoolchildren. How bad is the Turner portrait of the U.S.S.R.?

—The Kremlin used to belong to the czars. "Now, it belongs to the people."

—What did Lenin face when he took over Russia? His party "needed to mold a new kind of citizen, one who would embody all the virtues of the socialist ethic—clean-limbed, right-thinking and dedicated to the state. The kind of model superperson that would be a shining example to all."

—What is the goal of communism? "A highly developed people, giving freely all they can to a society and in return taking back all they need."

—How has the Soviet Union dealt with its artists? "Just outside of Moscow, living in the most amazing grace, is an enclave of top Russian artists. [These] princes of literature have their homes in this Russian Beverly Hills."

—Is there freedom of religion in the Soviet Union? Forgawdsakes. "Atheist though the state may be, freedom to worship as you please is enshrined in the Soviet constitution."

—But haven't the Soviet Union's managers in fact failed to create an advanced society? Horsefeathers. "It's modernization on a grand scale—a great success."

—Didn't a dozen million citizens perish in Siberia as the result of the policy of Gulag? Siberia "used to be a one-way ticket to exile; it's now a chance for young Soviets to do something for their country, make some extra money, maybe even start a whole new life."

—Don't Soviet history books lie about everything? Well, "increasingly, Soviets feel it is essential for the young, indeed everyone, to have an honest account of their own history."

—Could it be that all this time, all these years, our thoughts about Lenin and Stalin and Khrushchev and Brezhnev and Andropov were mistaken? "The longer you're here, the more you discover how many wrong ideas you have about the Soviets."

Ted Turner was accosted about this travesty on his own *Crossfire* feature. Pat Buchanan put it to him that this was the most concentrated pack of lies about the Soviet Union in one package since a broadcast by Goebbels on the Jews. His answer? "I wanted to go over there and paint a beautiful portrait of the Soviet Union." Pressed to explain the distortions, he just said it again. "Well, that's true, that's absolutely true, we went over there to paint a portrait, we painted a portrait, and I'm not going to apologize for it."

The wonderful irony is that when this beautiful portrait of the Soviet Union was exhibited *in* the Soviet Union, the Soviet government ran a disclaimer, criticizing the program for failing to describe the harsh realities of the Soviet Union.

This was all too much for L. Brent Bozell III, chairman of the Media Research Center in Washington, who wrote to the Encyclopaedia Britannica distributors, and got back from Mr. Michael Jirasek, who is "manager, communications services," the dumbest letter of the year. Jirasek's position is that whatever is told inadequately by the movie gets corrected by educational reading matter that accompanies it. So? Make a movie about how wonderful life was under Adolf Hitler in Germany, distribute it to all the schoolchildren, and then expose them to some light reading taking exception to this position. The Kremlin should give Turner the Order of Stalin, except that the Kremlin would be embarrassed to associate Stalin with Turner's ideas of Stalin.

—WFB   JULY 15, 1988

Come Undressed As You Are

It is axiomatic that the underworlder will by ostentatious public benefactions seek the approval of the same community he systematically despoils. Mafia boss Joe Bananas supporting the local church. Billy Sol Estes hosting a Boy Scout picnic. Louis B. Mayer contributing to an institute of higher learning. No one has practiced the art of civic diversion more prodigiously than Hugh Hefner, founder of *Playboy* magazine and godfather of the sexual revolution. His formula was as straightforward as the advertisements in *Playboy* for sexually stimulating paraphernalia: make a lot of money by pandering to the sexual appetite, elevating it to primacy—then spend part of that money co-seducing critics or potential critics.

Years ago Harvard theologian Harvey Cox wrote an essay on *Playboy*, denominating it the single most brazen assault on the human female as a person in general circulation. What seemed like moments later, the same scholar found himself writing earnest essays for *Playboy*; and before long he forgot all about his mission to identify *Playboy* for what it essentially is: an organ that seeks to justify the superordination of sex over all other considerations—loyalty to family, any principle of self-discipline, any respect for privacy, or for chastity or modesty. *Sex omnia vincit*, Hugh Hefner's magazine told us, issue after issue.

Really, I wonder if anyone in the future can ever again take seriously the Anti-Defamation League. Here is an organization "dedicated to the combating of prejudice and discrimination against Jews and other minorities, and to the protection and extension of our democratic system for the benefit of all Americans." "The League," the brochure continues, "works with the various institutions of our society, public and private, religious and secular, to achieve these ends." And it is celebrating later this month its First Amendment Freedoms Award by giving a dinner-dance in honor of—Hugh M. Hefner.

About the honoree the ADL says, with an apparently straight face, that he "began with little more than a unique idea for a magazine" (nude women, jokes about copulation, and advice on how to seduce young girls) "and a philosophy of social change." (The "philosophy," quite simply, that the gratification of the male sexual impulse is to be achieved without any second thought to the possible effect on (a) the girl, (b) her family, (c) your family, (d) any code of self-restraint.) "The empire he founded has had a far-reaching impact, not only on the publishing industry, but on the mores of American society as well." That is correct. Any serious disciple of Hugh Hefner would not hesitate to purr anti-Semitic lovelies into the ears of his bunny, if that was what was required to effect seduction.

The Anti-Defamation League has, in the past, surrendered to temptations alien to its splendidly commendable purpose, namely to focus public attention on, and bring obloquy to, acts of racial discrimination. It meddled actively in the presidential campaign of 1964, endeavoring to scare its clientele into believing that Senator Goldwater was an ogre of sorts, backed by fanatics. Its current director, Mr. Nathan Perlmutter, is a man of high sensibility, gentle, firm, discriminating, a scholarly man long associated with Brandeis University. One notes that he is charging $250 a plate to guests who seek the privilege of joining with him to honor Hugh Hefner.

The tawdriness of the symbolism is driven home. Even as Hugh Hefner sells pictures of parted pudenda in order to make the dollar, a nickel of which he donates to institutions devoted to the rights of Nazis to march in Skokie, and of fellow pornographers to hawk their wares, the ADL raises money to combat discrimination by honoring the principal agent of the kind of selflessness that deprives racial toleration of the ultimate sanction. This sanction rests on a profound belief in the sanctity of the individual, yes, even that of the nubile girl. Take away from the struggle for racial toleration the profound spiritual commitment to the idea of a higher law, and the code against anti-Semitism becomes a mere matter of social convenience, the kind of upwardly mobile patter one is taught in the pages of *Playboy* to imitate, on the order of wearing Dior handkerchiefs or Gucci loafers.

Racial toleration draws its principal strength from the proposition that we are all brothers, created equal by God. The *Playboy* philosophy measures human worth by bustline and genital energy. The affair will be celebrated, appropriately enough, in Hollywood, at the Century Plaza Hotel. The invitation specifies "black tie." Well, if the guests arrive wearing only a black tie, that will be more than some of the guests wear at Hef's other parties.

—WFB   SEPTEMBER 6, 1980

Exit Mr. Shawn

It shouldn't be hard to understand the two points of view. On the one hand the frenetic undertow of competition, and the feeling that that which must eventually happen (the retirement of Mr. Shawn) should perhaps be accelerated (to accommodate anxious business and editorial pressures). That is the point of view of management, and management's concern for quality of leadership is documented by its choice of a successor, a bookish, imaginative editor, Robert Gottlieb, in some ways not unlike his legendary predecessor. When asked some time ago what were his concerns, he replied that they were his work, his reading, his family, and the ballet. He is not encumbered, in his ascendancy from editor of Knopf to editor of *The New Yorker,* by any shortage of skills or taste. His difficulty, which will probably be short-lived, is his lack of consanguinity. He was not (the objection from the second point of view) a member of the *New Yorker* family.

In a perfect world, Mr. Shawn would have lived forever. Not that there was always satisfaction: Inasmuch as Mr. Shawn's whole world was *The New Yorker,* sometimes *The New Yorker* read as though it was edited only for those whose whole world would be *The New Yorker.* But his traits were for that very reason unique: Caring only for his creature, he gave everything within his power to give, and the creeping asphyxiation of the long, leisurely time for the written arts that is a function of this hectic century was something the century would need to worry about, because Mr. Shawn would not. His ways were his ways, and those who worked with him—worked for him—knew that they had experienced true singularity in a world bent on Procrusteanism.

—WFB   FEBRUARY 13, 1987

DEFEAT OF CLAY, AMONG OTHERS

Time magazine's witty headline ("Defeat of Clay") gives the bare-bones story: Clay Felker lost control of *New York* magazine in 1976 . . . vowed it wouldn't happen again . . . bought *Esquire* . . . lost money . . . lost more money . . . began giving up stock for money . . . couldn't finally get more financing. . . . A Swedish conglomerate has combined with an outfit in Tennessee that publishes a giveaway, ad-oriented, ad-soaked journal for young people, is taking over. . . . "I never even *heard* of the [new owners]," wailed *Esquire's* ace political reporter Richard Reeves. . . . New management is expected to transform the mag into a "service-oriented" journal. . . . Lotsa ads.

And not very much journalism.

One reflects on the magazine which, during the thirties, published Scott Fitzgerald and Ernest Hemingway.

Last December, Editor Clay Felker called in a young writer, one of the Roving Editors thus described on his masthead. FLASH! How about a really good piece on the King of Spain? People don't really *know* much about him. Go to Spain. Interview him. Interview everybody who knows him. Interview *everybody.* Get a *good* piece.

The writer goes to Spain, spends six weeks questioning the whole bloody Spanish establishment—prime ministers, opposition leaders, dukes, bishops, cardinals, rejected pretenders, taxi drivers—finally sees The Man himself, threads his way through a marvelously candid interview given off the record.

The writer uncovers an incredible historical footnote, heretofore unpublished: Franco got it into his head, not so long ago, that the Bourbons never really *understood* Spain, so he communicates secretly with Dr. Otto von Habsburg, who if things had gone differently in World War I would today be the emperor of Austria-Hungary; and Franco says: How would you like to be the king of Spain? Dr. Habsburg says, No thanks, I'm not much for taking other people's crowns, but thanks for asking.

The young man sweats back to New York and in ten days reduces it all to six thousand words. He has spent two months on the story. His expenses come to $2900. His salary is $830 per fortnight. Add it all up and it comes to about a dollar per word. Worth it? Every penny, I say: but *Esquire* lost four million dollars last year, doing that sort of thing; and the new owners are not likely to indulge such extravagant curiosities, let alone cultivate them.

The young writer was hired by *Esquire* six months before Clay Felker bought it. He had made a good impression on the editor-in-chief, and six months after being hired, fresh out of college, he was appointed Managing Editor. He cabled the news of his promotion to his father, who at the time was working his way around the Baltic on a cruise ship as an "enrichment lecturer." The father was very proud, and when he got back to New York, he escorted his son to the most expensive restaurant in New York for a private father-son celebration.

On that occasion, the young man, whose loyalties had clearly been involuted by his new responsibility, brazenly advised his father that the fee *Esquire* had contracted to pay for Old Dad's next scheduled piece—was too high! Old Dad mobilized all his reserves of authority, which by all accounts are formidable, and said to his son, "If you pursue this line of discussion, I shall be required to reduce your allowance." Managing Editors are not often exposed to such definitive intimidations.

Where do the writers go, in the ever-diminishing world of serious journalism? *The New Yorker* is still there, thank God; and *Harper's,* the *Atlantic.* The new *Life* runs some, but not a lot of copy; ditto the born-again *Look.* The skin mags buy some pretty expensive fig leaves. And there are the journals of opinion. A generation ago, *Esquire* apart, there was the *Saturday Evening Post, Collier's, Liberty,* a huge *Life* mag which serialized Churchill, a huge *Look,* which serialized William Manchester.

It may be true that Felker has "feet of Clay." But the bigger point is that there is less and less space in magazines willing to lay out six thousand dollars for a *really* good piece about the king of Spain. Besides, where is my son to go now for a job?

—WFB   MAY 3, 1979

Editor's Footnote

Christopher Buckley went on to other accomplishments beyond reducing WFB's fee. He is editor of *Forbes's* bright publication *FYI;* regularly writes humorous essays for *The New Yorker;* and has published several highly regarded and popular books.

———

New Guard, *New York Times*

We do not disguise that beyond the reach of memory, we at *National Review* have used the *New York Times* as our very favorite pincushion. Much of this the paper has earned, particularly in its editorial pages where, especially under the leadership of an editor providentially retired several years ago, the *Times* was militantly, not to say disreputably, tone-deaf, showing an enthusiasm for such disparate calamities as Fidel Castro and John Lindsay.

But the *New York Times* even then was a very great newspaper, with a profound sense of its responsibility to cover the news, even if the temptation, often, was to do so tendentiously, as when Barry Goldwater ran for President. But the news last weekend of a shifting of the guard brings to mind how heavily indebted all readers of the *New York Times,* and all readers of readers of the *New York Times,* are to A. M. Rosenthal for the extraordinary vision he brought to the paper, which he dominated (save only the editorial pages) for almost twenty years. The brightness of the Gray Lady, its appetite for the news, for features, for supplements, the sheer universality of its coverage make it the outstanding newspaper in the world. It is sad that Mr. Rosenthal is retiring, but reassuring to know that the traditions he accepted and reinforced will be maintained by his successors.

Mr. Rosenthal once noted that it is not easy for the editor of the *New York Times* to move through the city with any sense of security, as the *Times* is blamed for everything that goes wrong. (It should be blamed for only about half of what goes wrong.) He cited to the editor of this journal an example: One evening, after a very long day at work, he eased into his bed and pulled out the freshest issue of *National Review,* opened it, and read in the lead editorial, "Abe? Abe Rosenthal! Are you listening, goddammit? That story you published last week about . . ." *Requiescat in pace.* Abe Rosenthal will write two columns per week for the Op-Ed page; Arthur Gelb, his gifted associate, will serve as managing editor; and Max Frankel, from the editorial page he substantially rescued, will be the new boss. Best wishes to them all. Goddammit.

—WFB   NOVEMBER 7, 1986

Dear Mr. Buckley:

A few years ago [the newspaperman] Bob Considine wrote from Nairobi that he "never knew until this trip that 'hippopotamus' means river horse in Latin." We must, however, make allowances for Bob. Being a liberal, he labors under the misapprehension that history began with the French Revolution and is probably totally unaware of the existence of Classical Greek.

However, in your column of today's date in the *San Antonio Light* I read: "An acting President cannot be made to feel like Macbeth's uncle, the successor king, sleeping in incestuous sheets."

Referring you to *Hamlet*, Act I, Scene 2, Lines 156 and 157, I remind you that I have adduced an excuse for Bob, but I would like to hear yours.

Sincerely,

MURL J. MANLOVE

SAN ANTONIO, TEXAS

Dear Mr. Manlove:

Come on. I am perfectly capable of typing out the sentence, "When Washington delivered his Gettysburg address . . ." I mean, that kind of thing happens. When it does, it should be caught (a) by me, when I reread my column; failing that (b) by my office, if the column is on that day traveling to the syndicate via my office; (c) by the syndicate before it sends it out to the newspapers; (d) by the newspaper editor before sending it to be set; (e) by the proofreader on reading proof. It is safer, when a fail-safe mechanism as elaborate as this fails, to assume that all human systems are capable of concerted carelessness, than that the entire editorial structure of American journalism has lapsed into historical or literary amnesia. Cordially,

—WFB   MARCH I, 1974

What's So Bad About Writing Fast?

If, during spring term at Yale University in 1949 you wandered diagonally across the campus noticing here and there an undergraduate with impacted sleeplessness under his eyes and coarse yellow touches of fear on his cheeks, you were looking at members of a masochistic set who had enrolled in a course called Daily Themes. No Carthusian novitiate embarked on a bout of mortification of the flesh suffered more than the students of Daily Themes, whose single assignment, in addition to attending two lectures per week, was to write a 500-to-600-word piece of descriptive prose every day, and to submit it before midnight (into a large box outside a classroom). Sundays were the only exception (this was before the Warren Court outlawed Sunday).

For anyone graduated from Daily Themes who went on to write, in journalism or in fiction or wherever, the notion that a burden of 500 words per day is the stuff of nightmares is laughable. But caution: 500 words a day is what Graham Greene writes, and Nabokov wrote 180 words per day, devoting to their composition four or five hours. But at that rate, Graham Greene and Nabokov couldn't qualify for a job as reporters on the *New York Times*. Theirs is high-quality stuff, to speak lightly of great writing. But Georges Simenon is also considered a great writer, at least by those who elected him to the French Academy, and he writes books in a week or so. Dr. Johnson wrote *Rasselas,* his philosophical romance, in nine days. And Trollope . . . we'll save Trollope.

I am fired up on the subject because, to use a familiar formulation, they have been kicking me around a lot; it has got out that I write fast, which is qualifiedly true. In this august journal [the *New York Times Book Review*] on January 5, Morton Kondracke of *Newsweek* took it all the way: "He [me—WFB] reportedly knocks out his column in twenty minutes flat— three times a week for 260 newspapers. That is too little time for serious contemplation of difficult subjects."

Now that is a declaration of war, and I respond massively.

To begin with: it is axiomatic, in cognitive science, that there is no necessary correlation between profundity of thought and length of time spent on thought. JFK is reported to have spent fifteen hours per day for six days before deciding exactly how to respond to the missile crisis, but it can still be argued that his initial impulse on being informed that the Soviet Union had deployed nuclear missiles in Cuba (bomb the hell out of the missile sites?) might have been the strategically sounder course. This is not an argument against deliberation, merely against the suggestion that to think longer (endlessly?) about a subject is necessarily to probe it more fruitfully.

Mr. Kondracke, for reasons that would require more than twenty minutes to fathom, refers to composing columns in twenty minutes "flat." Does he mean to suggest that I have a stopwatch which rings on the twentieth minute? Or did he perhaps mean to say that I have been known to write a column in twenty minutes? Very different. He then goes on, in quite another connection, to cite "one of the best columns" in my new book—without thinking to ask: How long did it take him to write that particular column?

The chronological criterion, you see, is without validity. Every few years, I bring out a collection of previously published work, and this of course requires me to reread everything I have done in order to make that season's selections. It transpires that it is impossible to distinguish a column written very quickly from a column written very slowly. Perhaps that is because none is written very slowly. A column that requires two hours to write is one which was interrupted by phone calls or the need to check a fact. I write fast—but not, I'd maintain, remarkably fast. If Mr. Kondracke thinks it intellectually risky to write 750 words in twenty minutes, what must he think about people who speak 750 words in five minutes, as he often does on television?

The subject comes up now so regularly in reviews of my work that I did a little methodical research on my upcoming novel. I began my writing (in Switzerland, removed from routine interruption) at about 5 P.M., and wrote usually for two hours. I did that for forty-five working days (the stretch was interrupted by a week in the United States, catching up on editorial and television obligations). I then devoted the first ten days in July to revising the manuscript. On these days I worked on the manuscript an average of six hours per day, including retyping. We have now a grand total: 90 plus 60, or 150 hours. My novels are about 70,000 words, so that averaged out to roughly 500 words per hour.

Anthony Trollope rose at five every morning, drank his tea, performed his toilette and looked at the work done the preceding day. He would then begin to write at six. He set himself the task of writing 250 words every fifteen minutes for three and one-half hours. Indeed it is somewhere recorded that if he had not, at the end of fifteen minutes, written the required 250 words he would simply "speed up" the next quarter-hour, because he was most emphatic in his insistence on his personally imposed daily quota: 3,500 words.

Now the advantages Trollope enjoys over me are enumerable and nonenumerable. I write only about the former, and oddly enough they are negative advantages. He needed to write by hand, having no alternative. I use a word processor. Before beginning this article, I tested my speed on this instrument and discovered that I type more slowly than I had imagined. Still, it comes out at eighty words per minute. So that if Trollope had had an IBM, he'd have written, in three and one-half hours at my typing speed, not 3,500 words but 16,800 words per day.

Ah, you say, but could anyone think that fast? The answer is, sure people can think that fast. How did you suppose extemporaneous speeches get made? Erle Stanley Gardner dictated his detective novels nonstop to a series of secretaries, having previously pasted about in his studio 3-by-5 cards reminding him at exactly what hour the dog barked, the telephone rang, the murderer coughed. He knew where he was going, the plot was framed in his mind, and it became now only an act of extrusion. Margaret Coit wrote in her biography of John C. Calhoun that his memorable speeches were composed not in his study but while he was outdoors, plowing the fields on his plantation. He would return then to his study and write out what he had framed in his mind. His writing was an act of transcription. I own the holograph of Albert Jay Nock's marvelous book on Jefferson, and there are fewer corrections on an average page than I write into a typical column. Clearly Nock knew exactly what he wished to say and how to say it; prodigious rewriting was, accordingly, unnecessary.

Having said this, I acknowledge that I do not know exactly what I am going to say, or exactly how I am going to say it. And in my novels, I can say flatly, as Mr. Kondracke would have me say it, that I really do not have any idea where they are going—which ought not to surprise anyone familiar with the nonstop exigencies of soap opera writing or of comic strip writing or, for that matter, of regular Sunday sermons. It is not necessary to know how your protagonist will get out of a jam into which you put him. It requires only that you have confidence that you will be able to get him out of that jam. When you begin to write a column on, let us say, the reaction of Western Europe to President Reagan's call for a boycott of Libya, it is not necessary that you should know *exactly* how you will say what you will end up saying. You are, while writing, drawing on huge reserves: of opinion, prejudice, priorities, presumptions, data, ironies, drama, histrionics. And these reserves you enhance during practically the entire course of the day, and it doesn't matter all that much if a particular hour is not devoted to considering problems of foreign policy. You can spend an hour playing the piano and develop your capacity to think, even to create; and certainly you can grasp more keenly, while doing so, your feel for priorities.

The matter of music flushes out an interesting point: Why is it that critics who find it arresting that a column can be written in twenty minutes, a book in 150 hours, do not appear to find it remarkable that a typical graduate of Juilliard can memorize a prelude and fugue from "The Well-Tempered Clavier" in an hour or two? It would take me six months to memorize one of those *números*. And mind, we're not talking here about the *Guinness Book of World Records* types. Isaac Asimov belongs in *Guinness . . .* but surely not an author who averages a mere 500 words per hour, or who occasionally writes a column at one-third his typing speed!

There are phenomenal memories in the world. Claudio Arrau is said to hold in his memory music for forty recitals, two and a half hours each. *That* is phenomenal. Ralph Kirkpatrick, the late harpsichordist, actually told me that he had not played the "Goldberg" Variations for twenty years before playing it to a full house in New Haven in the spring of 1950. *That* is phenomenal. Winston Churchill is said to have memorized all of "Paradise Lost" in a week, and throughout his life he is reported to have been able to memorize his speeches after a couple of readings. (I have a speech I have delivered fifty times, and could not recite one paragraph of it by heart.)

So cut it out, Kondracke. I am, I fully grant, a phenomenon, but not because of any speed in composition. I asked myself the other day, Who else, on so many issues, has been so right so much of the time? I couldn't think of anyone. And I devoted to the exercise twenty minutes. Flat.

—WFB   FEBRUARY 19, 1986

Chapter 12

A Columnist on Column Writing— and on Choosing Carefully Your Words and Your Opponents

At times, the tension between writers dueling in public almost snaps the bonds of friendship that, in many cases, lie beneath. Buckley's jousts with Professor John Kenneth Galbraith over the years—and they *are* friends— reminds one of the desirability of picking worthy adversaries. I have often thought that (as WFB suggested to Kilpatrick) they could take their act on the road. As indeed they have done, or at least in print.

The touchiness and testiness between WFB and another regular opponent—a regular guest on *Firing Line*—threaten to stretch on into the next century.

THE VIOLATION OF ARTHUR

Just after Mr. Kennedy's inauguration, I met with Professor Arthur Schlesinger, Jr., historian and dogmatic theologian for Americans for Democratic Action, in public debate in Boston on the subject of the welfare state. It was on that occasion that Mr. Schlesinger, countering some point or other I had made, announced that the "best defense against communism is the welfare state." Now everybody expects that professors will say foolish things from time to time, but Professor Schlesinger had just then taken leave of Harvard to accept a position as special assistant to the fledgling President of the United States, so that a great deal of publicity was given to that remarkable statement. A decent interval should have elapsed before an egghead academician would presume to press such homeopathic nonsense about how to deal with communism on practical men of exalted station but the assembly was sobered on witnessing the professor's grand entry into the lecture hall, twenty minutes late, escorted by screeching police cars—it obviously hadn't taken long for Mr. Schlesinger to acquire princely habits.

And along with them, it is my sad duty here to report, he seems to have lost—an occupational risk for humble folk who suddenly find themselves supping with the great—whatever sense of humor he once possessed.

Schlesinger had been accustomed to such fawning audiences as he regularly came upon at Harvard and elsewhere in the academic world, where they preach academic freedom and practice liberal indoctrination; and was quite visibly disconcerted on discovering from the audience's reaction that one half of those present were quite adamantly opposed to his views and those of the New Frontiersmen. Under the circumstances, he thought to curry the opposition's favor by handing me, as their spokesman of the evening, a most redolent bouquet. Quoth Arthur: "Mr. Buckley has a facility for rhetoric which I envy, as well as a wit which I seek clumsily and vainly to emulate." The crowd (or my half of it) purred with pleasure. As an old debater, I knew exactly what he was up to, and determined, when my turn came to rebut, to say something equally oleaginous about Arthur. But I had only fifteen minutes before getting up to speak during which to compose a compliment, and I guess my imagination failed me—I forget.

And indeed I forgot about the whole incident until a couple of months ago when I received a letter from a lady in Boston who had been there that night. She cited Mr. Schlesinger's cream puff to illustrate his exemplary "fairness to the opposite political camp." It happened that at just that moment I was supposed to furnish my publishers with some quotations for the jacket of my new book, *Rumbles Left and Right.* I thought it would be mad fun to include the words of Arthur Schlesinger—you know, sort of the literary oxymoron of the year.

Well sir, you'd have thought this was the biggest swindle since the Donation of Constantine. A few weeks ago, while minding my own business, I received a frantic telegram from my publisher announcing that Arthur Schlesinger, having seen the blurb in an advertisement for my book in *National Review,* demanded to know where and when he had said any such thing about me. I wired back: "MY OFFICE HAS COPY OF ORIGINAL TAPE. TELL ARTHUR *THAT'LL* TEACH HIM TO USE UNCTION IN POLITICAL DEBATE BUT NOT TO TAKE IT SO HARD: NO ONE BELIEVES ANYTHING HE SAYS ANYWAY." Needless to say, I sent a copy of the telegram to Mr. Schlesinger, with the postscript: "Dear Arthur: I am at work on a new book which, however, will not be completed until the spring of 1964, giving you plenty of time to compose a new puff for it. Regards." And then, on the upper left-hand corner of the letter, properly addressed to Mr. Schlesinger at his august quarters (The White House, Washington, D.C.), I wrote, "Wm. 'Envy His Rhetoric!' Buckley," with my return address.

That, apparently, did it. Before even Arthur could say "I-believe-in Free-Speech," the firm of Messrs. Greenbaum, Wolff and Ernst let it be known to my publisher and to *National Review* that they would demand an apology—or Schlesinger would sue. Now there is a very good case to be made for everyone apologizing who has ever quoted Arthur Schlesinger; but isn't it droll to be asked to apologize *to* Schlesinger for quoting *from* Schlesinger? Messrs. G., W. & E. have solemnly announced that I have "invaded Mr. Schlesinger's privacy . . ." A most interesting complaint, considering that Mr. Schlesinger's words had been uttered before an audience of fifteen hundred or so, before television and radio, and before members of the press and the wire services. For someone who wants what he says to be kept private . . . that's a strange way to go about it, wouldn't you say? . . .

Ah well, it is a mad world. But I shall certainly put in for next year's Freedom Award. On the grounds that the more time Schlesinger devotes to me, the less time he has left over to devote to public affairs.

—WFB   MARCH 30, 1963

———

The brouhaha continued, with less haha. An exchange with lawyers and several parting shots followed, though, as often with Buckley, the shots were neither fatal nor intended as such.

———

Schlesinger *vs.* Buckley *et al.*

Mr. Arthur Schlesinger has told the press he does *not* intend to sue Putnam's or *National Review* or William Buckley for their outrageous decision to quote his sentences on the dust jacket of *Rumbles Left and Right*. So WFB wrote to Messrs. Greenbaum, Wolff and Ernst and asked, Is it all off? To which they replied, in effect, Never mind what Arthur said to the press, we will hold you "fully responsible" for "any further use of the quotation by anyone in conjunction with the promotion, sale or advertising of" *Rumbles Left and Right* . . . Our letter to the lawyers had included a P.S.: "While you are at it, would you be so kind as to ask Mr. Schlesinger to okay the following translation of his quotation into French: '*Monsieur Buckley a une facilité de rhetorique que j'envie de même qu'un bel esprit que je tâche maladroitement d'imiter et sans succés.*' " But the lawyers' reply ignored the request . . . Mr. Schlesinger, by the way, told *Newsweek* he had said the words in "ironic derision." We propose to announce, shortly, the availability of a 45 rpm recording of Mr. Schlesinger saying all those nice things about Mr. Buckley . . . By the way, did you know that Mr. Schlesinger finds *National Review* "entertaining reading"? Well, he does. He said so. Same debate. Context? "I think we are all charmed by the characteristically delightful mixture of fantasy and hyperbole which Mr. Buckley has served us, and which makes his magazine such entertaining reading." Tell your Liberal friends! *Schlesinger finds National Review entertaining reading!* Never mind his pixyish phrase, "mixture of fantasy and hyperbole"—he was just being ironically derisive. . . . Being mustered: National Committee to Secure Privacy for Arthur Schlesinger, Jr. . . . A columnist, Mr. Wm. Hogan of the *San Francisco Chronicle,* reviewed *Rumbles* two weeks ago, before the brawl was made public. . . . Gist of review: Buckley is awful, everybody he disapproves of is wonderful, and everybody he likes is almost as awful as Buckley, though not quite. And then (. . . So help us, we didn't put him up to it), "Even Arthur Schlesinger, Jr., another of Buckley Jr.'s arch enemies, has been quoted on his fellow essayist: 'He has a facility for rhetoric [etc., etc.]' No question about it—he is one of the most suave and challenging writers around." Ho! ho! ho! Er. Harrumph! Attenshun greenbaum! Wolff! Ernst! Sue that man Hogan! (Not to be continued.)

—WFB   april 30, 1963

Exchanges with Schlesinger followed over the years—some funny, some a touch acrimonious—but the historian and sometime political figure continued to be one of Buckley's favorite adversaries. None can claim service in such a long-running dogfight, however, as that between WFB and John Kenneth Galbraith. In the next column, WFB reports on what happens when writers on holiday gather in one small village with a hard-pressed bookstore.

The Great Cadonau War

gstaad, switzerland.—Gstaad is a sleepy little town that bustles two or three months per year, when people descend on it in great numbers, most of them to ski or to look at the skiers, or to drink with them. Everyone runs into everyone at Cadonau's, which is where one picks up the daily edition of the *International Herald Tribune,* paint supplies, Scotch tape, stationery—and, occasionally, a book.

Madame Cadonau's window is a showcase for a few recently published books which are there in three languages, available for the occasional tourist in Gstaad who knows how to read. The saga of the past few months has to do with my looking into the showcase to find prominently displayed David Niven's bestseller, *The Moon's a Balloon.* Mr. Niven is a local resident who is very highly regarded. It came as something of a blow to the professional writers in residence when Mr. Niven managed to dash off a superbly written bestseller. The comment of the playwright George Axelrod was dead on: "How dare he write so well? Do I go about playing British colonels?" Fortunately, Mr. Niven is not a professionally qualified skier—otherwise he would be intolerable.

I felt no resentment at all against the display of his book. But just next to it was another book by a famous local resident—*War, Economics, and Laughter,* by John Kenneth Galbraith. Bad enough, I thought, to pollute this unspoiled Alpine retreat by displaying a book by Mr. Galbraith, but altogether intolerable in light of the fact that a chapter in it is devoted to the disparagement of a classic on municipal government written by a third distinguished writer-in-residence of the area, to wit, me.

Added to this slight was the mysterious nonappearance of my own recently published book, a lacuna which Madame Cadonau embarrassedly explained on the grounds that the book, though ordered months ago, had not arrived presumably because of the New York dock strike. I replied that New York's longshoremen are distinctly my kind of people, and I could not imagine their consenting to load the innocent bottoms of Liberian transports with books by Galbraith, and declining to ease their conscience by supplying them with my own. I called New York and had air-expressed six copies to Madame Cadonau, and then went to China.

I returned to find, in the window, all the old entries, plus a paperback of Mr. Galbraith's *Ambassador's Journal.* I thereupon collected from an old trunk a copy of my anthology of conservative writing, and handed it, wordlessly, to Madame Cadonau, who dutifully shoehorned it into her feverish window. The next day, I saw there a copy of *The New Industrial State*—in German, which is the kind of thing that happens when Galbraith decides to pull rank. I wired New York and got hold of the single extant copy, in German, of a book I had a hand in writing eighteen years ago on Senator McCarthy, which desiring not to lose it (there were only eighty-seven copies printed), I priced at a level beyond the reach even of the ski set of Gstaad.

At this point it had become necessary to retire from the window *Everything You Always Wanted to Know About Sex,* by Dr. Reuben, and everything you didn't want to know about sex by Harold Robbins. Everyone has been moved out except of course David Niven, and now the showcase has in it the original doctoral dissertation of Professor Galbraith, written in 1936 and entitled, "Economic Reasons Why the Government of South Vietnam Cannot Last Another Fortnight." That one was hard to beat, but I have written to Buckingham Palace for the original of a letter I dispatched to King George when Mr. Galbraith was a sophomore at college.

Late last night, a tall, lean man with a lock of graying hair was spotted going into the back door of Madame Cadonau's, so I have today written to Dr. Kissinger to ask him please to make a secret visit to Madame Cadonau, who has for days now refused to move from her upstairs apartment, and to promise mutual de-escalation and the repatriation of all American incunabula, as tensions diminish. I believe in taking the initiative, where peace is concerned.

                                        —WFB   MARCH 14, 1972

———

Buckley, the columnist, occasionally makes a mistake or is charged with having made one, and at times his responses make you glad he made the mistake, for the reward of what ensues.

———

Explain *Why* You Get Up in the Morning!

As a columnist myself, I try to keep in mind that as often as not it is as easy to do the natural thing as the unnatural thing, and that therefore it makes sense to be reasonably sure that the man on whom you have trained your sights is in fact acting inexplicably, before closing your finger on the trigger. Drew Pearson types need to operate on a quite different assumption, namely that a public figure will go out of his way in order to betray his trust. Okay. So? So it pays to remember that Drew Pearson types are doing what comes naturally to them when they ascribe venal motives to their victims, venal motives being the gas on which they fuel their engines.

My brothers Evans and Novak are not, by and large, Drew Pearson types, but occasionally they feel the tug, most recently at my expense. They say that Washington is buzzing over my role as "bard" for Frank Shakespeare, the Director of the United States Information Agency, because I have been "singing his praises with the help of the taxpayers' money." Altogether disreputable, they suggest, inasmuch as I am a member of the President's Advisory Commission on Information, charged under the law with "conducting forthright appraisals of USIA policies."

The criticism is in two parts.

One: Money. Yes, I *have* traveled "at the taxpayers' expense," which is how they always phrase it when they want to taint a use of public money.

The three trips in question, one to Vienna, one to Russia, a third to Vietnam, were taken at the instigation of Mr. Shakespeare. After two of those trips, I reported my findings to the President, at his request. After one of those trips, I was called to testify before a congressional committee, to report my findings, which I did, and got from the Democratic chairman of that committee his most effusive thanks.

Mr. Jack Anderson last summer complained that my air travel was paid during these trips even though I wrote columns as I traveled. I advised his assistant, who was kind enough to call me on the telephone, that that was indeed true. But when I am asked by a government agency to go somewhere for purposes prescribed by it, I shall damned well charge the government for fare. My philanthropy is my time. The commission's members are unpaid.

Two: Messrs. Evans and Novak take Jack Anderson's complaint a step further. Their complaint isn't that I write columns when I travel for the USIA (I write columns wherever I am, that being what my contract requires), but that when I travel, I write "glowingly" about the USIA. Consider, those of you who are interested in the uses of rhetoric, the following sentence from E & N: "When Buckley was attacked in the press for using taxpayers' money to travel the world and write encomiums for the head of the agency he oversees . . ." Tricky? (a) The "press" never "attacked" me, Jack Anderson did, and there is, thank God, still a difference. (b) Anderson's attack wasn't that I traveled in order to write encomiums of the agency, but that I wrote anything at all. But never mind, E & N have insinuated their point.

Now, as to the impropriety of writing "encomiums" on the Director of USIA, (a) In fact I never wrote one, (b) I have written two columns about Mr. Shakespeare. The first I wrote while in Vienna. The subject? Shakespeare's wonderful performance in Vienna? The glories of meeting with USIA's choir boys in Vienna? No, the subject was the attack on him by Joe McGinniss in the book *The Selling of the President,* which was published while I was in Vienna, in which Mr. McGinniss suggested that Mr. Shakespeare's views on communism were naïve. Inasmuch as Mr. Shakespeare's views on communism are exactly the same as my own, I tend to the conclusion that they are not naïve. Therefore I defended Shakespeare.

The other column I have written in defense of Mr. Shakespeare was when he was the object of a considerable attack by *Pravda* a few weeks ago. I wrote that column in New York City, and I did not charge the depreciation on my typewriter to the USIA.

All of which is awesomely trivial . . . if there is an effective anti-Communist who has *not* been praised by me, do me the favor, and send me his name. I shall then write about him. And Anderson, Evans and

Novak will construct an evil motivation, so that you may understand why I did as I did.

—WFB   JANUARY 5, 1971

The Ethics of Junketing

My friend Mr. Mike Wallace, a gentleman who is given to protracted concern with scruple, called recently in his diligent way to inquire what are my rules concerning "junkets," by which he means trips paid for by someone else. He proposes to do a television program on the subject, and I am grateful to him for his maieutic inquiry about my own views, which had not crystallized.

1. When a columnist is invited on a trip, he should begin by asking whether the host expects that his guest will write about the trip. Obviously if you are invited, say, to look in at the opening of Disney World, your hosts expect that you will write about Disney World. If you are invited (as I along with 1,000 others were) to travel in great luxury to witness the dedication of a new refining plant in a distant arctic archipelago, your host clearly does not expect that you will write about the plant.

2. In the second case, then, there is obviously no inhibition in accepting the invitation. In the first, you need to say to yourself: if I find that Disney World is a great bust, will I feel altogether free to say so notwithstanding that the trip down was paid for, as also the hotel bill? That question is only coped with by the injunction: to thine own self be true. But here a qualification is appropriate. Going to Florida and back is not a very big deal, in this peripatetic age. So that the indebtedness of the visiting journalist is not really as heavy as, say, a trip to, well, Mozambique, to examine the policies of the Portuguese government there.

3. Here the situation becomes more complex, and more interesting. On the one hand there are newspapers that pridefully insist that no journalist should travel to a foreign country at that country's expense because implicit obligations are incurred. That point of view is defensible.

But there is another point of view. It is a part of a journalist's duty to move about, and to report to his readers on what he sees. Most often he will use his own money to pay the fare. But—and here are more sub-qualifications—sometimes (a) the trip is too expensive to justify the amount of time the journalist reasons he can devote to the subject (how many columns can one write about Mozambique?); and (b) sometimes the journalist is simply not certain whether the trip will produce anything interesting enough to justify the trip.

It is my opinion that in such circumstances the journalist should feel free to accept the round-trip fare, cutting his potential losses to his own time.

But once again he must know that he will feel free to write as he sees the situation, without any inhibition deriving from the auspices. This is especially difficult because one often tends to lean over backward to establish one's analytical independence, and that is as unjust as to shill. To say the problem is easily solved by simply avoiding the temptation is to take the easy way out.

Some examples, from my personal experience:

I traveled, at the expense of South Africa and the Portuguese Government, eleven years ago, to South Africa and Mozambique. I wrote three columns, and a long essay-piece. Where I came out on the general subject of South African domestic policies is, I suppose, best situated by saying that a pro-South African committee in the United States made reprints of my essay, while the government of South Africa refused to distribute it.

I traveled over one hectic weekend, at the expense of the government of Northern Ireland, to view the situation there just before Orangeman's Day. It was an excruciatingly uncomfortable trip of seventy-two hours. I wrote three columns, in which I find not a hint of servility to my hosts.

I traveled, at the expense of the United States Government, from New Zealand to the Antarctic, and stayed there five days, visiting the South Pole and writing about U.S. operations there. This is one for the naturalists, and though I treasure the experience, I would not undergo it again, even to bring peace with honor to the nations that contend there for scientific advancement.

The general impression is that such jaunts are offered daily to columnists. That has not been my experience. Of course, it is possible that from afar they smell in me that incorruptibility that causes the angels and the saints to chant my name.

—WFB   DECEMBER 25, 1973
[CHRISTMAS]

COLUMNISTS ARE PEOPLE

People who write newspaper columns are also people, and that is a great, but unexpungeable, distraction. It is sometimes useful to be a people, in addition to a newspaper columnist—there is no other way, for instance, to have a family, or to drink good wine, or engage avocationally in other practices than writing a column. But let me, just this one time, share my problems with you as a fellow people, giving four examples.

1. A fortnight ago, a tape was played at the Watergate trial. The voice of President Nixon came in loud and clear, talking to Haldeman, discussing clemency for Howard Hunt. He said: "We'll build, we'll build that son-of-a-bitch up, like nobody's business. We'll have Buckley write a column and say, you know, that he, that he should have clemency . . ."

Within a very few minutes, my office reached me at the airport en route to Boston. The newspapers had begun to call in, asking the obvious question: Was Mr. Buckley approached? Does he have any comment? I dictated over the telephone two sentences that were then given by my office to the *New York Post,* the *New York Times,* and the Associated Press: "At no time did any member of the Nixon Administration approach me. Besides, I don't need to be reminded to write columns urging clemency even for sons-of-bitches, as Mr. Nixon has every reason to know from personal experience."

The next morning, the charge was carried very conspicuously in the *Boston Globe*—together with my retort, which I also saw in the New York papers and in *Time* magazine. Notwithstanding, I have received much mail asking why I was silent on the subject raised at the Watergate trial. And two large newspapers have carried letters by readers suggesting that I have been an appendage of the Nixon Administration—without any comment from the editor bringing to the writer's attention my brief reply. One more example of the difficulty of catching up with a misleading story:

2. A month ago, I wrote a column on the now famous [Arthur] Goldberg book by Victor Lasky, in which I expressed the view—having now read the book—that although it was of course hostile to Justice Goldberg, it was far from being libelous. I remarked that the only distortion in it was Lasky's statement that Mr. Goldberg was the worst public speaker in the State of New York, since in fact he was the worst in the country. I received a letter from a journalist who covered the campaign advising me that it was going the rounds of the boys in the bus toward the end, that "if Goldberg gives one more speech, Rockefeller will carry Canada." Mr. Goldberg called me on the telephone and was extremely amiable, and made no criticism of the book, merely of its provenance.

I did not note, in my column, that I am the chairman of the board of the parent company that owned the company (Arlington House) that published the Goldberg book. I did not do this for two reasons. The first was that when the book was first discussed, my position in the corporate hierarchy was widely identified, so that I proceeded on the happy or, if you prefer, unhappy assumption that most people knew about it. The second reason is that never having heard of the book before, I was in no way implicated in the decision to publish it. But if I had mentioned my corporate affiliation in the column, I'd have had to go on to make the connecting point, and this struck me, on balance, as unnecessarily self-concerned. Result: a big article in *Editor & Publisher* on whether my omission of my connection was ethically correct. You decide.

3. Maybe four or five times a year, I am greatly struck by an article or analysis published in *National Review.* Now I am the editor-in-chief of

National Review, and its sole owner. So when I mention the article, I give the name of the author—but leave out the name of the magazine where the article was published, lest it should appear that I am attempting to advertise my impecunious but magnificent journal (150 East 35th Street, New York 10016—$12 per year). Then I get mail asking me how could I have been so sloppy as to fail to give the name of the journal where the article I wrote about appeared. . . .

Finally, (4), there is no way to avoid writing, occasionally, about the doings and sayings of James Lane Buckley. How should I identify him? As "My brother the senator"? That has the obvious disadvantage of calling attention to myself, and the less obvious disadvantage of snuggling up against the cognate cliché, "my son the doctor." So, I resolved to refer to him as "the sainted junior senator from New York." Hyperbole is a form of self-effacement; but I still get a letter or two, complaining. These I answer by expressing great surprise that the reader is unaware of the beatific character of the junior senator from New York. But there, now, you share my problems this one time, and I shan't ask you soon again to share them. Many thanks.

—WFB   DECEMBER 5, 1974

Dear Mr. B.:

If you wrote the enclosed column, I'll change my religion from Catholic to atheist, my Republican affiliation to liberal—and I'll even eat the goddam newspaper. Well???????

> Faithfully,
> AL PACETTA
> VERO BEACH, FLA.

Dear Mr. Pacetta: I am happy to be the instrument of retaining your religious and political faiths and the good order of your stomach: No, I did not write it. Sometimes newspapers run me under Art Buchwald's logo, and AB under my logo, the cumulative result of which is to make me seem funnier than I am, and him wiser than he is. But I don't even recognize the columnist whose wild meanderings appeared in the *Vero Beach Press-Journal* (Oct. 16) under my name. Cordially,

—WFB   DECEMBER 5, 1986

STUCK?

It is conceivably of interest to the world out there what happens when a columnist gets stuck . . .

You see, poring over a table of figures, I wrote yesterday a careful piece announcing certain conclusions about the nature of economic distribution that I thought astonishing. Indeed they proved to be. Later that day, at a social function, I accosted a very bright gentleman, head of a big banking house in New York, and announced my findings to him. Startled is not quite the word to describe his reaction. He said I was quite simply wrong. Not possible, I said, citing the source of my figures.

Half an hour ago, when my researcher got to the office, I telephoned and told her that, just to be sure, she might check. Ten minutes later she rang to say that the gentleman who had put the chart together intended that it should be read—well, upside down is the best way to put it. The difficulty then—and it happens to columnists every now and then, though I don't remember in twenty years its coming quite so close—is how to write interestingly on no notice whatever, running (in this case) between engagements in Chicago, live appearances, one more or less on top of another, which cannot be put off. The question is whether, in the interstices, I can meet my professional obligations to this newspaper.

Once, two or three years ago, I was doing a program with the amiable Mr. Gene Shalit of NBC. Everything went swimmingly. Too swimmingly. Because he played me like a cobra, undulating hypnotically this way, that way, as I gradually lost any sense of caution. He said then: "How do you know what to write about, when you write a column?" I found myself saying, "Gene, when you have been at the profession for long enough, you can, if in a bind, close your eyes and point to the front page of the *New York Times,* and whatever story you are fingering when you open your eyes—you can write a column on that story."

"Yes"—Shalit struck—"I think I remember that column."

Victor Borge documented the art of improvisation as practiced by a musician. During his great one-man show he neared the end, turned to the audience and asked for volunteers to pronounce any one of the first seven letters of the alphabet. He would point to one and then to another, until he had a series: A G E F B D C. These, of course, correspond to musical notes. He would sit down and tap the notes out in consecutive order. Then he would vest a little rhythm into the sequence, and suddenly a tune emerged. This tune he played out in the style, respectively, of Bach, Mozart, Schumann, Chopin, Brahms, Liszt, Gershwin. A smash exhibition of improvisatory powers.

But a scribbler cannot easily duplicate a musician's powers—though I suppose a poet, or the versifier, could do so. Write a piece, without the opportunity to research, on this morning's stories on the front page of the *Chicago Tribune:* "Embassy Raiders Release Four More." Well, you could go on a bit about international terrorism, but we've done that. "Cut U.S. Deficits/IMF Nations Ask." Not bad, actually. Representatives of the nations of the world meet in Toronto to accuse the United States of economic malpractices, such as deficit spending and inflation. You could play with that, but you would need to dig up the corresponding figures of our critics. It would be fun if one of those were a representative of Mexico. Or Brazil. Or Argentina. Or Great Britain. But you see the problem.

"Israel Demands Security Zone/In Lebanon As Tensions Grow." Oh no! Not another column on Israel and Lebanon. You cannot do that to the American-speaking world. Not after a dozen columns on the subject during the past dozen weeks. And, finally, "Health Hazard Waste Heads for Chicago." No, that won't play even in Peoria, which is near enough to Chicago and probably shares Chicago's concerns.

So you sit—you have max twelve, fourteen minutes, and you think: What on earth can I write about? It is a pickle, and so you sit down and write a column about human nature or the United Nations or John Kenneth Galbraith, all of them, always, live wires.

—WFB   SEPTEMBER 11, 1982

From *Overdrive*

George Will once told me how deeply he loves to write. "I wake in the morning," he explained to me, "and I ask myself: 'Is this one of the days I have to write a column?' And if the answer is 'Yes,' I rise a happy man." I, on the other hand, wake neither particularly happy nor unhappy, but to the extent that my mood is affected by the question whether I need to write a column that morning, the impact of Monday-Wednesday-Friday is definitely negative. Because I do not like to write, for the simple reason that writing is extremely hard work, and I do not "like" extremely hard work.

I work for other reasons, about which mostly dull people write, dully. (I have discerned that those who are given to the formulation, "I am one of those people who . . ." would generally be safest concluding the sentence, ". . . bore other people.") Is it some aspect of a sense of duty that I feel? Moral evangelism? A fear of uselessness? A fear that it is wrong to suppress useful, here defined extramorally as merchandisable, talent? I do resist introspection, though I cannot claim to have "guarded" against it, because even to say that would suppose that the temptation to do so was there, which it isn't. Indeed, these very words are prompted by an imperative handed to me by my friend and editor Sam Vaughan, the least imperious of men: but curiosity is, in such circumstances, his professional business. Why do I do so much? I expect that the promptings issue from a subtle dialectical counterpoint. Of what? Well, the call of *recta ratio,* and the fear of boredom. What is *recta ratio?* The appeal of generic Latin terms (*habeas corpus, nihil obstat, malum prohibitum*) derives in part because the language is indeed dead and therefore unmoved by idiomatic fashion. In part, however, it is owing to the complementary character of its tantalizing inscrutability. It is just faintly defenseless; so that one can, for instance, interpret a Latin term—use it metaphorically, even—without any decisive fear of plebiscitarian denial. We know that the term translates to "right (rightly) reason(ed)," and that the Scholastics used it to suggest the intellectual instrument by which men might reason progressively at least to the existence of God, at most to how, under His aegis, they should govern themselves in all major matters, avoiding the major vices, exercising discipline, seeking virtue. The search for virtue is probably best drowned out by *commotion,* and this my life is full of. It is easier to stay up late working for hours than to take one tenth the time to inquire into the question whether the work is worth performing.

And then, as I say, that other, the fear of boredom. Thoreau is known for his compulsion, day by day, to discover more and more things he could be without. But I have enough of everything material, at least measured by ordinary standards. But not the reliance to do without distraction; so that I would not cross the street without a magazine or paperback, lest the traffic should immobilize me for more than ten seconds. The unexamined life may not be worth living, in which case I will concede that mine is not worth living. But excepting my own life, I do seek to examine, and certainly I dilate upon, public questions I deem insufficiently examined.

I was saying that I do not enjoy writing. I envy those who do. John Chamberlain once told me that if he has not written during the day he will not sleep, and it is only when he wonders why he cannot fall asleep that he remembers that he has not written during that day; and so he rises, and writes. John Chamberlain is as incapable of affectation as Muhammad Ali of self-effacement. It is simply the case that some people like to sit down hour after hour and write, and with some of them the disease is so aggravated that it doesn't particularly matter whether what they write will be published. . . .

It is inevitable, even in a book where the focus is on words, that a writer's tools of the trade will come up. Here is Buckley the columnist on such instruments in his (and our) pre-computer phase.

WHAT'S GOING ON?

Aboard a cruising vessel bound for China a few months ago I unpacked an aluminum suitcase in which I had stored my cassettes, player, and portable typewriter. The typewriter was gone! There is no panic to equal that of the journalist caught without his typewriter, and accordingly I rushed back down the gangway, asked a guide where I might buy a typewriter, was directed to a department store nearby. An escalator plotted me through the crowd up to the third floor and there my eyes feasted on a counter-load of typewriters. I grabbed a sturdy-looking red portable, pausing only to establish that the lettering sequence was conventional. Back on board, I tapped out a few lines on it to discover that it was as near to being a totally satisfactory portable as the old Royal on which I was weaned—and my memory was jarred.

I first heard the word "obsolescent" when at school, in England, at age thirteen. A master (he was a Jesuit priest) had informed a class of older boys (age fourteen) that American car manufacturers engaged in "planned obsolescence." I took this as an affront on my homeland and demanded an explanation, and was given a kindly and abstruse explanation, which was the first time I looked up the meaning of the word "jesuitical."

Flash forward thirty years to a taxi driver in Hartford, Connecticut, who, having helped stow my bags at the station, noticed my Olivetti portable. For many years, he said, he had worked at the Royal typewriter factory but, he said, he had given up his job in disgust over the deteriorating standards of workmanship. I told him I had had a most splendid Royal portable for ten years beginning at age fifteen, which had been stolen in Mexico, and that ever since I had wandered like the Flying Dutchman from portable to portable. The Olivetti was nice to handle, but was as fragile as a soufflé, that I had gone through a dozen of them. He clucked his misgivings about American technology, and I thought of the obsolescence I had first heard about in 1938.

A year ago, I stopped at an airline newsstand to buy a copy of *Time* magazine, putting down my Olivetti to reach into my wallet. After pocketing the change, I leaned down to pick up the typewriter—which, however, was not there. It had been stolen, a venture in planned obsolescence perfected in New York City. I was bound for Cambridge, Massachusetts, to do battle with the big dragon Professor Galbraith, whose lovely secretary, a closet Republican, volunteered to help me. But there are no portable Olivettis in Cambridge, and so she came up with a Swiss Hermes, a small machine that requires the finger action of a pneumatic jackhammer, not bad for writing a speech that penetrates Galbraithian goulash, but not quite the right thing for flights of fancy. That was the machine missing in Kobe, Japan, when Providence put me in the hands of the Brother Valiant 413 ($80 FOB Kobe, Japan).

Why is it that what had been so securely American—the fine, reliable, relatively inexpensive machine—is disappearing? The idea behind planned obsolescence in Detroit, if that is what it was, was to cause you to buy another American car every three years or so. But American typewriters that drive you to Japanese typewriters via Italian and Swiss typewriters would seem to be making an economically unconsummated point. Goodness knows it did not used to be that way. The Woodstock typewriter used by Alger Hiss was still functioning ten years after it had been used to transcribe half of America's defense secrets for the benefit of Mr. Hiss's spymasters.

At home I used, for years, serenely and with pleasure, a Royal Standard I bought in my freshman year in college, in 1946. Are we the victims of nefarious economic design? The kind of thing Ralph Nader, or Michael Harrington, or the boys and girls who write for *The Nation* magazine, would like to think about American enterprise? Again, it would not appear to make sense, any more than it would make sense, having eaten one McDonald's hamburger, to resolve to move over to Burger King.

It is very sad, whatever the explanation. At age fifty-seven, I'd have a harder time talking back to that Jesuit priest than I did at age thirteen.

—WFB   JANUARY 1, 1983

Memo to: Bill
From: Priscilla

The *Christian Science Monitor* (March 13) reports you are looking after *NR*'s interests while airborne. See attached: (Headline: "Today's High-Flying Businessman: Have Typewriter, Will Travel." ". . . According to a longtime TWA flight attendant I know, no business traveler is quite so capable of wrapping himself in a six-mile-high cocoon as William F. Buckley Jr. 'I had Mr. Buckley on a transatlantic flight,' she said, 'and he had what looked like a month's worth of work beside him, piled all the way up in his lap. I noticed he didn't speak to the man beside him, he was so totally engrossed. When he got up to stretch his legs, the other man called me over. He said he couldn't find his shoes under the pile of Mr. Buckley's discarded papers. We finally found one and then another, but it wasn't his shoe. Sure enough, when Mr. Buckley came back he was wearing the other man's shoe on one of his feet.' ")

Memo to: Priscilla
From: Bill

Now I know why I was limping when I arrived in Geneva! XXX Bill
         —WFB   MAY 4, 1984

———

Buckley has long since left the ranks of the typewriter users and has been for years an enthusiastic computer user—and pusher. Years back, he put in my lap when we were working in Switzerland a little jewel of an early Epson laptop, taught me the commands for SAVE and for BACKSPACE, which, as computer nerds know, also means ERASE, but does not say so. (Computer keyboards are still under the influence of engineers whose first language is logarithm—see: they don't even know how to spell *rhythm*—not in English or even Japanese.) I proceeded to type my notes about his manuscript-in-progress. The next day he said, delighted with his computer's ability to count (all right, *compute*), "You wrote eleven thousand words!" He also loves the instant feather touch by which he can summon up his built-in dictionary and thesaurus. I was dazzled properly and still am, especially by Buckley's ability to stay at the cutting edge of word processing, where a new "annual" model is produced every month.*

Next, he writes of an encounter with a Teletype machine and then of the word processor and those who would criticize its use, making what is, for him, a natural reference to other types of keyboards, the piano's and the harpsichord's, with which he is intimately at home.

———

SHOP TALK

I have been asked over the years, in person and by correspondence, about the mechanics of column writing, and today is a good day to give some details of the craft and its engineering.

Why today? Because columnists whose material goes to the newspapers by mail are hit by a circumstance, the kind of thing that happens, oh, a half-dozen times every year. On Monday, I wrote a column outlining the problems of the U.S. Government in respect of Libya, and what might usefully be done about them. On Tuesday night, President Reagan came out with his own ideas on the subject, so to speak scooping me. I don't

* Recently, WFB combined two loves by writing the bilingual introduction to a new book, *De DOS a Windows,* an *Introduccion a las computadoras personales*—a basic introduction to personal computers for Spanish-speakers, by Jaime A. Restrepo (Random House, 1996).

suggest that the analysis sent out by this pundit on Monday is useless or even anachronized by the President's press conference, merely that if the columnist had known exactly what the President was going to say, the column would have addressed his remarks, rather than go out self-launched.

You see, there are two flotillas of pundits. The first set is, so to speak, on the scene. These pundits write their columns minutes or at most hours after the event they write about, and their copy goes to client papers by wire. A James Reston, for instance, will appear in Wednesday morning's newspaper reporting on Tuesday night's presidential press conference. Such types have the advantage of instant communication.

The second flotilla moves in a stately gait for massive bombing after the front-line forces have undertaken their initial action. We have the disadvantage of coming in late, but then we have the countervailing advantage of surveying the scene a day or so after the arrival of the shock troops, and selecting our targets more deliberately.

Columns and the paraphernalia that go with them (research, correspondence, etc.) are subject to vicissitudes, common and not so common. In Moscow once I found that the only way I could possibly meet my deadline was to borrow the *New York Times*'s Teletype machine. Having done so, I faced the problem that I did not know how to operate it, or rather that operating it, given my unfamiliarity, was taking me about a half-hour per sentence. Taking pity on me, *New York Times* correspondent Bernard Gwertzman sighed, eased me out of my seat, and in a few minutes dispatched my column to New York. Bernard Gwertzman figures in my last will and testament; and, no doubt, he remembers the high point of his political education while in Moscow.

Getting material from faraway places can be as easy as popping a salted peanut, or it can present quite extraordinary difficulties. Answering two hundred to three hundred letters and dictating notes on a few matters of interest consumed most of three days' working time aboard a sailboat during the Christmas holidays, and a friend in St. Maarten was entrusted with two large plastic sacks, each one with the relevant ninety-minute cassette for transcription in New York. Three days later, a hysterical telephone call from New York advised me that the sacks had arrived, but not the cassettes.

One fumed over wretched pilferers who would steal a two-dollar cassette onto which to pipe one more abomination by Boy George, but lo, three days later it transpired that for reasons known only to God and some officious post office bureaucrat in Miami, the cassettes had been extracted and sent back to St. Maarten, presumably because they were suspected of containing dope, or instructions to Libyan hit men. Never mind, my friend in St. Maarten reassured me over the telephone to the Dominican

Republic, he would see to it that the very next day his houseguest would take the tapes to New York.

But going the next day to fetch his houseguest for their last lunch together before the flight, my friend found the bathroom door locked. Worried, he finally broke it open, and his houseguest was in the tub, quite dead.

Requiescat in pacem, to be sure; but there was also the problem of the cassettes, and his guest (it was Mr. Sam Spiegel, the—late—movie mogul) had already packed his bags, requiring my friend to undertake a morbid search until he discovered the two cassettes, in one of which were notes dictated after an interview with the president of the Dominican Republic, which would serve as background detail for a newspaper column.

Which, for reasons now divulged, appeared a few days later than originally scheduled. That's the way it is.

—WFB   JANUARY 11, 1986

On Some of the Tools of Learning

Since it has become everybody's business to reform education, permit from this corner a word about the mechanics of learning. Many years ago I asked the dean of my alma mater why no credit was given for the mastery of typing or shorthand, and he replied beneficently, "There is no body of knowledge in typing." Quite right: It is not a three-dimensional discipline, on the order of poetry or physics, but it is the principal means by which John communicates with Jane or, for that matter, with the world at large.

Typing reached a new age with the discovery of the chip. It is fashionable to condescend to word processing. Never mind. It is to the writer, whether professional or amateur, what the tractor is to the farmer. And those who rail against it do so for the most practical reason: They have not mastered its use. They strive for metaphysical formulations to justify their hidden little secret (sloth and fear). But those of us with X-ray vision: We know, we know.

Consider the recent denunciation of word processing by the poet Louis Simpson, done for the *New York Times.* When Milton described the obstruction of Lucifer ("Whence and what art thou, execrable shape,/That dar'st, though grim and terrible, advance/Thy miscreated front athwart my way/To yonder gates?") he spoke no less scornfully than Mr. Simpson of the word processor. Listen:

"Poets do have to make changes, but they cannot think so; they must think that the next word and phrase will be perfect. At times, and these are the happiest, they have the feeling that words are being given to them with absolute finality. The word processor works directly against this feeling; it tells you your writing is not final. And it enables you to think you are writing when you are not, when you are only making notes or the outline of a poem you may write at a later time. But then you will feel no need to write it."

To accept Mr. Simpson's thesis is to suppose that writers (and poets) always feel that the language of the moment is lapidary, never mind that, when detoxified, they proceed to make changes. The easiest way to handle Mr. Simpson's miscreated affront is to remind him that words engraved onto a computer's memory are everlastingly there if that is the writer's election, but that they are vaporized instantly and handily if that becomes the writer's election.

If it should happen that someone prefers to compose using a pencil, the proper attitude toward him is simply to look to one side, as one would do if one came upon a writer who could only compose with a teddy bear on his desk. The word processor is very soon discovered by the writer to be something on the order of overdrive in an automobile: like shifting from first gear, into overdrive, that's what it feels like. Like swimming in a pool infinitely long, so that you need never turn around. Aahh!

Just as schools and colleges should encourage students in word processing, they should encourage the mastery of touch-typing, which permits the user to turn his head to one side, reading material he is simultaneously typing, without looking at the keyboard.

The prejudice against learning by heart those thirty little keys is one of the great mysteries of the world. The great Rosalyn Tureck, who can play from memory all the keyboard works of Johann Sebastian Bach, leans over her typewriter and, I kid you not, hunts and pecks. Even though she can sit down and play the 27th Goldberg without missing a note, she never bothered to learn that, on a typewriter, the order is, Q W E R T Y. . . . It is a note of minor historical interest, offered by the fine computer popularizer Peter McWilliams, that the typewriter keyboard reflects the deficient technology of a hundred years ago. When the typewriter was invented, keys could not be got to move as quickly as fingers, so that the configuration of characters was done to slow the typist down.

Let our teachers encourage the use of the tools of learning, and forswear nonsense about how Shakespeare would have written flatly if he had had a word processor. It is likelier that he'd have written eight more masterpieces, one of them at the expense of Luddites.

—WFB   JANUARY 19, 1988

SEE YOU LATER

ST. THOMAS, VIRGIN ISLANDS—Syndicated columnists are given two weeks off every year. And this, I note in passing, is by no means a venerable convention (in my case, the vacation came only after my fifth year in the trade). Moreover, there have been columnists who as a matter of principle never took a vacation, lest their public discover that life was possible, nay even keener, and more joyous, without the columnist's lucubrations.

The late George Sokolsky wrote six columns a week for King Features, and then a seventh for the local Sunday paper. When he learned that he had to have his appendix out, he carefully composed columns ahead based on all the variables in the arts of prognosis: two columns in the event everything went smoothly; four columns in the event of complications; six columns in the event of major complications. I asked him, on hearing the story, whether he wrote a seventh column in the event of terminal complications, but he replied that his interest in his worldly constituency was only coextensive with his life on earth.

Mine isn't: when I go, I intend to hector the Almighty even as, episodically, I do from here, to look after my friends and (most of) my enemies. But I confess to being uncomfortable at taking my two weeks together, instead of separating them as is my practice (one week in the winter, one in the summer). Still, I am setting sail on a splendid racing vessel, from here to Bermuda to the Azores, and to Spain. The second leg of my journey will keep me incommunicado (at sea) for eleven days, in the unusual posture of being only on the receiving end of the world's events. During that period President Carter, Senator Kennedy, the airlines, the people who spend their days profaning the English of King James, may misbehave safely in the knowledge that there will be no reproach from me. It is horrifying to meditate what enormity the White House will execute, I having advertised my isolation. On the other hand, if President Carter is determined to make me one of the boat people, I am splendidly well ahead of the game: I need only to sail on.

But sail on to where? Ah, there's the rub, as the poet intuited four hundred years ago. Where can we go if distress should come to America? There is only Switzerland, but nature so arranged it so that you cannot sail to Switzerland, and this would not be the season to rely on U.S. naval helicopters to pick up my boat and ferry it into Lake Geneva. Accordingly, I adjure my Lords, secular and spiritual, not to be too licentious while I am gone.

What shall I concern myself with? Well, the exact time of day. I really must know—no kidding—exactly what the time is. I wear a chronometer which for several years lost exactly one second per week. Even folk as disorganized as I can cope with such retrogressions, and I happily set it right every Christmas and every Fourth of July, and I always knew what time it was. But in an idiotic fit of hubris, I returned it to the clockmaker reminding him that my watch was guaranteed not to gain or lose more than twelve seconds per year. It has never been quite right since. So—well, I have a computer I navigate with, and it has an inbuilt chronometer. It keeps excellent time. But, you see, excellent time will not do—you need the exact time. So, I also have a little radio (thirty-six dollars at Radio Shack) which is supposed to bring in WWV from Fort Collins, Colorado, which vouchsafes to all the ships at sea the exact time. Mostly the little radio brings in that signal. Every now and then it does not. In which case I ask my sailing companion Danny for the time, and his watch is pretty reliable. Dick Clurman's cheap little Casio keeps disgustingly good time. And I can tell from friend Reggie's sly smile that he believes, in a pinch, he can come up with the time.

I need sun. Not to darken my skin, because in fact the doctor says that sun is the enemy of fair skin and I must now use something called Total Eclipse No. 15. I need the sun, and the time, to discover which way to point in order to effect a rendezvous at the Azores. If in this matter I should fail, the reader may deduce, two weeks hence, that I am absent without leave. The moon is getting lean right now, but will flower again; and when it is half-bright, it gives you a horizon, and on some magical moments you can combine that horizon with the North Star, and before you know it, you have your latitude, even as Columbus had that, and only that, with little idea of the time, and yet managed to discover our wonderful country.

The chances, then, are overwhelming that, like MacArthur, I shall return. In the meantime, the Republic is on probation.

—WFB   JUNE 12, 1980

Chapter 13

Man of
Letters

As is evident throughout this book, WFB is not only a man of letters in the larger sense, but a man who receives a great many missives and does his best to answer them *(missives* and *missiles* are both apt in this case). His mailbag, with his dictating machine and his computer, goes where he goes. Two notices over a long period of time give inadvertent witness to the volume and flow of his correspondence.

Memo to: Unknown, and unknowable, correspondents
   From: WFB
     Re: A missing briefcase

On December 12, a briefcase crammed full with correspondence for the most part as yet unread (I had been traveling) was lost somewhere between La Guardia Airport and Miami International Airport. Heroic efforts at retrieval have been unavailing. The result: 100 to 150 communications addressed to WFB are scheduled to go unacknowledged and, worse, unread. If you chance to be the author of one of these, pray send a copy.

—JANUARY 20, 1978

> STOLEN. From WFB's car, one seabagful of unanswered mail (three to four hundred letters) including a dozen unread manuscripts. Date of theft, December 16. The bag could have contained letters dating back to the first week in November. There is no record of such letters, and WFB greatly regrets any inadvertent failure to reply. There is a record in the office of the mss. and in due course the authors will be advised.

FEBRUARY 8, 1985

These are real letters, not the slippery faxes which seem to demand instant response, or E-mail, which calls for the same, only faster. (My favorite reaction to such "labor-saving" devices was the line uttered by one electronically oppressed man in *New York* magazine, I believe: "The fax has changed my life!" he wrote excitedly. And in more somber voice added: "It's shortened it.")

In any case, letters are part of the sum and substance of Buckley's life and he answers almost all—from children, antagonists, friends, strangers, loved ones, etc.—with virtually the same courtesy and verve.

In earlier collections, he has given glimpses of the traffic, as in this excerpt from *Cruising Speed* (1971).

. . . I have a telegram from a young playwright: "Dear Mr. Buckley. The soul of a secular nation is its theater. Our theater is all but dead. I send you a modern classic tragedy and you are too busy and important to read it. How disgusting." Frances Bronson, my secretary, was very much annoyed by the telegram, because only five days earlier she had sent a letter to Peter Glenville that I had dictated. "I would not normally send along a manuscript, but I am so fetched by the vigor and grace of the letter that accompanied it (I attach it) that I wonder if you could possibly tell me whether you think it has a chance?" Frances heatedly wrote out a telegram which she proposed to send, rebuking the playwright for his impatience. I told her not to send it, because I react against declamatory rudeness that is coercive in intent—obviously the playwright thought that his telegram would get him some action. (The following week Peter told me that the author was talented but the play, in his opinion, was not ready for commercial production. I assume he is a very young man, I said, the telegram in mind. "If he isn't," Peter replied, "then you will have to counsel him to stop writing plays.")

. . . I wrote to a friend in Switzerland: "It occurs to me that you have sought by your silence to communicate your displeasure with me. I find that too bad, particularly since I am by all odds the nicest man I know. However, I do think that in order to save us embarrassment, we ought to know ahead of time whether on my return to Switzerland [where I spend February and March] we are supposed, on happening upon each other, to exchange only Averted Gazes, because my Averted Gaze is a little rusty, and needs some practicing up. Or, we can resume our amiable relationship, wherein you admire my prose, I admire your art, and we agree to leave moot the question of your business acumen. Why don't we leave it this way, that if I do not hear from you in response to this letter, I shall regretfully assume that the former is your election? My love to the girls [his wife, daughter, and dog, who is Rowley's* second cousin]."

There are the routine requests, all of which I regularly resolve to handle with form letters, but how to compose a form letter adequate to the resources of some writers, particularly the very young ones? "Well, here I am again. Yes sir, it takes more than a broken typewriter to keep this kid down. This is my third letter to you . . . But gee-wiz golly-darn Mr. Buckley, when are you going to answer my letters? To totally ignore a seventeen-year-old high school conservative, I must warn you, could prove to be dangerous. We are not only relatively rare but also very sensitive. After all if you keep ignoring my letters I might get the idea you don't want young people in the conservative movement. Wouldn't that be terrible? (The answer is 'yes'). But if you ignore me you are ignoring more than a young conservative. Your [sic] ignoring a young conservative from Indiana. A Cardinal Sin! . . . But Hark! All is not lost. And to prove to you I am not really sore I am going to give you this chance to make-up with me and the state of Indiana (both of whom have been ignored too long). You, Mr. Buckley, are cordially invited to be the guest speaker at our high school's Good Government Day program . . . Please understand that Key Club is a service organization for high school boys and as such we wouldn't be able to pay the high price that I know you normally get . . ."

He gets a non-form letter, the key sentence of which is, "Whenever you are disposed to be sore at me, try to remember that *National Review* is available to you for five or six dollars a year in part because of activities I

* One of the Buckleys' dogs.—Ed.

undertake which result in my having to answer rather briefly notes from such pleasant people as yourself, and say no to nonpaying invitations to speak." . . . A form letter suffices for "I am writing a term paper in high school about Communism in America. I would appreciate it if you would send me some information about this subject. My teacher told me that you are a conservative who is probably a strong anti-Communist." *The teacher would not have got a form letter.* . . . The *Notre Dame Lawyer* wants a review of Ramsey Clark's book *Crime in America:* "Upon publication of a review, we would be glad to send you fifty complimentary copies of the review, and a one-year subscription to the *Lawyer.*" I have always thought that the most genial of all form letters is the one that suggests that the correspondent did not get through, so that he won't therefore feel that his persuasiveness was met and resisted. Whence, "Mr. Buckley has asked me to interdict all requests for interviews, articles, reviews, etc., for the next period—probably about six months, as he is drastically in arrears on commitments he has already made. I hope you will understand that to take on any further commitments at this point simply means failing to keep those he has already made. Thank you for writing. Very truly yours, Frances Bronson." . . . Then, what is about as hard a sell as I ever get, from the student government head of DePauw an elaborate wind-up: "Surely this letter will rank among the very oddest of the wide and weird assortment which no doubt floats your way each week. I am writing to attempt to persuade you to accept a speaking engagement here. Please hear me out—if it's of any consequence, I've shown you the same courtesy countless times in your columns and books, in spite of profound philosophical disagreements." Then about DePauw, and how important it is. But, however good the education at DePauw, there is "one glaring defect: the absence of an even reasonable articulate conservative spokesman." The letter goes on. "It is entirely possible—nay, probable—that the overwhelming majority of DePauw students graduating in the last decade have *never heard* so much as a syllable from an intelligent conservative." And a little guarded flattery. "Do not think me a flatterer [the word "flatterer" comes out charmingly home-typed, which I always like: something like "flatterer"]; *you* know you are intelligent—why should I pretend [sic] *I* don't? To these people the term conservatism (please forgive this unavoidable use of labels) conjures up images of Hoosier anti-communist hysteria or (worse) the editorial pages of the *Chicago Tribune* and *Indianapolis Star,* intimately connected with this institution—on both of which many students here have been spoon-fed from infancy.

"The deleterious effects of this homogenized diet are several: slow-witted conservative students here are imbued with the fusiest sorts of ideas about American society and are rendered utterly incapable of defending themselves intellectually against even a mediocre liberal spokesman. (Let us face facts: it does not require overwhelming philosophical utensils to make intellectual puree out of the grade triple-Z grist cranked out by the *Tribune* and *Star*.) Perceptive conservative students become either bored with or nauseated by such drivel and abandon the conservative cause for the better articulated, more sophisticated, and more popular liberal theses available in abundance through the media and other sources (e.g., university faculty). Liberal students all along the intelligence gradient acquire a sense of smugness and self-righteousness, and grow intellectually paunchy due to a dearth of skillful conservative sparring partners.

"We are not a wealthy organization. We can afford very little beyond your travel and associated expenses, plus perhaps a small honorarium (no doubt a pittance compared to what you could usually command). However we can promise a capacity turn-out, excellent coverage by the mass media, and unlimited flexibility—you can pick any date you wish. *Please,* give this a moment's consideration." . . . I did, of course, and decided not to take on the student body president of DePauw University on the question of the triple-Z incapacity of the chief editorial writers of the *Chicago Tribune* and the *Indianapolis Star,* both of them Phi Beta Kappas from rather exacting universities; that kind of argument one simply hasn't time for. "Your letter touched me," I wrote. "I say that quite sincerely. But you must consider my situation. I work overtime so as to be able to send *National Review* to anybody who wants it for approximately $12.00 per year. [The disparity in the cited cost is because, for students, we have a crazy-rate system, which reduces the subscription price by a couple of dollars.] It costs us approximately $20 a year to produce it. The difference is made up by fund appeals and my own activities as a lecturer. The obvious answer to your generic question is: If your fellow students have any intellectual curiosity at all, they will pick up *National Review* at a very small cost to them. If they want me personally, what they want is theater. [A deucedly good point, what?] For theater, I charge—and remit my earnings to *National Review.* I don't like to say it because it sounds self-serving, but there are over five hundred applications from colleges willing to pay the full fee [I exaggerate. More like two hundred], and it would not be fair to penalize *National Review* by patronizing DePauw, however much I am inclined to do so as a result of your own eloquence. It is not the same thing, but I would be very happy if you would lunch with me next time you come to New York."

No answer would ever come to my answer; that often happens. The kids are, a lot of them, first-rate at turning on the charm when they want something. And then, win or lose, they deploy their charm elsewhere. I believe in thank-you letters, and I have a tickler-system that reminds me when a delinquent institution writes to me for a speech, or article. The all-time offenders are the graduate students, who manage to get free speeches from you as you succumb to their sycophantic embraces, and then you never hear from them again, like the girl in any de Maupassant story. Ah, but I have learned, have I learned. The Dean of the Graduate School at Princeton, an irresistible liberal of charming habits, now calls in the student lecture head, or that is my impression, and dictates to him the thank-you letter he is to send me after my dutiful appearances there, free gratis, every couple of years, a murderous habit I fell into in the fifties, before I got around to composing my super-form letters. *I am waiting to be asked back by a certain organization at Harvard . . .*

———

At times, letters arrive which are deeply touching:

———

Dear Mr. Buckley:

In the fall of 1986, Captain Paul J. Weaver and I arrived at Hurlburt Field, Florida, prepared to learn how to operate our new aircraft, the AC-130H Spectre Gunship. Aviators rarely discuss anything other than flying, but Paul was unique in his interests and breadth of knowledge. Our conversations quickly moved to politics.

Paul was passionately conservative, and as our conversations progressed, I realized he was extremely well read on the issues of the day, and I was not. He suggested a subscription to *National Review* and I shall forever be in his debt.

Paul was equally passionate in his respect and love for your magazine, your columns, and most of all *Firing Line.* He was one of your greatest unknown admirers.

On January 31, 1991, Major Weaver was the aircraft commander of a gunship, Spirit 03, engaged with enemy forces during the battle of Khafji. He and his crew of thirteen were desperately searching for an Iraqi surface-to-surface missile site that was threatening U.S. Marines in the area. Numerous anti-aircraft-artillery sites were reported to the crew by two gunships exiting the area, but they elected to stay and support the Marines.

Spirit 03 was shot down that morning and all fourteen aboard were lost. I don't know if you knew any of America's casualties personally, but one of them knew you very well. In Paul Weaver, America has lost a great patriot and warrior, and you, a faithful follower.

I thought you should know.

Sincerely,

CHARLES G. MCMILLAN

CAPTAIN

USAF

EDWARDS AFB, CALIF.

Dear Captain McMillan: I am profoundly moved; and I extend you, his friend, our condolences, even as we share your pride in our friend. Gratefully,

—WFB   MAY 27, 1991

———

But if someone really wants to take Buckley on by letter or column or book, he can expect a polite barrage back. And he should be prepared to stay the course—or face the most serious response of all: silence.

———

Memo to: Bill
From: Priscilla
Did you catch Herb Caen's latest?

How Little We Know

SLICE OF WRY: Maxwell Arnold suggests that William Buckley Jr., fairest flower of the right wing, is an odd choice to act as host of the TV series based on Evelyn Waugh's classic English novel, "Brideshead Revisited" (tonight's installment is on KQED at 9). On Page 543 of "The Letters of Evelyn Waugh," we find the author writing to Tom Driberg on June 6, 1960. After congratulating him on a magazine article about right-wing movements, Waugh asks Driberg, "Can you tell me: did you in your researches come across the name of Wm. F. Buckley Jr., editor of a New York, neo-McCarthy magazine named *National Review?* He has been showing me great & unsought attention lately & your article made me curious. Has he been supernally 'guided' to bore me? It would explain him" . . . If anything can.

★   ★   ★

Herb Caen
San Francisco Chronicle
Dear Herbert:

The item on Brideshead, Waugh, and me was understandable fun. Though perhaps a little skepticism would have been in order, even as I'd have shown skepticism toward any writer who pronounced that "Herb Caen is a bore." We are other things. The letter, Waugh to Driberg, was an inside joke. Waugh had just finished reading a book by me the last chapter of which is an attack on Driberg. Following the letter you quoted were several not listed by the anthologist, Mr. Amory, for reasons unknown. Mr. Waugh also went on to submit a piece to *National Review* and write a book review for us. His last letter to me I quote:

Combe Florey House, Combe Florey, Nr. Taunton 2nd April 63
Dear Mr. Buckley:

Very many thanks for *Rumbles.* [*Rumbles Left and Right* by WFB, New York, Putnam's, 1962].

Some of the essays were familiar to me from *National Review.* I reread them with the same zest as those which were new. You have the very rare gift of captivating the reader's attention in controversies in which he has no direct concern. I congratulate you on the collection. At your best you remind me of Belloc; at your second best of Randolph Churchill.

. . . Please accept my greetings for Easter (which I shall be spending in Rome).

Yours sincerely,
EVELYN WAUGH

Herb, I thought the world of Evelyn Waugh, but sometimes when I think of what he wrote about me, I blush. Yours cordially,

BILL

—MARCH 5, 1982

Mr. Mark Amory
Ticknor & Fields
London

Dear Mr. Amory:

I'm not sure why I put off writing to you for so long. Perhaps it was my general admiration for the job you did in editing the letters of Mr. Evelyn Waugh [*The Letters of Evelyn Waugh*, edited by Mark Amory, Ticknor & Fields, 1980].

But now, with yet another smirking allusion [see "Notes & Asides," March 5] to the low opinion Waugh had of me, my magazine, and my abilities (this one in New York, following similar references in Los Angeles and San Francisco), I must ask you for an explanation.

1. I enclose a copy of the San Francisco column by Mr. Herb Caen. I enclose a copy of the letter I then addressed to Mr. Caen.

2. I enclose a copy of the feature "Notes & Asides" from *National Review,* November 14, 1980. I should have addressed a copy of that feature to you at the time, so that I'd have had access to your explanation for the missing letters, EW to WFB.

3. My confusion is reinforced by the acknowledgments in your book. Apparently I gave you permission to enter my files and to take from them copies of letters from EW to me. When the book came out, I asked the Yale University Library, which keeps my papers, to give me in turn copies of letters from EW to WFB. I instantly received the entire set published in the *National Review* feature. It is, I should think, logical to conclude that you were in possession of the identical set. Why then did you not, even if you elected not to publish any of his subsequent letters to me, mention in a footnote that Mr. Waugh was friendly to me, and to my journal? I am most anxious for your explanation, as it will facilitate my handling of my critics, who are greatly enjoying themselves on this point.

I am sending a copy of this letter and enclosures to Auberon Waugh, not in the spirit of intimidation, but because, as an old personal friend, I would not want him to be surprised that there was contention, so to speak, in the family.

Yours faithfully,
WM. F. BUCKLEY, JR.

Combe Florey House
Somerset, England

Dear Bill:

Thank you for sending me your correspondence with Mark Amory. I am sorry that he seems to be making cheap capital from the few rude references to you in my Father's correspondence. If he had known you better there would probably have been more of them, but that would not mean that he held you in anything but the greatest esteem. He always spoke of you with admiration, as I remember, and was delighted when I started writing for you many years ago.

The problem with opening anyone's letters or diaries is that one is bound to find unkind references to friends, relations, and even strangers which the writer would never have intended to see published. It was a difficulty which I met particularly in the Diaries, by a blanket policy of publishing everything. There were many extraordinarily rude references to myself and other members of the family, both in the Diaries and in the Letters. My policy was to hide nothing simply on the grounds that it would have been rather a despicable thing to discriminate. We all write unkind jokes and even deeply wounding remarks about our best friends in circumstances where we do not expect them to read them. One just has to learn not to take offense. But I am sorry that people are using these references to embarrass you. The only policy in my experience is to rise above it all. One of the joys of journalism is that everybody forgets it within a week or two.

Mark Amory is a very old friend of mine, but of course he is a Liberal. His mother decided to stand as Liberal candidate while he was at Oxford, and the result is to be found in a little-read novel of mine called *Path of Dalliance* where she appears as Mrs. Sligger. I am sure that no malice is intended, merely the impulsive journalistic urge to make jokes.

Have you ever been to Combe Florey? I hope we may tempt you down here one day. I practically never move nowadays except for twice-yearly pilgrimages to the Far East, but it would be lovely to see you again, when you are in England. I was in Cuba two weeks ago and brooded on the terrible struggle in your breast between patriotism and appreciation of good cigars which you somehow solved by leaving a box of Cuban cigars in my house in Wiltshire. There is a fast train service from London if ever you are tempted.

All the best.

Yours ever,
BRON
[AUBERON WAUGH]

Dear Mr. Buckley:

When I asked for letters from Evelyn Waugh, I was indeed sent the complete set and I am sorry to have returned evil for good. I edited ruthlessly on grounds of interest or amusement, fairness coming a poor third.

Certainly your relationship with Waugh was distorted as a result. His rudeness about you was clearly meant to cheer up Driberg, an old friend whose book you had criticized. My explanation will not seem strong to you but was for me: to put in corrective footnotes throughout would have been laborious, dull to read, and lead into the tricky, almost impossible, area of deciding how much of what Waugh said he meant.

You have my sympathy and my apologies for the resulting annoyance but I see that they are not much good to you.

Yours sincerely,

MARK AMORY

Dear Auberon:

I attach this note to my letter [not here reproduced] to you, as I have just seen Mark Amory's letter, a copy of which I enclose. I have decided it doesn't require an answer.

As ever,

BILL   —NOVEMBER 23, 1982

One wonderful letter-writer appreciates another, for a regular exchange of letters is like a continuing conversation.

EVELYN WAUGH AND LADY DIANA COOPER, CORRESPONDENTS

Everybody knows who Evelyn Waugh was. Not so Diana Cooper, to whom Waugh wrote about three hundred letters from 1932 until he died in 1966, twenty years before her own death at a very advanced age. One way to begin to situate her is to note the wedding presents she received in 1919 when, as the beautiful young daughter of the Duchess of Rutland, she married the penniless, untitled Duff Cooper: "The King and Queen gave a blue enamel and diamond brooch bearing their own initials; Queen Alexandra a diamond-and-ruby pendant; the French Ambassador a gold ewer for incense-burning; the Princess of Monaco a diamond ring; Lord Wimborne a William and Mary gold dressing-case; King Manuel a gold sugar-sifter; Lord Beaverbrook a motor car; Dame Nellie Melba a writing-table." (The list of wedding gifts, as Philip Ziegler reports in his biography *Diana Cooper,* occupied eighty-eight pages of a large notebook.)

Lady Diana Cooper was, then, socially noticeable. By the time Waugh met her, she had been a screen actress and also played on the stage. In the late 1950s she turned to writing, producing three volumes of memoirs; Waugh wrote that he thought them "a single work of art, one of the great autobiographies of the century." Lady Diana's granddaughter, Artemis Cooper, provides samples of these expressive skills in *The Letters of Evelyn Waugh and Diana Cooper,* as when Lady Diana addressed Waugh severely (she often did so) following Duff Cooper's death, just after the midnight that brought in the new year, 1954:

> You have never, I think, known real Grief—panic, melancholia, mad-ness, night-sweats, we've all known for most of our lives—you and me par-ticularly. I'm not sure you know human love in the way I do. You have faith and mysticism—intense inner interests—a diverting, virile mind—gusto for vengeance and destruction if necessary, a fancy—a gospel.
>
> What you can't imagine is a creature with a certain iridescent aura and nothing within but a beating frightened heart built round and for Duff. . . . For two days I am quite alone—in these empty rooms with one thought one prayer—'let it end now'—an absurd feminine desire to die in the same way exactly as Duff. [I have now a] fearlessness of death—so let it come now before custom of living disinclines me for dying.

But such grief was not characteristic. Diana Cooper loved people and traveling and adventures and fun—and she loved Evelyn Waugh, though one surmises that they were happier when planning to see each other than when in each other's company. The dour Waugh ("I am an insensitive lout") was relentlessly adoring. Among Lady Diana's attractions were her blue blood and her tendency to move about "grand architecture"—bring-ing him "delight. . . . Still more the aesthetic joy of seeing you in your proper setting of luxury and splendour. Still more, and incomparably more, the happiness to know that you have kept a warm place for me in your heart all through my ice age. I love you."

But she didn't *always* bring him delight. "Baby" (as he called her) could irritate Waugh by what she said or by her occasional bouts of silence or by misinterpreting his catechisms. "You know perfectly well," she reassured him after one such misunderstanding, "you have no Baby as loyal as this Baby and that if you believe anything else you are very foolish. I thought, if you want to know, that you did it to irritate—or rather from Irritabil-ity's possession. It's an unexorcisable demon. . . . O dear how sad it all is."

In the big 1980 volume of his letters edited by Mark Amory it was made clear, as only Waugh could make things clear, that he considered it the burden—the very function, the *raison d'être*—of the correspondent *to inform and to entertain.* He was lavish in discharge of this duty. Thus he tells Lady Diana of a visit to Hilaire Belloc: "Two civil and pretty grandsons received us. Sherry in the hall. Then a long wait for Belloc. Shuffling and stumping. Then an awful smell like the wolves at the zoo, then entry. A tramp, covered in garbage. A sweet, wise, mad face. An awful black growth like a truffle under one eye. First words: 'Old age is a curious thing. It leaves a man crawling like a beetle while his mind is as strong and young as ever.' Second words (rather disconcerting, because I have met him twenty times or more since you first introduced us . . .): 'It is a pleasure to make your acquaintance, sir.' "

Belloc was very nearly unique in eliciting something like awe. Mostly Waugh's world was populated by lesser creatures, such as those he came upon in his travels. During a cruise of the Mediterranean in the fall of 1933 he undertook, one by one, to describe his traveling companions. Miss Marjorie Glasgow was, for example, "a very rich young lady whom I had met before on account of her mother giving parties I used to go to before I became fastidious. She was the leader of the left-wing nudists. She was attended by three naked Counts, one Polish, one Belgian and one Italian, one carried her gramophone, another her backgammon board and the third her sunbathing mattress."

He was especially fine when transmitting hilarities in the matter-of-fact tones of the schoolteacher: "I wish you had come to Goa. It is really a very singular place. . . . At the moment it is full of pilgrims from all over India and Ceylon—the descendants of people Francis Xavier preached to without knowing their language. . . . Did you know that when F.X. went to Japan he asked the word for God and they told him the Japanese for [penis] so he spent weeks preaching phallic worship without knowing it."

Evelyn Waugh depended on his friends, especially when traveling—which was much of the time—for news of the kind he most wanted. "Please keep writing and tell me about the general election and who is sleeping with whom and so on." He spoke of vacations, but never seemed to let up. It isn't widely recognized how very much he worked, how copiously he produced. He proffered as the reason for writing the sheer need for the income to care for his wife and six children, athwart the predatory hands of a socialist government. "I cannot with the utmost economy live on less than £5,000 a year and I have to earn £62,000 to spend that and I am getting too old and downcast to earn it," he wrote in December 1951, surveying his crowded household. His children were all very well, but children were very simply "defective adults." He was "glad to possess" his own, but got "little pleasure from their use—like first editions." He found it comfortable to be comprehensive in his dislikes—"Hate everyone except you and Maimie"—even if he knew that was somehow wrong, and could make himself write: "I am full of regret for failures in gratitude and patience and service and that has made me think of my failures towards all I love. . . . Please . . . believe always in my love."

It is well known that Evelyn Waugh rejoiced in the upper class, in particular the titled nobility, however ironic his oblique references to this fixation ("After I left you I went to play dominoes with the poor"). Anyone wishing to document this affinity will lean heavily on the comprehensive footnotes appended to these letters by Artemis Cooper, the talented and industrious editor of this intricate volume. Here one runs into—or else that is the sensation—just about every titled person in Britain; somehow they all manage to figure in Waugh-Cooper colloquies. The footnote for Waugh's mother-in-law reads: "She was born the Hon. Mary Vesey, and married Aubrey Herbert M.P. (1880–1923) in 1910. Aubrey Herbert, who was twice offered the throne of Albania, was a half brother of the fifth Earl of Carnarvon (the patron of Howard Carter, who discovered the tomb of Tutankhamun)."

Lady Diana does not disappoint this appetite or conceal its mannerisms. "Will it be soon" that Waugh pays another visit? she wonders. "I fear the hols are over and you are happy at home. The house is warm and there are no guests for bed or board. You could do your [diet] here—no cook, no maître d'hotel, no one who can read or write. Pierro who puts 'CRI' for gruyère. Jacqueline—my life, my memory—is off with a garagiste to be knocked about by a frog husband, her place is taken by a Czech child—utterly unlearned. Antoinette, the Polish milker, is in command—she can't even make herself plain—but cooks with originality and charm. . . . Louise has had her lung out and is like a roebuck in spring. Phyllis, and my dearest sister Marjorie, to say nothing of Viola Tree and Clarissa's mother, might all have been saved most hideous deaths [from lung cancer]." There is nothing to do, nobody to go out with that one would care to go out with. "There is no sap in Nature—nor in me. Spiritless, not in pain or acute melancholy I languish chilly—not happily resigned."

It has long been my own reading of Waugh that his delight in the festoonery of the titled class was merely a perverse aspect of his resentful co-optation by a populist history-on-the-march that disregarded the forms he revered: in religion, the old Roman Catholic Church; in society, the standards of decorum and behavior that marked, if not so much the separation of classes, the acknowledgment of the idea of class. That the upper classes had long since lost any meritocratic credentials he seldom paused to notice. What Waugh bothered with was the loss of his privacy. "The only human relationships I abide are intimacy, formality and servility. What is horrible here [England] and in America is familiarity. That doesn't exist in Asia." And again, "I live in a world which seems to me to deteriorate daily before my eyes." But his problem, he knew, was also personal: "How right you are about not losing friends. . . . I lose mine fast. . . . You find something agreeable in almost everyone. I am put off by anything not wholly agreeable."

Diana Cooper was one exception. Not that she was always reliably agreeable. ("If only you could treat friends," he chided, "as something to be enjoyed in themselves not as companions in adventure.") But she was a lifelong source of joy for Waugh, the quality of which is transmitted by these letters to readers who knew neither of them, and presumably care little for their workaday concerns. Waugh wrote that "it ought always to be disappointing to meet an artist; if his work is not something otherwise invisible in him he can't have the real motive for work. Artists to be heard and not seen." But in his triumphantly readable letters Waugh tells us otherwise—though, granted, we experience him in the written word with the kind of safety that would not have protected us when experiencing him in person.

I have jocularly ventured for some years now that a dispositive proof of the existence of the Holy Spirit is that Evelyn Waugh died just after attending church on Easter Sunday in 1966, immediately after which the convention was introduced in the Catholic Mass of the sign of peace, a moment when worshipers are bid to shake hands with fellow worshipers to their right, to their left, in the pew ahead and in the pew behind. Such an exercise could not have coexisted with Evelyn Waugh, defender of the faith. Either he had to go, or else the ritual had to be postponed. The Holy Spirit made His choice. Waugh went, but not before having a certain satisfaction at the expense of the Cardinal most responsible for the "reforms" of the Second Vatican Council:

Combe Florey
7 February 1965

Darling

. . . Nice to go to Rome. They are destroying all that was superficially attractive about my Church. It is a great sorrow to me and for once undeserved.

If you see Cardinal Bea spit in his eye.

All love

BO

To which Lady Diana replied:

> 10 Warwick Avenue
> [postmarked March 7, 1965]
>   Can you imagine the luck—I went up in a tiny lift with Cardinal Bea in full canonicals preceded by two candles—so with a spluttered greeting I was able to spit in his eye for you. . . .
>
> PUG

These letters are a great exotic flower in modern literature.

—WFB

Chapter 14

Usage IV: Oh, What's the Usage?

Buckley and one of his discoveries, a young writer who became the formidable author, teacher, and syndicated columnist Garry Wills, no longer make beautiful music together, but they still correspond. Wills, for example, wrote a complaining letter to protest someone's substitution in a piece he wrote of *mesocephalic* for *mesomphalic,* feeling no need to apologize for having used the word in the first place.

In the exchange that follows, WFB, after a passing reference to Wills, picks up a criticism of something Buckley has written from a respected critic and friend—and thereby triggers a flood of exegesis, response, and counter-response.

———

One Sentence

Inasmuch as I am encouraged by my colleagues to fill this space as I please, I take liberties. Or do I? What follows is primarily of interest to syntacticians. How many of them are there? Not many. But—ah!—how many voyeurs? What follows is interesting, also, to students of friendship, nothing less than an assiduous case of which could have prompted the redoubtable Professor Hugh Kenner to such heroic efforts to demonstrate the demerits of a single English sentence. . . .

HK to WFB Sept. 19, 1968

. . . Garry [Wills] under pressure tends to deliquescent metaphor (vide his Miami piece, *NR*), as does WFB to filigree syntax (vide current *Esquire,* first sentence, which while it parses . . . resembles less a tensioned intricacy in the mode of M. Eiffel than it does a toddler's first efforts with Tinkertoy). . . .

WFB to HK Oct. 1

. . . You are surely wrong about that lead sentence? I re-read it, found it springy and tight.

HK to WFB Oct. 15

. . . about that *Esquire* lead: it reads in my copy:
"Robert F. Kennedy had a way of saying things loosely, and it may be that that is among the reasons why so many people invested so much idealism in him, it being in the idealistic (as distinguished from the analytical) mode to make large and good-sounding generalities, like the generality he spoke on April 5 after the assassination of Martin Luther King, two months exactly before his own assassination."
"Springy and tight" my foot. Those aren't springs, they're bits of Scotch tape. Have your syntactic DNA checked for mutations; it just isn't governing the wild forces of growth as of yore.

WFB to HK Oct. 17

Come on now, you are a goddam professor of English, so stop name-calling and get to work. . . .

HK to WFB Oct. 25

. . . Okay, that sentence:
One way of putting the problem is that it's not discernibly heading anywhere; it ambles along, stuffing more and more odds & ends into its elastic bag, until it simply decides to sit down. Mr. Niemeyer has ridiculed my interest in syntactic energy, countering my regret that Johann Sebastian Bach should be taking out the garbage with his pleasure that it's being taken out, whazzamatter, don't I want a tidy house? Yet I revert to the con-

cept: something, something corresponding to tension and relaxation, to the turn of the key and the swing of the door, to departure from and return to the tonic, makes us willing to accept the necessity of a long sentence being one sentence and not three spliced by mispunctuation. Back to the exhibit: if there were a period after "loosely" no one would feel that a flight had been arrested in mid-course. Or after "him," or after "generalities." I think one test of the long sentence is that if it's stopped before it's over the reader should sense the incompleteness. This is sometimes a matter of formal grammar: if we start with "because" the reader won't accept a full stop until he's been accorded a principal clause. It's sometimes just a matter of promising in the opening words or by the opening cadence (a device of Gibbon's) some amplitude of concern the reader expects to see implemented. But here the offer to develop the proposition that RFK had a way of saying things loosely creates no syntactic expectation because it's capable of standing as a sentence by itself; nor does it retrospectively command the rest of the sentence, because the sentence has managed to end not with an amplification of RFK's looseness but with a triplicated irrelevancy about the date.

"Robert F. Kennedy had a way of saying things loosely: large and good-sounding generalities which being in the idealistic (as distinguished from the analytical) mode help explain why so many people invested so much idealism in him: generalities like the one Martin Luther King's assassination prompted him to utter on April 5, just two months, as it happened, before he was assassinated himself."

A possible improvement, if one *must* include all those components. The main difference is that by putting the colon after "loosely" one gives notice that the opening clause will preside over the remainder, not simply join to the next section of track. Then repeat of "generalities" to hitch the peroration to the second member. And rearrangement of terminal items keeps the mention of King and *l'affaire* Sirhan from sounding like doodles irrelevantly prompted by "April 5." I do not offer the improved version as anything but an exercise; I wasn't writing the article and haven't in my blood the points you anticipated making, so all I can manage is a piece of engineering.

I do not fuss about your occasional sentences to preserve a professorial edge. I merely call attention to dangers when I chance to see them. You revise carefully, I know, and it never hurts to have a few explicit criteria of revision. One is the rationale of the long sentence, as above (and failing that rationale, or failing time to adequate one's drafts to the rationale, vita being brevis and deadlines being yesterday, one ought, I think, to cut spaghetti into shorter sentences where natural stopping places occur). Another is that grammatical lint is best picked: in my suggested version I've avoided "that that," "reasons why" (your ear had told you to eschew yet a third "that"), and "it being." These all have rhetorical uses, as colloquialisms bounced off girders, but strung along in a row like old peanut shells they suggest WFB just plain improvising while he awaits a glimpse of daylight, and suggest to *les* Dwight Macdonalds that the Scrambled Egghead Method is to talk till one figures out what one is saying. This method is of course frequently necessary, and inoffensive, *viva voce,* say on TV, but its appearance should be avoided in print.

WFB to HK Nov. 4

. . . I worry about that confounded sentence, as one worries upon failing to appreciate something which one is prepared to postulate as good, to wit your criticism of it. I shan't even apologize for belaboring the point, because I know that you will know that by talking back, I am proving that I have not put you to such inconvenience merely for my own amusement.

"*Robert Kennedy had a way of saying things loosely*" followed by the colon you suggest means to me that I am about to demonstrate my allegation, or give an example of it. Followed by a period, the lilt of the sentence is, it seems to me, self-consciously dramatic, as in "John F. Kennedy had a way of seducing women." Followed by a comma, I thought it to be leading rather gradually to a point I did not want for a while yet, until the mood set in, to crystallize: whence, "*, and it may be that that is among the reasons why so many people invested so much idealism in him*"—again, if the period had come here, I'd have attempted, or so it strikes me, a stolen base, and the reader would have been annoyed by the intimation that I have proved my point; or that I infer that the reader will merely permit me to asseverate it. When, i.e. by way of further explanation, begging the reader's indulgence so to speak, "*, it being in the idealistic (as distinguished from the analytical) mode to make large and good-sounding generalities*"—department of amplification, not without—yet—the example I am about to furnish, and spend several hundred words confuting, "*, like the generality he spoke on April 5, after the assassination of Martin Luther King*" surely writing about what Kennedy said about another man's assassination a few days after Kennedy's own assassination (which is when I wrote this article), gives a certain spooky suspense, which is ratified, Robert-Louis-Stevenson-wise, with the adverbial clause "*, two months exactly before his own assassination.*" That last I take to be a fair substitute for "two months exactly, as it happened, before his own assassination." Seems to me that, although the sentence is long it is not impossibly long, and that although the commas appear somehow to be loose and thoughtless linkages they are justified by their meiotic contribution to the plot I am contriving. Hell, it merely disturbs me that while I *understand* your generic points, my ear does not grant them a preemptive relevance in this instance; and I repeat, that I worry because undoubtedly you are right and I wrong. Anyway, I shall remember the generic advice. Believe. Me. Pal.

HK to WFB Nov. 7

. . . Not to wrangle, I'd make a final suggestion: that your inability to relate my comments, which you follow, to the sentence, the intentions of which you expound convincingly, is perhaps based on this, that you're not reading the printed sentence but hearing yourself speak it. By pause, by suspension, by inflection, by variation of tone and pace, you could make the "little plot" you speak of sing. The written language provides no notation for such controls, and your intention as graphed by printed words leaves the reader too much to supply, and too many options for supplying the wrong tacit commentary, e.g., that WFB is standing in an open space scattering peanut shells.

We have no such public style as Pope could posit, and vary from minutely, in an aesthetic of microscopic inappropriatenesses. We have instead the convention that the writer creates his operating conventions *de novo.* "Robert Kennedy had a way of saying things loosely."—followed by a hypothetical period, you say, its lilt is self-consciously dramatic. Yes, but those are the very first words of a long essay; we are just tuning in to station WFB; his eschewal of the self-consciously dramatic is not yet an operative principle; and one of the options open to us is to suppose that a dramatic opening was intended but muffed by a fault of punctuation. I think your rebuttal to my statement that the sentence could be terminated by a period at several points without creating a sense of incompleteness consists in an appeal to nuances of taste: it would make nuanced differences to cut it off here or here. So it would. But the reader hasn't yet a feel for the governing structure of taste in the piece before him. *Especially* in an opening, the reader would be well served by a syntactic tension, as inevitable as gravitation on an inclined plane, which makes it essential that the sentence incorporate, as it proceeds, the members it does, or else fall down. . . . *Mais passons.*

WFB *urbi et orbe,* Jan. 1, 1969: Who's right?

Kenner v. Buckley

Herewith my response to the well-aimed point from Professor Kenner ["Notes & Asides," Jan. 14]:

> *Syntactic energy is drained*
> *While pondering a thought.*
> *It's more important to have gained*
> *In logic than been caught*
> *By cadence, which could well ensnare*
> *The ruminating process.*
> *Professor, Sir, I couldn't care:*
> *Less.*

POLLY WILLIAMS

MOUNTAINSIDE, N.J.

Professor Kenner offers Mr. Buckley an "out" through his remark that the written language contains no notation for the subtle controls of pause, suspension, inflection, variation of tone and pace, which WFB would have required to make his *Esquire* lead "sing." Certainly I must agree with him that the sentence as WFB has written it and punctuated it does not sing; in fact, I had to reread it a couple of times to pin down its proposition. Unfortunately, Professor Kenner's edition singeth not itself, though it burns with a cold, gem-like flame.

There is an alternative course, though I'm sure the editors of *Esquire* might have been more than a little startled to see it adopted by WFB. It is, to utilize *all* the flexibility, all the nuances, of modern notation . . . to adapt and adopt the conventions of punctuation displayed by Cummings, Pound (particularly Pound—ain't he loverly?), and others in poetry, by Tennessee Williams in his plays and by William Faulkner in his prose, plays, and poetry.

RALPH D. COPELAND

LOCK HAVEN, PA.

The lamentable fact is that Wm. F., like the late Robt. F., has a way of saying things loosely, especially when he is writing about the late Robt. F., there being something contagious even in the recollection of the hard little Boston moptop who declaimed in the same flat accents for the brotherhood of man and the bugging of Jimmy Hoffa, whose enmity Kennedy craved as a crocodile feeds on barracuda steak.

It was a bum sentence, Bill. But you are still the greatest editor in the world.

JAMES JACKSON KILPATRICK

ALEXANDRIA, VA.

Dear Mr. Buckley:

At first I couldn't believe. Then, others confirmed. Our usually precise hero had slipped. On *Firing Line* he had lapsed into saying: *a number of.*

Thus, I'm impelled to point out—as I've done to Presidents, *N. Y. Times* editors, TV anchorpersons & others—that this three-word combination has been defined as "a meaningless phrase used by lazy writers & speakers" . . . has a variety of alternatives such as few, many, dozens, scores, etc. . . . & frequently can be eliminated without effect on a message's import.

Ban this inanity from publishing & politics & there'd be a vast saving of natural resources—forests, oil, coal & energy—currently wasted on its reproduction & dissemination. There also would be ancillary benefits including smaller newspapers (fewer hernias from handling Sunday editions), briefer newscasts &, conceivably, an occasional political speech that makes sense.

Of greater significance would be the spread of the addiction to literature:

> *Think of the poetry lost*
> *Had the phrase been used by Robert Frost,*
> *Lord Tennyson & Mr. Browning,*
> *Or in songs we enjoy singing.*
> *People would think Tennyson mad*
> *For: ". . . rode a number of lads."*
> *And Browning, feet of clay*
> *For: ". . . I love thee a number of ways."*
> *Plus, what of the cost to Frost*
> *For: ". . . I have a number of promises to keep & a*
> *   number of miles to go before I sleep"?*
> *And who'd want to dance with one's love*
> *To "Tea for a Number Of"*
> *Or join a singalong*
> *Of "A Number of Frenchmen Can't Be Wrong"?*
> *But all would wish a whammy*
> *On both Al Jolson & his "Mammy"*
> *For: "I'd walk a number of miles for a number of*
> *   your smiles."*

Please, kind sir, seek to provide a better example.

Sincerely,

ALEX W. BURGER

NEW ROCHELLE, N.Y.

Dear Mr. Burger: How do you handle the need to communicate, "A number of the odd-numbered series was revealed as the key to the missing formula?" Or should one simply abandon the search for the formula? Many thanks,

—WFB   OCTOBER 19, 1984

To the Editor:

In a recent issue of *National Review,* a reader takes Mr. Buckley to task for using the phrase "a number of," calling it strictly meaningless. It is the critic himself who is at fault for not knowing an idiom when he sees one. As far back as 1380, Wyclif wrote: "In the Church above in heaven is a number of great saints." Bacon in 1626 says that water lilies have roots in the ground "and so do a number of other herbs that grow in ponds." The phrase has the clear meaning of *several,* a word that in our day tends to sound formal—hence the frequent and unambiguous recourse to "a number of."

To require logic of an idiom is waste of time—the critic might as well have said that "a good number" is a foolish expression because numbers are neither good nor bad. Yet "a number of" is not entirely unexplainable. It clearly implies that the thing described is not absent or even unique: a number*ing* is possible. Note that the adjective *numerous,* which is literally the same as "a number of," goes idiomatically in the other direction and means "a great many."

JACQUES BARZUN
NEW YORK, N.Y.   JANUARY 11, 1985

The Editor
The Baltimore Sun
Baltimore, Md.

Dear Sir:

I have two objections to your editorial, "Buckley, *ex Cathedra*" (September 24).

You write of my calling Reagan's refusal to lay down tariffs to protect U.S. steel "the correct Christian decision," and you ask, "We trust that Jewish, Moslem, Hindu, and Buddhist teachings on the religious aspects of international commerce in steel were considered and dismissed as 'incorrect.'"

If you will consult Webster III, you will find that under "syn." for the adjective *Christian* is given, "decent, civilized." The example cited is, "act in a Christian fashion."

And then you write, "William F. Buckley, Jr., whose elegant arrogance and affectation of a British accent has won him fame and fortune . . ." You should have written, "William F. Buckley, Jr., whose elegant arrogance and affectation of a British accent *have* won him fame and fortune . . ." You see, arrogance and affectation being separate modifiers, they require the use of the plural verb.

Yours faithfully,

WM. F. BUCKLEY, JR.   FEBRUARY 8, 1985

Dear Mr. Buckley:

I enjoyed reading your response to the editor of the *Baltimore Sun* ["Notes & Asides," Feb. 8]. In pointing out his egregious grammatical error, however, you happened to commit one slight faux pas yourself. In the sentence "William F. Buckley, Jr., whose elegant arrogance and affectation of a British accent have won him fame and fortune . . ." arrogance and affectation are not modifiers; they are subjects (abstract nouns) of a modifying clause. Indeed they give the appearance of acting as modifiers (much, so my liberal colleagues assure me, the way Ed Meese can give the appearance of acting improperly). Furthermore, in your sentence "You see, arrogance and affectation being separate modifiers, they require the use of a plural verb," the word *they* is a redundant subject—though I find the usage stylistically apropos, considering its intended affectation.

Forgive me, Bill. This is what's become of the mind of an associate professor of English who has been forced to teach rudimentary grammar to his college students.

Sincerely,

RICHARD ORODENKER

PEIRCE JUNIOR COLLEGE

PHILADELPHIA, PA.

Dear Professor Orodenker: That's quite all right, quite all right, I understand the pedantic imperative. By the way, the device used above is called an anacoluthon. Cordially,

—WFB   MAY 17, 1985

Dear Mr. Buckley:

I recently read, with great interest, your article appearing in *Harper's* on "Giving Yale to Connecticut."

In that article you said: "if mind and conscience led them to the conclusion, they would be not only free, but compelled to decide . . ."

I assume that your use of the construction "not only . . . but . . ." is a form of "not only . . . but *also* . . ." If so, how can someone who is free also be compelled? If not, what did you intend to say?

Otherwise keep up the good work.

Sincerely yours,
SCOTT BREWER
SUNY AT STONYBROOK, N.Y.

Dear Mr. Brewer: What I wrote is a contraction of "not only free, but [assuming your mind and conscience are in working order] compelled to [etc.]." Any time. And thanks very much. Cordially,

—WFB   APRIL 16, 1982

Dear Mr. Buckley:
Some years ago, in correspondence, a gentleman prominent in the "peace" movement made one point on which I had to agree he was absolutely correct. I pass the lesson on to you, since the Dec. 1 *NR* (e.g., the editorial "Peking Duck") contains the same mistake in your own ordinarily impeccable prose. The fact is, words such as "escapee" and "attendee" should never be used in their vulgar senses. The ending "-ee" strictly means that the subject is acted on, not acting. Thus, in a jailbreak, the convicts getting away are escapers, the jailers are escapees. If a person has fleas, they are his attenders, he is their attendee.

I need not point out to you the importance of conserving precision in language. But I might say that, on occasion, the deft interjection of this particular point in debate can be useful in confounding the ungodly, including those in the "peace" movement.

POUL ANDERSON
ORINDA, CALIF.

Dear Mr. Buckley:
Re the first sentence of one of M. Stanton Evans's "Lawmakers" columns, which began: "Lincoln said it: . . . 'When you see eye-beams hoisted . . .' "???

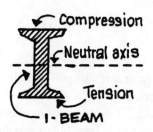

I am familiar with "I" beams (but I don't think Lincoln was)—first in cast iron and then steel, and rarely used in wood houses. Lincoln saw beams, girders, rafters, etc., but what the hell is an eye-beam except that

which you fix on some blonde in a bikini? Elucidate for a very ancient architect.

FRANK ROEHR
WILSONVILLE, ORE.

Dear Mr. Roehr: The use of "eye" for "I" is common in telegraphic communications, as in: "Please ship me four eye-beams before eye go nuts." Cordially,

—WFB   JULY 24, 1981

Dear Mr. Buckley:

I have stumbled too long over the clumsy locutions journalists use for the way bureaucrats speak, e.g., *bureauspeak, bureaucratese.* I propose the following as euphonious and descriptive:

> **bureaulalia 1.** speech, esp. of functionaries, connoting progress while concealing its lack; **2.** mental disorder of one claiming to aid the commonweal, while feeding on it, often ravenously (*from* bureau: any government rathole, + lalia [Greek]: defective speech)

Are you able to give this word your endorsement? If so, a plug in the magazine would make our public discourse more sonorous.

Sincerely yours,
DENNIS R. KELLEY
GLENVIEW, ILL.

Dear Mr. Kelley: I can give your word exposure, but not my endorsement; sorry. It's pedantic, and wouldn't flow into the vocabulary, leaning as it does on a Greek word that no one is familiar with—except, presumably, Greeks. Cordially,

—WFB

Dear Mr. Buckley:

Although I no longer subscribe to your journal, every Christmas I would give a subscription to Hazel Overland, my grandmother. Although she did not always agree with your politics, she enjoyed your writing and loved your God. I recall how she raved about your pilgrimage to Lourdes. My grandmother died on Easter Sunday. They said it was peaceful. I'm glad. I'm also thankful for all the enjoyable moments you gave my grandmother during her last years on Earth.

Sincerely,
JOSEPH HOLPER
DEKALB, ILL.

Dear Mr. Holper: Many thanks, and may your grandmother R.I.P. By the way, it's *our* God, you know. Cordially,

—WFB   JUNE 13, 1994

Dear Mr. Buckley:

You have a maddening habit of using the words "England" and "Britain" interchangeably; most recently in the column based on your interview of Mr. Kinnock. You present a scenario in which the Soviets "take out Cardiff," and the U.S. President asks whether he should issue an ultimatum to the Soviet Union to "leave England alone"—as if Cardiff were part of England.

Listen: England is England. England plus Scotland and Wales is Britain (Great Britain, if you prefer). Britain plus Northern Ireland is the United Kingdom.

It would be wrong to go to Cardiff or to Glasgow and remark to the locals, "It's nice to be in England." Moreover, it would be most inadvisable.

Sincerely,

RICHARD R. DOBSON
EDITOR OF THE EDITORIAL PAGE
MINOT DAILY NEWS
MINOT, N.D.

Dear Mr. Dobson: Does that mean I can't say anymore, Oh, to be in Cardiff, now that April's here? Cordially,

—WFB   AUGUST 20, 1982

Dear Mr. Buckley:

Am a bit annoyed because two, maybe three, times in *NR* I have seen "transpired" used as a synonym for happened. I almost swear I saw it so used in one of your columns. Possible? Naw!

I still use the essay on language you did for the American Heritage Dictionary* and would by inference swear that you would rub the bugger out on every occasion. Do I infer too much?

Sincerely,

(MR.) CONNIE MACK REA
ENGLISH DEPARTMENT
CALIFORNIA UNIVERSITY OF PENNSYLVANIA
CALIFORNIA, PA.

---

* See chapter 16, "Passing in Review."

Dear Mr. Rea: Thanks for your act of faith, which is by the way justified. I'd as soon slit my throat as misuse *transpire*. If it was misused by others in these sacred glades, let's hope that this way of telling them satisfies all relevant diplomatic requirements. Cordially,

—WFB   JULY 20, 1992

Chapter 15

On Fiction

Buckley—at an age when many men are thinking of consolidating their gains, taking no new risks, and settling for doing well what they already know how to do—turned to fiction. In this introduction to *The Blackford Oakes Reader* (Andrews and McMeel, 1995), he gives his version of how the novels came about.

BLACKFORD OAKES: AN INTRODUCTION

I take the opportunity to answer some of the questions most often put to me as the author of the ten novels featuring Blackford Oakes. A question that continues to intrigue is: What is it that, at age fifty, beckoned me to write fiction?

It's a brief story, rather mundane, but it has its charm. I had for many years been in touch with Samuel Vaughan, then of Doubleday, a gentle, bright, shrewd man of letters who suggested we lunch and said he'd bring along two friends. It developed that they too were associates of Doubleday. The agenda for the lunch never materialized formally, though at some point, Sam asked if I had recently read any action thriller I thought especially well of and I said, Yes, I read *Day of the Jackal* last week and thought it tremendous. "Why don't you try writing a novel?" he said. I answered, as I remember, "Sam, why don't you play a trumpet concerto?" The conversation proceeded, pleasantly and aimlessly, and the next morning I found on my desk a proposed contract to write a novel for Doubleday.

I was titillated by the entrepreneurial initiative of my friend Sam, but it happened that that very day, the newspapers carried the story of William Safire. He had turned in, to Morrow, his volume on Richard Nixon, for which an advance commitment had been made to pay him $250,000. What the news story told us was that William Morrow had rejected his manuscript on the grounds that it was not "satisfactory."

Now what everybody who knows anything knew, indeed knows, is that Bill Safire does not submit "unsatisfactory" manuscripts. What was "unsatisfactory," in the summer of 1975, was Richard Nixon. He had a year before left office, the first American President to be run out of town so to speak with wet towels. The publishing company was taking an unseemly advantage of that little phrase in the publisher's contract that specifies that the writer's manuscript has to be "satisfactory" and that the publisher is the sole judge of whether that criterion has been met.

Accordingly I wrote to Sam Vaughan and said, Well sure, I'll try to write a novel, but how about this: You pay me up front one third of the advance and I write one hundred pages. I send these to you, and you then say after reading them: "Go ahead"—in which case you are committed to paying me the balance of the advance. Or else you say, "It was a fun idea, but kindly abort immediately"—in which case I'll have become an ex-novelist before ever becoming a novelist. . . . As it turned out, it was all very good news. *Saving the Queen* appeared on the best-seller list one week before its official publication date, and stayed there for thirteen weeks.

What was the novel about? Well, it featured one Blackford Oakes.

I am occasionally asked about the genesis of Blackford Oakes, the protagonist of my novels.

He was a kind of distillate. I arrived in Switzerland with only a single idea in mind, and that idea was to commit literary iconoclasm: I would write a book in which the good guys and the bad guys were actually distinguishable from one another. I took a deep breath and further resolved that the good guys would be—the Americans!

I had recently seen a movie called *Three Days of the Condor.* Perhaps you will remember that Robert Redford, a CIA agent of Restless Intelligence, working in a CIA front in New York City called the American Literary Historical Society, goes out one day to buy a hamburger, and returns to the CIA brownstone to find all nine of his colleagues quite dead. Murdered. By pistols firing ice pellets. In due course we discover that the Mr. Big who ordered the killings isn't a robber or a member of the Mafia or of the KGB. He is very high up in the government of the United States. Indeed, if the movie had endured another half hour, by the law of compound interest the viewer would have been satisfied only on discovering that the evil spirit behind the killing of Robert Redford's CIA colleagues was the President of the United States; or, to be really dramatic and reach all the way up to the highest vault in the national pantheon, maybe Ralph Nader.

Thus the movie went, deep in suspense. Mr. Big, who had ordered the mass killings, might have been exposed, finally, as a conventional double agent: posing as an American patriot, but actually a spy working for the Soviet Union. It transpired, however, that the man who ordered the slaughter was a one hundred percent American, period. And there was nothing at all unusual about him in the movie. His decision to eliminate all those nice people at the American Literary Historical Society was entirely routine. He did so because they were about to stumble on a secret, contingent CIA operation—by following a lead turned up by Robert Redford's Restless Intelligence.

So finally, in a dramatic sidewalk confrontation, Mr. Big's deputy—on instructions from Mr. Big—explains to Redford that the unfortunate killings were motivated by high patriotism: they were a necessary safeguard against the discovery of a top secret plan to protect America against a contingent shortage of oil. Stressing the importance of keeping Redford's knowledge secret, the deputy invites Redford to come back into the Agency, no hard feelings, and simply accept the imperatives of real life . . . of an intelligence agent in the modern world.

But Redford, taking off his glasses in anticipation of heady thought, says, "No, *never*. This very day, I have disclosed everything to . . ." The camera slithers up to a marquee above the two men and you see the logo of . . . *The New York Times*. The director of *Three Days of the Condor* neglected only to emblazon on it, "Daniel Ellsberg Slept Here."

The deputy reacts like the witch come in contact with water. He snarls and shivers and slinks away after muttering half-desperately: *"Maybe they won't print it!"* But Redford has by now seeded the audience with his Restless Intelligence, and we all know that *The New York Times will* print it, and thus we shall all be free.

The film's production notes stated, "Over a year ago, Stanley Schneider, Robert Redford, Sidney Pollack, and Dino de Laurentiis decided to create a film that would reflect the climate of America in the aftermath of the Watergate crisis."

"The climate of America" is a pretty broad term. They really meant, "the climate of America" as seen by Jane Fonda, the Institute for Policy Studies, and *The Nation* magazine. One recalls Will Rogers returning, in 1927, from the Soviet Union, where he had witnessed a communal bath at which the bathers were nude.

"Did you see all of Russia?" a reporter asked.

"No," Rogers said, weighing his answer carefully. "But I saw all of parts of Russia."

Redford-Pollack-de Laurentiis had shown us the climate in all of parts of America. It was very cold out there.

And so I thought to attempt to write a book in which it was never left in doubt that the CIA, for all the complaints about its performance, is, when all is said and done, not persuasively likened to the KGB.

I was myself an agent of the CIA, for nine months beginning in 1951 when I left college. I do not confuse my admiration for the mission of the CIA with its overall effectiveness. A few years after leaving the CIA I published [as noted earlier] in *National Review* an editorial paragraph that read, "The attempted assassination of Sukarno in Jakarta last week had all the earmarks of a CIA operation. Everyone in the room was killed except Sukarno."

The point I sought to make, and continued to do so in subsequent novels, is that the CIA, whatever its failures, sought, during those long years in the struggle for the world, to advance the honorable alternative. When I wrote, it wasn't only Robert Redford who was however obliquely traducing the work of our central intelligence agency. He had starred in a movie the point of which was that the CIA is a corrupt and bloody-minded secret instrument of an amoral government, and that it routinely embarks on stratagems that beggar moral justification. Many others were making similar points in every branch of the media: in novels of the recent past, novels by Graham Greene, and John le Carré,* and Len Deighton, for instance. The point, really, was that there wasn't all that much to choose from in a contest between the KGB and the CIA. Both organizations, it was fashionable to believe, were defined by their practices. I said to Johnny Carson, when on his program he raised just that question, that to say that the CIA and the KGB engage in similar practices is the equivalent of saying that the man who pushes an old lady into the path of a hurtling bus is not to be distinguished from the man who pushes an old lady out of the way of a hurtling bus, on the grounds that, after all, in both cases someone is pushing an old lady around.

The novelistic urge of the great ideological egalitarians who wrote books under such titles as *The Ugly American* had been to invest in their Western protagonists appropriately disfiguring personal characteristics. So that the American (or British) spy had become, conglomerately, a

* See review of le Carré in chapter 16, "Passing in Review."

paunchy, alcoholic, late-middle-aged cuckold—moreover, an agent who late at night, well along in booze, ruminates to the effect that, when all is said and done, who really was to judge so indecipherable a question as whether the United States was all that much better than the Soviet Union? The KGB and the CIA really engage in the same kind of thing, and what they do defines them, not why they do it, right?

When I sat down, a yellow sheet of paper in my typewriter, to begin writing that first novel, it suddenly occurred to me that it would need a protagonist. By the end of the afternoon I had created Blackford Oakes, the principal character in *Saving the Queen.*

A year later, the editor of *Vogue* magazine wrote to me to say that many reviewers had denominated Blackford Oakes as being "quintessentially" American. She invited me to explain, explicitly, what was the "American look." I thought to reject the invitation, because I resist the very notion of quintessentiality, as here invoked. It seems to me an image that runs into its inherent incredibility. You will remember that F. P. Adams once said that the average American is a little above average.

The reason you cannot have the quintessential American is the very same reason you cannot have a quintessential apple pie, or indeed a quintessential anything that is composed of so many ingredients. In all composites there has got to be an arrangement of attributes, and no such arrangement can project one quality to the point of distorting others. This is true even in the matter of physical beauty. An absolutely perfect nose has the effect of satellizing the other features of a human face; a beautiful face is a comprehensive achievement.

So anyway, Blackford Oakes is not the quintessential American, but I fancy he is *distinctively* American, and the first feature of the distinctively American male is, I think, spontaneity, a freshness of sorts born of curiosity and enterprise and native wit.

Would you believe that three days after meeting her, Blackford Oakes was in bed with the queen of England? (Not, I hasten to elucidate, the incumbent queen. Blackford Oakes, as the distinctive American, is a young man of taste, who sleeps only with fictitious queens, thereby avoiding international incidents.) There was something yes, distinctively, wonderfully American, it struck me, about bedding down a British queen: a kind of arrant yet lovable presumption. But always on the understanding that it be done decorously, and that there was no aftertaste of the gigolo in the encounter. Moreover, in my novel the queen was the seducer, Blackford the seduced.

I remember with some trepidation—even now, almost twenty years later—the day that my novel came out in London. The first questioner at the televised exchange was, no less, the editor of *The Economist,* Andrew

Knight, and he asked me a question I thought quite un-English in its lack of circumspection: "Mr. Buckley, would you like to sleep with the queen?"

Now such a question poses quite awful responsibilities. Just to begin with, I am a married man. And then, there being a most conspicuous incumbent queen, one could hardly wrinkle up one's nose as if the question evoked the vision of an evening with Queen Victoria on her diamond jubilee. The American with taste has to guard against any lack of gallantry, so that the first order of business became the assertion of an emancipating perspective, which would escort Queen Elizabeth II gently out of the room, lest she be embarrassed. This I hoped to accomplish by saying, just a little sleepily, as Blackford Oakes might have done, "*Which* queen?"— and then quickly, before the interrogator could lug his incumbent monarch back into the smoker—"Judging from historical experience, I would need to consult my lawyer before risking an affair with *any* British queen."

The American male must be tactful, and tact is most generally accomplished by changing the subject without its appearing that you have done so as a rebuke. It worked, and another aspect of my novel came before the house, the character of Blackford Oakes.

He appears on the scene at age twenty-two, a veteran of the war. So I stuck him in Yale, which gave me the advantage of being able to write about a familiar few acres. It has been observed by several critics that Blackford Oakes emerged with characteristics associated, in the literature, with Yale men.

Like what?

Principally, I suppose, self-confidence; a certain worldliness that is neither bookish nor in any sense of the word anti-intellectual. Blackford Oakes is an engineer by training, the kind of engineer who learns how to build bridges, and his nonroyal girlfriend is studying for her Ph.D. and doing her doctorate on Jane Austen. *She* is not expected to dwell in conversation on her own specialty, let alone show any curiosity about how to build bridges. The American look wears quite offhandedly its special proficiencies: If one is a lawyer, one does not go about talking like Oliver Wendell Holmes, any more than Charles Lindbergh went about sounding like Charles Lindbergh. Though Blackford quite rightly shows a qualified, if not extensive, curiosity about Jane Austen, and probably has read (actually, reread: one never reads Jane Austen, one only *rereads* her) *Pride and Prejudice,* and his girlfriend has no objection to the profession of engineering.

Now Blackford Oakes is physically handsome, in a sense a metaphor for his ideals. Here I took something of a chance. I decided not only to make him routinely good looking, but to make him startlingly so. I don't mean startling in the sense that, let us say, Elizabeth Taylor is startlingly beautiful. It is hard to imagine a male counterpart for what we understand as pulchritude. An extremely handsome man is not the *equivalent* of an extremely beautiful woman, he is her complement, and that is very important to bear in mind in probing the American look—which is not, for example, the same thing as the Italian look. When Schopenhauer exclaimed that a sixteen-year-old girl is the "smash triumph of nature," he made a cosmic statement that could only have been made about the female sex.

So that when I decided that Blackford Oakes should be startlingly handsome, it was required that he be that in a distinctively American way, and what does *that* mean? Well it doesn't mean you look like Mickey Rooney, obviously. But it doesn't mean you have to look like Tyrone Power, either. I think the startlingly handsome American male is not made so by the regularity of his features, however necessary that regularity may be, but by the special quality of his expression. It has to be for this reason that, flipping past the male models exhibited in the advertising sections of the local newspaper or of *Esquire* magazine, one seldom finds oneself pausing to think: That man is startlingly handsome. But such an impression *is* taken away, from time to time, from a personal encounter, or even from a candid photograph. Because the American look, in the startlingly handsome man, requires animation, but tempered by a certain shyness; a reserve.

I thought of Billy Budd. I have long since forgotten just how Melville actually described him, but Melville communicated that Billy Budd was startlingly handsome. But looks aside, his distinctiveness was not that of Blackford Oakes. Billy Budd is practically an eponym for innocence, purity. Oakes, though far removed from jadedness, is worldly. And then, and then . . .

Billy Budd, alas, is humorless. Correction: not *alas*. "Do not go about as a demagogue, urging a triangle to break out of the prison of its three sides," G. K. Chesterton warned us, "because if you succeed, its life will come to a lamentable end." Give Billy Budd a sense of humor and he shatters in front of you into thousands of little pieces, which you can never reconstruct. Blackford Oakes doesn't go about like Wilfrid Sheed's protagonist in *Transatlantic Blues,* or John Gregory Dunne's in *True Confessions,* being hilariously mordant. The American look here is a leavened sarcasm. But careful, now: Escalate sarcasm and you break through the clouds into the ice-cold of nihilism. The American must *believe.* However discreetly or understatedly. Blackford Oakes believed. He tended to divulge his beliefs in a kind of slouchy, oblique way. But at the margin he was, well—an American, with Judeo-Christian predilections; and he knew, as with the clothes he wore so casually, that he was snug as such; that, like his easygoing sweater and trousers, they—fitted him. As did the ideals, and even most of the practices, of his country.

I remember with delight reading a review of that first novel, published in *The Kansas City Star,* written by a professor of English from the University of Missouri, I think it was. I had never heard of the gentleman, but he made it quite clear that he had spent a considerable part of his adult life abominating me and my works and my opinions. He was manifestly distressed at not quite disliking my first novel, which he proceeded to describe. He salved his conscience by concluding, "The hero of *Saving the Queen,* Mr. Blackford Oakes, is tall, handsome, witty, agreeable, compassionate and likable, from which at least we can take comfort in knowing that the book is not autobiographical."

There arose, as a practical matter, the responsibility of recreating in fiction men who have been very much alive in recent history, and investing in them conspicuous attributes for which they were well known.

Consider, for instance, the proud, patrician, sarcastic Dean Acheson, Secretary of State under Harry Truman. He is an adamant critic of the Republican Party, the party of his old friend Allen Dulles, the Director of the Central Intelligence Agency who, one afternoon in 1953, soon after Truman was replaced by President Eisenhower, comes to call on him to confer about a looming crisis in West Germany:

> Allen Dulles had missed the day-to-day analysis of international events—mordant, clairvoyant—of this infuriating man, with whom he had been officially associated, until the last election, in the administration of President Truman. Now Mr. Acheson had just published a book, called *A Democrat Looks at His Party,* in which he had calmly announced that the principal distinction between a Republican and a Democrat is that Democrats tend to be bright, and Republicans tend to be stupid.
>
> "It's just that easy," he now teased his guest while tea was being poured. "You mustn't be offended by this, Allen. Besides, you must find it consoling that your people will stay in power a good long time."

There was a special tone of mock resignation in Acheson's observation.

> "In some discursive reading the other day I found interesting corroboration for this thesis. It is from a speech by John Stuart Mill delivered, I believe, in the British parliament."

With his left hand, Acheson extends his teacup to the maid who refilled it as he adjusted his glasses with his right hand.

"Mill said"—Acheson reads now from a book—" 'I never meant to say that the Conservatives are generally stupid. I meant to say that stupid people are generally Conservative. I believe that is so obviously and universally admitted a principle' "—the Secretary raised his eyebrows in tribute to the majesty of First Principles—" 'that I hardly think any gentleman will deny it. Suppose any party, in addition to whatever share it may possess of the ability of the community, had nearly the whole of its stupidity, that party must'—take heart, Allen—'by the laws of its constitution be the stupidest party; and I do not see why honorable gentlemen should see that position as at all offensive to them, for it ensures their being always an extremely powerful party.' " Dean Acheson smiled with great satisfaction, and looked up again, as if to acknowledge, reverently, yet another providential insight.

Here, then, was an attempt to recreate theoretically, if you like, a dominant impulse in a dominating American character of the fifties. I would write a dozen such vignettes in the novels that lay ahead. I needed, for instance, to cope with John Fitzgerald Kennedy. How to do so? I elected the device of the soliloquy. Talking to himself. He is all alone in the Oval Office, at the end of a day, a few minutes before he is summoned upstairs to prepare for a state dinner. Listen. . . .

I've got just one hour before I need to go upstairs to dress for the state dinner for what's-his-name, the little hypocrite. Allen Dulles told me he's stolen maybe forty, maybe fifty million bucks, and he is always poor-mouthing about his people. Damn right they're poor. He stays in power another ten years, what's-his-name (I must make it a serious point to get his name straight before the state dinner—why aren't they all called Gonzalez? I mean, most of them are as it is)—ten more years and his "people" will have nothing at all left.

Ah, but if only the worst problems were Latin American. Latin America. Chiquita Banana, da-da-da da-da. How does it go?

. . . But I'm putting off what I need to concentrate on. More hard thought on Khrushchev, the bastard, and Berlin. I can't remember whether Dad told me that all Communist chiefs of state, like all American businessmen, were s.o.b.'s. Maybe he thought I'd simply take that for granted.

Two weeks from now I'll have met with Khrushchev . . . Is it possible to count the number of hours I've spent studying Khrushchev? With Dean Acheson, for instance? Good old Dean, he wants just one little world war before he dies . . . What do they say about Khrushchev? Pretty much the same thing. I've studied the minutes of: God! Geneva summit, 1955. Camp David summit, 1959. And Paris summit, 1960. Khrushchev aborted the damned thing on account of our U-2 flight! That was vintage Khrushchev, right? Complaining about espionage! Especially the press conference he gave when he stopped over in Vienna. Said maybe Ike was just a little cuckoo . . .

Brings up an interesting point. One of the things I have to ask myself is: How far do I let him go? I mean, if he starts to scream and yell, what do I do in the cause of Peace with Honor? God, I wish that phrase had never been coined. Fact is, you don't often get both at the same time.

Okay, so what's he up to? Seriously, what is he up to? Jack old boy, I mean, Mr. President old boy, let's start that at the other end. What's he *not* up to?

Well, he's not up to beginning a nuclear war. Among other things, Poppa Marx wouldn't like that. A nuclear war with maybe only Patagonians left over isn't going to do much to validate the Marxist theory of class struggle. Okay, at what point do we start dropping nuclear bombs? A hell of a question to ask, but I'm the one who's going to decide.

Khrushchev is sort of unique, they all say. But so are all Soviet chiefs of state. That's the way they talk, the way they behave.

Well by God, that's not the way they're going to talk to me! Screw summit conferences.

No, that's the wrong word. Don't want to say anything unfriendly about screwing.

To hell with summit conferences.

If Khrushchev is just being Khrushchev, then the boys have got to weigh whether just being Khrushchev is the best way to advance their cause. And the only means they have to measure that is me. How do I react? That's the question. How does John Fitzgerald Kennedy, President of the United States, maximum leader of the imperialist powers, react? And what will I come up with, in my search for something we can give them, that we can do without?

The special telephone on his desk rang, to which, at the other end, only one person had access.

"I'm coming, dear."

. . . The second book confronted a dilemma. What to do about the inspiring young West German nobleman who in 1953 was emerging as the probable victor of impending national elections on a platform of reuniting Germany at any cost? Stalin had communicated to Eisenhower: Get rid of that man, or—prepare for a Russian invasion of Germany.

What to do?

Stained Glass, I happily recall, went on to win the American Book Award as the best mystery story of the year. I like to think it was not the narrative suspense that overwhelmed the judges. What the book did was to pose the central question of counterintelligence and espionage as conducted by a free society.

The decision had finally been reached, in Washington, to accede to the demands of the Kremlin and to assassinate my fictional West German, Count Axel Wintergrin, whose startling rise to power threatened a world war.

And so the execution—rigged as an electrical accident, at the count's old Gothic castle—was arranged. Blackford Oakes supervised the plan (even though, at the end, he refused to take a personal hand in its consummation). And so the gallant and idealistic young German politician, who might seriously have challenged the Russian hegemony, was dead. And a devoted legend about him was born, so that every year, around the reconstructed thirteenth-century family chapel, larger and larger crowds gathered to commemorate the anniversary of his death. On the tenth anniversary, Blackford Oakes, the count's executioner, was discreetly present in the chapel and he spotted, traveling incognito, the man who, by coded telegraph ten years ago, had given him that awful, terminal command to proceed with the execution: It was retired CIA chief Allen Dulles.

By now—ten years later—it was retrospectively clear that Stalin would not have reacted to a political victory by Wintergrin by moving into Europe. So that the execution, in hindsight, had been a most gruesome mistake strategically, its moral hideousness quite apart.

Walking back to his car in the parking lot, after the memorial services, Blackford Oakes espied the man, the head of the agency for which he worked, but a man he had never laid eyes on before today. Inflamed by the memories evoked during the ceremony mourning the young man he had put to death, Oakes suddenly—impulsively—approaches the car of Allen Dulles. The text reads . . .

He waited until the old man had unlocked the door at the driver's side and entered. He knocked on the window opposite. Surprised, but without hesitation the old man reached over and tripped open the door handle. Blackford opened the door, got in, and closed it. Sitting with his hands on the steering wheel, Dulles turned his head. Blackford did not extend his hand. He said simply,

"I am Blackford Oakes."

"I see." Allen Dulles did not go through the formality of introducing himself.

There was a pause.

"Well, Mr. Dulles, did we do the right thing in 1952?"

"Mr. Oakes, the question you asked, I do not permit myself to explore, not under any circumstances."

"Why not?"

"Because in this world, if you let them, the ambiguists will kill you."

"The ambiguists, as you call them, were dead right about Count Wintergrin."

"You are asking me to break my rule."

Blackford replied: "Excuse me, sir, but is your goddamn rule more important than Wintergrin and his cause?"

"Actually," said Dulles, "it is. Or, if you prefer, put it this way, Oakes: I have no alternative than to believe it is more important. And I hope you will understand, because if you do it will be easier. If you do not, you are still too inexperienced to discuss these matters with me."

"I don't want it to be easier for me." Oakes turned now to look directly at the man whose will had governed Blackford's own for ten years. He found himself raising his voice, something he never did. "Wintergrin was the great hope for the West. The great opportunity. The incarnation of western idealism. You made me . . ."

He stopped. Already ashamed of a formulation that stripped him of his manhood. Nobody had forced Blackford to lead Axel Wintergrin to the execution chamber.

He changed, as quickly as possible, the arrangement of his thought. "You lost a great chance."

Dulles was now aroused. He lit his pipe with jagged movements of his hands.

"I believe you are right. I believe Wintergrin was right. The Russians, I believe, would not in fact have moved. But do you want to know something I don't believe?" His voice was strained.

Blackford was silent.

"I don't believe the lesson to draw is that we must not act because, in acting, we may prove to be wrong. And I know"—his eyes turned to meet Blackford's—"that you know that Axel Wintergrin thought so too."

There was nothing more to say. Impulsively, Blackford extended his hand, and Dulles took it.

When I finished that book, and before I had given it a title, I wrote to an old friend—we had met in 1954—to say, "Henry, I have written a book, the narrative of which is set forth in the accompanying blurb written by the publisher. I should like to dedicate it to you, and perhaps to call the book *Détente*. But I would not want to do this if it would cause you any embarrassment."

Henry Kissinger wrote back, "Dear Bill: Many thanks, but I think the book, which I look forward to reading, would best be inscribed to someone else while I am Secretary of State. If you wish to dedicate your next novel to me, I would be very grateful. Provided it isn't on the subject of Cyprus."

Well, Blackford Oakes has not visited Cyprus. After his terrible mission in Germany he was in Paris, in *Who's On First,* where he faced a moral dilemma that got him fired.

He was next seen (*Marco Polo, If You Can*) in the Lubyanka Prison in Moscow, condemned to death after his U-2 plane was shot down over southwest Asia, a constituent episode in a great master plot designed to accelerate crystallizing differences between Khrushchev's Soviet Union and Mao's China.

He went then, in *The Story of Henri Tod,* to Berlin, where he immobilized himself, rather than abort a patriotic attempt by West German patriots to frustrate the Soviet creation of the Berlin Wall.

In *See You Later Alligator,* Blackford Oakes was in Cuba, negotiating, at the direction of President Kennedy, with Che Guevera a possible détente. At one point in the story he declines to obey abrupt orders from Washington to abort his mission and return home.

In *High Jinx* he was in London, on assignment to penetrate the leak of highly secret documents which foretold the slaughter of the men sent out to liberate Albania.

In *Mongoose, R.I.P.,* we learned that the Russians, retreating from Cuba after the missile crisis, had left one missile secretly in place, programmed to land in Dallas. Fidel Castro had planned for the missile to be fired at Dallas—on November 22, 1963, when President Kennedy would be there.

In *Tucker's Last Stand,* the protagonist—yes, an American intelligence officer—turns over our critical plans on how to block the Ho Chi Minh trail to his girlfriend, even after he learns that she is an agent, working for the enemy. Blackford Oakes finds himself powerless to intervene.

And in *A Very Private Plot,* Blackford Oakes has to report to President Reagan that there is an entirely native plot afoot in Moscow to assassinate Gorbachev. And how does Reagan react? With excruciating difficulty.

In the first novel I guess it is correct to say that I intuitively got the idea that the novel should frame a single person (primarily). That person's character and experiences should illuminate the story. In *Saving the Queen* it was Blackford himself, at school in England, developing a character and a knowledge of Britain and its institutions that he would come to lean on only six years later.

In *Stained Glass* I sought to portray a young, aristocratic German idealist, to tell what he did when Hitler took Germany to war, how he comported himself during the war years and immediately after, as the dream consolidated in his mind: that his mission would be to deliver his country from the post-Hitler tyranny.

In *Who's On First* I felt the need to convey something of the feeling of life in Gulag. I had read Solzhenitsyn and sought to explore what life was like for two dissenting scientists during the last few years of Stalin, and what it was like to emerge from Gulag and confront the challenge of servitude to the new Soviet masters.

In *The Story of Henri Tod* I focused on a young Jewish boy, in hiding with his family from Hitler, spirited away to Great Britain, cut off from a younger sister with whom he had been inseparable, and the hardening of a resolve, like that of the aristocratic young count in *Stained Glass,* to lift the iron curtain that divided Berlin.

In the two Cuban-set novels I focused on a young Spaniard, lured to the Communists after the civil war. He was the object of a quixotic effort to rob a bank which resulted in years of imprisonment, followed by a devoted apprenticeship to the Party—which dispatched him to Mexico to take part in the assassination of Leon Trotsky. He found himself a party to the (historically correct) assassination of Soviet ambassador Oumansky—and his own wife.

And *A Very Private Plot* gives us a portrait of a young Ukrainian growing up under the Communist lash, a prodigy at school, sent to the Afghanistan front where, viewing the carnage, a slow resolve within him consolidates. He decides, quietly, that he will assassinate Gorbachev.

Some of the portraits lean directly on history. They are the kernel of the ten novels, and are here set down for the first time unencumbered.

Well, the Cold War ended. Blackford Oakes, in a few flash-forward scenes in *Plot,* is seventy years old. The time had come to pack it in. The novels will, it is my judgment, survive, for reasons I leave it to others to indite. The purpose of this volume is to extract from each one of them one portrait, perhaps memorable.

I have taken care to isolate the portraits in this volume so that they stand on their own two legs. No reader need know anything that happened before in that novel or, for that matter, anything that happened subsequently. . . .

I pray that the reader will enjoy even languorously the animations here collected. . . .

Entertainment and distraction are the objective. The educational objective in the novels has been to make the point, so difficult for so many Westerners to comprehend, that counterintelligence and espionage, conducted under Western auspices, weren't exercises in conventional political geometry. They were—they are—a moral art.

Consider one hypothetical dilemma and reason backward, from the particular to the generality. I give you a question and ask that you wrestle with it, confining yourself, if you can, within the maxims of the conventional morality.

Is it wrong to effect the execution of a chief of a state with which you are not at war?

Yes, it is wrong to do so.

Is it wrong to countenance a destructive event of such magnitude as conceivably to trigger a world war?

Yes, it is wrong.

What then do you call it when it appears to rational men that the second injunction cannot be observed save by defying the first?

Scene: Uganda. Colonel Idi Amin has got possession of a nuclear bomb and plans at midnight to dispatch a low-flying plane to drop that bomb on Jerusalem. A CIA agent in the field communicates to Washington that Idi Amin will lie between the crosshairs of the agent's rifle at the airport before the bomber is dispatched. Should he squeeze the trigger?

There are those, and Blackford Oakes was one of them, who would address that morally wrenching point by saying two things: (1) As to the particular question, yes, authorize the agent to shoot, in order to abort the destruction of Jerusalem and all that might then follow. But (2), do not then require as a condition of this decision that laws or rules be set down that embody the distinction. It isn't possible to write such judgments into law, no more than to specify to the artist the exact arrangement of circumstances that call for a daub of Prussian blue or, to the composer, the exact harmonic situation that benefits from rules that admit the striking of an A-augmented eleventh chord.

Blackford Oakes lived in an age when what mattered most was the survival of one of two systems. Us and Them—that was the difference that mattered. The failure by beneficiaries of life in the free world to recognize what it was that we had here, over against what it would have been had our lives been transformed so that we too might live under totalitarianism, amounted to moral and intellectual nihilism. This was far more incriminating of our culture than any transgression against eristic scruples of the kind that preoccupied so many of our moralists who inveighed against the protocols of the CIA and MI-6.

Blackford Oakes had weaknesses spiritual and corporeal. But a basic assumption guided him. It was that the survival of everything we cherish depended on the survival of the culture of liberty; and that this hung on our willingness to defend this extraordinary country of ours, so awfully mixed up so much of the time, so schizophrenic in our understanding of ourselves and our purposes, so crazily indulgent in our legion of wildly ungovernable miscreants. Yet, without ever saying so in so many words, Oakes thought this country the finest bloom of nationhood in all recorded time, worth the risk, which he so often took, of life and limb.

He did all that, but he recognized also that a vital part of America's singularity is its capacity to give pleasure, which it is the primary aim of the Oakes novels to do.

—WFB

The resulting novel sequence was a phenomenon. Blackford Oakes entered the language as a well-known (if not well-understood) character, and almost every one of the novels was a best-seller, until WFB ended the series of novels at ten. The following is a sample of the kind of expanded attention Buckley awards to at least one new major character in each novel.

ERIKA CHADINOFF

The parents of her friends in America would make references to her "privileged" upbringing and now and then would imply, not without admiration, and not without envy, that she had been spoiled. Sometimes over a weekend visit or vacation, Erika's hosts, in the effusive style of the forties, would push Erika forward to exhibit one of her accomplishments, even as they might ask an older brother to show off a card trick. Erika went through the usual stages: she would be shy, she would be recalcitrant, she would use evasive tactics, but after her third year at the Ethel Walker School in Simsbury, Connecticut, she surprised everybody who knew her. Her fat friend Alice begged her after dinner one night to play on the piano excerpts from the first movement of the Grieg A-Minor Concerto, which Erika had played before the entire school at the annual concert only the week before—accompanied by the school piano teacher, who knew very little about music, but that didn't matter because it was recorded and rerecorded that in her youth she had actually studied under Clara Schumann. Erika surprised Alice, and rather dismayed Alice's parents, who went once every summer to the Lewisohn Stadium when Alexander Smallens did *Porgy and Bess* and thought themselves thereby to have acquitted a full year's responsibility to music, by getting up without demurral and proceeding through twenty-two minutes of music, stopping only to sing at the top of her husky voice the parts written by Grieg for the missing orchestra.

"You certainly are a privileged young girl," Alice's mother said admiringly while the father, fearful that his daughter would suggest that Erika play an encore—had Grieg written another concerto? he worried . . . everyone knew that Mozart had written over, was it four hundred concertos?—clapped loudly, looked at his watch, and said as a treat he would drive them all to the late movie with Bob Hope and Bing Crosby off and away on the Road to Morocco. The girls went happily to get their coats and Erika had time in the car to muse over her privileged upbringing, in

Germany and England, before coming to the United States three years before at age thirteen.

Of course, being the daughter of Dimitri and Anna Chadinoff *was* a privilege, this she did not deny, though she wondered—she truly wondered—what her parents would have done about her if she had not been . . . clever. She had picked up that word in England and thereafter used it—there being no satisfactory American substitute, as she told Alice. Her friends supposed that her early memories of Germany were of intellectuals and artists coming to her parents' elegant apartment to eat stuffed goose and read aloud each other's poems and short stories and argue long into the night the meaning of a fable by Pushkin. What Erika in fact remembered was the awful physical discomforts and the utter indifference of her father to them. She was very young when she learned that something called "money" was terribly important. When her mother looked into her handbag, either there was money in it or there was not money in it. In the former event Erika would eat dinner, in the latter event she would not. Beginning in midafternoon, Erika would find that her attention was substantially given over to the question, Would there be money that night when her mother opened her handbag? Her mother, though not as stoical as her father, was twice as vague. If, on opening her handbag, she had pulled out a diamond necklace, she'd have said, "Dimitri, dear, I apparently have a diamond necklace here I hadn't reckoned on." Dimitri would have said, "That's fine, my dear," which he would also have said if his wife had announced that she had found an armadillo in her handbag.

Her mother did concern herself for Erika, and in the especially cold winter of 1936, washed dishes at the corner restaurant in return for bread and potatoes left over at the end of the evening's meal. Sometimes Erika had her dinner at one in the morning on her mother's return. Sometimes there was food left over from the night before. But sometimes there was no food at all. During these daily struggles her father was always reading or writing. He had access to the public library and spent much of his time there, often taking Erika because that way she could be warm. It was troublesome to do this at first because the guard at the door announced that the library was not a nursery in which to keep little girls. Dimitri Chadinoff asked just when could children be brought into the library, and the answer was: When they are old enough to read. Dimitri turned around, took Erika home, and was with her for three days, interrupted only when Erika could no longer stay awake. On the fourth day, triumphantly, he led her back and was stopped at the same entrance by the same guard. Calmly, Dimitri made his announcement. The guard leaned over from his high desk, put a newspaper into the girl's hands and, pointing to the headline, said: "Read this, little girl." Her face solemn, Erika read, haltingly, but without error: "Roosevelt Sweeps Country/Dems Control Both Houses." She was three years old.

Her father showed no particular pride in his daughter, then or later when, at age seven, she earned a few pennies by drilling two dull teen-age boys, sons of a noble family, in English; or when Anna's friend Valerian Bibikoff, a fellow expatriate from Russia who taught piano and gave lessons to Erika, reported that the girl was singularly talented. Her father was as surprised as if he had been informed that his daughter was remarkable because she had ten fingers. He showed displeasure as rarely as he showed pleasure. When, freshly arrived in England, Erika returned to their flat to say she had made friends at school with the daughter of the Soviet military attaché, Dimitri looked down at her from his desk and told her that he would just as soon she did not associate with the children of barbarians.

"Why are they barbarians?" Erika asked in French, that being the only language spoken at the Chadinoff household on Thursdays (Monday, German; Tuesday, English; Wednesday, Italian; Thursday, French; Friday, Saturday, and Sunday any language save the language spoken in the country being inhabited).

"They are barbarians," said Dimitri Chadinoff, "because they wish to obliterate everything important that human beings have learned about how to treat each other in three thousand years."

"Why do they want to obliterate it?"—Erika had no difficulty with unusual words. Her problem, at school, was in learning that some words *were* unusual: she had to study them attentively and learn to use them with great discretion, or preferably not at all, since at home they were used as nonchalantly as kitchen utensils. She got off to a bad start her first day at Blessed Sir Thomas More's School in Cadogan Square by asking a girl whether the policies of the school were "latitudinarian." It was years before she could explain to anyone—the solemn Paul, at the Sorbonne—that she had been guilty of affectation throughout much of her youth only by searching out simple substitute words for those that occurred to her naturally.

"They want to obliterate it," said her father, "because they are bewitched by the secular superstition of communism, which is a huge enterprise that will settle for nothing less than bringing misery to all the people of the world."

"Why should they want to bring misery to all the people of the world?" Erika repeated her father's formulation piously.

"It isn't that they want to bring misery, though some do. They strut up and down in their baggy clothes swinging golden chains from their vests as if the keys to happiness were attached. All they have succeeded in doing is killing and torturing people and promising to do as much to people fortunate enough not to live in Russia during this period. To think that they have done it to Russia, the most beautiful land in the world," said Dimitri Chadinoff, and Anna agreed, recalling how the weather would be now in their native hills outside St. Petersburg.

"Did they take away all your money?" Erika wanted to know.

"Yes, they took away all our money."

Such an indifference as Dimitri Chadinoff's to money had not been seen since the natives begged St. Francis to accept a copper if only to have the pleasure of giving it away. But he did not deign to express from where, in the hierarchy of Soviet offenses, the loss of the family money had come. *Infra dignitate.* Erika, a thoughtful girl, assumed that her father was correct but promised herself one day to think the matter over more exhaustively, and turned to her homework in mathematics, which she was always pleased to express her concern with because she knew it was the single subject in which neither her father nor her mother could help her.

"What exactly is an integer? I don't understand."

"Ask your teacher. He's getting well paid," said her father.

Well, not so well paid by modern standards, but the school was well staffed and now Dimitri was making five pounds per week translating for a London publisher on a piecemeal basis, and that same publisher had sent out Chadinoff's fresh translation of Pushkin to be assessed by scholars at Oxford and Cambridge. "I could advise you," Chadinoff wrote to his editor, "which of the scholars at Cambridge and Oxford are competent to evaluate my work, but I suppose that if you agreed to accept my judgment in the matter the entire enterprise would be circular. Anyway, for the record the only man at either university who has the necessary background is Adam Sokolin at Cambridge. He studied under my old tutor, who beat some sense into him thirty years ago. Sokolin has done good work on Pushkin, from which we may safely conclude that he will not get very far in Cambridge." The editor took the letter by the corner, his fingers raised as if carrying a dead rat by the tail, walked into the office of his superior, dropped it on his desk and asked: "Have I your permission to tell this egomaniac to go and peddle his Pushkin elsewhere?"

The next day, manuscript back in hand, Chadinoff sent it to the Harvard University Press. The following day, the London publisher dropped him as a part-time editor and then, after Erika had gone to sleep, Anna took Dimitri aside and, even though it was Tuesday, spoke to him in Russian and said that they had to do something to bring in some money, that all their friends and relatives were equally impoverished, that there was no money for the next week's rent, nor for the next month's school bills for Erika.

Well, said Dimitri—ever so slightly disposed to point out, by twiddling his fingers on the open page of his book, that Anna had interrupted his reading—did she have any suggestions?

Yes, she said, she had recently been talking to her friend Selnikov (former colonel in the Czar's prime equestrian unit). Poor Sergei Babevich had not only himself and his wife to look after but three daughters and a son. He had taken a position as a maître d'hôtel at a medium-priced restaurant where a knowledge of several languages was useful. "The trouble with you, dear Dimitri, is that your knowledge of food is really not very refined. You could write a scholarly book about the feasts of Lucullus, but you would not be able to distinguish the actual food from fish and chips at Lyons. So I have another idea."

Dimitri had sat without any show of emotion thus far. "Well?"

Anna couldn't, at first, remember what her other idea was, and Dimitri waited. Finally the newspaper caught her eye.

"Ah yes. There is an advertisement in the paper for a concierge. He must be presentable—here." She reached for the paper, shuffling through to the marked section. "Presentable, must be fluent in French and German. Some Italian and Spanish desirable. References."

Dimitri took the job. His hours were from one until midnight. He would sleep until six and then resume his own work. Erika was not permitted to see her father at the hotel during working hours. Once she decided mischievously to do so. She was small for twelve years, so that her head only just reached the counter. She had on a friend's hat, and her light-brown hair was knotted under it. She put on spectacles and, carrying a handbag, she said in a little girl's voice, imitating her father's own imperious accent and speaking in German: "Concierge, please get me a sleeper to the Finland Station!" Dimitri permitted himself a smile, and then in Russian said to her: "Get yourself out of here, Rikushka, before I invite the manager to paddle your behind." She went out roaring, and told her mother, who laughed, and then said not, ever, to do such a thing again. The following morning, when she went off to school, she found tucked into her notebook, in her father's unmistakable hand, a fable dedicated to her. It was called "The Little Girl Who Took the Train to the Finland Station, and Woke Up Lenin." That day, she thought, she was closer to her father than she had ever been before.

When the letter came from the Harvard University Press, Chadinoff was pleased, but not particularly surprised. He knew his Pushkin was superior. But he was surprised a month later to be invited by the Department of Slavic and Romance Languages to go to Harvard to lecture during the spring term. Chadinoff replied that, thanks very much, he would be happy to do so, and able to do so inasmuch as his job as concierge at the

Basil Street Hotel required him to give only three weeks' notice, and February was still three months away.

They made reservations for the tenth of December on the S.S. *Mount Vernon,* and it was well that they did, because after the seventh of December, which was the day of Pearl Harbor, no reservations were accepted save for returning residents of the United States. Chadinoff and his family carried Nansen passports, and his excited wife and daughter were apprehensive, up until the moment the gangplank was lifted, about having to yield their room to returning U.S. residents.

During the commotion Erika, snugly dressed in a white skirt, peasant blouse, and tweed jacket, excitedly accosted a tall, handsome blond boy—at least two years older, she judged—wearing an English public-school blazer, chewing an apple, and affecting the ways of the cosmopolitan traveler.

"Do you think we will pull out on time?" she began the conversation.

"Oh, sure," he said. She was surprised his accent was American. "They always pull out on time. Especially when there are submarines."

"Why should a ship be punctual for the sake of the submarines?"

Blackford Oakes looked at her pert face, and frank, inquisitive eyes accented by her austerely coiled braids. "Because"—he spoke just a little less casually than before—"there are escort vessels, and it is quite a muddle if every boat decides for itself when to start out."

She did not answer, but looked at her lumpy watch. She would wait—for what, later at Smith College, the philosophy professor would tell her is called "empirical verification." And, in fact, at exactly one forty-five in the afternoon the gangplank was pulled, the whistles and horns blew, the crowd at the pier interrupted its waving and yelling, and her parents rejoined her. Before skipping off she turned to the boy, munching a fresh apple and looking very self-satisfied.

"You were right."

He smiled—it was a splendid smile, warm, animated. He reached into the brown paper bag and said, "Here, have an apple." She looked up at her mother, who nodded her head, so she took it and said, "Thank you," and then with her free hand grabbed her straw hat, which almost blew away as the great steamship slid out of the lee of the quay.

By the time Erika was sixteen her father was well known in the academic world and now held down a chair at Brown University, delivering learned, acidulous, witty lectures that would become famous. There was now money enough to pay the tuitions at the Ethel Walker School and, later, Smith College, and in her senior year her father gave her a secondhand car which Erika rejoiced in, traveling about New England tirelessly, to celebrate the end of gas rationing. She took on every challenge, competing for the classics prize, the philosophy prize, winning one, placing second in the other. In her junior year the dean had called her in to ask whether she would consider *not* competing for the Russian, German, French, and Italian prizes. She had won them all in her freshman and sophomore years, and now the teachers were finding it hard to persuade anyone to compete against so certain a winner. Erika said she would have to consult with her father, whose instructions to her had been to enter every competition. He wrote back and told his daughter that, noblesse oblige, she should allow other girls a chance at the prizes, but if she wanted to compete for the big Prix Giscard she might focus her energies on winning it. This prize went annually to four girls selected from applicants throughout the country to study in Paris, all expenses paid, and its renewal, now that the war was over, had recently been advertised.

Erika competed and won without much difficulty, and without causing resentment. Though serious by nature, she could participate in gaiety and do so convincingly. Her friends now accepted matter-of-factly her prolix virtuosity and had long since ceased to think anything about it. She was like the boy or girl at graduation whose name recurs and recurs and who has to walk up to the headmaster fifteen times before he is done collecting the silver: Best Athlete, Best Student Leader, Best Scholar—Best Prig, often as not. But Erika got on well with her friends, all of whom assumed that she would either go on to become a professor of almost anything, or else that a very gallant and very rich man, desiring a beautiful girl of exotic manner and prodigious attainments, would take her off and make her duchess of something where she would preside over salons for a couple of generations of Princes of Wales. At home the night before leaving, in the comfortable house in Providence exploding with books and order, she actually managed to catch her mother's and father's attention at dinner by saying, "Are you glad we won the war, Father?"

Chadinoff, dressed in his velvet smoking jacket, finished chewing what he had in his mouth.

"I am glad we won. I am sorry *they* won. I am sorry that they now occupy Eastern Europe. I predict they will still occupy Eastern Europe one, maybe two years from now."

Erika remembered the night her father so greatly embarrassed her during her last year at Ethel Walker, before two friends spending the weekend in Providence. It was the critical weekend when at first Stalingrad was reported captured by the Germans, and then the Russians were reported holding out. As the radio reports came in the girls cheered on all the news of Russian advances and hissed all the news of German advances. It soon became uncomfortably clear that their host, Professor Dimitri Chadinoff, was unmistakably cheering the other side. Alice, who was well known for her ingenuous candor, looked up during the late morning and said, "Professor Chadinoff, are you pro-Nazi?"

"No, Alice," said Chadinoff. "Permit me, are you pro-Communist?"

"Why, no," said Alice.

"Very well, then?" Chadinoff's eyebrows lifted, and he was evidently prepared to change the subject.

"But we are at war with the Nazis."

"Who is 'We'?" Chadinoff replied.

"Well, Americans . . ." Then she gasped. She hadn't thought about it before. She turned to Erika, hoping for help. But Erika's father was in charge.

"We carry Nansen passports, Alice. They are a kind of diplomatic Man-Without-a-Country passports. We are grateful to the United States for its hospitality and express our gratitude by paying exactly the same taxes we would be paying if we had been born and raised in Topeka, Kansas. We have not taken any oath to support America's foreign policy and, my dear Alice, if truth were told, no one's reputation for intelligence could survive the taking of such an oath."

Alice was a fair student of biology, a little backward in languages, including English, so she thought at least she could charm the famous linguist by trotting up a phrase from her Ethel Walker School French: "Well, Professor, *chacun à son goût.*"

"*Chacun à sa bêtise,*" Professor Chadinoff retorted and returned to his reading.

That afternoon, when her guests were dressing for the Brown-Yale football game, Erika pleaded illness, sending her date off alone to the game. She then turned to her father as she had never done before and, fire in her eyes and a great ball of resentment in her stomach, she blurted out: "I think what you did to Alice was disgusting! Doesn't it matter to you that one million—*one million*—Russians have died in the last two months defending Stalingrad? They can't be as mad as you are at communism for having taken away *their* landed estates!" She flung the door shut, went up to her room, locked the door, and wept. She wept fitfully through the afternoon and her intelligence alerted her, after a while, that her discomposure was deeply rooted. She did not know exactly what was the cause or causes of it, and now, three years later, she still did not know. Characteristically, neither her father nor her mother had ever again alluded to the incident.

This time she said, "Father, do you believe in God?"

"No. But I believe in some of the things attributed to God."

"Like what?"

"Like the Ten Commandments. Most of the Ten Commandments. One or two are arguable, explained by Jewish cultural idiosyncrasies."

"What do you believe in?"

"I believe in the life of the mind, and in human fancy, and in the everlasting struggle against vulgarity."

"What do you mean, you believe in *the struggle against vulgarity*? Does that mean you believe that that struggle is going to happen, or does that mean that you believe that that struggle is worth winning?"

"It is obviously worth winning. But it will never be won. That is why I qualify it by calling it an everlasting struggle."

"The Communists believe more than you do."

"That is certainly correct. So do African witch doctors."

Her mother was following the argument, but was now distracted by something, and she could not remember what it was. She had mistakenly begun the meal by serving the chocolate soufflé because she had found that, by misreckoning, it was done when they sat down, and obviously would not wait, whereas the lamb would.

"As a matter of fact," broke in Anna Chadinoff, her points of reference not immediately clear either to her husband or to her daughter, "lamb will wait very nearly indefinitely."

"What did you say, Anna?"

"I said that lamb would wait very nearly indefinitely."

"Do you mean, like the everlasting struggle?"

"What do you mean by that, dear?"

Chadinoff, knowing when the door was finally closed on any possibility of nexus, pronounced the chocolate soufflé quite excellent, and wondered whether they would now be served kippered herring.

No, Anna said. Now there would be lamb. And Chadinoff then understood. Erika understood. God, if he existed, now understood. Erika thought that, really, her parents were quite splendid, but how wonderful it would be to be gone from them for a while: for a long while, she thought that night.

Erika arrived in Paris in the awful, depressed postwar season three years after the war. She was loaded down with letters from her father and mother commending her to the attentions of their numerous friends in the expatriate world. She began dutifully with the first names on the list: Mr. and Mrs. Valerian Sverdlov. Mme. Sverdlov was a niece of Tolstoy; her husband had commanded a czarist cavalry regiment; both had known Erika's parents since childhood and both greeted her warmly once communication was effected.

This proved difficult because although Erika rang the telephone number her father had given her and, after a few days during which there was never an answer, checked it against the telephone book to find it correct, *still* there was no answer. So she sent a letter and got back a prompt invitation to come to tea, which the following day she did. Mr. Sverdlov, quite bald, with a mustache, bad teeth, pink cheeks and twinkling eyes, was always laughing, and he rejoiced at seeing his beloved Chadinoff's daughter, rejoiced at being able to speak in Russian to her, and several times emptied his glass of vodka to celebrate the general celebration. His wife, though more reserved, was also warm. She worked as a tutor in Russian and found now in the postwar world a considerably increased demand for her services. Beginning the following week, Valerian would return to his job as driver of an American Express tourist bus. Erika was faintly surprised to learn this, but then reminded herself that, until a few years ago, her father worked as a concierge and her mother as a dishwasher.

When she alluded to the difficulty in getting through to the Sverdlovs on the telephone, he laughed and laughed and said several times that the French were the *silliest* people in the *whole* world. You see—he adopted a conspiratorial voice—I was a *collaborator*! Yes! I worked for the Germans! One day I traveled with the German Army as far as St. Petersburg. Not *into* St. Petersburg, but as *far* as St. Petersburg—and there—he stood theatrically, and waved his arm forward, "there from the hilltop I could see— my house. My father's house. My grandfather's house. Where your father played with me when we were boys."

But, he said, that was as far as they had got. Russian resistance proved effective and the retreat began. He returned to Paris and resumed his clerical work as translator of Russian war documents and radio communications—it was understood he would work only against the Soviets.

"Now," he said with delight to Erika, who struggled to conceal her chagrin at her father's friend's collaborationist activity but little by little was caught up by his ebullience—"now," he said, "the French know that I was a collaborator. And *they* know that *I* know that *they* know that I was a collaborator. But!"—he stood again and howled with glee, his mustache high over his white, crooked teeth, his wispy hair tousled, cheeks pink with mirth and stimulation—"they cannot prove it. And the reason they cannot prove it is that before the Germans left, I said to Colonel Strassbourg: 'My dear Colonel, you can have very little use for my file in Berlin, so be a good chicken and let me have it.' And he did, and I burned it, right there"—he pointed to the shabby little fireplace with the four pieces of coal warming, or trying to warm, the whole apartment.

"So what do these silly Frenchmen do? They take away my telephone! They do not tell me: 'Mr. Sverdlov, you are a traitor, and we cannot send you to jail, and we cannot send you to the firing squad, so we are going to take away your telephone.' No. They just disconnect it. Everything else is the same. And when I ask about it they just shrug their shoulders and say I must wait!" He laughed at this trivialization of treason, although of course he too, Erika knew, would have used the same arguments her father used about the Nansen passport, so she did not catechize him. She enjoyed him most unabashedly, and he offered to take her the next Monday to Chartres; and, on the bus, where he wore a chauffeur's cap without any apparent self-consciousness, he buoyantly situated her in the seat directly across from him and they chatted as he drove.

When, like her parents, he had run out of money, he had applied to American Express for a job as a bus driver, stressing his knowledge of French (perfect), German (excellent), English (shaky), and then he qualified his application by saying he would be interested in only a single route: to Chartres. His employer was puzzled until Sverdlov explained that the cathedral at Chartres was the most beautiful sight in the world, more beautiful even than any sight in Russia, and if he was destined to drive a bus every day he might as well drive it to the most beautiful sight in the world.

"Why not?" he exclaimed, his whole face and shoulders rising in interrogation. When after a month the dispatcher told him that that day he would have to drive the bus to the cathedral at Rheims, Sverdlov said that under no circumstances would he go to Rheims—the cathedral there, for all its reputation and pretensions, being simply inadequate. American Express tried suggesting that he was, in fact, under no obligation to join the tourists in the cathedral, but Sverdlov was so affronted by the implied mechanization of his role, American Express quickly retreated, undisposed to discipline the driver who was the favorite of the tourists. By now, even after the war's long interruption, his title to Chartres was secure and no one would question it, he said happily. Later, in a whisper, he told Erika that after seeing the cathedral, he would take her to a little Russian delicatessen where they would have some vodka and some cheese and sausage while the other tourists had their regular lunch.

Erika's reaction, on seeing the cathedral, gratified Sverdlov: she found it was everything Henry Adams said it was—in the book she was assigned to read by one of her art professors at Smith—and other things that Henry Adams had failed to say it was. She asked Sverdlov, whom now she was told to call Valerian Babeyevich, whether he had read Adams's book on Mont St. Michel and Chartres, and he replied that he had not, that he did not want to read about the cathedral, only look at it. Erika mused that her father, who would much prefer reading about a cathedral to seeing it, would scarcely approve of Valerian's attitude: and in the course of the afternoon she discovered that Valerian really knew nothing about her father's career except, vaguely, that he had become a success of sorts in America.

"When he writes me letters"—Valerian laughed, as he tipped his fifth jigger glass of vodka down his throat—"he writes about obscure poets or writers he has discovered, and always he forgets to tell me about Anna and his darling and beautiful daughter."

He looked at his watch and said that they must go back to the bus now, the tourists would be assembling as instructed. He insisted to Erika on paying the bill, which proved painless when the old Russian shopkeeper in turn insisted on refusing payment from his old friend, who had brought that day such an "elegant"—he bowed to Erika—"and beautiful daughter of an old friend."

From the American Express bus terminal it was a short walk to the apartment Erika rented at Rue Montalembert: a bedroom, study/living room/dining room, kitchen, and bath—for thirty-five U.S. dollars per month, on the Left Bank almost but not quite overlooking the river. From there she could walk to the Sorbonne, and did now regularly, even though the weather had turned cold, attending classes in philosophy and the history of art. The classrooms were cold and dirty, the students poorly dressed, and on the faces of many of the boys there was a premature gauntness of expression. Erika noticed a sharp divergence in the attitude of the students. Half, perhaps more than half, diligently took notes on what the instructor said, particularly in the class taught by Jean-Paul Sartre, who when he spoke did so with a precisionist nonchalance, a quiet and perfect engine of volubility whose words, transcribed, could have formed completed chapters of books, indeed regularly did so. But other students, though they might make a note occasionally, were studiedly skeptical, as if to communicate to the instructor that no presumptive respect was owed either to him or to the words he spoke. During the exchanges these students, when they said anything at all, tended to challenge this or that generality of the teacher, or ask whether, by this inflection, he had meant to say such and such. M. Argoud, who had written a history of art, answered questions, however provocative, neither with indignation nor with servility. If the question was barbed he would ignore those parts of it that were provocative, giving unadorned answers to whatever was left. "Would you not say, M. Argoud, that you slip into confusion when you suggest there are similarities between the theoretical defenses of abstractionism and of primitivism?"

"The similarities to which I alluded are listed in the chapter on Braque in my book."

Next question.

M. Argoud did not care for his students, and did not care if his students cared for him. But he would do what he had contracted to do so that as quickly as possible he might get back to his own work. He broke his rhythm on one occasion to notice Erika, with her tweed skirt, blouse, and sweater, her full bosom—perhaps she reminded him of something Braque had said, or painted, or loved? Erika looked at the teacher, still young but utterly unconcerned. If he could look ten years younger by snapping his fingers, she thought, he would probably not take the trouble. But to inquire into the authenticity of a Del Sarto in a museum, he had devoted seven months—and came up calmly with the pronouncement that it was a forgery. Erika guessed that, on the whole, M. Argoud would probably prefer coming up with a forgery than with an original: the whole exercise would somehow reinforce his misanthropic inclinations.

Except, of course, for Paul. M. Argoud obviously cared for Paul. Paul's (infrequent) questions were answered in a tone of voice distinctly different. M. Argoud was even seen, on at least one occasion, talking casually with Paul in the cold, high-ceilinged corridor. Since Paul was young and beautiful and intense, Erika wondered whether the relationship was unnatural, but when Paul sat next to her in the cafeteria one day at lunch and they fell to talking she discovered that Paul Massot was François Argoud's stepbrother and that they had belonged to the same guerrilla unit during the resistance. Both had been tortured in the same cellar at the same time, she would learn weeks later when she and Paul were lovers, and Paul whispered to her early one morning, stroking her breasts with his chin, that if he had known her then, he'd have probably told them everything, done anything, espoused any creed, incurred any risk, performed any treachery, lest they deprive him of her—his—Erika, no one else's, ever, ever—his rhythms were matching now the words, and her responses were elatedly fused to his own, as he repeated the word, ever, ever, ever, ever, ever, more excitedly, more quickly, almost shouting now, as she closed her eyes and moaned, then opened them to observe her beautiful Paul, EVER!

Whenever he left her apartment, whether to fetch a book in the library or perform an errand or check the mailbox, there was prolonged discussion. Exactly how long would he be gone?

Twelve minutes?

That was too long, Erika said, and Paul would agree. And he would say that perhaps if he ran both ways he could manage it in eleven minutes. As often as not, Erika would suggest that the safest way to handle the problem would be for both of them to leave together. His solemn young face would light up with pleasure and, taking her hand, he would open the door, pausing on the stairway, now for a passionate, now for a tender kiss.

Paul Massot's stepfather, the elder Argoud, had died during the war. Since he wasn't shot by the Nazis and did not die in a military prison, he didn't qualify for the Vermork; but he was listed officially as a "casualty" of the war because, suffering from diabetes, he was medically undernourished owing to scarcities that were an undisputed result of the war; so that his impoverished widow, Paul's mother, received a little pension on which Paul now drew a few francs every month to finish the studies interrupted when, at seventeen, he withdrew from the university to devote himself to the resistance.

He had gone then, instinctively, to his austere, normally unapproachable half-brother, older by eight years, with whom he associated during the nearly three years before the American troops, General Leclerc heading the procession, entered Paris. There were long, tedious hours of joint activity. On one occasion, Argoud and Paul were responsible for checking the movements of a Gestapo official. They huddled in a single room across the street with their stopwatches and notebooks, clocking the monster's goings and comings for nearly three months. In the long stretches of inactivity Argoud undertook two missions, the first to teach his half-brother something about the esthetic history of the world: it would prove, before long, a substantial history of the Renaissance. And the second, to convince Paul that the only hope for humanity lay in acknowledging the truths of Marxist analysis and historiography and in backing the Soviet Union's lonely, and acknowledgedly often brutal, efforts to export to the world that which only Russia was experiencing.

Paul knew about Erika's background and had even read some of the works by Chadinoff, whose fame had come to France. Neither he nor she was perturbed by Chadinoff's reactionary politics. Why should one expect Chadinoff to feel or reason otherwise? Paul said. How natural! If it were *easy* for the world to accept communism, it would have done so by now. The forces aligned in opposition to communism aren't merely those specifically identified by Marx. There are all those other accretions of man: his nostalgia, his fear of the unknown, his conservative temptation to resist change.

"But, Paul, there *are* other things." They were at dinner, in their favorite restaurant where, unless instructed otherwise, the waiter brought them the same appetizer, the same entrées, the same house wine, and the same bill, but no longer any cigarettes (Paul having told Erika she must give up smoking), which came to seventy-five U.S. cents apiece. "There's the suffering in Russia."

"There has been suffering everywhere. Look at the suffering in Germany and Italy. Even in the United States, one hundred years advanced over Russia industrially, they could not manage their Depression. Stalin is not a gentle man, and he has made many mistakes, and will make other mistakes. But unlike the Catholic Church, the Marxists do not claim infallibility for their leader. We claim only that history has imposed a responsibility on him, and we must help him discharge that responsibility. There is no way of getting around the fact, Erika, that millions of Russians fought for Stalin and for their country: and no one disguised from them that they were fighting for communism. Of course it has been bitter and hard. And it will be harder and more bitter if we are to prevent the forces in opposition from gainsaying the effort of all those years, all those lives, because"—he dug into his meatloaf with his knife; he never used a fork—"that is exactly what will happen if, just because the formal fighting is over, we think of ourselves as other than at war."

Erika heard the arguments but could not say, really, that she had listened to them. All through her life she had resisted only that one intellectual challenge, an examination of the ideology that had banished and impoverished her father. She did not, really, want to go into the arguments now, though she would if Paul wanted her to. She would do anything Paul wanted her to. She could not imagine that it was possible to know such joy as she knew, whether at the table listening to him, seeing his straight dark hair fallen over his brow, his sad brown eyes, his pointed and delicate mouth deftly retrieving the morsels of food from the knife, his long, tapered fingers, explaining his position to her, sensitive to every sound, every inflection, or in bed during those long bouts of ardor and tranquillity. Or sitting next to him, listening to his unprepossessing but acknowledgedly brilliant half-brother. She could admire her father, but she could not ever really *believe* in him. In Paul she believed—entirely. And she knew that she would never betray him. If it should happen, in a final philosophical revelation, that his ideology was wrong, and the contrary of it right, it would matter far less that she had taken the wrong course, than that she had followed him. He was her ideology, her idyll, her lover, her friend, her counselor, her Paul, forever forever forever.

"Do you understand what I'm talking about?"

"I understand what I need to understand. If you want me to study Marxism, of course I'll study Marxism. And"—she smiled at him—"I'll even win the Marxist Prize if you want me to."

No, he did not want her to study Marxism, he said. He would like it if she read Marx, but that didn't matter so much; he, Paul, would tell her everything she needed to know about politics. What he did not want was for her to associate openly with Marxists, because that would put her in the way of unnecessary harassments. The anti-Communist French were mobilizing against the French Communists, and there were divisions already even among men and women who had worked together during the resistance. The Croix de Feu, which drew from the militant wing of the anti-Communist coalition, were talking violence. The forces of American fascism were everywhere. There was no need to alert anyone, save his own special friends, to her new political allegiance. He himself had been careful not to enroll in the Party, and not to attend any of its official functions—François, though himself an active Party member, had so counseled him.

And thus it was left, during that golden autumn. One day every week he was away, by himself, pursuing duties which, he told her, he could neither neglect nor explain. One other evening per week he required her to share with his political intimates, who, after the briefest experience with her, were all of them happy that Paul, whose star was so manifestly ascendant, had found so accomplished and lovely a companion. She liked especially Gerard, and when one day he actually stopped smoking long enough to make it possible to see through the smoke to his wry face, she was surprised to notice how much he looked like her own father, though younger of course. He presided over the meetings, which is what they really were, and there was a worldliness but also a spirituality in his analysis of the French contemporary scene that touched Erika, which she found wanting in her own father. Gerard was especially kind to Erika and one day surprised her by addressing her in a Russian which, though clearly not native, betrayed a convincing knowledge of Russia, a knowledge the details of which Erika did not feel free to probe; these were, after all, clandestine meetings. She did not know Gerard's surname, nor where he lived.

It had proved difficult to locate Gerard, but finally Erika succeeded in doing so, exactly one week after the day when, groceries in hand, she had opened the door, exhilarated at the prospect of seeing Paul lying there as she so regularly came on him, dressed only in his undershorts, reading easily in the dim light. He was there exactly as she had anticipated, but the book rested flat on his olive-skinned chest and his head was slightly turned, by a bullet that had entered his brain.

Erika was released from the hospital just in time to attend the funeral three days later. Scant attention was given to the extraordinary shooting—execution?—of young Paul Massot. Paris was inured to death and terror, after five years of it. The detectives came, but eventually they left, without formal findings. Still white when she tapped the doorknob of Gerard's apartment, she waited, and Gerard came and, on opening the door, beheld a grown woman ten days after knowing her as a university schoolgirl.

"Who did it?" she asked.

"I don't know," he said.

"You do know"—she looked him in the eyes, and the psychic pressure was greater than the torturer's that nightmare night in 1944. He yielded.

"It was almost certainly the work of the Croix de Feu. Paul was assigned to penetrate the organization." Gerard held out his arms to her but she was past tears, and simply took his extended hand in hers and said good-bye, and told him that if ever he needed her services, he might have them.

In 1988 the editor of the *Paris Review,* George Plimpton, asked Buckley to sit for the sort of lengthy author interview for which that literary journal has become well known. Buckley agreed, on condition that I conduct the questioning.

We did the interview—actually several interviews, done several ways—with, after a long period, several additional questions by Plimpton, and turned it in. After eight years, the interview has just appeared in the *Paris Review.*

The prefatory biography and scene-setting are by the editor of this book.

William F. Buckley, Jr.
The Art of Fiction

William Frank Buckley, Jr., founder, editor, and now editor-at-large of the *National Review;* author, lecturer, and host of Public Television's *Firing Line,* the longest-running serious TV talk show, was born in New York City on November 24, 1925. His early schooling was in England and France. He graduated from the Millbrook School in N.Y., studied at the University of Mexico, and took a B.A. with honors at Yale in 1950, where he had fenced, debated, was Class Day Orator, and chairman of the *Yale Daily News.*

Drafted into the Army as an infantry private in 1944, he was discharged as a 2nd Lieutenant in 1946. From 1947 to 1951, Buckley taught Spanish at Yale and in 1952 became associate editor of the *American Mercury.* Then he resigned to do freelance writing. In 1955, he started his own magazine and is generally held to be responsible for assembling a coherent, responsible, modern Conservative movement in the United States. In 1962, he began a syndicated weekly column, which continues; in 1965 ran for Mayor of New York; in 1966 began hosting his weekly television show.

He was Lecturer at the New School, was a member of a Presidential Advisory Commission on the USIA, and in 1973 was appointed by the president as a public delegate to the UN.

He has received 36 honorary degrees and sixteen awards in journalism, literature, television (an Emmy). His latest, the Presidential Medal of Freedom, was awarded in 1991.

From his first, *God and Man at Yale*, in 1951, to his most recent, the novel *Brothers No More* (1995), he has written 36 books and contributed to nine others, including volumes on intellectuals, Catholicism, the Beatles, etc. It was at fifty that he first turned to fiction, producing *Saving the Queen* (1976) and in 1980 won the American Book Award for Best Mystery (*Stained Glass*). After ten novels featuring his hero, CIA agent Blackford Oakes, he produced his eleventh novel, *Brothers No More*, taking a new tack.

Any attempt to catch William F. Buckley, Jr., in one place at one time must fail to catch the essence of a man in motion. Interviewing Buckley at his most characteristic offers several choices; the interviewer took them all. He can be caught on the move, which means most of the time; or in repose, which usually means at work in other ways. This "interview" is the result of a series of exchanges over a period of time. The settings were as varied as Buckley's interests and attachments.

His weekdays are crowded with traveling, writing, lecturing, etc., and his weekends are reserved for Pat (Mrs. Buckley), family, and friends, and yet always and everywhere, some form of creative work. The cars are parked outside, including a middle-aging Volvo, and a stretch limo, which he has recommended for its efficiency to others (in *Overdrive*), attracting considerable criticism. It serves as a rolling office, complete with phone (he had one early), computer, etc., and is frequently completed as well with Mrs. Buckley, three King Charles spaniels, and household staff, and is driven by a large, protective man called Jerry.

The family's main house, in Stamford, Connecticut, is a large, comfortable old establishment with a stucco exterior, painted a surprising purple, surrounded by flower and herb gardens, tended carefully by Mrs. Buckley, and it is a house filled with flowered cushions and eccentric bathrooms. Books and framed photographs are everywhere. Part of the talks took place in the music room, which houses a harpsichord, bookshelves, a projection screen television set, and audio equipment. A Bosendorfer piano is visible within the house, used over the years for concerts by Buckley's friends like Rosalyn Tureck, the virtuoso harpsichordist; Dick Wellstood, the jazz pianist; and Buckley himself. Outside the big glass windows, beyond a sloping lawn, is Long Island Sound, one of Buckley's favorite sailing grounds.

Buckley's office is in the capacious garage, and overflows with papers, computer equipment, books. Over the garage is a small apartment where the Buckleys' son, Christopher, the novelist, humorist, and editor, has done some of his own writing.

The principal setting for our talks was in the Buckleys' pied-à-terre, off Park Avenue in Manhattan, an elegant place, with most of the conversa-

tions conducted in the Red Room. This serves as Pat Buckley's city office—she is a formidable fund-raiser for good causes, most of them in the
arts—and as library, small sitting room, bar, etc. Outside, in the foyer, is a
harpsichord at which arriving visitors are likely to find the master of the
house practicing or playing for his own enjoyment.

It is a true Buckley place, handsome but not staid, warmly hospitable.
Evidences of their enthusiasms are everywhere: again, photographs,
books, as well as paintings, picked out by small spotlights; a candlelit dining room; and a long salon for entertaining, with the aid of the Buckleys'
largely Hispanic staff. Much of the daily small talk in the house is in Spanish, with English almost a second language.

Other exchanges took place by telephone, from his car, by letters, faxes,
and E-mail, some from the Buckleys' winter place near Gstaad, Switzerland, . . . and once from the Concorde on the way to Sri Lanka, on which
plane he was leading a round-the-world tour group and which had recently suffered "the humiliating loss of one-third of its tail after takeoff
from Sydney."

Despite his peripatetic existence, Buckley, an unfailingly gracious man,
with a wry smile and a quick laugh, gives full attention to questions, as if
he had all the time in the world. He just uses well all the time in his world.

The first two interviews took place in the afternoons of December 12
and 14, 1988.

INTERVIEWER: What sort of things had you been writing before the novels?
You tend to group your previous books into categories, yes?

BUCKLEY: The most obvious, I suppose, are the collections of columns, articles and essays, four or five of those before my
first novel. There were two or three offbeat books: a book
on the United Nations and the term I served there. A book
on running for mayor of New York. A book on crossing
the Atlantic, which has the ocean as *mise-en-scène,* and
then a sort of autobiographical book on a week in my life,
Cruising Speed. So when you suggested that I write a novel,
I had at that point published twelve or fifteen nonfiction
books.

INTERVIEWER: I remember your saying you might like to try a novel one
day. The word "Forsythe" came up and I thought your reference was to the *Forsyte Saga,* which was then on television . . . as well as in the literature. You said, No, like
Frederick Forsyth.

BUCKLEY: Well, my memory of it was that I had just read *The Day of the Jackal* and admired it hugely. That the reader should know exactly how it ended and nevertheless still pant his way with excitement through three hundred pages—I thought that was really a splendid accomplishment. I remember saying something along the lines of, If I were to write a book of fiction, I'd like to have a whack at something of that nature.

INTERVIEWER: So you liked the challenge of writing about an occurrence in contemporary history where the reader knew the outcome and . . .

BUCKLEY: Yes, although I proceeded not to do so. That is, *Saving the Queen* did not have a predictable and well-known outcome, though some of the succeeding novels did. However, I have this problem—perhaps some people would think my problem is greater than that—which is that I have never succeeded in pre-structuring a book. I've never started a novel knowing what the end is going to be. When I get about halfway through—and I go into this only because I assume it's of some technical interest to other writers—I then need to stop and force myself to figure out how the Gordian knot is going to be severed, because at this point there are a lot of characters and dramatic questions that need to be consummated. Some people feel that a book comes out better written that way—i.e., if the author himself doesn't know what's going to be in Chapter Two when he writes Chapter One, Chapter Two might then be more freshly minted and read that way. I'm skeptical. It seems to me that a thoroughly competent operator would sit down and think of what's going to be in Chapter One through Chapter Forty, and simply move ahead. What I do at the end of an afternoon's work is write two or three lines on what I think is the direction of the narrative, and where we might logically go the next day.

INTERVIEWER: If you stop yourself halfway through—almost as "Ellery Queen" used to stop three quarters of the way through and say, Now that you have all the clues necessary for a solution, what is the solution?—is there a tendency then to load too much resolution into the end of a book?

BUCKLEY: I think that's a danger. It's what I hope I've avoided, in part because I'm very easily bored, and therefore if I can keep myself awake from chapter to chapter, I assume I can keep other people awake. That is why I don't reserve all the dynamite for the end. This may be the moment to say that in all of my novels, to the extent that I have a rule, it is to devote a very long chapter, close to the beginning, to the development of a single character. In Book One it's Blackford Oakes, which is natural. In Book Two, *Stained Glass,* it was Erika, a Soviet agent. I lifted her as though Vladimir Nabokov had a daughter, not his son, Dimitri. I confided my invention to Nabokov which perhaps precipitated his death. He didn't live to read the book, but he was very enthusiastic, as you remember, about the first book, and his widow liked *Stained Glass.* In any event, I've always felt that the extensive development of one character gives the book a kind of beef that it doesn't otherwise have. That's the only regimen to which I willingly subscribe and towards which I naturally drift.

INTERVIEWER: One of the questions about your novels is: How much is true, and how much is invented?

BUCKLEY: Well, I poach on history to the extent that I can. For instance, when I was in the CIA it was reported to me that the evidence was overwhelming that the destruction of Constantin Oumansky's airplane—he was the Soviet ambassador to Mexico—was an act of sabotage, ordered by Stalin. Stalin was killing people capriciously anyway in those days, so it was inherently believable. On the other hand, as I remember, Oumansky lived for a few hours after the plane came down, so the explosion wasn't very efficient. Thus there's a school of thought that sees it as a genuine accident. But for a novel I don't trouble myself about matters of that kind. That is to say, if something was in fact a coincidence, but might have been an act of treachery, I don't hesitate to decide which is more convenient for the purpose of the narrative. The books are, after all, introduced as works of fiction. Everybody knew that Charles de Gaulle was going to survive the OAS, and everybody knows that Kennedy is not going to survive the twenty-second of November, 1963, and everybody knows that the Berlin Wall is going to rise. Even so, I attempt to create suspense around such episodes.

And manifestly, succeed. The books get heavy criticism, positive and negative, but no one says, Why read a book in which you know what's going to happen?

INTERVIEWER: Still, it's a nice challenge of art to put yourself up against that.

BUCKLEY: Sure. And I owe that idea to Forsyth.

INTERVIEWER: In the patterns you've developed, one of them is the unspoken premise: This is the way it *might* have been behind that great event that we all know about.

BUCKLEY: That's right. I found myself attracted to this idea of exploring historical data and visiting my own imagination on them. The very successful book on the death of Kennedy written by Don DeLillo—*Libra*—does, of course, that. In a sense overcomplicated and ineffectively ambitious in some of its sections, it's a magnificent piece of work, in my judgment. As long as the reader isn't persuaded that you are trying, via fiction, an act of historical revisionism, I don't think you meet any hard resistance.

INTERVIEWER: So the reader will go with you in a combination of invention and known history, but won't accept so cheerfully an editorial.

BUCKLEY: Yes. Of course, I think it probably depends also on how contentious the theme is. For about twenty-five years, dozens of books were published to the effect that Roosevelt was responsible for Pearl Harbor. Never mind whether he *was,* in a sense, or was not, I think that if during that period a novel pressing his guilt had been written, there would have been a certain amount of polemical resentment. If one were to write today a novel about a senator from Massachusetts and a young woman in Chappaquiddick, and how he drowned her or deserted her or whatever—readers would tend, under those circumstances, to think of it as more effort to make the case against Teddy Kennedy, rather than as a work of fiction.

INTERVIEWER: There seems to be a period that has to elapse before you can safely . . .

BUCKLEY: I think so. At this point I think you can speculate about the death of JFK and not get into trouble. Like Sacco and Vanzetti.

INTERVIEWER: You consciously stayed away from that event for a long time.

BUCKLEY: Until novel Number Eight. *Mongoose, R.I.P.* flatly says that although Oswald took the initiative in suggesting that he intended to try to assassinate the President, Castro, without acting specifically as an accomplice, urged him to proceed.

INTERVIEWER: To go back for a moment to the one character you chose to develop at length, do you decide as you're writing your way into the novel which character you will give a full history, or do you decide that before you write?

BUCKLEY: Again, I sometimes don't know who the character is going to be until I've launched the book, but I'm consciously looking for a target of opportunity. For instance, in *Stained Glass* I decided that the Soviet woman spy, who is acting as a translator and interpreter for Count Wintergrin, the protagonist, was the logical person to have a complex background. So I made up the daughter of Nabokov and went through her whole childhood and love life and her apostasy from the West.

INTERVIEWER: The Cold War is an essential handicap . . .

BUCKLEY: I hate to use the word in this context, but I must––these are novels that *celebrate* the Cold War. I don't think that's a paradox that affronts, any more than, say, a novelist who celebrates a world war. But my novels "celebrate" the Cold War, and therefore the passions awakened by this titanic struggle are really a narrative obligation. The fact of the matter is that in our time—in my adult lifetime—somewhere between fifty and sixty million people were killed by *other* causes than as a result of war or pestilence. And most cases—the great exception being the victims of Hitler—were the victims of the Communists. Now that struggle is sometimes made to look like a microcosmic difference, say some slight difference of opinion between Alger Hiss and Whittaker Chambers. In fact, it was a typhoon that roared across the land—across bureaucracies, academia, laboratories, chancelleries. One week after Gorbachev was here in New York, I find myself using the past tense about the Cold War, which shows you how easily co-opted I am. But the Cold War is the great political drama of the twentieth century, and there is extraordinarily little literature about it written in the novel form. There are great exposés—*The God That Failed, The Gulag Archipelago*. But if you think about the American scene, there isn't really an abundant literature, is there?

INTERVIEWER: Why do you think this is so?

BUCKLEY: I think that there's a sort of feeling that much of the conflict has been an *alien* experience. Of course, there are those New York intellectuals who are exceptions. I remember one middle-aged man who came to *National Review* a couple of weeks ago and said that when he was growing up he thought the two political parties in the United States were the Communist Party and the Trotskyist! That was all his mother and father ever talked about. Irving Kristol will tell you that the fights at CCNY were always on this or that modality of communism. But on the whole it has not been a national experience. When you think of Updike or Bellow or Walker Percy, and the tangentiality of their involvement in the Cold War, there isn't really a hot concern for it. It must be because our novelists disdain such arguments as grubby, or because they think that it's an ideological quarrel with no genuine intellectual interest for the mature person. But of course it has been the great struggle of our time. For that reason I think of my novels as entertainment but also designed to illustrate important problems in that setting. It means a lot to me to say this: when I set out to explore the scene, I was determined to avoid one thing, and that is the kind of ambiguity for which Graham Greene and to a certain extent Le Carré became famous. There you will find that the agent of the West is, in the first place, almost necessarily unappealing physically. He drinks too much, he screws too much and he's always being cuckolded. Then, at some dramatic moment there is the conversation or the moment of reflection in which the reader is asked to contemplate the difficulty in asserting that there *is* a qualitative difference between Them and Us. This I wanted to avoid. So I was searching, really, for a little bit of the purity of Melville's Billy Budd in Blackford Oakes. Billy Budd has no sense of humor, and without a sense of humor you can't be genuinely American . . . I made him almost spectacularly good-looking in defiant reaction to these semi-disfigured characters that Greene and Le Carré and Len Deighton specialize in. I got a little tired of that after Novel Three or Four, so I didn't belabor the point as much.

INTERVIEWER: Your reference to Graham Greene. Does he matter to you, or figure in your . . . ?

BUCKLEY: Graham Greene has always struck me as being at war with himself. He has impulses which he sometimes examines with a compulsive sense to dissect them, as though only an autopsy would do to dissect their nature. He is a Christian more or less *malgré soi*. He is a Christian because he can't quite prevent it. And therefore he spends most of his time belittling Christianity and Christians. He *hates* the United States, and his hatred is in part I suppose a reaction by some finely calibrated people to American vulgarity. But with him it's so compulsive it drives him almost to like people who are professional enemies of the United States. And since the most conspicuous critic of the United States in this part of the world during the last twenty-five years has been Fidel Castro, he ends up being, God help us, pro-Castro. He once gave the answer—it might have been in the *Paris Review,* I forget—to the question, "What is the word you least like in English?" "America." And he set out to prove it. Given the refinement of his mind, it's always been a mystery to me that he should be so besotted in his opposition to that towards which he naturally inclines—Christianity and all that Christianity bespeaks—in order to identify himself with those he sees as the little man? Okay, but when the little man is such a person as Fidel Castro or Daniel Ortega? It all defies analysis.

INTERVIEWER: Who else among the people practicing this kind of fiction do you pay attention to?

BUCKLEY: Well, I'm not a systematic reader. I read a little bit of everything. I've never studied the achievement of any particular author seeking to inform myself comprehensively of his technique or of his point. I occasionally run into stuff that deeply impresses me. For instance, Updike's *The Coup,* which I reviewed for *New York* magazine.* It astonishes me that it is so little recognized. It's *the* brilliant put-down of

---

* See chapter 16, "Passing in Review."

Marxist Third World nativism. It truly is. And hilarious. It's a successor to *Black Mischief,* but done in that distinctively Gothic style of Updike's—very different from the opéra bouffe with which Evelyn Waugh went at that subject fifty years ago. And then I think that Walker Percy's *Love in the Ruins* is another *1984.* An exquisite extrapolation of what life might be like if we don't dominate technology, and yield to totalitarian imperatives. He combined in it humor with a deep and often conscious explanation of human psychology via this vinous character—the doctor—who dominates the novel so convincingly.

INTERVIEWER: Somehow, for some unannounced reason, we are talking about Christian novelists. I'm struck by this only because the much-remarked phenomenon of the nineteen-fifties, sixties and seventies has been—certainly in America—the Jewish novel, or the novelist who writes from background in Jewry.

BUCKLEY: That reminds me that along about nineteen fifty-one or two—whenever it was that Graham Greene wrote *The Love Affair* [*The End of the Affair*]—one critic said, "If Mr. Greene continues . . . if he writes one more book like this, he must thereafter be evaluated as a "*Catholic* novelist." He didn't say "Christian novelist." And indeed Greene's succeeding book was a rather sharp departure. It occurs to me that the point you really make is more nearly about *Christians* who write novels, not Christian novelists. Chesterton, Belloc, and Morris *were* Christian novelists. But Updike is a Christian who writes novels. A reading of his work wouldn't permit you to decoct from it, with any sense of certainty, that the author was a professing Christian. I don't think from *Love in the Ruins* you could guess Walker Percy was a Catholic.

INTERVIEWER: I was thinking about your own deep religious faith.

BUCKLEY: Well, yes. I'm a professing Christian, and every now and then I take pains to let the reader in on the fact that so is Blackford Oakes. On the other hand, it would be hard, I think, to pronounce my books as "Christian novels" unless you were to go so far as to say that any novel that acknowledges epistemological self-assurance to the point of permitting us to say, *They're wrong and you're right,* has got to trace to that sense of certitude that is distinctively Christian.

INTERVIEWER: Yes, you're certainly not *preaching* in the novels. Blackford Oakes occasionally prays, which is just as natural to him as breathing, but his Christianity doesn't color everything. I was just wondering whether the Christians who write novels have become an underground sect, as Christians were at the outset.

BUCKLEY: I think to a significant extent they have. Raymond Williams—the late British novelist—was the last novelist I can think of offhand who was a flat-out Christian novelist. Am I wrong?

INTERVIEWER: Frederick Buechner has been plying his trade as a Christian novelist. George Garrett—his big novels are set in the Elizabethan era, but they're written with Christianity very much alive and at issue. And, at times, include spies. I wonder if spying and religion are in some way natural literary bedmates.

BUCKLEY: Well, isn't it safe to say that people who pursue the Communist objective—certainly early on—were motivated by ideological convictions which were almost religious in nature? Religious in the sense that they called for sacrifice and for the acceptance of historicism. That became less and less so as fewer and fewer people of moral intelligence actually believed in Leninism and communism. What they then believed in was Russian expansionism, and they became mere agents of the Soviet Union . . .

INTERVIEWER: So it began with religious fervor which supplanted what traditional religion might have been for some.

BUCKLEY: I think so. These days it would be hard to find somebody in his twenties comparable to Whittaker Chambers in his twenties. This doesn't mean that there aren't still Communists—Angela Davis is a very noisy Communist, but she's shallow. But there isn't really a sense of life in the catacombs, the kind of thing you had in the twenties and thirties, when people like Malcolm Muggeridge (until his early epiphany) were, temporarily, in thrall to the idea of the collectivist state.

INTERVIEWER: Do you think that in a time when the visible attachment of many people to formal religious institutions has been waning that there has been a corresponding attraction to other causes?

BUCKLEY: Yes, I do. And for that reason it is not easy to command a large public. Most writers want a large public, and tend for that reason not to write religious novels. And explicitly religious—God, it's been so long since I've read one!—an explicitly religious novel would be looked on merely as a period piece.

INTERVIEWER: How do you handle the technical stuff in the novel? Do you do your own research?

BUCKLEY: I am very unmechanical. I remember once, halfway through writing *Stained Glass,* I had to fly back to New York from Switzerland to do two or three episodes of *Firing Line* to catch up. I called my electrician in Stamford and I didn't have a lot of time; so I just said, "Could you please tell me how to execute somebody with electricity?" Well, he was sort of dumbfounded.

INTERVIEWER: He doesn't make house calls of that kind?

BUCKLEY: That's right. And he hadn't really given it much thought. He sort of muttered a couple of utterly unusable things like, "Put him in a bathtub and have him fix electricity." So I mentioned this in a letter to a historian at the University of San Jose. He wrote back and said, I must introduce you to my friend, Alfred Aya. Aya turned out to be a bachelor, aged then about fifty-five, who worked for the telephone company. As my historian described him, at heart a physicist—and more. When he was six years old and traveled with his parents, he would inevitably disappear for four or five minutes in the hotel, and from that moment on anybody who pushed "UP" on the elevator went down, and anybody who pushed "DOWN" went up. Aya loves challenges. So I wrote him a letter and said: Look, I've got this problem. . . . He gave me the idea of executing him via this device—what I call Chromoscope—which was entirely plausible. Later, he gave me all the information I needed to write satellite scenes in the novel that dealt with the U-2, including how to make the thing appear to be coming down, and how to destroy it, etc., etc. I remember when I came to the nuclear missile question—at this point we communicated with each other via MCI because he's an MCI nut, as am I—so I shot him a message via computer. Here's the problem: there's one nuclear weapon left in Cuba, and I have to know what it looks like. I must know what is needed to fire it, what is needed to redirect it to a target other than the one prescribed for it. And twenty-four hours later, I had a twenty-nine-thousand-word reply from him. Absolutely astonishing. Which made me—temporarily—one of the world's foremost authorities on how to handle a single nuclear bomb.

INTERVIEWER: Does he give you any credit for helping him work off aggressions?

BUCKLEY: He's absolutely delighted to help.

INTERVIEWER: What else is your system of research, since there is so much fact?

BUCKLEY: Wherever there is something concerning which I have a factual doubt, I put in a double parenthesis, which is a code to the librarian at *National Review*, who moonlights on my books, to check that, so she often will find five or six or seven hundred of those in the course of a novel. And she then copes.

INTERVIEWER: Are you aware of the category they now call the techno-thriller, like the novels of Tom Clancy and so on?

BUCKLEY: Well, I know Tom Clancy.

INTERVIEWER: I just wondered whether these writers who make a fetish out of hardware have influenced you?

BUCKLEY: No, except that I admire when it's done skillfully. For instance, Frederick Forsyth, in the book mentioned earlier, describes the assembly of the rifle with which he's going to attempt the assassination; I like the neatness with which he names the various parts. I have a book called *What's What*, in which you can look up "shoe" and find out exactly what you call this part of one, or that, etc.

INTERVIEWER: Now, famously, you write, *everywhere*. You write in New York at *National Review;* you write in New York in your home; you write in Connecticut in your home; you write in the car, you write in planes, you write presumably in hotels. Is it only your novel-writing that is done in Switzerland?

BUCKLEY: In order not to break the rhythm, I almost always write a chapter on the airplane from Switzerland to here when I come back for my television work. Working on a novel, I like to write every day so as not to break it up. There are two nights when I cannot do it. Those are the nights when I am preparing for the television the following day. But I try not to miss more than two nights.

INTERVIEWER: Do you think when a novelist begins a novel, he has to live the novel . . . that you have begun to become one or more of the characters, and you don't want to be interrupted playing those roles any more than an actor wants to be interrupted . . .

BUCKLEY: Oh, I am *feverishly* opposed to that idea. I've seen people wreck their lives trying to do it. I know the MacDowell Colony and Breadloaf and such are pretty successful, but I also know that some people seclude themselves to write and become alcoholics precisely because they have nothing else to do. I have a close friend who has that problem, because when he sets out to write a novel, he wants to clear the decks. Nothing would drive me battier than to do *just* a novel over the course of an entire month. I have only x ergs of purely creative energy, and when I'm out of those, what in the hell do I do then?

When one sets out to write a book, I do believe one should attack it two or three hours a day, every day, without fail. You mustn't interrupt it to do a week's lecture tour or whatever. On the other hand, don't ever devote the entire day to doing just that, or the chances are you'll get bored with it, or simply run out of energy. But I'm glad you asked me that question, because I feel so strongly about it. I'd like to see more novels *not* written by people who have all the time in the world to write them.

INTERVIEWER: As an editor I spend half of my life trying to persuade people who think they should write books that they don't have to give up careers and certainly not family in order to write a book. They do have to find time—they have to make time—but they don't necessarily have to jump ship.

BUCKLEY: It seems so marvelous when you realize that and can say, Look, fifteen hundred words a day and you've got a book in six weeks.

INTERVIEWER: Now when you wrote your first novel, I found it a surprise—an agreeable surprise because I somehow thought it would be in homage to writers you liked . . .

BUCKLEY: Imitative? I don't have the skill to imitate. For instance, I admire people who can come up with a touch of a foreign accent. I just don't know how. There may be a school somewhere—Cornell?—that teaches you how to do that. And if I thought I could go somewhere for a half-day and learn how to make a character sound like a Spaniard, I would. My son has that skill, marvelously developed. I can't do it. And I can't in speaking either. I sometimes call somebody and don't want to be recognized, but I don't know how to do it. And I don't know how to write like anybody else.

INTERVIEWER: As your editor, I didn't think you'd write a page-turner. I thought, as I've said, that you would write a clever novel, an intelligent novel, maybe ideologically weighted. What I didn't see coming was the novel that moves ahead. I wondered if that comes at least in part from the fact that you write fast?

BUCKLEY: Well, perhaps in part. But mostly, it's my terribly overdeveloped faculty against boredom. I was introduced into the White House Fellows annual lunch affair by a man who had done some research on my books and he picked up a line I had forgotten. "Mr. Buckley," he said, "has written that he gets bored winding his watch." True, I was greatly relieved when they developed the quartz. I never *just* brush my teeth—I'm reading and brushing my teeth at the same time—so, if something bores me, then it's certainly going to bore somebody else.

   I live a hectic life. Someone once asked me if I ever could lay aside my Christian scruples so as to have a mistress, and I said, "I really don't have the time."

INTERVIEWER: You once said to me that you are not particularly reflective, or thoughtful, and you said, I think, it is perhaps because you're so compulsively busy. How can you write a novel with as many parts and qualities, as many components, as many subplots and themes as you do, and still say that you're not thoughtful, not reflective?

BUCKLEY: Well, what that takes is hard concentration. I don't think that people who are very busy are for that reason diluting the attention that they give to what they are doing when they are doing it. For instance Churchill in his wonderful essay on painting said when he's painting that's *all* he's thinking about. When I'm painting, that's *all* I'm thinking about. I happen to be a lousy painter, I should admit instantly, but I enjoy it, and I concentrate on it. Sometimes, going up in the lift with, say, Doris Brynner, a ski-mate, who's a wonderful listener, I'll say, Now I've got to the point where I've got this problem, and this girl has to come out alive. On the other hand, she's going to be in the Lubyanka . . . that kind of thing, and just saying it helps. I only really think when I'm writing or talking. I suppose it's a gift of extemporaneity. But also, added to that method, I think is the usual one. When you reach a knotty problem in your novel, you sometimes have to sit back in your chair and think, What am I going to do next? I don't want to give the impression that I simply keep using my fingers.

INTERVIEWER: Reviewers have noticed, and it has always intrigued me, that you write your enemies so well that it sometimes seems as if you characterize them better than *our* guys—the good guys. Your portraits of Castro, of Che Guevara, of Khrushchev, Beria, and so on, are all close, pores and all . . .

BUCKLEY: Nobody can possibly like the Beria that I depicted.

INTERVIEWER: No, I don't mean it's necessary to *like* them, but you give them so much color. Blackford sometimes pales—and I suspect this is your intention—by comparison to the roster of heavies.

BUCKLEY: Well, exposure to these historical characters is almost always limited. In the first book in which Khrushchev appears, he makes, I think, two appearances. Therefore you take the essence of Khrushchev and give it to the reader and the reader is grateful, because it *is* the essence of what we know or can imagine about him. If you had to write four hundred and fifty pages about Khrushchev, you'd run the danger of etiolation. I think I've read enough about these characters to have some idea of what they're like. I depended heavily on Carlos Franke when I wrote about Castro and Che Guevara. Guevara was a very magnetic human being. Cruel, and entirely obsessed, but nevertheless attractive. Fidel Castro is more attractive to ten thousand people than he is to ten people, whereas Che Guevara was the other way around. I think I captured Castro well, but I'm equally pleased with the portraits I've drawn of Americans. The Dulles brothers, and Dean Acheson . . .

INTERVIEWER: Let's speak for a moment of the amount you write and the presumed speed at which you write, novels and everything else. Do you have any models or inspirations who helped you to this sustained burst of intellectual and creative activity?

BUCKLEY: I'm not sure I'm all that fast or all that productive. Take, for example, Trollope. He'd rise at five-thirty, do his toilette, and have his breakfast, all by six. He would then begin writing, and he had a notepad which had been indexed to indicate intervals of two hundred and fifty words. He would force himself to write two hundred and fifty words per fifteen minutes. Now, if at the end of fifteen minutes he hadn't reached one of those little marks on his page, he would write faster. And if he passed the goal in fifteen minutes he would write more slowly! And he wrote that way for three hours—three thousand words a day.

INTERVIEWER: Do you approve?

BUCKLEY: If you were told to write a cantata every Sunday, and you got what Bach got out of it, how could you disapprove of it?

INTERVIEWER: Do you keep to a particular standard with your work?

BUCKLEY: It's true about everybody, that some stuff is better than other stuff. But I don't release anything that isn't roughly speaking—I say roughly speaking—as good as it can be. If I reread, say, my column, a third time, I probably would make a couple of changes. I'm aware of people who create both, so to speak, the "quality stuff," and the "non-quality stuff," who think nothing of writing two or three pulp novels per year. Bernard De Voto was that way. I don't do that and I'm not sure I could. What I write—especially the books—needs a lot of work. So I always resent critics who find themselves saying, "Mr. Buckley's novels look as though they were written with one eye on the in-flight movie."

INTERVIEWER: Nobody's been clever enough to say that.

BUCKLEY: Sheppard in *Time* magazine did. Who, by the way, has often praised my books. So it would be odd, I think, for someone who has reached age sixty-three, which I have, writing as much as I do without being able to discipline himself.

INTERVIEWER: Although you don't measure it out like Trollope, nevertheless you know you have so many days and weeks in February and March in which to write a novel.

BUCKLEY: Well, I'm much slower than Trollope . . . and never mind the differences in quality. If Trollope had given himself, say, six hours instead of three, would his novels have been that much better? I don't know that anybody could reach that conclusion. But then he took three hours to write three thousand words, which is very fast writing when using a pencil, but not fast at all when you're using a word processor.

INTERVIEWER: It should change the statistics.

BUCKLEY: When I sit down to start writing every day in Switzerland—which is usually about a quarter to five to about seven fifteen, two and a half hours—it's inconceivable to me that I would write less than fifteen hundred words during that time. That's much slower than Trollope, even though I have faster tools. So although I write fast, I'm not a phenomenally fast writer.

Speechwriters get told by the President that he's going to declare war the next day and please draft an appropriate speech. And they do it. Or, Tom Wicker. I've seen him write ten thousand words following one day's trial proceedings, and all that stuff will appear in the *New York Times.* Now it's not belletrism, but it's good journalistic craftsmanship.

INTERVIEWER: There's no automatic merit in being fast or slow. Whatever works, works. Georges Simenon, who was a phenomenon of production, always got himself in shape to write each novel. I hate to mention this in your presence, but he usually wrote his novels in seven or eight days. He had a physical beforehand—I think perhaps particularly for blood pressure—and then went into a kind of trance and wrote the novel, and then was ordered by his doctor to go off and take a vacation.

BUCKLEY: I'll go you one better. Rotzan Isogner, who does not go to sleep until he has finished the book.

INTERVIEWER: You've said more than once that you find writing is hard work . . .

BUCKLEY: But how would the reader know? That doesn't solve it at all. Writing, if it's done at all, has got to yield net satisfaction. But that satisfaction is long after the foreplay. I'm not saying that I wish I were otherwise engaged professionally. I'm simply saying that writing is terribly hard work. But it doesn't follow at all that because it's hard work, it's odd that it's done so quickly. I think that's quite natural. If writing is pain, which it is to me, it should follow that the more painful the exercise is, the more quickly you want to get on with it. The obvious analogy, I suppose, would be an execution. For years they've been trying to figure out how to execute a person more quickly, so that he feels less protracted pain.

That's a *reductio ad absurdum,* but in any event, if your living depends on writing a piece of journalism every day, and you find writing painful work, you're obviously much better off developing the facility to execute it in an hour rather than ten hours.

INTERVIEWER: Your workroom in Switzerland. What is that like?

BUCKLEY: Well, it's a converted children's playroom. I have my desk and my reference library at one end; there's the harpsichord and gramophone, and there's a Ping-Pong table . . . on which all the paints are . . .

INTERVIEWER: Do you play music while you're writing? Do you write to Scarlatti, or to Bach, or—

BUCKLEY: Do I play? . . . Oh, my goodness! Heavens, yes! I thought you meant, did I play myself? Occasionally, I get up and— you know, in a moment of boredom or whatever—and hit a few notes. But the answer is, Yes, I have the record player on most of the time. Also, in Switzerland, one of the better socialized institutions—but I love it—is that you can, for a few francs per month, attach to your telephone a little music-box device which gives you six channels, one of them a good music channel.

INTERVIEWER: Is there any link between what you're writing and what you're listening to?

BUCKLEY: No, none whatever.

INTERVIEWER: So you could play Fats Waller one time and Beethoven an-
                    other?

BUCKLEY: I don't play jazz when I write. I don't know why but I just
                    plain don't. But I do when I paint.

INTERVIEWER: What about revising?

BUCKLEY: Of all the work I do, it's the work I look forward to most—
                    rewriting. I genuinely, *genuinely* enjoy that—especially
                    with the invention of the word processor, which makes it
                    mechanically so neat.

INTERVIEWER: So partly it's the technological joy of working with these
                    instruments?

BUCKLEY: Yes.

INTERVIEWER: You're a computer maven, you've been through all the
                    known stages of man with regard to writing and its instru-
                    ments. You presumably started writing by hand or, as some
                    people would insist, with a quill pen, yes?

BUCKLEY: Well, I did in this sense: until I was writing every day for
                    the *Yale Daily News,* as its editor, I would write by hand
                    and then type, so the typewritten copy would be draft
                    number two. It happens that my handwriting is sort of
                    malformed. In fact, my father, when I was fifteen years old,
                    sent me a typewriter with the instructions: (a) learn to use
                    it, and (b) never write to him in longhand again. So I
                    learned the touch-type system, and by the time I was, I
                    guess twenty-three, it wouldn't occur to me to write any-
                    thing by hand. In fact, I was so unhappy doing so that I
                    would ask my professors' permission, on the honor system,
                    to type an exam instead of writing it. And with one excep-
                    tion, they all said, Sure. I'd take one of those blue books
                    into the next room and type away.

INTERVIEWER: About vocabulary: you get criticized, or satirized, for your
                    use of arcane words. Are you conscious of reining in your
                    vocabulary when you're writing a novel?

BUCKLEY: No, I don't think I am. In the novels, there's less obvious
                    analysis than in nonfiction work. I'm attached to the convic-

tion that sometimes the word that you want has an in-built rhythm that's useful. And there are some words that are onomatopoeic, and when they are, they too can be very useful. Let me give you a concrete example. This morning, I wrote about Arafat's speech, and the coverage of the speech, which consumed most of the television news last night. This had to do with the question, Did he or did he not live up to the demands of the State Department that he denounce violence absolutely, agree to abide by the relevant resolutions of the United Nations Security Council, and acknowledge the existence of Israel? Now all the commentators said, Well he skirted the subject; his language was sometimes ambiguous. I concluded that he had more nearly consummated his inherent pledge—"however *anfractuous* the language." Now the word came to me not only as a useful word but also as a *necessary* word. I first ran into that word in a review by Dwight Macdonald of Norman Mailer's book on the Pentagon (*Armies of the Night*), and I didn't know what it meant; I couldn't figure it out by internal inspection, so I looked it up. And that's *exactly* the word to describe Arafat's discussion of Israel's existence. There is an example of where one could use the word "ambiguous," but that extra syllable makes it sound just a little bit more "windy."

I remember once in a debate with Gore Vidal at which [TV talk show host] David Susskind was deriding me in San Francisco, 1964. I used the word "irenic," which didn't disturb Vidal, of course. So after it was over, Susskind said, "What's irenic?" I said, "Well, you know, sort of serene, sort of peaceful." "Well, why didn't you say serene or peaceful?" And I said, "Because the other word is a better fit." At this point believe it or not, Vidal, who was on Susskind's side a hundred percent during the exchange, said, "You know the trouble with you, David, is that you don't learn anything, ever."

INTERVIEWER: Irenic is a nice word.

BUCKLEY: And again onomatopoeic. So, in defending the use of these words, I begin by asking the question: Why were they invented? They must have been invented because there was, as the economist put it, "a felt need" for them. That is to say, there came a moment at which a writer felt that the existing inventory didn't quite do what he wanted it to do.

These words were originally used because somebody with a sensitive ear felt the need for them. . . .

INTERVIEWER: "Anfractuous" is a more vigorous, almost violent word.

BUCKLEY: Yes. It suggests a little hint of the serpentine, a little bit the impenetrable going around and around. So therefore why not use it? Years ago, the review of *God and Man at Yale,* again by *Time* magazine, referred to my "apopemtic" book on leaving Yale. So, of course I looked it up, because I didn't know what it meant, and it's different from "valedictorian," because an "apopemptic" speech, if memory serves, is usually what the ruler gives to the pilgrims en route somewhere. His sort of final message and advice. So the writer on *Time,* whoever he was in 1951, was making a very shrewd difference between "valedictory"—I'm leaving Yale—and giving Yale my parting advice; in effect, *Time* set me up as if I were the ruler of Yale, giving my subjects my advice. Very nice. So occasionally I use "apopemtic," and when I use it, it's strictly when I want that tiny little difference in inflection, which is worth making.

INTERVIEWER: You once said you used the words you know.

BUCKLEY: A good point. Everybody knows words that other people don't know. Reading *The Coup,* I found twenty-six words in it I didn't know. I listed them in a column, and there were great hoots in my office because everybody knew quite a lot of them. . . .

INTERVIEWER: So words are put into your vocabulary by other writers?

BUCKLEY: Yes. I'm offended by people who suggest—and some have—that I spend my evenings with dictionaries . . . There are certain words that I couldn't bring myself to use, not because they aren't instrumentally useful, but because they just look too inventionistic. How they got there, one never quite knows. A lot of them are sort of medical.

INTERVIEWER: So, for those who might have thought your use of language elitist, you have quite the reverse view. You trust your reader either to know it or look it up, or go over it like a smooth ski jump.

BUCKLEY: The reader can say, I don't care, it's not worth my time. But there's no reason why he should deprive other people grateful for that augmented chord, which gives them pleasure. Did you know that forty percent of the words used by Shakespeare were by him used only once? I've never read a satisfactory explanation of the seventeenth-century capacity to understand the stuff we hear with some sense of strain. Shakespeare used a total of twenty-eight thousand words; most of them were within reach of the audience. And when you consider that books by Newman were serialized as recently as a hundred years ago. The *Apologia* was serialized and upped the circulation of a London daily. Imagine serializing the *Apologia* today. Or take the difference between a Lincoln-Douglas debate and a Kennedy-Nixon debate. . . . Lincoln, in that rich, biblical vocabulary of his, was not at all self-conscious about using a wide vocabulary.

I've never seen a test, though I'd like to see it done, that would scan, say, three or four pages of the current issue of the *New York Times,* and three or four pages of a hundred years ago of, say, the *Tribune,* and find out what the so-called Fry Index reveals.

INTERVIEWER: The Fry Index?

BUCKLEY: The Fry Index is the average number of syllables per word and the average number of words per sentence.

INTERVIEWER: In writing fiction, your vocabulary is nevertheless somewhat constrained by the fact that you are limited to the words that your characters would use?

BUCKLEY: Absolutely. Except that one of my characters is a Ph.D., and I remember on one occasion she used the word "syllepsis." Christopher Lehmann-Haupt wrote, "Mr. Buckley's character doesn't even know how correctly to use the word 'syllepsis,' she really meant . . . " Anyway, he gave me a wonderful opportunity, since a second printing was coming out right away, to go back and rewrite the dialogue to have her say, "syllepsis—a word the correct meaning of which is not even acknowledged by the *New York Times* critics."

INTERVIEWER: To shift a bit, in a conversation with Louis Auchincloss you asked, Why do people take less satisfaction from novels than they used to do?

BUCKLEY: Well, I mentioned television as the principal time consumer, and it just plain is. It's established statistically that

the average American has the television set turned on between thirty-five and thirty-nine hours per week.

INTERVIEWER: If people derive fewer rewards from novels than they used
to, does this reflect something about the novels themselves,
rather than the competition for time?

BUCKLEY: Well, it certainly can. It can also suggest that the passive intelligence is less resourceful than it used to be. My favorite
book at age nine was called *The Magic of Oz*. If you could
correctly pronounce a string of consonants, you could turn
yourself into a giraffe. I can't imagine a nine-year-old today
being engrossed—being *diverted,* let alone being engrossed
by that because he would want to see it happening on the
screen.

INTERVIEWER: He'd want to see dancing consonants.

BUCKLEY: That's right.

INTERVIEWER: People have traditionally turned to novels, at least some, for
a way to get a grip on the world; a way to see the order in the
chaos. Have we gone past that period; is it that many novels
are not so avidly consumed because they provide small delights, they don't provide epiphanies, or grand epiphanies?

BUCKLEY: Well, I have to reflect on that. We spoke about the scarcity
of, say, the Christian novel, and to that extent one is probably justified in talking about the absence of great spiritual
themes. By the same notion there isn't the eschatological
novel in which one has a sense of achieving order, as for
instance *A Tale of Two Cities* did, i.e., persuade the reader
that what he had read and vicariously experienced was a
narrative *beneath* the order of things—the gods. Now, all
experiences tend to become more individuated. But then
of course all larger experiences are solipsistic. And for that
reason I think reading the many contemporary novels you
get some of that feeling of, Where in the hell have I been
that it was worthwhile going to?

INTERVIEWER: People either accuse you, or are interested in the Blackford
Oakes novels, because they think you're writing about
yourself.

BUCKLEY: Of course, it becomes very easy if one takes the obvious
profile. You begin with the fact that we were both born the

same year and went to Yale at approximately the same
time. Now, I made him a Yale graduate—I think it was the
class of 1951—for sheer reasons of personal sloth. I was in
the class of 1950, so that I knew that I could coast on my
knowledge of the scene without having to go and visit a
fresh college and see how things happened there. Then, for
the same reason, i.e., sloth, I made him an undercover
agent of the CIA, so that I could give the identical training
I had received and know that it was absolutely legitimate.
So that much was, if you like, autobiographical . . . if you
can say it's autobiographical that two different people went
to Yale and to the CIA. . . . But beyond that, people who
want to sustain the parallel have a tough time. In the first
place he's an engineer, a Protestant. He has a sweetheart
whom he has yet to marry—I married when I was twenty-
four years old. He's a pilot which I was not. He signed up
in the CIA as a *profession* which I didn't. I knew I was only
going to be temporary and I'd quit after nine months. He's
not a writer. There's a little touch of James Bond in his experiences, which there never was in mine, which were very
sedentary. To be sure, it is quite true that he's conservative.
In fact for the fun of it, I have him read *National Review*
and occasionally read stuff of mine and Whittaker Chambers and so on. And he's also pro-American. And we're
both bright, sure.

INTERVIEWER: And you're both admirers of Bill Buckley.

BUCKLEY: Exactly! Though sometimes he kind of lags behind a little
bit.

INTERVIEWER: About Blackford Oakes again: there are some sort of serious disagreements about your style. Just running barefoot
through some of these critical notices, I see: "Oakes is as
bloodless as well-done English roast beef"—that's a reviewer in Florida—versus Broyard in the *New York Times*:
"In every respect he is a welcome relief from the unroman-
tic superiority and disengagement of a James Bond. Beneath this Cold War there beats a warm heart." Then we
get from another reviewer: "Blackie has a distinctive personality"—and from another lines like: "A flat character
and an annoying name dropper." You attract lines like: "A

Rambo with a Yale degree" and all sorts of things. This character of yours seems to be capable of stirring up a lot of confusing and conflicting opinions. Maybe that's biographical.

BUCKLEY: Well, yes, I have a feeling—I hate to say it, but I have a feeling this is mostly a confusing of things about me. I simply decline to believe that two or three of those things said about Blackford Oakes would have been said if the books had been written by Mary Gordon, say. They just wouldn't have said it—and they wouldn't have *thought* it. Now, whether they convinced themselves that this was so, or whether they feel the stereotypical compulsion to say it must be so because I wrote it, I don't know. I've never asked anybody. I'd like to think that Anatole Broyard is not easily seduced—at least not by me!—and I like to think that Blackford Oakes is an interesting human being. True, in certain of the novels he plays a relatively minor and flat role. But never quite as minor as people have sometimes charged.

INTERVIEWER: You seem to attract reviews which don't have much to do with the book at hand.

BUCKLEY: My son Christopher thinks I suffer from overexposure, and I'm sure he's right. I'd like to think some of my books would have done better if they had been published under an assumed name, so that people wouldn't feel they had to do the Buckley bit before talking about the book. It's especially true in England, by the way, although I'm underexposed in England in the sense that I'm not all over the place. Some aspects of my situation as a novelist are probably unique. Gore Vidal is very public in his experiences, but he's episodic. He goes away for a year and a half— thank God!—and then he writes his books and then he comes back and publicizes them. Norman Mailer, during his *Village Voice* period, and right after, was almost always in the news, not for something he said or for a position he had taken, about which people ceased caring, but about something he had done. You know, urinated in the Pentagon, or married his seventh wife, or got drunk at his fiftieth birthday, that kind of thing. But I assault the public three times a week in the column, and once a week on television, and every fortnight if they elect to read the *National Review.* So that's kind of a hard battering ram for people disposed to be impatient, either as critics or as consumers, of a novel written by me.

INTERVIEWER: That puts your critics to a particular test—that is, to detach themselves.

BUCKLEY: Anatole Broyard has been very attentive and receptive, and so has Lehmann-Haupt. Between them they've reviewed almost everything I've written.

INTERVIEWER: Did you say once that when you decided to write a novel, John Braine sent you a book on how to write a novel?

BUCKLEY: We were friends. John Braine was born again, politically. This was along around 1957 or '58 when he ceased to be an angry young man, and became an early deplorer of the excesses with which we became familiar in the sixties and seventies. So he used to write me regularly, and I had lunch with him once or twice in London; he was on my television program, along with Kingsley Amis. But then he—he was a little bit moody, and then he sort of stopped writing his letters. There wasn't any implicit act of hostility—I just had the feeling he wasn't writing his twenty-five people per week, that kind of thing. But when I sent him a letter saying that I was going to write a novel, he said, Well, I wrote a book on how to write a novel, and here it is. So I read it.

INTERVIEWER: Was it helpful?

BUCKLEY: I remember only one thing—which doesn't mean that I wasn't influenced by a hundred things in it—but he said that the reading public expects one coincidence, and is cheated if it isn't given one, but scorns two.

INTERVIEWER: Is there anyone or anything you would never write about?

BUCKLEY: I wouldn't write anything that I was simply not at home with. I wouldn't write a Western novel, for instance. I'm not sure I'd want to write *Advise and Consent*—the inside-the-Senate type of novel . . .

INTERVIEWER: Why don't you think about writing a novel like Tom Wolfe's—the novel of manners, of certain strata of society, of the mixture of social and political and business life. You have the keen observer's eye, and maybe not quite the same rapier instinct that Tom has for the false note, and—

BUCKLEY: And certainly not his descriptive powers, or his talent for caricature. Because those are indispensable weapons. For the first few chapters of *Bonfire,* I underlined just his descriptions of people's clothes, and in a million years I couldn't achieve that.

INTERVIEWER: It's true, there are no caricatures in your novels that I can think of. Tempting as it must have been to do so with some of the darker figures in those novels.

BUCKLEY: Well, some people thought the Queen was. I didn't think so. I thought she was a somewhat Dickensian, original creation. I'm really quite serious. The fact that she's terribly sharp-tongued, and terribly sarcastic; terribly aware of the fact that she's nominally sovereign, and actually powerless, I think adds to the credibility of her character. I would love to see her on the stage. As would have been done by Bette Davis.

INTERVIEWER: It's amusing to think back on how difficult it was for your agents to find publication in England for *Saving the Queen* because of your sacrilege in having Blackford Oakes bed down with her, even though a fictional queen.

BUCKLEY: And I have no doubt that not only killed that book in England, but probably inhibited its successors also.

INTERVIEWER: Have the novels been any kind of turning point? What have they meant to you? I have a feeling you took on the first one as a challenge—you wanted to test yourself against the form, and have some fun, which you certainly did—and then?

BUCKLEY: I did find that there were reserves of creative energy that I was simply unaware of. Obviously, as a nonfiction analyst, one has to think resourcefully, but if, let's say in the novel I'm depicting a Soviet prison train going from Moscow to Siberia, I've got to create something that can hold the reader's attention during that journey. The answer became: You can do that. And it's kind of nice to figure out that you *can* do that . . . create a story that carries you from there.

Of Buckley's eleven novels to date—ten of them concerned with Blackford Oakes, the CIA and the Cold War—the second, *Stained Glass*, occupies a special place. For years, it was *the* best-seller among his best-selling novels. More serious, less a jape than his debut novel, *Saving the Queen*, though all his novels are at bottom serious entertainments, it seems to convey a special feeling for its tragic hero—a German count, not Oakes—and for the unavoidable, undeclared human predicaments of that war in the shadows.

Invited by the Actors Theatre of Louisville, Kentucky, to contribute to their new playwrights program, the Humana Festival of new American plays—a commendable effort to get writers accomplished in other forms to try writing for the theater—WFB's play was produced in March–April 1989. Here is how their bulletin described the novel and introduced their interview.

Among his many books are eight novels which follow the adventures of the dashing Blackford Oakes, American secret agent, through an array of international intrigues and political hotbeds. Buckley has adapted his play from the second work in the series, *Stained Glass* . . .

In *Stained Glass,* Oakes is undercover in 1953 West Germany, as an engineer rebuilding a chapel. There, his assignment is to keep tabs on Count Alex Wintergrin, a charismatic leader seeking to reunite East and West Germany and quickly gaining popular support, to the dismay of both Washington and Moscow. Oakes soon becomes caught in the middle of Cold War détente and faces a moral dilemma: whether to obey his CIA orders and eliminate Wintergrin, or to follow his personal allegiance to a leader he respects as "the most admirable man alive." In a conversation with his Soviet espionage counterpart, Oakes expresses the confusion of his predicament: "Our people agreed to his 'elimination'—what a Sunday-suited word, his elimination—because *you* gave us no alternative. *That's* the official view of it. God knows it isn't my view of it."

An Interview with the Playwright

Why did you accept a commission from Actors Theatre to write a play?
Well, I hadn't done one before, and I thought it would be interesting to try it.

Had you thought about writing one before?
No, I hadn't . . . though my son had produced a play the summer before, at Williamstown, and he thought it was an exhilarating experience. So I thought, well, I'll try it.

And how did you find it, writing a play?
Writing a play was very difficult, very novel, in the sense that after a day's work I had no idea if I had done anything particularly good. Obviously, if you are a professional playwright, you develop enough experience to coach you on whether you are moving in a right direction or in a bad direction. I can do that in a novel or in nonfiction, but not yet in a play. It was very illuminating to me to have the thing read professionally. Then I got some idea of what it was that I had performed. It made a tremendous difference.

From your various novels why did you choose to adapt Stained Glass?
It seemed to me to have a high dramatic potential, and also one that didn't require visits to six planets in two acts; most of the action is concentrated right there. To the extent that it isn't, you can *make* it happen there. Now, I had a wildly permissive letter which said in effect that anything you write we can produce, but my son warned me against excesses of that kind.

The Blackford Oakes character and the series of novels he appears in certainly make for some dramatic material. I'm surprised that we haven't seen any movies. Has Hollywood ever been interested in making films of your novels?
Yes, they dart in and out, they're doing that right now. There was a big hiatus as a result of the financial failure of Robert Redford's CIA film, *The Day of the Condor,* some years ago. They lost their shirt on that, so no one would touch a spy film. Anyway, this will be the first venture in non-book form. Several screenplays have been written, not by me, but by others of various of the novels, but none of them have been produced.

You're known as a very prolific writer, and you seem to move quite easily from political essays to books on sailing and novels. At the end of the process of writing Stained Glass, *did you find yourself more comfortable with playwriting?*
Yes, by the time I sat down with the script a couple of months later to look at it again and rewrite it, I found I had achieved a perspective that I didn't have the very first night I started in. That may have been simply the passage of time, also comments on draft one from one or two people, especially my son, who had had some dramatic experiences. So it's fair to say the missing perspective began to crystallize—the idea of communicating with an audience exclusively through spoken words, without the reliance on nonspoken words which novelists rely on very heavily.

Do you find that it's easier to make a political point in writing a play instead of an editorial or novel?

The availability of another voice—so to speak, a Greek chorus sitting in your pocket to be trotted out anytime you want—can't be discounted. It's obviously advantageous. On the other hand, the stage has the overwhelming advantage of the utterly direct experience with a listener who is engrossed, or who is supposed to be engrossed—he is a captive audience for a couple of hours—so *that* obviously gives you a dramatic purchase on the stage that you don't have in the passive material. What I'm trying to say is the advantage of the novelist is the one I've exploited, having written eight novels and only one play.

In the play we get a sense that the U.S. is buckling under, giving in to pressure from Stalin. Do you feel that the U.S. allowed itself to be intimidated, and could have more strongly opposed the Soviet occupation of Eastern Europe?

Absolutely. In that respect a lot of renowned strategists agree that from Yalta on, until we started to wake up, we did really nothing. The Marshall plan was an important economic step, and NATO was an important economic step, but we in effect sat around while the Soviet Union developed hydrogen bombs and crystallized its hold on Eastern Europe. It's of course wildly ironic when you consider the reason we went to war was to save Poland's freedom in 1939.

In the play we get the sense that the reason for the Americans' intimidation is fear. Why did we sit around letting the Soviets develop hydrogen bombs?

The big example is 1956 when the Soviets moved into Hungary and Eisenhower had an opportunity to do something or not do something. He opted to do nothing. In doing that he more or less documented the fact that as long as they stayed behind their own frontiers they were absolutely safe. *Stained Glass* foresees the fear felt by Western leaders every time an ultimatum was handed down by Stalin.

East-West relations have changed since 1952 and since 1978, when you wrote Stained Glass. *In the age of Gorbachev and glasnost, what point does* Stained Glass *make about East-West relations?*

In *Stained Glass,* set in 1953, Stalin was still head of the Soviet Union. He was succeeded by a troika, which became Khrushchev; the violence of Khrushchev was documented in his oppression of running tanks over students in Czechoslovakia. Khrushchev denounced Stalin and then Brezhnev came in. He denounced Khrushchev. And now Gorbachev just denounced Brezhnev. But none of them denounced Lenin, and we're still dealing with a country whose huge, huge overhead is inexplicable except in terms of wanting to dominate the politics of the world. We've had all these ups and downs of détente and friendship and summit conferences, but the substantive causes of antagonism have not dissipated and won't dissipate until they renounce that part of Lenin that says, 'Go out and make the world a huge socialist state, which you will serve as a motherland.' They've got a lot of problems that distract them from doing that right now, of course, but none of the elements of the drama of *Stained Glass* is in any way affected by what's happened since.

What about the reunification of the two Germanys, is that a dead issue?
It's pretty dead, and it's not really an issue concerning which there's even German solidarity. The East Germans are afraid of the West Germans, and the West Germans are not absolutely sure that East Germany can be assimilated, and all the surrounding countries who twice in this century have been mauled by united Germany are in no particular hurry to patch them up. Clemenceau uttered a great line at Versailles. He said, "I love Germany so much I think there should be more of them."

In the play, Rufus makes a point that the end can at times be justified by the means. That reminded me of Darkness at Noon, *in which the excesses under Stalinist oppression could be justified by referring to its historical goals. What's the difference, with Rufus talking about U.S. covert action—*
Rufus was saying, Don't use the cliché "The end does not justify the means" because the end *very often* justifies the means. The correct statement is, "The end does not justify *any* means." We had a first-strike potential against the Soviet Union in 1953—we didn't use it, we didn't think of using it, quite correctly. If there is a single lesson to be learned from the eight novels I've written it is that there is a world of difference between *their* doing something and *our* doing something because the motives in both cases are entirely different. They want to maintain their slave state, we want to defend free people from being enslaved by them.

So when the U.S. plays dirty in terms of manipulating a nation's elections (as in Stained Glass) *and that sort of thing, it's because the Russians play dirty—?*
No, it's to save them from the Russians. Italy would have gone Communist in 1948 if we hadn't gone in there and spent millions of dollars and, as you put it, manipulated the vote. I wish to hell we'd manipulated the vote in Germany before Hitler got in, but the answer is what are we trying to accomplish? We're not trying to enslave somebody, we're trying to keep them free. We haven't dominated Italian politics since then, we left them on their own, but meanwhile they were free to act on their own rather than free to act as their Communist boss would have told them to do—as Stalin would've told them to do. . . .

This is a central point in your play; what place does personal morality have in government service?

We were reminded at Nuremberg that personal morality *at some point* transcends any loyalty to the state so that if the state were to say, you, I give you instructions to kill all Jews, or all Catholics or all blacks, you say just, I'm not going to do it. So there is always a surviving role for the conscience in any state, notwithstanding a presumptive obligation to obey orders.

Is that the case in Stained Glass?

Yes, Blackford Oakes reserves for himself a tiny little area of independent action and he says Okay, I work for the CIA, I acknowledge that the commander in chief thinks there's a danger of a world war, and under the circumstances I don't consider this a Nuremberg type of event, but let someone else do the actual pulling of the trigger. Now I don't necessarily defend that . . .

What is the significance of the chapel to you in the play?

It was a metaphor in the novel as it is in the play: the desire by Count Wintergrin to reconstitute the chapel fused in his spirit and his imagination with his desire to reintegrate Germany. They were part of the same dream. . . .

—THOMAS AUGST

Chapter 16

Passing in Review

All authors, perhaps especially those few who profess not to read their reviews, would like to talk (scream?) back at some of those who review their latest works. Prudence, caution, and publishers suggest otherwise. Bill Buckley more than once has dared to review his reviewers. This is either a bold and courageous maneuver or a kamikaze impulse. Asked to write an introduction to the paperback edition of the nonfiction book, *Overdrive* (Little, Brown & Company, Boston and Toronto, 1984), he wrote what follows, slightly abridged. WFB suggested that the reader could read the "Introductory Epilogue" before reading the book or after reading the book, or skip it entirely (he has suggested skipping when writing the inevitable chapter on navigation that adorns, or afflicts, each of his sailing narratives, sensitive to the fact that not every reader will be as enthralled by the techniques of navigation as he).

He gives more space to quoting the attacks on his book (and him personally) than to his ripostes or to his favorable reviews, most of them summed up in a footnote. Once again, he charges when he sees red and he most enjoys those negative reviewers who are clever—see the splendid parody in the following—not those who would merely tear him limb from limo.

INTRODUCTORY EPILOGUE

When Ray Roberts, who is my editor for a paperback edition of *Overdrive,* asked if I would write an introduction to it I agreed right away ... I thought the reviews of it worth going over with some thought, hoping that such a study would interest readers, and knowing that it would interest me. There are over a hundred of these (*Overdrive* was handled intensively by the critical press) and they say something about the book but also about the culture in which they cropped up.

I begin, in search of focus, with a chronology. I reveal in the text of *Overdrive* when exactly it occurred to me (quite suddenly) to write this book, a journal of that particular week in my life. I had done such a book ten years earlier. It was here and there suggested by some critics that I had dreamed up a way to discharge an obligation to my publisher. In fact, the contrary is the case because when I decided to write this book I needed to get my publisher's agreement to postpone a commitment I had already made. ...

It took me as many weeks to complete, almost exactly, as any of my other books, including my novels. It was suggested by one critic (you will see) that I more or less dictated scraps of this and that into a machine, presumably while skiing in February. Other critics, however, did not challenge that the book was written with care.

When I returned to New York, the manuscript complete except for the fine-tuning I do in July, I sent a letter to the editor of *The New Yorker,* Mr. William Shawn. I told him I thought it unlikely he would want to see my new book, given that I used exactly the same formula I had used ten years before in writing *Cruising Speed,* which *The New Yorker* had excerpted. Mr. Shawn replied that he would like to read *Overdrive,* which he subsequently bought.

It happened that the task of editing *Cruising Speed*'s excerpts fell to Mr. Shawn, if it can be said that anything at *The New Yorker* "falls" to Mr. Shawn. In any event, I had the extraordinary experience of working with him, he going over every sentence. When we lunched together one day I remember that a substantial part of our meeting was concerned with my habit of placing commas in unconventional places. This finally drew from Mr. Shawn, over the telephone, what I take it must be the sharpest kind of reproach the gentleman ever permits himself: "I am afraid, Mr. Buckley, that you do not really know the proper use of the comma." If St. Peter had declared me unfit to enter the Kingdom of God, I could not have felt more searingly the reproach, delivered in Mr. Shawn's inimitable manner. I hardly intend to suggest that he is otherwise permissive, though he sticks firmly, after *The New Yorker* makes the first-draft selection, to his determination to let authors whose works are being excerpted signify what they wish included, what excluded. Merely that he is meticulous. "I want *you* to be pleased with what we publish," he said to me. I have had a wonderful relationship with *The New Yorker,* having submitted five book manuscripts to Mr. Shawn, and received five acceptances.

I did not again work directly with Mr. Shawn. My next editor, William Whitworth, also demanding, and thorough, and civil, is now the editor of the *Atlantic Monthly.* The succeeding editor was Patrick Crow, a genial, surefooted, relaxed and amusing man who does not for a moment attempt to conceal that Mr. Shawn is *the* editor of *The New Yorker,* who reviews every controversial decision made during the many hours spent between the author and his *New Yorker* editor. When the author especially pleads for inclusion of a passage to which Mr. Shawn unwaveringly objects, what happens is that Mr. Shawn calls the author up and patiently explains why he is opposed to the inclusion of that passage. This author always relented. I would do anything for Mr. Shawn save join the Communist Party, and I am happy that it is unlikely he will ever ask me to do so.

All of this is by way of background, given that some critics (a) concluded that I expanded by force-feeding into a book (about 75,000 words long) what I had written for *The New Yorker* (the *New Yorker's* version ran about 45,000 words); while others (b) pretended to flirt with the idea that Mr. Shawn had coaxed me into writing a self-parody, that he had acted as an editorial *agent provocateur*—a reading of Mr. Shawn wildly ignorant of the kind of person he is; leaving also (c) a few critics who, though reviewing my book, obviously had not read it, having clearly read only the excerpts published in *The New Yorker.* One critic especially comes to mind, who warned, "Readers seeking the tart side of Mr. Buckley will be disappointed." The tart side of Mr. Buckley is well represented in the book, less so in *The New Yorker* excerpts because Mr. Shawn explained to me over the telephone, after I had pitched for the inclusion of one very tart episode, that *The New Yorker* does not have a letters column in which editorial targets can fire back, and that therefore he feels it morally important to avoid anything that might be thought as hit-and-run.

In due course (January, February 1983), the *New Yorker* excerpts were published, and the reaction to them was, well, out of the ordinary. The *Washington Post's* Curt Suplee reported joyously in his column, "That incessant scrunching noise you keep hearing to the north is Wm. F. Buckley Jr. attempting to squeeze his ego between the covers of the *New Yorker.* The behemoth first half of his two-part personal journal makes Proust look positively laconic. Buckley maunders along like Macaulay on Quaaludes about his house, limo, kids and friends, gloating and quoting his snappiest ripostes . . . *And yet you can't put the damn thing down!* Odd anecdotes bob up in the verbal spew (e.g., the time a typo in his column made it seem as if Pat Boone and his wife were wild about porno movies). The rhythm becomes hypnotic and . . . is there such a thing as smug-o-lepsy?"

I think I can only describe the reaction of *Newsweek* as hysterical. Before the *New Yorker*'s ink was dry, Mr. Gene Lyons published an excoriation in high tushery of indignation ("So who is this preposterous snob?"). Not satisfied with this, *Newsweek* then published letters from readers for whom the mere mention of my name is obviously emetic. And not content with *that,* *Newsweek* then published a piece speculating on who might be the successor to William Shawn when he retires as editor of *The New Yorker,* including reference to unnamed critics' concern over Mr. Shawn's wilting powers, as witness that he had published the "self-indulgent" journals of Mr. Buckley. (The three assaults prompted me to write to *Newsweek* to observe that I hoped their obsessive concern over my self-indulgent journals had not got in the way of their enjoyment of the two-million-dollar party *Newsweek* had given itself in New York to celebrate its fiftieth anniversary. The letter was published, but in bowdlerized form.)

Now, leading up to publication of the book and fired by *The New Yorker,* came the parody-makers. There was one by Jon Carroll of the *San Francisco Chronicle* which was quite funny, burlesquing among other things my occasional use of Latin phrases. He had me referring to "Nihil Obstat, our Cuban-American cook," summoning my "Honduran-American driver, Pari Passu," sailing my "71-foot sloop, Malum In Sea," and using the services of my "ever efficient secretary, Gloria Mundi." There was another treatment by Richard Cohen of the *Washington Post,* good-natured and clever. Another in the *New York Review of Books,* some of it very funny, and still another in the *New Republic.*

I have elected to publish here in full the parody I thought funniest. It was written for the University of Chicago daily, the *Chicago Maroon,* by an undergraduate, David Brooks, the week before I went there as a visiting fellow. I put it all here in part because it is exuberantly readable but also because it communicates the nature of the irritation felt by some of the readers of the *New Yorker* articles. He touches, in the manner of the parodist, on themes that would be sustained by many of the critics when the book came out in August.

The Greatest Story Ever Told

William Freemarket Buckley was born on December 25, 1935 in a little town called Bethlehem. He was baptized an Episcopalian on December 28 and admitted to Yale University on the 30th.

Buckley spent most of his infancy working on his memoirs. By the time he had learned how to talk he had finished three volumes: *The World Before*

Buckley, which traced the history of the world prior to his conception; *The Seeds of Utopia,* which outlined his effect on world events during the nine months of his gestation; and *The Glorious Dawn,* which described the profound ramifications of his birth on the social order.

Buckley attended nursery school at the School of Soft Knocks, majoring in Art History. His thesis, "A Comparison of Michelangelo's David and My Own Mirror" won the Arthur C. Clarke award for Precocious Criticism and brought him to the attention of world luminaries.

His next bit of schooling was done at Exeter, where he majored in Pre-Yale.

Buckley's education was interrupted by World War II, during which he became the only six-year-old to fight in Guadalcanal and to land on the beaches of Normandy. Combat occupied much of his time during the period, but in between battles he was able to help out on the Manhattan Project, offer advice at Yalta, and design the Marshall Plan. His account of the war, *Buckley Versus Germany,* perched atop the *New York Times* Best Seller List for three years.

Upon his return to Exeter, Buckley found that schoolwork no longer challenged him. He transferred his energies to track, crew, polo, golf, tennis, mountain climbing, debate, stock brokerage, learning the world's languages, playing his harpsichord and, of course, writing his memoirs. By this time he had finished his ninth volume, *The Politics of Puberty,* which analyzed angst in the international arena and gave advice on how to pick up women. A friend at the time, Percy Rockefeller-Vanderbilt III, remembered, "Everybody liked Bill at Exeter. His ability to change water into wine added to his popularity."

The years at Exeter were followed by the climax of his life, the Yale years. While at Yale he majored in everything and wrote the bestseller, *God and Me at Yale,* which was followed by *God and Me at Home,* and finally, *God and Me at the Movies.*

His extracurricular activities at Yale included editing the *Yale Daily News,* serving as President of the University, and chairing the committee to have Yale moved from New Haven to Mount Olympus. He also proved the existence of God by uttering the Cartesian formula, "I think, therefore I am."

While a senior, Buckley founded the publications which would become his life's work: one was a journal of politics entitled *The National Buckley,* and the other was a literary magazine called *The Buckley Review.* Later, he would merge the two publications into what is now known as *The Buckley Buckley.*

On the day of graduation, Buckley married Miss Honoria Haight-Ashbury and fathered a son and a daughter (Honoria helped) both of whom would be named Yale.

As any of you who read *The New Yorker* know, life for Mr. Buckley since then has been anything but dull. On any given morning he will consult with a handful of national leaders and the Pope, write another novel in the adventure series, "Bill Buckley, Private Eye," chat with a bevy of Academy Award winners, write a few syndicated columns, and tape an edition of his TV show, "Firing Pin." He also tames a wild horse, chops down trees to reduce U.S. oil imports, and descrambles some top secret Soviet spy transmissions.

In the afternoons he is in the habit of going into crowded rooms and making everybody else feel inferior. The evenings are reserved for extended bouts of name-dropping.

Last year, needing a break from his hectic fast-lane life, Buckley sailed across the Atlantic in his yacht, the HMS *Armsrace,* and wrote a book entitled *Atlantic High.* In one particularly riveting scene, the *Armsrace* runs out of gas in the middle of the ocean and Buckley is forced to walk the rest of the way.

Buckley has received numerous honorary degrees, including an M.B.A., an Ll.D., a Ph.D., an M.D. and an L.H.D., all of them from Yale, of course.

During his two days at this University, Mr. Buckley will meet with students, attend classes, deliver a lecture and write four books.

So that as the countdown approached for the publication of *Overdrive,* one had the feeling that pens were being taken to the smithies to be sharpened. My son Christopher has a sensitive ear for these matters and advised me to batten down the hatches: I had seriously provoked, he warned me, substantial members of the critical community. And sure enough, his Farmer's Almanac proved reliable because the flak from the most conspicuous critical quarters (the *New York Times,* the *Washington Post,* the *New York Review of Books,* the *New Republic, The Nation, Atlantic,* and *Harper's*) was instantaneous, and heavy. These critics were uniformly . . . upset, might be the generic word to describe their emotions. They expressed themselves differently and at different lengths, ranging from the four-thousand-word review by John Gregory Dunne in the *New York Review of Books,* to the two-sentence review in the *Atlantic Monthly.* They found the book variously boring, boorish, presumptuous, vain, arrogant, illiterate, solipsistic, and other things.

The Virginia Kirkus Service, a prepublication bulletin designed for bookstores and libraries, summarized that "most readers will probably find this [book] tedious at best, sleekly loathsome at worst." The writing is "sloppy." An example of the kind of thing one finds in it is that at one point I ask myself why I labor, and answer, " 'the call of *recta ratio,*' and 'the fear of boredom.' He then goes on, patronizingly, to explain what *recta ratio* means." I think this means either that everybody already knows what *recta ratio* means, or that if not everybody knows what it means, an author should not explain the meaning, as to do so is patronizing. Writing for the *New York Times,* novelist Nora Ephron was oh so scornful. "He has written a book about money," was her principal finding. She imputed anti-Semitism (ever so deftly, but more readers would catch that than the meaning of *recta ratio*) and insensitivity to the suffering of my friends all in a single sentence: (". . . it's appalling that Mr. Buckley should mention Shylock when discussing *National Review's* landlord or discourse so blithely on the physical infirmities of his friends"). And closed by suggesting that my affectations might best be understood by using a little ethnic imagination ("The English used to say, give an Irishman a horse and he'll vote Tory, but never mind").

So certain was Miss Ephron that much would be made of the fact that I get about in a chauffeur-driven limousine that she led off with it, . . . to wit:

> I cannot imagine that anyone who reviews this book will fail to mention the part about the limousine, so I may as well begin with it. Only a few pages into *Overdrive,* WFB gets into his limousine . . . and the occasion inspires him to reveal the circumstances under which he had the car custom-built. "What happened," he writes, "was that three years ago when it came time to turn in my previous car, which had done over 150,000 miles, the Cadillac people had come up with an austerity-model limousine, fit for two short people, preferably to ride to a funeral in. The dividing glass between the driver and driven was not automatic, there was no separate control for heat or air conditioning in the back, and the jump seats admitted only two. . . . This simply would not do: I use the car constantly, require the room, privacy, and my own temperature gauge. . . . There was, as usual, a market solution. You go out (this was in 1978) and buy a plain old Cadillac. You deliver it to a gentleman in Texarkana [I should have said Ft. Smith, Arkansas]. He chops it in two, and installs whatever you want. Cost? Interesting: within one thousand dollars of the regular limousine, and I actually don't remember which side."

Don't you see, Miss Ephron asks, "the story of the limousine is *emblematic*"? (My italics.)

My colleague Joe Sobran, on seeing Miss Ephron's review, sent me a memorandum: "Dear Bill, The critical reaction is interesting: Nora Ephron calls it 'a book about money,' when it's her *review* that's about money. I can't imagine you dwelling on the subject as she does; for that matter, I can't imagine you writing about your worst enemy as she writes about her ex-husband. Wonderful to hear such a woman lecture on poor taste, vulgarity, the nouveau riche. . . . My impression was that you can only be nouveau riche for the short-term; she seems to want to make you out as *second-generation* nouveau riche. She sees bigotry in a Shake-spearean tag, then proceeds to make a crack about the Irish which the *Times* wouldn't tolerate about just *any* ethnic group."

Grace Lichtenstein, writing for the *Washington Post*, leaned heavily on the tease that William Shawn was pulling a fast one. "When parts of this book first appeared in *The New Yorker*, I thought it was a joke, a Buckley parody of how some leftist might view Buckley's preoccupation with material possessions and his aristocratic lifestyle. Alas, it is not an intentional parody, although there are, swimming in this sea of trivia, some amusing anecdotes. . . ." Again, the business about my obsession with wealth, the slouchiness of my writing style; and then, to preserve her credentials as an even-minded critic, "Now let me tell you the most awful part of *Overdrive*. After plowing through a third of it I realized . . . I was also (deep breath here) [her deep breath] quite envious. I mean, who wouldn't want a stretch limo in which to dictate one's letters? [etc., extending to a cook and a chauffeur]—plebeian clod that I am," said Miss Lichtenstein, teasing us, because we are all supposed to know she is not *really* a plebeian clod.

Harper's took pretty much the same line, done by Rhoda Koenig, and the *Atlantic Monthly* saved space with a two-line review. "Mr. Buckley has assumed that a move by move record of one week in his bustling life, together with such recollections, reflections, and droppable names as occur to him en route, will be of benefit to the public. Ah, well, to err is human, and Mr. Buckley is not divine." . . .

The *San Francisco Chronicle* also elected a short dismissal, by Patricia Holt. "Buckley has produced an overdone, overwritten, overblown 'personal documentary' whose preview in *The New Yorker* earlier this year provoked a brilliant sendup by Jon Carroll in these pages. Better to read that column than waste your time with this book." The revelation to the citizens of San Francisco that an editor of the *San Francisco Chronicle* was actually concerned about wasting their time was apparently met with such exuberant skepticism that *Overdrive* became, in that city, a modest best-seller.

The attack in the *New York Review of Books* was hefty and unexpected, this because its author, John Gregory Dunne, an acquaintance of long standing, had written to me after the *New Yorker* articles had been published to say in a pleasant context that he had "inhaled" the *New Yorker* pieces and looked forward to the book treatment. Usually, if you hear that something you created had been "inhaled," you are likely to conclude something other than that your friend had been bowled over by a mephitic encounter. In any event, when Mr. Dunne's attack was published, the editor Robert Silvers punctiliously offered me space to reply.

The gravamen of Mr. Dunne's objections was, really, my technicolored view of life. Unhappily, the descriptions he gave of episodes touched on in the book justified his criticisms of them. If I were to write that Hamlet was a man who never could make up his mind and therefore manages to bore us to death I am, as a reviewer, fully protected—except against anybody who proceeds to read *Hamlet*. In my reply to the *New York Review of Books* I was concrete in the matter, excerpting exactly Dunne's description of one episode in the book (my quarrel with the *Boston Globe*) and then describing the episode itself. Mr. Dunne's version will live as a locus classicus of distortion. (Locus Classicus, I should say for the benefit of Jon Carroll, is my Shangri-la.)

A week after seeing Dunne's review I received a letter: "If they ever listen [to what you wrote] (which must be a question) you will teach them not to take the sacred elixir of life and splash it all over the roadside, as they are too prone to do." That was the comment on *Overdrive* by Louis Auchincloss. Lance Morrow (I anticipate my narrative) wrote, "I was just thinking about your book again, and about several exceptionally stupid reviews of it that I read. It seems to me that there was some massive point-missing going on there, but I can't quite account for it. Well, maybe I can at that."

Not easy. *People* magazine said of it, "Less self-confident men would be embarrassed to flaunt themselves so openly, but Buckley is obviously never shy." By contrast, Mr. Dunne was complaining: "[Buckley] is really not very giving of himself." *People* magazine would shrink to four pages if the editors suddenly found it "embarrassing" to express a curiosity about People ten times more inquisitive than any I would consent to satisfy. But Dunne was relentless in at once protesting the lack of profundity, while trivializing or ignoring what is there. Thus (in pursuit of the general vision of my hedonism), "[Buckley] spends every February and March skiing in Switzerland." That was on the order of my reporting, "Mr. Dunne spends every morning brushing his teeth." (My skiing occupies as much of my day in Switzerland as Mr. Dunne's stair-climbing does his days in Los Angeles.)

But oh how he worries about me! . . . I closed my letter to the *New York Review of Books* by quoting Dunne's final strictures . . . :

"The show has been on the road too long," Dunne pronounced. "Mr. Buckley has spread himself so thin that he has begun to repeat himself, repeatedly. *Overdrive* is *Cruising Speed* redux as last year's *Atlantic High* is *Airborne* redux. As might be expected, Mr. Buckley is unrepentant." I answered, "As well complain that I edit a 28-year-old magazine which will celebrate the fourth of July again on the fourth of July. I have written a dozen non-fiction books, six novels, and a few books that are not routinely classified, though they are, by some, glibly dismissed. In 1985, I shall write a book called *Pacific High*, patterned after the first two. The literary technique explored in *Cruising Speed* . . . is so majestically successful I intend to repeat it ten years hence, and ten years after that. At which point I shall be happy to review John Gregory Dunne's *True Confessions IV*, inasmuch as I am certain there will be great wit in it, as there was in its progenitor; as also in *True Confessions Redux*, published last year. [My reference was to his novel *Dutch Shea Jr.*] I promise in my next book to scratch up a friend about whom I can say something truly unpleasant if Greg Dunne promises in *his* next book to come up with a murdered woman who doesn't have a votive candle [as he had written] protruding from her vagina."

But others viewed *Overdrive* very differently. Take, for instance, the question of snobbery. A number of critics came gleefully to the conclusion that *Overdrive* was the work of a snob. Mr. Charlie Slack of the *Chattanooga Times* said it quaintly: "To call William F. Buckley Jr. a snob is to call the U.S.S. Nimitz a boat, the Sahara Desert a sandbox." The charge, widely if less picturesquely framed, struck the sensitive ear of *Time* essayist Lance Morrow. Now Morrow was himself disturbed by what he apparently deemed an unnecessary elongation in this book of hedonistic passages . . . "Buckley luxuriates in his amenities a bit too much, and one hears . . . in his prose the happy sigh of a man sinking into a hot bath." But he scotches conclusively, in a striking passage, the correlations so widely drawn about people who luxuriate in soapsuds. "So his enemies [note the *mot juste*] try to dismiss him as Marie Antoinette in a pimpmobile. They portray him as, among other things, a terrible, terminal snob. To make the accusation is to misunderstand both William F. Buckley, Jr., and the nature of snobbery. Buckley is an expansive character who is almost indiscriminately democratic in the range of his friends and interests. He glows with intimidating self-assurance. The true snob sometimes has an air of pugnacious, overbearing self-satisfaction, but it is usually mere front. The snob is frequently a grand porch with no mansion attached, a Potemkin affair. The essence of snobbery is not real self-assurance but its opposite, a deep apprehension that the jungles of vulgarity are too close, that they will creep up and reclaim the soul and drag it back down into its native squalor, back to the Velveeta and the doubleknits."

Closely related to the charge of snobbishness was that of arrogance (egotism, vanity, what you will). The reporter for *Palm Beach Life*, who should be familiar with the phenomenon, wrote, "His book is outrageous in its egotism," he concluded, "but amusing withal. Treat yourself to it."

Phillip Seib, writing in the *Dallas Morning News,* took arrogance for granted but ventured an explanation: "A certain arrogance is essential if one is to publish what Buckley calls 'a personal documentary.' " The trouble with that extenuation, as far as an author is concerned, is that it gives such comfort as you would get from reading, "Mr. Joseph Blackburn, who traverses Niagara Falls on a tightrope, is said to be a damned fool. But who else but a damned fool would be expected to traverse Niagara Falls on a tightrope?"

Thomas Fox of the *Memphis Commercial Appeal* evidently thought he caught it all when he pronounced *Overdrive* "nothing more than the product of a smug exhibitionist who likes to wave his ego in public," while Peter Richmond, writing for the *Miami Herald,* gritted his teeth: *Overdrive* "may be the most egregious example of the abuse of literary license since Jack Kerouac, well into fame, actually published 250 pages of his dreams." The publisher of *The New Republic,* James Glassman, wrote in *USA Today* that *Overdrive* was "an act of sheer gall" but he quickly gave an individuated explanation for it. "My theory is that Buckley wrote *Overdrive* as proof of his own security in social and literary matters. He must have known that the literati would make fun of the book, but he wrote it anyway, just to flout them." That is an interesting insight, but it fails to explain why I should go out of my way to slight so many critics in this special way, since I tend to do so routinely in so many other ways. And it is incorrect to say that I expected anything like the reaction *Overdrive* got. . . .

Pamela Marsh of *The Christian Science Monitor* said that, really, it was worse than sheer arrogance. "Add to that his obvious relish in what seems an overwhelming arrogance—he is in fact proud of his pride." That tends to ask for more thought than one is routinely prepared to give to such facile statements, unless they come in from philosophers. (Let's see: John is proud to be an American. John is proud of his pride in being an American. How about: John is proud of his pride in his pride in being an American. I wonder if Miss Marsh ever thought of that? Ever *worried* about that?)

Doug Fellman, a student writing for *The Hopkins Newsletter,* tried to be reasonable about the whole thing: "Naturally, some persons will complain that Buckley, in recording his life in such a journal, is committing an act of great egotism and conceit. Yet the autobiography is a common and accepted form of biography, and Buckley simply chooses to record his life in the present and as an excerpt." But untuned objections were everywhere. *Booklist* said comprehensively that, for some readers, *Overdrive* would prove "a cross section of everything that is wrong with America, from elitism to Reaganomics." The *Cleveland Plain Dealer* found "the private Buckley who appears in this book . . . laced with pride, unflinchingly materialistic and self-centered—all in all, a popinjay."

I (happen to) prefer temperamental reactions to the lorgnetted sort of thing *Overdrive* drew from what one might call The Social Justice Set. I especially preferred Miss (Ms. would here be safer, I suppose) Carolyn See of the *Los Angeles Times,* who saw the author of *Overdrive* as "an American institution . . . lounging elegantly in his talk-show chair, driving Norman Mailer into a conniption fit, teasing and torturing Gore Vidal until he just can't take any more, driving at least 49 percent of the viewing audience into a state of mind that can't really be described in words, but it involves lurching up out of your chair, burying your hands in your hair and shrieking 'Yuuggh! Turn it off! Make him go away!' " There's no quiche in Ms. See's diet, 100 percent All Bran.*

The refrain on the matter of wealth was widespread, the popular corollary of which was to [comment on] insouciance with respect to poverty, as (Ann Morrissett Davidson, *Philadelphia Inquirer*) for instance: "But there is something rather beguiling and even enviable about this over-driven patrician and his way of life. Perhaps it is his apparently blithe blindness to most of the world's miseries." The patronizing explanation is both sweet and deadly. Jack the Ripper just didn't know it was wrong to strangle ladies, don't you see?

Two weighty voices, however distinct, came in from the Big Leagues.†

One of them Eliot Fremont-Smith of the *Village Voice,* the other Norman Podhoretz, the editor of *Commentary.* Fremont-Smith, in voicing qualified approval of the book and its author, is a prominent liberal who found himself teeming with things to say.‡

He began with the novel point that those who harp on the theme of the privileged life of the author of *Overdrive* tend to neglect a not insignificant point. "I think of *his* dilemma. No public figure I know of has been so chided by people he likes or is willing to admire or takes it with such aplomb." He insisted that *Overdrive* was ultimately a book about friendship. "Friends are more important, indeed all important. *Overdrive* is a record and celebration of connection, of how association (memories, locales, daily working intercourse, surprise, pleasure) improves the soul and

---

* Sometimes such wholesome antagonists go on to blush. Ms. See concluded her colorful review, "Buckley shows us a brittle, acerbic, duty-bound, 'silly,' 'conservative' semi-fudd, with a heart as vast and varicolored and wonderful to watch as a 1930s jukebox."

† I am grateful to a score of critics whose reviews, appearing in newspapers and magazines that seldom penetrate the Eastern Seaboard Establishment's switchboard, were understanding in every case, in some cases even encouraging, in a few even affectionate.

‡ His task was concededly complicated by a personal friendship, recently formed.

perhaps the cause of civilization and bestows grace on all and sundry, by no means least of all" on the author. Fremont-Smith, unlike the automatons who approached the book with floodlights in search of Social Justice and a hemorrhaging psyche, had eyes for *detail* (of which, in many reviews, there was a total absence). "He . . . discourses on Bach and Scarlatti with the likes of . . . Fernando Valenti and Rosalyn Tureck, and also mediates between them (the sections on music and the ego requirements of great performers are among the funniest, most scrupulous, and moving in the book)."

F-S becomes concrete, and it is interesting to reflect here on observations by one critic, alongside observations by two others.

On what I wrote in *Overdrive* about homosexuality, Fremont-Smith: "His riff on homosexuality, for notorious example [of my occasional waywardness], seems deliberately blind to all sorts of subtleties he should, at his age, with his antennae, be less innocent of."

On my treatment of homosexuality, Franz Oppenheimer in the *American Spectator:* "Another pernicious myth touched upon in *Overdrive* is the supposed biological and hereditary nature of homosexuality. . . . My father, who practiced psychiatry, first in Germany and after his emigration in San Francisco, collected substantial evidence in support of Buckley's impression that homosexuality is a disease that can be cured. During my father's entire professional life he endeavored to find a true 'biological,' i.e., an incurable homosexual. He never did."

And then at a personal, more evaluative level, referring to a eulogy and a testimonial I gave in my book, Fremont-Smith:

"[In *Overdrive,*] love is couched in courtly encomiums that are heartfelt but nevertheless embarrass."

Norman Podhoretz: "He is so good at delivering tributes that one would choose him above all others (well, perhaps not above Daniel P. Moynihan) to deliver the eulogy at one's own funeral, or better still, the speech in one's honor on some appropriate occasion. There are samples of both kinds of speeches in *Overdrive* and they are, without exception, masterpieces of the extremely difficult art of praise." Some say tomayto; which of course is to be preferred.

Fremont-Smith, finally, declines to accept my implied proposition that the literary form I adopted (one week in the life of X) is generally viable. He rejects the notion that the form is widely useful. Rather, he insists that it must be taken as a singular phenomenon. "Two questions [in fact] arise: a) How is all this activity possible? b) Can we stand it? Particularly, can we stand Buckley's glorying in it? . . . basically *Overdrive* is a log—not a how-to-do-it but how-has-it-been-done in a particular frame of time by one particular energy."

Norman Podhoretz . . . in November led the Book Review section of *Commentary* with an answer to the critics of *Overdrive*, interrupting a long silence as an active book reviewer. I am moved by the self-pride abundantly so designated in quotes already cited—but above all by feelings of gratitude most readers in my position would, I think, understand—to quote from this review. Podhoretz began, no less:

"The first thing to say about *Overdrive* is that it is a dazzling book. The second thing to say is that it has generally been greeted with extreme hostility."

Podhoretz went on to examine the causes of such hostility, discarding routine ideological antagonism as a satisfactory answer. "I do not believe that the injustice done to *Overdrive* can be explained in strictly political terms. Something deeper and more interesting is at work here." What that is is not easily distilled, though I will have a few thoughts on the subject at the end of this essay.

To those who declaimed first against the insubstantiality of *Overdrive* and then against the craftsmanship, like the woman who thought it should have been subtitled "Dictated but not read," Podhoretz replied: "The material is fascinating in itself and all Buckley's virtues as a writer are called forth in the recording of it. The prose flows smoothly and elegantly, its formality tempered with colloquial touches that somehow never jar, its mischievous wit coexisting in surprisingly comfortable congruence with its high rhetorical solemnities, its narrative pace sure-footed enough to accommodate detours and flashbacks without losing the necessary forward momentum." (Compare Grace Lichtenstein in the *Washington Post*: "What Buckley needed was a snappy rewrite by an experienced *People* hand. . . .") Podhoretz, who does not like to give ground, dealt defiantly with the matter of Money: "I for one do not doubt that the delight Buckley takes in his privileges is an exemplary spiritual virtue. If I do have a doubt, it concerns the extent of this delight. I mean, is he always so cheerful? Does he never suffer from anxiety?" (Eliot Fremont-Smith was more direct on this point: "In the book, Buckley has exquisite sandwiches but never takes a pee.") I wrote to Mr. F-S that I had trained myself never to pee, but he has not answered this letter, nor publicly celebrated my achievement.

(". . . What I was most struck by were the parts in which you tell us what you have to be sober about," my colleague Richard Brookhiser wrote me.)

To Mr. Podhoretz, I take the opportunity to say that I thought the shadows were there, in *Overdrive,* and that if they were not discernible to him, I do not know what is the appropriate reaction. Angst, in this volume, would not work.

Well, then. I have before me page after page of excerpts from reviews that make interesting observations. But economy requires that I put aside these notes and conclude. I do so by probing two questions, one concrete, and in its own way heuristic, the second general and critical.

The first is the matter of the limousine and the prominence it was given.

There was remarkably less fuss about my limousine when it figured in *Cruising Speed.* What, then, was the provocative difference between my *1970* limousine and my *1981* limousine? Hard scrutiny of the reviews suggests that the second *having been "custom-made"* caused it to be marginally insufferable. This is very interesting, especially so since the offended reviewers did not (many of them) hesitate to quote my narrative, in which, as Miss Ephron has reminded us, I revealed that, in 1978, buying a limousine with roughly the same features as the traditional, i.e., pre-austerity, limousine, cost approximately the same as the regular commercial limousine now being offered by the Cadillac company.

What then was it about the customizing that so inflamed?—that caused the *New York Times Book Review* critic to begin her review by concluding that *everyone* would focus on the limousine, whereafter she proceeded to devote almost one-third of her review to it?

Is it—I explore the question again—simply, the economic point? That a limousine is expensive? If so, isn't it odd to weigh in so heavily on this, given that a limousine costs only about twice what a Ford sedan costs? It does not require that one belittle the figure to ask: Why is it, when other finery of affluence is there to choose from, that a limousine is so conspicuous? I explain, in *Overdrive,* how I spend my days; and it quickly becomes obvious that it would no more be feasible to spend my days as they are spent in the absence of a car and driver than it would be to run a taxi service without taxis. Without going over a time sheet, in the week I recorded I would guess that eight hours of work resulted from being driven rather than driving. What is it that especially affects so many about this particular auxiliary to one's commercial life? The cost of it?

But that is hardly rational. Well then, is it the point that one ought not to expect rationality in a review of how one American (this American) leads his life if his *modus vivendi* is judged obnoxious? I say it is irrational because hardly anyone bothered, in reviewing *Overdrive,* to dilate on his objections to extravagances even when clearly unrelated to productivity. E.g., owning and maintaining a 36-foot sailing auxiliary which (by the way) costs three times what a limousine costs (ask any of the hundred thousand Americans who have one). I own a grand piano worth more than my limo; used less, and mutilated more. Or consider articles of un-questioned and unmitigated professional uselessness, like a thirty-three-year accumulation of one's wife's jewelry. . . . What *is* it about a limousine?

Sometime after the first dozen reviews appeared, I lunched with Sam Vaughan of Doubleday and told him I was astonished by the intensity of the concentration on the matter of my limousine, which at this point I was tempted to paint khaki. Sam observed that typical luxuries go largely unobserved, but that a chauffeur-driven car is the single most provocative possession of the modern urban American. "Everyone," he expanded, "no matter who, has been caught on a street corner in the rain, waiting for a bus, or trying to hail a taxi. And inevitably they will see a limousine slide by, with the lumpen-bourgeois figure in the back seat, maybe smoking a cigar; maybe even reading *The Wall Street Journal.* That is the generically offensive act in the big cities."* A good point, if the idea is to explain the spastic hostility toward limousine owners. Not, I think, a sufficient point to understand the peculiar emphasis put on the limo in some of the re-views.

I think that of the several points raised in opposing the book, this con-crete point puzzled me the most. I dwell on it because American culture has tended to be guided—not finally, but substantially—by utilitarian criteria. Does John Appleseed produce more using a tractor than a horse-drawn plow? Does Tom Wicker perform more efficiently using a typewriter, and going on to a word processor, than with a pencil? Why isn't the utilitarian coefficient dispositive in the matter of a limousine? Is it because the critic cannot distinguish between the limousine *qua* limousine, i.e., a luxury ve-hicle associated with inaugurations, weddings, and funerals, and the lim-ousine as mobile office? If so, there are two problems, the first the failure of the critical intelligence. The second, whether the envious view, trans-formed to resentment on that rainy day, on the sidewalks of New York, of the man comfortable in his limousine isn't, to use Miss Ephron's freighted word, "emblematic" of a public, rather than a private, disorder.

The second point touches on the corrosive use of the word "gleeful" to describe a reaction to one's material situation. I have especially in mind, because it was so frequently adduced by reviewers, my reference to a swim-ming pool. What I said about it parenthetically—words (if I may say so, gleefully reproduced)—was that it is "the most beautiful indoor swim-ming pool this side of Pompeii."

---

* After lunch, Buckley, ever generous, offered me a lift in his limo back to my office. "Are you crazy?" I said, ever paranoid, waving him off.—Ed.

Now I found it odd that several reviewers of obvious intelligence bridled at this. . . . In doing so it seems to me, on hard reflection, that they must have understood me to be saying something different from what I intended to say, so that the fault is either mine or theirs, and it is worth inquiring: Whose?

My indoor swimming pool is of modest dimensions (I give them, in *Overdrive*). In the book, as a matter of course, I acknowledge the architect who designed the pool, and the artist I engaged to give me a mosaic pattern to decorate it. My delight, therefore, was clearly not with my own doing, but with theirs. I cannot imagine resenting any expression of pleasure uttered by the man who, having, say, commissioned the Parthenon, goes on to describe it in his diary (presciently) as "the most beautiful pre-Christian temple ever constructed." What would he have been saying that a rational, self-respecting critic could object to? Mine was the voice of acclamation: a celebration of the architect, and of the artist: hardly of the author who accumulated the money with which to pay them.

But how odd, so widespread a reaction at an expression of delight at others' competence and artistry (many made as much of my reference to an "exquisite" sandwich made by our cook). Isn't it the job of the critic to distinguish between a compliment slyly paid ostensibly to someone else, actually to oneself, and a genuine compliment? Or are the critics reading self-congratulations by the man who had the wit to commission the pool, and the taste to appreciate the singularly well-made sandwich? That surely is reaching, isn't it? Would a reviewer single out a diarist's encomium on the performance of a visiting artist as an effort to draw attention to the author's piano? Or to his leverage on the artist?

I focus, finally, on what appears to have been a highly provocative literary proposition, namely my contention that a scrupulous journal of a week in an individual's life is at least a literary form worth thinking about, at best a literary idea worth celebrating. Many years ago the editor of the humor quarterly *Monocle* (it was Victor Navasky, now editor of *The Nation*) asked me to do a review of the work of the columnist Murray Kempton. I replied that he was asking me for the equivalent of a review of the work of Walter Lippmann, never mind that it would be more fun. Was I supposed to go back and read, or rather reread, fifteen years of Murray Kempton in order to write three thousand words?

I came up with a formula that satisfied Navasky, satisfied me, and planted, I think, the idea that blossomed, if that word is not too tendentious, in *Cruising Speed* and, now, *Overdrive*. Why not take a week of columns by Murray Kempton—next week's columns, say—and talk your way through them? He was writing five times a week back then, so that the chances were on your side that you would catch Murray Kempton reacting to a satisfactory range of challenges, phenomena, provocations, scandals, whatever. Enough to acquaint the reader with the moods (penetrating), style (incomparable), and thought (unreliable) of Murray Kempton.

It worked, in my judgment.

And so does it work, again in my judgment, on a larger scale in *Overdrive*.

To ask and quickly answer the most sensitive question, let me simply blurt it out:

Not everyone can write such a book. . . .

William Murchison, the columnist from Dallas, Texas, wrote, "Few indeed are the authors who could bring off such an enterprise as this. A week, literally speaking, with Ralph Nader; or Walter Mondale; or Phil Donahue; or General Westmoreland! To think of it is to weep."

Now Mr. Murchison has a point here, but not of the kind that should cause the egalitarian furies to howl.

We seem to concede, without any problem, that only people who are technically qualified can satisfactorily perform on the piano before an audience. So we concede, again without any apparent problem, that unless one deftly uses paint and canvas, one ought not to expect to be able to merchandise one's art. I do not see why there should be so much difficulty in applying the same implicit criteria in order to distinguish what one might call the "performing writer." Perhaps the problem exists at all only because very few people without the technique to bring it off would undertake to play the "Flight of the Bumblebee" on the piano. Not many weekend painters would expect to sell their canvases even to the very little galleries.

By contrast, everybody—writes. And, in writing, there is progressive fluency that approaches artistry. No one can say exactly where the line is, but it is to comply with the requirements of the full disclosure laws to admit: it would probably separate those who, using this standard, could, and could not, publish their journals, only the former being "performing writers." Okay. So why should it be difficult to accept the proposition that, from a writer, one expects work of a distinctive quality, even as one would from a painter or musician or plumber? If one managed that problem, one would cope with the preliminary objection to a journal based on a single week in a person's life: The person needs to be a writer.

But if the writer *is* qualified, what besides that does the reader, in order to be satisfied, require?

The reader would want an interesting sensibility. What is in process, in such an undertaking, is a literary self-portrait. I say "literary" only because the author's reactions are sometimes limned with operative emphasis on *the way* in which the reactions are expressed: and what then happens is that you collect, one by one, the little colored dots which, when they are, however chaotically, assembled, leave you with a mosaic, at best a pointillist portrait of—one human being.

Why should you care to have a self-portrait, as done, for instance, by William F. Buckley, Jr.—or by Groucho Marx? Or by Kay Graham?

Because, I think, self-portraits of many people can be interesting. If they work, they amuse. Enlighten. Explain. They provoke. And—I cling to the point—although the formal autobiography lets the actor stage his life and thought with more regard for conventional architectural prominences, the week's journal has complementary advantages. If I were offered today the alternative of reading an autobiography of Walter Lippmann, tracking his career, with which I am routinely familiar, or another comprehending his activity and his thought hour by hour during a single week, I *think*—I'm not sure—I might not lose by choosing the former. Remember that the supplementary alternative isn't necessarily excluded.

A book like *Overdrive* written by Ralph Nader? Well—who knows? He has not, true, achieved his reputation as a writer. . . . On the other hand, if he had the training to carry it off, would I be interested in reading a journal of a week in Ralph Nader's life? My own answer is, Yes: I would. So would I—I mean it—a week in the life of Phil Donahue. In fact, I would sleep outside the bookstore, waiting to put my hands on such a book, if it were such a book. It would take only one or two other explorers to set the form in concrete. Murray Kempton comes to mind as ideal. Or Patrick Moynihan. Or how about Jesse Jackson? If he would speak Honest Injun, as I do.

I regret many things about the reception of *Overdrive,* though I am obliged to record here two qualifiers. The first is that the book has been a solid, if not spectacular, entrepreneurial success. The second is that the book has generated an extraordinary amount of mail from strangers, strangers who, after reading it, thought to write to me, their motives varied. The volume of that mail I was unprepared for—the reach of *The New Yorker* always astonishes me; I think no book I have written (with one exception) has got such a response—but overwhelmingly grateful, for what I take to be the sense communicated of a common and joyful search for serenity, in which the readers appear to have been helped. (One wrote, "Rambling, idiosyncratic, amused, cranky, occasionally flamboyant— your observations and recollections were most enjoyable testaments to a vital life. You actually believe *something:* Something old, something blue, with flecks of tweed, patches on the elbows, old Nantucket and Martha's Vineyard before everyone else came, in short: the right way of doing things." Another: "In a confusing world, I must express my gratitude . . .") For that reason, among others already given, I regret the facile dismissal of the literary form by some reviewers (there were exceptions: *Time*'s Roger Rosenblatt wrote, "I think you've invented a genre. Pepys on speed, but better") who, in their haste to disparage, did not give sufficient thought to the potential uses of such a form by people whose thought and careers they would read about with less resistance. I hope, before I die, to see others using this form. I said airily that in ten years I intended to write a sequel to *Cruising Speed* and *Overdrive,* and ten years after *that,* a fourth journal. The prospect of this will cause a disturbing number of people to wish me . . . retired sooner, rather than later. But I caution them against strategic optimism in these matters. My limousine has miles to go before I sleep.

A critic who is also a friend has particular potency. Here, excerpts as "Kilpo" tries to get Buckley to cease and desist from breaking the Seventh Rule, which might be defined as the "you'all" commandment:

How Not to Write Dialect
by James J. Kilpatrick

In his hilarious essay on the literary offenses of James Fenimore Cooper—an essay that every novelist should read—Mark Twain laid down eighteen rules that govern the writing of romantic fiction. This was Rule No. 7:

"It requires that when a personage talks like an illustrated, gilt-edged, tree-calf, hand-tooled, seven-dollar Friendship's Offering in the beginning of a paragraph, he shall not talk like a Negro minstrel in the end of it."

I was reminded of Rule 7 the other day in reading William F. Buckley's new novel, *Tucker's Last Stand.* It is the ninth in his series starring CIA agent Blackford Oakes, and it is Buckley at his best. Believe me, his best is very good indeed.

But—you could feel the "but" coming—but my beloved friend neglected Rule 7. One of his principal characters is President Lyndon Johnson. Buckley undertook to capture the President's speech. He might with equal success have attempted to catch a soap bubble in a butterfly net.

Thus we observe that sometimes Lyndon says "I," and sometimes Lyndon says "Ah." On Page 147 the President is thinking of sending a note to Hanoi: "Ah know we never done it before. That's one of the reasons I want to do it now." Over the course of two pages, Lyndon says "Ah" six times and "I" nine times.

In Buckley's dialectal spelling, Johnson sometimes says "an" and then inexplicably reverts to "and." The President drops a *g* in "talkin' " and "confusin' " but sounds the consonant in "telling" and "going." In the same fashion, Barry Goldwater sometimes says "them" and sometimes says " 'em." All the other characters speak like Oxford dons.

The trouble is that the rendering of speech is a fearfully difficult task, in part because most of us vary our speech patterns to the occasion at hand. Lyndon Johnson was no exception. When he was in his molasses mode, seeking to cajole a waffling senator, he spoke as if he had a ripe plum in his mouth. On other occasions, when the cactus juice was flowing, he spoke Texan. I would not attempt to reproduce Lyndon's nasalities. He had a large nose, packed with resonant cavities, and the sound chambers did odd things to his speech.

Let it be said that Bill Buckley, as always, is in distinguished company. Not long ago I had occasion to reread Robert Louis Stevenson's *Kidnapped.* It remains a great yarn. Early in the novel David Balfour befriends Alan Breck. Alas, Stevenson could not decide whether Alan says "you" or "ye." Sometimes Alan speaks in "hoot, mon" Scottish, and sometimes not.

Owen Wister also neglected Rule 7. Off and on throughout *The Virginian*, Wister spelled "you" as "yu." It is not clear why he used this peculiar orthography, for 99 percent of English-speaking people pronounce "you" as "yu." On one page the hero says "an'." On the same page he says "and." . . .

A few writers have looked at the challenge of dialect and brought it off. Twain himself had a fine record of consistency. Huck Finn speaks in the same voice, and in the same spelling, throughout the novel. William Faulkner accurately caught the cadence and verbal structure of much black speech.

Dialectal writing demands more than an ear for individual words. There are regional vocabularies as well as regional accents. In some parts of the country the hour of 9:45 is a quarter to ten, in others it is a quarter of ten. Many Southerners carry groceries in a tote bag; Midwesterners carry groceries in a sack . . . Mastering these nuances is the work of a lifetime.

Sometimes, I know, the impulse to write dialect is overwhelming. Let me offer a word of sound advice: When the impulse strikes you, lie down until it goes away.

—MAY 12, 1991

To the Editor
American Spectator
Bloomington, Indiana

Your reviewer, Mr. Joseph Shattan, writes about me (*Who's On First*, by William F. Buckley, Jr.; June 1980), "The Yale-educated Mr. Oakes is no mere fop. On the contrary, he was trained as a nuclear physicist, he gained renown as a fighter-pilot during World War II, and he reads the geopolitical works of James Burnham for relaxation. Fluent in many tongues and related to—among other luminaries—the Queen of England, the young Oakes is at once effortlessly cosmopolitan and deeply patriotic." Elsewhere, Mr. Shattan advises us that he read Mr. Buckley's book about me in a single sitting. Could that have been the trouble?

You see, I took my degree at Yale in mechanical engineering, not nuclear physics. It is true that I fought in the war and knocked down two Nazi planes, but I took sick, and didn't therefore have the opportunity to gain renown, though I appreciate Mr. Shattan's assumption that, had my health stood up, I'd have shortened the war. It is true that I have read the works of James Burnham, hardly true that I read them "for relaxation." It is more nearly true that they are to be read as realistic substitutes for horror stories. And, then, unhappily, I am not a polyglot. I made a considerable effort in the spring and summer of 1952 to achieve a limited fluency in German. But my French, as Mr. Buckley pointed out, is at the level of *savez-vous-planter-les-choux.* I am mystified at the news that I am related to the Queen of England. It is correct that Mr. Buckley penetrated my penetration, but he never suggested that I am related to the Queen, though perhaps he knows something about me I don't know, not surprisingly since he is a very clever fellow.

Mr. Shattan shouldn't feel too bad, however. The reviewer for the *New York Times,* Newgate Callendar, pronounced me a "devout Catholic," which certainly qualifies him as a sleuth inasmuch as my mother is Episcopalian, my father Presbyterian, and I am somewhere in between. To be sure, I have a great admiration for Catholics, some of whom are among my closest friends; but I am mystified at how this datum was derived from anything Mr. Buckley, a careful writer though given, I think, occasionally, to euphuism, wrote. My regards to Mr. Shattan.

BLACKFORD OAKES

LANGLEY, VA.   OCTOBER 3, 1980

Perhaps one of the most effective ways to stretch one's neck out in search of a chopping block is for a novelist to review other novelists, a wordsmith to review a dictionary, etc. Naturally, Bill Buckley sails into such situations, chin jutting, eyes gleaming, a strange half-smile playing around his lips. This is from *The New York Times Book Review,* December 19, 1971.

The Oxford English Dictionary
The Compact Edition of the Oxford English Dictionary. Complete Text Reproduced Micrographically. 4,116 pp. New York: Oxford University Press. Two Vols., boxed. $75.

The Oxford English Dictionary was the moon-landing project of the English people, and if Sidney Webb, who was born the year the project was conceived and reached seventy the year it was completed, did not denounce it as a dreadful extravagance in an age when poverty was abundant in the groaning industrial areas of England, it can only have been because he forgot to do so. The enterprise resulted—to use the words of its publishers in connection with the new edition—in "the most prestigious book ever published," even as the moon landing is almost indisputably the most prestigious scientific enterprise ever consummated. Of course, scientific achievement, like an athletic one, is obsolescent in a sense quite different from a cultural achievement. The man who ran the four-minute mile knew that he was not being given tenure as a world record holder. The men who contributed to the O.E.D. achieved a more certain satisfaction.

Not exactly like the individual artist, who defies "improvement" in any measurable sense. But halfway there; far enough to raise the question, on which I shall touch in due course: Why isn't the O.E.D. a *continuing* masterpiece?

It could only have been a sense of historical excitement that kept successive lexicographers working over a period of seventy years to achieve this dictionary, that kept at least one compositor busy during the whole of his working life setting type for this dictionary which was printed in sections that sold for twelve shillings and sixpence each, beginning twenty-five years after the project was conceived, on into 1928. Each of the twelve volumes required anywhere from three to ten years to complete, depending on such variables as whether an editor (at the peak there were three working simultaneously) died, or whether England was fighting a particularly engrossing war, or whatever.

There were moments of doubt and even of panic, as when the whole of it was offered to Cambridge University, which sniffed it away, even as Yale disdained Mr. Harkness's colleges only to discover that Harvard instantly and greedily accepted them. But eventually the thing was done, and a set of the volumes was presented one each to the chiefs of state of the great English-speaking powers, King George V and President Calvin Coolidge, that they should know better their common philological patrimony.

Incidentally, there were American scholars involved in the project, and generous acknowledgment is made of their contributions. Indeed, the principal editor, Dr. James Murray, adjourned the meiotic tradition of his countrymen to say, as early as 1880, that he had discovered in Americans "an ideal love for the English language as a glorious heritage and a pride in being intimate with its grand memories, such as . . . is rare indeed in Englishmen toward their own tongue; and from this I draw the most certain inferences as to the lead which Americans must at no distant date take in English scholarship." Dr. Murray was, of course, correct: The study of linguistics is all but a protected American industry.

And it was the idea of an American, Mr. Albert Boni, head of the Readex Microprint Corporation, to take the entire O.E.D. and bring it out in two volumes. This involved shrinking thirteen volumes, not twelve. The editors brought out the supplemental volume in 1928 to deal with words that had come into being too late to be included in the previous volumes—it was too expensive to collate the new words typographically. And, as lagniappe, they threw in a list of "spurious words" the scholars had come upon in dictionaries dead and extant, which impostors had got into them as the result of typographical or other errors (sample: "*Depectible, a.* Error in Johnson's Dict. and some later Dicts. for *Depertible*") and finally, the Supplement gives the long list of books cited in the great dictionary.

The principal motive for bringing out the new edition is of course to reduce the cost of the dictionary to the reader. The original costs three hundred dollars, so that the current edition of two volumes is if not quite two-thirteenths of the price of the entire set, a large step (at seventy-five dollars) in that direction. Most human eyes will need a little help, and that is tactfully furnished—a magnifying glass mounted on a wooden rectangle a few inches by a few inches, along the base of which lies a groove whose purpose is nowhere explained. If it is intended somehow to permit the reader to manipulate the glass, as a periscope, by remote control, I must report that the motor, or drive shaft, or whatever, was missing from my set. No matter, there are other and better magnifying glasses on the market, and very strong eyeglasses will do.

The economy apart, there is the advantage of space saved, and the general feeling of accessibility that comes from dealing with two instead of thirteen volumes. I am surprised that the publishers neglected to provide a lettered thumb index, but I installed my own without much trouble. The books are well bound and the pages fall open easily, without crowding—four of the original appearing in each page of the miniaturized volumes, which total 4,116 pages. I cannot imagine that anyone who has the money will put off the purchase of a set; or that anyone who hasn't the money will put off borrowing to buy the set. That is the way I feel about it, and if you are a doubter, stay with me for just a moment.

The dictionary is best described by its own editors. They explain, for instance, that they did not include words that had become obsolete by 1150 A.D., giving the reasons why. Beyond that, ". . . it is the aim of the Dictionary to deal with all the common words of speech and literature, and with all words which approach these in character; the limits being extended farther in the domain of science and philosophy, which naturally passes into that of literature than in that of slang or cant, which touches the colloquial. In scientific and technical terminology, the aim has been to include *all words English in form* . . . except those of which an explanation would be unintelligible to any but the specialist; and such words, not English in form, as either are in general use, like *Hippopotamus, Geranium, Aluminium, Focus, Stratum, Bronchitis,* or belong to the more familiar language of science, as *Mammalia, Lepidoptera, Invertebrata.*"

The thought given to the arrangement of the words bore exotic fruit, beyond anything for which mere catalogues are useful. The richness of the work is suggested in the passage that gives the thinking of the editors on how to deal with *Combinations:*

"Under this term are included all collocations of simple words in which the separate spelling of each word is retained, whether they are formally connected by the hyphen, or virtually by the unity of their signification. The formal union and the actual by no means coincide; not only is the use of the hyphen a matter of indifference in an immense number of cases, but in many where it is habitually used, the combination implies no unity of signification; while others, in which there is a distinct unity or special-ization of meaning, are not hyphened. The primary use of the hyphen is *grammatical:* it implies either that the syntactic relation between two words is closer than if they stood side by side without it, or that the rela-tion is a *less usual* one than that which would at first sight suggest itself to us, if we saw the two words standing unconnected. Thus, in the three sen-tences, '*After consideration* had been given to the proposal, it was duly ac-cepted,' '*After consideration* the proposal was accepted,' '*After-consideration* had shown him his mistake,' we have *first* no immediate syntactic relation between *after* (conjunctive adverb) and *consideration; secondly,* the relation of preposition and object; *thirdly,* the relation of attribute and substantive, closer than the first, less usual than the second, (since *after* is more com-monly a preposition than an adjective). But *after-consideration* is not really a single word, any more than *subsequent consideration, fuller consideration;* the hyphen being merely a convenient help to the sense, which would be clearly expressed in speech by the different phrase-accentuation of *a'fter consideration* and *a'fter considera"tion.* And as this 'help to the sense' is not always equally necessary, nor its need equally appreciated in the same place, it is impossible that its use should be uniform. Nevertheless *after-consideration,* as used above, is on the way to become a single word, which *reconsideration* (chiefly because *re-* is not a separate word, but also because we have *reconsider*) is reckoned to be; and indeed *close grammatical relation* constantly accompanies close union of sense, so that in many combina-tions the hyphen becomes an expression of this unification of sense. When this unification and specialization has [?] proceeded so far that we no longer analyze the combination into its elements, but take it in as a whole, as in *blackberry, postman, newspaper,* pronouncing it in speech with a sin-gle accent, the hyphen is usually omitted, and the fully developed com-pound is written as a single word."

Is that not beautiful? One can read it again and again, once for the analysis, again as philosophy, twice more for the music; and there isn't an entry in the dictionary that does not present itself as manifestly the object of the lovingcare (note, no hyphen) these grave, and lively, and penetrat-ing craftsmen gave us; and, no doubt, when the volumes were received by the critics, and for years after, workmen sat as nervously as Mission Con-trol in Houston, lest error be found, or the tiniest miscalibration, such as might propel a future statesman towards war instead of peace. As far as I

know, their principal humiliation lay in having omitted the word APPEN-
DIX, which had to wait to debut in the Supplementary Volume. It is rumored that, buried deep in the dictionary, is a SPURIOUS WORD of the
editors' super-secret devising, so that their grandchildren might know the
contemporary estate of plagiarism. If it is true, the identity of the word is
a well-kept secret.

The limitations of the O.E.D. are I should think unavoidable. There
are a great many words one needs to know about which simply aren't
there, so that one always has to have another dictionary—a more contemporary dictionary—at hand. And then, here and there one comes across
anti-metaphorical rigidity. For instance, ENTROPY is not permitted, in the
O.E.D., to stray out of its thermodynamic cage, so that one gets no hint
of Webster's 4th meaning, "The ultimate state reached in the degradation
of the matter and energy of the universe. . . ."

The Compact Edition, now that it is done, strikes one as so obviously
a useful idea, one cannot imagine why it wasn't done before. So, now, a
proposal for the next edition. Probably two stout volumes of supplementary words could be listed, if the successors to the editors who laid down
their burden in 1928 were to address themselves to the word explosion of
the succeeding four decades. No doubt the enterprise hasn't been revived
because the economic cost of typographical collation is discouraging.
But—but—these days we have the computer printout! Why not an edition of the O.E.D., made current say every ten years, in which the new
words are fed alphabetically into place on the master tape. The user would
buy the tape, which would come in a unit that would look like a portable
typewriter, a small screen perched on top of the carriage. Whereupon—
you guessed it—you would need merely to type out the word you wished
to explore, and there you'd have it, illuminated on the screen. The O.E.D.,
as a continuing masterpiece. The O.E.D. needs updating even as the census does, and the Encyclopaedia Britannica, and the ingenuity of the publishers in bringing out the current Compact Edition ought not to be
terminal (lest we reach ENTROPY). But even now, there is no literary excitement quite like the ownership of these volumes, the experiencing of
which is like having been out there in the early morning at Cape Kennedy,
and seeing the missile stagger up, knowing that it will travel all the way to
the moon.

Dear Mr. Buckley:

Some scabrous lout has written me a postcard from Israel without providing a return address and thus unfairly avoiding counterattack.

This is the message, in its entirety, the writer a stranger to me:

"Dear John:

"First of course 'Shalom!', huh? Next, darn, darn, darn but my new 'The Concise Oxford Dictionary' doesn't carry (perhaps among others) such words as 'yare,' 'pica' (as used by you), 'pygal,' 'porpentine.' 'Glistering,' yes—but hell, you could have used glistening, huh?"

John, one Bill Buckley is enough.

"Shalom!

—S. W. HARRIS"

I would have begun my reply with the observation that the new Concise Oxford must be very new and indeed concise and gone on from there to some dizzying height of sarcasm. Instead, I am drunk with frustration and in such condition have before me two Buckleys.

Shalom!

JOHN MCPHEE
The New Yorker

Dear Mr. McPhee:
Dear Mr. McPhee: Drunk with *what?*
Drunk with *what?*

WFB

WFB   JANUARY 20, 1978

Asked to debate in print another member of the American Heritage Usage Panel, WFB takes the negative side on the question of permissiveness.*

What is it that brings verbal "acceptability"? It is suggested that usage should be the "chief" determinant. It occurs to me that the two sentences just now composed could not communicate what they now do save that precision in definition and inflection is still possible; and precision is still possible precisely because mere usage, however prolonged, does not baptize. Providence in due course sometimes accepts into its bosom sinners, but usually only after time served in the antechambers. And how will we know just when that dispensation is granted? Well, to answer that only in part in jest: by asking me.

Why me?

* Re: *American Heritage Dictionary*, Second College Edition, 1982.

[As noted earlier,] I had a colleague at *National Review*, a professor of political science at Yale University given to rather endearing narcissism, and another colleague, a lady of scrupulous editorial rigor, the kind who would write "If it be true that . . ." Suzanne La Follette was always approaching Willmoore Kendall, open dictionary in hand, spectacles perched over the end of her nose, to substantiate the illegitimacy of a particular usage by Kendall. After a half dozen of these encounters Kendall, exasperated, commented: "Don't you *see*, Suzanne, when people get around to writing dictionaries, they come to people like *me* to find out what to put *in* them."

I don't know a better penetration of the point. *"People like me."* At once, in Kendall's statement, one discerns the statesmanship of lexicography, which is on the one hand to authorize change, on the other to deny change's plebiscitary presumptions. Or, more exactly, to confine the constituency of change; to insist that only such as Kendall are consulted. It doesn't matter if 99 percent of the American people say "spokesperson." Only if Kendall—and I—agree will it become "acceptable."

That word is in quotation marks to emphasize that it does not automatically convey exactly what it is that actually *happens* when acceptability is achieved. There is a sense in which a great many things become "acceptable" by the fact of their high incidence—for instance, lying and adultery. But the words manage to retain a pejorative impact because the deeds they denote are defined outside a purely democratic sociology. The *presumption* is against lying, as it is against adultery, which is less than to pronounce that lying and adultery are absolutely in all circumstances forbidden (though Immanuel Kant, for instance, always rejects the lie, and strict-constructionist Christianity, adultery). What is implied by the surviving pejorative is that *dispensations* are especially granted—ad hoc, ad personam. If the pejorative were bled out of the acts of lying and adultery, then the words would lose their moral dimension; the prevailing practices of society's citizens would determine the acceptability of the terms *lying* and *adultery*. That the pejorative survives surely tells us that intuitively people, recognizing their own weaknesses as such, do not wish the moral criteria to change. In short, acceptability is by no means routinely achieved merely by democratic affirmation.

And then I ask, What exactly is meant by the "chief" determinant of "acceptability"? What is it intended that the qualifier "chief" should convey? How is "chief" here defined? Is it intended to be conclusive? Or is it merely intended to invert the presumptions? Does it intend to convey that if the majority use "spokesperson," it becomes "acceptable" practice to do so? Or merely that if the majority indeed do so, objectors need to shoulder the burden of making a case for continuing illegitimacy? The resolution, we can see, hedges, both in the use of "acceptability" and in the use of the qualifier "chief." And understandably so, because although the Miss La Follettes of this world cannot be permitted to freeze a language in its tracks, when changes are authorized they must be authorized by the Kendalls of this world. The remaining question, then, is: Why?

Because, as is frequently pointed out by science, human progress is achieved by the taking of exact measurements. Language is inherently inexact, but even though the objective is asymptotically approached, it remains the objective; and such exactitude as language *is* capable of is a casualty of careless usage. But if carelessness is to be deplored, by whom will it be deplored? By those who judge it to be careless. And what are they to consult, in their anxiety, if not a dictionary? That dictionary may, in certain of its declarations, be held to be obsolete. But make sure that it is the Kendalls of this world who judge it so, because they are expertly trained and congenitally gifted. They know how to take careful measurements, and they use the language to do this.

How else?

Language is an aesthetic as well as an analytical tool. And to slur language is as painful to the well-tempered ear as to slur music. In music the individualist seeks to introduce a new modality. He may emerge as a great artist, or he may be held to be witless; juries will judge. Usually, in serious music, a genuinely new style requires fifty years to win acceptance. In language some words have been paying court to the admissions committee for centuries, while thousands upon thousands have simply given up. Some win almost immediate acceptance. But the question is always, acceptance by whom?

Vulgar, Slang, Regional, Nonstandard, Informal: most new meanings or uses need to work their way against that upstream drag; and resistance should be formal, i.e., embodied in a dictionary prepared to accept but also prepared to deny.

Lexicographers are sufficiently conversant with their craft to make judgments, yea, even unto designating a word, or a usage, *illiterate.* The other way is mobocratic, undifferentiated. And what is the purpose of a *guide* to usage if not—as required—to exclude? The negative function of a dictionary is a part of its function. It is not a sign of arrogance for the king to rule. That is what he is there for.

1982

Other panelists weigh in on other issues. One such deals with the acceptability of individuals and their redefinitions, at times of a brevity approaching scandal.

Dear Mr. Buckley:

You will, I know, be interested, as a member of the Usage Panel of the American Heritage Dictionary, in a copy of my letter to the editor of that dictionary. I reproduced its definitions of "dictator," "leader," "statesman," and "premier." And then: "I think you'll agree, especially in the light of definition 1.b. [a tyrant] that the term 'dictator' has a pejorative connotation . . . the terms 'leader,' 'statesman,' and 'premier,' on the other hand, are not at all pejorative. Quite the reverse.

"Keeping all this in mind, contrast the two biographical descriptions:

> *Mussolini, Benito.* 'Il Duce.' 1883–1945. Italian Fascist dictator (1922–45); assassinated.
> *Hitler, Adolf.* 1889–1945. Austrian-born German Nazi dictator.

with the five biographical descriptions:

> *Stalin, Joseph.* 1879–1953. Soviet Communist revolutionary leader.
> *Trotsky, Leon.* 1879–1940. Russian revolutionary and Soviet statesman; assassinated.
> *Mao Zedong* also *Tse-tung.* 1893–1976. Chinese Communist leader.
> *Castro, Fidel.* b. 1927. Cuban revolutionary premier (since 1959).
> *Pol Pot.* b. 1928. Cambodian political leader.

I would appreciate hearing from you on this subject."

Sincerely yours,
DAVID R. JEFFRIES
SAN FRANCISCO, CALIF.

Dear Mr. Jeffries: Nice going. Let me know what the people at American Heritage say. Cordially,

—WFB   FEBRUARY 5, 1990

Permissive or not, it is just a short hop for Buckley from debating the contents of a dictionary to praising its accessibility. *Home Office Computing* magazine billed this short essay with the line "An Electronic Dictionary Fuels a Well-Known Writer's Love of Language." In it, the author speaks of two pleasures: (1) word processing, which, as I've said, for the computer-happy Buckley is perhaps *the* greatest invention, exceeding even sliced bread; and (2) dictionaries.

MINCING WORDS

Ever since computers entered—and in some respects came to dominate—my life, I have from time to time, quite accidentally, tripped upon a program that caused a glint in the eye of the possessor. I also found that he or she wasn't always all that eager to communicate the discovery. It can be that way with a special joke: Some people just don't want to toss it around indiscriminately, perhaps on the grounds that a universal knowledge of it would cause it to lose its flavor.

It was through such experiences, plus the comprehensive generosity of one or two experts, that I came upon programs that had the effect on me I'd have expected if I were in sixteenth-century Peru and someone suddenly said: "Here, why don't you try this when you move all those rocks around? It's called a wheel."

About two years ago someone casually mentioned the American Heritage Dictionary. Years before I had bought the Oxford English Dictionary on one CD and paid an appalling nine hundred bucks for it. But it isn't that often that you build up the etymological hunger that absolutely requires you to know when, under the scrutiny of lexicographers, was the first use of *bacterial* (1872). And to check it out meant a considerable interruption in your work, or at least in my work, because I can't simultaneously view my screen and my CD. What happened is that I neglected the OED, and indeed sometimes went to the volumes, rather than bother with the CD version.

Along came this retiring soul who said to me that, really, I should get the AHD. What he was talking about, he said, was fifteen floppy disks that you could enter as a subdirectory in your hard drive and instruct your working program to stand by to access it. What then happens, he said, is that you can with one (or two) keystrokes stare at the dictionary meaning of the word you have just finished typing.

"How long does that take?" I wanted to know.

"How fast is your computer?"

"I have a 486."

"It will take about a tenth of a second."

I got the AHD but, even as I installed it, I found myself wondering whether it would be a kid's version of a dictionary. . . .

You will have guessed it is nothing of the sort. There are 361,000 entries in this magical device. If you choose, you can call in the thesaurus. You spelled it *thesorus*? A column of fifteen words on the right gives you the nearest thing to what you were looking for. The AHD is also a mini-encyclopedia. When was Xerxes? 519–465 B.C.

I was so struck by the AHD's effective displacement in my life of the major dictionaries (OED, Webster III), I began to record the words I asked the meaning of which it did not have. Here is the fruit of two years' labor: *seakindly, apopemptic, outrance, angelism, jesuitry, roadkill, ipsedixitism, potvaliant,* and *instantiate.* Two years' search!

My opinion for years has been that the nonusers of word processing simply have to be abandoned.... But then I think of my AHD. It changes your habits by enticing you to look up quite ordinary words, to reflect on their etymologies, or usages, or whatever. I mean, I don't have idle hours to spare, but I can give you a tenth of a second any time—just try me. And don't think you can dismiss me as flushed with wedding-night enthusiasm. I remind you, it was a full two years ago I found this, the greatest clerical blessing of my lifetime, excepting only Word Processing, the King of Kings.

The other day, I was in a radio exchange with the senior U.S. liberal, Professor Arthur Schlesinger, Jr., who in a casual survey of technology stunned me by saying that, in his judgment, "word processing is the greatest invention in modern history." Suddenly I was face-to-face with the flip side of Paradise. That means, doesn't it, that Professor Schlesinger will write more than he would do otherwise?

—WFB   APRIL, 1996

Now Buckley takes on other writers, including Mailer and Le Carré, Henry James and Updike, with sometimes surprising results. The first column goes back thirty-plus years.

NAKED AND HALF ALIVE

Do you know who Norman Mailer is? He complains bitterly because he supposes you do not, and the right *not* to know Norman Mailer is *not* an American right, however free is this land of the brave. Gore Vidal (do you know who he is? Surely. He's been on television) wrote a couple of years ago that the lack of public response is "at the center of Mailer's desperation, [for] he is a public writer, not a private artist; he wants to influence those who are alive at this time, but they will not notice him even when he is good."

With the result, suggests Vidal, that Mailer has become a teensy-weensy bit of an exhibitionist, striking garish public poses with the aim of luring people into his tent, where, where ... "Mailer is forever shouting at us that he is about to tell us something we must know or has just told us something revelatory and we failed to hear him or that he will, God grant his poor abused brain and body just one more chance, get through to us so that we will *know*. . . . *Anything* to get (the public's) attention, and finally (and this could be his tragedy) so much energy is spent in getting the indifferent ear to listen that when the time comes for him to speak there may be not enough strength or creative imagination left him to say what he *knows*."

Now this sounds like a first-class literary feud, does it not, and in a way it is, Mailer having previously written that, alas, his competitor Vidal has yet to write "a single novel which is more successful than not." Yet they are friends, and, on balance, admire each other's work, but these literary cats are that way when they talk about each other, which is not to say we must dismiss what they have to say. Vidal is quite right about Mailer—he doesn't know what it is he wants to say, but his desperate anxiety to say it, fired by his incandescent moral energy, makes him very much worth watching, if only he could come up with something to say.

If you have not yet placed him, Mailer is the celebrated author of *The Naked and the Dead, The Deer Park,* and *Barbary Shore,* and crowned king of the philosophy of hipsterism, which is the philosophy of a sort of rhythmic detachment from an agonized and agonizing world. The hip are a brotherhood of nonproductive sensual self-seekers, a brotherhood in the same sense of Ayn Rand's brotherhood who take over the world in *Atlas Shrugged*—except that the latter are producers, men of iron will and fist, who bring the world to heel; while Mailer's hipsters construct a world of their own, refusing to live in this grisly world on its own terms.

One of the remarkable things about the modern age is the number of sensitive men who march forward determined to resynthesize all of human experience and give to us a wholly new worldview. Such people sometimes have difficulty being heard, in which case they do not do too much mischief; sometimes they are heard, like Karl Marx, and there is hell to pay. These neoterics begin on the flat assumption that the philosophical patrimony of the Western world is useless, and square. God is dead! Nietzsche announced. God is dying! Mailer corrects him. It is of course the duty of creative men to add to our store of knowledge and accommodate new experience and contingencies. But the boys to worry about are those who want to start completely afresh—who want, in the words of the disgusted back-bencher, to "send a man to the guillotine to do away with a case of dandruff." "How shall I go about founding a new religion?" the young man asked Voltaire. "Go and get yourself crucified," Voltaire answered, "then rise again on the third day." On reading Mailer one has no doubt he might be prepared to do just that, save possibly for fear that during those three days our Maker might persuade him to stay around and stew awhile. But Norman Mailer will never cease trying.

The American conservative is often accused of being complacent in his essential philosophy, and the fact of the matter is that is true, he is. He believes that the cluster of truths which are loosely referred to as our "Judeo-Christian tradition" are—well, are truths, and that while our age must ingeniously improvise on them to meet such apocalyptic demands as face us, there is no need to start afresh, and chase about wildly through hipsterism and existentialism and humanism and Freudianism and communism and fascism and objectivism and what have you, just to say you've got the blackboard clean. What the tormented Mr. Mailer needs so sorely is the grace that hit the young Chesterton with such force early in his lifetime, making him a fountainhead of wisdom and joy. "I am the man," he recalled, "who with the utmost daring discovered what had been discovered before. I did try to found a heresy of my own; and when I had put the last touches to it, I discovered that it was orthodoxy."

—WFB   SEPTEMBER 23, 1962

Which leads, three years later, to a form of appreciation.

LIFE GOES TO NORMAN MAILER

The life and art of Mr. Norman Mailer are discussed all over the pages of *Life* magazine this week by an intelligent and gifted writer, Mr. Brock Brower, who had the sense to acknowledge even before setting out on his twelve-page journey that he doesn't know (and neither does Mr. Mailer) what in fact is the goal of Mr. Mailer's "reckless quest." The heavy recognition of Mr. Mailer by the editors of *Life* is final confirmation that he is big on the literary scene—and more: that he is big on the American scene, for reasons that most critics do not know how to explain but, by their friendly activity in trying, go so far as to acknowledge that the Quest to Explain Norman Mailer is itself worthwhile.

And indeed it is. He is probably the single best known living American writer, only second to John Dos Passos. It doesn't mean his books have sold as well as Erskine Caldwell's or John Steinbeck's, merely that far more of the people who read Mailer's books wonder about who he is, and what he is trying to get at, than ever have on reading Caldwell or Steinbeck.

Mailer is interesting in two respects. The first—and here is why I love him as an artist—is that he makes the most beautiful metaphors in the business, as many as a dozen of them on a single page worth anthologizing.

The second reason why he is interesting is that to many who read him hungrily (and perhaps too seriously) he represents present-day America. He expresses their feelings that America today is shivering in desolation and hopelessness, is looking for her identity after a period of self-alienation marked by a couple of world wars, a depression and a cyclonic advance through technology and automation.

It was Mailer who developed the cult of the hipster—the truly modern American who lets the bleary world go by doing whatever it bloody well likes, because nothing it does can upset the hipsters' inexhaustible cool. It isn't that Mr. Mailer's characters are without passion; on the contrary they tend to be so highly strung that no matter how gently you stroke them, they emit twangy sharp tones. It is that the workaday pressures of civilization don't affect them. They aren't influenced very much by tradition, or by the venerable arguments for continence and moderation, or by the recognition that other people's existences and hopes abut against our own ambitions and self-concern.

In every categorical sense, Norman Mailer is an utter and hopeless mess. If there is an intellectual in the United States who talks more predictable nonsense on the subject of foreign policy, I will pay a week's wages not to have to hear him.

On the domestic scene, he is a so-so socialist. So-so because even though he finds he can float only in the cool waters of the left, he is transparently unhappy, really, as a socialist, although he is more docile toward that barren religion than toward any other. As a citizen, he is wild, defying not only those starched conventions that are there primarily to stick out your tongue at, but the other conventions, the real McCoys: those that are there to increase the small chance we have, whether as children or as adults, for a little domestic tranquillity.

As a philosopher, however, Mailer is—dare I say it?—in his own fashion, a conservative. Wrestling in the twentieth century with the hegemonies of government and ideology, the conservative tends to side with the individualist. In his savage novels, Mailer's titanic struggles are sustained by the resources of his own spirit (plus booze). In his most recent novel, *An American Dream*, a hero as screwy as Mr. Mailer lurches from Gomorrah to hell and back, but always depends on himself to get out of the jam.

Mr. Mailer is properly denounced by philosophical taxonomists as a solipsist—a man for whom reality is confined to himself and his own experience. Still, it is a relief—sort of a halfway house to the proper blend of the individual and tradition—to read a novel in which the protagonist doesn't depend for his salvation on life rafts cast out into the sea of hope by Marx, Freud, or U Thant.

I confess that Mr. Mailer's tours through the nightspots of hell are not my idea of recreation, even with pad and pencil in hand to jot down what one has learned about Things. I do not enjoy spelunking in human depravity, nor do I wish my machine around to tape-record the emunctory noises of psychic or physical human excesses. Even so, there is hope in Norman Mailer's turbulent motions.

—WFB   SEPTEMBER 25, 1965

The King Must Die, by Mary Renault (Pantheon, $4.50), is the story of the legendary Theseus, who, though heir to the nascent kingdom of Athens, went off to Crete with the fifteen young Athenians who every year were tearfully yielded up to die a bloody death, to sate the bloodlust of the Minotaur. Miss Renault on Greece has been compared to Robert Graves on Rome. But she is even better, more light-footed, self-effacing; and she writes about the most innocent, the most enchanting age in history. Mary Renault is as much a part of ancient Greece as Helen Waddell is a part of the Middle Ages, and she evokes her period with equal skill. She has the total sensual perception to distinguish, and the poetic skill to make readily distinguishable, the generative matrix of everything in Grecian life—the religion, the sport, the love, the wine, the discourse, the battle; and clearly she loves beauty as the Greeks did, with all her heart and mind. Miss Renault accepts the discipline proper to one who writes a historical novel. Her imagery is that of the period: in this case confined to the rudimentary properties of taste and smell that were Homer's only tools. And look what she has done! In the mountain of work of the sprawling, uninhibited writers of what Clifton Fadiman aptly calls the Unedited Generation there is not the evocative power of one of Mary Renault's finished paragraphs.

W. F. BUCKLEY, JR.   OCTOBER 11, 1958

———

And embedded in this appreciation of Tom Wolfe is WFB on what would come to be called political correctness—back in 1970.

———

MAU-MAUING WOLFE

Those of you who are not aware of Tom Wolfe should—really—do your best to acquaint yourselves with him. For one thing, he is probably the most skillful writer in America. I mean by that that he can do more things with words than anyone else: a greater variety of things. He is like the pianist Henry Scott, who can play the "Flight of the Bumblebee" while wearing mittens. That is of course stunt stuff, but Wolfe, the virtuoso, does not depend alone on his flashy cadenzas. He can do anything. Meanwhile he is a leading figure in the New Journalism, which weds the craft of the novelist to the obligations of the journalist. And on top of that, he has written a very very controversial book, for which he has been publicly excommunicated from the company of the orthodox by the bishops who preside over the *New York Review of Books.*

Mr. Wolfe was born in Richmond, Virginia, in 1931, and took his B.A. at Washington and Lee University. His principal enthusiasm at college was baseball, in which he hoped to become a professional. He failed and, dropping out, went to Yale, taking there a doctorate in American Studies. He worked briefly as a copyboy for the *New York Daily News,* principally because an editor there desired the experience of having a Ph.D. bring him his Coca-Colas. Then the *Washington Post,* then the *Herald Tribune,* and now he is an editor of *New York* magazine. His articles, published there and in *Esquire,* are regularly compiled into books with crazy titles. The first was *The Kandy-Kolored Tangerine-Flake Streamline Baby;* then there was *The Pump House Gang* and *The Electric Kool-Aid Acid Test.* And, now, *Radical Chic and Mau-Mauing the Flak Catchers,* the first part of which is about the famous party that Leonard Bernstein threw to raise money for the Black Panthers who had been indicted for conspiring to bomb a few department stores, presumably racist department stores, in New York City, during Eastertide.

Well sir, what happened shouldn't happen to an honest hangman, let alone an artist. What Mr. Wolfe did in his book was *make fun* of Bernstein et al., and if you have never been told, you *must not make fun* of Bernstein et al. when what hangs in the balance is Bernstein's moral prestige plus the integrity of Black Protest; learn the lesson now. Tom Wolfe, although thoroughly apolitical, focused on the paradoxes involved in the spilling of Black Rage over the extra-porous sensibilities of an antimacassar liberal, who has been trained to salivate over the plight of any Negro, even one whose cause is the absolute right of Black Panthers to commit revolution, bomb department-store buildings, and rage against the Jews while they are at it.

Anyway . . . Tom Wolfe is an unfortunate victim of ideological ire. His wit attracts the witless among the critics. For instance? Well, here is Wolfe, talking about how some of the black militants in San Francisco succeeded in terrorizing Poverty Program types into giving them money, namely by frightening them. "There was one genius in the art of confrontation who had mau-mauing down to what you could term a laboratory science. He had it figured out so he didn't even have to bring his boys downtown in person. He would just show up with a crocus sack full of revolvers, ice picks, fish knives, switchblades, hatchets, blackjacks, gravity knives, straight razors, hand grenades, blow guns, bazookas, Molotov cocktails, tank rippers, unbelievable stuff, and he'd dump it all out on somebody's shiny walnut conference table. He'd say, 'These are some of the things I took off my boys last night . . .' "

This is the kind of thing that is met (by Mr. Jason Epstein of the *New York Review of Books*) with such embarrassing moral pith-and-moment phrases as that Mr. Wolfe is "cruel and shallow," that his "sin is a lack of compassion," that his is an "intellectual weakness" because he "finds himself beyond his depth, frailties that commonly accompany moments of great personal or public stress," and so on and so forth: Cotton Mather reviewing Peter Pan.

Tom Wolfe will survive the humorless of this world—that or else the world will not, should not, survive. If he feels down, after such reviews as Mr. Epstein's, he can go back and reread Karl Shapiro's that appeared in *Book World* after his previous book: "Let us . . . pay homage to Tom Wolfe right off the bat. He has given us the finest mug shots of the soi-disant revolutionaries we shall see in a long time. He has pinned their little wriggling personae to the bulletin board for all to gape upon. He has performed necessary acts of vilification with a superb aristocratic cool. He is a master of intonation and an extrapolator who can put to shame the regnant sociologists of guilt and hedonism. . . . Tom Wolfe is more than brilliant . . . Tom Wolfe is a goddam joy."

Read his book, and see if you don't agree.

—WFB   DECEMBER 24, 1970

TERROR AND A WOMAN

The Little Drummer Girl. By John le Carré. Alfred A. Knopf.

The beginning of John le Carré's new book is, for a spy thriller, entirely orthodox: There is a bombing, a bombing by a terrorist. Where? Near Bonn, but the location does not matter. There have been so many others, in Zurich, in Leyden, here and there. It matters only that the victim was an Israeli. Although the reader spends time in Bonn and in Tel Aviv and in Vienna, Munich, Mykonos, London, it matters hardly at all, except that the ambiance of these places is an invitation for Mr. Le Carré to use his palette. The places are simply where the terrorist strikes, or where the antiterrorists are collected.

It becomes instantly apparent that we are in the hands of a writer of great powers. In the very first paragraph of *The Little Drummer Girl* he reveals the skill with which he can write in shorthand: "It was the Bad Godesberg incident that gave the proof. . . . Before Bad Godesberg, there had been growing suspicion; a lot of it. But the high quality of the planning, as against the poor quality of the bomb, turned the suspicion into certainty. Sooner or later, they say in the trade, a man will sign his name."

And then Mr. Le Carré informs the reader that he is in no hurry at all; he has all the time in the world. So he gives us a little belletrism, and that also works. He describes the residential diplomatic area in which the bombing took place: "The fronts of some of the houses were already half obscured by dense plantations of conifers, which, if they ever grow to proper size, will presumably one day plunge the whole area into a Grimm's fairy-tale blackout." There is the "patently nationalistic" look of some of the dwellings. "The Norwegian Ambassador's residence, for example, just around the corner from the Drosselstrasse, is an austere, redbricked farmhouse lifted straight from the stockbroker hinterlands of Oslo. The Egyptian consulate, up the other end, has the forlorn air of an Alexandrian villa fallen on hard times. Mournful Arab music issues from it, and its windows are permanently shuttered against the skirmishing North African heat."

We are very quickly aware that we are reading not Dashiell Hammett but someone much more like Lawrence Durrell. The author does not forget his duty. There is sleuthing galore ahead of the reader; and, in the end, the Palestinian terrorist is emphatically dead. But the momentum of the story is not ended with his death. There is left—the girl. The instrument of the Israeli antiterrorists. An English actress named Charlie, she is permanently changed by the complex role imposed on her—to be faithful at once to the Israeli and the Palestinian causes. And she is in love with the most mysterious character to have appeared in recent fiction, whose flesh-and-blood reification Mr. Le Carré flatly refuses to give us. His name is Joseph, and other than the Israeli superspy Schulmann, the English actress Charlie and, however briefly, the Palestinian superterrorist Khalil, there is only Joseph seriously to ponder. At first he is merely a will-o'-the-wisp, and one is not entirely certain that he actually exists. Then he is incorporated formally into the plot, his persona on the one hand central, on the other hand continuingly elusive. And when finally only he exists for Charlie, after the entrapment, after Khalil is gone, the magnetism is enormous. The emotional tension of the postlude elevates it into a full fourth act. A wonderful achievement.

Mr. Le Carré's novel is certainly the most mature, inventive and powerful book about terrorists-come-to-life this reader has experienced. It transcends the genre by reason of the will and the interests of the author. The story line interests him but does not dominate him. He is interested in writing interestingly about things interesting and not interesting. Terrorism and counterterrorism, intelligence work and espionage are, then, merely the vehicle for a book about love, anomie, cruelty, determination and love of country. *The Little Drummer Girl* is about spies as *Madame Bovary* is about adultery or *Crime and Punishment* about crime. Mr. Le Carré easily establishes that he is not beholden to the form he elects to use. This book will permanently raise him out of the espionage league, narrowly viewed.

I venture this judgment even though I am not familiar with all of his preceding books. Indeed I remember discarding one of them as too steep, in my cursory scouting of its first couple of chapters, to be worth climbing, pending the judgment of others I had confidence in that the view would be worth the effort. *Drummer Girl* has here and there passages that demand diligent reading. And sometimes Mr. Le Carré is drawn, annoyingly, to nondeclarative narrative. Disdain for narrative rigidity is probably closer. There is something of John Fowles in his style, in the liberties he gives himself to wander about as he likes, to dwell at any length that grips him or amuses him, serenely confident as he is that we will be, respectively, gripped and amused—and if not, we should go read other people's books. But he succeeds, almost always, because he is naturally expressive, dominant and in turn dominating in his use of language. And so the liberties he takes tend to be accepted as a part of his tapestry—even if, looked at discretely, they can be, as I say, annoying and even logically dissonant.

Here is an example. The Israeli Schulmann, determined to track down the Palestinian Khalil, has decided (most implausibly) on the attractive instrument for the entrapment—the touring actress, half-gypsy, half flower child, Charlie. And so he kidnaps her and begins a brain-washing operation that in most circumstances would cause the reader to smile with condescending incredulity. Consider the girl being interrogated thoroughly so that the supersleuth can learn literally all he can about her, the better to manipulate the penetration of the terrorist network.

It is known that Charlie's childhood home was taken by creditors when her father was caught up in embezzlement, and the supersleuth presses her for details of the episode: "Charlie, we recognize that this is very painful for you, but we ask you to continue in your own words. We have the van. We see your possessions leaving the house. What else do we see?"

"My pony."

"They took that too?"

"I told you already."

"With the furniture? In the same van?"

"No, a separate one. Don't be bloody silly."

"So there were two vans. Both at the same time? Or one after the other?"

"I don't remember."

Charlie was quite right. The questioner was being bloody silly. But wait.

About the same man who could ask bloody silly questions, Mr. Le Carré can write, "When Schulmann smiled, the wrinkles that flew into his face had been made by centuries of water flowing down the same rock paths and his eyes clamped narrow like a Chinaman's. Then, long after him, his sidekick smiled, echoing some twisted inner meaning. . . . When Schulmann talked, he fired off conflicting ideas like a spread of bullets, then waited to see which ones went home and which came back at him. The sidekick's voice followed like a stretcher party, softly collecting the dead." People who merit such description can be forgiven occasional silliness.

Is there a message in *Drummer Girl*? Yes. A quite earnest one. It is that the intensity with which the Israelis defend what they have got can only be understood if one understands the intensity with which the Palestinians resent what it is that they have lost. The Israelis triumph in the novel, even as they do in life. But Mr. Le Carré is careful to even up the moral odds. I have in the past been discomfited by trendy ventures in ideological egalitarianism, such that the reader ends by finding the Communist spy and the Western spy equally weak, equally heroic; and perhaps the ambiguist in Mr. Le Carré would overcome him in any exercise in which the alternative was moral polarization. But having acknowledged that this may be in John le Carré a temperamental weakness, reflecting the clutch of ambiguity rather than any ultimate fear of moral fine-tuning, one must go on to acknowledge that he permits the Palestinian point to be made with rare and convincing eloquence.

He is a very powerful writer. His entertainment is of a high order. He gives pleasure in his use of language. And his moral focus is interesting and provocative.

—WFB   MARCH 13, 1983

Now and then, Buckley does a movie review—and once again is way out ahead in predicting the tastelessness to which some moviemakers will eventually sink, well after this view of *The Right Stuff*.

THE ALMOST RIGHT STUFF

A few things should be said about the movie *The Right Stuff*, which is coming in with the biggest bang since *Gone With the Wind*.

The first is that seeing it is not an experience comparable to reading Tom Wolfe's book. This is a point especially relevant given that the producers tried very hard, spared no expense and were wonderfully ingenious. The best example of their relative failure is the reception for the astronauts given at the Houston Astrodome. In the book, four or five of the most hilarious pages in modern social commentary describe an event that is at once vulgar, boisterous and poignant. In the movie all the humor is gone, and we are exposed merely to the celebration of vulgarity, which, next to the conquest of space, is what the movie mostly focuses on. Tom Wolfe's genius brings to the study of almost every situation the leavening humor that makes tolerable—well, makes America tolerable.

And speaking of America, *The Right Stuff* is oddly unaware of it. It is always possible, if you are willing to put all collective human ventures under a microscope, to see only discrete personal acts. The movie gives us men who are merely brave, ambitious and competitive. The notion that they were in any way animated by national pride would have struck the director as quaint. Indeed, wherever it becomes necessary to bring in the good old U.S.A., there is a smell of chauvinism and sleaziness.

There can't have been a more obnoxious human being than *The Right Stuff*'s Lyndon Johnson since, well, the real Lyndon Johnson. Jack Kennedy makes boilerplate talks about the challenge to America, various senators are depicted worrying about the political implications of it all—America, in the movie, is a sideshow. In the book, however lightly done, America is, really, the main event. The astronauts were up to something different from Evel Knievel's flamboyant assaults on gravity.

Mind you, it is a wonderful spectacular, with superb acting and direction, and memorable characterizations. You begin with the impact of the loneliness of a remote air base (Edwards, in California) where, out of eyesight, great feats are accomplished. Chuck Yeager, the legendary test pilot, is wonderfully depicted by actor-author Sam Shepard. It is routine, at Edwards, to ride horses wildly (nice juxtaposition, the frontiersmen, old and new), drink up a vat of beer, pursue your woman (all of them marvelously drawn), perhaps break a rib or two because of your earthly recklessness. And then—the next day—you get into the cockpit, chew your gum, get dropped from the mother ship, and break the sound barrier.

A couple of weeks later, the other man at the bar has gone Mach 1.3, so you know that, maybe tomorrow, maybe in a week or two, you will have to go for Mach 1.4. Let's drink to that. And an important point to stress: In those days there were no parades, no publicity, no big contracts with *Life* magazine, because all this was, you see, secret stuff. Shh, get away from that telephone, boy, freedom of the press is one thing, national security is one thing better.

But then we discover the need for great funding. And that spigot can only be turned on by capturing the public imagination. So the flyboys—a brand new set—go public. And when the astronauts went public, they went all the way. It was much harder on them than merely reaching the moon.

But here, again, a complaint. There is one scene—it is in the sequence of physical ordeals to which the astronauts were subjected by the medical examiners before being certified—so glaringly unnecessary as to bring forth from the audience only that nervous laughter that conceals embarrassment. The sheer tastelessness of it defies understanding. Perhaps cinema verité is going to require tomorrow's cameras to depict human beings in the act of excretion.

It is sad to reflect that these are the tastemakers; that what individual directors of individual movies do is said to dictate today's folkways, tomorrow's mores. I have not studied the circuitry of audience resentment, and do not therefore know how a general disgust is communicated. The scene is hardly enough to bring on a substantial rejection of an otherwise entertaining and engrossing narrative. But it is a great blotch in the memory.

Go see it. And then, to remind yourself of the unique power of the written word, read, or reread, Tom Wolfe's book. There is no substitute for that wonderful experience.

—WFB   OCTOBER 10, 1983

Hollywood Piety

Let me be done with it and say that the movie *True Confessions* is (in an opinion with which men may with impunity differ) awful; whereas the book of the same title from which it is taken is (in an opinion with which no man may safely differ) rich as Rabelais, haunting, evocative, synaesthetically sensational. In the movie, Robert De Niro is badly miscast. He is never entirely convincing, and words are put in his mouth ("I've packed up my bags," when he announces he has cancer) that one wouldn't have thought wild horses could have dragged from the typewriters of the talented screenwriters. The scenes are one cliché mounted joylessly on another, so that the unfolding of each reminds you progressively of the weakness of the predecessor. But I am not here to criticize the movie—rather to remark the ease with which Hollywood now handles the theme of the thoroughly disreputable priest, though the priest in *True Confessions* isn't actually all that hateful, no more is his boss the cardinal; nor, for that matter, is his brother Tom, the driven, cynical policeman.

Monsignor Desmond Spellacy is ambitious. In his dealings with the cardinal he is somewhere between docile and servile. He is bright enough to know what's really going on, and that what's really going on shouldn't really go on, because Mother Church in Los Angeles has no business giving one of those annual medals ("Catholic Citizen of the Year," or whatever) to a big, beefy, repulsive character, no matter how much money he has given for the construction of parochial schools, if it is known among the cognoscenti (1949 was before Vatican II outlawed Latin) that said character had got rich by pimping, is probably still connected with organized crime, and regularly devotes himself to the easier part of that biblical injunction to go out and multiply. What fascinates—or is supposed to do so—is the cultural departure in protocol.

It used to be that Hollywood priests were Bing Crosby, going his way, and making ours lighter; or Spencer Tracy, telling the dead-end kid he was a good boy after all, with transmutational effect; or Hollywood nuns were Ingrid Bergman, raising money for the bells of St. Mary's and, while at it, tingling the chimes within the human spirit. Most people, I should think, knew that this was romance; that in real life Bing Crosby neglected his children, Spencer Tracy kept a mistress, etc.

But the theatrical convention was there: that all priests behave in such a way as to dare emulation. Between the Fifties and the Seventies no professional class (save possibly investigative journalists) was presumptively supposed to be engaged in altruistic activity. Ben Stein wrote a book (*The View from Sunset Boulevard*) about a year in Hollywood during which he had come upon not a single "good" businessman, or "good" military officer in the pulp-forests he had seen produced for television and the movies. If John Gregory Dunne had sat down to write a book about a priest who behaved like Mother Teresa, not even with the aid of his talented wife, Joan Didion, would he have been invited to make a movie based on his discovery. The priestly calling is a theatrical victim of an age of skepticism; and it isn't entirely unreasonable that the theatergoer should take this in stride. For one thing there are all those thousands of priests and nuns who have been "laicized," a desertion no man may judge harshly whose own faith, whether in God, marriage, country, or politics, has ever been shaken. But desertion it was: i.e., one pledged one's life to a calling, most spiritual in aspect—and after a while the public recognized you as the fellow drinking beer with the wife or girlfriend while watching Monday night football, waiting your turn at the bowling alley. The stereotype of tenacious Franciscan asceticism is irretrievably gone.

And then, too, there was the ideologization of religion. It's easier, among Catholic clergy, to pick a fight over whether to send arms to the rebels in Nicaragua than whether the Shroud of Turin bears the marks of an extra-worldly implosion.

So that John Gregory Dunne's colorful story about priests who have one eye on ambition, and cardinals who leave it to God to forgive the means by which the local philanthropists accumulated their money in the first place, isn't likely to disrupt the rhythm of the movie audience munching its popcorn. The book, by the way, is infinitely more shocking than the movie: but this was so not because the clergy were proved human, but because the language, particularly of the cop and his sidekick, is textured with a blend of profanity and obscenity which almost everywhere (I think of one or two lapses) transports the imagination to a delight unsullied by the ultimate moral corruption. True corruption is what happens when you are asked to believe that as between right and wrong, there really aren't any differences. It is one thing to discover that the pious priest was really Elmer Gantry all over again. Something else to read in the *Playboy* philosophy that philandering is good because anything that *feels* good *is* good—except maybe lynching uppity niggers. (*Playboy*—and Hollywood—feel they have to draw the line somewhere.) The book *True Confessions* shocks by color and an irreverence that knows itself to be that. You could fit every Christian martyr in the chasm between *True Confessions* and *Last Exit from Brooklyn*.

The cultural difference is worth noting, however. Thirty years ago there was plenty of sin going on. In the Eurasian continent more people were killed probably than in three millennia of recorded history. However, for a period, however brief, in popular culture benign presumptions were indulged. Just as rabbis were "wise," priests were "benevolent." Drank a little too much, like Barry Fitzgerald maybe, but good fellows, professionally devoted to philanthropy of sorts. The viewer was only occasionally teased into examining the underlying dogmatic solemnity of it all.

The Spanish, twenty-five years ago, brought out a discreet little venture in evangelism, as charming as *The Hobbit*. A little orphan boy, living in the monastery, whisked away bread and an occasional apple to feed the disconsolate crucifix in the attic, where, at mealtime, before the dazed stare of the child, the incarnation was reenacted, day after day at 6 P.M.— till the monks, counting lost apples, broke the reverie (*Marcelino, Pan y Vino*).

At the hot end of the electric theological prod, the viewer could see a dazzling blend of faith triumphant over sacrilege (*Le Défroqué*). Without faith there cannot, of course, be sacrilege: and here we had the sometime priest, become agnostic professor of philosophy, dining with his young protégé, who had stayed true to their once-common faith and was now, freshly ordained, in the priesthood. In the noisy, bibulous tavern crowded with hedonists three violinists carry about the huge five-liter tankard of wine, playing noisily and accelerando gypsy-rhythmed catalysts to frenzy, while one at a time guests chug-a-lug, the leader so far having emptied only a fifth of the seemingly bottomless barrel.

It is now routinely refilled, and the violinists place it on the next table down, where the earnest young priest is talking affectionately with his apostate mentor. The audience is distracted—and at just that moment the ex-priest, driven to black-mass exhibitionism, quietly intones, within the hearing only of his young, freshly consecrated friend, the transubstantiating incantation: *Hic est enim Calix Sanguinis mei . . . For this is the Chalice of my Blood . . .* The violinists, unaware, resume the routine. The young priest, dazed by his knowledge that apostate priests are not shorn of their sacramental powers, lifts the tankard—the blood of Christ—to his lips. He begins to drink . . . the crowd goes wilder . . . the violinists sweat . . . the professor is alarmed . . . Now he has emptied the tankard; the crowd is delirious with admiration. . . . The young priest, stumbling outdoors to the cheers of the crowd, succumbs and dies. Flash forward to the funeral. It is being conducted by the professor. Dressed in clerical garb. Returned to the faith. Nobody who saw *Le Défroqué* will forget it.

True Confessions (the movie, not the book) is unlikely to be denounced even by the Legion of Decency. Catholics don't have an Anti-Defamation League, for one thing; for another, there isn't anything there that is truly sacrilegious. Some priests will visit brothels as long as lust is given a fighting chance on earth, and it is the organizing Christian proposition that even Christ was tempted. The Catholic Church is the inspiration for great utterances, even as it has provoked resonant denunciations. G. K. Chesterton, face to face with his time's version of Hollywood agnosticism, concluded a major book by writing that "there are an infinity of angles at which one falls, only one at which one stands. . . . To have avoided them all has been one whirling adventure; and in my vision, the heavenly chariot flies thundering through the ages, the dull heresies sprawling and prostrate, the wild truth reeling but erect."

Those who will be shocked by *True Confessions* may—or may not—achieve perspective by reminding themselves that a century ago Charles Kingsley was writing such witty stuff as, "The Roman religion . . . for some time past, [has] been making men not better men, but worse. We must face, we must conceive honestly for ourselves, the deep demoralization which had been brought on in Europe by the dogma that the Pope of Rome had the power of creating right and wrong; that not only truth and falsehood, but morality and immorality, depended on his setting his seal to a bit of parchment."

Now that's the kind of anti-Papist stuff that makes Hollywood's *True Confessions* taste like no-cal Popsicle. But—a note to all those who seek to offend, or to be offended: Caution! Kingsley, above, brought forth Newman's *Apologia pro Vita Sua,* the crushing masterpiece that British news-paper readers lined up to buy when it was serialized, a book that devas-tated Kingsley, leaving that urbane, witty skeptic to sound like the village atheist. Impiety breeds piety. I don't know what the movie version of *True Confessions* will bring on, but pending that dreadnaught, you are vouch-safed these little words, good for just enough life-sufficiency to keep you afloat until the genuine article comes along.

—SEPTEMBER 18, 1981

On one occasion, Mr. Buckley, just as he has done self-interviews, did a self-review (in his own magazine), a temptation every novelist, budding or other, will understand.

Saving the Queen. By William F. Buckley, Jr. Doubleday.

Mr. Buckley's first novel features an attractive hero (American, young, handsome, patriotic, sassy); an irresistible Queen (of England; never, in the novel, confused with the incumbent); a great crisis of state (American hydrogen-bomb development secrets are being leaked to Stalin); a super-secret mission (the hero has to find out who the leak is, the suspects hav-ing narrowed to the Prime Minister of England and the Queen of England); a dalliance with the Queen (she is described by the *Washington Post* reviewer: "If you will try to imagine a woman who looks like a young Grace Kelly, has the mischievousness of an Alice Roosevelt Longworth, the wit of an early Dorothy Parker, the sweetness of Dorothy in the *Wiz-ard of Oz,* and the breeding of, well, the Queen of England, you will get the picture [of the fictional Queen Caroline]."); a theatrical duel with the traitor (fought over the skies of England, the Queen and the military no-bility innocently looking on); an ironic eulogy delivered at St. George's Chapel, Windsor Castle (by the killer, in praise of the traitor); and, in an epilogue, the frustration of the Rockefeller Commission investigating the CIA (by the hero, invoking a privilege not enumerated in the Bill of Rights; a common-law privilege, so to speak). Since the book's appear-ance, the author has repeatedly been asked whether the novel is autobio-graphical. His answers have sometimes appeared evasive, although he readily admits to having served briefly as a deep-cover agent in the CIA after leaving college. Asked if, like his hero, he was treated sadistically at a British public school, he has answered that no, while at school in England as a boy he was beloved, then as now, of everyone. Asked to reply to the charge that everyone in his novel speaks like himself, he has remarked that this is a weakness he has in common with Jane Austen. Criticized in the *New York Times* for a scene that "reads like the Hardy Boys at a brothel," he replied that, speaking for himself, he would be delighted to read a chapter depicting the behavior of the Hardy Boys at a brothel. Asked why his hero, however amusing, departs so abruptly from the stereotype of Greene, Le Carré, et al., the author observed that not all American spies wear dirty underwear, or toss and turn at night wondering whether maybe Stalin wasn't right after all. Asked whether he has in mind a plot for a future novel, he was—once again—evasive, admitting only that he had mused on the theme of a novel based on a great novelist who consumed his talent worrying about mundane world affairs.

WILLIAM F. BUCKLEY, JR.   FEBRUARY 20, 1976

A self-review was called for many times when a reviewer reviewed Buckley rather than the book at hand and what was in it. The steady success of the Blackford Oakes novels was often dampened when splashed or spat on by a reviewer who could not free himself or herself from a political agenda or when a reviewer ignorantly confused Oakes with the author. Even the sailing books called forth reviews, which meant that sometimes, a fella needed a friend.

To the Editor
The Washington Post
Washington, D.C.

The review of William F. Buckley Jr.'s *WindFall* was not criticism but a kind of street crime, gratuitously violent, filled with envy and something like hatred. Buckley wrote a wonderful book about friendship, sailing, fatherhood, and getting on in years. Why did you publish such strange, disgraceful ranting about it?

Sincerely,
LANCE MORROW
(SENIOR EDITOR, *TIME* MAGAZINE)

Dear Lance:
Many thanks for sending along your letter reproaching the *Washington Post* for the sick-unpleasant review of my *WindFall*. But if you want to see a *real* killer review, get a load of this!

Planning to Read *WindFall*?

Mr. Buckley has written another of those autobiographical day-by-day books, if you can stand it, which I can't. The vehicle this time is a trans-Atlantic sailing trip (westbound) in which he does everything he can to liken himself to Christopher Columbus whom (come to think of it) he somewhat resembles, both gentlemen being vain, arrogant, and imperious. Those readers who have labored through his other sailing books (*Airborne, Atlantic High, Racing Through Paradise*) will recognize the usual sights and smells. Elaborate cuisine, a boatful of indentured servants/mates/captains, enough to keep Mr. Buckley out of serious trouble. (He goes through one storm which he all but likens to the 1938 hurricane, and after having done everything a good sailor shouldn't do, delivers a lecture at the end of the chapter about what he ought to have done about the storm, which ought to have included not to write about it.)

The book is an attempt to weave great meaning out of quotidian events. Thus his subtitle is "The End of the Affair." Ho ho, are we going to get from Buckley, the chauvinist Christian, some sort of an envoi to a departed mistress? Not at all; his "affair" has been with his magazine (*National Review*), which by everyone's reckoning has vastly improved since his departure as Editor-in-Chief; with ocean crossing (this is his fourth voyage, hence Ocean Four); and with his son, who to the evident surprise of Mr. Buckley actually outgrew, at something like age thirty-five, filial servitude to the Mahster.

One hopes, reading along, to find safe passage from the overweening concern of the author with himself. One is best off abandoning hope at the beginning of "Book One," since in that way one can shield oneself from frustration. Mr. Buckley is bedeviled (*mot juste?*—as he might put it?) by himself. Whatever concerns him, he is determined to inflict upon his audience. Do you care how close Altair and Vega are together, in degrees and minutes measured from the horizon, in mid-November? Well, you had better care, because if you do not, you are going to be wasting more time than most people have available to read trivial books.

Or—this is my favorite in Mr. Buckley's inventory of effronteries—are you interested in how he prepared in his youth for his hilariously unsuccessful avocation as an amateur musician? Well, there are pages and *pages* on this subject, including detailed accounts of several appearances with symphony orchestras evidently broke enough to bring him in for benefit concerts, satisfied that Mr. Buckley will attract idolatrous crowds, which he will, except if there happens to be among them anyone who knows anything about music. We go through a Q&A previously published in the *New York Times* about why he consented to play with the Phoenix Symphony Orchestra in 1989, which is inexplicable enough, alongside which the only thing more inexplicable is his evident conviction that his reasons are of public interest.

The first of the three "books" is simply a compilation of material Mr. Buckley has placed in yacht journals over recent years. They have in common only that the author is the hero in every situation, ranging from the decision to shut down one engine on a power yacht so that he can be heard more easily by his guests, to his decision to settle for smaller and smaller boats as the years go by. At this point one wishes he would settle for a boat he could blow about in his bathtub, the trouble being that he would almost certainly write a book about it: *Ocean Five: The Art of Traversing a Truly Large Bathtub in a Tiny, Frail Boat,* by Horatio Selfhornblower Buckley.

Pretty tough stuff, no? But rather witty in its savagery, I like to think—since I composed the above review, as a lark, one year ago, and sent it to my editor as warning that this is the direction The Enemy would take. . . .

Most cordial regards,

BILL   AUGUST 3, 1992

Interesting reviewing results when one prolific writer, intoxicated with language—and a self-reviewer, too—reviews another.

You've Had Your Time

The Second Part of the Confessions. By Anthony Burgess. Grove Weidenfeld.

Anthony Burgess is an insistent literary presence who comes at us from every direction and who has just now published the second volume in an autobiography that is scheduled to go to a third volume—on the assumption that he will die sometime soon, say before the millennium (he thinks this likely: "I cannot keep myself healthy—too many bad habits deeply ingrained, cardiac bronchitis like the orchestra of death tuning up under water"). Otherwise, there is sure to be a fourth, so compulsive is his productive energy.

Those whose ear responds only faintly to the mention of Anthony Burgess will recognize him as the author of *A Clockwork Orange,* a book that achieved immortality when Stanley Kubrick made a movie of it. (On that novel, Mr. Burgess quotes a critic who wrote of it, and him: "Anthony Burgess is a literary smart aleck whose novel *A Clockwork Orange* last year achieved a *succès d'estime* with critics like William Burroughs, who mistook his muddle of sadism, teddyboyism, jive talk and Berlitz Russian for social philosophy.")

Better-informed readers know that Mr. Burgess has written many books, including nonfiction. A few know that he is also professionally concerned with music and phonetics, and that he is a lapsed Roman Catholic who wrote the screenplay for Franco Zeffirelli's *Jesus of Nazareth.*

It helps, in reading *You've Had Your Time,* to prepare yourself for Mr. Burgess's level of candor, which is pronounced without being exhibitionistic. And, one adds hastily, the documentation of his sexual biography is perfunctory, in contrast to Volume One (*Little Wilson and Big God*), although he is not engaged in concealing anything that interests him. Moreover, he is chronically broke, and he is hardly unaware of the nexus between sexual candor and sales. ("When book-buyers buy books, they look for sex, violence and hard information. They get these from Arthur Hailey, whose characters discuss problems of hotel management while committing adultery before being beaten up.")

Accordingly, the reader must not be put off by casual reference to his polymathic pursuits, which as they come in at us, chapter after chapter, sometimes page after page, yield up finally a pointillist portrait of the man whose autobiography we are reading: "I assessed works on anthropology and sociology and structuralism in a variety of languages . . . and was paid a guinea per report." "By the end of 1961 I had published seven novels and a history of English literature." "I was paid . . . £3,000 for writing the history of a great metropolitan real property corporation." "In 1964, I tried to celebrate the quatercentenary by publicly reciting Shakespeare in Elizabethan phonemes." "Like Dr. Johnson, I would write on anything. I even became an abortive lexicographer." "I was able to write a long article on Shakespeare and music for the *Musical Times* and to give a talk on the same subject, with musical illustrations, in the BBC's *Music Magazine.*"

"Verse is for learning by heart, and that is what a literary education should mostly consist of. I know the whole of Hopkins by heart, a good deal of Marvell, many of Pound's Cantos and most of Eliot. Also the lyrics of Lorenz Hart and Cole Porter." "I proposed some day to write a novel from the viewpoint of a homosexual and achieved this in 1980." "Giuseppe Gioacchino Belli was the great master of the dialect and a scholarly recorder of the filth and blasphemy. He wrote 2,279 sonnets in Romanesco, and one of my tasks became the translation of some of these into Lancashire English." "I had for some time past toyed with the notion of writing a Regency novel, a kind of Jane Austen parody, which should follow the pattern of a Mozart symphony." "After the success of *Cyrano de Bergerac,* he [the director of the play] wanted another new translation of a classic play, and he first proposed *Peer Gynt* . . . I began to work on my Norwegian." "Later we [Mr. Burgess and the composer Stanley Silverman] were to work together on a production of *Oedipus Tyrannus* in my translation."

"I had a novel in mind, one based on the structuralist theories of Claude Lévi-Strauss, but [his publisher] grew gloomy when I gave him an outline. It is unwise ever to give a publisher an outline, unless that outline is a catalogue of modes of fornication: it is like playing the proposed themes of a symphony with one finger." "I could take over [he had been offered] the chair of the retiring Lionel Trilling at Columbia." "I then started drafting a musical version of *Ulysses*. I had no piano at the time . . . and had to rely on my inner ear to assess its tonalities." "The Russian translation [of *A Clockwork Orange*] I read with interest." "I took the New Testament [to the film site of *Jesus of Nazareth*] in Greek, in order to get a fresh or original look at it." "I have started to read Hebrew." "This was in connection with the performance of a work of mine in Geneva, a twenty-five-minute composition for two flutes, two oboes, two clarinets, two bassoons, one horn, one trumpet, timpani, piano, vibraphone, xylophone and glockenspiel."

In the book's last page he resolves to "dig myself deeper into Europe with an opera based on the life of Sigmund Freud." Do not suppose that such challenges are glibly met. For instance, on the Freud opera there is the problem of the baritone's libretto, which will be set in Viennese German. *But*—"I do not know whether this can be done. It will be hard to find a baritone willing to stop singing halfway through because Freud's voice has been stilled by cancer of the jaw. Anna Freud, soprano, takes over from him, and, in a final fantasy before death, he recovers the tones of a denouncing prophet to smash the tables of the law upon cowering Jung, Adler, Rank and Ferenczi. It seems to me that here we have a golden opportunity to use atonality and profound dissonance to represent the workings of the unconscious, while conscious action can be conveyed through the tonalism of Mahlerian music, café waltzes, bands in the park."

Now if the above has bored you, you were not meant to read *You've Had Your Time*. But I am reminded that I was once required ever so gently to tell a lady on my left that she ought to consider the possibility that if indeed Bach bores her, it is her problem, not his. The reader is, however, entitled to ask: is there a human narrative under this truckload of cultural petit point? Not a whole lot, to tell the truth, but some.

At the beginning, a doctor tells Mr. Burgess (at the age of forty-one) that he has one year to live, and so he resolves to write two thousand words per day to accumulate a little money for his imminent widow. That many words a day "means a yearly total of 730,000. Step up the rate and, without undue effort, you can reach a million. This ought to mean ten novels of 100,000 words each." He didn't meet his goal: "I was not able to achieve more than five and a half novels of very moderate size." Later he adds: "I do not boast about the quality of my work, but I may be permitted to pride myself on the gift of steady application." He can do a lot more than that, by my standards. In talking about the Roman *scippatori,* those youthful bandits on Vespas who career by you and snatch purses and briefcases, he records that one summer "I wrote a book on the language of James Joyce, I carried it in its Gucci case towards a Xerox shop to be copied, but it was *scippato* on the way. The typescript was presumably fluttered into the Tiber or Tevere and the case sold for a few thousand lire." Causing him to do what? Go off to a monastery for the rest of his life? Commit suicide? Not at all. "I had to write the book again, not with too much resentment: it was probably better the second time." Mr. Burgess is not like ordinary people. Not even like ordinary writers.

He does not die, but his wife (who never reads his books and is never boring) mostly drinks gin and dies for having overdone it, and he is more shocked than pained. But lo, a one-night stand with an Italian academician, it transpires, bore hidden fruit, and she appears on the scene with their four-year-old son. The author is taken by the woman, for which reason, and also to save the boy from bastardy, they are married. The ensuing chapters take us to Malta, Italy and New York.

Everywhere they go Mr. Burgess has experiences worth recording—if the recorder is as observant and as gifted as Mr. Burgess . . . as a writer, [he] is not universally admired. He quotes liberally his critical detractors: "A viscous verbiage . . . which is the swag-bellied offspring of decay," or (my favorite) "It would be helpful if Mr. Burgess would indicate whether these poems are meant to be good or bad." He amuses himself by reviewing one of his own novels under a pseudonym, from which review he quotes: "This is, in many ways, a dirty book. It is full of bowel-blasts and flatulent borborygmus, emetic meals . . . and halitosis." On the whole he is at war with the critical community, primarily because critics do not help the author cure his own weaknesses, primarily because they (we) cannot spot these weaknesses, or if we can, cannot prescribe for them.

Anthony Burgess flees England eventually, in part because the cultural implications of the class system there forbid him access to readers who might otherwise celebrate his achievements, and partly because he finds life under socialism asphyxiative. He is accused by a tabloid of behaving like the rat who leaves a sinking ship, to which he comments that "rats are wise to leave sinking ships." And he succeeds, imperfectly, in putting England out of mind; but, one is here and there reminded ("I was always ready to call on my abandoned faith when I lacked the courage to make my own moral decisions") he has not succeeded altogether as a lapsed

Catholic. He continues to wonder about hell and about purgatory and though he is oppressed by many problems, he has the satisfaction of knowing what they are, and fights, to quote the phrase, "against the dying of the light," because his mortality means not only "works never to be written, it is a matter of things unlearned."

Is he happy? One would think it impudent to ask Mr. Burgess so private a question. He surprises us by asking it of himself: "Am I happy? Probably not." But he has certainly earned his keep, and the reader's time.

—APRIL 28, 1991

NEW YORK TIMES BOOK REVIEW

Two inspired, practically perfect matchups of book to reviewer were commissioned by the editors of *The New York Times Book Review*. The first, an assignment for WFB to review the massive two-volume work of Henry James on the subject of travel; the other a book by two unknown authors on sailing, about which more later.

HENRY JAMES: COLLECTED TRAVEL WRITINGS

Great Britain and America: English Hours, The American Scene, Other Travels. By Henry James. Edited by Richard Howard. The Library of America.

HENRY JAMES: COLLECTED TRAVEL WRITINGS

The Continent: A Little Tour in France, Italian Hours, Other Travels. By Henry James. Edited by Richard Howard. The Library of America.

It fair takes your breath away. Page after page, chapter after chapter; cities, towns, villages, churches, monuments, in country after country, described and probed by a belletrist with a mighty, enchanted caduceus in hand. He uses it to crown in elaborate liturgical ceremony the glories of man and nature, but also to squirt ice water on those aspects of the world and its inhabitants that are not, well, not according to Henry James. And, manifestly, he has all the time in the world at his disposal.

But then what accumulates is more than most readers have time for, even though we must all marvel at what we read. In 1897, when in his mid-fifties, Henry James complained of soreness in his wrist. This can hardly surprise us. (He thenceforward dictated to a secretary.) In 1909, he burned forty years' worth of letters and papers, and one can't seriously suppose that he found the time to reread them before burning them—not at the pace at which he wrote and in the hours left over from his work. A year later, he spoke of having had "a sort of nervous breakdown." Might this have been a reaction to the consuming demands of his creative curiosity? Five years after that, he decided to make his expatriation official and so became a British subject. The following year, in 1916, he was dead, at seventy-two. A prodigious talent, and a most industrious artisan. Perhaps his biographer, Leon Edel, has calculated the size of his total output. The Library of America's two tightly formatted volumes of his *Collected Travel Writings* (*Great Britain and America* and *The Continent*) I estimate at about three quarters of a million words. Approximately the size of a nine-hundred-page issue of *Time* magazine, back when *Time* printed mostly text.

He was very famous, though not very rich. (Edith Wharton sneaked a few thousand pounds into his bank account.) He was the gregarious bachelor, fiercely conventional, who recorded that he had dined out 105 times in one London social season. During the Civil War, when he was studying law at Harvard, he grew a beard. When he was fifty-seven, he got rid of it, because it had turned white. He was close to his siblings; his brother William, the preeminent philosopher, was as famous as he. He spent time with Flaubert, Zola, Stevenson, Maupassant, Conrad, Browning, Kipling, Shaw and Wells, and wrote enduring novels, including *The Wings of the Dove, The Portrait of a Lady* and *The Ambassadors*. As a gift to celebrate his seventieth birthday, his friends gave him his portrait, done by Sargent. King George V gave him the Order of Merit, an award reserved for the very few, the mightiest in talent and achievement. His novels transformed the model, with their stream of consciousness and their literary hauteur— as much so as, a generation later, Hemingway's would do, in a very different mode.

What runs through the mind, then, of the reader of these travel pieces? Two things. The first is that nobody, except for Eagle Scouts in graduate schools, is going to read the entire text. The second? You can close your eyes and open either volume at any page and find yourself reading prose so resplendent it will sweep you off your feet. Yet after a while, after a long while, you will recognize that, really, you have to come down to earth because there are so many other things to do. And besides, if you stay with him for too long, in that engrossing, scented, colored, brilliant, absorbing world, you feel strung out, feel something like hanging moss.

For instance? In his incessant travels, one day he leaves Italy to go to Germany. Henry James does not gad about the world with his mind shut or his pen locked in his drawer. As he once put it, "I have it on my conscience to make a note of my excursion." So how does one square things with one's conscience upon traveling to Germany from Italy? One ruminates on the differences between the two countries. Read how Henry James does it, and abandon any hope of competing with him:

"A few weeks ago I left Italy in that really demoralized condition into which Italy throws those confiding spirits who give her unlimited leave to please them. Beauty, I had come to believe, was an exclusively Italian possession, the human face was not worth looking at unless redeemed by an Italian smile, nor the human voice worth listening to unless attuned to Italian vowels. A landscape was no landscape without vines festooned to fig-trees swaying in a hot wind—a mountain a hideous excrescence unless melting off into a Tuscan haze. But now that I have absolutely exchanged vines and figs for corn and cabbages, and violet Apennines for the homely plain of Frankfurt, and liquids for gutturals, and the Italian smile for the German grin, I am much better contented than I could have ventured to expect. I have shifted my standard of beauty, but it still commands a glimpse of the divine idea."

As one might put it today, "*That's* what I call being transported!"

James's little paeans are not easily duplicated, even those that are, so to speak, given *en passant*. Walking through the streets of Eton one summer in the 1880s his mind turns to Winchester, the home of another great public school. He recalls "the courts of the old college, empty and silent in the eventide; the mellow light on the battered walls; the great green meadows, where the little clear-voiced boys made gigantic shadows; the neighborhood of the old cathedral city, with its admirable church, where early kings are buried—all this seemed to make a charming background for boyish lives, and to offer a provision of tender, picturesque memories to the grown man who has passed through it." This little recollection, mind you, only for the purpose of reassuring us that "Eton, of a clear June evening, must be quite as good, or indeed a great deal better."

The contrasts are sharply drawn. There is the other face of England, as seen aboard a steamer cruising the "sordid river-front" in London. "For miles and miles you see nothing but the sooty backs of warehouses, or perhaps they are the sooty faces: in buildings so utterly expressionless it is impossible to distinguish. They stand massed together on the banks of the wide turbid stream, which is fortunately of too opaque a quality to reflect the dismal image. . . . The river is almost black, and is covered with black barges; above the black housetops, from among the far-stretching docks and basins, rises a dusky wilderness of masts. The little puffing steamer is dingy and gritty—it belches a sable cloud that keeps you company as you go. In this carboniferous shower your companions, who belong chiefly, indeed, to the classes bereft of luster, assume an harmonious grayness; and the whole picture, glazed over with the glutinous London mist, becomes a masterly composition."

In 1904, Henry James had been away from America for twenty years. The death of his parents in 1882 was one reason for not returning; then, too, "the Atlantic voyage" could be counted "even with the ocean in a fairly good humor, an emphatic zero in the sum of one's better experience." And so he gave us extensive impressions of what he saw ("If one is bent upon observation nothing . . . is trivial"). James is now acknowledged as an expatriate. He is a little bit disoriented: "It is of extreme interest to be reminded . . . that it takes an endless amount of history to make even a little tradition, and an endless amount of tradition to make even a little taste, and an endless amount of taste, by the same token, to make even a little tranquillity. Tranquillity results largely from taste tactfully applied, taste lighted above all by experience and possessed of a clue for its labyrinth."

Yet James's fondness for England, though vividly expressed, is not, I concluded after reading his tributes to New England, Italy, France and Germany, by any means exclusive. But, then, wherever he travels, the critical eye is alert: "I had just come in, and, having attended to the distribution of my luggage, sat down to consider my habitation." And so there is, almost always, perspective, so often leavening. And he can be severe. About Geneva he writes that its "moral tone" is "epigrammatically, but on the whole justly, indicated by the fact, recently related to me by a discriminating friend, that, meeting one day in the street a placard of the theater, superscribed *Bouffes-Genevois,* he burst into irrepressible laughter. To appreciate the irony of the phrase one must have lived long enough in Geneva to suffer from the want of humor in the local atmosphere, and the absence, as well, of that esthetic character which is begotten of a generous view of life."

O.K. But what about the Swiss in general? They have, we are informed, "apparently, an insensibility to comeliness or purity of form—a partiality to the clumsy, coarse, and prosaic, which one might almost interpret as a calculated offset to their great treasure of natural beauty, or at least as an instinctive protest of the national genius for frugality."

About the English, James was hardly the sycophant. In these travel writings he trains his eyes on national characteristics. He thinks it supremely a British endowment that they are a people disposed to let people alone. (Seventy-five years later, Anthony Burgess would leave England because, under socialism, he complained that they no longer left people alone.) James observes a political demonstration of a kind that, in countries of volatile temperament, would very likely have caused some consternation. Not so in England, because of this "practice of letting people alone," of "the frank good sense and the frank good humor and even the frank good taste of it."

He will permit himself in specific circumstances to be adulatory. In respect of the ancient rivalry between Oxford and Cambridge, Henry James might have instructed Solomon: "If Oxford were not the finest thing in England the case would be clearer for Cambridge. . . . Oxford lends sweetness to labor and dignity to leisure. When I say Oxford I mean Cambridge, for a stray savage is not the least obliged to know the difference, and it suddenly strikes me as being both very pedantic and very good-natured in him to pretend to know it."

Since his formal mandate in these pieces, many of them written for *The Nation*, was to talk of travel, he talks of the people the traveler comes upon. He compares the Brit to the Yankee in what are, strictly speaking, sociological asides:

"The English have more time than we, they have more money, and they have a much higher relish for active leisure. . . . A large appetite for holidays, the ability not only to take them but to know what to do with them when taken, is the sign of a robust people, and judged by this measure we Americans are sadly inexpert. Such holidays as we take are taken very often in Europe, where it is sometimes noticeable that our privilege is rather heavy on our hands."

Concerning the deportment of travelers, of "tourists," as we would now describe them, James is not unaffected by class prejudices, which is not to say that he should have been. On the one hand, he is easygoingly tolerant about young-blood licentiousness at the races at Epsom, commenting on "a coach drawn up beside the one on which I had a place," in which "a party of opulent young men were passing from stage to stage of the higher beatitude with a zeal which excited my admiration." However, on British women of another class than those who sat in coaches at Epsom getting drunk, he hands down opinions that achieve credibility by the authority with which they are stated. The reader doesn't think of James as motivated by snobbishness, and he is not condescending or in any way bent on inducing contempt. He is pronouncing on how people are. "She is useful, robust, prolific, excellently fitted to play the somewhat arduous part allotted to her in the great scheme of English civilization," he says of the working-class British woman, "but she has not those graces which enable her to lend herself easily to the decoration of life."

Elsewhere, he is, by his standards, blunt on the matter of some habits of the British on holiday: "You must give up the idea of going to sit somewhere in the open air, to eat an ice and listen to a band of music. You will find neither the seat, the ice, nor the band; but on the other hand, faithful at once to your interest and your detachment, you may supply the place of these delights by a little private meditation on the deep-lying causes of the English indifference to them." Why? Well, he says, just think about it. "In such reflections nothing is idle—every grain of testimony counts; and one need therefore not be accused of jumping too suddenly from small things to great if one traces a connection between the absence of ices and music and the essentially hierarchical plan of English society. This hierarchical plan of English society is the great and ever-present fact to the mind of a stranger: there is hardly a detail of life that does not in some degree betray it."

James acknowledges his own preferences, his tastes, but he is not an epicurean or a snob, and in any case he was writing well before the age when tastes were transformed into social prejudices. But he unhesitatingly acknowledges a concern over human behavior and the implications of its neglect. Thus on British tourists visiting Westminster Abbey: "When I reached the Abbey I found a dense group of people about the entrance, but I squeezed my way through them and succeeded in reaching the threshold. Beyond this it was impossible to advance, and I may add that it was not desirable. I put my nose into the church and promptly withdrew it. The crowd was terribly compact, and beneath the Gothic arches the odor was not that of incense."

Did this reaction disturb him? "You feel yourself at times in danger of thinking meanly of the human personality; numerosity, as it were, swallows up quality, and the perpetual sense of other elbows and knees begets a yearning for the desert."

But in one essay Henry James, the great doctor of social manners, makes the definitive point. "It was, I think, the element of gentility that most impressed me. I know that the word I have just ventured to use is under the ban of contemporary taste; so I may as well say outright that I regard it as indispensable in almost any attempt at portraiture of English manners."

On his return to America, James isolated the special difficulty of American women of the affluent class in constituting a link in a social hierarchy. He observes that this is in part because they themselves lack truly institutional caste but also because there is a void in the next station up. American "ladies of the tiaras," lacking any access to royal courts, might instead settle for appearances at operas, "these occasions offering the only approach to the implication of the tiara known, so to speak, to the American law. Yet even here there would have been no one for them, in congruity and consistency, to curtsey to—their only possible course becoming thus, it would seem, to make obeisance, clingingly, to each other. This truth points again the effect of a picture poor in the male presence; for to what male presence of native growth is it thinkable that the wearer of an American tiara *should* curtsey?"

James is particularly rewarding in these copious travel writings when he engages his empirical strengths as an observer with his metaphysical imagination. He is, for instance, unable to discern the reason that affluent Americans at the turn of the century simply ignored the capacity of their clubs to accommodate that which clubs were so especially useful for, a neglect the clubs tended to share with the mansions of the wealthy:

"The American club struck me everywhere, oddly, considering the busy people who employ it, as much less an institution for attending to one's correspondence than others I had had knowledge of; generally destitute, in fact, of copious and various appliances for that purpose. There is such a thing as the imagination of the writing-table, and I nowhere, save in a few private houses, came upon its fruits; to which I must add that this is the one connection in which the provision for ease has not an extraordinary amplitude, an amplitude unequaled anywhere else." The American house, "with almost no one of its indoor parts distinguishable from any other is an affliction against which he has to learn betimes to brace himself."

Would he have said as much about contemporary arrangements? But, to begin with, there is very little club life in modern America, and the typical American who sets out to burn forty years of correspondence will not cause flame enough to heat a cup of tea.

Sometimes, whether plodding or coasting along these journals—and which of the two you find yourself reading can be a reflection as much of your own mood as of the caliber of James's performance—you might screech with impatience. As when you come upon constructions so periphrastic as to approach caricature:

"As for the author of that great chronicle which never is but always to be read"—it is not clear from the context whose journal James is referring to—"you may take your coffee of a morning in the little garden in which he wrote *finis* to his immortal work—and if the coffee is good enough to administer a fillip to your fancy, perhaps you may yet hear the faint reverberation among the trees of the long, long breath with which he must have laid down his pen."

Though one admires the filigree of it, if you wrap yourself in it too massively, you run the risk of choking. As in: "And what shall I say of the color of Wroxton Abbey, which we visited last in order and which in the thickening twilight, as we approached its great ivy-muffled face, laid on the mind the burden of its felicity?"

What we will say, Mr. James, is that you are a bloody genius, but sometimes you are too much. Too much in *this* day and age. Henry James's *Collected Travel Writings* are for long ocean trips and for monasteries, and for those happy to feel the great velveted halls of another, more deliberative age.

—WFB   DECEMBER 12, 1993

The other bit of casting now seems perfectly obvious: a book on sailing? Get Buckley, super-literate, a zealot on the sport, witty, etc. But the irony was that *The New York Times* had just decided to give up cover reviews in its book supplement and to give over the covers to art and a preview of what was within. So Buckley's review of an unheralded little book was the last front-page review in what the book trade refers to as the TBR.

Few knew the *Times's* motive in eliminating the cover review—to get people to look inside, for example? Anyhow, there was in the air in other quarters some suspicion that print had lost its punch, that "position" didn't matter much anymore. Time was when the cover of *Time* meant virtually certain best-sellerdom, if devoted to a book or author; when a review in the daily *New York Times* was among the most potent forces attracting attention, pro or con, to a new book; when the cover of the *TBR* was akin to the Book-of-the-Week Award. But these and similar sources weren't causing the phone to ring as much as it did in the past.

Then, Buckley, almost anachronistically, wrote his review.

My Old Man and the Sea: A Father and Son Sail Around Cape Horn. By David Hays and Daniel Hays. Algonquin Books of Chapel Hill.

The story is of a voyage done ten years ago on a sailboat by a father (David, as he is everywhere designated, was fifty-four) and his son (Dan, twenty-four). *Sparrow* is 25 feet long. Dan sailed it mostly single-handed from New London, Connecticut, to Jamaica (seventy-eight days), where his father joined him. Together they sailed through the Panama Canal and on to the Galápagos Islands, then Easter Island—and then around the Horn to the Falkland Islands. From there David flew home and Dan soloed *Sparrow* back to New London, putting in at Montevideo, Rio de

Janeiro and Antigua. The entire passage took 317 days, during which the boat traveled 17,000 miles. The account of the passage, related in alternating sections by father and son, will be read with delight one hundred years from now.

What prompted it all? "The voyage was my idea," David writes. " 'Let's do the big one, Dan,' I said. 'The Horn.'

" 'Where's that, Dad?' he asked.

" 'What had I wrought?' "

Answer: a captivatingly unusual and gifted son, as *My Old Man and the Sea* makes clear. Daniel Hays knew very well what and where the Horn is and what it signifies. But he was only twenty back then, a nonchalant college student, breezy, a little cheeky. David Hays served as artistic director of the National Theater of the Deaf (and continues to do so) and is an obsessive sailor. He had taken Dan out for his first sail at the age of three.

"Why Cape Horn?" David asked himself. "Maybe because I grew up sailing with my father and brother and with salts who whispered the great name the way elderly aunts whisper *cancer*. 'The Horn can be tranquil,' one sailor said, but 'The Horn' was whispered."

It took them two years, nights, weekends, hours before breakfast, all summer long, to prepare the 25-foot *Sparrow*. Why so small a boat? "Because this is as big a boat as we could afford to perfect, as we understood that inexact word," David writes. "Dan and I shared a desire for a boat that one of us could strip of canvas in less than a minute in suddenly bad winds."

On arriving in Jamaica, Dan passed judgment on *Sparrow*—"this perfect boat, which I made and sailed." ("She feels big below without an engine," David notes. "There's something perversely snug about being that tight to the water, to every wrinkle in its skin, like a chip of wood or a corked bottle.") "Everything below," Dan noted in his journal, "that is not attached is encased. . . . My theory is that *Sparrow* will be rolled over completely and since I hate mess, I didn't want to clean up afterward as well as prevent her from sinking. Actually Dad and I disagree about messes. . . . But we agree about wanting to sink neatly."

Dan had an unexpected companion: Tiger, a red-and-white kitten all but dumped on board, at the moment of leaving, by a friend. It would become a great romance, Dan and Tiger: "Tiger steps off the cabin top onto my shoulder, nestles into my jacket and settles right on my chest. He looks up. 'Whatcha doing?'

" 'Writing about this very moment,' I say.

" 'Am I in it?' he says, chewing the edge of my notebook."

Yes, Dan says, and threatens to edit the cat out if a certain misbehavior is repeated. "He closes his eyes and smiles, knowing he can and I won't."

The boat is of course self-steering, and Dan's skills as a celestial navigator are highly developed. But without an engine, without radar, the responsibilities of piloting heighten. "I fall asleep on deck for a couple of hours," Dan notes. "I wake as *Sparrow* lifts and a loud roar—not from any direction but all around—fills my ears. I jerk up and see a beach and house looming directly ahead. Waves are breaking *on the beach* only 50 yards from *Sparrow*'s bow! . . . I envision *Sparrow* as she would have been: lying on her side, waves and sand crashing on us. My home, on a beach."

He can see the headline: "BOY WRECKS FATHER'S YACHT ON CALM NIGHT, DRINKING SUSPECTED."

Dan is resourceful. "I love being self-sufficient. To me that has always meant having the right *stuff* for any emergency." He lists the contents of his car back home, approximately 200 items, including 200 feet of parachute cord and a copy of *Winnie the Pooh:* "I mean, you could drop me in the middle of Africa with my car and I'd either drive out or set up an entire new Western civilization based on consumption."

Page after page the observations, of father as well as son, engross the reader by what they choose to observe and by how they do so, always letting us hear the music of the sea and of their company. "After dinner we swim," Dan writes, "making ourselves seem angels of glow light with the phosphorescent creatures—water fireflies—that our arms and legs disturb."

They spend a full week in Panama, going over every square inch of *Sparrow* with a fine-tooth comb. Many miles out, flying fish plop into the cockpit. "We've had a few, and they were good," Dan writes. "I thought briefly of how right it is—even natural—to gather protein from the sea, how insignificant this creature is—so abundant in the ocean that he randomly flew into my boat—out where the word 'vast' does not describe—does not even begin to pull the strings of thought into existence of how big the sea is. I let him go. Maybe to atone for past murders, injuries to life, or maybe because I want to later on justify what I will do, as if there were a karma currency. I feel happy."

He woke two mornings later to a vision of big waves: "During the night there were many squalls and the seas built to over 12 feet. They are long slow rollers like passionate sex and locomotives. I can see the horizon only for a moment when we balance at the crest—then we slide into a blue valley."

The father admires his son's skills. "Dan had hardly ever steered by tiller, but his skill was marvelous, undoubtedly honed by hours of handling the joystick in video-game parlors. He looked possessed. Horsemen have their centaurs, why don't we sailors have a name for the half-man, half-boat that Dan was at that moment?"

David had wondered what it would be like to spend one hundred days "rarely more than three feet apart" from his son in such circumstances. When Dan went off to Washington State to college, David wrote to him every day. "I needed it," David recalls. "He didn't." He spotted now in his athletic son "for the first time, in just a flicker across his face, his distress that I was becoming old." And occasionally Dan squirms: "We're balancing on a tightrope. On one side is our love as father and son, on the other is the way we work as a grown-up team. And the tightrope, woven from a web of all the things that have happened, holds us up."

There was no problem of boredom. "We always had chatter," David writes, "a lifetime of shared projects, as much to talk about as an old married couple, and no awe." And Tiger was an unending joy for Dan: "Tiger and I are so cool—he'll jump in from the hatch, landing expertly on the foul-weather-gear bin. I'm leaning against it, writing and wearing headphones, and I feel him thump land. I immediately turn to touch noses with him. 'Getting any?' he asks. 'Yah, as much as you!' He turns and goes off to cat fantasy."

Sparrow makes ready to leave Galápagos for Easter Island, where wife/mother Leonora will be with them for a week before they set out for Cape Horn. Dan evidently thinks the moment appropriate to send his mother a letter, sort of balancing the books. David had recalled one scene between mother and son, years ago. "Dan, even at eleven, hated to see that self-destruction," David writes of his wife's smoking and Dan's complaint about it one night at supper. " 'My son,' said Leonora. . . . 'I smoke. That's the way I am, Dan, that's the real me, and you just have to live with it.' Dan thought for a moment, then reached over and snatched the cigarette out of her mouth and dropped it into her glass of wine. She started to yell and he said, calmly, 'I just put out your cigarette in your wine. That's me. That's the way I am, the real me, your son.' "

So now the son writes to his mother. "Dear Mom, Did I ever ask you to forgive me for being such a jerk . . . for so many years?" he says in a joyful mix of conceit and submission. "I would like to be forgiven. I want you to know that I forgive you for all the things that I thought/think you did to me. I do. You are hereby forgiven and O.K. as you are. I still have trouble there—I always want people to be how I think they should be to be happier. . . . You're O.K. with me and I love you very much. Love, Dan." Father and son arrive at Easter Island twenty-seven days later, and when they meet the plane bringing in Leonora, "Mom comes bounding off the plane, with the instinct gear set at high, immediately tucking in my shirt," Dan writes. As usual I'm a little embarrassed as she introduces me to half the people on the plane as 'the most beautiful child ever.' I'm eight years old, again."

Now only Cape Horn matters. "One day," David records, "I sewed for fourteen hours to make a canvas envelope to hold our life ring." At sea, he surveyed the scene and drew from it a kind of heroic satisfaction: "My cup of chocolate would be wedged into the corner of the fence that rims the stove, which also swung with the lamp and the shadows. Forward, in the peak of the boat, a string hammock that held rolls of paper towels, spare line, and the spare paddle to the Navik [steering gear] would also be moving, barely seen except as its extended shadow, and the whole side of the boat seemed to breathe as we moved. It was never quiet, but the whooshes, the thumps, and even the thuds were mellow."

He recalls voyages past: "We would hover a moment and then fall forward in slow motion into troughs too deep and dark to see their bottoms, troughs that brought to mind nightmares of bared rocks at the bottom of black waterless pits. You could imagine plunging down and being shattered into a million bits of wood and steel and bone. We fell and splintered the water into a thousand white birds that burst like ducks from the water."

They spy the Horn. Dan: "Day 178. . . . I'm too excited to sleep. To see land after twenty-four days at sea. I'd planned to put on my wet suit and swim away to get a picture of *Sparrow* in front of the Horn, but when we are actually there the thought raises the hairs on my teeth. Dad agrees. He had thought of going up to it—I guess for forty years—and now he's too awed and wants to leave it to itself."

But they had made the passage, survived.

The ride to the Falklands was rough and cold. David had written that his abiding terror was of rising to see his son gone, swept out to sea (the rule was always to be tethered to the lifeline). That didn't happen to Dan (though he came close), but on Day 200 he rose and looked about the tiny boat: "I can't find Tiger: he's not on board."

He writes Leonora: "Dear Mom, Gloomy day—last night, Tiger fell overboard and all day my head's been full of images of him—there's this vacuum where he was—there's no meowing, purring, cuddling or playing. So many things in that sweet fur. He's been on for ten thousand miles exactly, so I guess he was a ten-thousand-mile cat—one thousand miles for each life and one extra because he was so loving. Dismal." He usually finds a good side in bad events, he writes. "But here, not much comes up. Mortality sucks. Love, Dan." That elegy is enduringly beautiful.

What happened, along the way to the Horn, was that the father recognized the earned seniority of the son and got out of the way, to the extent that's possible in a boat the size of *Sparrow*. He made Dan captain. "What changed? A year after the voyage, my wife, Leonora, asked me who my ideal person was. 'You know,' she said, 'a hero, growing up.' The faces flickered in front of my eyes—Abraham Lincoln, my father, Judge Brandeis, Lou Gehrig, Franklin Delano Roosevelt, Arturo Toscanini, my older brother, my father.

" 'My son,' I blurted out and started to cry."

My Old Man and the Sea will do that to everyone who reads it, will make you cry and smile and exult, even. It is an engrossingly beautiful tale of adventure of the spirit, aboard a little boat that dared great deeds.

JULY 23, 1995

―――

WFB had called Algonquin, ordered copies of the book as gifts, said he would review it. Christopher Lehmann-Haupt also praised the book in the daily *New York Times,* as did the reviewers for *Sail,* and *Eco Traveller,* and *Yankee.* By August 1995 the book had been through nine printings, by November had some 117,500 copies in print, was on *The New York Times* best-seller list, and stayed there for three months. It had become the first best-seller (but not the first good book) from Algonquin in Chapel Hill.

―――

As with Le Carré, with whom he has political differences, Buckley finds much to praise in the work of John Updike, who has powers of description that WFB claims not to have, meanwhile sacrificing sheer narrative drive, which to Buckley, as with more overtly popular novelists, is a major goal. In the case of Le Carré and Updike, it is the marvelous play of language itself which animates Buckley's admiration. A subtle, perhaps, but nice distinction in a field where novelist-reviewers are apt to praise only the kind of books they themselves write.

This review appeared in *New York* magazine.

―――

The Coup. By John Updike. Knopf.

The piano people have taken to letting down a gauze curtain to prevent the judges from being influenced by the persona of the contestant. That way, you simply sit and listen, oblivious of musically extrinsic factors. If one did not know, and went through *The Coup,* it would I think drive the reader mad guessing the name of its author. Except that geniuses collaborate only on behalf of Medici, and they are dead, one would think that this novel was written by Antoine de Saint-Exupéry, to whom descriptions of the wind, the sand, and the stars were assigned; Lawrence Durrell (smells, sensuality); Gabriel García Márquez (tribal life); Mary Renault (exotic evocation); and Vladimir Nabokov (philological radiance). If one goes on to ask the question, Would one want to read a single novel composed by these writers, the answer is: John Updike proves that the answer is yes, *God* yes.

The Coup is not to be missed, and it doesn't terribly matter whether you read it from the beginning, or backward, or every other page, though there are no bad pages in it, provided you go in recognizing that John Updike would rather describe than narrate. The muzzle velocity of some of the action in this novel validates the law of Zeno that an arrow shot at the wall opposite will never reach there for having forever to cut the intervening distance in halves. But one does not mind, because every verbal distraction is felicitous ("After the loss of Sheba [the girl], such a fall [the coup] followed as one segment of a telescope brings with it another, slightly smaller. No one to blow me, no one to bow to me. *Takbir!*"). Well, sometimes there is an admixture of verbal virtuosity and leg-pull, as when the protagonist, the mad black superliterate colonel, determined that his vast parched country shall perish from starvation rather than admit U.S. bubble gum, reproaches his lieutenant for not having shot up a bunch of vaguely irksome black and Arab tourists. He threatens the lieutenant with imperialism: "You will be Xed out by Exxon, engulfed by Gulf, crushed by the U.S., disenfranchised by France. . . ." Hmm.

In this book *everybody* is fluent, poetic. Styron's Nat Turner was illiterate by contrast with Updike's corporals. But there is rhythmic wit everywhere. The black attendant at the drugstore of the border town where Western technology is insinuated behind the colonel's back replies to the disguised dictator (the colonel travels everywhere anonymously) when asked if there is a soda fountain,

> "Such frills went out of modern use years ago when the minimum wage for soda jerks went sky high. You are living in the past, it seems. A machine that vends cans of soft drinks purrs in the rear of the store, next to the rack of plastic eggs holding gossamer panty hose. Take care, my friend, not to drop the pull-tab, once removed, back into the can. Several customers of mine have choked to death in that manner. We call it the Death of the Last Drop."

John Updike once said, on being reproached for having given up a formula so successful when he wrote *The Centaur,* that there is no point in reiterating a success (even as Thoreau abandoned his factory after consummating the definitive pencil). And so he rolls on with his experiments, playing this time with Africa, ideologues, racism. Does he harbor strategic political designs? On occasion he sounds as though he were Malcolm X avenging Evelyn Waugh's *Black Mischief.* Thus, attending a college in the

Middle West before returning to Africa to take power, the protagonist lunches with his girl friend's father, who slugs a little whiskey and decides patronizingly to talk to the black foreigner as though he were fully grown . . .

> "Feelicks, if I'm not being too personal, what's your major going to be at McCarthy [College]?"
>
> "Freshmen are not required to declare, but I had thought Government, with a minor in French Literature."
>
> "French Literature, what the hell use would that be to your people? . . ."
>
> "In the strange climate of my native land, Mr. Cunningham, the literature the French brought us may transplant better than the political institutions. There is a dryness in Racine, a harshness in Villon, that suits our case."

There *is* a narrative—of a fanatic brought down by forces not so different from those he so eloquently and ingeniously despises, but forces which have a peculiar faculty for finding ways to feed people who would otherwise starve; and therefore, not altogether bad. What happens to the fictitious country of Kush after they get rid of the colonel is a vulgar fecundity, not to be confused with John Updike's, which is all mead.

—WFB   DECEMBER 18, 1978

Chapter 17

On Saying Good-bye (or) The Art of the Obituary & the Eulogy

Said *Time:* "A good obituary is always hard to write. Celebrating well-lived lives, marking the passage of exemplary men and women—this is a journalistic task with a whiff of the sacred about it." (*Time* magazine, October 2, 1995)

In WFB's case the task is not just journalistic, but a final act of friendship and in some cases love. Even the deaths of his antagonists bring out the courtesies of the man. He never disguises their differences but buries them with the deceased.

Buckley's usually brief obits are as much a feature of his magazine, his writing, and his character as the "Notes & Asides" columns. In finding the right language with which to say farewell, he puts words to a noble purpose.

These examples are limited to only those persons whose lives were, at least in part, remarkable for their writing. WFB does not write most of them as mini-biographical sketches, preferring instead to strive for essence rather than comprehensive treatment—with notable exceptions.

E. E. CUMMINGS, R.I.P.

As in the case of so many artists, what first brought e. e. cummings to public attention was a novel outward trait that over the years proved to have only minor inward meaning: the decapitalizations, especially of the first person singular pronoun and his own name. His oddities of punctuation, syntax and word-splitting were more serious, for through them he aimed at, and sometimes achieved, a kind of verbal analogue of the multi-dimensional simultaneity of certain paintings of Picasso and other twentieth-century artists—an effect which, curiously enough, Cummings never sought in his own rather straightforward paintings. Cummings's eccentricities, in life and in art, were never trivial because they were among the means that he found to define himself as a free individual in a society that makes this so difficult and continuous a task. Like William Faulkner, Cummings never succumbed to any of the political ideologies that periodically swept the intellectuals; and, though he knew and was known by everyone in literature and the arts, he stayed remarkably clear even of the changing literary cliques and fashions. He hated despotism and war—his splendid novel, *The Enormous Room,* written after his experience as ambulance driver and internee in World War I, was a breathtaking commentary on both—but he was not afraid of them. He was a true poet and a true man, and we honor his memory.

—WFB   SEPTEMBER 25, 1962

TRUMAN CAPOTE, R.I.P.

In Cold Blood, a nonfiction "novel" about two murderers, was probably Truman Capote's best book. Here he was able to apply his literary talents to the presentation of material derived from the external world, which excused him from having to imagine it. He did not have a powerful novelistic imagination, and in this, at least, he resembled Norman Mailer, whose *In Cold Blood* was *The Executioner's Song,* Mailer's best book.

Capote emerged at twenty-three with *Other Voices, Other Rooms,* emerged as a writer and as a personality. The photograph on the dust jacket, depicting a tiny androgynous dandy, reclining, with a blond doe's stare, established the identity. His prose style, which some admired and for which he himself claimed a great deal, reinforced that idea. It was off-beat in its focus on odd details, consistently alienated, and "fragrant"—music for chameleons indeed.

In his later years he had calamitous drug and alcohol problems, not so unusual for writers, and it is useless to try to diagnose his state of mind. Perhaps he had stretched his minor talent as far as it could go; perhaps, in his social life, he was, in Barbara Gordon's phrase, dancing as fast as he could. He died last week in Los Angeles, at the age of fifty-nine.

—WFB   SEPTEMBER 21, 1984

Stewart Alsop, R.I.P.

"A dying man needs to die, as a sleepy man needs to sleep, and there comes a time when it is wrong, as well as useless, to resist." These words—from Stewart Alsop's account of his own fatal illness, *Stay of Execution*—have been quoted endlessly in the days since he died, and their simple eloquence is of that kind that affects the hearer immediately and permanently. That is typical of his writing: gently penetrating, frank and critical, yet somehow comforting and even—despite his professed agnosticism—pious. Describing himself as a New Deal liberal, he took his subsequent positions cautiously, never drawn into partisan or ideological wars, his acuity and wide sympathies giving him an uncommon instinct for the political crux of an issue. If he usually wound up defending the status quo, it was because he knew how necessary to social harmony a status quo is, and because he never descried a more humane one on the horizon. Nobody spoke better for the liberal establishment, or better embodied what virtues it has.

—WFB   JUNE 21, 1974

In writing of his mother, Bill backs off from brevity, understandably.

Aloise Steiner Buckley, R.I.P.

She bore ten children, nine of whom have written for this journal, or worked for it, or both, and that earns her, I think, this half-acre of space normally devoted to those whose contributions are in the public mode. Hers were not. If ever she wrote a letter to a newspaper, we don't remember it, and if she wrote to a congressman or senator, it was probably to say that she wished him well, and would pray for him as she did regularly for her country. If she had lived one day more, she'd have reached her ninetieth birthday. Perhaps somewhere else one woman has walked through so many years charming so many people by her warmth and diffidence and humor and faith. I wish I might have known her, too.

ASB was born in New Orleans, her ancestors having come there from Switzerland some time before the Civil War. She attended Sophie Newcomb College but left after her second year in order to become a nurse, her intention being to go spiritedly to the front, Over there, Over there. But when the young aspiring nurses were given a test to ascertain whether they could cope with the sight of blood and mayhem, she fainted, and was disqualified. A year later she married a prominent thirty-six-year-old Texas-born attorney who lived and practiced in Mexico City, with which she had had ties because her aunt lived there.

She never lived again in New Orleans, her husband taking her, after his exile from Mexico (for backing an unsuccessful revolution that sought to restore religious liberty), to Europe, where his business led him. They had bought a house in Sharon, Connecticut, and in due course returned there. The great house where she brought us up still stands, condominiums now. But the call of the South was strong, and in the mid-thirties they restored an ante-bellum house in Camden, South Carolina. There she was wonderfully content, making others happy by her vivacity, her delicate beauty, her habit of seeing the best in everyone, the humorous spark in her eye. She never lost a Southern innocence in which her sisters even more conspicuously shared. One of her daughters was delighted on overhearing an exchange between her and her freshly widowed sister who had for fifty years been married to a New Orleans doctor and was this morning, seated on the porch, completing a medical questionnaire, checking this query, exxing the other. She turned to Mother and asked, "Darling, as girls did we have gonorrhea?"

Her cosmopolitanism was unmistakably Made-in-America. She spoke fluent French and Spanish with undiluted inaccuracy. My father, who loved her more even than he loved to tease her, and whose knowledge of Spanish was faultless, once remarked that in forty years she had never once placed a masculine article in front of a masculine noun, or a feminine article in front of a feminine noun, except on one occasion when she accidentally stumbled on the correct sequence, whereupon she stopped—unheard of in her case, so fluently did she aggress against the language—and corrected herself by changing the article: the result being that she spoke, in Spanish, of the latest encyclical of Pius XII, the Potato of Rome (*"Pio XII, la Papa de Roma"*). She would smile, and laugh compassionately, as though the joke had been at someone else's expense, and perhaps play a little with her pearls, just above the piece of lace she always wore in the V of the soft dresses that covered her diminutive frame.

There were rules she lived by, chief among them those she understood God to have specified, though she outdid Him in her accent on good cheer. And although Father was the unchallenged source of authority at home, she was unchallengeably in charge of arrangements in a house crowded with ten children and as many tutors, servants, and assistants. In the very late thirties her children ranged in age from one to twenty-one, and an in-built sense of the appropriate parietal arrangements governed the hour at which each of us should be back from wherever we were—away at the movies, or at a dance, or hearing Frank Sinatra sing in Pawling. The convention was inflexible. On returning, each of us would push, on one of the house's intercoms, the button that said, "ASB." The conversation, whether at ten when she was still awake, or at two when she had been two hours asleep, was always the same: "It's me, Mother." "Good night, darling." If—as hardly ever happened—it became truly late, and her mind had not recorded the repatriation of all ten of us, she would rise, and walk to the room of the missing child. If there, she would return to sleep, and remonstrate the next day on the forgotten telephone call. If not there, she would wait up, and demand an explanation.

Her anxiety to do the will of God was more than ritual. I wrote to her once early in 1963. Much of our youth had been spent in South Carolina, and the cultural coordinates of our household were Southern. But the times required that we look Southern conventions like Jim Crow hard in the face, and so I asked her how she could reconcile Christian fraternity with the separation of the races, a convention as natural in the South for a hundred years after the Civil War as women's suffrage became natural after their emancipation, and she wrote, "My darling Bill: This is not an answer to your letter, for I cannot answer it too quickly. It came this morning, and, of course, I went as soon as possible to the Blessed Sacrament in our quiet, beautiful little church here. And, dear Bill, I prayed *so* hard for *humility* and for wisdom and for guidance from the Holy Spirit. I know He will help me to answer your questions as He thinks they should be answered. I must pray longer before I do this."

A few years earlier she had raised her glass on my father's seventy-fifth birthday, to say: "Darling, here's to fifteen more years together, and then we'll both go." But my father died three years later. Her grief was profound, and she emerged from it through the solvent of prayer, her belief in submission to a divine order, and her irrepressible delight in her family, and friends. A few years later her daughter Maureen died at age thirty-one, and she struggled to fight her desolation, though not with complete success. Her oldest daughter, Aloïse, died three years later. And then, three months ago, her son John.

She was by then in a comfortable retirement home, totally absentminded; she knew us all, but was vague about when last she had seen us, or where, and was given to making references, every now and then, to her husband, "Will," and the trip they planned next week to Paris, or Mexico.

But she sensed what had happened, and instructed her nurse (she was endearingly under the impression that she owned the establishment in which she had a suite) to drive her to the cemetery, and there, unknown to us until later that afternoon, she saw from her car, at the edge of an assembly of cars, her oldest son lowered into the earth. He had been visiting her every day, often taking her to a local restaurant for lunch, and her grief was, by her standards, convulsive; but she did not break her record—she never broke it—which was never, ever to complain, because, she explained, she could never repay God the favors He had done her, no matter what tribulations she might need to suffer.

Ten years ago, my wife and I arrived in Sharon from New York much later than we had expected, and Mother had given up waiting for us, so we went directly up to the guest room. There was a little slip of blue paper on the bed lamp, another on the door to the bathroom, a third on the mirror. They were: love notes, on her 3 × 5 notepaper, inscribed "Mrs. William F. Buckley." Little valentines of welcome, as though we had circled the globe. There was no sensation to match the timbre of her pleasure on hearing from you when you called her on the telephone, or the vibration of her embrace when she laid eyes on you. Some things truly are unique.

Five days before she died—one week having gone by without her having said anything, though she clutched the hands of her children and grandchildren as they came to visit, came to say good-bye—the nurse brought her from the bathroom to the armchair and—inflexible rule— put on her lipstick, and the touch of rouge, and the pearls. Suddenly, and for the first time since the terminal descent began a fortnight earlier, she reached out for her mirror. With effort she raised it in front of her face, and then said, a teasing smile on her face as she turned to the nurse, "Isn't it amazing that anyone so old can be so beautiful?" The answer, clearly, was, Yes, it was amazing that anyone could be so beautiful.

—WFB   APRIL 19, 1985

V.N.—R.I.P.

The cover of this magazine had gone to press when word came in that Vladimir Nabokov was dead. I am sorry—not for the impiety; sorry that VN will not see the cover . . . , which he'd have enjoyed. He'd have seen this issue days ahead of most Americans, because he received *National Review* by airmail, and had done so for several years. And when we would meet, which was every year, for lunch or dinner, he never failed to express pleasure with the magazine. In February, when I last saw him, he came down in the elevator, big, hunched, with his cane, carefully observed by Vera, white-haired, with the ivory skin and delicate features and beautiful face. VN was carrying a book, which he tendered me with some embarrassment—because it was inscribed. In one of his books, a collection of interviews and random fare, given over not insubstantially to the celebration of his favorite crotchets, he had said that one of the things he *never* did was inscribe books.

Last year, called back unexpectedly to New York, I missed our annual reunion. Since then I had sent him my two most recent books, and about these he now expressed hospitable enthusiasm as we sat down at his table in the corner of the elegant dining room of the most adamantly unchanged hotel in Europe: I cannot imagine, for all its recent architectural modernization, that the Montreux-Palace was any different before the Russian revolution.

He had been very ill, he said, and was saved by the dogged intervention of his son, Dmitri, who at the hospital ordered ministrations the poor doctors had not thought of—isn't that right, Vera? Almost right—Vera is a stickler for precision. But he was writing again, back to the old schedule. What was that schedule? (I knew, but knew he liked to tell it.) Up in the morning about six, read the papers and a few journals, then cook breakfast for Vera in the warren of little rooms where they had lived for seventeen years. After that he would begin writing, and would write all morning long, usually standing, on the cards he had specially cut to a size that suited him (he wrote on both sides, and collated them finally into books). Then a light lunch, then a walk, then a nap, and, in nimbler days, a little butterfly-chasing or tennis, then back to his writing until dinner time. Seven hours of writing, and he would produce 175 words. [What words!] Then dinner, and book reading, perhaps a game of Scrabble in Russian. A very dull life, he said chortling with pleasure, and then asking questions about America, deploring the infelicitous Russian prose of Solzhenitsyn, assuring me that I was wrong in saying he had attended the inaugural meeting of the Congress for Cultural Freedom—he had never attended *any* organizational meeting of anything—isn't that right, Vera? This time she nods her head and tells him to get on with the business of ordering from the menu. He describes with a fluent synoptic virtuosity the literary scene, the political scene, inflation, bad French, cupiditous publishers, the exciting breakthrough in his son's operatic career, and what am I working on now?

A novel, and you're in it.

What was that?

You and Vera are in it. You have a daughter, and she becomes a Communist agent.

He is more amused by this than Vera, but not all *that* amused. Of course I'll send it to you, I beam. He laughs—much of the time he is laughing. How long will it take you to drive to the airport in Geneva?

My taxi told me it takes "un petit heure."

Une petite heure [he is the professor]: that means fifty minutes. We shall have to eat quickly. He reminisces about his declination of my bid to go on *Firing Line*. It would have taken me *two weeks* of preparation, he says almost proudly, reminding me of his well-known rule against improvising.

Every word he ever spoke before an audience had been written out and memorized, he assured me—isn't that right, Vera? Well no, he would answer questions in class extemporaneously. Well *obviously!* He laughed. He could hardly program his students to ask questions to which he had the answers prepared! I demur: his extemporaneous style is fine, just fine; ah, he says, but before an audience, or before one of those . . . television . . . cameras, he would freeze. He ordered a brandy, and in a few minutes we rose, and he and Vera and I walked ever so slowly to the door. "As long as Western civilization survives," Christopher Lehmann-Haupt wrote in the *Times* last Tuesday, "his reputation is safe. Indeed, he will probably emerge as one of the greatest artists our century has produced." I said goodbye warmly, embracing Vera, taking his hand, knowing that probably I would never see again—never mind the artist—this wonderful human being.

—WFB   JULY 22, 1977

CLARE BOOTHE LUCE, R.I.P.

I first laid eyes on her in 1948. She was delivering the Keynote Address to the Republican Convention, and she said of Henry Wallace, who was running for President on the Progressive ticket, that he was "Joe Stalin's Mortimer Snerd."* They all rocked with laughter, and the critics, of course, bit her again.

I first met her at her quarters, on Fifth Avenue. She had telephoned and asked if I could come by to discuss the worsening crisis under President Diem in South Vietnam. I was there at four and she opened the door with paint brushes in one hand. I told her by all means to finish what she was doing before we got down to the problems of Southeast Asia, and so she led me happily to her atelier, but instead of herself painting, she undertook to teach me there and then how to use acrylics, launching me in a mute inglorious career. Two months later there came in the mail at my office a big manuscript pulsating with scorn and indignation over the treatment of President Diem by Washington, with special focus on Diem's sister-in-law, Madame Nhu. She called it "The Lady's Not for Burning." I put the article on the cover of the next issue of *National Review* and had a startled call from the press editor of *Newsweek*. He wished to know how it came about that . . . Clare Boothe Luce . . . was writing for . . . *National Review*. I told him solemnly (I could manage a hidden smile, since we were speaking by telephone): *tous les beaux esprits se rencontrent*—roughly translated, that beautiful spirits seek each other out. The following day, Presi-

---

* A corn-fed dummy, used by the ventriloquist Edgar Bergen.—Ed.

dent Diem and his brother, the Dragon Lady's husband, were murdered. The only happy result of that Byzantine mess, for me, was that I was never again out of touch with Clare Boothe Luce, for whom, months ago, my wife and I scheduled a dinner—at her request—to be held here, in New York, on September twenty-ninth, two weeks before she died.

I have thought a lot about her in the past few days and weeks. The last time we stayed with her in Honolulu we were met at the airport by her gardener, Tom. There were twelve of us for dinner. We were seated in her lanai, being served cocktails, while Tom was quietly lighting the outdoor gas lamps. Suddenly he fell. In minutes the ambulance arrived. Surrounded by Clare's anxious, silent guests, Tom was given artificial respiration. Clare gripped my hand and whispered to me: "Tom is going to die." There was dumb grief in her voice; and absolute finality. Two hours later, the hospital confirmed that Tom was dead. Clare said goodnight to her guests, and departed to keep the widow company.

Clare knew when an act was done. In so many respects, she was always a woman resigned.

I think back on her career . . . Look, you are a young, beautiful woman. Pearl Harbor was only yesterday, and you have spent several months poking about disconsolate Allied fronts in Asia and the Mideast. You have written a long analysis, cruelly objective, about Allied disorder, infinitely embarrassing to the Allies and correspondingly useful to the Axis powers. On the last leg of your journey, a sharp-eyed British customs officer in Trinidad insists on examining your papers. His eyes pass over your journal, he reads in it, snaps it shut, and calls in British security, which packs you off under house arrest. What do you do?

Well, if you are Clare Boothe Luce, you get in touch with the American consulate, and the American consulate gets a message through to your husband, Henry Luce. Mr. Luce calls General Donovan, the head of U.S. Intelligence. General Donovan arranges to appoint you *retroactively* an intelligence official of the United States Government. The British agree to let you fly to New York, and there they turn your report over to the British ambassador. He is so shaken by it that he instantly advises Winston Churchill of its contents. Churchill pauses from the war effort to cable back his regards to Clare, who meanwhile has been asked by the Joint Chiefs of Staff to brief them on her analyses, which, suitably bowdlerized, appear in successive issues of *Life* magazine and are a journalistic sensation.

Thus passeth a week in the life of the deceased.

The excitement and the glamour, the distinctions and the awards, a range of successes unequaled by any other American woman. But ten years later she was writing not about tanks and planes, but about the saints. She began coquettishly by quoting Ambrose Bierce, who had defined a saint as a "dead sinner, revised and edited."

But quickly, Clare Luce's tone of voice altered. She wrote that perspectives are very changed now. "Augustine," she said, "came into a pagan world turning to Christianity, as we have come into a Christian world turning towards paganism."

St. Augustine fascinated her. She wrote that "he explored his interior sufferings with the same passionate zeal with which he had explored exterior pleasures, and he quailed to the depths of his being at the [projected] cost of reforming himself. 'These petty toys of toys,' "—she quoted him—" 'these vanities of vanities, my long-time fascinations, still held me. They plucked at the garment of my flesh, and murmured caressingly: Dost thou cast us off? From this moment shall this delight or that be no more lawful for thee forever?' Habit," Clare Luce commented, "whispered insistently in his ear: 'Dost thou think that thou canst live without these things?' And Augustine, haunted by Truth, hounded by Love, harried by Grace, 'had nothing at all to answer but those dull and dreary words: Anon, anon; or Presently, or, Leave me alone but a little while. . . .' "

Clare Luce knew that it was truly miserable to fail to enjoy some of life's pleasures. When asked which priest she wished to confess to on entering the Catholic Church, she had said, "Just bring me someone who has seen the rise and fall of empires." But some years later, told by someone how utterly admirable were the characters of Clare's play, *The Women*, she replied in writing, "The women who inspired this play deserved to be smacked across the head with a meat axe and that, I flatter myself, is exactly what I smacked them with. They are vulgar and dirty-minded and alien to grace, and I would not, if I could, which I hasten to say I cannot, cross their obscenities with a wit which is foreign to them and gild their futilities with the glamour which by birth and breeding and performance they do not possess." So much for the beautiful people.

"Stooping a dozen times a day quietly"—Clare Luce was writing now about another saint, St. Thérèse of Lisieux—"she picked up and carried the splinters of the cross that strewed her path as they strew ours. And when she had gathered them all up, she had the material of a cross of no inconsiderable weight. The 'little way of the Cross' is not 'the way of a little cross.' "

One of Clare's biographers, a friend since childhood, wrote five years ago about a trip with her, visiting first the Citadel in Charleston, and then

Mepkin—"which used to be the Luces' southern retreat. . . . Here," Wilfrid Sheed wrote, "the welcome is very effusive, in the manner of priests in old movies . . . and it looks for an uneasy moment as if they are buttering up the patron.

"But Trappists are tricky. Being released from almost perpetual silence by guests, the talk bubbles out gratefully like fizz from a bottle. As this subsides, they turn out to be quite urbane and judicious talkers. . . . They genuinely seem to love Clare," and "she considered them her last family. I have never seen her more relaxed."

". . . After her daughter's death," Sheed continued, "Clare could no longer bear to go [to Mepkin] for pleasure, and [giving the estate away to a religious order] was an ingenious way of keeping it and letting it go at the same time. The expansionist abbot of Gethsemani, Kentucky, . . . was only too happy to take it, and I dimly remember the Luces' ironic discussion of this back in 1949 while the deal was being completed. They were onto the abbot's game but did not think less of a priest for being a shrewd businessman. And what better way to retire the place that her daughter, Ann Brokaw, had loved more than any other in the world?

"Clare immediately moved both her daughter's and her mother's remains to Mepkin, where they now share adjoining graves. And then, to everybody's surprise, it turned out sometime later that Presbyterian Harry had decided to join them, and he was buried in the middle, after a nervous ecumenical service. The cost-conscious abbot of the moment suggested a double tombstone with Clare's name on it too, cutting off, as she noted, all possibilities of future husbands or new religions"—at this point she must have given off that wonderful, wry nasal laugh.

Last Wednesday, in Washington, Clare's doctor confided to the White House that Clare would not live out the week, and that no doubt she would be pleased by a telephone call. The President called that night. Her attendant announced to her who it was who was calling. Clare Boothe Luce shook her head. You see, she would not speak to anyone she could not simultaneously entertain, and she could no longer do this. The call was diplomatically turned aside. The performer knew she had given her last performance, but at least she had never failed.

And then last Sunday, her tombstone at Mepkin no longer sat over an empty grave. She is there with Harry. Over the grave is—"a shady tree sculpted above the names, and to either side her mother, Ann Clare, and her daughter, Ann Clare, in a grove of oak and cypress and Spanish moss running down to the Cooper River."

When Bill Sheed wrote those lines, five years ago, he quoted Abbot Anthony telling him quietly as they walked away, "She's taking it pretty well this year. She's usually very disturbed by this."

Clare Luce, now at Mepkin finally, is no longer disturbed. It is only we who are disturbed, Hank Luce above all, and her friends: disconsolate, and sad, so sad without her, yet happy for her, embarked finally, after stooping so many times, to pick up so many splinters, on her way to the Cross.

—WFB   SEPTEMBER 6, 1987

ALAN PATON, R.I.P.

"In 1948 a book was published with a bewildering title, by an unknown author, on a theme alien to American concerns. The book became the central cultural document of South Africa, where it sold more copies than any other volume save the Bible. *Cry, the Beloved Country* is free of bitterness, telling the story of a fraternal bond between a black minister tormented by the sins of his son and his sister, and a white man."

With these words, in May 1977, I began my introduction of Alan Paton, on *Firing Line.* It struck me, after the hour was done, that a great fatigue was on him: that he had grown old, as some of the prophets grew old, under the pressures of a noncompliant world. Alan Paton stayed active in politics, as head of the Liberal Party (which favored the universal franchise). When he left the party, he also left politics, confining himself to criticism of his country's policies, as also criticism of nostrums favored by other foes of apartheid (Paton consistently opposed economic sanctions).

Last week's *Time* magazine published an incomplete essay by Paton, incomplete because he was taken to the hospital before finishing it. But *Time* gives us what he did write, and Paton began by saying, "I have lost my surefootedness. . . . I do not now feel happy walking among the coarse hummocks of a grassy hill. . . . When I was a young student of seventeen or eighteen, I remember crossing the Umsindusi River . . . on the stepping-stones. I didn't walk, I ran. Today I would fall into the river at the first stone. I have grown very lethargic." And then he quoted four lyrical sentences from one of his books, introducing them with the sigh, "I shall never again write such words as these."

Twenty years ago Bennett Cerf, the founder and publisher of Random House, told me that he kept two young women busy reading fiction books sent to Random House over the transom. "In thirty years, we've only published two titles that came in that way." Why don't you cancel the operation? I asked. "Because one of those books was *Cry, the Beloved Country.*" About the author of that book one could only say that he had reason to be fatigued, and that he had earned eternal rest.

—WFB   MAY 13, 1988

R.I.P. Reginald Stoops, 1925–1988

The following eulogy by WFB was one of three delivered at Trinity Episcopal Church in Newport, R.I., on September 16, 1988. Reginald Stoops served informally as a scientific adviser to NR.

"But how otherwise did you enjoy the evening, Mrs. Lincoln?" has become gallows humor. Even so, it was the line that came to mind on Wednesday morning when Christo* called me and gave me the news. His second sentence—perhaps his training as a journalist prompted it—was, "It happened at 11:22." My eyes turned to a gaudy new chronometer sitting on my desk, guaranteed not to lose more than seven-tenths of one second in one year. The exact time was 11:45.

Ten days ago I told Reggie that our navigational worries at sea over the exact time were ended, that whenever we set out to cross Long Island Sound—or Narragansett Bay—or the Atlantic Ocean—we would never again have to worry about exactly what time it was in Greenwich, England. He said that he longed to see the new clock—our studied fantasy about the months and years we would sail together after his freak illness never flagged in our thirty brief conversations during the past two months. I commented that no doubt he would insist on taking my chronometer apart and ridding it of that seven-tenths of one second annual problematic. I went on to ask him what his weight was today, and he said 137 pounds, which permitted me to say that we would have no further excuse for singling out Danny Merritt to go up to the masthead; and he laughed his gentle laugh, and said with that little hoarseness I was becoming used to, "I guess you're right. On the other hand"—his voice registered now a trace of curiosity—"they're giving me something to make me fatter, so don't count on it." I didn't count on it, because of course I knew; he by then knew it, and he knew that I knew it, and so it goes.

I knew it even back on the eve of his marriage, in June, as a few others did, who managed more successfully than I to internalize that knowledge. But on Wednesday, thinking back to Mrs. Lincoln, I forced myself to think not about what had happened at 11:22 on that morning, but about what happened during all the years I had known him. Was it one hundred nights or was it one thousand and one nights that we shared, in fine and awful circumstances, the cockpit of a boat, and I experienced the soft delights of his understated company? Oh yes, he could drive grown men to tears with the deliberateness of his reactions. Rehearsing an emergency drill, the second night of our Pacific crossing, Dick Clurman asked him

---

* Christopher Buckley.

where the lifesavers were stored. He reacted as if he had been asked to give a brief definition of the Fourth Dimension. The pause, the slight clearing of the throat, the innocent look of a man accosted by an angular question: but followed by the exhilarating frankness of his innocent reply ("I'm not quite sure at this point"). In the book from which that passage comes, I quoted from Christopher's journal. He had written, a few days before we landed in New Guinea, "You find out on a trip like this who you can *absolutely* depend on. And really, the answer is, Pup and I agreed, that the person who is absolutely dependable in every situation is Reggie."

"We didn't mean"—I added in my book—"that anyone on board had ever broken the inflexible rule of interpersonal courtesy, merely that Reg is a critical mass of intelligence, good nature, and composure. He has never complained about anything." A year later, at a reunion of the crew, he presented us all with T-shirts on which the entire paragraph I have quoted was reproduced in DRINK COCA-COLA sized type.

"*He has never complained about anything,*" I reminded myself on Wednesday, thinking back first on the pleasures he had got from life, and then of the pleasure he had given to everyone who experienced him.

But the climax was ahead of him, when those words were written, co-inciding—providence can be that way: providence has its elfin ways—coinciding with the beginning of the last stages of his illness. Given the human predicament, one can only with dumb hesitation rail against the God Who, at one and the same time, took his life, but also gave him the supreme gift, the woman he married, who did more than all of science's opiates to make those three months endurable; to make that, para-doxically, a period of unparalleled happiness.

When finally I brought myself to visit him other than on the telephone, face to face, it was just before midnight Monday, and we embraced, after his very best friend, my son Christopher, had kissed him on the forehead. He pronounced my name and managed a smile. I looked at his fine face and thought back this time to another moment of great strain. It was mid-March in 1957. The little dinghy in which we had set out to retrieve a duck blind a mile in front of my house on Long Island Sound had upset, and we realized, suddenly, that our lives hung on our ability to swim, in our heavy winter clothing, in freezing water, to a promontory a half mile away. For a full minute we could not judge whether we were making head-way against the northerly wind, but we were. Gradually, painfully, we made progress. Fifty yards from land he looked at me and said, "Go ahead. I can't make it." I could not help him with my frozen hands, but I sang raucously to him, and I prayed with unfeigned imperiousness, ordering him to continue to beat his arms, however limply, against the waves. In five more minutes we were there, crawling on our stomachs to shelter.

What brought this to mind was the infinite dignity on his frozen countenance that afternoon, thirty-one years ago, which I saw again, on Monday night, on his pallid, skeletal face: struggling to live almost as a matter of good manners, but resigned to die; determined only that he would never complain, never let go that fierce dignity which he carried in good times and bad times, drunk or sober, exhausted or animated, in sickness and in health.

I had a bouncy friend who once managed a witticism. "When I get to St. Peter," he said, "I'm going to ask him to take me to the man who invented the dry martini. Because I just want to say, 'Thanks.' "

I am a Christian who, believing that our Redeemer lives, knows that one day I'll be once again in his company, on that endless journey in the peace he now enjoys. When that time comes for me, as for others here, I shan't forget to say, as in my prayers I have said so often during the last days, Thanks. Thanks for the long play that came before that fatal bullet struck him down. Thanks, everlastingly, for the memory, everlasting.

—WFB

Alec Waugh, R.I.P.

When this journal was very young we approached Alec Waugh to serve as travel editor, a position he immediately accepted. We were flattered by this act of recognition, and our admiration of Mr. Waugh was only slightly diminished when we came to learn that his practice was never, ever to turn down a literary commission from anyone, at any time. Whence his copious production—fifty books, and fifty times fifty times fifty (if that is technically possible) articles. Six days out of seven spent in writing, which however never got in the way of his unimpeachable good manners, good humor, and good taste. Unlike his brother, he sought primarily to please, and with one or two exceptions (e.g., his very first book, *The Loom of Youth,* written at age nineteen, in which he revealed the homosexual element in British public-school life) succeeded in doing so. He pleased us greatly, personally and professionally, and so we join in mourning his death, at eighty-three, in Tampa.

—WFB   OCTOBER 2, 1981

Raymond Aron, R.I.P.

Before the *nouveaux philosophes,* before the French intelligentsia discovered Solzhenitsyn and, through him, that strange and thitherto-uncharted country, the Soviet Union, Raymond Aron knew the score. *The Opium of the Intellectuals,* a front-and-center assault on Marxism, appeared twenty-eight years ago. Aron was already fifty. He had been a schoolmate of Jean-Paul Sartre. But unlike Sartre and most other French intellectuals of this century, he did not cleave to any ideological sect, whether of the far right or the Communist left. He remained that increasingly rare thing, a classical European liberal, defending freedom against its totalitarian enemies. Among his last public pronouncements was a call for the deployment of the Pershing and cruise missiles. His memoirs—oh, say, his fortieth book—top the best-seller lists. French scholarship and journalism lose a keen and steady voice.

—WFB　　　NOVEMBER 11, 1983

The following is WFB's remembrance of another Aloise, his sister. We reproduce both, partly because of this Aloise's wonderful way with words—her own and of those around her. (This is written with his sister, Priscilla.)

ALOISE B. HEATH, R.I.P.

"For her," an august and worldly professor of the social sciences called in when the word leaked out that she was in coma, "I have to confess I have said a prayer, for the first time in many years even though I never met her." His prayer, and others, were unavailing. Aloise Buckley Heath died on Monday January 16, ten days after an unsuccessful operation which was performed a few hours after she had complained of a bad headache and was driven, by her husband, to the hospital in Hartford. Unconsciousness and partial paralysis gradually set in and when the doctor did operate it was only because, as he put it, he would have done so on his own wife under similar circumstances—he gave her only one or two chances out of one hundred. And then a few minutes later when he actually observed the damage done by the cerebral hemorrhage, he simply stitched her back together and waited, as the family did—her husband, her ten children, her mother, her eight brothers and sisters—for the inevitable end. It came later than the young doctors had predicted. "They don't realize," said one doctor, "that at forty-eight the heart is strong. It goes right on beating, for a while, a good while.

"What happened to her brain is the kind of thing that usually happens to people in their late sixties or seventies. That's why she isn't dead—yet. But there won't be any pain, any consciousness." She was buried at St. Bernard's Cemetery, in Sharon, Connecticut, on Wednesday, January 18, alongside two of her sisters, who had died at age three days, and thirty-one years. At the service, said as she would have wanted, in Latin, a memorial card was distributed, a small photograph, the dates of birth and death on one side, and on the other a passage from François Mauriac's *Ce Que Je Crois* that she had seen and expressed admiration for—as a young girl she had been schooled in France, and she knew the language as a native—only a month before. Mauriac wrote: "*Faites, Mon Dieu, que je me recueille dans la paix de votre présence, afin que quand mon heure sera venue, je passe par une transition presque insensible, de vous à vous, de vous, pain vivant, pain des hommes, à vous amour vivant déjà possédé par ceux de mes biens-aimés qui se sont endormis avant moi dans votre amour.*"—"Grant, O Lord, that I might commune in the peace of Your presence, so that when my hour is come, I shall pass through a transition all but insensible, from You to You; from You, the Living Bread, the Bread of Man, to you, the Living Love, already possessed by those of my beloved ones who, in that love, have gone before me to sleep."

"Though I never met her," one reader wrote, "I felt along with thousands of *National Review* readers, I'm sure, the force of her personality; her vibrant, joyous spirit sang out of her seasonal articles for *National Review.*" "Of all the writers on your magazine, over the past eleven years," an attorney wrote, "she must surely have been the most lovable." And from a minister: "My wife, my children, and I feel something of a personal loss in the death. . . . As she has on several occasions in the past, she added to the joy of our Christmas celebration with her most recent article, [giving us] that sense of thankful and lighthearted appreciation of the mercies of God which we are trying to nurture in those whom He has given us to love."

Aloise Heath wrote for the very first issue of *National Review,* and had an article in the issue that was on the stands when she took sick. She did not, however, write frequently. There was of course the handicap of her motherhood of ten children, and the very special care she took of them. Besides that she was notoriously disorganized, so much so that generations of editors clamored, unsuccessfully, for her articles, and when she died, she had on her desk, as usual unanswered, a letter from the editor of a prominent monthly, begging for her copy. She had excited, at Smith College, the admiring attention of the academicians, as sharply distinguished from the administrators who at one point got so fed up with her dilatory habits as to suspend her for a year (she graduated with the class of 1941, instead of 1940)—a lever against her which unfortunately no editor inherited. But the professors gave her all the ritual honors of a very bright young writer. She was married in 1942 and got around to writing an article about her first child five years later. It was published in the *Ladies' Home Journal,* and with her check for five hundred dollars she bought expensive presents for all her brothers and sisters, resolved to write regularly, and didn't, not even when the agent for Somerset Maugham—who thus announced himself—offered to handle her material. She was always acquiescent; she would agree to write anything in the world any editor asked her to write, and simply did not do so—she was too busy with her growing family. She did produce a piece for *NR* at Christmas-time, the ordeal of whose parturition was an annual agony—bits and pieces would come in by notepaper, telegram, telephone. But they were the most applauded pieces we ever published, even though they seldom touched on politics (one reader suggested we get Aloise Heath to write *all* of *every* issue). Seldom, but not never . . .

She complained in one of them that her children had been over-politicalized. For instance "the kindergartner of unshakable opinion—what we can't shake in Janet is her firm opinion announced thirty seconds after she heard of the President's assassination last year that Senator Goldwater shot him. 'Janet, you *mustn't* say that!' her horrified older brothers and sisters exclaim when the subject comes up from time to time. 'I won't. I won't tell *anyone*,' she reassures them. 'Shall it be our two's secret?' "

Janet wasn't the only problem. A year later there was Timothy, with his paraplegic leg: "Six-year-old Timothy, who has been standing aloofly in the background watching you with great concentration, has apparently now accepted you. He whispers in my ear that he something important to tell you. I transmit the message and Timothy stands before you shortly and informs you somberly that his message is about Communism. The Communists, he thinks you ought to know, are against us and we are against Communists, and they plan to beat us up but, man, are they going to be surprised, because they don't even *know* about Timothy Heath yet! And with modest pride, Terrible Timothy sticks one skinny little leg in the air and shows you his heavy brace and boot. 'One kick with *that* foot,' he grits from clenched teeth; and while you ponder the appalling fate in store for the Communists, Tim smiles and the serious little face breaks into whole galaxies of twinkles and dimples. . . ."

And there was always, in the household, the problem of distinguishing politics and theology. Sometimes, she admitted, she was herself responsible for the confusion. Let her speak for herself on the matter of Mrs. Major and her eternal soul. . . . "Did I really tell Timothy that Tommy Major's mother was going to Hell because she voted for Johnson? No. *I did not*. Once and for all.

"What happened was this. One day Timothy said: 'Would you go to Hell if you voted for Johnson?'

"I said: 'Do you mean me or do you mean people? If you mean me, the answer is yes because I'm an educated voter and I'd be committing a mortal sin if I voted for him. If you mean "people," no, because they are not as smart as your dear, dear, mother, you lucky boy.' Tim looked at me gravely. 'Will Tommy's mother go to Hell? She's going to vote for Johnson.'

" 'Oh, I don't think so, Tim,' I said, not terribly interested in the whole subject. 'She doesn't know enough to know what she's voting for. But wouldn't she be surprised if she *did* go to Hell!'

"It was then that I made my big mistake. You remember those lovely warm days last fall. Well, they affect me very badly. They increase my euphoria to the point of mania. I was near the piano while I talked to Tim and I sat down and played and sang, '*Tommy's mother went to Hell/On the Donkey ticket/Now she knows a Johnson vote/Is very, very wicked.*' Timothy thought it was charming and rushed out to collect his friends Brian and Billy to hear it. Billy called in his sister Beth who was playing with Pammy Shepherd from the next street over. In about ten minutes there were over a dozen children in the house bawling out at the top of their lungs the news that 'Tommy's Mother went to Hell.' And what was I doing? Big fat fool that I am. I was sitting there at the piano bawling it out with them and playing different versions of the piano accompaniment and setting up duets and interesting arrangements and in general behaving not at all like a woman whose living room windows face onto the Major driveway. And that's absolutely all there is to it.

"I don't blame her for thinking it was a rehearsal. I don't even blame the children for telephoning her the next few days and nights to sing it. I drummed it into their heads so hard, they probably still can't think of another tune. And that I swear is the whole story. It is absolutely what happened. And don't believe any other version."

But her madcap problems were not usually political. She was sharply observant and therefore sharply critical; the curse of the whole class of the pretentious, because she had a jeweler's eye for cant, for silliness (which, however, if it was unaffected, she loved), for hokum, political and nonpolitical. One of her weapons was literalness. She wrote several times with vast amusement about some of the practical problems posed by writers in ladies' magazines. There was the article warning the wife against "Becoming Less Appealing," which cautioned against making long social telephone calls, or "talking more loudly than her husband." "In certain isolated circumstances," she mused, "doing so would be justified; chronic laryngitis on the part of the husband, for instance; or the case of a man who might be worried about *his* Becoming Less Appealing, and therefore refusing to talk more loudly than his wife at the very same identical moment that his wife refused to talk more loudly than her husband. We can all see where *this* sort of situation would end, I am sure."

And there was the article that caught her eye, instructing wives on how to be more romantic with their husbands: "There was a *very* moving love scene (in the article) in the course of which a woman stood 'with her hands clasped on Loren's neck, her red hair pressed against his chin, her lips ardently uplifted.' The trouble is, when *I* clasp *my* hands on my husband's neck, press my interestingly graying hair against his chin and ardently uplift *my* lips, all I get is a mouthful of Adam's apple."

She was as amused by all aspects of language. Traveling in France with her sister Priscilla she found herself stuck in the elevator. "I cried: 'To the help!', which is what you cry when you are trapped in an Alpine pass in a blizzard at midnight and wolves are attacking you; and Priscilla shouted: 'The ascendor does not march!', which means that the elevator isn't working. After a while, pausing for a cigarette, we noticed the sign on the door. 'By means of a telephonic apparatus which finds itself at the interior of the ascendor, *ladies* and *gentlemen*,' the sign said pointedly, 'may inform the concierge with all calm that a mechanical anomaly has passed itself.' There is more to this message than meets the eye, we found. And you will find, if you try to say *'Anomalie mécanique'* *without* all calm."

Her strength was the children she loved—to the extent, she always made clear, that that was possible for anyone who truly understands children. One time she received a letter from an irrepressibly attractive and utterly impossible thirteen-year-old boy, friend of one of her sons, asking her whether she would recommend him to a school into which he sought admittance. (The entire, hilarious correspondence caught the eye of the *Reader's Digest,* which published it in its entirety.) She wrote, copy to the applicant, to the headmaster: ". . . [Peter] is more sophisticated today than three years ago, when, at the age of ten, he frequently urged me not to get my liver in a quiver. Today, when Peter and I have what he refers to as 'a difference of opinion,' he retires with complete equanimity to his own back yard until such time as my ill-humor subsides. My change of mood is apparently picked up by Peter's extrasensory perception within the hour, for whenever I decide that the time has come for forgiving and forgetting, he appears at my front door within fifteen minutes, to assure me *he* has forgiven and forgotten. By way of proof (penance?) he then resumes without rancor his status as our daily visitor. . . ."

She knew children, and knew the duty of the parent to try to dominate children, but knew also the limits of any such ambition, children being— children. "If they start throwing books at each other," she wrote in a piece about carpools, "it is best to park the car on the side of the road and exhibit emotional stability until they've stopped. Even this is unnecessary if the books are being thrown by Fourth, Fifth, or Sixth Form boys. Their aim is invariably excellent, and you are in no danger whatsoever. Occasionally there may be stationed on one of your carpool routes a policeman who does not like it when a child sticks his head out of the car and shouts:

'What's old pennies made of?' and all the others shriek, '*Dirty Copper!*' At least he doesn't like it twice a day for nine months of the year, which is when the children like it. If this should be the case, humor him. I myself find that the easiest thing to do is to work out a detour around him, though I understand some mothers make the children stop it."

But she always found her own children (and everyone else's), whatever the generic menace, individually fascinating, individually challenging, individually superior. "Timothy is five years old. He is small, handsome, stern, rather conceited, we suspect; and he has the kind of passion for accuracy which so unduly prolongs even the simplest of bedtime stories. When he comes home from kindergarten, we meet; we do not reune, as did his poor be-momméd eldest brother and I twelve years ago. Nor do I ask for a detailed accounting of Timothy's morning; I say 'Have fun?' and then I say 'That's good!' before he answers . . ."

". . . Timothy was home from school with a cold, and we were glad to see each other, so to speak. We sat alone together in the kitchen, over a plateful of plums, and I said as a gesture of friendship: 'Tim, what's two and two?' Between Heaths, this is not a question; it is the opening gambit of an old routine which ends in 'What's twelve and twelve?' to which the (always) killingly funny answer is, 'Twenty-four. Shut your mouth and say no more.' Furthermore, it is Timothy's absolutely favorite joke: so I felt a little rebuffed when he asked gravely: 'What's two?' "

And thus was his mother introduced to the New Math, in which numbers are second-class citizens, and it all depends on colored rods ("Spare Me the Rods," Dec. 31, 1963).

Always she insisted on the realisms. There was the Christmas when she announced to her children that they would attempt a Trapp Family Christmas, the distinguishing feature of which was that each child would select another child (by ballot) as his special protégé (*Christkindl*), and proceed to shower (anonymously) special favors upon him or her until Christmas day when the *Christkindl*'s benefactor would identify himself. The idea was heroically launched. But her children didn't appear to be exactly Trapp-minded. . . .

"That afternoon they were all in the coat closet (well they *were*, that's all. They *like* the coat closet) making out their Christmas lists. Pam, who can spell, was helping the ones who can't write; and Alison, who is magic, was helping the ones who can't talk. I had my ear at the crack, listening, because I'm still trying to hear one of those childhood conversations whose innocent candor tears at your heartstrings. You've read about them, I'm sure. What I heard was my dear little ones calculating how much more each of them would get for Christmas if they didn't have so many brothers and sisters. They named, giving reasons therefor, their choice—those they would gladly do without. They catalogued the children they would trade for hockey skates or an electric organ with four octaves, or seven Betsey-Wetsies with seven different-colored hairs. From what I could hear through the crack, *nobody* kept Buckley and Timothy, which is understandable, but not nice. . . ."

Undaunted, she went on with her resolute plans for a Trapp Family Christmas.

"I didn't see how the *Christkindl* custom could go wrong, though. I *still* don't. In the Trapp family, everyone writes his name on a piece of paper and the papers are put in a basket which is passed around as soon as the children have finished singing: '*Ye heavens, dew drop from above.*' Everybody picks a name from the basket, and the pickee, if you follow me, becomes the picker's secret *Christkindl,* and the idea is, you do your *Christkindl* a good turn every day until Christmas without ever letting him know who you are. . . ." But at her house it was, as usual, chaotic . . . the children found themselves picking themselves, or prematurely divulging their identities, or whatever. Finally, she contrived a means by which the children would pick out their *Christkindl,* and be picked out. It was not altogether democratic, and by no means left to chance. She reserved a *droit de mère:* All the children were *given* a specified piece of paper. "The baby ate her paper; but it was all right, because I knew whose name she had eaten. I had arranged for us to draw each other, because we're in love. Everybody was getting pretty tense, not to mention bloody, until one of them—I haven't asked which—found a solution: every Sunday now, they each buy seven penny lollipops, and every night they slip a lollipop under their *Christkindl*'s pillow. Well, I *know* that doesn't sound so terribly spiritual, but it's better than what they used to do. What they used to do was steal each other's lollipops. I wouldn't want anybody to think that the baby and I have sunk to such a mundane relationship, though. We haven't had to change our routine at all. Every morning my *Christkindl* allows me to rock her a little; and every evening I rock my *Christkindl* a little."

The last Christmas, never daunted, she had experimented with group singing which meant the children as a body, rather than as individuals; and that, as ever, was something else again, and, as ever, she wrote about it hypnotically . . .

"Gay my children unquestionably are. They rollick into the house from school, burst into paroxysms of laughter at the extraordinary coincidence of their reunion from various carpools, plan their far-flung wickednesses in gales of muffled giggles, are scolded with eyes twinkling above insufficiently suppressed grins, and fall asleep in the midst of a choked chuckle at 8, 9 or 10 P.M., according to whether their bedtime was at 7, 8, or 9. . . .

"One of the reasons—I say one of the reasons because I could easily think of another if I put my mind to it—that I kept on having babies for years after all my classmates had worked up to president of the state *PTA* was that I always thought a big family would be such fun at Christmas. Which who doesn't, including people like me, who know? I know why my husband Ben has the Spirit of Christmas around Thanksgiving and the Spirit of Ash Wednesday around Christmas. I keep telling him I know. 'I know,' I say. 'I know. I know. I know.'

"I know we always get more glitter and glue on the floor than on the candles and that I never remember to wipe it up until the dining-room carpet is permanently (though interestingly) spangled. I know I look absolutely insane, crawling around in the snow for weeks before Christmas, putting candy canes on window sills and then galloping madly off into the dark, jingling sleighbells and shouting 'Ho! Ho! Ho!' I know the newsboy would rather have two dollar bills than a $1.95 flashlight wrapped in green paper and silver ribbon, with 'MERVYN' spelled out in red Scotch tape. I know no one can eat those Cut'n'Bake cookies after the children have decorated them with green sugar and cinnamon hearts (Christmas tree) and then with more cinnamon hearts and melted marshmallow (Santa Claus) and then with more melted marshmallow and pink crayon (angel). I know it's un-Gesell and not even altogether Spock to look a ten-year-old square in the eye and say: 'But Sweetie, how should *I* know why Polly's Santa Claus is really her father? Maybe her father *has* to be her Santa Claus, poor little thing! Maybe Santa Claus just doesn't *like* Polly. Did you ever think of that?' . . ."

Stuff and nonsense? Well . . . "Some day,"—she wrote on Christmas, 1964, taking off with her striking literary skill on the ladies'-type magazines that tell you how to be a perfect wife, promising, in her own caricature, to be "even more emetic"—but somehow accomplishing something quite different. She wrote: "Some day, though, I will have a fling at becoming a perfect woman, nobly planned, which, the way I dope it out, means spending absolute hours making love your whole existence, and keeping silent in the churches, and weeping while men work, and trying to be a better smoke than a good cigar, and constantly widening the gap between your price and rubies', and being good and letting who will be clever, and while your babes around you cling, showing Wordsworth how divine a thing a woman may be made.

"In my case, though, it will have to be while my grandbabies around me cling, because right now, and for the next fourteen and a quarter years, I'm going to be too busy. . . ." Celebrating Christmas in the usual way.

On Christmas Eve last, with only twelve and one half years to go, she was busy, at the apogee of her yearly cycle, stuffing the stockings of her children with candies and puzzles and games and toys, when she stretched out under the tree and slept. This was not totally unusual for her. But the difference was when she woke an hour later. She did not resume her duty, her joy—though there were still four stockings left to fill. She went, without saying a word, to bed; and so her husband and oldest child, astonished, worried, finished the work of the Christmas-maker extraordinary. She didn't know what it was that had happened, and the doctors didn't seem to know, and two weeks later the Christmases were, for her, forever ended. And little Janet, her *Christkindl* of the year of the Trapps, when she got the news, responded that "Nothing will ever be fun again"; which is exactly how others felt, who knew her when we were all children together.

—WFB JR.

—PLB   FEBRUARY 7, 1967

A special place is reserved in Bill Buckley's affection for those who helped him start, develop, and refine his magazine.

WILLIAM F. RICKENBACKER, R.I.P.

He first surfaced for us at *National Review* when he challenged the government of the United States. The Census Bureau had gone to work collecting its data in 1960, and Bill Rickenbacker received what they called the Long Form, designed to elicit detailed information, the better to complete the decennial inquiry into how many Americans were living where, earning what, doing what, living how. Bill looked at the form, put it in his wastebasket, and addressed one of his inimitable letters to the secretary of commerce, whom he addressed as Dear Snoopchief, denouncing the long form as an invasion of his privacy. C. Dickerman Williams, *National Review*'s distinguished lawyer, undertook his defense. He lost, was fined $100, and put on one day's probation: and at the end of the succeeding decade, tasted finally the fruit of his struggle when the Commerce Department announced that the long form would be completed only by those U.S. citizens who wished to complete it.

Rickenbacker came then to *National Review* as a senior editor, and life was wonderful in his company. He retreated after eight years or so, went into business for himself, wrote eight books, and continued his studies of music, of languages, and of the canon of Western thought.

But he never lost touch with us, and in 1991, with Linda Bridges, he published the book *The Art of Persuasion*. A few years ago, responding to a rebuke for his failure to visit New York more often, he wrote me, "I too wish I could move around a bit more, but I seem to have simplified my life a good deal in recent years. Three or four hours a day at the old piano will nail a fellow down good and hard. But I have dreams, dreams in full color, not to mention aroma, of lunch at Paone's [the reference is to the restaurant around the corner, heavily patronized by *National Review*], which, by the way, why doesn't somebody burn it down and rebuild it up here in God's country?"

. . . Bill, in his letter, went on about his schedule. "Now I'm moving steadily through the fifteen volumes of the collected utterance and effusions of Edmund Burke, and the more I see of him the less I trust him. He keeps reminding me of Everett Dirksen—not that Dirksen ever reminded me of Burke."

Bill was a professionally qualified pianist. "I've recorded," he wrote me, "to my satisfaction, four short pieces of our great teacher, the Bach of Bachs, Schubert comes next, and then a dollop of Chopin. I find this project far more difficult than it was twenty-five years ago. Two trends have been in play: my standards have risen, and my physical capacity has fallen. When I piled up my airplane and broke a dozen bones including my right wrist, I didn't advance the cause; my right hand, if I don't pay good attention, is still in danger of being shouted down by the unruly Bolshevik in my left—a faction that gathered its preternatural strength during ten years of intensive club-gripping on the golf course." He had been captain of the golf team at Harvard. And, like his father, Captain Eddie, he flew, until glaucoma stopped him.

His curiosity was boundless. "Did you see my Unamuno in the current *Modern Age?*" The reference was to an essay he had just published. "Next comes Ortega y Gasset. I've read twenty-one volumes of his and am now organizing my notes. I'll probably have sixty pages of notes in preparation for an eight-page piece. I don't think the name for that is scholarship; more like idle dithering."

It seemed endless, his curiosity. "I've been studying Hebrew *very* hard and loving it all the way. A wonderful language. Since college days I've wanted to read the Psalms in Hebrew; now I shall."

He was not altogether a recluse. A couple of years ago he consented to address my brother Reid's public-speaking school in South Carolina. Reid asked how he should introduce Bill's speech. He sent me a copy of Bill's suggested titles:

—How I Spent My Summer
—What the North Wind Said
—Counselor Said I Couldn't Eat Dinner Till I Wrote Home
—Why I Hate My Sis

—Legalization of Crime: Pros & Cons

—Was Mozart Queer?

—The Bartender's Guide to the Upstairs Maid

—Merde! Golfing Decorum in Postwar France

—Are Lasers Protected under the Fourth Amendment?

—Public Speaking Minus One: A Tape Cassette of Wild but Intermittent Applause, with Stretches of Silence to Be Filled with Remarks by the Apprentice Orator

—Sexual Repression in Emily Dickinson's Punctuation

—Why I Am Running for President (applause)

—Why Dead White Males Don't Laugh

—Do Hydrogen and Oxygen Look like Water? I Ask You!: Chemistry Disrobed and Shown to Be the Fraud It Is

He kept in touch with his friends. When *National Review*'s ex-publisher Bill Rusher had his bypass operation, Rickenbacker wrote to me, "I heard from Claire [Bill Rusher's secretary] on Monday that his bypass was sextuple, which I thought pretty damned good for a bachelor, and look forward to sending him something cheerful as soon as they take the chopsticks out of his nostrils."

And his concern for public affairs was alive as ever. "There has been some talk of flying the flag at half mast," he wrote me, "until the Court's decision [permitting the burning of the flag] is nullified, but I don't think a gesture of mourning is in order when the battle has hardly begun. Instead, I'm flying my own flag at full mast, but upside down, in the international signal of distress. A flag that has been abandoned by its own country is certainly in distress, and I intend to fly mine upside down until the Court turns right side up."

He enjoyed always the exuberant flash of muscle that interrupted, and gave perspective to, his serenity. "I have been a grandfather for five days now and I am growing crotchety. I have told both my boys and both my stepsons that the first one calls me gramps gets a knee in the groin but I doubt if I'll be safe much longer."

Though that was in 1990, he was right—not much longer. It was last fall that the cancer came. But after the operation, he wrote to soothe me. ". . . my moribundity is no more serious than anyone else's of similar time in grade. The so-called treatment, which is in reality, as I need not tell you, . . . a form of Florentine poisoning, offers the advective cruelty of the absence of wine. Anyway I now have two Sanskrit grammars, a matched pair, and will present one copy to [his doctor] when next I see her, which I fear will be on Monday. My hope is that she with her wise Velázquez-brown eyes will find a way to administer my Sanskrit intravenously, with a dash of curry and the faintest after-aroma of popadams. (Do you remember when our mothers could buy popadams in large flat tins from India, the cakes packed between green tobacco leaves?)"

And, only a week later, a letter describing his doctor, whom he much admired. But half way down the page, "EGGS ON FACE DEPT. When I sent you the copy of her letter, I failed to proofread her copy with care, and discovered only later that when she says she may extend a certain life span by two or three months, she means *years*. I double-checked her on this. So relax, mon vieux: it will be longer than you think before your life and property shall be safe."

The doctor was right the first time. But Bill went on with his work. "I've been having fun writing my study of three-letter words. Since the emphasis is on their history and not their definition or use, I have elbow room in the definitions. 'Gun' for instance, which has a very peculiar etymology, I define as 'A metallic pipe through which missiles, which have been excited by chemical explosions in their fundaments, are hurled airmail to their recipients.' For the kind of people who like that sort of thing that's the sort of thing those people will like. . . .

Bill had for a while been reading religious literature, and now he wrote, "I'm reading the Pope's book. I bought a copy for each of my boys, gave one to Tommy, and held one back to read myself before giving it to Jamie. I should buy a third, because I want the book at my elbow always. It's so drenched in wisdom and experience and devotion that I can't take it in in one reading. I read sentence after sentence two or three times. What a man! Among the great souls of history, I say."

A month later I spoke with Nancy on the telephone. She had difficulty in speaking, but told me Bill had been given three or four days more to live. I asked whether I should write to him. Yes, she said, giving me the fax number. I had never before written or spoken to someone on his deathbed, to whom circumspection was no longer possible. So I wrote to my dear and gifted friend,

"Wm, [This was our protocol, dating back three decades: All letters from one to the other would begin, Wm, and be signed, Wm]

"This is not the season to be jolly. Miracles do happen, Evelyn Waugh wrote in *National Review,* 'but it is presumptuous to anticipate them.' It will happen to us all, I brightly observe, but you should feel first the satisfaction of knowing that soon you will be in God's hand, with perhaps just a taste of Purgatory for the editorial you wrote when Bobby was killed, though I here and now vouchsafe you the indulgence I merited on declining to publish it. Second, the satisfaction of being with that wonderful Nancy in your tribulation, and third, the knowledge that those who have known you count it a singular blessing to have experienced you. I send my prayers, and my eternal affection. Wm."

In fact he lived three weeks more and, before losing the use of his writing hand, indited his own obituary, two paragraphs of biographical data, and the closing sentences, "A bug or two showed up last fall and began to do what a bug does best, namely, to make a joke out of life's spruce intentions, and to provide a daily wage or two for journalists, whose business it is not my duty as a Christian to inquire into. Sometime between when this ink and mine go dry the bugs will have had their day. He leaves behind him his wife and two devoted sons, two daughters-in-law, three grandchildren, a beloved sister, an unfinished manuscript or two, and a heart filled with blessings."

May he rest in peace.

—WFB   APRIL 17, 1995

JOHN CHAMBERLAIN, R.I.P.

Late one afternoon in the fall of 1955, on the eve of the appearance of the first issue of *National Review,* something people more loftily situated would have called a "summit conference" was set in New York City, for which purpose a tiny suite in the Commodore Hotel was engaged. Tensions—ideological and personal—had arisen, and the fleeting presence in New York of Whittaker Chambers, who had dangled before us in an altogether self-effacing way the prospect that he might come out of retirement to join the fledgling enterprise, prompted me to bring the principals together for a meeting which had no specific agenda, being designed primarily to reaffirm the common purpose. As I think back on it, two of the five people present were born troublemakers. To say this about someone is not to dismiss him as merely that: Socrates was a troublemaker, so was Thomas Edison. But troublemaking was not what was primarily needed to distill unity, and so, one half hour after the meeting began, things were not going smoothly.

And then, when it was nearly six o'clock and I thought I detected in Chambers a look of terminal exasperation, John Chamberlain showed up, briefcase in one hand, a pair of figure skates in the other. He mumbled (he almost always mumbled) his apology . . . He had booked the practice time at the ice rink for himself and his daughters . . . The early afternoon editorial meeting had been protracted, the traffic difficult . . . No thanks, he didn't want anything to drink—was there any iced tea? He stole a second or two to catch up on Whittaker's family, and then sat back to participate in a conference—which had been transformed by his presence at it.

When a few days later Chambers wrote, he remarked the sheer "goodness" of John Chamberlain, a quality that no man or woman, living or dead, has ever to my knowledge disputed.

At the time a sharp difference had arisen, not between me and John Chamberlain, but between Willi Schlamm and John's wife, Peggy (R.I.P.). Schlamm viewed the projected magazine as a magnetic field, professional affiliation with which could no more be denied by the few to whom the call was tendered than a call to serve as one of the Twelve Apostles. Poor Peggy would not stand for it: John was then serving as an editor of *Barron's* magazine and as a writer for *The Wall Street Journal.* Before that he had been with *The Freeman,* before that with *Life,* before that *Fortune,* before that the *New York Times.* In each of these enterprises he had achieved singularity. He had two daughters not yet grown up. How could anyone reasonably ask that now, in middle age, he detach himself from a secure position to throw in with *National Review*—an enterprise whose working capital would not have seen *Life* magazine through a single issue, or *Barron's* through a dozen, and whose editor-in-chief was not long out of school?

I like to remind myself that I did not figure even indirectly in the protracted negotiation, respecting, as I did, not only the eminence of John Chamberlain, but also the altogether understandable desire of his wife for just a little economic security. But Willi was very nearly (nothing ever proved so conclusively shocking to Willi) struck dumb with shock, the thought that *National Review* might be created without John Chamberlain as a senior editor. That was one of the clouds that hung over that late-afternoon discussion, in which Willmoore Kendall exploited every opportunity to add fuel to the fire, principally by the device of suggesting that for *some* people security means *everything;* the kind of thing John did not wish to hear, among other reasons because it so inexactly reflected his own priorities—he was concerned not with security, but with domestic tranquillity.

So it went, and in one form or another the tensions continued, though they never proved crippling. John settled the problem by moonlighting—as lead reviewer for *National Review.* But I learned then, during that tense afternoon, the joy of a definitively pacific presence. Ours might have been a meeting to discuss whether to dump the bomb on Hiroshima; and John Chamberlain's presence would have brought to such a meeting, whatever its outcome, a sense of inner peace, manliness, and self-confidence.

There are stories John never told, even in his memoirs published a dozen years ago. That was characteristic. Bertrand de Jouvenel once told me, at a luncheon devoted to discussing our common friend Willmoore Kendall, that any subject at all is more interesting than oneself. I am not absolutely convinced that this is so—because some people know no other subject so thoroughly as themselves. But with John Chamberlain self-neglect was an attribute not of manners, but of personality. When *National Review* started up, six weeks after our Commodore summit, he would come in to the office every week (the magazine was then a weekly), sit down at whatever typewriter was free, and type out the lead book review with that quiet confidence exhibited by sea captains when they extricate their huge liners from their hectic municipal ships to begin an ocean voyage. After forty-five minutes or so a definitive book review was done; and John would, quietly, leave, lest he disrupt the office.

In those days "the office" consisted of six or seven cubicles, each one with desk and typewriter. Most of *NR*'s top editorial staffers—James Burnham, Willi Schlamm, Willmoore Kendall, Whittaker Chambers, Frank Meyer—from the beginning on, served only part time, so that at any given moment at least one cubicle was unoccupied, though seldom the same one. Four or five months into the magazine's life a young graduate of Smith, age twenty-four, serving in the circulation department, complained to her classmate, my sister Maureen, that the repairman who came once a week to check the typewriters had not once serviced her own. We couldn't wait to tell John Chamberlain, the delinquent typewriter repairman, when he came in the following Tuesday. He laughed heartily, then sat down to write an illuminating review of the entire fictional work of Mary McCarthy.

I never saw him, during the 1930s, slide into his chair at the *New York Times* to write his daily book reviews, many of them masterpieces of the form. Nor at *Fortune,* where he would return from two weeks on the road to write what he called a "long piece," which would prove the definitive article on this or that intricate problem of management or labor. Nor at *Life,* where he presided over the editorial page that was Henry Luce's personal cockpit, from which he spoke out, through John, to God and man in authoritative, not to say authoritarian, accents. But I decline to believe that in any of these roles, or in any of the myriad others he filled—as professor at Columbia, as dean of journalism at Troy State University in Alabama, as a book writer or a columnist—John Chamberlain ever did anything more disruptive than merely greet whoever stood in the way, and amble over to wherever the nearest typewriter was, there to execute his craft: maintaining standards as high as any set by any critical contemporary.

Because John Chamberlain could not sing off key. And the combination of a gentle nature and a hard Yankee mind brought forth prose pure and lasting. His was a voice of reason, from an affable man, unacquainted with affectation, deeply committed to the cause of his country and to liberty. He believed the fate of his country co-extensive with that of civilization; and, certainly, with that of his two daughters from his first marriage, and of his son—a young poet—from his second, to the enchanting Ernestine, to whom he went soon after Peggy's untimely death.

John Chamberlain's memoirs were surely the most soft-throated in the literature of men who took passionate political positions. As a young man who had demonstrated his prowess as a critic (William Lyon Phelps called him the "finest critic of his generation"), and as a political thinker manifestly addicted to progress, he wrote his book *A Farewell to Reform,* in which he seemed to give up on organic change, suggesting the advantages of radical alternatives. But his idealism was never superordinated to his intelligence, and in the balance of that decade of the thirties, and then in that of the forties, Chamberlain never ceased to look at the data, which carefully he integrated in his productive mind. Along the line (he tells us) he read three books, so to speak at one gulp—and the refractory little tumblers closed, after which he became what is now denominated a "conservative." The books in question, by the three furies of modern libertarianism—Isabel Paterson, Rose Wilder Lane, Ayn Rand—provided the needed cement. After that, he ceased to be surprised by evidence, now become redundant, evidence that the marketplace really works, really performs social functions, really helps live human beings with live problems.

His writings told the story of his journey through this century. His calmness and lucidity, his acquiescent handling of experience, free of ideological entanglement, provoked in the reader the kind of confidence that John Chamberlain throughout his long life provoked in his friends. But his friendships would never run any risk of corrupting the purity of his ongoing search, through poetry, fiction, economic texts, corporate reports, and—yes—seed catalogues, for just the right formulation of what may be acknowledged as the American proposition. He sought an equilibrium of forces that would foster the best that could be got out of the jealous, contentious, self-indulgent, uproarious breed of men and women that have made so exciting a world here, giving issue, in one of America's finest moments, to a splendid man.

I last saw him at a little party given in a noisy New York hotel to celebrate his ninetieth birthday. My sister Priscilla sat next to him, and I was with the proud and lovely Ernestine. I reflected on my first meeting with him. He came to the little house in which I had written *God and Man at Yale,* the manuscript of which had been sent him by the publisher Henry Regnery. It was inconceivable to me that he would consent to write an introduction to a book so disruptive in the circles in which he lived. The purpose of his call—he was the editorial-page editor of *Life*—was to say, Yes, he would write the introduction. We were friends for forty-five years, during all of which we knew his goodness. The staff of *National Review* joins in extending our sympathy to his wife and family.

—WFB

MAY 1, 1995

———

And on a final note of friendship—eternal friendship, which underlies so much of Buckley's choice of words—these words were spoken at the memorial service for Richard M. Clurman, journalist, public servant, master of the genuinely curious, genuinely helpful gesture, at Temple Emanu-El on May 20, 1996, in New York City.

———

RICHARD M. CLURMAN, R.I.P.

Three years ago, one evening in July, he asked whether I'd cross the ocean again in 1995, what would have been the fifth such venture, done at five-year intervals beginning in 1975. "I'm prepared to go," he told me. I suppose I smiled; it was dark on the veranda when he spoke. I told him I doubted my crew could be mobilized for one more such trip, and just the right crew was indispensable. He had done with me two Atlantic crossings, one Pacific crossing. He was an instant celebrity for his ineptitudes at sea, done in high spirit with a wonderful, persistent incomprehension of what was the job at hand. He was the object of hilarious ridicule in my son's published journal—and he loved it all, even as Christopher loved him; even when, while discoursing concentratedly on matters of state, he would drop his cigarette ash into Christopher's wine glass, or very nearly set fire in the galley when trying to light the stove. He thrived on the cheerful raillery of his companions, but on one occasion thought to say to me, in a voice unaccustomedly low: "I'm good at other things."

He hardly needed to remind me. Yes, and from everything he was good at he drew lessons, little maxims of professional and extra-professional life of great cumulative impact, instantly imparted to all his friends, at the least suggestion from them, or from their situation, that they needed help, or instruction. It is awesome to extrapolate from one's own experience of his goodness the sum of what he did for others.

When Osborn Elliott, on Shirley's [Mrs. Clurman] behalf, asked me to say something today I went right to my desk, but I found it impossible to imagine his absence from the scene. Was it true that there would be no message from him tomorrow on our E-mail circuit? That we would not be dining together during the week, or sharing a tenth Christmas together? In the strangest sense, the answer is, No, it isn't impossible that we will continue as companions, because his companionship left indelible traces: how to work, how to read, how to love.

It came to me last Thursday when just after midnight my son reached me at the hotel, that I have always subconsciously looked out for the total Christian, and when I found him, he turned out to be a non-practicing Jew. It will require the balance of my own lifetime to requite what he gave to me.

—WFB

Appendix

A Buckley Lexicon

For some years, the author, at a publisher's request, has been drawing up his own word lists, defined by him and illustrated with examples drawn from his published works, somewhat like a one-man French Academy writing his own dictionary.

They were initiated by the ingenious firm of Andrews and McMeel, which each year publishes a calendar titled *William F. Buckley, Jr.'s 365 Words You'd Like to Know*. Perhaps you would like to know them too, or, more likely, perhaps you know them already and would like to confirm or contest WFB's definitions or usage.

This is a decidedly informal compendium (one section ends with words starting with the letter *i*, for reasons we can't explain), but they all are part of WFB's working vocabulary.

Lexicon I—1991

The following words are taken from *Mongoose, R.I.P.*, by William F. Buckley, Jr., Random House, 1987:

affect (verb) *To pretend; to give the impression of; to feign.*
When Larry Fillmore told his superior in the Agency that he had become engaged, he was told that on no account could he reveal to his fiancée what his actual affiliation was, that he must continue to **affect** to be a Foreign Service trainee. (p. 149)

anomalous (adjective) *Unusual in context; abnormal.*

A U-2 flight, doing its twice-a-week run over Cuba, had yielded an **anomalous** picture taken over San Cristóbal. (p. 267)

arcane (adjective) *Very unusual; the kind of thing generally known only to scholars.*

There were some difficulties, mostly revolving about Spanish translations for **arcane** Russian terminology. Happily most nuclear language relies heavily on Greek and Latin roots and it never proved impossible finally to communicate everything Pushkin wanted to communicate. (p. 274)

ascetic (adjective) *Disposed to do without luxuries; austere.*

Faith Partridge was an **ascetic** woman, in part by nature, in part by necessity; she needed to hold together a household headed by a free-lance writer whose work was mostly rejected, which rejections drove him to despondent drink, even as his occasional acceptances drove him to festive drink. (p. 90)

attenuate (verb) *To stretch out; prolong.*

That was the rumor that caught Cubela's attention and that led, after two months' excruciatingly **attenuated** probing of contacts, to the first communication between Rolando Cubela and Rufus. (p. 160)

auspices (noun) *The umbrella under which you operate; the patronage.*

No questions. No nothing. But perhaps all that would happen in Havana?

Indeed it did, although the **auspices** were unexpected. (p. 198)

avuncular (adjective) *The kind of thing you'd expect of an uncle; benevolent.*

"I was class of 1918." He smiled his warm, **avuncular** smile. "It's hard for old fogies like me to think of women at Yale, though I know they've always been in the graduate school." (p. 96)

badinage (noun) *Light conversation; banter.*

Anthony said something or other, lapsing into **badinage,** and they signed off. (p. 75)

beatific (adjective) *Exalting; radiant; suggesting a special blessedness.*

Her smile was **beatific,** and now she took the glass of sherry, but before she had finished it, her eyes closed. Maria took it from her hand, and Doña Leonarda slept. (p. 126)

bursary (noun) *The arrangement by which students do work for the school or college in return for a remission of a part of their tuition or room and board.*

Sally worked at Vassar ten hours every week as a **bursary** student. (p. 92)

caudillo (noun) *A Latin American dictator, usually self-installed.*

The Americans still thought Castro a banana-republic **caudillo.** (p. 242)

chimera (noun) *An imagined idea, person, or fancy, unusually impractical, romantic.*

Turning his head abeam, the constellation his eyes fixed on had splashes of starry hair that shimmered, and eyes to steer by, and lips set in a pensive, seductive mode. He felt a luff in the sail, snapped his head forward to the mast, and quickly located his navigational star. He had wandered high on his course, while looking back at that **chimera** over Mexico. (p. 81)

communization (noun) *The transformation of a person or movement into complicity with communism, sometimes voluntary, sometimes forced.*

Dr. Alvaro Nueces had turned against Castro in 1960, protesting the **communization** of the 26th of July Movement. (p. 132)

construe (verb) *To put a certain meaning on something; to understand something in a particular way.*

Tamayo might be given an opening to **construe** a conversational jog in an unexpected way. (p. 207)

contiguous (adjective) *Immediately adjacent, in time or location.*
Lindsay Bradford was now engaged in conversation with a **contiguous** beer drinker. (p. 100)

coterie (noun) *A small group of people bound together by common interests or loyalties.*
Lieutenant Gallardo was in charge of the little **coterie** of bodyguards that surrounded Castro wherever he went. (p. 229)

cryptic (adjective) *Having a hidden meaning, perhaps even impenetrable.*
Consuelo stood by the window of his office in downtown Mexico City after receiving the **cryptic** telegram from Miami. The assignment he had received from Rolando Cubela was startling. (p. 172)

diapasonal (adjective) *A musical term which suggests fully orchestrated; full; harmonious.*
The documents they were given to read were in many respects lurid, melodramatic—preposterous even, so their exchanges were not always in the **diapasonal** mode when one of the young CIA agents would interrupt his reading to make a comment or ask a question. (p. 4)

didactic (adjective) *Characteristic of the teacher, whether in manner, or arrangement, or posture.*
"I am glad to hear your Spanish is so good, Blacky. And I, Professor Sally Partridge, am competent to test how good it is." She appeared briefly in the doorway in her dressing gown, affecting her **didactic** posture at the lectern. (p. 30)

dreadnought (noun) *A heavily armed battleship, connoting that nothing can stop it (or you).*
With my Kaypro 386, plus Path-Minder, plus Desq View, plus SideKick, plus Daniel Shurman of Humanware to make sense of it all, I am something of a **dreadnought** on a word processor. (p. 321)

epiphany (noun) *The illuminating meaning of an experience; the sudden penetration of a heretofore elusive truth.*
As he tapped out his message, the **epiphany** crystallized. His redemptive mission was incandescently clear. He, Rolando Cubela, would kill Fidel Castro. (pp. 137–38)

epochal (adjective) *Extremely important, likely to affect future events or the understanding of them.*
During the tumultuous month since being told he would be returning to Cuba on an important mission, he had been given intensive training. And then had come the **epochal** briefing the day before his departure, delivered by Malinovsky himself. (p. 253)

expiate (verb) *To make up for; atone for.*
During those ninety days he came to terms with himself. He decided that he could not **expiate** the sin he had committed against an innocent man until he had undertaken a great and heroic task of redemption. (p. 131)

expostulate (verb) *To plead earnestly in an effort to persuade or correct.*
That afternoon, Nicolai Pushkin shouted himself hoarse and spent himself to the point of exhaustion. His thickly built guard did nothing while Pushkin **expostulated**, except to read, seated at his desk, his comic book. (p. 270)

extrinsic (adjective) *Unrelated to the person or matter or idea at hand; extraneous.*
Maria later realized that she reached maturity only that day, at that moment: she felt a concern entirely **extrinsic** to her own interests. (p. 126)

extrude (verb) *To disgorge; push out; thrust out.*
She looked up at a young, bearded man who, **extruding** the envelope from her hand, said to her politely but firmly, "*Seguridad, Señorita.*" (p. 198)

fastidious (adjective) *Fussy about details; meticulous.*
Among other assets, Maria Raja had a second passport. Her mother, a refugee from Hitler's Hungary, was above all things **fastidious** about security arrangements. (p. 120)

furtive (adjective) *Stealthy; surreptitious; hidden.*
Fidel Castro had got out of the habit of **furtive** midnight meetings, far removed from the handy personal and political apparatus he had got so used to which, with the push of a button, would get him a world leader on the telephone. (p. 239)

hector (verb) *To fuss over insistently, intending to press a point.*
Blackford had made a passing effort to detoxify Sally during senior year at Yale, but hadn't since **hectored** her (or anybody else) on the subject of smoking. (p. 186)

hew (verb) *To cling; to adhere; to hold tightly to.*
As often as not Anthony would take the opportunity to **hew** to the lewd, low road. (p. 74)

hirsute (adjective) *Hairy; covered with hair.*
Fidel was of course **hirsute**, while Rolando had only the trace of a shadow. He wondered whether to shave, as he would do if he were going to a social engagement, or to leave his chin as it was. (p. 19)

histrionic (adjective) *Theatrical; stagey.*
Usually the two men were alone when Tamayo reported his commission had been completed. When that was so, they would both break out into raucous laughter after their **histrionic** exchange. (p. 161)

honorific (noun) *Titles or other forms designed to suggest titles or honors earned or received.*
There were those who believed that no one in memory would ever outshine the brilliant young Luís Miguel, dressed now like an Italian movie star, with a tiny palette of colors below his handkerchief pocket, the flora and fauna of Latin American **honorifics**. (p. 86)

husbandry (noun) *The careful, non-spendthrift management of your money.*
Faith Partridge's **husbandry** did not make her lose all perspective. (p. 90)

ideologize (verb) *To absorb within a system, so as to make it a part of that system, even if the fit isn't very good.*
Che Guevara's concern with medicine was by now almost totally **ideologized**. He cared less how to cure someone suffering from a burst appendix than that the treatment should be the responsibility of the state. (p. 129)

idiomatic (adjective) *Verbally informal.*
"The principal liquid asset is the ten thousand dollars paid by the government when your brother was killed. Faith—your mother—managed to get your father's signature on that check"—Cam Beckett was a family friend as well as attorney, and Sally did not resent his **idiomatic** references to the family situation. (p. 95)

imperturbable (adjective) *Resolutely calm; unshakable; collected.*
The official Castro of tonight, Che reflected, bore little resemblance to the **imperturbable** private Castro of Sierra Maestra. (p. 233)

indigent (adjective) *Poor; impoverished.*
Señora Cubela begged him to stay and eat something, quietly convinced that so distinguished a visitor would not share a meal in such **indigent** surroundings. (p. 175)

internecine (adjective) *Mutually damaging; wounding.*
Stalin had singular historical problems to confront, from the **internecine** question of succession after the death of Lenin, to the dogged resistance of the kulak class, to the war by Hitler. (p. 205)

inveigh (verb) *To protest, in a dogged way; to make vehement, protracted objection.*
One day Castro stormed into a radio station, seizing the microphone and **inveighing** against Batista and praising freedom and democracy and social justice and anti-imperialism for a full ten minutes while his companions kept watch for the police. (p. 18)

jocularity (noun) *Sense of fun; mirthfulness.*

Pano took the rest of his beer slowly. All the usual **jocularity** faded from his face. (p. 171)

limn (verb) *To become visible, traceable, detectable as to features or form.*

Young Jesús Ferrer, with his cosmopolitan background, his derring-do in the mountains, gradually **limned** into the consciousness of the press. (p. 213)

lubricity (noun) *Tendency to sexual stimulation; salacious.*

Blackford remonstrated every now and then when Anthony's **lubricity** got out of hand. "You are like a lot of Englishmen," Blackford once told Anthony. "They learn about sex later than we do and freeze into a Freudian first gear whenever anything remotely suggestive comes up."

lurid (adjective) *Gruesome; horrifying; causing shock or horror.*

The documents they were given to read were in many respects **lurid**, melodramatic—preposterous even, so their exchanges were not always in the diapasonal mode when one of the young CIA agents would interrupt his reading to make a comment or ask a question. (p. 4)

manifestly (adverb) *Obviously; self-revealingly.*

Sally looked at the party-dressed, self-assured, animated young lawyer, like Antonio in his early thirties; probably—no, **manifestly**—more than a lawyer to Antonio. (p. 85)

manifold (adjective) *Various; multiple; of many kinds.*

The following day Olga Kirov walked into the Cuban Embassy, explained that the Señorita Rincona was expecting her, and was admitted into a special reception area, heavily armed because of the **manifold** requirements associated with Fidel Castro's visit. (p. 181)

miff (verb) *To offend; annoy.*

"Is it your guess," Ruth probed, "that Castro would shrug his shoulders if she got **miffed**?" (p. 152)

monitory (adjective) *Warning; admonitory.*

When the censor, at the special request of the Russian-Cuban interpreter, promised a quick reading of the letter to Major Kirov from his wife, he checked his files routinely, and spotted the **monitory** marking. (p. 182)

moribund (adjective) *Deathly; about to die; having to do with death.*

When there was someone else in the room on unrelated business, Castro and Tamayo would satisfy themselves, after the **moribund** dialogue, with an oblique cross-glance, an exchanged wink. (p. 161)

multifarious (adjective) *Many and various; diverse.*

Castro liked it when his intimates joined him in exploring the **multifarious** reefs around Cuba. (p. 225)

nomenclature (noun) *A vocabulary associated with an art, or science, or discipline.*

Rolando had not got used to the brevity of revolutionary **nomenclature** and found it difficult to say "*Buenas noches, Paco*" to a man twice his age. (p. 20)

obtrude (verb) *To thrust out; push forward.*

"Your husband is at San Cristóbal," the interpreter said, a smile **obtruding** her creased face. (p. 180)

officious (adjective) *Showing bureaucratic attention; offering unnecessary and perhaps unwanted advice and services.*

She was surprised when, at the airport in Mexico, a middle-aged man, portly and **officious** (he bellowed out instructions to the porter who accompanied him), approached her at the gate of her flight, his diplomatic badge, pinned conspicuously above his breast pocket, permitting him into the inspection compound. (p. 197)

oleaginous (adjective) *Unctuous; oily; affected.*

On the second evening of his state visit in Moscow, Fidel Castro had been carried away by an **oleaginous** toast in his honor delivered by Soviet President Leonid Brezhnev. (p. 177)

palpably (adverb) *Obviously; transparently; perceptibly.*

She moved, for the first year or so, **palpably** under a shadow and it wasn't until the end of the spring term that her irrepressibly buoyant roommate unearthed the cause of Sally's melancholy and set out to do something about it. (p. 92)

patently (adverb) *Obviously; manifestly; plainly.*

Kirov plied Tamayo with questions of theoretical concern to students of Marxism-Leninism and, **patently,** of immediate concern to him. (p. 204)

penumbral (adjective) *Shadowy; done under the cover of darkness; concealed.*

Consuelo had engaged in interesting enterprises, most of them concerning Mexicans, often Mexicans seeking ways, legal and **penumbral,** of taking out of Mexico sums of money accumulated by political activity. (p. 172)

peroration (noun) *The closing part of a speech.*

The effect of Fidel's **peroration** was slightly marred by Che's aside, directed not so much at Castro directly as to the assembly. "Well, our independence would perhaps be more convincing if we relied less completely than we are forced to do on Soviet economic and military favors." (p. 141)

perquisites (noun) *Those advantages in a job or in a position that aren't a part of your formal contract.*

Perhaps she was simply doing a job, a job that not only paid well but gave her important **perquisites** in Castro's Cuba—access, for instance, to Diplotiendas, where the select few could buy coffee and extra-conventional luxuries, such as a bar of scented soap imported from Canada, or a chocolate bar. (p. 130)

piquancy (noun) *Something attractively offbeat; provocative.*

M'Lou could always make Sally laugh—that had never been a problem. Sally reacted instantly to humor, as to **piquancy.** (p. 92)

precocity (noun) *Early intellectual or artistic development.*

She walked over to her slender neighbor, whose lined face suggested an age greater than the sixty-one she acknowledged when making one of her frequent references to the **precocity** of her important son. (p. 125)

preternaturally (adverb) *Extremely; more than one would think natural.*

In less than fifteen minutes, Blackford felt **preternaturally** at home with the young Cuban designated by Rufus to be his right hand. (p. 34)

promulgate (verb) *To issue a new law or regulation.*

When Rolando Cubela concluded that he had the mandate—to execute Fidel Castro—he was prepared to be ever so cautious in his plans. Nothing reckless. After a month's deliberation, Cubela had it down on paper—in his mind:

1) Castro's death—it must be absolutely assured.

2) A plausible new Cuban government—instantly **promulgated.** (p. 156)

punctilio (noun) *Highly formal observance of formalities.*

"You wonder about me, Pano?" Blackford said.

"I need to wonder about *todo el mundo,* the whole world. My professional *puntillo*—how do you say that, my friend?"

"**Punctilio.** Okay, Pano, but it is only right, then, that we should wonder about each other. Whom do you want to hear from about me?" (p. 41)

putatively (adverb) *Supposedly; ostensibly; reputedly.*

It didn't surprise Sally that Art was talking not to old friends, **putatively** interested in Art Shaeffer, football tactician, but to undergraduates he had never met before. (p. 99)

quixotic (adjective) *Idealistic and impractical. The word comes from Don Quixote, who tilted at windmills, fancying them an enemy overcome.*
Haydee Santamaria was the sister of the brave man tortured to death during the Moncado fiasco of 1953, when Castro led the **quixotic** charge against the well-fortified barracks at Santiago de Cuba. (p. 132)

refectory (noun) *Eating quarters, usually of religious orders.*
The room across the courtyard from the entrance, on the second floor, above what used to be the chapel and was now the printing office from which Castro's instructions flowed out to his subjects, had been the monks' **refectory**. (p. 226)

remonstrate (verb) *To argue rebukingly.*
Blackford knew better than to **remonstrate** on the theme of the Elusive Distinction. (p. 171)

riposte (noun) *A bouncy reply; usually provocative.*
Blackford thought back on the agonies of the Bruderschaft, and for a moment said, reverently, nothing by way of **riposte**. This quickly communicated a hint of resistance to her. He got back into his customary role, the succubus of her taunts. (p. 31)

robustly (adverb) *Unapologetically frank, open, vigorous.*
On entering the **robustly** Victorian Fence Club, to which he had been elected as an undergraduate at about the time of Pearl Harbor, Art's spirits quickly revived. (p. 98)

sagacity (noun) *Wisdom; soundness of judgment.*
Pedrito nodded his head vigorously, in extravagant recognition of her **sagacity**, and they strolled back toward the little knots of Mexican family friends. (pp. 85–86)

sectarian (adjective) *Divisively attached to one faction within a church, ideology, or political party.*
"Khrushchev, we are admiring of the Soviet Union, we are grateful for the aid you are giving us to realize our own socialist revolution, but we cannot be conscripted into the ranks of your **sectarian** wars against Mao," Castro declaimed. (p. 140)

solecism (noun) *A breach of the formal rules, usually of syntax.*
When lunch was served, the rabbinically disguised Oakes, rather than commit any inadvertent dietary **solecism**, ate nothing, and so emerged from the plane, with his false passport, hungry. (p. 211)

somnambulist (noun) *A sleepwalker.*
To the left and right were cell doors with small apertures at eye level. The only sounds were the occasional moans and what sounded like **somnambulists'** soliloquies. (pp. 134–35)

squalid (adjective) *Squat, dirty, or wretched in appearance.*
The elm trees were budding on Vassar's neat green campus in the **squalid** city on the day the envelope arrived. (p. 94)

subterfuge (noun) *A deception.*
"It is inconceivable that Khrushchev should have authorized any such **subterfuge** without—well, without my authorization," Castro said. (p. 143)

surreptitious (adjective) *Hidden; out of sight; clandestine.*
Ingenio Tamayo was a mean-spirited man—who very much enjoyed performing Fidel Castro's highly **surreptitious** commissions primarily because they called for the discreet elimination of someone Castro did not wish officially to detain and execute. (p. 161)

sycophantic (adjective) *The manner of someone who seeks to gain favor by flattery.*
Castro laughed. He laughed uproariously. Such a laugh as demands of subordinates **sycophantic** acquiescence. (p. 22)

tumultuous (adjective) *Violently agitated; uproarious.*

During the **tumultuous** month since being told he would be returning to Cuba on an important mission, he had been given intensive training. (p. 253)

valedictory (noun) *Farewell; that which is said in the course of ending a speech or bidding good-bye.*

Fidel Castro had never succeeded in expunging from his own or others' use the traditional Cuban **valedictory** that one should go forward with God. (p. 146)

verisimilitude (noun) *Authenticity; the appearance of being the genuine article.*

Fidel explained, his voice now conversational, "The repetition? 'A most terrible, a most horrible accident?' As a writer, I would not engage in such crude repetitions. But here, it gives **verisimilitude** to the heat with which I am speaking." (p. 295)

vernacular (noun) *The language spoken in the informal idiom of a trade or profession; informal idiom.*

He reiterated—it had to be a native Soviet. No Cuban, never mind his training in Russian, could master the kind of **vernacular** the Kremlin would expect to receive in telexes from the field, the bureaucratic accretions, the idiomatic twists and turns. (p. 275)

volubly (adverb) *Talkatively.*

Betancourt, who had early on sided enthusiastically with Castro and his insurgency, was by now **volubly** disgusted with what Castro had done to his country. (p. 157)

voluptuarian (adjective) *Lustful; sensuous.*

Anthony leaned forward, got up to stir the log fire, and sat down again, his face radiant in what, under entirely different circumstances, Blackford had once referred to as "your lewd, **voluptuarian** smile." (p. 5)

williwaw (noun) *A gust of cold wind; a mini-gale.*

When the anti-Semitic williwaw of the mid-thirties suddenly threatened to grow to Typhonic force, young Astra led her widowed mother to meet her river friend, the elderly policeman with a fondness for the children who played along the river's verdant banks. (p. 121)

The following words are taken from Mr. Buckley's syndicated column, "On the Right":

---

aberration (noun) *Deviation from the truth or a moral standard, from the natural state, or from a normal type.*

Now Jeane Kirkpatrick is my sister and Pat Buchanan my brother, and if I have ever differed from their foreign policy analyses it can only have been in a moment of **aberration**. (5/4/89)

abortifacient (noun) *A drug or any agent that induces abortion.*

The choicers are now saying that the Griswold decision must be understood as permitting not merely physical barriers to impregnation, but also **abortifacients**. (4/28/89)

abrogate (verb) *To rescind; abolish by official action.*

It would be quite mistaken to **abrogate** the treaty in reaction to these infractions: Nothing would more quickly propel the three quarters of the Panamanian community that dislikes Noriega to return to his fold. (5/16/89)

accretion (noun) *Something that has been added that doesn't necessarily belong.*

The minimum wage is an **accretion** of the New Deal that is not publicly defended by any serious economist. (6/15/89)

aegis (noun) *The direction, control, supervision.*

The key to stopping the erosion of Eastern's assets under the **aegis** of the judge who seems to have the power to conduct either an autopsy or a revivification is, of course, the unions. (6/16/89)

albescent (adjective) *Becoming white, i.e., shining out more conspicuously.*

Nobody knows how Congress is going to leave Social Security and the other entitlement programs untouched and come up with $50 billion or so to save the savings and loans, which we are informed need to be saved because the alternative—letting them fail—is more costly in the long run because Congress has insured the depositors against harm. And there is the **albescent** matter of a United States with (a) no nuclear weapons facilities, and (b) a lot of unmanageable toxic nuclear waste material. (1/6/89)

analogue (noun) *Something similar; another version of the same thing.*

They speak of Sen. Joseph McCarthy paralyzing the Foreign Service: Will history give us any **analogue** more indicative of the power of superstition than that of the antinuclear lobbyists over the development of nuclear power? (7/25/89)

angst (noun) *A kind of perpetual, even neurotic state of anxiety.*

One artist sought to explain his **angst** by sticking a crucifix in a jar of urine. That this exhibit should be financed by taxpayers is a proposition Senator Helms had no difficulty taking on. (7/28/89)

animadversion (noun) *An unfriendly reference, statement, criticism.*

The machinists of Eastern Airlines tend to slur off into **animadversions** on the management of Frank Lorenzo, whose personality poses no threat to Perry Como's. (3/9/89)

anneal (verb) *To strengthen; toughen.*

The myth of Napoleon suffered mortal wounds. It required three more years to put him away permanently, but the resolve to do so was **annealed**. This time they'll probably award Gorbachev not a lifetime on St. Helena, but a Nobel Peace Prize. Machiavelli can be taken too far. (2/9/89)

arbiter elegantiae (noun) *The person who rules on matters of fashion, protocol, taste.*

Professor Arthur Schlesinger, who is the **arbiter elegantiae** of liberal fashion, wrote a few months ago that only bigots would vote against Jesse Jackson. (1/20/89)

arrant (adjective) *Naked, unmitigated.*

Soviet television is showing only pictures of Chinese students attacking Chinese soldiers. And the Soviet press quote only Chinese officials' statements in which the student protesters emerge as "counterrevolutionaries" guilty of sadistic killing of patriotic soldiers.

Any excuses for this kind of behavior are **arrant** Bolshevism of the old school. (6/8/89)

asseveration (noun) *An assertion made in very positive form; a solemn assertion.*

Dr. Robert DuPont gave the impression that he had disposed of any question (as to whether drugs ought to be legalized) before the house by his initial **asseveration**. To wit, "Name me one politician in the United States who has run successfully for political office who believes in legalizing drugs." (2/23/89)

Attican (adjective) *Athenian in its classical simplicity, elegance.*

We should all be in favor of short speeches. But if we're going to set up an **Attican** theatrical background to commemorate the moment of the Soviet departure from Afghanistan, why doesn't General Gromov use up his one minute and seven seconds to fire a bullet into his head? (2/9/89)

avatar (noun) *A high priest; a semi-god; an incarnate authority.*

There was talk by the **avatars** of a free press charging cowardice and betrayal of common responsibilities to defend the First Amendment. (2/28/89)

banality (noun) *Something obvious; repetitious; lacking in originality.*

In Warsaw President Bush told the press, "There are times in diplomacy when a certain delicacy is called for." Putting that on the front page [in *The New York Times*] could have been the work of a sly reporter whose only defense against **banality** is to print it. (7/11/89)

bellicose (adjective) *Characterized by military hostility; provocatively warlike.*

The closeness of de Gaulle and Adenauer was a historical monument to the possibilities of trans-**bellicose** life. (2/24/89)

bellwether (noun) *The guide by which one measures other data.*

The current airline industry load factor (i.e., the percentage of filled seats) is between 65 percent and 75 percent. And the **bellwether** price of a ticket (economy class, non-super saver) is greatly inflated. (6/30/89)

beneficently (adverb) *Kindly; charitably.*

Many years ago I asked the dean of my alma mater why no credit was given for the mastery of typing or shorthand and he replied **beneficently,** "There is no body of knowledge in typing." (1/19/89)

Brobdingnagian (adjective) *Huge. The word is from Jonathan Swift's imaginary country, inhabited by giants, in* Gulliver's Travels.

Finally the Khomeini cried uncle, and, at age eighty-eight, set out to attempt to bring to Iran a small measure of the growing prosperity it was experiencing even while feeding the Peacock Throne the gold, frankincense and the myrrh it had taken to consuming with such **Brobdingnagian** appetite. (2/22/89)

bull (noun) *An authoritative declaration or statement.*

Adult men and women, staring hard at a clause in the Constitution of the United States that forbids an establishment of religion and recognizing no reasonable nexus between that prohibition and the recital at their local public school of a public prayer jointly formulated by rabbis, ministers, and priests, receive on Monday what might be called a juridical **bull** from the Supreme Court, and on Tuesday there is compliance. (6/29/89)

burden (noun) *The central theme; the principal idea.*

The front-page story (the *New York Times,* July 24) is headlined, "H.U.D. Approved Rent Subsidies/After Coors Wrote the Secretary." From the headline alone, the **burden** of the story is communicated. (7/27/89)

Cartesian (adjective) *Relating to the philosopher Descartes, who specified direct and logical forms of thought and analysis.*

In an idle moment during a holiday, I searched the wave band of a portable radio in quest of something to listen to. None of the twenty or so options relayed classical music. It required only a little **Cartesian** *gelandesprung* to alight at the conclusion that it is the responsibility of the government to maintain monuments that are man-made, as well as those given us by nature. (2/7/89)

catechizing (verb) *Severe questioning designed to illuminate moral guilt.*

Tony Coelho, who has spent much of his adult life **catechizing** Republicans, fled office rather than submit to a public study of whether he has himself been submitting to the standards he has preached. (6/2/89)

cavil (noun) *A quibble; a frivolous objection.*

The **cavil** that Beethoven doesn't need looking after since his records sell by the trainload isn't at all satisfying to someone spelunking through radio channels in search of Beethoven. (2/7/89)

chiliastic (adjective) *Relating to the Second Coming; having to do with the reappearance of Christ on earth.*

That the existence of the Congress of People's Deputies, or of the Supreme Soviet, should have meaning at all is positively **chiliastic** in its implications. (6/1/89)

cloying (adjective) *The special taste you get when something is repeated, or heard, or seen so often that it loses its original flavor and becomes simply boring.*
The lawyers are of course active, as also the anti–capital punishment organizations; but lawyers and generic opponents of capital punishment have a way of **cloying**—they sometimes leave the impression they'd have freed Jack the Ripper—and indeed they kept Ted Bundy alive for ten years. (8/11/89)

commonweal (noun) *The common interest; the good-better society.*
The idea of a vote governed by an ethos of the **commonweal**—a voter's fiduciary obligation to vote not alone for his narrow best interest, but for the public interest—is substantially lost sight of as candidates gather together money from the lobbyists and settle down to lifetimes in the House of Representatives. (6/22/89)

contumely (noun) *Disdain; expression of contempt, dislike, hatred.*
Has Michael Milken, in his revolutionary lifetime, re-situated the ethical norms of business conduct in such a way as to earn universal **contumely**? (9/28/89)

credenda (noun) *The constituent elements of what forms your belief, in religion, politics, whatever.*
Imagine a reformist pope who questions the authenticity of the Bible, and you have some idea of the philosophical and spiritual problems that Gorbachev faces. He cannot deny the **credenda** of the Soviet state without denying at the same time his own legitimacy. (5/4/89)

danseur (noun) *The male dancer in a ballet group; often used to suggest said dancer's exhibitionistic impulses.*
George Bush was in Brussels deciding that he would, for once, take the arms control show away from the world's premier **danseur,** Mikhail Gorbachev. (6/1/89)

decoct (verb) *To figure out by deduction what the true meaning is of a statement, a symbol, an oblique communication.*
It isn't easy to **decoct** the machinists' message from the picket signs or from public pronouncements. (3/9/89)

demagogue (noun) *Someone who appeals for public support by saying, or promising, that which most appeals to the crowd, or mob, he is addressing.*
Noriega is an effective **demagogue**. And—always a winner in Latin America—he has defied the United States of America and got away with it. (5/9/89)

deracination (noun) *Cutting off cultural and institutional and ethnic ties, leaving the individual, or tribe, or nation without its traditional support system.*
A European figure so august that ladies curtsy when they are presented to him was telling the table at which we all sat about the great mischief being done by the missionaries in Venezuela who move in on native tribes and totally break down their cultural order, resulting in **deracination** and chaos. (3/14/89)

disingenuous (adjective) *You know what is true, but you argue as though you didn't know it, because you want to make a point that serves your interests.*
Congressional retaliation is based on attempting to fix in the public mind that the President anticipated revenues of ABC, a growth rate of XYZ, and interest rates of GHI—and that these were defective as predictions and **disingenuous** in conception. (2/21/89)

disinterested (adjective) *A position taken—political, moral, analytical—which has no bearing on the position that would suit your own personal interests, because your interests are simply not involved.*
They seek to dramatize a point that choicers should force themselves to acknowledge is entirely **disinterested,** even as demonstrators for civil rights were fighting not for themselves, but for others. (7/20/89)

dithyrambic (adjective) *A truly exaggerated exercise in praising something or somebody.*
In recent weeks we found ourselves interrupted in our **dithyrambic** praise for democracy when the guy in El Salvador whom we did not like won. (5/9/89)

dulcet (adjective) *Done in quiet, sweet, soft tones.*
The question arises of the fear of a united Germany, a fear widely expressed, if mostly in **dulcet** tones, by Europeans east and west of Berlin. (8/10/89)

ecumenical (adjective) *A position that has the backing of more than one faction, political, theological, or scientific.*
Two ideas are current, neither of them the property of conservatives or of liberals. It is an **ecumenical** mix, with some conservatives arguing that the show is up for world communism, some liberals arguing that it is much too early to tell. (6/8/89)

egregious (adjective) *Flagrant; distinctively presumptuous, horrible.*
Recent amendments to the Constitution have merely codified popular passions. But (save for the largely irrelevant exception) there has been no constitutional amendment the purpose of which was to revise the interpretations of a Supreme Court, notwithstanding **egregious** provocations by the Court, most recently during the '50s and '60s when it became commonplace to refer to the "Warren Revolution." (6/29/89)

envoi (noun) *The final communication; valedictory; send-off.*
The portrait of Ronald and Nancy Reagan done by Mike Wallace for *60 Minutes* was their **envoi** to the republic on their presidency. (1/17/89)

epigoni (noun) *Close followers, given to imitating, or being bound by, the star they become the creatures of.*
William Winpisinger, the president of the striking (Eastern Airlines) machinists, is a socialist and is quick to put a class struggle aspect on any labor-management division, and indeed Mr. Winpisinger lost no chance to do this. And the **epigoni** jumped in. Sure enough, there was Jesse Jackson joining the picketers. (3/9/89)

eremitical (adjective) *Characteristic of the hermit; far removed from ordinary life and considerations.*
To say that Mrs. Jones is unbiased in the matter of Colonel North because she was unaware of him, notwithstanding that Colonel North dominated the news in the press, on radio, and on television for about three weeks two springs ago, isn't to come up with a fine mind that missed the entire episode because she was absorbed in **eremitical** pursuits. (2/3/89)

eschatological (adjective) *Pertaining to the ultimate ends of life, existence.*
It became clear—years ago, for the perceptive; only recently, for the true believers—that communism does not work, i.e., communism does not bring on the redemptive **eschatological** paradise predicted by Marx, does not ease the burden of the worker, and does not reduce the power of the state. (3/2/89)

eschew (verb) *To turn down; ignore; disdain; do without.*
The United States has two sovereign responsibilities at this point. The first is to maintain our guard. The second is to **eschew** any invitations to finance the economic rehabilitation of the Soviet Union. (6/1/89)

estop (verb) *To put an end to; bar; prohibit.*
Is it suggested that a defense secretary who had been to a cocktail party, or even one who had gone to bed drunk, would **estop** the flow of instructions from the President? (3/7/89)

evanesce (verb) *Gradually to disappear.*
Marx and Engels promulgated the view that if you eliminate private property, all derivative vices **evanesce**. (3/30/89)

excogitation (noun) *Something thought up and said or written or pronounced. There is an implication of derision, or contempt, when the word is used.*

Roe *v.* Wade was a lousy decision, perhaps even an indefensible act of constitutional **excogitation,** and the choicers know that they are safest by not asking the Court to look again at this century's version of the Dred Scott decision. (1/19/89)

ex officio (adverb) *"In virtue of the office" is the literal translation. What it designates is the power of the pope, in Catholic dogma, to pronounce finally on questions of religion and morals.*

About a year ago, Senator Nunn suddenly announced that the stricter of two plausible versions of the ABM ban on testing was the correct one, and I swear it was like the pope pronouncing **ex officio** on a question of dogma. (2/16/89)

fatuous (adjective) *Silly; thoughtless; inane.*

So much for Tom Wicker's **fatuous** attempt to make his frantic point that the fate of Owen Lattimore is now being visited on Tom Foley by the ass in the Republican National Committee who wrote a silly memo from which only silly people would conclude that the charge was made that Tom Foley is gay. (6/9/89)

ferula (noun) *A cane, or rod, used as an instrument of punishment. Usually a flat piece of wood, sometimes encased in leather.*

Since it is pre-decided that the Bush Administration will not advocate the legalization of drugs, the Bennett basket is going to have to be chock-full of **ferula** with which to beat offenders. (6/27/89)

flaunt (verb) *To exhibit with the view to attracting attention.*

Successful men are not necessarily ascetic men, and although a public is within its rights in declining to elevate to the presidency a candidate who **flaunts** his immorality, it is simply mistaken to suppose that failed marriages and occasional draughts of good spirits ruin the night of our kindly and gentle nation any more than they ruined the wedding at Cana. (2/16/89)

fons et origo (noun) *The source. Literally, the fountain and origin.*

Mikhail Gorbachev can criticize Constantin Chernenko and Leonid Brezhnev—and Brezhnev can criticize Nikita Khrushchev, who criticized Stalin; but no one will criticize the **fons et origo** of all that poison, Lenin. (5/26/89)

fungible (adjective) *Two things that are fungible will intermix without difficulty. Some things are not fungible, e.g., oil and water.*

Although the age of computers and satellites and television dishes has done much to circulate ideas hitherto pockmarked in totalitarian cavities, in fact knowledge isn't all that **fungible.** (6/8/89)

fusilier (noun) *Rifleman; soldier armed with a fusil (musket).*

Deng Xiaoping is seized, in Karl Wittfogel's phrase, with the megalomania of the aging despot, and rather than acknowledge the right of his citizens peaceably to assemble in order to petition the government for a redress of grievances, he shoots them; and, tomorrow, may hang those his **fusiliers** missed. (6/6/89)

fustian (adjective) *Overblown; pompous; wordy.*

The only thing we can reasonably do isn't, at this point, **fustian** retaliation. (6/6/89)

gerrymander (noun) *An electoral district carved up without regard to demographic symmetry, intending to fortify a particular political party at the expense of another political party. The word is also used as a (transitive) verb.*

The fat and rich Democratic **gerrymanders** are going to find a dragon waiting for them when they rev up for the decennial hanky-panky. Those interested in self-government should side with the dragon, Newt Gingrich. (3/24/89)

gravitas (noun) *The kind of solemnity one associates with kings, bishops, and wise men. The word in Latin was used in Rome to designate the mien of thoughtful, civic-minded, wise men.*

The key figure, of course, is Senator Nunn, around whose judgments **gravitas** closes in like clouds gathering around a prophet. (2/16/89)

hegemonic (adjective) *Preponderant influence and authority, to the point of excluding other influence.*

In order to maintain the pressure that orients the Soviet Union and China toward reform in the first instance, we need to continue to roam those quarters of the world where the Soviet Union continues to exercise **hegemonic** influence. (8/1/89)

hegemony (noun) *Preponderant influence or authority; leadership; dominance.*

Since Moscow is still willing to pay $14 million per day to continue to support Fidel Castro, Daniel Ortega reasonably hopes to hang on to that incremental Soviet subvention necessary to eliminate any possibility that the tatterdemalion contras will ever seriously challenge the Marxist **hegemony** in Nicaragua. (2/14/89)

impute (verb) *To attribute accusingly, often unjustly.*

I assume that a communist is a pro-communist, though Tom Wicker sometimes acts as though it would be an act of McCarthyism to **impute** pro-communism to Joseph Stalin, let alone Mikhail Gorbachev. (7/13/89)

———

The following words are taken from *On the Firing Line: The Public Life of Our Public Figures,* by William F. Buckley, Jr., Random House, 1989:

———

abominate (verb) *To loath; detest.*

I had never heard of the gentleman, a professor of English from the University of Missouri, who wrote a review of *Saving the Queen* for the *Kansas City Star.* He made it quite clear that he had spent a considerable part of his adult life **abominating** me and my works and my opinions. He was manifestly distressed at not quite disliking my first novel. (p. 420)

abstruse (adjective) *Difficult; difficult to understand, to penetrate the meaning of.*

Here is a man [Cardinal Arns of São Paulo] who studied literature at the Sorbonne, where he achieved his doctorate; who taught petrology and didactics at highly respected universities; who has written twenty-five books, including **abstruse** treatises on medieval literature. (p. 34)

accretion (noun) *An addition to the original law, idea, concept, institution, which is not necessarily a legitimate part of the original.*

WFB: You say that the rights of lawyers and priests should extend to journalists.

ABRAMS: As a general matter, yes. There are some differences, but as a general matter, yes, I—

WFB: That's sort of a revolutionary **accretion** and yet, in asserting that point, you tend to do so as an exegete of the Constitution rather than as somebody who wants to amend it. (p. 198)

afflatus (noun) *A creative impulse; a divine warrant or inspiration.*

As Muhammad Ali explained, "I was the onliest boxer in history people asked questions like a senator." But then he was touched by the **afflatus** of Elijah Mohammed. . . . (p. 94)

altruistic (adjective) *An act motivated by concern for others, rather than for oneself.*

WFB: (*addressing a question to George Gilder*) I am determined to build a cheaper mousetrap in order to get your patronage and to line my pocket. But since in the course of creating a cheaper mousetrap I have made it possible for you to purchase one, I have committed an objectively **altruistic** act for selfish motives. Now, why do you assume there is an incompatibility between those two concepts? (p. 297)

ameliorate (verb) *To improve; make better.*

To suggest that politics is not the solution is to endanger political careers. It is not a subject directly addressed by Jean-François Revel—the difficulty in achieving the desired circulation of thought, for the purpose of **ameliorating** such problems as race relations in such a country as the United States. (p. 325)

animadversion (noun) *An unkind, critical remark.*

It seems to me that if you are going to take legendary auspices for current attitudes, you will find ten **animadversions** on man for every one on woman in literature. (p. 440)

animadvert (verb) *To remark or comment critically, usually with strong disapproval or censure.*

John Kenneth Galbraith asked me just when major corporations had lost 85 percent of their value: and I evaded an answer (I did not have the data in the front of my memory; and in any event, I had exaggerated the effect of the Dow Jones dip of 1969–70 by **animadverting** one of JKG's books, suggesting that its collapse had coincided with that of the market). Manifestly, I did not get away with this, and ought not to have done. (p. 22)

anomaly (noun) *Deviation from the normal or common order, form, or rule; abnormality.*

The "conservatives" in the Kremlin are those who desire a return of Stalinism. Sometimes the **anomalies** bite back. *The New York Times* ran a sober account from Moscow about a crackdown by "Kremlin conservatives" against the importation of foreign books. One of the proscribed titles was *The Conscience of a Conservative* by Barry Goldwater. (p. 168)

antinomian (adjective) *Opposed to, defiant of, or rejecting moral law.*

William Kunstler was probably the best-known of the lawyers who identified themselves with dissent, and who sought a kind of **antinomian** liberty for dissenters. (p. 97)

apostasy (noun) *Defection from one's faith, political or religious.*

I was left to infer that while serving as a courier, Whittaker Chambers was proving to his case officer his utter reliability (subject, of course, to **apostasy** from the Communist movement). (p. 405)

asceticism (noun) *Rigorous self-discipline, severe abstinence, austerity.*

Bauhaus was the name given to a compound of architects gathered together after the First World War in Germany to remark the general desolation, which they sought to shrive by a kind of architectural **asceticism** noted for a cleanness of line, an absence of ornamentation, the blandness of color, and the "honesty" of generic building materials. (p. 263)

banausic (adjective) *Of purely mechanical interest or purpose.*

Al Lowenstein was the original activist, such was his impatience with the sluggishness of justice, so that his rhythms were more often than not disharmonious with those that govern the practical, **banausic** councils of this world. (p. 433)

bowdlerized (verb) *Shrunk, with the purpose of expurgating titillating bits. After Thomas Bowdler (1754–1824. R.I.P.)*

Churchill pauses from the war effort to cable back his regards to Mrs. Luce, who meanwhile has been asked by the Joint Chiefs of Staff to brief them on her analyses, which, suitably **bowdlerized,** appear in successive issues of *Life* magazine and are a journalistic sensation. (p. 444)

cognate (adjective) *Related to each other; analogous.*

Freedom of the press, freedom of speech—these **cognate** liberties are, of course, routinely construed to extend not only to journalism but also to expression of a more subtle kind, namely, artistic expression. (p. 201)

condign (adjective) *Deserved; appropriate; adequate.*

ABRAMS: A reporter, Paul Branzburg, was called to testify in front of a grand jury, and he took the position that he should not have to testify about material he had learned in confidence. The Supreme Court held five to four that he did have to testify. Mr. Branzburg subsequently left the state, and so far as I know has not returned to Kentucky.

WFB: Is that **condign** punishment? (p. 196)

congeries (noun) *A collection; accumulation; aggregation.*

I have seen only two political firestorms that resulted in sharp and immediate political response. The first was the sentencing of William Calley, the anti-hero of My Lai. The crowd simply insisted his penalty was inordinate, insisted on this for a **congeries** of reasons, primarily a frustration with the length and conduct of the Vietnam war. (p. 152)

contumacious (adjective) *Obstinately disobedient; rebellious; challenging the law.*

Francis Plimpton wrote to me, I replied, and toward the end of our correspondence he asked me to make publicly plain his own feeling about **contumacious** lawyers. (p. 102)

cosmology (noun) *A view of the origin, structure, and (often) purposes of the universe.*

Jeff Greenfield wrote a withering piece for the *Yale Alumni Magazine* about an appearance I made at Yale which had begun with a press conference and went on to a formal speech. His piece was a stretch of arrant scorn for my thought, logic, diction, and **cosmology**. (p. 171)

coterminously (adverb) *Contained within the same period; coextensive.*

Allen Dulles was head of the CIA for nine years. During that period, and as a matter of fact since then, he and the CIA are criticized more or less **coterminously**: Allen Dulles was the CIA incarnate. (p. 411)

defi (noun) *A challenge; rejection of.*

Tom Wolfe had published *The Painted Word*, a **defi** hurled in the face of the art critics, challenging their taste, questioning their originality, and lamenting their power. (p. 262)

derogation (noun) *Disparagement; belittling.*

(*WFB posing a question to Allen Dulles*) What is your opinion of the continued **derogation** of the intelligence function? Why should the CIA be made a—a sort of general laughing stock? (p. 412)

desideratum (noun) *That which is desired; the better, or even perfect, state.*

Jesse Jackson began by saying that for a black, his blackness is forever the supreme fact of life. In saying so, without suggesting that he lamented this priority, he moved very far from Martin Luther King's Dream, in which color made no difference: colorblindness isn't a **desideratum** for Jackson. (p. 313)

dialectical (adjective) *The interactive action between one view and a contradictory view.*

You cannot argue effectively with anyone whose position is removed from your own by more than one **dialectical** unit. (p. 365)

dilate (verb) *To write, or speak about, at great or greater, length.*

(*WFB speaking to Mortimer Adler*) You begin by reaching a very interesting conclusion which I would like to hear you **dilate** on, namely that it doesn't really matter whether there was a prime mover [i.e., a force that created the first earthly thing]. (p. 451)

dyspeptic (adjective) *Bitter; morose; spastic.*

George Gilder was working for the *New Leader* magazine, having graduated from Harvard a few years earlier. In **dyspeptic** protest against the Republican Party's nomination of Barry Goldwater, he and a friend had written a book called *The Party That Lost Its Head*—i.e., the GOP, by nominating Goldwater. (p. 299)

egalitarian (noun) *Equalist; one who believes in the doctrine of equalizing the political and economic condition of everyone.*

The novelistic urge of the great ideological **egalitarians** who write books with such titles as *The Ugly American* has been to invest in their protagonist in the CIA appropriately disfiguring personal characteristics. (p. 418)

epicene (adjective) *Sexless; lacking in vigor, virility.*

To spend one hour with a principal British political figure without any critical attention being given to the leaders of the Labour Party or to his critics within the Conservative Party would make for an **epicene** hour. (p. 282)

epistemological (adjective) *The philosophical discipline that has to do with learning; how we learn.*

Is it correct or incorrect to view the adversary process as an **epistemological** process? Will it lead us to the truth, or is it more likely to be described as something which leads us to the only bearable means by which we will agree to proceed in deciding whether to put this guy in jail or not? (p. 232)

eponym (noun) *A person whose name gave meaning to a word that became common. In the case of Billy Budd—as cited.*

Billy Budd is practically an **eponym** for—innocence; purity. (p. 419)

eristic (adjective) *Finely argumentative; taking logic and argument to extreme lengths.*

Any failure by beneficiaries of the free world to recognize what it is that we have here, over against what it is that they (the Communist world) would impose on us, amounts to a moral and intellectual nihilism: far more incriminating of our culture than any transgression against **eristic** scruples of the kind that preoccupy so many of our moralists. (p. 420)

exiguous (adjective) *Scant; meager.*

Five years later, the general prosperity of commercial television edged *Firing Line* over toward public broadcasting (commercial television could not afford to give up the revenue a program like *Firing Line,* with its **exiguous** ratings, displaced). (p. xxxii)

extirpate (verb) *To wrench out; destroy; exterminate; remove any traces of.*

In his late crazy days, as distinguished from his early crazy days, Mao Tse-tung decided that Mozart and Beethoven were great public enemies of the revolution and sought to **extirpate** them and others from the inventory of music the Chinese were permitted to listen to. (p. 327)

gainsay (verb) *To deny; ignore; overlook.*

It was not true that the liberal element within the Republican Party was willing to hand the party over to the right. There was no **gainsaying** the political influence of such prominent Republican liberals as Senator Charles Mathias. (p. 159)

gravamen (noun) *The central point of a complaint; the heart of an accusation or objection.*

The **gravamen** of James Baldwin's complaint was that the *Times*'s publication had aborted the publication by *Playboy* magazine of Baldwin's speech, imposing a financial sacrifice on him of the $10,000 he had been told *Playboy* would pay him. (p. 54)

gregarious (adjective) *Seeking and enjoying the company of others.*

[Clare Boothe Luce] became ill. She was alternately reclusive and **gregarious** in the six months that were left. (p. 442)

homiletic (adjective) *Of the nature of a sermon; having the intention of edifying morally.*
REAGAN: Do you mean, bad as Congress has been all this time with praying, they want us to take it now without praying?
WFB: I think that what you said is so **homiletic** it might itself be unconstitutional. (p. 190)

imposture (noun) *A fake; a substitute of an unreal for the real; an act of deception.*
At the U.N., you regularly hear the totalitarians proclaim that genuine freedom is social and economic security. For that reason, there is "freedom" in East Germany, but not in West Germany. The argument is philosophically an **imposture**—just to begin with—because "freedom" is properly defined as an absence of constraint from man-made impediments. (p. 361)

ineffaceably (adverb) *Impossible to deny or erase.*
It becomes relevant here to bear in mind that [Clare Boothe Luce] was always, necessarily, **ineffaceably**, a very attractive woman, no matter how hard she strove to make a theoretical cultural case forbidding any distinction between men and women. (p. 436)

inimical (adjective) *Injurious; unfriendly to; harmful.*
The resistance to private-sector enterprise as **inimical** to abstract democracy is thoroughly ingrained in many who think themselves especially sensitive in their understanding. (p. 135)

interstitial (adjective) *Coming in the small narrow spaces between the principal parts.*
Professor Donald MacKay is a physicist and a Christian. The remarkable exchange between him and Professor B. F. Skinner I present here with **interstitial** comment because what both men say repays more reflection than the pace of their spoken exchange permits. (p. 82)

invidiously (adverb) *Intending to be critical; at the expense of.*
(*WFB speaking of Roy Cohn*) He shows his adamant loyalty to the FBI, well-sheltered contempt for the character of Martin Luther King, and scorn for hypocritical comparative judgments, he accuses the accuser, and he ends with a mom-and-pop defense of a favorite government agency. I say this, by the way, **invidiously**. (p. 409)

irredentist (adjective) *Having to do with the claim by a nation to lands that once belonged to it.*
While formally going along with Peking in its insistence of sovereignty, we maintained, in effect, diplomatic representation in Taiwan. Meanwhile, the graduated liberal reforms of Chiang Ching-kuo combined with the industry and energy of the people of Taiwan to nurture an evolutionized super-minipower. And direct **irredentist** pressure from the mainland lessened. (p. 336)

laconically (adverb) *With the use of few, rather than many, words; succinctly.*
Professor Galbraith, I'd be most grateful if you would answer my questions directly and **laconically**. (p. 72)

latitudinarianism (noun) *Broadmindedness; permissiveness.*
The feds shrewdly decided to try Harry Reems in Memphis, Tennessee, a venue not given to **latitudinarianism** in matters of obscenity. (p. 204)

licentiousness (noun) *The disregard of accepted standards of meaning, behavior, analysis.*
The terminological **licentiousness** of the day is very striking. In his book Paul Johnson quotes Castro as saying, "Of course we're a democratic society. We have a democracy every day, inasmuch as we're expressing the will of the people." It's that kind of word-play which is the essence, as Orwell told us in another connection, of totalitarianism. (p. 389)

millenarian (noun) *The person who believes that perfection is coming for us down the line, for reasons biological, political, or theological.*

PAUL JOHNSON: Broadly speaking, there are two types of people. One is the person who believes in God. The other is the type who says, "I don't believe in God. I don't believe in an afterlife. It's all nonsense. This life is the only one we've got, and we have to try to improve it, and I don't believe that human—"

WFB: The **millenarian**?

JOHNSON: Yes. "—I don't accept that human nature is permanently imperfect. It can be perfected." (p. 449)

mimetic (adjective) *Imitative.*

WOLFE: In domestic architecture there was constant guerrilla warfare and rebellions and so forth. But not in great public structures.

WFB: What does that tell us about the response of public men—this sort of **mimetic** response as against the relative individualism of the consumer?

WOLFE: In this country, in the midst of what could certainly be called the American Century, we remain the most obedient in matters of the arts—we remain the most obedient little colonial subjects of Europe. (p. 265)

mollify (verb) *To quiet; soothe; lessen.*

Do I understand you, Mr. Reagan, to say that the actual role attempted by, say, President Johnson during the riots of his administration might have exacerbated the situation rather than helped to **mollify** it? (p. 181)

morphology (noun) *The study of the nature of a word, thought, movement, including its causes and its composition.*

Firing Line continued to deal with much else, but, inevitably, spent time in the sixties on The Sixties: on its culture, its **morphology**, and its implications. (p. 3)

nascent (adjective) *Aborning; about to be.*

I had persuaded Steve Allen in the course of a discursive afternoon that the logic of his adamant stand against nuclear weapons committed him to backing a preemptive strike against the **nascent** nuclear-bomb facilities of Red China (as we used to call it). (p. 235)

nuanced (adjective) *Given to slight, delicate, subtle degrees of meaning, explanation, analysis.*

Firing Line is a **nuanced** program, and a thorough knowledge of English is required to do justice to subtle thought. (p. 334)

nugatory (adjective) *Trifling; of little importance.*

It has always seemed to me that the correct balance of police power and individual rights should reflect the crime rate. The interdiction by the airlines of terrorist weapons, conducted at the expense of every American who steps foot on an airplane, can be demonstrated statistically to be **nugatory** in its accomplishments. (p. 230)

obloquy (noun) *Hatred; loathing; discrimination; ostracism.*

The Scarlet Letter was designed to stimulate public **obloquy**. The AIDS tattoo is designed for private protection. If our society is generally threatened, then in order to fight AIDS we need the civil equivalent of universal military training. (p. 212)

oligopolistically (adverb) *In the manner of a small group of agents who control the market.*

(*Speaking of OPEC*) Thirteen governments **oligopolistically** took hold of a great reservoir of the supply of oil and quadrupled its prices overnight. (p. 70)

penchant (noun) *Tendency; inclination; liking for.*

George McGovern is a formidable opponent, a crowd-pleaser with a populist-analytical **penchant** that has carried him a long way, though when he ran for President, he was rejected by forty-nine states. (p. 139)

peroration (noun) *The closing part of a speech.*

After the debate was over I shook McGovern's hand and whispered to him, "George, that **peroration** is as good as when I first heard you use it at Dartmouth in 1957." "Yes," he agreed. "Very effective, isn't it?" (p. 58)

petrology (noun) *The study of the source of a discipline, most commonly, the fathers of the Christian faith.*

Here is a man [Cardinal Arns of São Paulo] who studied literature at the Sorbonne, where he achieved his doctorate; who taught **petrology** and didactics at highly respected universities; who has written twenty-five books, including abstruse treatises on medieval literature. (p. 34)

phlogistonic (adjective) *Heat-producing; combustible.*

Far from demanding with increasing truculence the diplomatic reincorporation of Taiwan, the government of Deng simply let the **phlogistonic** question cool. (p. 336)

piquant (adjective) *Something attractively offbeat; provocative.*

I was amused that Alan Dershowitz revealed on the program that he himself had never seen the movie *Deep Throat*. That was a **piquant** touch: it enabled him to say, in effect, "I am defending a man for taking part in a movie. What is in that movie is so irrelevant to the defense I shall not even bother to view it." (p. 205)

polemical (adjective) *Argumentative; intending to make a point at variance with that of your opponent.*

[Clare Boothe Luce] always had an answer to any question at the tip of her tongue. Though this, I came to know, was **polemical** training; she was often dissatisfied, after consulting her private intellectual conscience, with the answer she gave. (p. 157)

prescind (verb) *To pull out; abstract; disengage.*

(*Speaking to* The New York Times's *super-journalist Fox Butterfield*) On this matter of the economic improvement of the average Chinese life, may I ask, have you found that there is a considerable tendency to **prescind** from the passage of time improvements in literacy or in health or in food consumption? (p. 329)

proclivity (noun) *An inclination; propensity; leaning.*

One thinks again of Jean-François Revel and his indictment—the **proclivity** of democracies to dissipate energies out of a sense of guilt. (p. 407)

Procrusteanize (verb) *To produce conformity by ruthless means. After Procrustes, a mythical Greek giant, who stretched or shortened captives to make them fit his beds exactly.*

Firing Line does not **Procrusteanize** a guest's formal vocabulary. (p. 82)

proximate (adjective) *The nearest cause; the most direct agent of change.*

Mr. Al Lowenstein is generally regarded as the **proximate** agent of the whole [Eugene] McCarthy phenomenon. (p. 425)

prurient (adjective) *That which seeks out sexual stimulation.*

In 1972, when Harry Reems made *Deep Throat*, the courts were being guided by the Roth standard. That decision, handed down by Justice Brennan in 1957, held that something was obscene if it appealed exclusively to the **prurient** interest and had no "redeeming social importance." (p. 204)

puerile (adjective) *Childish.*

A young man was once a guest of *Firing Line* for the sole reason that he had become, at age twenty-seven or thereabouts, the de facto manager of the mind and body of Bertrand Russell. Here was this **puerile** ideologue sending out invitations in Lord Russell's name to statesmen and scholars the world over to attend a War Crimes Trial of Americans for pursuing an objective in Vietnam, quoting Lord Russell to the effect that there were no differences between the United States and the Nazis. (p. 278)

quietus (noun) *An end; the death of.*

The ABM treaty put a **quietus** on U.S. defensive technology: We even dismantled a protective ring of antinuclear defense missiles planted in the area of Wyoming, and did not trouble to avail ourselves of the option to construct a ring of defensive weapons around Washington, D.C. (p. 388)

quintessence (noun) *The essence of; a pure, typical form of.*

The editor of *Vogue* invited me to explain, explicitly, the "American look" since so many reviewers had denominated Blackford Oakes as being "quintessentially" American. I thought to reject the invitation, because I reject the very notion of **quintessence** as here applied. (p. 419)

quotidian (adjective) *Recurring daily.*

I introduced candidate Ronald Reagan in January 1980 with a view to provoking his critics. And I toyed, with the advocate's delight, with the **quotidian** criticisms of Mr. Reagan. (p. 180)

rapacious (adjective) *Greedy; ravenous.*

Tom Wolfe records the **rapacious** success of the Bauhaus school, which within a generation had captured almost the whole of the American architectural academy, bequeathing us such megatonnage as, say, the World Trade Center. (p. 263)

ratiocination (noun) *Systematic thought.*

It has occurred to me (after modest **ratiocination**) that style is, really, a matter of timing. (p. 279)

recidivist (adjective) *Of the kind committed before; back to the old business.*

Prisons are bursting at the seams, with over 200,000 more criminals inhabiting quarters than our prisons were designed for, resulting in a gruesome intensification of the awful experience in prison and a resulting increase in **recidivist** crime. (p. 249)

rectitude (noun) *Uprightness (here used sarcastically); righteousness.*

Taiwan was even denied its athletes' participation in the Olympics in Canada, a seizure of diplomatic **rectitude** that did not affect Prime Minister Pierre Trudeau at the expense of any Soviet satellite, though Russia's de facto rule over the Baltic states is at least as questionable—or at least as offensive—as Taiwan's dream of ruling over China. (p. 335)

regnant (adjective) *The predominating meaning, figure, concept.*

"Are you against labor unions?" an indignant Harriet Pilpel asked Professor Thomas Sowell on *Firing Line.*

Professor Sowell replied, "You asked what were some of the factors that stood in the way of black economic progress and I said that one of them was the labor union. That is a fact, and I'm simply reporting facts, not prejudices." How do you handle such a man, if your political career is staked out on the **regnant** cliché? (p. 319)

reticulation (noun) *Networking, i.e., figuring out diagrammatically where everything is, or should be—so many paces to the right, so many paces up, down, etc.*

Hoffa appeared to believe that the proper organizing principle for [prison] reform was segregation. [Inmates] should be carefully segregated according to age, the nature of the offense, and temperament. One got the feeling that all these **reticulations**, finely drawn, would have isolated James Hoffa as the sole occupant of one federal prison. (p. 243)

rubric (noun) *The governing license; the sponsoring idea, concept, protocol.*

The **rubric** that year of [Jesse Jackson's] PUSH convention was "Black America: An Economic Common Market." (p. 313)

ruminate (verb) *To let the mind dwell on and develop; disport with.*

One **ruminates** on the analysis, the idealism, the inventiveness, the disillusion, the demoralization expressed by Professor Thomas Sowell. (p. 325)

solipsism (noun) *The idea that, actually, only you exist. (From "just oneself")*

Doesn't it strike you as possibly the case that the twentieth century, where the intellectual and romantic odysseys usually begin from yourself and end up with yourself, becomes therefore the age of **solipsism**? (p. 262)

stentorian (adjective) *Loud; declaratory; emphatic.*

I can hear even now the vibrancy of [Norman Thomas's] voice and the **stentorian** tones of the preacher denouncing the sinner. . . . His then current crusade was to save Vietnam and the United States Marines from each other. (p. 4)

synecdoche (noun) *The single example, in place of the whole. The one, for the many.*

LUCE: The Old Testament myth of the Garden of Eden has aroused the ire of women feminists for generations. God creates heaven and earth in this legend in Genesis. He then creates man; man shares in the spirit of God.

WFB: Man the male or man the **synecdoche** for human beings? (p. 439)

tautology (noun) *The statement of that which is obvious, and therefore does not need restating; redundant.*

Now, the fact that six times as many shootings occur in houses that have guns as don't have guns seems to me—well, the **tautology** is, you obviously can't have a shooting where you don't have guns. (p. 215)

tendentiously (adverb) *Stated in such a way as to promote a cause; not impartial.*

In his opening statement, John Kenneth Galbraith got about as much as one can possibly hope to get from twelve minutes: rapport with the audience; a broad statement of his position, **tendentiously** given; a sense of wisdom and of realism; and a bite or two to show the audience that the speaker has plenty of ginger, and knows just where, as required, to stick it. (p. 65)

tocsin (noun) *A bell used to sound an alarm or a general summons.*

Michael Harrington published a book, *The Other America.* The book described a portion of the American population beset by tormenting poverty. Its thesis was brought to the attention of President Kennedy on November 19, 1963. The book sounded the **tocsin** for massive federal action to "make war" on poverty. (p. 306)

trenchant (adjective) *Forceful; tightly constructed.*

Norman Podhoretz was associated with the left in American politics until some time in the late sixties, when he gradually, but with that **trenchant** willpower which even his critics acknowledge, changed his mind. Since then he has been a penetrating critic of disorderly thought and romantic views of the Soviet Union. (p. 112)

truculent (adjective) *Combative; vitriolic.*

Firing Line programs have almost always been governed, temperamentally, by the attitude and behavior of the guest. Norman Thomas was a highly **truculent** debater (a running distemper was a part of his public persona). (p. 10)

vaticination (noun) *A prediction; prophecy.*

(*WFB speaking on* Firing Line *with Norman Thomas*) Because in point of fact, if you don't mind, rather than simply—automatically—accept your **vaticinations,** I'd like to point out that in Korea, we did actually stop the aggressor. (p. 5)

Weltanschauung (noun) *The German word, widely used, to denote one's world-philosophy, the sum of one's essential views (on politics, theology).*

People are curious about the Impossible Guest. I could name but won't the guest whose entire knowledge of life filled eight minutes, so that when the ninth came along, he simply recycled his *Weltanschauung* for the next eight minutes. (p. 43)

The following are *more* words taken from Mr. Buckley's syndicated column, "On the Right":

---

auto da fé (noun) *The ritual accompanying the execution of a heretic, used especially in connection with the Inquisition.*

Here was a modern **auto da fé**: not for countenancing heresy, but for denouncing it. (9/21/89)

booboisie (noun) *The dumb class. The term is H. L. Mencken's, and he self-evidently took pleasure in suggesting that the dumb class was composed substantially of the bourgeoisie, normally thought of as the hardworking middle class.*

The critics of those who joined Senator Jesse Helms in protesting the use of public money to finance the "art" of Robert Mapplethorpe and Andres Serrano did a hell of a job of caterwauling about the provincialism of the **booboisie** who protested the exhibitions. (9/21/89)

candor (noun) *Directness of expression.*

It appears that Mayor Koch's most ingratiating quality, an unquenchable thirst for **candor,** was what finally did him in. (9/14/89)

covenant (noun) *A rather solemn agreement, designed as binding.*

There is one aspect to the tax turmoil that asks for reflection. It is the unfortunate breach of the 1986 **covenant** at which time it was generally agreed that the tax committees of Congress would simply let things alone for a while and see how it all worked out. (9/22/89)

dysgenically (adverb) *Genetic profusion of a kind thought inimical to public interests. Thus Dr. William Shockley spoke of the "dysgenic" effect of the greater rate of black population growth.*

Israel does not like the fact that most Russian Jews express a wish to settle down not in Israel but in the United States because it needs a Jewish population to guard against being **dysgenically** overwhelmed by Arabs who procreate with the speed of light. (10/3/89)

indolence (noun) *Laziness; a failure to accept responsibility.*

Children need to feel at a very early age the whiplash of **indolence**: long dull lives washing dishes and seeing television movies of non–Third World countries such as Japan and West Germany with thriving populations. (9/26/89)

inimical (adjective) *Unfriendly; hostile.*

We should be careful when we say we do not "claim the right to order the politics of Nicaragua." The politics of Nicaragua are very much our concern when they are co-opted by a foreign power **inimical** to the best interests of the United States and the Nicaraguan people. (3/28/89)

iniquitous (adjective) *Sinful; evil; wrongful.*

There were those who, reviewing the work of Owen Lattimore, which included eleven days of interrogation by the chief counsel of a Senate committee, came to certain conclusions about him that Tom Wicker suggests were surrealistic at best, **iniquitous** at worst. (7/13/89)

internecine (adjective) *Mutually destructive; harmful.*

It is gradually dawning on the population that the war against Iraq was won by Iraq, if it can be said that there are winners of encounters so **internecine.**

interstice (noun) *A space, usually little, that intervenes between solid matter.*

Under Stalin, a list long but not indefinitely long was drawn up of prohibited activities. Anything not prohibited could be engaged in. That left little **interstices** within which to maneuver. (3/30/89)

intractable (adjective) *Unmovable; inflexible; difficult to lead.*

Is the Brezhnev doctrine really dead if the retreat from Afghanistan is nothing more than an unprofitable collision with a major and **intractable** force? (5/12/89)

junket (verb and noun) *To travel as a congressman or public official at public expense, ostensibly on business, actually on a pleasure trip.*

Members of the judiciary do not send a million letters without postage, do not **junket** around the world, do not get free massages or whatever in the exercise room of the House of Representatives. (2/10/89)

lacuna (noun) *The missing item, datum; the hole in someone's learning.*

Ten years ago a longtime friend of Sidney Hook confided in me the most wonderfully humanizing story of the **lacuna** in Hook's knowledge. (7/21/89)

laggard (adjective) *Slow to act, to respond, to react.*

We are **laggard** on that [deterrent] front and we face a concrete problem in Europe given the tergiversation of Helmut Kohl on the modernizing of the remaining nuclear missiles in West Germany. (2/22/89)

lagniappe (noun) *A gratuitous little gift, in any form, e.g., a free liqueur at a restaurant after dinner.*

Drugstore cowboys walk out into the street, hail the mob, and tell them to come in for free ice cream cones. That is how the Bush administration clearly understands Gorbachev's **lagniappe** when he offered to destroy 500 missiles, 2.5 percent of his inventory, reducing the threat to export glasnostian Bolshevism by a factor of nothing, these missiles having been redundant for years. (5/18/89)

lèse majesté (noun) *An offense against the sovereign; whence an indignity at the expense of the reigning authority.*

When Newt Gingrich took time off to insist that evasion of the reelection finance laws ought to apply not only to lowly congressmen but also to the speaker of the House, he faced a barrage of shocked fraternity brothers unaccustomed to violations of the law of *lèse majesté.* (3/24/89)

libertarian (adjective) *The political philosophy that stresses the absolute right of the individual to make his own decisions, unobstructed by the state.*

Conservatives raised on **libertarian** principles have long since remarked that any invasion of the sacred No Trespassing sign puts you on the slippery slope toward collectivist capitulation. (2/7/89)

literati (noun, plural) *The literate, educated class.*

What proved most curious is that there was a substantial lobby that night, among the **literati** of Louisville, for every position concerning the drug problem. (3/23/89)

lodestar (noun) *The guiding force, star; the focus of attention, inspiration.*

Kissinger Associates would almost certainly not succeed as a partnership of 100 retired Foreign Service officers: The relationship to the **lodestar** becomes too attenuated. (3/17/89)

lotus (noun) *The mythical Greek fruit, the eating of which induced torpid satisfaction, pleasure, forgetfulness of duty.*

The mood is out there, and we are tasting the **lotus** in the green pastures of peace. (9/29/89)

Luddite (adjective) *Pertaining to the nineteenth-century movement that disapproved of labor-saving devices. Hence, opposed to technological progress.*

We, the government, will protect you—even as we protect bank depositors—against lawsuits the effect of which is to enrich the legal participants, protect nobody against a threat not yet perceived, and wrench the United States into a **Luddite** gear which, had such a thing happened two generations ago, would have been the equivalent of forbidding the flight of airplanes on the grounds that one of them would lose its wings and fall on Aunt Minnie. (7/25/89)

manifestly (adverb) *Made obvious by its own appearance; self-evidently.*
 We are invited to believe that if John Tower participates in any of the activities engaged in by Alexander the Great, Napoleon and General Grant, he is **manifestly** unfit to serve. (2/16/89)

metaphysical (adjective) *Beyond measurement; transcendent; supersensible.*
 Those who rail against it do so for the most practical reason: They have not mastered its use. They strive for **metaphysical** formulations to justify their hidden little secret (sloth and fear). (1/19/88)

miscegenetic (adjective) *Having to do with the mixture of the races; here used as suggesting a mixture of East and West.*
 The new policy would say to the Soviet Union: Look, the big dream—the ideological conquest of the world—isn't going to happen. Not only is it not going to happen, other things aren't going to happen—namely a permanent, **miscegenetic** annexation of Eastern Europe by you. So let's make a deal. (8/10/89)

moot (adjective) *Rendered irrelevant by circumstances; no longer of practical significance.*
 Suddenly we discover that the FBI knows somebody or some people who have seen John Tower under the influence; but, in any event, the whole question became **moot** when he made his public pledge to give up drinking altogether, if confirmed. (3/10/89)

nabob (noun) *An important character, whether by reason of heredity, power, or wealth.*
 Henry Kissinger has an inclination to know who are the movers and shakers. To suggest that this is on the order of a movie starlet wanting to know the industry's **nabobs** is entirely to misunderstand the point. (3/17/89)

nefarious (adjective) *Disreputable; unethical; detestable.*
 The feds charge insider trading and a number of other activities, some of them **nefarious,** some of them—well, that is one of the reasons so many people are interested in Mr. Milken. (9/28/89)

obsequious (adjective) *Fawning; servile; sycophantic.*
 Even if one accepted Castro's figures, the progress in his country cannot match the progress in other Caribbean nations, so what is there to celebrate, save the hope that the day will come when the mere mention of Castro's name calls to mind not only massive torture, political prisoners and a docile, **obsequious** press, but also a lifeless society, fallen behind in general welfare. (1/3/89)

obverse (noun) *The other, opposite side (in a coin, the obverse of tails is heads).*
 The business of finding twelve jurors in Washington, D.C., who so to speak never heard of Colonel Oliver North assumes ludicrous proportions, something like the **obverse** of Diogenes' search for an honest man. (2/3/89)

pander (verb) *To truckle to someone's desires, usually disreputable—e.g., lust, greed, power hunger.*
 Would it be possible to institute death as the penalty for drug merchants? Would the court prohibit the execution of drug merchants who had **pandered** to minors? (6/27/89)

peregrination (noun) *A voyage from place to place to place; voyaging about, especially including foreign countries.*
 Conceivably one could find life on Mars—nice old ladies and gentlemen who could tell us that Jesus Christ was a planetary figure of parochial dimension, and by doing so spare the Christian world the awful overhead of all those priests, and nuns, and papal **peregrinations,** and missions, and cemeteries. (7/25/89)

perfervid (adjective) *Excessively, unbalancedly ardent.*
 If what the optimists are saying is that a wave of reason is sweeping over the world, how do we account for the **perfervid** worship of the Ayatollah Khomeini the day he was buried? (6/8/89)

perfidy (noun) *Deceit; treachery.*

Any effort to pursue an investigation into allegations that the plane that brought down in flames Pakistan leader Zia was sabotaged by sophisticated Soviet chemical explosives was blocked. By the Soviets? No no no, you don't understand. By the United States. Why expose Soviet **perfidy** when détente is at an exhilarating boil? (2/9/89)

periphrastic (adjective) *Ornately long-winded; given to profuse formulations.*

Three cheers for Senator Jesse Helms. As ever, he tends to get to the point of a difficult question with carrier-pigeon directness, leaving many of his sophisticated critics lost in **periphrastic** meaninglessness. (7/28/89)

perspicacious (adjective) *Analytically or visually acute.*

Up until a few years ago, Paris did not permit anyone to publish or to sell the works of the Marquis de Sade. Simone de Beauvoir wrote a book on de Sade in which she stressed the historical and **perspicacious** passages in de Sade, to which the appropriate comment is, "Aha." (7/28/89)

pettifoggery (noun) *Little-mindedness; bureaucratic absorption with silly little details.*

To tell the members of the federal judiciary that they cannot get a raise even sufficient to cope with inflation is **pettifoggery** of an ignoble sort. (2/10/89)

phantasmagoria (noun) *An ongoing vision, nightmare, fantasy.*

The Chinese communists are not likely to renounce their **phantasmagoria** explicitly, nor to sacrifice what they call socialist centrism. (3/21/89)

platonic (adjective) *Otherworldly.*

The **platonic** ideal of the unbiased juror presumes a quarrel in which there hasn't been significant national involvement. (2/3/89)

plebiscite (noun) *A submission of a proposed new law, or whatever, for a vote by the people.*

It was a very splashy and moving open letter, signed by 170 writers, actors and artists, urging Fidel Castro to hold a **plebiscite** on his rule. (1/3/89)

polemical (adjective) *An argument designed to damage someone else's position; disputation, as hand-to-hand combat.*

M.I.T. Professor Lawrence Lidsky predicts that inherently safe nuclear plants that can produce electricity at less than one-half the cost of current reactors are unlikely to come along for twenty years or so, because existing forces stand by their **polemical** guns. (1/12/89)

prescience (noun) *The faculty of being able to see ahead.*

We are talking on the eve of near-universal access to the atom bomb. There is little doubt but that the Iraqis would now have it, save for the boldness and **prescience** of the Israelis. (2/22/89)

prodigality (noun) *Extravagance; reckless spending.*

Newt Gingrich had warmed up on Tip O'Neill, whose genial **prodigality** with the people's purse was accepted as the good-old-boy way of doing things. (3/24/89)

propitiate (verb) *To appease, conciliate.*

Last Sunday's (London) *Times* reveals that the publishers Viking Penguin, who bought Mr. Rushdie's novel, are negotiating with Britain's Moslem leaders. The objective is to **propitiate** them, and to get from them some sort of peace offering that can be waved across the Mediterranean to the Moslem world. (2/28/89)

provincialism (noun) *A narrow, usually uneducated, concern for what lies immediately about you, as distinguished from farseeing, urban, cosmopolitan.*

It isn't a sign of **provincialism** to say that it makes more sense to spend excess dollars on developing domestic fuel options than on inquiring into the flora and fauna of Mars. (7/25/89)

proximate (adjective) *Pertaining to the immediately preceding event, or push, or causative factor.*

It is not to give in to economic determinism to reflect on the **proximate** pressures bringing about these reforms [in South Africa]. (2/21/89)

punctilio (noun) *The concern for form, manners, appearance.*

The story of the Bay of Pigs is told again and again. But always in the telling of it, by modern chroniclers, one tends to lose sight of the bloody landscape, so distracted are we by democratic **punctilio**. (1/24/89)

pundit (noun) *A wise man, but often used sarcastically. Columnists, for instance, are regularly referred to as "pundits" who "opine"—usually by people who disagree with their punditry.*

Now while George Bush is President, no subordinate is going to come out in favor of legalizing the sale of drugs, the culture shock being as it is. Such proposals are here and there made by a **pundit**, or a mad libertarian, or a fatalist. (3/3/89)

putative (adjective) *Supposed; ostensible; reputed.*

Much will happen in the weeks and months ahead in conference between the Senate and the House of Representatives, and Senator Helms would be well counseled to exclude from his proscription any **putative** work of art more than fifty years old. This would distinguish the Rodins from the Mapplethorpes. (7/28/89)

renascent (adjective) *Born again; recrudescent.*

Effective leadership needs to be shown by the bankruptcy judge, who if properly guided buys the long-term prospects for creditors, which are improved by a **renascent** airline rather than by the sale of its nuts and bolts. (6/16/89)

revivification (noun) *The rebirth; the invigoration of; the injection of life into.*

The key to stopping the erosion of Eastern's assets under the aegis of the judge who seems to have the power to conduct either an autopsy or a **revivification** is, of course, the unions. (6/16/89)

rubric (noun) *The governing license; the sponsoring idea, concept, protocol.*

The business of being tried by your peers, which is the governing **rubric** in these matters, makes you begin to wonder whether there isn't a bearing between finding Colonel North's "peer" and deciding what it is that he is being tried for. (2/3/89)

salient (noun) *The cutting point; the apex of the military formation, or of an argument.*

President Bush has not confronted the massed will of the Soviet government in any crisis. This doesn't mean that such a will won't materialize, and won't present a crisis. The most obvious **salient** here is West Germany. (5/2/89)

sate (verb) *To overfill to the point of glutting; cloying.*

What is it that tempers the appetite of Mikhail Gorbachev for bloody expansionism? Answer: There is no evidence that his appetite is tempered, but much evidence that his appetite cannot be **sated** because of what George Bush might call "the economic thing." (3/21/89)

satyagraha (noun) *The pressing of a political or moral position through the doctrine of passive disobedience. Associated with Gandhi.*

Of course, China is the great melodramatic event of the political decade, practicing the **satyagraha** of Gandhi on a massive scale, with tanks being deployed, not in unison to march against the masses, but pointing at each other, on the eve of what became a great civil war. (6/8/89)

schismatic (noun) *A deviant (usually religious); unlike the heretic, the schismatic still belongs to the old communion, but is separated from its core authority.*

Is Swaggert's deviant lechery characteristic of evangelical Protestantism? Is Khomeini's genocidal search for **schismatics** and blasphemers a correct transcription of the word of Allah? Is an excommunicated Mormon paradoxically an example of the practicing Mormon? (2/16/89)

sclerosis (noun) *Hardening of the tissue owing to neglect or overburdening. The metaphor suggests inactivity to the point of sluggishness, owing to years of inattention or bureaucratic overhead.*

Gorbachev hasn't repealed all those accretions of state socialism. To do so would pit him against every Comrade Ulanov who clings to his position of authority. Besides which, the market needs a little time to extrude three generations of compacted **sclerosis.** (5/4/89)

sclerotic (adjective) *The adjectival form to express "sclerosis," above.*

When you meet with Mr. Milken, you meet at the same time with his lawyer and with a couple of aides. The situation is not for that reason **sclerotic.** (9/28/89)

sinologist (noun) *A student of Chinese history, culture, language.*

Novelist and **sinologist** Robert Elegant writes: "Regarding the recent controversy about the emperor of Japan, I should like to quote from an interview that he gave to Bernard Krisher of *Newsweek*." (2/24/89)

strictures (noun, plural) *The demands, restrictions, requirements of.*

Mr. Bush disappoints his American supporters by failing, once he had left China and was unbound by the **strictures** of diplomacy, to remark sadly on the continuing low estate of human rights in China. (3/2/89)

stultification (noun) *The act or process of invalidation; immobilization; being rendered useless.*

In Brazil, inflation brings unemployment, **stultification** and grinding poverty. (3/21/89)

superannuation (noun) *Becoming useless, because of age.*

I have mentioned that a study last summer reveals that there is a greater turnover in the House of Lords (from **superannuation**) than there is in the House of Representatives (where 99 percent of the incumbents who ran for office were returned to office last November). (3/24/89)

suppurating (adjective) *Generating pus; giving out poison.*

In Leningrad the successor to Romanov was defeated—even though he ran unopposed—thus documenting the failure of communism to transform human nature. Now that is an official part of the Soviet record. And nothing *Pravda* can do to bury the results of the vote can hide the **suppurating** sore: Marxist man is a human badly clothed and underfed. (3/30/89)

symbiosis (noun) *The profitable coexistence of two organisms, to their mutal advantage.*

The counsel to President Truman began by advising him that the president had no authority to engage in secret intelligence work in peacetime, but later, under pressure, revised this opinion to the effect that if a president OKs a secret enterprise and Congress provides the funds for carrying it out, the **symbiosis** between these two acts breeds a little constitutional baby, through artificial insemination. (1/24/89)

tabula rasa (noun) *(From the Latin, "clean slate.") The condition of the mind before it is exposed to anything; total innocence, blankness.*

What Judge Gerhard Gesell and the defendants appear to be looking for is Seven Truly Ignorant Washingtonians, who will approach the question of Colonel North, guilty or innocent, **tabula rasa**—with absolutely unformed opinions. (2/3/89)

tendentious (adjective) *Stated in such a way as to promote a cause; not impartial.*

I pause here to remark that the series is politically **tendentious.** It is a plain matter of record that Bobby Kennedy was the man who authorized the taping of Dr. King. (1/24/89)

tergiversation (noun) *Reversal of opinion; backsliding.*

We are laggard on that [deterrent] front and we face a concrete problem in Europe given the **tergiversation** of Helmut Kohl on the modernizing of the remaining nuclear missiles in West Germany. (5/12/89)

transubstantiate (verb) *To change into another substance; transform; transmute.*

Surely a society that has the power to conscript, and in many cases send [men] to their deaths in defense of that flag and its citizens, has also the right to guard against desecrating the flag that symbolizes, even it if does not **transubstantiate,** their ideals. (6/23/89)

trinitarian (adjective) *Having three parts; threefold; usually referring to the Christian belief in the Trinity. Opposite of Unitarian.*

Now the intricacies of the alleged crime of Salman Rushdie are read for the most part by Westerners for whom discussion of whether the word "prostitute" can conceivably characterize the prophet's wives, or whether the term "Mahmoud" can ever be used to refer to the prophet is about as engaging to Christians and Jews as discussions of the **trinitarian** God of the Christians engage the Moslem world. (2/22/89)

troth (noun) *One's pledged word.*

We should not have been surprised when the spokesman for Castro carefully explained to us that the **troth** had been plighted by the Cuban people thirty years ago once and for all: In the Marxist world there is no retreat from history. (1/3/89)

turpitude (noun) *Corruption; evildoing; iniquity.*

Neither Ronald Brown nor other victims of Republican **turpitude** specify what it is that Republicans did to Wright that Democrats didn't also do to Wright, given the ethics panel's bipartisan vote. (6/2/89)

unshirted (adjective) *Undiluted; unsparing; undisguised.*

Charles Murray, Manhattan Institute author of *Losing Ground,* urges President Bush to give **unshirted** hell to the critics of private education. (1/27/89)

usurpation (noun) *The wrongful assumption of power.*

A constitutional amendment, done athwart the will of the Court for the first time in modern history, would accomplish more than simply bringing relief to the majority who consider themselves victims of judicial **usurpation.** (6/29/89)

velleity (noun) *A slight, i.e., nonfervent wish, much as one might have a velleity for a Popsicle.*

People get annoyed when you use words that do not come trippingly off the tongue of Oprah Winfrey, but how else than to designate it as a **velleity** would you describe President Bush's fair-weather call for landing some people on Mars? (7/25/89)

venal (adjective) *Corrupt; susceptible of being bought.*

Here is what the *New York Times* invites the reader to think. Joe Coors is a wealthy brewer from Colorado and is known to be a hot conservative. It is especially ironic under the circumstances that he should be the **venal** influence peddlar. (7/27/89)

vermiform (adjective) *By derivation, "wormlike"; used almost exclusively to suggest "useless," even as some human organs are thought of as vermiform appendices, e.g., the appendix.*

The other day, historian Arthur Schlesinger, Jr., was lamenting the very institution of vice president, on the grounds that he was not really elected by the people; rather, he is a **vermiform** appendix of the presidential nominee, who comes to life only when the president dies or is shot. (1/6/89)

vulgarian (noun and adjective) *A person of vulgar habits, mind, manners, dress, or behavior.*

All of this adulation, which reaches even into the demonstrators' square, was for a man (Mao Tse-tung) at once the total **vulgarian;** and the Brobdingnagian dictator, a kind of King Kong poet. (5/26/89)

winnow (verb) *To separate, seeking the better, or the best; to analyze, with the same purpose in mind.*

When the anti-federalists mobilized during the days the Constitution was being discussed, they enunciated what was to become the Bill of Rights. This list of rights included Provision No. 7 which was both more wordy and more absolute than what **winnowed** down into the Second Amendment. (7/18/89)

xenophobia (noun) *A hatred, fear, or suspicion of that which is foreign, or of foreigners.*

A factor not to be dismissed is the **xenophobia** of a great power (China) that for a century and a half was a plaything of the younger sons of European noblemen. (5/23/89)

LEXICON II—1992

ab initio (Latin) *From the beginning.*

He had begun Latin, last year, at Greyburn, and had been trained *ab initio* in the English sequence. (From *Saving the Queen*, p. 63, Doubleday & Company, 1976)

ad hominem (adjective) *Marked by an attack on an opponent's character rather than by answer to his contention.*

Beame was so clearly above that kind of suspicion that an insinuation to that effect was never even raised, not even in a campaign desperate for issues and gluttonous for *ad hominem* argument. (From *The Unmaking of a Mayor*, p. 282, The Viking Press, 1966)

ad libitum (adverb) *In accordance with one's wishes; ad lib.*

To have proposed abortions *ad libitum* was, quite simply, unthinkable for a politician. (From *Cruising Speed*, p. 234, G. P. Putnam's Sons, 1971)

abattoir (noun) *Slaughterhouse.*

I wondered amusedly and intensively, what could J. K. Galbraith be up to, revealing these thoughts as we approached the **abattoir**, the Cambridge Union? (From *Cruising Speed*, p. 155, G. P. Putnam's Sons, 1971)

aberrant (noun) *A person whose behavior departs substantially from the standards for behavior in his group.*

It is not unlikely that this book, upon its appearance, will be branded as the product of an **aberrant** who takes the Wrong Side, i.e., the side that disagrees with the "liberals." (From *God and Man at Yale*, p. 140, Regnery Books, 1986)

ablutions (noun) *The washing of one's body or part of it.*

Several witnesses noted the license number, and the California authorities had it within minutes, leaving it a mystery why there was no one there at his apartment to greet Edgar Smith when he drove in to perform the identical **ablutions** of nineteen years earlier—an effort to remove the blood from his person and clothing. (From *Right Reason*, p. 197, Doubleday & Company, 1985)

accession (noun) *Something added, as to a collection or formal group.*

Abbie Hoffman is not the King of England, but the point of course is that he seeks a kind of metaphorical **accession** to the throne by the use of any means. (From *Cruising Speed*, p. 208, G. P. Putnam's Sons, 1971)

acerbic (adjective) *Sharply or bitingly ironic.*

His only apparent extracurricular involvements were an occasional letter to the *Yale Daily News*, **acerbic**, polished, and conclusive in the sense of unfailingly suggesting that any contrary opinion should not presume to expect from him any rebuttal. (From *Saving the Queen*, p. 11, Doubleday & Company, 1976)

acidulous (adjective) *Biting, caustic, harsh.*

By May 14, 1981, Edgar Smith had become, in the **acidulous** words used by one commentator, "the most honored murderer of his generation." (From *Right Reason,* p. 189, Doubleday & Company, 1985)

adjudication (noun) *A formal ruling by a tribunal.*

So how do we make the final **adjudication**? Why not use a Democratic measurement of the Misery Index? Under Mr. Carter, the Misery Index stood at 19.8. Under Mr. Reagan, at this moment, it is 15.8. (From *Right Reason,* p. 94, Doubleday & Company, 1985)

affectation (noun) *A manner of speech or behavior not natural to one's actual personality or capabilities.*

He had intended to ask Anthony whether "10:36" was an **affectation**, but forgot, and accordingly took pains to be punctual. (From *Saving the Queen,* p. 18, Doubleday & Company, 1976)

a fortiori (adverb) *All the more convincingly; with greater reason; with still more convincing force.*

A mother, while obviously exercising de facto authority over the survival of the fetus, is nevertheless legally and **a fortiori** morally nothing more than the custodian of the fetus whose insulation against abuse ought to be guaranteed by the state. (From *Cruising Speed,* p. 241, G. P. Putnam's Sons, 1971)

agglomeration (noun) *An indiscriminately formed mass.*

Yale's mission is not articulate except in so far as an **agglomeration** of words about enlightened thought and action, freedom and democracy, serve to define the mission of Yale. (From *God and Man at Yale,* p. 223, Regnery Books, 1986)

agglutinate (verb) *To unite or combine into a group or mass.*

The clerk uttered the workaday incantation in the humdrum cadences of the professional waterboy at court. The procedure is everywhere the same. The speed must be routinized, and accelerated, like liturgical responses, the phrases **agglutinated**, yet somehow audible. (From *Saving the Queen,* p. 245, Doubleday & Company, 1976)

altruistic (adjective) *A disinterested consideration of, regard for, or devotion to others' interests.*

It could in fairness be said that all the money thus solicited goes straight to the student in one form or another. In the last analysis, it is being solicited for **altruistic** purposes. (From *God and Man at Yale,* p. 134, Regnery Books, 1986)

anarchic (adjective) *Tending toward anarchy; lawless, rebellious.*

The policeman was relieved when the young man suddenly strode off, because his build, though slim, was pronouncedly athletic, and deep in his eyes there was an **anarchic** stubbornness, which policemen detailed to guarding the Soviet legation were experienced enough to spot. (From *Saving the Queen,* p. 17, Doubleday & Company, 1976)

anathema (noun) *A vigorous denunciation.*

I ask reasonable observers to look out for evasive and irrelevant answers, for rebuttal by epithet, for flowery **anathemas**. (From *God and Man at Yale,* p. 140, Regnery Books, 1986)

Anglophilia (noun) *A particularly unreasoned admiration of or partiality for England or English ways.*

Helen had long since become accustomed to Blackford's desire to meet everyone, which she attributed to natural gregariousness, and a galloping **Anglophilia**. (From *Saving the Queen,* p. 128, Doubleday & Company, 1976)

animus (noun) *Ill will, antagonism, or hostility, usually controlled, but deep-seated and sometimes virulent.*

The anti-American **animus** was not really all that transparent until just before the punishment began, and on through the ferocity of it and the hideously redundant final blows. (From *Saving the Queen,* p. 79, Doubleday & Company, 1976)

anomie (noun) *A state of rootlessness in which normative standards of conduct and belief have weakened or disappeared; a similar condition in an individual, commonly characterized by personal disorientation, anxiety, and social isolation.*

Edgar Smith had walked out of Trenton into the more incapacitating bonds of **anomie**. (From *Right Reason*, p. 195, Doubleday & Company, 1985)

antipodal (adjective) *Opposed; widely different.*

More academic and philosophical attention has been devoted in the last fifty years to the flowering of Marxist thought and life under Marxism. Still, it is astonishing how little thought is given to the great residual paradox expressed in the **antipodal** manifestos of our time. (From *Right Reason*, p. 228, Doubleday & Company, 1985)

aperçu (noun) *A brief glimpse or immediate impression, especially an intuitive insight.*

Professor Edward Luttwak came up several years ago with a hauntingly bright **aperçu** calculated to distinguish between Mao man and Soviet man. (From *Right Reason*, p. 275, Doubleday & Company, 1985)

apodictically (adverb) *Expressing necessary truth; with absolute certainty.*

The prediction (mine) that the two major candidates would differ from one another only in the appoggiaturas was, it turned out, correct. The *New York Times* made the point **apodictically**. (From *The Unmaking of a Mayor*, p. 169, The Viking Press, 1966)

a posteriori (adjective) *Arriving at a principled conclusion as a result of an examination of the facts; reasoning from the particular to the generality.*

Will the historians trained in **a posteriori** sleuthing say to us one day, "Kennedy got this insight from the history of Walpole that Galbraith gave him to read"? Did JFK read it? (From *Cruising Speed*, p. 94, G. P. Putnam's Sons, 1971)

appoggiatura (noun) *An accessory embellishing note or notes preceding an essential melodic note or tone.*

He knew not to expect any explanation of how the mission had been accomplished— these romantic **appoggiaturas** on the mechanics of the spy business were peculiarly the anxiety of the Americans and the British. (From *Saving the Queen*, p. 237, Doubleday & Company, 1976)

apriorism (noun) *Reasoning from principles to particulars; thus, if free speech is right, the person who exercises it is right.*

Nothing is more futile—or, for that matter, more anticonservative—than to indulge the heresy of extreme **apriorism**. (From *The Unmaking of a Mayor*, p. 261, The Viking Press, 1966)

arcana (noun) *Secret or mysterious knowledge or information known only to the initiate.*

Truman Capote was something of a lay criminologist, appearing on talk shows, explaining such terms as "sociopath," "psychopath," and other **arcana** of penological psychology. (From *Right Reason*, p. 186, Doubleday & Company, 1985)

artifice (noun) *A wily or artful stratagem; guile.*

Oakes flushed, doodling on his pad, conscious that everyone was looking at him, unlearned in the **artifices** of appearing indifferent. (From *Saving the Queen*, p. 63, Doubleday & Company, 1976)

aspersion (noun) *The act of calumniating; defamation.*

I mention Robert Kennedy without **aspersion** of any kind—on the contrary; because his foes and his friends agree that he felt deeply, and it is at least the public understanding that he was not merely a practicing Catholic but a believing Christian. (From *Cruising Speed*, p. 160, G. P. Putnam's Sons, 1971)

aspirant (noun) *One who is ambitious of advancement or attainment.*

Quite possibly the **aspirant** mayor, in order to get himself elected, would need to make precisely those commitments to the old order which preclude the very actions needed to overcome those crises. (From *The Unmaking of a Mayor,* p. 29, The Viking Press, 1966)

asseveratively (adverb) *With positive or emphatic affirmation.*

I am going to devote my time today to setting forth one or two propositions, some of which I tender **asseveratively,** others—well, inquisitively. (From *Right Reason,* p. 112, Doubleday & Company, 1985)

assiduously (adverb) *Marked by constant, unremitting attention or by persistent, energetic application.*

Robert Price resisted, his contention being that Lindsay's candidacy was best served by flatly ignoring his Conservative opponent, which Lindsay proceeded **assiduously** to do. (From *The Unmaking of a Mayor,* p. 160, The Viking Press, 1966)

assonant (adjective) *Marked by resemblance of sound in words or syllables; resemblance.*

In Garry Trudeau's "Doonesbury," the reader is well nourished, all the more so since there is all that wonderful **assonant** humor and derision in midstrip: indeed, not infrequently the true climaxes come in the penultimate panel, and the rest is lagniappe. (From *Right Reason,* p. 385, Doubleday & Company, 1985)

asymptotically (adverb) *Getting closer and closer to a goal, but never quite reaching it.*

The ceremony reaches cyclical heights of debauchery every few years as the management struggles, **asymptotically,** towards the goal of fully anesthetizing the losers' pain. (From *Cruising Speed,* p. 221, G. P. Putnam's Sons, 1971)

banal (adjective) *Lacking originality, freshness, or novelty; failing to stimulate, appeal, or arrest attention.*

He begins to recount his misgivings about American society, the war, the draft, the profit system, the educational establishment. My answers are diffuse, **banal,** and repetitious. (From *Cruising Speed,* p. 224, G. P. Putnam's Sons, 1971)

bawdy (adjective) *Obscene, lewd, indecent, smutty.*

In undermining religion through **bawdy** and slapstick humor, through circumspect allusions and emotive innuendos, Professor Kennedy is guilty of an injustice to and an imposition upon his students and the University. (From *God and Man at Yale,* p. 15, Regnery Books, 1986)

beleaguered (adjective) *Hemmed in; bottled up: subjected to oppressive or grievous forces; harassed.*

What power did the Mayor of New York, or the **beleaguered** publishers, have to come to the aid of the public—in the wake of a generation's legislation granting special immunities to the labor unions who are free to conspire together in restraint of free trade? (From *The Unmaking of a Mayor,* p. 106, The Viking Press, 1966)

belletristic (adjective) *Relating to the writing of belles lettres; speech or writing that consciously or unconsciously is more concerned with literary quality than with meaning.*

The special idealism of the youth who went to college or completed college during the postwar years seized on collective fancies. When these fell apart, they fell back to the paunch liberalism of the fifties, dressed up by the **belletristic** politics of Adlai Stevenson. The end came in Dallas. (From *Cruising Speed,* p. 92, G. P. Putnam's Sons, 1971)

Benthamite (noun) *After Jeremy Bentham, principal architect of utilitarian philosophy: one who adheres to the theory that the morality of any act is determined by its utility, and that pleasure and pain are the ultimate standards of right and wrong.*

The problem is to weigh the voting strength of all the categories and formulate a program that least dissatisfies the least crowded and least powerful categories: and the victory is supposed to go to the most successful **Benthamite** in the race. (From *The Unmaking of a Mayor,* p. 4, The Viking Press, 1966)

bestir (verb) *To stir up; rouse into brisk, vigorous action.*

If the alumni wish secular and collectivist influences to prevail at Yale, that is their privilege. What is more, if that is what they want, they need **bestir** themselves very little. (From *God and Man at Yale,* p. 114, Regnery Books, 1986)

bifurcate (verb) *To branch or separate into two parts.*

Yale shouldn't be turned over to the state because there are great historical presumptions that from time to time the interests of the state and those of civilization will **bifurcate,** and unless there is independence, the cause of civilization is neglected. (From *God and Man at Yale,* p. 1, Regnery Books, 1986)

blasé (adjective) *Apathetic to pleasure or life; indifferent as a result of excessive indulgence or enjoyment.*

I was asked whether I would consent to a public demonstration staged outside my office urging me to run. I was flabbergasted, but sought to act **blasé** about the whole thing. (From *The Unmaking of a Mayor,* p. 103, The Viking Press, 1966)

boiserie (noun) *Carved wood paneling.*

The dinner, discreetly served in the Queen's Drawing Room, in the candlelight with the crystal **boiserie** effect and, always, the soft light, its Fauvist colors standing out in the mortuary of regal ancestors. (From *Saving the Queen,* p. 189, Doubleday & Company, 1976)

bombastic (adjective) *Pretentious, inflated.*

Anthony was incapable of pomposity. He cared more about effective relief for those who suffered than about **bombastic** relief for those who formed committees. (From *Saving the Queen,* p. 10, Doubleday & Company, 1976)

breviary (noun) *An ecclesiastical book containing the daily prayers or canonical prayers for the canonical hours.*

St. James's was dark except for candles on both sides of the sanctuary, the four dim lights overhead for tracing the aisles and the pews, the light inadequate for reading one's missal or **breviary.** (From *Saving the Queen,* p. 209, Doubleday & Company, 1976)

bugaboo (noun) *A source of concern, especially something that causes fear or distress often out of proportion to its actual importance.*

As for the **bugaboo** that an element of internal debt is being passed on to future generations, it is "unmistakably false." (From *God and Man at Yale,* p. 70, Regnery Books, 1986)

bumptiousness (noun) *The quality of one who is presumptuously, obtusely, and often noisily self-assertive.*

After it was all over, the student body president approached me with a wonderful combination of diffidence and **bumptiousness,** to say that he disapproved of the pig-bit, but that I was not to mistake this for approval of anything I had said, presumably not even the passage in my speech in which I deplored race prejudice. (From *Cruising Speed,* p. 71, G. P. Putnam's Sons, 1971)

cacoëthes (noun) *An uncontrollable desire.*

I wink noisily at Rosalyn (Tureck) and suggest that WHO KNOWS, the liqueur might just conceivably give her a case of **cacoëthes** piano-itis. (From *Cruising Speed,* p. 143, G. P. Putnam's Sons, 1971)

caliper (verb) *To measure by or as if by calipers, an instrument having two legs or jaws that can be adjusted to determine thickness, diameter, etc.*

Granted that the frame of the Cardinal's letter was melodramatic, and that the melodrama is inhospitable to distinction: even so—call it feticide and **caliper** as you will the differences exquisite between feticide and murder on the moral scale. (From *Cruising Speed,* p. 240, G. P. Putnam's Sons, 1971)

callow (adjective) *Lacking in adult sophistication, experience, perception, or judgment.*
Trust influenced Blackford from the time they were at school together in England just before the war, and Trust was in the fifth form and Blackford a **callow** third-former. (From *Saving the Queen*, p. 10, Doubleday & Company, 1976)

cant (adjective) *The expression or repetition of conventional, trite, or unconsidered ideas or sentiments.*
Boris old boy, although I am entirely committed to our cause, I find the repetition of the **cant** phrases of communism altogether depressing. (From *Saving the Queen*, p. 153, Doubleday & Company, 1976)

caravanserai (noun) *An inn in Near or Far Eastern countries where caravans rest at night; usually a large bare building surrounding a court.*
Although Tito was prepared to spend cold nights in the trenches with his troops, he was manifestly happier in the **caravanserai** of the mighty. (From *Right Reason*, p. 392, Doubleday & Company, 1985)

Catonically (adverb) *In connection to Marcus Porcius Cato (149 B.C.), Roman statesman, or Marcus Porcius Cato (46 B.C.), Roman Stoic philosopher, both celebrated for austerity: repeated injunctions, or warnings, or predictions (e.g., "Delada Carthago est," Marcus Porcius Cato's "Carthage must be destroyed.").*
I haughtily, and indeed just a little sadly, remind Pat that Horrible Foo has, as, **Catonically**, I had always warned her he would, proved to be a wicked, wicked dog. (From *Cruising Speed*, p. 145, G. P. Putnam's Sons, 1971)

centripetalization (noun) *The process by which things proceed in a direction toward a center axis.*
It was obvious to the conservatives who grouped together after the Second World War that the **centripetalization** of power simply had to be arrested. (From *Cruising Speed*, p. 91, G. P. Putnam's Sons, 1971)

chiding (noun) *Reproof, rebuke.*
Johnny turned to Blackford. "You and your goddam . . . continence." . . . [He] got orotund when he was tight, and Blackford smiled at the familiar **chiding.** (From *Saving the Queen*, p. 7, Doubleday & Company, 1976)

chivalrous (adjective) *Marked by honor, fairness, generosity, and kindliness especially to foes, the weak and lowly, and the vanquished according to knightly tradition.*
Let us move towards a **chivalrous** candor, based on a respect for the essential equality of human beings, which recognizes reality, and speaks to reality. (From *The Unmaking of a Mayor*, p. 156, The Viking Press, 1966)

circumlocutory (adjective) *Marked by or exhibiting the use of an unnecessarily large number of words to express an idea; using indirect or roundabout expression.*
Smith was recalling to himself that he had taken great, **circumlocutory** pains never actually to deny his guilt directly to those who had most intimately befriended him. (From *Right Reason*, p. 202, Doubleday & Company, 1985)

clerisy (noun) *The well-educated or learned class; intelligentsia.*
The impact of the scientific developments that have absorbed the moral energies of our bishops and of the American **clerisy** in general prompts questions more basic than the question of selective conscientious objection. (From *Right Reason*, p. 117, Doubleday & Company, 1985)

coadjutor (noun) *A helper, assistant.*
"The Republican party," said Nelson Rockefeller—Lindsay's **coadjutor** in New York modern Republicanism—in the summer of 1963, "is the party of Lincoln." (From *The Unmaking of a Mayor*, p. 80, The Viking Press, 1966)

coda (noun) *A concluding portion of a musical, literary, or dramatic work, usually a portion or scene that rounds off or integrates preceding themes or ideas; anything that serves to round out, conclude, or summarize yet has an interest of its own.*

Ah, the ideological **coda**, how it afflicts us all! And how paralyzingly sad that someone who can muse over the desirability of converting New York into an independent state should, having climbed to such a peak, schuss down the same old slope, when the mountains beckon him on to new, exhilarating runs. (From *The Unmaking of a Mayor*, p. 39, The Viking Press, 1966)

codicil (noun) *A provision, as of a document, made subsequently to and appended to the original.*

"Do you mean, m-m-ma'am," the Prime Minister said to Queen Caroline, "those held in Great Britain by the United States, pursuant to the **codicils** of the NATO Treaty? Or d-d-do you mean those bombs over which we have total authority?" (From *Saving the Queen*, p. 99, Doubleday & Company, 1976)

cogency (noun) *The quality or state of appealing persuasively to the mind or reason.*

A young man cannot automatically be condemned for having acted frivolously if he sets out to weigh the demands of loyalty to this country's government against the **cogency** of the military objective he is being conscripted to risk his life for. (From *Right Reason*, p. 117, Doubleday & Company, 1985)

colloquy (noun) *A high-level, serious discussion.*

The Liberal Party's deliberations—which are a **colloquy** between Mr. David Dubinsky and Mr. Alex Rose—are copiously reported; and Adlai Stevenson, John Kennedy, and Lyndon Johnson all appeared in person to accept the Party's endorsement at great big to-dos. (From *The Unmaking of a Mayor*, p. 51, The Viking Press, 1966)

colonic (adjective) *Having to do with the colon. [A high-colonic medical examination reaches up into the large intestine.]*

"I never went to Yale, Blacky, so I can't answer those high-**colonic** questions." (From *Saving the Queen*, p. 218, Doubleday & Company, 1976)

comity (noun) *Friendly civility, mutual consideration.*

The American President, the British Prime Minister and the Soviet despot make dispositions involving millions of people for the sake of temporary geopolitical **comity**. (From *Saving the Queen*, p. 198, Doubleday & Company, 1976)

complaisant (adjective) *Marked by an inclination to please or oblige or by courteous agreeability.*

Thorton Wilder had first to step over the body; he smiled at me as if he had negotiated a mud-puddle. The Master who followed Mr. Wilder smiled as well. His was less **complaisant**. (From *Cruising Speed*, p. 223, G. P. Putnam's Sons, 1971)

complementary (adjective) *Suggestive of completing or perfecting; mutually dependent: supplementing and being supplemented in return.*

Lindsay emphasized certain themes, foremost among them his own liberalism and his aloofness from the Republican Party. He developed a **complementary** theme, namely the necessity of saving New York City from the curse of reaction. (From *The Unmaking of a Mayor*, p. 286, The Viking Press, 1966)

concatenation (noun) *A series or order of things depending on each other as if linked together.*

José López Portillo, the people's friend who left Mexico with a foreign debt of $90 billion, before he left office built, in addition to houses for himself and each of his children, an astronomical observatory, useful for tracing friendly astrological **concatenations**, if indeed Sr. Portillo acquired all the money with which he built his houses by speculation. (From *Right Reason*, p. 297, Doubleday & Company, 1985)

concupiscent (adjective) *Lustful.*

The Protestant theologian Dean Fitch reminds us that we have recently entered upon the most acutely degenerate of the stages of civilization: The Age of Love of Self. For a period we loved God; then we loved rationalism; then we loved humanity; then science; now we love ourselves, and in that **concupiscent** love all else has ceased to exist. (From *Cruising Speed,* p. 179, G. P. Putnam's Sons, 1971)

confutation (noun) *The act or process of overwhelming by argument.*

It is necessary in making one's complaints against the society we intend to replace, to be vague and even disjointed. To be specific, or to be orderly, is once again to run the risk of orderly **confutation.** (From *Cruising Speed,* p. 213, G. P. Putnam's Sons, 1971)

consanguinity (noun) *The state of being related by blood or descended from a common ancestor; (thus) a close relationship or connection; affinity.*

John Lindsay might have waited until 1965 to oppose Jacob Javits in the primary, but such a move was out of the question by reason not only of political prudence but of ideological **consanguinity.** (From *The Unmaking of a Mayor,* p. 63, The Viking Press, 1966)

contemn (verb) *To view or treat with contempt as mean and despicable; reject with disdain.*

Samuelson would have us not only **contemn** the treatment of economics of such men as Jewkes, F. A. Hayek, Ropke, Anderson, Watt, and von Mises, we are also to doubt their motives. (From *God and Man at Yale,* p. 81, Regnery Books, 1986)

continence (noun) *Self-restraint from yielding to impulse or desire.*

Johnny, opening the window to reach for another can of beer, discovered with horror that there were none left; and reaching into the cigarette box, discovered that he had simultaneously run out of cigarettes. He turned to Blackford. "You and your goddam . . . **continence.**" (From *Saving the Queen,* p. 7, Doubleday & Company, 1976)

contravene (verb) *To go or act contrary to; obstruct the operation of; infringe, disregard; oppose in argument; contradict, dispute.*

It does not take political courage to **contravene** one's own religion, it takes moral infidelity, of which I do not propose to be guilty inasmuch as I put the moral order above the political order. (From *The Unmaking of a Mayor,* p. 180, The Viking Press, 1966)

controvert (verb) *To dispute or oppose by reasoning.*

I find it continuingly relevant, in a book on contemporary politics, to attempt to **controvert** controvertible misrepresentations. (From *The Unmaking of a Mayor,* p. 10, The Viking Press, 1966)

cordon sanitaire (noun) *A line designed to act as a buffer between two territories actually or potentially hostile to each other.*

We arrive [at Fillmore East to hear Virgil Fox, the organist, play Bach], and there are hippies and non-hippies trying to get in, a sellout. One young man ventures forward, do I have an extra ticket? I give him one of the two tickets, thinking to keep the second, under the circumstances, as **cordon sanitaire.** (From *Cruising Speed,* p. 51, G. P. Putnam's Sons, 1971)

Coventry (noun) *A state of ostracism or exclusion from the society of one's fellows.*

The irrepressible and irrational right-crackpot who advances an inanity—say that "Eisenhower and Kennedy have brought us to the brink of surrender"—is instantly identified as what he is, and the forces of opprobrium, social and intellectual, quickly maneuver to consign him to **Coventry.** (From *The Unmaking of a Mayor,* p. 307, The Viking Press, 1966)

cozen (verb) *(1) To deceive by artful wheedling or tricky dishonesty; (2) to beguile craftily: victimize by chicanery; (3) to act with artful deceit.*

It is easy to say that ideally you should stand still and be polite and attentive when addressed and **cozened** by the same man who that same morning berated you as a racist and hater. (From *The Unmaking of a Mayor,* p. 236, The Viking Press, 1966)

credo (noun) *A strongly held or frequently affirmed belief or conviction.*

The term "professionally competent," as used by the academic freedomites to describe a legitimate criterion of employment, can, under their **credo,** be meaningfully applied only to the "fact" aspect of teaching. (From *God and Man at Yale,* p. 146, Regnery Books, 1986)

credulous (adjective) *Ready or inclined to believe, especially on slight or uncertain evidence.*

I have no quarrel with Mr. Seymour, although I should be perhaps less categorical— enough so, for example, to allow me to express preference for a **credulous** Democrat over a profoundly convinced Communist. (From *God and Man at Yale,* p. 178, Regnery Books, 1986)

cudgels (noun) *"To take up the cudgels" is to enter into a vigorous contest.*

He says that he is not even sure whether, when his father dies, he will take up the **cudgels** of the House of Lords. (From *Saving the Queen,* p. 188, Doubleday & Company, 1976)

cursory (adjective) *Rapidly, often superficially, performed with scant attention to detail.*

His introduction in that subject at Maxwell Field ("How to be useful if shot down and incorporated in the resistance movement") was **cursory.** (From *Saving the Queen,* p. 32, Doubleday & Company, 1976)

cynosure (noun) *A center of attraction or interest.*

Blackford's classmates were already dribbling into the classroom and, alerted to the cause of the excitement, looked instantly at the **cynosure** on the blackboard and exploded in squeals of delight and ribaldry. (From *Saving the Queen,* p. 70, Doubleday & Company, 1976)

decorous (adjective) *Marked by propriety and good taste, especially in conduct, manners, or appearance.*

And how long are the professors willing to wait before a **decorous** opportunity presents itself for exposing the steady drive in the direction of collectivism that has gathered so much momentum at Yale over the past dozen years? (From *God and Man at Yale,* p. 104, Regnery Books, 1986)

deify (verb) *To glorify or exalt as of supreme worth or excellence.*

The Department of Economics is not alone in **deifying** collectivism. (From *God and Man at Yale,* p. 99, Regnery Books, 1986)

demurral (noun) *The act of taking exception.*

He permitted himself a smile as he shot out his trigger finger to the door, which was the director's way of saying, "Out"—to which there was no known **demurral.** (From *Saving the Queen,* p. 4, Doubleday & Company, 1976)

denouement (noun) *The final outcome, result, or unraveling of the main dramatic complication in a play.*

Blackford gave Joe the plot, but not the **denouement,** and as they were driving home Joe expressed himself as genuinely indignant at Iago, and Blackford told him that was a really good sign. (From *Saving the Queen,* p. 216, Doubleday & Company, 1976)

derogate (verb) *To make to seem lesser in esteem; disparage, decry.*

Salesmanship is nowadays **derogated,** the assumption being that a salesman is somebody who persuades you to do something you do not want to do. (From *Cruising Speed,* p. 129, G. P. Putnam's Sons, 1971)

desultorily (adverb) *Lacking steadiness, fixity, regularity, or continuity.*

However **desultorily,** his father always kept in touch with him, and the more easily as his son grew older, and the two, though apart, did not grow apart. (From *Saving the Queen,* p. 55, Doubleday & Company, 1976)

de trop (adjective) *Too much or too many; in the way; superfluous; unwanted.*

The swanks at PBS are pretty proud of their audiences, but an exchange in Latin would probably be thought **de trop.** (From *Right Reason,* p. 217, Doubleday & Company, 1985)

detumescence (noun) *The collapse of what was heretofore stiff, as in a penis.*

Surely it was with malice aforethought that he permitted the ash on his burning cigarette to grow to advanced **detumescence.** (From *Right Reason,* p. 435, Doubleday & Company, 1985)

devolve (verb) *(1) To cause to pass down, descend, be transferred, or changed; (2) to transfer from one person to another: hand down; (3) to pass by transmission or succession.*

John Lindsay was to stress repeatedly the nonpartisan nature of his own candidacy, assiduously cultivating the air of transcendence that **devolves** to a candidate too big for any single party. (From *The Unmaking of a Mayor,* p. 45, The Viking Press, 1966)

dialectic (noun) *Any systematic reasoning, exposition, or argument that juxtaposes opposed or contradictory ideas and seeks to resolve their conflict; play of ideas; cunning or hairsplitting disputation.*

It may be in fact that to bring up a particular subject before a particular audience results in a **dialectic** whose meaning is a function of time and place. (From *The Unmaking of a Mayor,* p. 25, The Viking Press, 1966)

dilettante (noun) *A person who cultivates an art or branch of knowledge as a pastime without pursuing it professionally.*

Professor Kirkland does not believe that academic freedom ought to protect the pedant, the **dilettante,** or the exhibitionist. (From *God and Man at Yale,* p. 143, Regnery Books, 1986)

discountenance (verb) *To put to shame; reject; abash, disconcert; refuse to look upon with favor.*

It is an interesting conjecture that the effect of the Republicans' closed shop is not only to **discountenance** a useful bloc of Republican voters but to discourage a potential flow of voters whose background is Democratic, and who might well view the Conservative Party as a way-station to a remodeled Republican Party. (From *The Unmaking of a Mayor,* p. 60, The Viking Press, 1966)

disjunction (noun) *The action of disjoining or condition of being disjoined; separation, disconnection, disunion.*

He [Jesse Jackson] is given to the most grating verbal rhetorical **disjunctions** in contemporary language. ("We're going from the outhouse to the White House." "They've got dope in the veins rather than hope in their brains.") (From *Right Reason,* p. 66, Doubleday & Company, 1985)

dislocation (noun) *A disruption of the established order.*

My host lightly probed me. I told him the truth, that I had heard the not so sotto voce impoliteness on the part of the student. He apologized for the social **dislocation,** and explained that the young man's father was a legislator who reversed himself and cast a deciding vote to relax the abortion law, in punishment for which he had failed of re-election, and that son was overwrought, particularly against conservative Catholics. (From *Cruising Speed,* p. 72, G. P. Putnam's Sons, 1971)

disquietude (noun) *Lack of peace or tranquillity.*
A man formally aligned on the other side of the political fence endorsing all your major platforms has the effect of relieving you of the **disquietude** that the existence of alternative approaches to government necessarily poses. (From *The Unmaking of a Mayor,* p. 99, The Viking Press, 1966)

dissimulation (noun) *Deception; hiding under a false appearance.*
Then there is someone who oscillates from sarcasm to **dissimulation.** You would think he had tipped his hand conclusively by beginning his letter, "Dear Mr. Pukely." (From *Cruising Speed,* p. 81, G. P. Putnam's Sons, 1971)

dissipation (noun) *Wasteful expenditures and intemperate living.*
What he is, is an undisciplined Catherine's wheel, whose columns read like angry and disordered reflections of the previous night's **dissipations.** (From *Right Reason,* p. 39, Doubleday & Company, 1985)

dittify (verb) *To turn into a ditty—a song or short poem, especially one of simple, unaffected character.*
"Remember: *Qui cogitat quod debet facere, solet conficere quod debet facere.*" Mr. Simon beamed as he attempted to **dittify** his maxim in English: "Those who think about their duty/Are those who end by doing their duty!" (From *Saving the Queen,* p. 64, Doubleday & Company, 1976)

doctrinaire (adjective) *Stubbornly devoted to some particular doctrine or theory without regard to practical considerations.*
Mr. Lindblom dislikes a **doctrinaire** attitude toward anything. He incessantly encourages the pragmatic approach to economics. It naturally follows that any reliance on absolutes, or any reference to indefeasible "rights" is unwarranted and anachronistic. (From *God and Man at Yale,* p. 91, Regnery Books, 1986)

dour (adjective) *Marked by sternness or severity.*
Georgianna opened the door, black and **dour** as ever, but instantly docile when Blackford said, "Georgy, lend me a dollar quickly." (From *Saving the Queen,* p. 53, Doubleday & Company, 1976)

dowdy (adjective) *Not modern in style; staid, shabby.*
She would never have got that **dowdy** kind of life with me, but that's what she wanted. (From *Saving the Queen,* p. 158, Doubleday & Company, 1976)

doxology (noun) *Praise to the Deity; thanksgiving for divine protection rendered anaphorically, i.e., repetitious in formulation. E.g., "Blessed be God/Blessed be His holy name/Blessed be His son Jesus."*
I would not expect in a serious conversation with a Cardinal about great affairs that he would punctuate his message with bits and pieces of Christian **doxology.** (From *Saving the Queen,* p. 153, Doubleday & Company, 1976)

dudgeon (noun) *A sullen, angry, or indignant humor.*
The Most Reverend Ernest Trevor Huddleston arrived at the makeshift studio at the nave of St. James's Church in Piccadilly in full Episcopal regalia, and in very high **dudgeon.** (From *On the Firing Line: The Public Life of Our Public Figures,* p. 345, Random House, 1989)

duplicity (noun) *Deception by pretending to entertain one set of feelings and acting under the influence of another.*
I have charged Yale with **duplicity** in her treatment of her alumni. (From *God and Man at Yale,* p. 134, Regnery Books, 1986)

dysphasia (noun) *Loss of or deficiency in the power to use or understand language caused by injury to or disease of the brain.*

REPORTER: But Mr. Lindsay said today that he never knew you at Yale at all—

WFB: Well, I'm surprised he said that because it's not true. If he is suffering from some sort of **dysphasia**, that would make a whole lot of his recent behavior understandable. (From *The Unmaking of a Mayor*, p. 262, The Viking Press, 1966)

eclectic (adjective) *Varied; reflecting different styles, doctrines, methods.*

Knowing Mr. Kennedy's appetite for **eclectic** reading matter, he gave him J. H. Plumb's *Sir Robert Walpole* and a volume of Betjeman's poems. (From *Cruising Speed*, p. 94, G. P. Putnam's Sons, 1971)

efface (verb) *To eliminate clear evidence of; to remove from cognizance, consideration, or memory.*

On those occasions when the Republican Party of New York has won municipal elections it has done so precisely by **effacing** any distinguishable characteristics of the Republican Party. (From *The Unmaking of a Mayor*, p. 42, The Viking Press, 1966)

efficacious (adjective) *Qualities that give power to bring about an intended result.*

I find it continuingly relevant, in a book on contemporary politics, to attempt to controvert controvertible misrepresentations because it is especially interesting to inquire whether they tend to be **efficacious** or not. (From *The Unmaking of a Mayor*, p. 10, The Viking Press, 1966)

effrontery (noun) *Act of shameless audacity and unblushing insolence.*

What they ought to be condemning is what I once called the special **effronteries** of the twentieth century. One of these—eastern seaboard liberalism—substituted ideology for metaphysics, causing the great void which the sensitive of whatever age feel so keenly. (From *Cruising Speed*, p. 93, G. P. Putnam's Sons, 1971)

egalitarianism (noun) *A belief that all men are equal in intrinsic worth and are entitled to equal access to the rights and privileges of their society; specifically, a social philosophy advocating the leveling of social, political, and economic inequalities.*

The adjacent fraternities are far gone in desuetude, for reasons nobody entirely understands, though everybody agrees they have something to do with the affluence-cum-**egalitarianism** paradox. (From *Cruising Speed*, p. 220, G. P. Putnam's Sons, 1971)

eleemosynary (adjective) *Of or relating to charity.*

I intended to probe the question whether an inverted kind of subsidy, to middle and big business, was going on under our **eleemosynary** noses—by encouraging, with social welfare schemes, a cheap labor market. (From *The Unmaking of a Mayor*, p. 36, The Viking Press, 1966)

elide (verb) *To suppress or alter at intermediate stages.*

When a politician has got so given to thinking of himself as a collectivity that he is capable of writing in his diary, "At 8 A.M., we got up and took a shower," he has **elided** from modesty to something else. (From *The Unmaking of a Mayor*, p. 85, The Viking Press, 1966)

elixir (noun) *A concoction held to be capable of prolonging life indefinitely; something that acts potently upon one, invigorating or filling with exuberant energy or cheer.*

The first course was an omelet of sour cream and tomatoes and **elixir**, unlike anything Black had ever tasted, and better. (From *Saving the Queen*, p. 114, Doubleday & Company, 1976)

empirical (adjective) *Originating in or based on observation.*

The **empirical** spirit is interesting both because it is organically American ("if it works, it's good"; "nothing succeeds like success") and because pride is a hugely important factor in the operation of governments, which after all are run by human beings. (From *Right Reason*, p. 80, Doubleday & Company, 1985)

enjambement (noun) *Continuation in prosody of the sense in a phrase beyond the end of a verse or couplet; the running over of a sentence from one line into another so that closely related words fall in different lines.*

" 'Against welfare,' says a woman supporter in a tall magenta hat, 'and not making New York a haven for . . . well . . .' She says no more." So writes *The New Yorker*. Now, great big grown-up people can effect the **enjambement** without strain. The lady in the magenta hat was anti-Black! (From *The Unmaking of a Mayor*, p. 236, The Viking Press, 1966)

enjoin (verb) *To direct, prescribe, or impose by order, typically authoritatively and compellingly.*

Assuming that the Yale graduate, a potential entrepreneur, is an inveterate, dauntless gambler and decides to run all these risks and launch his business, there are further considerations that his economists have **enjoined** him to keep in mind. (From *God and Man at Yale*, p. 84, Regnery Books, 1986)

enumerate (verb) *To relate one after another.*

The Declaration of Independence goes on to **enumerate** the grievances of the colonies. It is a stirring catalogue, but it finally reduces to the matter of the source of power, i.e., who should rule? (From *Cruising Speed*, p. 206, G. P. Putnam's Sons, 1971)

ephemera (noun) *Of transitory existence, interest, or importance.*

The whole thing [Mike Wallace's farewell interview with President and Mrs. Reagan on *60 Minutes*] seems a cheerful mix of nostalgia and **ephemera,** but the portrait was genuine and will be studied (or should be) by future biographers. (From Mr. Buckley's syndicated column, "On the Right")

equerry (noun) *One of the officers of the British royal household in the department of the master of the horse in regular attendance on the sovereign or another member of the royal family.*

An **equerry,** introducing himself genially, supervised turning the car over to a chauffeur, and Blackford's luggage to a footman. (From *Saving the Queen*, p. 165, Doubleday & Company, 1976)

eructation (noun) *A violent belching out or emitting.*

He knew that the center of their earth was heaving and fuming and causing great **eructations** of human misery in its writhing frustration over the failure of Soviet scientists to develop the hydrogen bomb at the same rate as the Americans. (From *Saving the Queen*, p. 104, Doubleday & Company, 1976)

erudite (adjective) *Possessing an extensive, often profound or recondite knowledge.*

"If you are not aware of it," said the Queen, "I am sure there are several members of this **erudite** company who will explain it to you." (From *Saving the Queen*, p. 168, Doubleday & Company, 1976)

espousal (noun) *A taking up or adopting as a cause or belief.*

Despite protestations that Professor Davis had failed to qualify for promotion, it was plain for all to see that he had been eased out because of his outspoken criticism of capitalism, his **espousal** of numerous left-wing causes, and his attacks on several large financial trusts and holding companies with which various members of the Yale Corporation were affiliated. (From *God and Man at Yale*, p. 149, Regnery Books, 1986)

eudaemonia (noun) *Happiness derived through a lifetime devoted to fulfilling moral obligations.*

Her doubts are of course shared by many who are discouraged by the failure of general education to achieve **eudaemonia.** (From *Cruising Speed*, p. 110, G. P. Putnam's Sons, 1971)

evocation (noun) *The act or fact of calling forth, out, or up; summoning, citation.*

Mr. Lindsay first discovered that the idea of taking positive action to relieve New York City of the curse of drug addiction can best be summed up in the haunting **evocation** of "concentration camps." (From *The Unmaking of a Mayor*, p. 164, The Viking Press, 1966)

ex cathedra (adverb) *Authoritative by virtue of or in the exercise of one's office, as with papal authority.*

The public is being trained, as regards the Supreme Court of the United States when it is interpreting the Constitution, to accept its ruling as if rendered **ex cathedra,** on questions of faith and morals. (From Mr. Buckley's syndicated column, "On the Right")

excretion (noun) *The process of eliminating useless, superfluous, or harmful matter.*

The conservative rejection of the John Birch Society, of the anarchists and other fanatics, was an act of **excretion** essential to political and intellectual hygiene. (From *Right Reason,* p. 220, Doubleday & Company, 1985)

execration (noun) *The act of cursing or denouncing.*

The Iranians, after they have done with the rituals of **execration,** are going to want that which is universally popular. Cars, rock music, Bloomingdale's. (From *Right Reason,* p. 72, Doubleday & Company, 1985)

exegete (noun) *A person skilled in critical explanation or analysis, especially of a text.*

WFB: You say that the rights of lawyers and priests should extend to journalists.

ABRAMS: As a general matter, yes. There are some differences, but as a general matter, yes, I—

WFB: That's a sort of a revolutionary accretion and yet, in asserting that point, you tend to do so as an **exegete** of the Constitution rather than as a somebody who wants to amend it. (From *On the Firing Line: The Public Life of Our Public Figures,* p. 198, Random House, 1989)

exigency (noun) *The hard requirements of a situation.*

We must bear in mind that the scholar has has not one but two functions. These pursuits are (1) scholarship, and (2) teaching. They are related solely by convenience, by tradition, and by economic **exigency.** (From *God and Man at Yale,* p. 182, Regnery Books, 1986)

exorcise (verb) *To get rid of the evil content of something.*

President Seymour had made a clarion call for a return to Christian values in 1937, but that did not **exorcise** the extreme secularism that characterized Yale at least during the last four years of his administration. (From *God and Man at Yale,* p. 43, Regnery Books, 1986)

expedient (noun) *Something that is suitable, practical, and efficient in achieving a particular end; fit, proper, or advantageous under the circumstances.*

I herewith request Mr. Charles Buckley to do me, and the voters of New York, the favor of ending the confusion by the simple **expedient** of changing his name. (From *The Unmaking of a Mayor,* p. 253, The Viking Press, 1966)

expunge (verb) *To obliterate completely; annihilate.*

"You, Comandante Fidel Castro," Kirov said, "are my sovereign. You, by your example in Cuba, will illuminate the Marxist movement throughout the world, and perhaps even **expunge** the cruel and barbaric Marxism being practiced in the Homeland of Lenin." (From *Mongoose, R.I.P.,* p. 243, Random House, 1987)

extirpate (verb) *To eradicate; destroy totally; wipe out; kill off; make extinct; exterminate.*

Teaching is not, for most of those who go into it, a priestly calling, a pledge made before God and Man to go out and **extirpate** ignorance from the globe. (From *The Unmaking of a Mayor,* p. 201, The Viking Press, 1966)

extuberance (noun) *Protuberance.*

Seville—At a little kiosk near the park is a child's mechanical rocking horse. You insert 25 pesetas, and for ten minutes your little boy or girl rocks around the clock, gasping with pleasure while holding on hard to the little wood **extuberances** that serve as bridles. (From *Right Reason,* p. 249, Doubleday & Company, 1985)

eyrie (noun) *A room or a dwelling placed high up; remote; isolated.*

Blackford was struck by the ornamental splendor of the scene, with the huge chandeliers, the gilt-red balcony, the steps behind him ascending to the regal **eyrie** whence Queen Caroline had descended. (From *Saving the Queen,* p. 131, Doubleday & Company, 1976)

fallacious (adjective) *Embodying or presenting a false or erroneous idea.*

The administration of Yale, and the president in particular, dwell from time to time on the merits of laissez-faire education, hinting that there exist some alumni with contrary notions—notions which are, of course, demonstrably **fallacious.** (From *God and Man at Yale,* p. 139, Regnery Books, 1986)

fasces (noun) *(1) A bundle of rods having among them an ax with the blade projecting, borne before Roman magistrates as a badge of authority in ancient Rome; (2) the authority symbolized by the fasces.*

Jimmy Jones had his **fasces,** and from all accounts they were liberally used to keep in line those whose restive intelligence or natural hedonism questioned the ideals or resisted the spartan regimen. (From *Right Reason,* p. 217, Doubleday & Company, 1985)

Fauvist (adjective) *Markedly vivid.*

A single early Picasso was lit by a shaft of soft light, its **Fauvist** colors standing out in the mortuary of regal ancestors. (From *Saving the Queen,* p. 189, Doubleday & Company, 1976)

fealty (noun) *The fidelity of a vassal or feudal tenant to his lord; faithfulness, allegiance.*

Congressman Lindsay voted with the Democrats a total of thirty-one times. As such, he was runner-up among liberal Republicans in the frequency of his **fealty** to Democrats-in-a-jam. (From *The Unmaking of a Mayor,* p. 70, The Viking Press, 1966)

fecundity (noun) *Fruitfulness; fertility.*

The story quotes me directly: "We do have similarities to the Kennedys," says Bill. "Our wealth, our **fecundity,** our Catholicism. Other than that, the comparison is engaging but misleading." (From *Cruising Speed,* p. 34, G. P. Putnam's Sons, 1971)

fetid (adjective) *Smelly, rotten.*

The Republican candidate for President should devote himself absolutely to making the atomization of the Marxist myth an official crusade, one to which we will attach ourselves as vigorously as if we were spreading the word of how to extirpate smallpox from the **fetid** corners of the world. (From *Right Reason,* p. 229, Doubleday & Company, 1985)

filigreed (adjective) *Adorned with a pattern or design resembling ornamental work of fine wire of gold, silver, or copper.*

"My dear Mr. Oakes," he read in a **filigreed** but authoritative hand that tilted sharply to the right. "I leave you to your researches during the morning and early afternoon." (From *Saving the Queen,* p. 181, Doubleday & Company, 1976)

flippant (adjective) *Treating or tending to treat with unsuitable levity that which is serious or to which respect is owing.*

References to genitalia are as effective in the classroom as they are at a bachelor party, and **flippant** allusions to sacrosanct subjects are as delightful from the podium as from the soapboxes of Hyde Park. (From *God and Man at Yale,* p. 15, Regnery Books, 1986)

flout (verb) *To treat with contempt; defile; mock.*

The problem with attempting eloquence at the United Nations is that that which is affirmed by all the surrounding moral maxims is regularly and systematically **flouted.** (From *Right Reason,* p. 214, Doubleday & Company, 1985)

forensic (adjective) *Rhetoric used to plead a point.*
There has been some dissatisfaction over the President's speech. Hardly surprising. It was a magnificent **forensic** performance. (From *Right Reason,* p. 100, Doubleday & Company, 1985)

fractious (adjective) *Tending to cause trouble (as by disobedience to an established order); hard to manage or unmanageable; refractory; unruly.*
Teenagers caught and convicted of felonies will be either put in jail or released in the recognizance of their parents. Said parents would have the right to surrender authority over **fractious** children by invoking probationary sentences. (From *The Unmaking of a Mayor,* p. 91, The Viking Press, 1966)

fulminator (noun) *One who denounces, sends forth censures or invectives.*
The 1,267 members of the freshman class of Yale University have been warned against the Moral Majority by President A. Bartlett Giamatti. And what a speech it was: Jerry Falwell, head of the Moral Majority, is said to be quite a **fulminator** himself. (From *Right Reason,* p. 48, Doubleday & Company, 1985)

fulsomeness (noun) *Copiousness, abundance so great as to become offensive.*
John Kennedy so oversold some of his own apostles on the general subject of his being the best qualified to serve as President of the United States that some of them went on to commit sins of **fulsomeness** which, one hopes, deeply embarrassed him. (From *The Unmaking of a Mayor,* p. 84, The Viking Press, 1966)

gambol (verb) *To bound or spring about as in dancing or play; skip about; frisk, cavort.*
"Not tomorrow," said Caroline. "Wouldn't do for me to **gambol** about the woods on my horse while they are lowering Queen Benedicta into the sod." (From *Saving the Queen,* p. 128, Doubleday & Company, 1976)

Gemütlichkeit (noun) (German) *Coziness; good nature, kindliness, cordiality.*
The loneliness of flight is not entirely overwhelmed by cabin movies, the drinks, the food, the ***Gemütlichkeit*** of shoulder-to-shoulder life. (From *Right Reason,* p. 95, Doubleday & Company, 1985)

Goo-gooism (noun) *(from the initials of* good government*) A reform movement in politics, especially in the era of Theodore Roosevelt—usually used disparagingly.*
If John Lindsay won, Republicans in Ohio and California would not be permitted to pass off his victory as meaningless, as merely a triumph of **Goo-gooism** in a jaded municipal situation. (From *The Unmaking of a Mayor,* p. 68, The Viking Press, 1966)

grandiloquence (noun) *Lofty, extravagantly colorful, pompous, or bombastic in style, manner, or language.*
Ramsey Clark is now and then just a little grandiose, e.g., "Dissent has been the principal catalyst in the alchemy of truth," which, substituting as it does "in the alchemy of" for the simpler "of," suffers not only from straitened **grandiloquence,** but from an edgy syntactical ineptitude. (From *Cruising Speed,* p. 121, G. P. Putnam's Sons, 1971)

guilelessly (adverb) *Innocently; naively; unsophisticated in manner.*
Professor Kennedy subverted the faith of numbers of students who, **guilelessly,** entered his course hoping to learn sociology and left with the impression that faith in God and the scientific approach to human problems are mutually exclusive. (From *God and Man at Yale,* p. 17, Regnery Books, 1986)

hagiographer (noun) *A writer of biography of an idealizing or idolizing character.*
"For John Lindsay, the device of playing up 'the candidate' rather than 'the party' has been startlingly successful." But as if to guard against the perils of an untoward de-Republicanization, the **hagiographer** cautiously adds: "He identified himself with Senator Javits, former Mayor La Guardia and others." (From *The Unmaking of a Mayor,* p. 72, The Viking Press, 1966)

hauteur (noun) *An assumption of superiority; an arrogant or condescending manner.*
Very soon after, we were back in Connecticut, and I strained to speak like Mortimer Snerd, so as to disguise from my friends the ignominy of my foreign experiences. The fashion is to comment on the **hauteur** of my diction. (From *Cruising Speed*, pp. 151–52, G. P. Putnam's Sons, 1971)

hebdomadal (adjective) *Meeting or appearing once a week; weekly.*
Sometime after Adlai Stevenson announced his candidacy for President in 1952, he telephoned his former wife and told her to prepare the "boys" to be picked up on Sunday. Sure enough, photographers were there to record the **hebdomadal** piety of Adlai Stevenson. (From *Right Reason*, p. 315, Doubleday & Company, 1985)

hegira (noun) *A journey or trip, especially when undertaken as a means of escaping from an undesirable or dangerous environment or as a means of arriving at a highly desirable destination.*
All of New York was wired to trip him up—local police, FBI, California sheriffs. In the interval, Edgar Smith undertook a **hegira**. He went deep into Pennsylvania, in search of a cemetery, he said later, at which he could meditate. (From *Right Reason*, p. 199, Doubleday & Company, 1985)

heterodoxy (noun) *An unorthodox opinion or doctrine.*
The president of the Conservative Book Club assigned *Message from Moscow* to readers, who reported back against it, on the grounds that the author's own prejudices were in favor of socialism; and such **heterodoxy** a small minority of CBC readers would not tolerate even as they would not have tolerated the distribution of *Animal Farm* in the light of Orwell's persistent inclination toward socialism. (From *Cruising Speed*, p. 48, G. P. Putnam's Sons, 1971)

heuristic (adjective) *(1) Providing aid or direction in the solution of a problem but otherwise unjustified or incapable of justification; (2) heightening curiosity about further scholarly or scientific exploration.*
Conservatives know that some human beings, as Albert Jay Nock stressed in his **heuristic** lectures at the University of Virginia, are educable, others only trainable. (From *The Unmaking of a Mayor*, p. 173, The Viking Press, 1966)

holographic (adjective) *Written in the hand of the person from whom it proceeds.*
A dotted line from the lips of the master led to a balloon, within which Blackford, imitating the **holographic** style of his teacher, who a few days earlier had explained the English evolution ("micturate") of Caesar's word to describe his soldiers' careless habits when emptying their bladders, indited the words: "Mingo, Mingere, Minxi, Mictum." (From *Saving the Queen*, p. 70, Doubleday & Company, 1976)

homily (noun) *A lecture or discussion on a moral theme.*
Senator Moynihan and Anthony Lewis charge that Ambassador Jeane Kirkpatrick and her legal adviser, Allan Gerson, are ignorant of the law. Moynihan added the **homily** that even though the Soviet Union does not abide by the law, that doesn't mean we shouldn't. (From *Right Reason*, p. 127, Doubleday & Company, 1985)

hortatory (adjective) *Using language intended to incite or to mobilize.*
The police reached the man, who had moments before jumped onto the stage and danced there naked, but poor Ken Galbraith, although he plowed a straight furrow through his **hortatory** address to the effect that the earth would open up and swallow us all if Nixon was reelected, was not able to engage the distracted audience. (From *Cruising Speed*, p. 58, G. P. Putnam's Sons, 1971)

hurly-burly (noun) *Confusion, turmoil, tumult, uproar.*
I never got around to it, in part because of the lack of time, in part because, of course, it would not, in the **hurly-burly**, have been publicly pondered. (From *The Unmaking of a Mayor*, p. 36, The Viking Press, 1966)

ignominious (adjective) *Marked by, full of, or characterized by disgrace or shame; dishonorable; deserving of shame.*

Mr. Leonard Hall added his voice to the chorus of breast-beaters after the **ignominious** defeat of Senator Goldwater. (From *The Unmaking of a Mayor,* p. 41, The Viking Press, 1966)

ignoratio elenchi (noun) *A fallacy in logic of supposing that the point at issue is proved or disproved by an argument which proves or disproves something not at issue.*

Lindsay ignored the challenge a half-dozen times, and finally replied to it by saying: "I don't know why you ask me to renounce Adam Clayton Powell, Jr., since Powell has come out for Mr. Beame." A classic example of what the logicians call *ignoratio elenchi.* (From *The Unmaking of a Mayor,* p. 271, The Viking Press, 1966)

impalpable (adjective) *Incapable of being felt by the touch.*

Boris knew to take the nearest church exit, keeping his eyes down, under no circumstances looking about him, lest his eyes fall on the intangible, **impalpable** Robinson. (From *Saving the Queen,* p. 208, Doubleday & Company, 1976)

impetuosity (noun) *Undisciplined thought or action.*

He has the faculty, where legal problems are concerned, of releasing, say every fifteen minutes or so, a gossamer blanket over your **impetuosities**. (From *Cruising Speed,* p. 116, G. P. Putnam's Sons, 1971)

implacable (adjective) *Incapable of appeasement or mitigation; inexorable.*

Castro kept both radio sets on, but after a while turned them down. There was the faint monotonic sound of people talking, from the one set and, from the other, the muted beat of the rock music, **implacable** in its cacophony. (From *Mongoose, R.I.P.,* p. 293, Random House, 1987)

importune (verb) *To press or urge with frequent or unreasonable requests or troublesome persistence.*

He wondered whether he would ever again feel so close a kinship as he had felt for the two men he had just now got killed. With morbid shame he recalled **importuning** them to request a transfer, after V-E Day, so that they could serve out the balance of their terms with him. (From *Saving the Queen,* p. 142, Doubleday & Company, 1976)

imputation (noun) *The act of laying the responsibility or blame for something falsely or unjustly.*

Blackford knew all about Meachey. He had led the Oxford Committee to protest the **imputation** of guilt to Stalin during the show trials in the late thirties. (From *Saving the Queen,* p. 92, Doubleday & Company, 1976)

incertitude (noun) *Absence of assurance or confidence.*

Either the Supreme Court will more or less laze up to different specific cases in different ways, leaving the question of what are and what aren't the rights of parties in dispute, in boundless **incertitude,** or else basic laws will have to be rewritten. (From *The Unmaking of a Mayor,* p. 198, The Viking Press, 1966)

inchoate (adjective) *Imperfectly formed or formulated.*

At Berkeley, that corporate sense of mission is as diffuse and **inchoate** as the resolute pluralism of California society. (From *God and Man at Yale,* p. 1, Regnery Books, 1986)

indefeasible (adjective) *Not capable of or not liable to being annulled or voided or undone.*

Mr. Lindblom dislikes a doctrinaire attitude toward anything. He incessantly encourages the pragmatic approach to economics. It naturally follows that any reliance on absolutes, or any reference to **indefeasible** "rights" is unwarranted and anachronistic. (From *God and Man at Yale,* p. 91, Regnery Books, 1986)

individuation (noun) *The process by which individuals in society become differentiated from one another.*

The kind of community Nisbet told us we all needed, and the kind that now Reich enjoins upon us, is inconceivable in the absence of **individuation;** and the individual is what happens when the state ceases to be taken for granted as the necessary instrument for human progress. (From *Cruising Speed,* p. 93, G. P. Putnam's Sons, 1971)

ineluctable (adjective) *Not to be avoided, changed, or resisted.*

The loose-jointedness of their mode leaves the revolutionists in a frame of mind at once romantic and diffuse, and the rest of us without the great weapon available to King Canute, who was able to contrive what would nowadays be called a Confrontation between—the **ineluctable** laws of nature and the superstitions of his subjects. (From *Cruising Speed,* p. 213, G. P. Putnam's Sons, 1971)

inept (adjective) *Lacking skill or aptitude for a particular role or task.*

A man gifted in research is not thereby gifted in the art of transmitting to the pupil his knowledge. This is periodically brought to mind in widespread student resentment at the retention by many universities of scholars who, while often distinguished in research, are miserably **inept** in teaching. (From *God and Man at Yale,* p. 182, Regnery Books, 1986)

inertia (noun) *Indisposition to motion, exertion, or action; inertness.*

For many teachers the prospect of commuting to disagreeable sections of the city, to grapple with **inertia,** indiscipline, and hostility, is not what they had in mind at all when deciding to teach. (From *The Unmaking of a Mayor,* p. 201, The Viking Press, 1966)

inexorable (adjective) *Not to be persuaded or moved by entreaty or prayer.*

The wisdom and indispensability of government action to regulate economy becomes the **inexorable** next step. (From *God and Man at Yale,* p. 67, Regnery Books, 1986)

inhere (verb) *To be a fixed element or attribute of; belong.*

States are amoral institutions. In a "state" **inheres** the authority to preserve itself. (From *Right Reason,* p. 247, Doubleday & Company, 1985)

in medias res (Latin) *Into the thick of it.*

Even then, blissfully distracted, he found himself wondering, **in medias res:** Would his future duties require him to . . . seduce women routinely? (From *Saving the Queen,* p. 14, Doubleday & Company, 1976)

insouciance (noun) *Lighthearted unconcern; nonchalance.*

The refrain on the matter of wealth was widespread, the popular corollary of which was to reason on to **insouciance** with respect to poverty as (Ann Davidon, *Philadelphia Inquirer*) for instance: "But there is something rather beguiling and even enviable about this overdriven patrician and his way of life. Perhaps it is his apparently blithe blindness to most of the world's miseries." (From *Right Reason,* p. 16, Doubleday & Company, 1985)

interloper (noun) *An unlawful intruder on a property or sphere of action; one that interferes or thrusts himself in wrongfully or officiously.*

I do not deny, and do not regret, that the general tendency of an opinion journal is to be particularly critical of any politician one considers as an **interloper** in one's own party. (From *The Unmaking of a Mayor,* p. 95, The Viking Press, 1966)

interposition (noun) *The actions of a state whereby its sovereignty is placed between its citizens and the federal government.*

I have a dream that one day the state of Alabama, whose governor's lips are presently dripping with the words of **interposition** and nullification, will be transformed. (From *Right Reason,* p. 63, Doubleday & Company, 1985)

intone (verb) *To utter in musical or prolonged tones; recite in singing tones or in a monotone.*
Black sternly discoursed on the illogic and immorality of the United States getting involved in a European war, recapitulating the phrases and paragraphs he had so often heard his father so earnestly **intone**. (From *Saving the Queen*, p. 52, Doubleday & Company, 1976)

intrinsically (adverb) *Inherently; having to do with its own nature, property. Thus, charity is intrinsically good.*
Now the idea of reinstating the IRA for everybody is **intrinsically** appealing. Any tax modification that reduces taxes on savings is appealing. (From Mr. Buckley's syndicated column, "On the Right")

intuit (verb) *To know or apprehend directly.*
Prosecutor Neely at this point **intuited** what Smith's strategy was. (From *Right Reason*, p. 201, Doubleday & Company, 1985)

inure (verb) *To reside in, be inherent in.*
What rights, then, **inure** to the country whose responsibility it is to safeguard the lives of its citizens? (From *Right Reason*, p. 78, Doubleday & Company, 1985)

invidious (adjective) *Detrimental to reputation, designed to denigrate.*
It is not intended as ethnically **invidious** to remark that history shows a propensity for violence in Latin America. (From *Right Reason*, p. 255, Doubleday & Company, 1985)

involuted (adjective) *Of an involved or complicated nature; abstruse, intricate.*
Recently Mr. Sargent Shriver said, "I am delighted to be in any cathedral where Mr. Adam Clayton Powell, Jr., is in the pulpit." Here is an **involuted** form of racism. It is short for: "Even though I know that Adam Clayton Powell, Jr., is a demagogue, whose power and reputation have been built on hatred between the races, I recognize he is a Black leader, and must treat him as though he were a qualified object of universal admiration." (From *The Unmaking of a Mayor*, p. 156, The Viking Press, 1966)

ipso facto (adverb) *By the very nature of the case.*
I do not mean to imply that simply because my viewpoint was not energetically circularized, the Council proved itself **ipso facto** ineffective. (From *God and Man at Yale*, p. 132, Regnery Books, 1986)

Jacobinical (adjective) *Of or relating to violent or revolutionary political extremism.*
At Columbia, Mr. Allard Lowenstein was hooted down and literally silenced for defending the right of Professor Herman Kahn to speak unmolested, and faculty members in that audience countenanced and even egged on the **Jacobinical** furies that ruled the crowd. (From *Cruising Speed*, p. 209, G. P. Putnam's Sons, 1971)

jape (noun) *Something designed to arouse amusement or laughter.*
"Oh," said Blacky, "so it was here that famous tryst took place?" Except that he was too stuffed with crème Chantilly, he'd have taken out his notebook, further to extend the historical **jape**. (From *Saving the Queen*, p. 117, Doubleday & Company, 1976)

jejune (adjective) *Devoid of substance, interest, significance.*
One of Edgar Smith's editorial contributions to the *Times* on prison reform had come out embarrassingly **jejune**. (From *Right Reason*, p. 194, Doubleday & Company, 1985)

jeremiad (noun) *A lamenting and denunciatory complaint: a dolorous tirade.*
Soaring taxes, inadequate police protection, irregular garbage collection, traffic congestion, the scarcity of low-cost housing: Great **jeremiads** can be written on each of these major deprivations which underwrite such a categorical disillusion as Mr. Richard Whalen's. (From *The Unmaking of a Mayor*, p. 30, The Viking Press, 1966)

juridical (adjective) *Of or relating to law in general or to jurisprudence.*
A call by the President for a declaration of war last November would have passed Congress overwhelmingly and, you betcha, with Senator Kennedy voting in favor. The de-

claration having passed, the **juridical** house is now in order. Not only the impounding of funds, which the President managed under an old law, but much more. (From *Right Reason,* p. 74, Doubleday & Company, 1985)

juxtapose (verb) *Place side by side.*

The device was to contrive wisps of frivolous conversation, à la *The Women,* and **juxtapose** them with horror stories from the Vietnamese battlefront (get it?), so as to effect a Stendhalian contrast that would Arouse the Conscience of Versailles. (From *Cruising Speed,* p. 83, G. P. Putnam's Sons, 1971)

kedge (verb) *To dig an anchor in securely.*

Mr. Rockefeller's composure, though temporarily adrift, quickly **kedged** up in that splendid self-assurance of investigating panel chairmen. (From *Saving the Queen,* p. 246, Doubleday & Company, 1976)

kite (verb) *To get money or credit by a kite, a check drawn against uncollected funds in a bank account; to create a false bank balance by manipulating deposit accounts.*

Excepting the fiscal deficit, which presumably cannot be **kited** indefinitely, things could probably stumble along much as before without causing New York City to close down its doors. (From *The Unmaking of a Mayor,* p. 28, The Viking Press, 1966)

languorous (adjective) *Producing or tending to produce a state of the body or mind caused by exhaustion or disease and characterized by a weak, sluggish feeling.*

History adduces now and again a morally **languorous** pope who was awakened from his slumbers (and many more popes who slept through it all) by morally energetic laymen, preferably saints. (From *Cruising Speed,* p. 242, G. P. Putnam's Sons, 1971)

lapidary (adjective) *Having the elegance and precision associated with inscriptions on stone.*

To accept Mr. Simpson's thesis is to suppose that writers (and poets) always feel that the language of the moment is **lapidary,** never mind that, when detoxified, they proceed to make changes. (From Mr. Buckley's syndicated column, "On the Right")

lasciviously (adverb) *Luxuriantly, wantonly.*

I had at the moment the campaign began no personal animus, certainly not a shred of that "personal disdain" which John Lindsay's biographer so **lasciviously** records. (From *The Unmaking of a Mayor,* p. 96, The Viking Press, 1966)

latently (adverb) *Dormantly, but usually capable of being evoked, expressed, or brought to light.*

Why would it make for good politics to endorse the impression that the New York City police force is **latently** sympathetic with the brutality shown under stress by the Selma police force? (From *The Unmaking of a Mayor,* p. 21, The Viking Press, 1966)

leech (verb) *To fasten onto, as a leech; feed on the blood or substance of.*

I once contributed to the impression that Beame was ordinary, or rather **leeched** on it, at a speech where I remarked that Mr. Beame constantly stressed that he was educated by the City of New York, "which fact should be obvious," I said; and I am ashamed of it. (From *The Unmaking of a Mayor,* p. 284, The Viking Press, 1966)

lineaments (noun) *An outline, feature, or contour of a body or figure; the distinguishing or characteristic feature of something immaterial.*

It was terribly clear from the visceral reactions of such people as Jackie Robinson that thousands of people were taking very special, even an acute, pleasure from believing that a sudden flash of light had exposed the **lineaments** of the wolf. (From *The Unmaking of a Mayor,* p. 22, The Viking Press, 1966)

longueur (noun) *An overlong passage, made dull or tedious.*

The **longeurs** in Trudeau's "Doonesbury" are sometimes almost teasingly didactic. (From *Right Reason,* p. 388, Doubleday & Company, 1985)

loquacious (adjective) *Given to excessive talking.*
Sometimes we spend as much as a half hour in conversation. He is, oddly, **loquacious**, and enjoys our intercourse. (From *Saving the Queen*, p. 109, Doubleday & Company, 1976)

lugubrious (adjective) *Mournful, sad, lachrymose.*
Jean-François Revel gave many **lugubrious** examples of the working of the Western mind. (From *On the Firing Line: The Public Life of Our Public Figures*, p. 120, Random House, 1989)

machicolation (noun) *An opening for shooting or dropping missiles upon assailants attacking below.*
"After the next war," the queen said cheerily, "when we shall all have exchanged hydrogen bombs, I should think these archives would be tremendously useful, since whoever is left over will be reduced to defending himself by the use of things like moats and **machicolations** and bows and arrows . . ." (From *Saving the Queen*, p. 171, Doubleday & Company, 1976)

magnanimous (adjective) *Generous, suggesting special inclinations to charity or philanthropy.*
Phil Donahue came up with an alternative suggestion that also commended itself to his audience—the Shah should undertake to return to Iran to face the punishment. (This **magnanimous** willingness to bring martyrdom to someone else recalls the wisecrack of 1939 to the effect that the British were prepared to fight to the last Frenchman.) (From *Right Reason*, p. 77, Doubleday & Company, 1985)

maladroitness (noun) *Lacking in shrewdness of execution, craft, or resourcefulness in coping with difficulty or danger.*
One can have no objections whatever to President Carter's mission, restricting our criticism to the **maladroitness** of its execution and the insufficiency of contingency planning. (From *Right Reason*, p. 79, Doubleday & Company, 1985)

malleable (adjective) *Open to outside forces or influences; urging a change in position, viewpoint.*
The courts are less **malleable** than they were even for Roosevelt. The Supreme Court gave him problems, and he tried to pack it, and eventually, got himself a court that would go along. (From *Right Reason*, p. 81, Doubleday & Company, 1985)

malversation (noun) *Corrupt administration.*
The Seabury disclosures that brought Fusion to the fore are not to be confused with the routine **malversations** of public officials. (From *The Unmaking of a Mayor*, p. 436, The Viking Press, 1966)

manumission (noun) *Formal emancipation from slavery.*
The dutiful Mr. Walter Cronkite closes his broadcast every night by citing the number of days in the infinitely prolonged negotiations having as their objective the hostages' release. The result of this kind of thing over a period of five months is that we are not one step closer to the **manumission** than we were on the fifth of last November. (From *Right Reason*, p. 76, Doubleday & Company, 1985)

mastodonic (adjective) *Something unusually, surrealistically large.*
But when you endeavor to shake the conviction that the **mastodonic** oil deposits that guard growlingly the outskirts of Bridgeport reflect the size of your own financial resources, a student at the University of Bridgeport displays amusement at my suggestion that it was neither factually not symbolically correct that I was there to argue the case for the Buckley oil interest in Bridgeport, *über alles*. (From *Cruising Speed*, p. 95, G. P. Putnam's Sons, 1971)

matriculate (verb) *To become admitted to membership in a body, society, or institution.*
Blackford completed his application for graduate school rather listlessly; convinced, correctly, that he would never **matriculate** during this bellicose season. (From *Saving the Queen*, p. 14, Doubleday & Company, 1976)

mete (verb) *To assign by measure; deal out; allot, apportion.*
Too many judges appear to have forgotten that the primary purpose of courts of justice is to assert the demands of the public order—by **meting** out convincing punishment to those who transgress against it. (From *The Unmaking of a Mayor*, p. 195, The Viking Press, 1966)

mien (noun) *The air or bearing of a person, especially as expressive of mood or personality.*
Black's final instructor had obviously spent much time in England. He was a gray man, his **mien**, hair, face, suit, shirt. (From *Saving the Queen*, p. 45, Doubleday & Company, 1976)

militate (verb) *To have weight or effect.*
The young graduate of Yale, the potential entrepreneur, must remember that money costs do not tally with social costs, and that therefore it is quite possible that the enterprise he is considering, regardless of its financial success, will **militate** against the social welfare. (From *God and Man at Yale*, p. 84, Regnery Books, 1986)

mollifying (adjective) *Making more agreeable; conciliatory; soothing.*
I have seen a variety of official answers to correspondents of Mr. Ober's general persuasion. Replies were **mollifying** in tone, but firm, and abundant in phrases like "freedom of speech" and "the great traditions of academic freedom." (From *God and Man at Yale*, p. 137, Regnery Books, 1986)

mordant (adjective) *Biting or caustic in thought, manner, or style; incisive; keen.*
Through it all, Smith had managed to put forward his case in an almost disinterested perspective. He was by turns **mordant**, judicious, inquisitive, impudent, amused. (From *Right Reason*, p. 190, Doubleday & Company, 1985)

mugwumpery (noun) *The views and practices of a mugwump, one who withdraws his support from a political group or organization: a regular member who bolts a party and adopts an independent position.*
Lindsay's biographer does not know how to handle the problem. On the one hand, Lindsay's transcendence of Republicanism must be presented as a statesmanlike projection of true Republican principle. On the other, a touch of **mugwumpery** is always charming. (From *The Unmaking of a Mayor*, p. 72, The Viking Press, 1966)

mulct (verb) *To leach from, gather up from, drain.*
In order for a nation to guard the common defense or look after the unfortunate, there has to be a certain residue. That residue can be **mulcted** from the masses, as in the Soviet Union, leaving them without the essential freedoms to engage in commerce or to blunt the sharp edges of life, or it can come out of what can reasonably be called a "surplus." (From *Right Reason*, p. 252, Doubleday & Company, 1985)

munificent (adjective) *Very liberal in giving or bestowing; lavish; characterized by great liberality or generosity.*
Many people come to New York because they are deluded, at least momentarily, into believing the myth of New York's **munificent** opportunities. (From *The Unmaking of a Mayor*, p. 37, The Viking Press, 1966)

muse (noun) *The creative spirit of an individual, the source of his inspiration.*
I would sooner risk the displeasure of a voter than I would that of my **muse**, who is more demanding. (From *The Unmaking of a Mayor*, p. 191, The Viking Press, 1966)

nepotistically (adverb) *Characterized by nepotism, favoritism shown to relatives.*
It had already been rumored that Blackford's selection to fly the new fighter had been **nepotistically** contrived. (From *Saving the Queen*, p. 222, Doubleday & Company, 1976)

nescience (noun) *The belief that nothing is establishable, provable.*
How is it that the president of a distinguished and cosmopolitan university tells us that God alone knows when human life begins? If you penetrate this rhetorical formula-

tion, you have a dimly obscured invitation to **nescience**. "God alone knows" is the safest way to say, "That-is-unknowable." Inasmuch as God is not invited to teach a regular course at Yale, Mr. Giamatti is saying in effect that the search for the answer to "When does life begin?" should be abandoned—because no one can tell. (From *Right Reason*, p. 49, Doubleday & Company, 1985)

nexus (noun) *Connection, interconnection, tie, link.*

Reason, conscience, and self-restraint are all that we have to rely upon, the burden resting on those who postulate a **nexus** between a sane position and an insane extension of it to make their demonstration. (From *The Unmaking of a Mayor*, p. 235, The Viking Press, 1966)

non grata (adjective) *Not approved; unwelcome.*

Others convey to the student who majors in sociology the definite impression that at best religion is **non grata** to the department, at worst it is the subject of relentless attack. (From *God and Man at Yale*, p. 18, Regnery Books, 1986)

numinous (adjective) *Divine, magical.*

Rosalyn Tureck sits down and pulls out that talismanic handkerchief, the fondling of which precedes the contact of her **numinous** fingers with the keyboard. (From *Cruising Speed*, p. 143, G. P. Putnam's Sons, 1971)

obduracy (noun) *The quality or state of being hard or resistant.*

I am not talking about someone who has familiarized himself sufficiently with the great scientific impasses that at various stages in the struggle to achieve the bomb have constituted roadblocks of historical **obduracy**. (From *Saving the Queen*, p. 147, Doubleday & Company, 1976)

obeisance (noun) *A movement of the body or other gesture made in token of respect or submission.*

Blackford rose, walked gravely to the lectern, and bowed with the faintly wooden truncation that becomes those ill at ease with the filigreed lengths of native **obeisances**, first to the Queen, then to the Archbishop. (From *Saving the Queen*, p. 242, Doubleday & Company, 1976)

objurgation (noun) *An act of decrying vehemently; castigation with harsh or violent language; harsh or violent reproof.*

Mrs. Gunning had, as chief organizer of the Parents and Taxpayers Association, been widely denounced, that being the cant **objurgation**, as an enemy of the Public Schools. (From *The Unmaking of a Mayor*, p. 261, The Viking Press, 1966)

oblation (noun) *Something offered or presented in worship or sacred service.*

I tell about the monk—the ex–circus hand—who, having no relevant skills, and having observed the artful **oblations** rendered by his brothers on the Feast Day of the Virgin, was spotted late that night, standing before her statue juggling his five weatherbeaten circus balls. (From *Cruising Speed*, p. 144, G. P. Putnam's Sons, 1971)

obverse (noun) *A counterpart necessarily involved in or answering to a fact or truth.*

The (conservative) Americans for Constitutional Action have their own poll—the **obverse** of the ADA's—which revealed that the median Republican voted with his party 86 percent of the time on issues of importance to conservatives. (From *The Unmaking of a Mayor*, p. 70, The Viking Press, 1966)

ochlocracy (noun) *Government by the mob; mob rule.*

She found it increasingly easy to achieve informality—to the dismay of her impossibly punctilious husband who desired **ochlocracy** abroad but, at home, to be paid homage even by the baboons at the zoo. (From *Saving the Queen*, p. 130, Doubleday & Company, 1976)

oenophile (noun) *A lover or connoisseur of wine.*

Blackford wondered where the **oenophiles'** journals were and thought Ellison must be a real sport to pass himself off as a winetaster, working in the sunkissed vineyards of Washington, D.C. (From *Saving the Queen*, p. 29, Doubleday & Company, 1976)

omnibus (adjective) *Of, relating to, or providing for many things at once.*

What we have is a great blur, an **omnibus** bill that goes everywhere from collecting taxes on tips at hamburger stands, to one that clips you extra on a phone call, to one that immobilizes one or another business merger because of changes in tax scheduling. (From *Right Reason*, p. 91, Doubleday & Company, 1985)

onus (noun) *Something (as a task, duty, responsibility) that involves considerable difficulty or annoyance; a burden.*

The probabilities are small that the cost of any modern government will reduce: which puts the **onus** back on the private sector to generate additional revenues, and ends us back with the question: Is the scarcity of public funds the major problem? (From *The Unmaking of a Mayor*, p. 32, The Viking Press, 1966)

opéra-bouffe (adjective) *Fit for a light comic opera characterized by parody or burlesque.*

"I persuaded a friend of mine from M.I.T. to go see the old gentleman. They hit it off and my friend is now hired," said Blackford with a feigned air of **opéra-bouffe** secretiveness. (From *Saving the Queen*, p. 171, Doubleday & Company, 1976)

opine (verb) *To give a formal opinion about.*

Pundits need to **opine** on developments in China while fearing that what we write on Monday will be obsolete on Tuesday. (From Mr. Buckley's syndicated column, "On the Right")

orotund (adjective) *Unduly strong in delivery or style.*

"You and your goddam . . . continence. I guess after graduation you'll go into training for the Graduate Engineering School lacrosse team and inflict on the next guy the necessity to go out into the wild night, in search of a normal room, with normal people, and normal supplies of the normal vices of this world."

Johnny got **orotund** when he was tight, and Blackford smiled at the familiar chiding. (From *Saving the Queen*, p. 7, Doubleday & Company, 1976)

ostracism (noun) *The exclusion by general consent from common privilege or social acceptance.*

What should happen is what should have happened when martial law was declared in Poland: a total economic, social, and cultural **ostracism** of the Soviet Union. (From *Right Reason*, p. 89, Doubleday & Company, 1985)

oxymoronic (adjective) *Relating to a combination for epigrammatic effect of contradictory or incongruous words.*

Michael Harrington's **oxymoronic** formulation—"coercion in favor of capitalists"— reminds us of the fashionable jargon in the commodity markets of the left (alas, not greatly changed). (From *God and Man at Yale*, p. xxxiv, Regnery Books, 1986)

palliative (noun) *Something that moderates the intensity of.*

Bowman and Bach's **palliatives** are mild by comparison with some of their brethren textbook writers who have molded the attitudes of so many students. (From *God and Man at Yale*, p. 52, Regnery Books, 1986)

pallid (adjective) *Lacking brightness or intensity.*

The truly extraordinary feature of our time isn't the faithlessness of the Western people; it is their utter, total ignorance of the Christian religion. They travel to Rishikesh to listen to **pallid** seventh-hand imitations of thoughts and words they never knew existed. (From *Cruising Speed*, p. 162, G. P. Putnam's Sons, 1971)

parabolically (adverb) *Expressed in the manner of a parable or figure; allegorically.*

It was easy to deny the rumor, that I had flown to Phoenix, Arizona, a few weeks earlier, there to meet with Barry Goldwater and Mrs. Clare Boothe Luce, since it was not true, not even **parabolically.** (From *The Unmaking of a Mayor,* p. 100, The Viking Press, 1966)

paradigm (noun) *An idealistic model.*

But Lenin had working for him not only the excitement of throwing over a dynasty, but of remaking a state around an ideological **paradigm** that excited everyone by its call to equality. (From *Right Reason,* p. 72, Doubleday & Company, 1985)

paralogist (noun) *One who uses reasoning that begs the question; one who uses a reasoning contrary to logical rules or formulas.*

A good debater is not necessarily an effective vote-getter: you can find a hole in your opponent's argument and thrill at the crystallization of a truth wrung out from a bloody dialogue—which may warm only you and your muse, while the smiling **paralogist** has made votes by the tens of thousands. (From *The Unmaking of a Mayor,* p. 272, The Viking Press, 1966)

parsimonious (adjective) *Excessively frugal.*

Eisenhower, as a young lieutenant, had had to train American soldiers using brooms as facsimiles for rifles, so **parsimonious** had the American isolationist Congress been toward the army. (From *Saving the Queen,* p. 184, Doubleday & Company, 1976)

partita (noun) *A set of musical variations.*

Rosalyn Tureck tells me that the note I sent her, likening Bach's E-minor **Partita** to *King Lear* was right on, that she had played the **partita** a thousand times, but always treated it with awe because she could not know what it would say to her this time around, even as *Lear* cannot be tuned by stroboscope. (From *Cruising Speed,* p. 142, G. P. Putnam's Sons, 1971)

paternalistic (adjective) *Relating to the practices of a government that undertakes to supply the needs or regulate the conduct of the governed in matters affecting them as individuals as well as in their relations to the state and to each other.*

The inflation that comes inevitably with government pump-priming soon catches up with the laborer, setting off a new deflationary spiral which can in turn only be counteracted by more coercive and **paternalistic** government policies. (From *God and Man at Yale,* p. 68, Regnery Books, 1986)

paucity (noun) *Smallness of quantity; dearth, scarcity.*

His subordinates complained with good and ill humor about everything, about the weather, the food, the hygienic facilities, the **paucity** of air cover, the stubbornness of Montgomery, the tenacity of the Germans. (From *Saving the Queen,* p. 140, Doubleday & Company, 1976)

pedagogical (adjective) *Characteristic of teaching.*

BORGES: I tried to teach my students not literature but the *love* of literature. I have taught many people the love of Old English.

WFB: And so there is a **pedagogical** art? It isn't simply a matter of—of exposure—you are indoctrinating your students? (From *On the Firing Line: The Public Life of Our Public Figures,* p. 275, Random House, 1989)

pejorative (noun) *Negative in inclination; critical.*

The term appeaser is used here not merely as a lazy **pejorative.** The appeaser tends to oppose a national draft, to oppose any increase in defense spending, to oppose economic boycotts, cultural boycotts, boycotts of athletic events. (From *Right Reason,* p. 101, Doubleday & Company, 1985)

penchant (noun) *A strong leaning or attraction; strong and continued inclination.*
Henry Regnery has passed along the principal executive responsibilities to his son-in-law, who is apolitical and resists, as financially unproductive, the **penchant** of his father-in-law for conservative-oriented books. (From *Cruising Speed,* p. 117, G. P. Putnam's Sons, 1971)

penury (noun) *Extreme poverty.*
In some measure, the educator is fortified by the knowledge that despite the trials and **penury** of his existence, he is shaping, more directly than members of any other profession, the destiny of the world. (From *God and Man at Yale,* p. 192, Regnery Books, 1986)

pertinacity (noun) *Unyielding persistence, often annoyingly perverse; stubborn inflexibility.*
Blackford muttered something about the **pertinacity** of the press. (From *Saving the Queen,* p. 230, Doubleday & Company, 1976)

phlegmatic (adjective) *Slow, stolid, unexcitable.*
"Frankly," said Black at dinner, to his aunt and her **phlegmatic** ever-silent husband, "the idea of going to school in England gives me the creeps." (From *Saving the Queen,* p. 55, Doubleday & Company, 1976)

pianissimo (adverb) *Very softly.*
Rufus's intensest emotions, like J. S. Bach's, were rendered **pianissimo**. (From *Saving the Queen,* p. 204, Doubleday & Company, 1976)

plenipotentiary (noun) *A person invested with full power to transact any business.*
Caroline drew closer to Perry. "I wish you were my minister **plenipotentiary**. I would trust you to do all these things for me, and then if anything at all went wrong, all I would have to do is simply behead you." (From *Saving the Queen,* p. 145, Doubleday & Company, 1976)

polyglot (noun) *Someone who speaks or writes several languages.*
If you can speak Spanish that easily, he persists, surely you can run through my book in French? **Polyglots** are that way, I find. They reach a point where every language silts up into a more or less recognizable vernacular. (From *Cruising Speed,* p. 49, G. P. Putnam's Sons, 1971)

pomposity (noun) *Ornately showy or pretentiously dignified demeanor, speech, or action.*
Anthony, though formal of speech, was incapable of **pomposity**. He cared more about effective relief for those who suffered than about bombastic relief for those who formed committees. (From *Saving the Queen,* p. 10, Doubleday & Company, 1976)

porcine (adjective) *Suggestive of swine.*
He talked about the necessity of replenishing his supply of French silk shirts, which heretofore were available only in America and other **porcine** countries. (From *Saving the Queen,* p. 156, Doubleday & Company, 1976)

portentous (adjective) *Exhibiting gravity or ponderousness; self-consciously weighty.*
"What matters is the nature of the Commonwealth."
"I have ideas about that," Caroline said. This sounded **portentous** so she added, "Everybody does . . ." (From *Saving the Queen,* p. 144, Doubleday & Company, 1976)

positivist (adjective) *Relating to the theory that rejects theology and metaphysics as being merely earlier imperfect modes of knowledge and instead holds that positive knowledge is based on natural phenomena and their properties and relations as verified by the empirical sciences.*
How much harm does *Playboy* do in fact, I have often asked myself, never getting much further than the presumptive disapproval of it, which I extend to any publica-

tion that declines to accept extra-personal or extra-**positivist** norms. (From *Cruising Speed,* p. 65, G. P. Putnam's Sons, 1971)

postprandial (adjective) *Occurring after a meal, especially after dinner.*
Sitting in the little drawing room of the Moscow apartment, Boris explained to his wife why they must retreat here for any intimate discussions, and routinely after dinner, when, he knew, the **postprandial** relaxation loosens the tongue. (From *Saving the Queen,* p. 106, Doubleday & Company, 1976)

postulate (noun) *A proposition advanced as axiomatic; an essential presupposition, condition, or premise; an underlying hypothesis or assumption.*
When scholars and statesmen disagreed on how to reconcile the **postulates** of America with the survival of slavery, it was to the Declaration of Independence that the abolitionists ideally repaired for guidance. Because the Declaration of Independence spoke of "self-evident" truths. Among them that men are born equal. (From *Cruising Speed,* p. 199, G. P. Putnam's Sons, 1971)

Potemkin (adjective) *(Referring to the Russian statesman who built fake villages along a route taken by Catherine the Great) Relating to creating an imposing façade or display designed to obscure or shield an unimposing or undesirable fact or condition.*
There is a little bit too much of the **Potemkin**-tour in the visit of some of the committees to the university. Appointments are set up for them, and they are put in touch with administration and faculty stalwarts. (From *God and Man at Yale,* p. 128, Regnery Books, 1986)

pragmatism (noun) *An American movement in philosophy founded by Peirce and James and marked by the doctrines that the meaning of conceptions is to be sought in their practical bearings, that the function of thought is as a guide to action, and that the truth is preeminently to be tested by the practical consequences of belief.*
Brief reference should be made to the substantial contribution to secularism that is being made at Yale and elsewhere by widespread academic reliance on relativism, **pragmatism,** and utilitarianism. (From *God and Man at Yale,* p. 25, Regnery Books, 1986)

prefecture (noun) *The office, position, jurisdiction, or term of office of a prefect.*
Though a prefect, Anthony was never a member of the **prefecture.** (From *Saving the Queen,* p. 11, Doubleday & Company, 1976)

prehensile (adjective) *Clutching greedily.*
Later that night, in Sally's car, they made love for the last time under the shadow of the West Rock. She was silent, but **prehensile.** (From *Saving the Queen,* p. 27, Doubleday & Company, 1976)

presumptive (adjective) *Apparent, presumed; based on inference.*
"This is a pretty good job," the Queen remarked. "I have inherited a lot of money, and a lot of junk, and a lot of perquisites, but there is something in it for everybody because of the **presumptive** necessity to worship something—somebody—worldly." (From *Saving the Queen,* p. 185, Doubleday & Company, 1976)

prevarication (noun) *A statement that deviates from or perverts the truth.*
Schlesinger dismissed the **prevarication** as part of the cover story, and confessed that he had not formulated an absolutely satisfactory ethic on the matter of lying to the press. (From *The Unmaking of a Mayor,* p. 101, The Viking Press, 1966)

probative (adjective) *Serving to prove; substantiating.*
With Presidents one proceeds more cautiously, because it is not the business of friends, let alone subordinates, to quiz the President. In the first place, one simply doesn't. In the second, a skillful politician could turn away the question easily; and the interrogator gets no **probative** satisfaction. (From *Cruising Speed,* p. 94, G. P. Putnam's Sons, 1971)

probity (noun) *Uncompromising adherence to the highest principles and ideals; unimpeachable integrity.*

If the educational overseer is interested in the activity of scholarship, let him endow a research center (and let him not, as a man of intelligence and **probity**, stipulate what shall be the findings of research not yet undertaken). (From *God and Man at Yale*, p. 186, Regnery Books, 1986)

prodigy (noun) *An extraordinary, marvelous, or unusual accomplishment, deed, instance, or person.*

Crosstown traffic is bad, but a new traffic commissioner who performed **prodigies** in Baltimore is now in charge. (From *The Unmaking of a Mayor*, p. 31, The Viking Press, 1966)

profanation (noun) *Debasement or vulgarization, especially by misuse or disclosure.*

It is a **profanation** to advance on Kempton's thought with compass, scissors, and tape measure, and it is a sign of his special genius that he inevitably leaves his critics feeling like Philistines. (From *The Unmaking of a Mayor*, p. 199, The Viking Press, 1966)

propensity (noun) *Natural inclination; innate or inherent tendency.*

An economic justification for a redistribution of income is the Keynesian insistence that more money go to that group which has a higher **propensity** to consume, that is, the lower and middle income groups. (From *God and Man at Yale*, p. 54, Regnery Books, 1986)

prosaic (adjective) *Having a dull, flat, unimaginative quality of style or expression.*

I gathered from my own representative that Lindsay's press conferences tended to be **prosaic** affairs, repetitious, formalistic, called for purely personal exposure. (From *The Unmaking of a Mayor*, p. 266, The Viking Press, 1966)

proselytize (verb) *To convert from one religion, opinion, or party to another; to evangelize.*

Mr. Lovett teaches the Historical and Literary Aspects of the Old Testament, but he does not **proselytize** the Christian faith or teach religion at all. (From *God and Man at Yale*, p. 6, Regnery Books, 1986)

prosody (noun) *A method or style of versification.*

To pray during the gymnastic exercise of the modern mass, athwart a vernacular **prosody** that belongs in the Chamber of Literary Horrors, is an exercise in self-discipline achieved most easily by the blind and the deaf. (From *Right Reason*, p. 373, Doubleday & Company, 1985)

pro tanto (Latin) *To a certain extent; proportionately; commensurately.*

Communities blockwide or greater will be given **pro tanto** relief in their property taxes, sufficient to pay the local police bills. (From *The Unmaking of a Mayor*, p. 91, The Viking Press, 1966)

provenance (noun) *Place of origin.*

There was just the trace of an accent there, and Blackford could not guess its **provenance**, and of course would not have presumed to inquire. (From *Saving the Queen*, p. 33, Doubleday & Company, 1976)

psephologist (noun) *Someone who pursues the scientific study of elections.*

I announce that the **psephologists** have just completed a study that reveals that the participation of Princeton volunteers was the very thing that brought brother Jim [newly elected junior senator for New York] over the edge of victory. (From *Cruising Speed*, p. 76, G. P. Putnam's Sons, 1971)

purposive (adjective) *Tending to fulfill a conscious purpose or design.*

Individual rights of the sort that for generations were never supposed to be prey to government actions are cheerily disposed of as unjustifiable impedimenta in the way of **purposive** and enlightened state policies. (From *God and Man at Yale*, p. 79, Regnery Books, 1986)

putsch (noun) *A secretly plotted and suddenly executed attempt to overthrow a government or governing body.*

Mr. Adam Clayton Powell, Jr., would be objectionable as a leader whether he became leader following a city-wide **putsch,** or whether he became leader having got one hundred percent of the vote of his constituency. (From *The Unmaking of a Mayor,* p. 253, The Viking Press, 1966)

qua (preposition) *In the character, role, or capacity of; as.*

The Republicans were increasingly maneuvered into the position of believing in John Lindsay **qua** John Lindsay, as their shriveled justification for their original enthusiasm gave way under the weight of one after another entanglement with the same old crowd. (From *The Unmaking of a Mayor,* p. 44, The Viking Press, 1966)

querencia (noun) *An area in the arena taken by the bull because he feels safe there.*

Dulles stared at him silently, then turned to talk with Griswold. Black eased away toward Sally—his **querencia,** his love—to lick his wounds. (From *Saving the Queen,* p. 44, Doubleday & Company, 1976)

Rabelaisian (adjective) *Marked by gross, robust humor, extravagance of caricature, or bold naturalism.*

I remember the old "Truth or Consequences" game they used to play over the radio, which towards the end was coming up with consequences so extravagant as to satisfy **Rabelaisian** appetites for the absurd. (From *Cruising Speed,* p. 59, G. P. Putnam's Sons, 1971)

raffish (adjective) *Vulgar; showy.*

Maria wandered over to the entertainment district and was not entirely surprised to find herself talking with a **raffish** man who in his plushily upholstered office looked at her carefully, asked her matter-of-factly to disrobe, examined her again, focused lights on her from various angles, and agreed to employ her. (From *Mongoose, R.I.P.,* p. 122, Random House, 1987)

recondite (adjective) *Very difficult to understand and beyond the reach of ordinary comprehension and knowledge.*

There is a luxurious offering at Yale of courses in the **recondite** byways of human knowledge, wonderful to behold. (From *God and Man at Yale,* p. xlviii, Regnery Books, 1986)

redoubt (noun) *A small, defensive, secure place; stronghold.*

At places like Harvard, Yale, and Princeton lecturers run into difficulty, because these colleges are not accustomed to paying their speakers the commercial rates; and speakers tend to indulge them, in part out of tradition, in part out of a curiosity to have a look at what used to be the **redoubts** of social and intellectual patricians. (From *Cruising Speed,* p. 67, G. P. Putnam's Sons, 1971)

regicide (noun) *The killing or murder of a king.*

After the original *World-Telegram* story charging vandalism, rape, and **regicide,** the Conservative Party took the precaution of instructing its captains to telephone to inquire whether any complaints had actually been lodged. (From *The Unmaking of a Mayor,* p. 234, The Viking Press, 1966)

reification (noun) *The conversion of something abstract into something concrete.*

A gesture of recognition—of Martin Luther King's courage, of the galvanizing quality of a rhetoric that sought out a **reification** of the dream of brotherhood—is consistent with the ideals of the country, and a salute to a race of people greatly oppressed during much of U.S. history. (From *Right Reason,* pp. 375–76, Doubleday & Company, 1985)

rescind (verb) *To take back; annul, cancel.*

"I've a terrific idea!" said Blackford. "Why don't you kidnap the Queen, hypnotize her, then send her back and have her **rescind** her invitation to me to do the eulogy?" (From *Saving the Queen,* p. 234, Doubleday & Company, 1976)

res manet (Latin) *"There the matter rests."*

School dropouts under the age of fourteen will be sent to special vocational schools, whose administrators will be especially trained. Successful graduates of one year's experience will be qualified to reenter public schools. [*Res manet*] (From *The Unmaking of a Mayor*, p. 93, The Viking Press, 1966)

reticulation (noun) *A network; an arrangement of lines resembling a net.*

When a number of colleges and universities were given over to the thousand blooms of the youth revolution, many of the same people who sharpened their teeth on *God and Man at Yale* were preternaturally silent. They feasted on ideological **reticulation**. (From *God and Man at Yale*, p. xxxii, Regnery Books, 1986)

ribaldry (noun) *Language characterized by broad, indecent humor.*

Before we knew it, FBI chief J. Edgar Hoover was bugging motels in which Martin Luther King spent the night, which tapes resulted in vocal **ribaldry** not suitable for family cassettes. (From Mr. Buckley's syndicated column, "On the Right")

rodomontade (noun) *A vain, exaggerated boast; a bragging speech; empty bluster.*

I teased my brother Jim by sending him, framed, the headline in the *New York Post* the day after the election, "Buckley: 'I AM THE NEW POLITICS,'" getting back from him a winced note of pain at this lapidary record of what looked like a lapse into **rodomontade**. (From *Cruising Speed*, p. 121, G. P. Putnam's Sons, 1971)

rump (adjective) *Relating to a fragment or remainder; as (a) a parliament, committee, or other group carrying on in the name of the original body after the departure or expulsion of a large number of its members; (b) a small group usually claiming to be representative of a larger whole that arises independently or breaks off from a parent body.*

Mr. Lindsay's Republican Party is a **rump** affair, captive in his and others' hands, no more representative of the body of Republican thought than the Democratic Party in Mississippi is representative of the Democratic Party nationally. (From *The Unmaking of a Mayor*, p. 105, The Viking Press, 1966)

sacrosanct (adjective) *Most holy or sacred; inviolable.*

Here in England, three thousand miles away from America, Blackford found it a corporate affront that a **sacrosanct** master should feel free to belittle so great a man as Lindbergh. (From *Saving the Queen*, p. 65, Doubleday & Company, 1976)

salacious (adjective) *Marked by lecherousness or lewdness; lustful.*

The television reporters ask their own questions and always gravitate to the most **salacious** issues of the day, preferably personal. (From *The Unmaking of a Mayor*, p. 267, The Viking Press, 1966)

salutary (adjective) *Effecting or designed to effect an improvement; remedial.*

By age fifteen Rolando had decided he wished to go into an entirely different kind of life—bloody, yes, but bloody-**salutary**, not bloody-destructive. (From *Mongoose, R.I.P.*, p. 17, Random House, 1987)

salvific (adjective) *Having the intent to save or admit to salvation.*

If we undertake a systematic, devoted, evangelical effort to instruct the people of the world that the Soviet Union is animated not by a **salvific** ideology, but by a reactionary desire to kill and torture, intimidate and exploit others, for the benefit of its own recidivist national appetites for imperialism, we will have done, by peaceful means, what is so long overdue. (From *Right Reason*, p. 230, Doubleday & Company, 1985)

sanguinary (adjective) *Bloodthirsty, murderous.*

Let us concede that the death squads of San Salvador are composed primarily of sadistic opportunists who, taking cover in the civil war, pursue their acquisitive and **sanguinary** interests relatively unmolested because of the preoccupation of civil authority with that civil war. (From *Right Reason*, p. 305, Doubleday & Company, 1985)

saprophytic (adjective) *Obtaining nourishment osmotically from dead matter.*
If the modern politician's invocation of Lincoln is to be taken as other than opportunistic and **saprophytic,** the invoker must describe what it is about Lincoln that he understands to be the quintessential Lincoln. (From *The Unmaking of a Mayor,* p. 78, The Viking Press, 1966)

saraband (noun) *The music of the saraband, a stately court dance of the seventeenth and eighteenth centuries resembling the minuet and evolved from a quick Spanish dance of oriental origin.*
Rosalyn [Tureck] giggles her aristocratic warm giggle, leans over, and whispers that she will play me the **saraband** she knows I love. (From *Cruising Speed,* p. 143, G. P. Putnam's Sons, 1971)

schuss (noun) *A straight, high-speed run on skis.*
Ah, the ideological coda, how it afflicts us all! And how paralyzingly sad that someone who can muse over the desirability of converting New York into an independent state should, having climbed to such a peak, **schuss** down the same old slope, when the mountains beckon him on to new, exhilarating runs. (From *The Unmaking of a Mayor,* p. 39, The Viking Press, 1966)

scintilla (noun) *A barely perceptible manifestation; the slightest particle or trace.*
In the two years he had known her, Blackford had never seen in Sally a **scintilla** of curiosity about anything scientific. (From *Saving the Queen,* p. 26, Doubleday & Company, 1976)

sciolism (noun) *Superficial knowledge; a show of learning without substantial foundation.*
I wasn't sure enough of myself on the facts of Roger Bacon's life, so I didn't note down to challenge Clark on the point; and anyway, he who lives off the exposure of **sciolism** will die from the exposure of **sciolism.** (From *Cruising Speed,* p. 122, G. P. Putnam's Sons, 1971)

scurrility (noun) *Abusive language usually marked by coarse or indecent wording or innuendo, unjust denigration, or clownish jesting.*
I have seen libelers try to excuse their own **scurrilities** (what a wonderful word!) against me by pleading that I am a public figure, leaving open the question whether what was said about me was said with actual malice. (From *Cruising Speed,* p. 185, G. P. Putnam's Sons, 1971)

secularist (noun) *One who advocates a view of life or of any particular matter based on the premise that religion and religious considerations should be ignored or purposely excluded.*
Best equipped to challenge the **secularists** in the Department of Philosophy is Professor Robert L. Calhoun, an ordained minister vastly respected as a scholar, as a lecturer, and as a man. (From *God and Man at Yale,* p. 19, Regnery Books, 1986)

seemliness (noun) *The quality or state of conforming to accepted standards of good form or taste; propriety.*
Such Republican judges as there are, are there simply because judicial **seemliness** requires that a second party should be seen, if not heard—if only to provide those comfortable democratic delusions which are formally satisfying. (From *The Unmaking of a Mayor,* p. 40, The Viking Press, 1966)

seine (verb) *To fish out or pluck from the sea.*
The arraignment and the trial were conducted with the care and precision of an Apollo moon launch, and it is questionable whether even Edgar Smith will succeed in **seining** out of the experience reversible error. (From *Right Reason,* p. 210, Doubleday & Company, 1985)

sequester (verb) *To set apart; separate for a special purpose; remove, segregate.*
One can be compassionate for the president of the New York Stock Exchange who goes to jail for his greed, and for the rapist who is unable to control his lust. But it is

necessary to **sequester** the transgressors, whatever the genealogy of the aberrations. (From *The Unmaking of a Mayor*, p. 98, The Viking Press, 1966)

seriatim (adverb) *In a series; serially.*

A short, bright, engaging review of the day-in-the-life of each of the candidates appeared **seriatim** in *The New Yorker* during October. (From *The Unmaking of a Mayor*, p. 236, The Viking Press, 1966)

shibboleth (noun) *(1) A word or saying characteristically used by the adherents of a party, sect, or belief and usually regarded as empty of real meaning; (2) a commonplace saying or idea; platitude, truism.*

I appear before you as the only candidate for Mayor of New York who has not a word to say in defense of the proposition that New York ought to stay as big as it is, let alone grow bigger. Is there an argument in defense of this **shibboleth**? (From *The Unmaking of a Mayor*, p. 37, The Viking Press, 1966)

sloth (noun) *Disinclination to action or labor; sluggishness, laziness, idleness, indolence.*

Those who rail against the [microcomputer] chip do so for the most practical reason: They have not mastered its use. They strive for metaphysical formulations to justify their hidden little secret (**sloth** and fear). (From Mr. Buckley's syndicated column, "On the Right")

sonorous (adjective) *Marked by excessively heavy, high-flown, grandiloquent, or self-assured effect or style.*

I maintain that **sonorous** pretensions notwithstanding, Yale does subscribe to an orthodoxy: there are limits within which its faculty members must keep their opinions if they wish to be "tolerated." (From *God and Man at Yale*, p. 151, Regnery Books, 1986)

sophistry (noun) *Reasoning that is superficially plausible but actually fallacious.*

The guardians of this sustaining core of civilization have abdicated their responsibility to mankind. And what is more depressing, they have painted their surrender with flamboyant words and systematic **sophistry** in their efforts to persuade us that far better things are really in store for the world by virtue of their inactivity. (From *God and Man at Yale*, p. 193, Regnery Books, 1986)

soritical (adjective) *Of or relating to an abridged form of stating a series of syllogisms in a series of propositions so arranged that the predicate of each one that precedes forms the subject of each one that follows and the conclusion unites the subject of the first proposition with the predicate of the last proposition. For instance: $A = B$, $B = C$, $C = D$, $D = E$. Therefore, $A = E$.*

I remember suggesting to Dan Mahoney that I make the **soritical** leap and announce quite frankly that the defeat of Lindsay was an objective of the Conservative Party. (From *The Unmaking of a Mayor*, p. 301, The Viking Press, 1966)

sotto voce (adverb) *Under the breath; in an undertone.*

"Mr. Oakes, this is Mr. Allen Dulles, deputy director of the Central Intelligence Agency." Black shook hands, and then winked mysteriously and asked *sotto voce:* "How's tricks?" (From *Saving the Queen*, p. 44, Doubleday & Company, 1976)

specious (adjective) *Superficially beautiful or attractive or coveted, but not so in reality; apparently right and proper; superficially fair, just, or correct.*

Note well that Professor Kirkland raised no objection to the fact that what later was demonstrated to be a **specious** biological generalization was taught to several generations of students. (From *God and Man at Yale*, p. 153, Regnery Books, 1986)

splenetic (adjective) *Characterized by morose bad temper, sullen malevolence, or spiteful, peevish anger.*

The war engaged all the **splenetic** instincts of Khomeini, and he urged all Iran's young people to die in the ecstasy of a mission that transcribed God's will. (From Mr. Buckley's syndicated column, "On the Right")

stricture (noun) *Something that closely restrains or limits.*

I am confident that the scholar who holds her in esteem and the scholar who does not could both make their way into Yale. Does this mean that Yale, true to the **strictures** of academic freedom, is unconcerned about the teacher's values? (From *God and Man at Yale*, p. 147, Regnery Books, 1986)

suasion (noun) *The act or an instance of urging, convincing, or persuading.*

It is important that the college student's choice be his own, for it is all the more valuable to him if there has been no exterior **suasion** on behalf of one or the other protagonist. (From *God and Man at Yale*, p. 145, Regnery Books, 1986)

sub specie aeternitatis (adverb) (Latin) *Viewed under the aspects of the heavens; in its essential or universal form or nature.*

Political speculation is necessarily framed by the values that contemporary history composes. So that any distinction-making, however relevant *sub specie aeternitatis,* simply ought not to be attempted in addressing, for instance, six thousand policemen three weeks after the horrors of Selma, Alabama. (From *The Unmaking of a Mayor,* p. 26, The Viking Press, 1966)

succubus (noun) *An evil spirit, but the victim, or supine partner of, the aggressive incubus.*

Blackford thought back on the agonies of the Bruderschaft, and for a moment said, reverently, nothing by way of riposte. This quickly communicated a hint of resistance to her. He got back into his customary role, the **succubus** of her taunts. (From *Mongoose, R.I.P.,* p. 31, Random House, 1987)

sunder (verb) *To break or force apart, in two, or off from a whole; separate, usually by rending, cutting, or breaking, or by intervening time or space; sever.*

David Lindsay and Jim Buckley became fast friends at Yale, and of all the personal dislodgements of the campaign I am most grievously concerned over the possibility that it may have **sundered** that friendship. (From *The Unmaking of a Mayor,* p. 95, The Viking Press, 1966)

supererogatory (adjective) *Verbally redundant, superfluous.*

[On having been requested to send a seconding letter by the sponsor of Franklin Delano Roosevelt, Jr., to the New York Yacht Club] I would have thought that my own inclinations on the matter of his proposed membership would have been (a) **supererogatory;** or (b) ideologically suspect. (From *Cruising Speed,* p. 38, G. P. Putnam's Sons, 1971)

supernal (adjective) *Being or coming from above; that which emanates from heaven.*

On the main highway he stopped, sticking up his thumb with that **supernal** confidence of the young that he would not be kept waiting. (From *Saving the Queen,* p. 51, Doubleday & Company, 1976)

supine (adjective) *Lying, so to speak helplessly, on one's back; manifesting mental or moral lethargy; indifferent to one's duty or welfare or others' needs.*

No one not apathetic to the value issues of the day can in good conscience contribute to the ascendancy of ideas he considers destructive of the best in civilization. To do so is to be guilty of **supine** and unthinking fatalism of the sort that is the surest poison of democracy and the final abnegation of man's autonomy. (From *God and Man at Yale,* p. 196, Regnery Books, 1986)

surcease (noun) *Cessation; especially a temporary suspension, intermission, or respite.*

Having got the votes of men and women who, in this city, are unemployable, the politicians let them institutionalize themselves as social derelicts, at liberty to breed children who, suffering from inherited disadvantages, alternatively seek **surcease** in hyperstimulation and in indolence. (From *The Unmaking of a Mayor,* p. 38, The Viking Press, 1966)

synoptic (adjective) *Affording a general view of a whole, of what came before.*

In the creation of comic strips, there is the nagging mechanical—and therefore artistic—problem of reintroducing the reader to the **synoptic** point at which he was dropped the day before. (From *Right Reason*, p. 385, Doubleday & Company, 1985)

tacit (adjective) *Implied or indicated but not actually expressed.*

One must hope that the President's **tacit** approval of Dole's Bill was wrung from him in the middle of a coughing fit, during which Mr. Reagan could not collect his senses. (From *Right Reason*, p. 89, Doubleday & Company, 1985)

tangential (adjective) *Deviating widely and sometimes erratically; divergent; touching lightly or in the most tenuous way; incidental.*

Why did Wagner subtly underwrite the distorted newspaper accounts? The necessary answer, barring **tangential** motives of unscientific bearing, is—because to do so made good politics. (From *The Unmaking of a Mayor*, p. 21, The Viking Press, 1966)

tantamount (adjective) *Equivalent in value, significance, or effect.*

In most situations only penny-wise thinking and inherent dishonesty would lead to a prescription by the subsidizer as to the outcome of research. This would be **tantamount** to a cigarette company's granting money for research into cancer, with the stipulation that it shall not be discovered that tobacco is in any way conducive to the spread of the disease. (From *God and Man at Yale*, p. 190, Regnery Books, 1986)

tenet (noun) *A principle, dogma, belief, or doctrine generally held to be true; especially one held in common by members of an organization, group, movement, or profession.*

It seems unjust to employ pernicious techniques to undermine the **tenets** of Christianity. Most students are unaffected, but some, impressionable and malleable, lose faith in God. (From *God and Man at Yale*, p. 16, Regnery Books, 1986)

theocracy (noun) *Government of a state by theological doctrine.*

But the state (under the Shah) was not run as a **theocracy**, and one wonders therefore exactly what it is that the Ayatollah has in mind when he speaks of an Islamic republic. (From *Right Reason*, p. 72, Doubleday & Company, 1985)

tort-feasor (noun) *One who is guilty of a wrongful act; a wrongdoer; a trespasser.*

The relevant questions, after the shooting down of the Korean airliner, were: (1) How does one punish a punishable act? (Answer: By demanding reparations.) (2) How does one take reasonable steps to see to it that such an act is not committed again? (Answer: By getting assurances from the **tort-feasor**.) (From *Right Reason*, p. 102, Doubleday & Company, 1985)

traduce (verb) *To lower or disgrace the reputation of; expose to shame or blame by utterance of falsehood or misrepresentation.*

A hundred organizations would lash out against Yale. They would accuse her of **traducing** education, of violating freedom. (From *God and Man at Yale*, p. 226, Regnery Books, 1986)

troglodytic (adjective) *Relating to cave dwellers; dwelling in or involving residence in caves.*

His light suntan belied the **troglodytic** life spent plumbing the mysteries of spooks. (From *Saving the Queen*, p. 41, Doubleday & Company, 1976)

truncated (adjective) *Cut short.*

I try a **truncated** version of the talk I gave the night before, wondering whether I might just discover, in this new version, that it is better communicated short than long. (From *Cruising Speed*, p. 98, G. P. Putnam's Sons, 1971)

tumbril (noun) *A vehicle for carrying condemned persons (as, political prisoners during the French Revolution) to a place of execution.*

We're worried as hell over what Stalin is up to. A purge, maybe of classic proportions, is under way. The **tumbrils** are full and, as usual, full of his own past intimates. (From *Saving the Queen,* p. 122, Doubleday & Company, 1976)

tu quoque (adjective) *Referring to a retort charging an adversary with being or doing what he criticizes in others, as in: "So's your old man."*

At a meeting with the distinguished editors of a distinguished newspaper, the dark point was explicitly raised, and I knew there was no easy answer, save the old *tu quoque* argument. (From *The Unmaking of a Mayor,* p. 236, The Viking Press, 1966)

tutoyer (verb) *To address familiarly, from the French* tu *as distinguished from the more formal* vous.

I am, in public situations, disposed to formality. On *Firing Line,* even if I have **tutoyed** them for decades, I always refer to my guests as Mr., Mrs., or Miss So-and-So. (From *Cruising Speed,* p. 184, G. P. Putnam's Sons, 1971)

ultramontanist (noun) *One who favors greater supremacy of papal over national or diocesan authority in the Roman Catholic Church.*

Sister Elizabeth did not want Manhattanville to be referred to as a "Catholic college." Call Sister Elizabeth, I had asked Aggie Schmidt, an **ultramontanist** graduate of Manhattanville, and tell her we are going to have to discuss the question of Manhattanville's Catholicism on the program, because after all that's the kind of thing the program is about. (From *Cruising Speed,* p. 13, G. P. Putnam's Sons, 1971)

ululation (noun) *Howls or wails; cries of lamentation.*

The original idea [Kemp-Roth] was to reduce taxes evenhandedly. Since everyone knows that 10 percent of $100,000.00 is more than 10 percent of $10,000.00, the Reaganites should have been prepared for all that rhetoric about favoring the rich. But not having stressed the risks of excessive progressivity, they proved unready for it. Came then the big media **ululations** about the rich. (From *Right Reason,* p. 89, Doubleday & Company, 1985)

unctuous (adjective) *Revealing or marked by a smug, ingratiating, and false appearance or spirituality.*

I maintain that if you put every politician in New York who appears before you groveling and **unctuous** and prepared to turn the entire apparatus of New York and put it at your disposal on a silver tray—you will not substantially augment the happiness, the security, the sense of accomplishment of your own people. (From *The Unmaking of a Mayor,* p. 147, The Viking Press, 1966)

unmeeching (adjective) *Not cringing, sneaky, or whining in tone.*

Sometimes the politician will want to identify the demon, in which case the accusations are direct in reference and **unmeeching** in tone. (From *The Unmaking of a Mayor,* p. 21, The Viking Press, 1966)

untenable (adjective) *Unable to be defended or maintained.*

Opposition to the brand of collectivism espoused by Morgan or Tarshis or Samuelson is simply **untenable,** and what little recognition is given to that barely noticeable corps of economists who repudiate the collectivists' program is sometimes forthrightly savage. (From *God and Man at Yale,* p. 81, Regnery Books, 1986)

usurious (adjective) *Involving charging an unconscionable or exorbitant rate or amount of interest.*

A tricky diplomatic business, but the CAB recognized a responsibility to protect American consumers, and therefore acted favorably on a suit the effect of which could be to deny landing rights to foreign carriers that continued to extort from passengers the **usurious** rate. (From *Right Reason,* p. 46, Doubleday & Company, 1985)

vainglorious (adjective) *Marked by ostentation or excessive pride in one's achievements.*
To have mentioned in this book that I had been the co-chairman of an Inter-Faith Conference would have been irrelevant, perhaps even **vainglorious**. (From *God and Man at Yale,* p. xxiii, Regnery Books, 1986)

vapid (adjective) *Lacking flavor, zest, animation, or spirit.*
All the questions were the obvious ones, and it gave me a chance to formulate some of those **vapid** responses that are indispensable to the success of a constitutional monarch. (From *Saving the Queen,* p. 185, Doubleday & Company, 1976)

vestigial (adjective) *Remaining or surviving, however degenerate, atrophied, or imperfect.*
When the Poles declared martial law and a country of forty million people found itself without the **vestigial** liberties it had been exercising, there was an outcry. (From *Right Reason,* p. 97, Doubleday & Company, 1985)

viscous (adjective) *Having a ropy or glutinous consistency and the quality of sticking or adhering.*
I cannot think as the crow flies for very long, unless I am wrestling with somebody, or something, more **viscous** than my own runny thoughts. (From *Cruising Speed,* p. 183, G. P. Putnam's Sons, 1971)

vitiate (verb) *To impair the value or quality of.*
I asked Chiang Ching-kuo, the son of Chiang Kai-shek, whether there was any possibility that Taiwan might make an alliance with the Soviet Union at some point in the future, if necessary to substitute for **vitiating** Western support (President Carter had recently booted CCK's ambassador out of Washington, replacing him with China's). (From *On the Firing Line: The Public Life of Our Public Figures,* p. 334, Random House, 1989)

volatile (adjective) *Characterized by quick or unexpected changes; not steady or predictable.*
Pyotr Ivanovich was a **volatile** man who felt that genuine emotion cannot be communicated except by totalist vocal measures. (From *Saving the Queen,* p. 107, Doubleday & Company, 1976)

voluminous (adjective) *Filling or capable of filling a large volume or several volumes; profuse, exorbitant.*
We should face it that understanding the Russians isn't something we are ever likely to master. James Reston struggles valiantly in his column and says perhaps they shot down the Korean airliner because they were invaded by Napoleon. That's as good a guess as any. Even concentrated Soviet-watchers are surprised by the **voluminous** lies being told about the downing of KA flight 007. (From *Right Reason,* p. 99, Doubleday & Company, 1985)

votary (noun) *A sworn adherent; an ardent enthusiast; a devoted admirer; a disciple, fan.*
A senator might say, "We are going to do everything we can to help the Red Cross," by which he means he, his administrative assistants, his uncles and aunts, friends and **votaries** will jointly do what they all can for the Red Cross. (From *The Unmaking of a Mayor,* p. 85, The Viking Press, 1966)

vox populi (noun) *Popular sentiment.*
The Inquiring Photographer, a New York City institution which delivers the **vox populi** for the *New York Daily News,* asks questions of the people it interviews, the answers to which are often superficial or wrong-headed. (From *The Unmaking of a Mayor,* p. 238, The Viking Press, 1966)

warrant (verb) *To declare or maintain with little or no fear of being contradicted or belied; be certain; be sure that.*
"The collegers at Eton," said Mr. Alex-Hiller, "there on scholarships are selected from the poorer classes. This is not to say that there are brighter boys among the poor than among the rich."

"No, that doesn't say it, but I **warrant** it's true," said the queen. (From *Saving the Queen*, p. 168, Doubleday & Company, 1976)

Weltanschauungen (noun) *Philosophies of life; ideology; the plural form of* Weltanschauung.

The answers to The Inquiring Photographer, in twenty-five words or less, are not intended to be taken as conclusive transcriptions of the interviewee's ***Weltanschauungen***. (From *The Unmaking of a Mayor*, p. 238, The Viking Press, 1966)

whimsical (adjective) *Characterized by a capricious or eccentric idea.*

Smith's prison mates administered a thorough beating to the child-killer. Sure, Smith's companions thought the murder of a fifteen-year-old a repellent form of crime; but these nice discriminations, among men who mug and rape and kill, are **whimsical**. In their eyes, Edgar Smith's crime was that he had confessed guilt to a murder after maintaining his innocence for twenty years. (From *Right Reason*, p. 200, Doubleday & Company, 1985)

wreak (verb) *To bring about (harm); cause, inflict.*

Most of the analysts reasoned that here was a hard-planned, nationally subsidized, highly organized campaign to **wreak** vengeance on John Lindsay. (From *The Unmaking of a Mayor*, p. 100, The Viking Press, 1966)

LEXICON III—1993

abjure (verb) *To disclaim formally or disclaim upon oath.*

An insurrectionary movement dominated by men committed to Communist doctrine and methods who refused to **abjure** the use of force and terrorism to achieve their goals. (From "On the Right")

absolutized (verb) *Made absolute; converted to an absolute.*

Joyce's *Ulysses* was okayed by a federal court after a long struggle, and pretty soon so was *Lady Chatterley's Lover*, and since then, such a book as *American Psycho*, the First Amendment having been **absolutized** in its application. (From "On the Right")

accelerability (noun) *The capacity to speed up; potential for quickening.*

The **accelerability** of economic development by force of will (a premise of the Point Four Program) is an article of faith for leading liberal spokesmen. (From *Up from Liberalism*, p. 168, Stein & Day, 1984)

acumen (noun) *Acuteness of mind; keenness of perception; discernment or discrimination.*

I bet his students did, all right—if they called Mr. Root a fascist-by-association, they might well have earned a reward for showing high critical **acumen**. (From *Up from Liberalism*, p. 99, Stein & Day, 1984)

adamantine (adjective) *Unyielding, inflexible.*

He gave the relevant details of the life of Bertram Heath. He stressed the central role of Alistair Fleetwood as the formative influence in Bertram Heath's life. He underlined the **adamantine** refusal of Fleetwood to any interview concerning Bertram Heath. (From *High Jinx*, p. 153, Doubleday & Company, 1986)

adducing (verb) *Bringing forward (as an example, reason, proof) for consideration in a discussion, analysis, or contention; offering, presenting, citing. [Used in 1991 calendar in a different form, namely,* **adduce** *(v.)]*

How mischievous is the habit of **adducing** reasons behind everything that is done! I can unassailably delight in lobster and despise crabmeat so long as I refrain from giving reasons. (From *Rumbles Left and Right*, p. 33, G. P. Putnam's Sons, 1963)

ad rem (adjective) *Pertinent to the matter or person at issue; directed at the specific thing.*

Ad rem depersonalizations are necessary to social life, and are not any more inhumane intrinsically than the motions of the mother counting noses before deciding how much dinner to cook. (From *Rumbles Left and Right,* p. 132, G. P. Putnam's Sons, 1963)

adulator (noun) *One who praises effusively and slavishly, flatters excessively, fawns upon.*
Edward Bennett Williams introduced to the jury a man who happens to be a Communist Party-liner in international affairs and an **adulator** of Nikita Khrushchev. (From *Rumbles Left and Right,* p. 88, G. P. Putnam's Sons, 1963)

adumbrate (verb) *To foreshadow, symbolize, or prefigure in a not altogether conclusive or not immediately evident way; to give a sketchy representation of; to outline broadly, omitting details.*
What Richard Rovere resists so fiercely, for reasons he has not thought through, is the insinuation that what one might call the Liberal Establishment holds to a definable orthodoxy (his going on to **adumbrate** that orthodoxy was sheer brinksmanship). (From *Rumbles Left and Right,* p. 20, G. P. Putnam's Sons, 1963)

adventitious (adjective) *Coming from another source; added or appended extrinsically and not sharing original, essential, or intrinsic nature.*
You cannot accomplish the elimination of twenty-five million Xs by so simple an arrangement as multiplying by twenty-five million the **adventitious** elimination of a single X, effected in spontaneous circumstances. (From *Gratitude,* p. 80, Random House, 1990)

Aesopian (adjective) *Conveying an innocent meaning to an outsider but a concealed meaning to an informed member of a conspiracy or underground movement.*
A great deal depends on the question whether Saddam Hussein can think straight, because much of what has come from him, and goes out to him, is rendered in the **Aesopian** mode: stuff that says one thing but implies or seeks to imply another. (From "On the Right")

aggrandize (verb) *To make great or greater (as in power, honor, or wealth).*
We turned over to their Communist oppressors tens of millions not only by defaulting on our moral obligations and diminishing our identification with justice, but also by **aggrandizing** greatly the enemy's power. (From *Rumbles Left and Right,* p. 116, G. P. Putnam's Sons, 1963)

agnosticism (noun) *The doctrine that the existence or nature of any ultimate reality is unknown and probably unknowable or that any knowledge about matters of ultimate concern is impossible or improbable.*
The rhetorical impulses of the day are sluggish in the extreme; they place an immoderate emphasis on moderation, and promote a philosophical gentility, deriving from **agnosticism**, that permeates our moral intellectual life to its distinct disadvantage. (From *Up from Liberalism,* p. 55, Stein & Day, 1984)

allurement (noun) *Something that attracts or entices.*
A great arsenal of rights and perquisites and **allurements** and toys has been organized for the benefit of youth, and it has been questioned whether it does young people the good Americans wish for them to continue in the direction we have taken with respect to their growing years. (From *Gratitude,* p. 122, Random House, 1990)

ambient (adjective) *Surrounding on all sides; encompassing, enveloping.*
Here are some **ambient** data by which we gain perspective. It costs $35,000 per year to maintain a soldier in the army. It costs $30,000 per year to keep an inmate in jail. It costs $13,000 per year for each VISTA volunteer. It costs $20,000 per student for four years of ROTC. (From *Gratitude,* p. 128, Random House, 1990)

amenities (noun) *Social courtesies; pleasantries; civilities.*
They didn't exchange even routine goodbyes. The Director and his principal spymaster were not, really, friends. When there were **amenities** exchanged they tended to be formalistic. (From *High Jinx,* p. 34, Doubleday & Company, 1986)

amorphous (adjective) *(a) Without clearly drawn limits; not precisely indicated or established; (b) without definite nature or character; not allowing clear classification or analysis.*

The National Center for Policy Analysis, based in Dallas, has issued a report called "Tax Fairness: Myths and Reality" . . . which is as lucid and pointed as Goreism is convoluted and **amorphous**. (From "On the Right")

amulet (noun) *Charm often inscribed with a spell, magic incantation, or symbol and believed to protect the wearer against evil.*

The President should be given a line-item veto, sure, but those who think the budget deficit is as easy to solve as by giving the Chief Executive this **amulet** will have to think again. (From "On the Right")

anfractuous (adjective) *Full of twists and turns; winding; tortuous.*

Alistair Fleetwood had several reactions to what he had been told. Triumph, clearly: Unless he had drastically misunderstood the **anfractuous** message of Alice Goodyear Corbett, the Great God Beria had backed down and agreed to see him. (From *High Jinx*, p. 190, Doubleday & Company, 1986)

anthropomorphize (verb) *To attribute a human form or personality to forces or things greater than human.*

But it's also true that his was a critical as well as a symbolic (and telegenic) role, and that the American habit is to **anthropomorphize**—Napoleon, not his footsoldiers, is lionized. (From "On the Right")

antimacassar (noun) *A cover thrown over the backs or arms of chairs to protect them from Macassar hair oil or other soilage; thus, tidily, fussily old-fashioned.*

To the argument that in combat conditions it is a burden to provide two sets of washroom facilities, the pleaders for what they call women's rights argue to the effect that in combat situations, **antimacassar** niceties become simply irrelevant, and that, after all, even in the narrow confines of a foxhole, it is possible to make token adjustments. (From "On the Right")

antiquarian (adjective) *Of or belonging to the antiquities, the study of antiquities, or old times.*

The direction we must travel requires a broadmindedness that strikes us as **antiquarian** and callous. (From *Up from Liberalism*, p. 224, Stein & Day, 1984)

aphoristic (adjective) *Characterized by concise, artful, quotable statements or principles; terse and often ingenious formulations of truth or sentiment.*

As it happens, the camera in Hanover is zooming in on a disaffected young staffer, a Chinese-American who had twice been reprimanded by the staff of *The Dartmouth Review* for seeking to insert bawdy quotations into the page given over to reproducing **aphoristic** or amusing quotes. (From "On the Right")

apogee (noun) *The farthest or highest point.*

Clive Bell observed that the grandeur and nobility of the Allied cause [during World War I] "swelled in ever vaster proportions every time it was restated"—reaching its **apogee** in our explicitly formulated determination to make the world safe for democracy. (From *Up from Liberalism*, p. 148, Stein & Day, 1984)

arrogation (noun) *To claim or seize without right; appropriate to oneself arrogantly; ascribe or attribute without reason.*

In the long view of it, conservatives have tended to be suspicious of the **arrogation** of power by the Executive. (From "On the Right")

arterial (adjective) *Of or designating a route of transportation carrying a main flow with many branches.*

The street outside was a heavily used **arterial** road running into London. (From *High Jinx*, p. 50, Doubleday & Company, 1986)

artifact (noun) *A usually simple object showing human workmanship or modification, as distinguished from a natural object.*

It is encouraging when Professor Galbraith is struck rather by his craftsmanship than by the **artifact.** Michelangelo would have been entitled to admire anything he had sculpted, even gallows. (From *Up from Liberalism,* p. xi, Stein & Day, 1984)

asperity (noun) *Roughness of manner or temper.*

Brother Hildred asked "Leo" if he would like to visit the school's physics laboratory that afternoon. Tucker replied that he would not like to visit it this afternoon, tomorrow, next month, or next year. But quickly he recoiled from his apparent **asperity,** and simply said he did not wish to revisit any aspect of his past professional life. (From *Tucker's Last Stand,* p. 31, Random House, 1990)

atavistic (adjective) *The reappearance, after a considerable interval, of an organism or cultural habit. [Used in 1991 calendar in a different form, namely,* **atavist** *(noun)]*

When it becomes self-evident that biological, intellectual, cultural, and psychic similarities among races render social separation capricious and **atavistic,** then the myths will begin to fade, as they have done in respect of the Irish, the Italians, the Jews. (From *Rumbles Left and Right,* p. 96, G. P. Putnam's Sons, 1963)

athwart (preposition) *Across; from one side to another; against; in opposition to.*

Sometimes one is tempted to take a bucketful of that clayey mud resembling creamy peanut butter and drip it over the heads of the Luddite lobby that stands **athwart** progress yelling Stop! (From "On the Right")

atomistic (adjective) *An object or concept viewed as particles of the whole.*

I do not believe it is undignified to confess to having been critically influenced by a teacher, or a faculty, or a book; but the accent these days is so strong on **atomistic** intellectual independence that to suggest such a thing is highly inflammatory. (From *Up from Liberalism,* Stein & Day, 1984, p. 96.)

aught (noun) *One iota, zero, cipher.*

One irrepressible senior, who did not care **aught** for ideology, but was bent on cashing in on those political impulses, announced that after graduation he would launch a firm to take over the foreign policy of sovereign states. (From *Up from Liberalism,* p. 138, Stein & Day, 1984)

augur (verb) *To predict or foretell, especially from signs or omens.*

Every delegate found a copy of that letter under his door the next morning; this generated wild rumors, huge resentments, a divided convention, a divided Republican Party, and **augured** a defeat in November. (From *Tucker's Last Stand,* p. 126, Random House, 1990)

becket (noun) *A simple device for holding something in place, as a small grommet or a loop of rope with a knot at one end to catch in an eye at the other.*

Racing to Bermuda in 1956, we would wear out a helmsman every half hour, even with the aid of a **becket** made out of several strands of shock cord. (From *Rumbles Left and Right,* p. 174, G. P. Putnam's Sons, 1963)

belletrism (noun) *An interest in belles lettres to the neglect of more practical or informative literature; literary aestheticism. [Used in 1992 calendar in a different form, namely,* **belletristic** *(adjective)]*

Though Chambers was a passionately literary man, always the intellectual, insatiably and relentlessly curious, in the last analysis it was action, not **belletrism,** that moved him most deeply. (From *Rumbles Left and Right,* p. 148, G. P. Putnam's Sons, 1963)

beneficence (noun) *Active goodness or kindness. [Used in 1991 calendar in a different form, namely,* **beneficently** *(adverb)]*

It is prudent to take reasonable precautions against the abuse of a **beneficence**; but it is not correct to evaluate a beneficence on its abuse-potential. (From *Up from Liberalism*, p. 203, Stein & Day, 1984)

bereft (adjective) *Deprived, especially by death; stripped; dispossessed.*

Miss Sayers contends that the faculty for logical thought is a skill of which the entire contemporary generation has been **bereft**; I note, but do not press the point. (From *Up from Liberalism*, p. 37, Stein & Day, 1984)

billingsgate (noun) *Foul, vulgar, abusive talk (named after a fish market in London where such talk was routine).*

The student was drunk, it was way past midnight, he had descended into the campus yard and there began a racist **billingsgate** at the expense of blacks, Jews, and Catholics. (From "On the Right")

blighted (adjective) *Withered or destroyed; disappointed or frustrated.*

That and the obdurate superstition, more widespread than anything since the number thirteen was **blighted** as unlucky, that the rich are not paying their share of taxes. (From "On the Right")

bugbear (noun) *An object of irritation or source of dread or abhorrence; especially a continuing source of annoyance.*

[William Safire's] **bugbear** is the statement made last week jointly by Secretary of State James Baker and Soviet Foreign Minister Alexander Bessmertnykh, "The ministers continue to believe that a cessation of hostilities would be possible if Iraq would make an unequivocal commitment to withdraw from Kuwait." (From "On the Right")

buncombe (noun) *Talk that is empty, insincere, or merely for effect; humbug.*

Arafat's approach to a fresh plan in the Mideast was scorned by the government of Israel as so much diplomatic **buncombe**. (From "On the Right")

burin (noun) *An engraver's tool having a tempered steel shaft ground obliquely to a sharp point at one end and inserted into a handle at the other.*

Not so much in the service itself, then, as in the recall of service, engraved and re-engraved gently but insistently by a dozen **burins**, decade after decade, will the idea of rendering service become lodged in the moral memory. (From *Gratitude*, p. 154, Random House, 1990)

cadre (noun) *A nucleus or core group, especially of trained personnel or active members of an organization who are capable of assuming leadership or of training and indoctrinating others.*

Arafat, who looks like a gangster, often acted as one, and surrounded himself with a terrorist-minded **cadre** pleading the excuse that the Israelis deploy terrorists who need to be coped with. (From "On the Right")

caeteris paribus (adverbial phrase) (Latin) *"If all other relevant things remain unaltered."*

Life for the average citizen, **caeteris paribus**, is about the same, except that in Venezuela any dissenting political activity was forbidden, whereas in Mexico only meaningful political activity is forbidden. (From *Up from Liberalism*, p. 151, Stein & Day, 1984)

calumny (noun) *False charge or misrepresentation intended to blacken one's reputation; slander.*

The **calumny** Mr. Harriman attempted to pin on Mr. Rockefeller was that he would permit the Transit Authority to do the only thing the Transit Authority is permitted by law to do, namely, raise the fares. (From *Up from Liberalism*, p. 162, Stein & Day, 1984)

canard (noun) *A false or unfounded report or story; a groundless rumor or belief.*

There exists an obdurate superstition that the rich are not paying their share of taxes. This **canard** is spread by the Congressional Budget Office, which is a propaganda arm of the Democratic Party that ought to be indicted by the Food and Drug Administration for feeding the general population dangerous stimulants. (From "On the Right")

canon (noun) *A basic general principle or rule commonly accepted as true, valid, and fundamental.*

The **canon** of academic freedom is very clear: no one idea is to find corporate favor in educational institutions over another. (From *Up from Liberalism*, p. 93, Stein & Day, 1984)

capricious (adjective) *Given to changes of interest or attitude according to whims or passing fancies; not guided by steady judgment, intent, or purpose.*

What can be proved between competing crews on different boats? Not very much. There is a feature of ocean racing that can make a shambles of the whole thing. The poorest judgment can, under **capricious** circumstances, pay the handsomest rewards. (From *Rumbles Left and Right*, p. 171, G. P. Putnam's Sons, 1963)

carapace (noun) *A protective covering similar to a hard bony or chitinous outer covering such as the fused dorsal plates of a turtle.*

They sat around a table in a soundproofed, bug-proof room situated within a **carapace** especially designed to frustrate any efforts at electronic intrusion. (From *High Jinx*, p. 152, Doubleday & Company, 1986)

cartelization (noun) *The organization of an industry or commodity in one or more countries so as to dominate commerce.*

The refusal of the principal European nations to defy their farm blocs has suggested the possible **cartelization** of the European economy in the next year or two. (From "On the Right")

Carthaginian (adjective) *Totalist, as in the Roman destruction of Carthage in 146 B.C.*

And one has therefore to pause before proceeding to hold every Iraqi responsible for the crimes of Saddam Hussein and those front-line sadists who disgraced the irreducible maxims of human decency. To consign them all to perpetual poverty is **Carthaginian** in moral architecture, and we must desist from doing this. (From "On the Right")

Carthusian (adjective) *Austerely self-disciplined, self-denying; relating to the Carthusians, members of an austere religious order founded by St. Bruno in 1084.*

Since anyone who chooses to do anything other than become a **Carthusian** monk is almost certain to pay taxes, the prospect of relief from ten thousand dollars in taxes is both real and appropriate. (From *Gratitude*, p. 142, Random House, 1990)

catechetical (adjective) *Relying on questions and answers to inculcate orthodoxy.*

A sane man might seek to designate whatever figurative edifice shelters the household gods of American Liberalism, its high priests, its incense makers, and its **catechetical** press. (From *Rumbles Left and Right*, p. 21, G. P. Putnam's Sons, 1963)

caterwauling (verb) *Complaining loudly; screeching. [Used in 1991 calendar in a different form, namely, caterwaul (verb)]*

It is a story that has to do with all the **caterwauling** about nuclear waste and what to do with it. (From "On the Right")

cede (verb) *To give up, give over, grant, or concede, typically by treaty or negotiated pact.*

It is very dangerous to **cede** to a society the right to declare what are and what are not the freedoms worth exercising. (From *Up from Liberalism*, p. 210, Stein & Day, 1984)

centripetal (adjective) *Moving, proceeding, or acting in a direction toward a center or axis. [Used in 1992 calendar in a different form, namely, centripetalization (noun)]*

When stopped and everyone turns his eyes on me, I experience that mortification I always feel when I am the center of **centripetal** shafts of curiosity, resentment, perplexity. (From *Rumbles Left and Right*, p. 190, G. P. Putnam's Sons, 1963)

chattel (noun) *Movable item of personal property, such as a piece of furniture, an automobile, a head of livestock.*
It was for this reason, said Mr. Thomas, that he could speak so eloquently on the subject of the Dred Scott decision, which reduced human beings—Negroes—to **chattels**. (From "On the Right")

circumlocution (noun) *Indirect or roundabout expression. [Used in 1992 calendar in a different form, namely, **circumlocutory** (adjective)]*
She wanted to know what I was up to, and I told her about Vietnam, with the usual **circumlocutions**. (From *Tucker's Last Stand*, p. 88, Random House, 1990)

climacteric (adjective) *A decisive or critical period or stage in any course, career, or developmental process.*
The steel companies irked Murray Kempton by putting on a statistical passion play whose **climacteric** shows that if next summer the steel unions should go after and get higher wages, the American companies will no longer be able to compete with foreign steel companies. (From *Rumbles Left and Right*, p. 132, G. P. Putnam's Sons, 1963)

concert (verb) *To play or arrange by mutual agreement; to contrive or devise.*
I expect you will share your information with your superior. And if it becomes necessary, of course, the Prime Minister and the President will need to **concert** the postponements. (From *High Jinx*, p. 205, Doubleday & Company, 1986)

conduce (verb) *To lead or tend, especially with reference to a desirable result.*
I sense intuitively that while friendship does not necessarily grow out of experience shared, experience shared **conduces** to a bond from which friendship can grow. (From *Gratitude*, p. 161, Random House, 1990)

conflate (verb) *To bring together; collect, merge, fuse.*
Now, nobody is going to be able definitely to establish what happens for every million dollars a state spends on a national service program. Too many questions have to be **conflated** to permit a responsible prediction. (From *Gratitude*, p. 129, Random House, 1990)

confute (verb) *To overwhelm by argument. [Used in 1992 calendar in a different form, namely, **confutation** (noun)]*
Listening to Marshal Zhukov elaborate the virtues of communism, President Eisenhower found himself "very hard put to it" to **confute** him. (From *Up from Liberalism*, p. 192, Stein & Day, 1984)

contemporaneity (noun) *The quality or state of existing or occurring during the same time.*
They suffer, for one thing, from **contemporaneity**. What was allegedly done by the Democratic team is extremely current, whereas the Republicans came up with events some of which were three to eleven years old. (From "On the Right")

contraband (noun) *Goods or merchandise the importation, exportation, or sometimes possession of which is forbidden; also, smuggled goods.*
The trouble is, the Viets know that however much of the **contraband** they succeed in stopping at sea, the stuff is getting through. (From *Tucker's Last Stand*, p. 169, Random House, 1990)

convention (noun) *General agreement on or acceptance of certain practices or attitudes.*
Alice Goodyear Corbett (the **convention** had always been to use her full name, dating back to when, at age five, asked by a visiting Russian what her name was, she had answered, "*Moye imya* Alice Goodyear Corbett") had attended schools in Moscow from kindergarten. . . . (From *High Jinx*, p. 66, Doubleday & Company, 1986)

cooptation (noun) *Election or selection, usually to a body or group by vote of its own members.*
The **cooptation** of the unions by the bureaucracy forwarded fascism of various kinds, including the militant and ideological fascism of Mussolini's Italy in which the state

became precisely that object so correctly feared: the central unit of undifferentiated loyalty. (From *Gratitude,* p. 57, Random House, 1990)

cornucopia (noun) *An inexhaustible supply, variety.*

"Petit déjeuner, simple," she smiled at him, expressing admiration over the **cornucopia** he had ordered and was proceeding, with such wholesome pleasure, to devour. (From *Tucker's Last Stand,* p. 179, Random House, 1990)

cosmopolitanism (noun) *An excessive admiration and imitation of the cultural traits or achievement of others at the expense of the cultural identity or integrity of one's own land or region.*

Olga turned her head to one side and began to cry. She confessed that her parents had become afraid of having foreigners coming to their home, Comrade Stalin having pronounced recently on the dangers of **cosmopolitanism.** (From *High Jinx,* p. 67, Doubleday & Company, 1986)

Couéism (noun) *A system of psychotherapy based on optimistic autosuggestion; the founder is best remembered for his adage "Every day, and in every way, I am becoming better and better."*

The wreckage of two world wars fought for democracy is made up of the collapsed surrealisms of the ideologues, who succeeded finally in pushing **Couéism** right over the cliff. (From *Up from Liberalism,* p. 160, Stein & Day, 1984)

cryptographer (noun) *One adept in the art or process of writing in or deciphering secret code.*

Blackford Oakes reappeared at James Street early in the afternoon, and said to Trust that he would like to consult with an Agency **cryptographer.** (From *High Jinx,* p. 39, Doubleday & Company, 1986)

curio (noun) *Something arousing interest as being novel, rare, or bizarre.*

Why reissue the book? I think the reason for doing so is that it is a historical **curio,** and historical curios are often worth looking at, especially if they are unfamiliar to you. (From *Up from Liberalism,* p. xiii, Stein & Day, 1984)

declamation (noun) *A rhetorical speech; harangue.*

He is fiercely loyal to his family, while firm in insisting that he will not leave his fortune to the second generation as he doesn't believe in inherited wealth. That **declamation** drew a discreet wink from his devoted wife of forty-six years. (From "On the Right")

decrepitude (noun) *A state of ruin, dilapidation, or disrepair; lack of power; decay.*

If indeed the nation is united behind Mr. Eisenhower in this invitation to Mr. Khrushchev, then the nation is united behind an act of diplomatic sentimentality which can only confirm Khrushchev in the contempt he feels for the dissipated morale of a nation far gone, as the theorists of Marxism have all along contended, in **decrepitude.** (From *Rumbles Left and Right,* p. 35, G. P. Putnam's Sons, 1963)

démarche (noun) *A course of action; maneuver; a diplomatic representation or protest.*

He could not now report that his diplomatic initiative had worked in such a way as to give the Soviet Union the opportunity to use its great resources to stall the German **démarche** planned by the Western powers. (From *High Jinx,* p. 213, Doubleday & Company, 1986)

denature (verb) *To change the nature of; take natural qualities away from.*

What the Pope does say with such heartening fidelity is that socialism is an extravagant historical failure and—more—that socialism has a way of **denaturing** human beings by giving power to a central government which tends to use that power to suppress the individual and to come up with false gods for him to worship, like nationalized railroads (the example is mine, not His Holiness's). (From "On the Right")

denominate (verb) *To give a name to; call by a name; designate.*

"The Cold War is a part of the human condition for so long as you have two social phenomena which we can pretty safely **denominate** as constants." (From *Tucker's Last Stand,* p. 79, Random House, 1990)

deprecate (verb) *To disapprove of, often with mildness.*

It is a part of the Japanese tradition to exhibit great modesty, to disparage one's accomplishments, to **deprecate**, even, one's most sacred opinions. (From *Up from Liberalism*, p. 118, Stein & Day, 1984)

depreciate (verb) *To make to seem less valuable or important; to diminish in value.*

Sir Alistair said to Queen Caroline, "Ma'am, I cannot believe that you **depreciate** natural curiosity, even if you don't exhibit it." (From *High Jinx*, p. 61, Doubleday & Company, 1986)

deracinate (verb) *To separate from one's environment. [Used in 1991 calendar in a different form, namely, **deracination** (noun)]*

Randall Jarrell was saying Serious Things. He was describing a morally and intellectually **deracinated** environment in which students are encouraged to cut their ties to the world of standards and norms. (From *Up from Liberalism*, p. 124, Stein & Day, 1984)

desiccate (verb) *To drain of vitality, especially to divest of vigor, spirit, passion, or a capability of evoking mental or emotional excitement.*

I have suggested that the principal difficulties of the beginning ocean sailor are (1) the mystifying lack of expertise in much of what goes into ocean sailing; and (2) the tendency in some experts to **desiccate** the entire experience by stripping it of spontaneity, or wonder. (From *Rumbles Left and Right*, p. 173, G. P. Putnam's Sons, 1963)

determinism (noun) *The doctrine that all acts of the will result from causes which determine them in such a manner that man has no alternative modes of action.*

One needs to remind oneself that under Marxism-Leninism it is the people who are supposed to be the vehicle of historical **determinism**. It fits nowhere in Soviet doctrine for the people to assert themselves in favor of reforms which the Kremlin opposes. (From "On the Right")

detritus (noun) *Products of disintegration or wearing away; fragments or fragmentary materials.*

The experience would touch the young, temperamentally impatient with any thought of the other end of the life cycle, with the reality of old age; with the human side of the **detritus** whose ecological counterparts have almost exclusively occupied fashionable attention in recent years. (From *Gratitude*, p. 110, Random House, 1990)

detumesce (verb) *To subside from a state of swelling; to diminish in size. [Used in 1992 calendar in a different form, namely, **detumescence** (noun)]*

Brother Leo in his monastic cell consulted the diary he kept of his activities, and counted nine visits to the Alargo mansion to see Josefina Delafuente. He went to the chapel, and on his knees prayed most earnestly. He tried to distract himself, but the daemon would not **detumesce**. (From *Tucker's Last Stand*, p. 34, Random House, 1990)

deviationist (adjective) *Depart from the principles of an organization (as a political party) with which one is affiliated.*

One can say, "disciples of Communism, en bloc, follow the Moscow line." That is a responsible generalization, unaffected by the fact of schismatic flare-ups or **deviationist** sallies. (From *Up from Liberalism*, p. 38, Stein & Day, 1984)

devolution (noun) *Passing down from stage to stage; the passing of property, rights, authority, etc., from one person to another. [Used in 1992 calendar in a different form, namely, **devolve** (verb)]*

It is jarring to recall that as recently as during this century, Wales and even Scotland were discussing the kind of "**devolution**" that would have meant, in effect, self-rule. (From "On the Right")

dialectic (noun) *Any systematic reasoning, exposition, or argument that juxtaposes opposed or contradictory ideas and usually seeks to resolve their conflict; play of ideas; cunning or hairsplitting disputation.*

During those months, a fascinating **dialectic** went on. Herbert Matthews would write that American prestige was sinking in Cuba—on account of the aid the U.S. Government was giving to Batista. Our Ambassador in Havana meanwhile complained to the State Department of the demoralization of the Batista government—on account of our failure to provide aid. (From *Rumbles Left and Right*, p. 49, G. P. Putnam's Sons, 1963)

diaphanous (adjective) *Of such fine texture as to be transparent or translucent.*

Three hours later they were in the suite Hilda shared with Minerva: two bedrooms, the living room between them dimly lit by lamps covered in only barely **diaphanous** pink. (From *High Jinx*, p. 102, Doubleday & Company, 1986)

diminution (noun) *Diminishing; lessening; decrease.*

Ask then, would we be better off chucking the opposition to federalized medicine? If we did this, there would be, assuming the validity of the findings above, an instant **diminution** in costs. (From "On the Right")

discursive (adjective) *Wandering from one topic to another; rambling; desultory; digressive.*

[He is] a very old friend about whom I wrote in a **discursive** book that I think of him as the most wholesome young man I have ever known. (From "On the Right")

disestablishmentarian (noun) *An advocate of disestablishing or altering the existent state or national institution.*

The English Establishment rests on deeply embedded institutional commitments against which the Socialists, the angry young men, the **disestablishmentarians,** have railed and howled and wept altogether in vain. (From *Rumbles Left and Right*, p. 16, G. P. Putnam's Sons, 1963)

disfranchisement (noun) *The deprivation of a statutory or constitutional right, especially of the right to vote.*

To deprive him of his vote it becomes necessary to deprive others like him of their vote, hence what amounts to the virtual **disfranchisement** of the race in Southern communities that fear rule by a Negro majority. (From *Up from Liberalism*, p. 156, Stein & Day, 1984)

dislocative (adjective) *Causing confusion; causing to deviate from a normal or predicted course, situation, or relationship.*

Many people shrink from arguments over facts because facts are tedious, because they require a formal familiarity with the subject under discussion, and because they can be ideologically **dislocative.** (From *Up from Liberalism*, p. 61, Stein & Day, 1984)

dispossess (verb) *To remove from someone the possession especially of property or land; put out of occupancy; eject, oust.*

What we deplore is what Saddam Hussein went on to do. Where is the Democrat who was urging all along that we consummate Desert Storm by marching into Baghdad and **dispossessing** Saddam? (From "On the Right")

disquisition (noun) *A formal or systematic inquiry into or discussion of a subject; an elaborate analytical or explanatory essay or discussion.*

Bui Tin began one of his rambling, historical **disquisitions** on the history and culture of the region. (From *Tucker's Last Stand*, p. 239, Random House, 1990)

dissolute (noun) *A person lacking in moral restraint.*

One of the two technicians added that Heath seemed very bored with the work at hand, that he tended to arrive late for work in the morning, and that he had acquired a reputation for being something of a **dissolute,** patronizing the local bars, often with a girl. (From *High Jinx*, p. 117, Doubleday & Company, 1986)

dissonant (adjective) *Marked by a lack of agreement; incongruous, dissident, discrepant.*

Why has the same nation that implicitly endorsed the social boycott of Soviet leaders changed its mind so abruptly—to harmonize with so **dissonant** a change in position by our lackadaisical President? (From *Rumbles Left and Right*, p. 36, G. P. Putnam's Sons, 1963)

doyen (noun) *The senior male member of a body or group; one specifically or tacitly allowed to speak for the body or group.*

So well known is Herbert Matthews as **doyen** of utopian activists that when in June of 1959 a Nicaraguan rebel launched a revolt, he wired the news of it direct to Mr. Matthews at the *New York Times*—much as, a few years ago, a debutante-on-the-make might have wired the news of her engagement to Walter Winchell. (From *Rumbles Left and Right*, p. 51, G. P. Putnam's Sons, 1963)

dramaturgical (adjective) *Pertaining to the art of writing plays or producing them.*

It is somewhere recorded that, reciting a speech written for him by one of his entourage, which speech he had not even read over before delivering it, [Huey Long] reached a line in which he thought the trace of a tear theatrically appropriate, engineered that tear without any difficulty, and later on casually commented on his proficiency in these **dramaturgical** matters. (From "On the Right")

edify (verb) *To instruct and improve, especially in moral and religious knowledge; enlighten, elevate, uplift.*

Transform the Peace Corps into a body of evangelists for freedom, young men and women highly trained in the ways of Communist psychological warfare who could in behalf of freedom, analyze, argue, explain, and **edify**. (From *Rumbles Left and Right*, p. 116, G. P. Putnam's Sons, 1963)

effete (adjective) *Soft or decadent as a result of overrefinement of living conditions or laxity of mental or moral discipline.*

Etiquette is the first value only of the society that has no values, the **effete** society. An occasional disregard for the niceties may bring us face to face with certain facts from which man labors to shield himself. (From *Up from Liberalism*, p. 129, Stein & Day, 1984)

effulgence (noun) *Strong, radiant light; glorious splendor.*

Kenneth Tynan is not a reasoner and his story about appearing before the Senate Internal Security Subcommittee goes on with its poetic **effulgence**. (From *Rumbles Left and Right*, p. 73, G. P. Putnam's Sons, 1963)

effusion (noun) *Unrestrained expression of feelings; something that is poured out with little or no restraint, used especially of self-expression.*

Kenneth Tynan is a young man of letters well enough known among the literati in England because of his precocious **effusions** against the established order. (From *Rumbles Left and Right*, p. 69, G. P. Putnam's Sons, 1963)

élan (noun) (French: "spirit") *Enthusiastic vigor and liveliness.*

The aide pondered the communication, its rather special **élan**, and made the decision to put the whole dossier into the Director's In box. (From *High Jinx*, p. 177, Doubleday & Company, 1986)

elegy (noun) *A poem or song of lament for the dead.*

Milton wrote an **elegy** to a young man dead, and Bach wrote music searingly beautiful, his own tribute to a departed brother. One must suppose that Milton wept over his poetry, and Bach over his music. (From "On the Right")

emanation (noun) *A flowing forth; a quality or property issuing from a source.*

Although Harriet Pilpel was as sharp in debate as any Oxford Union killer, she managed a benevolent **emanation** that, I like to think, after twenty years of carpet-bombing exchanges with her, genuinely reflected her character. (From "On the Right")

emendation (noun) *The word or the matter substituted for incorrect or unsuitable matter.*

The new conservatives, many of whom go by the name of Modern Republicans, have not been very helpful. Their sin consists in permitting so many accretions, modifications, **emendations,** maculations, and qualifications that the original thing quite recedes from view. (From *Up from Liberalism,* p. 189, Stein & Day, 1984)

emplace (verb) *To put into position.*

The Israelis **emplaced** their nuclear-capable Jericho-2 missiles in hardened silos and in September 1988 mounted their first satellite launch. (From "On the Right")

encysted (adjective) *Enclosed in a cyst, capsule, or sac.*

Do we need to describe how bad the scene is in Detroit? It is the **encysted** home of unemployment and unrest, on account of unemployment plus the racial tensions that are engendered in communities in which whites and blacks vie for desperately needed jobs. (From "On the Right")

endemic (adjective) *Widespread; taking hold throughout a community or society.*

A great, indeed a massive, change was under way in America in the late fifties, the beginning of an **endemic** disenchantment with American liberalism. (From *Up from Liberalism,* p. xiii, Stein & Day, 1984)

engender (verb) *To bring into existence; give rise to.*

They spent a relaxed hour talking about this and that, with that odd sense of total relaxation **engendered** by the knowledge of great tension directly ahead. (From *High Jinx,* p. 13, Doubleday & Company, 1986)

ennobling (adjective) *Tending to elevate in degree or excellence.*

Whatever byways, on the road to this final Third Act, George Bush may have missed, this is the time to adjourn any complaints about them and to concentrate on an **ennobling** performance. (From "On the Right")

epicurean (adjective) *Suited to a person with refined taste, especially in food and wine.*

Blackford laughed. "This dinner is **epicurean** by comparison with what you poor English boys have to eat at your fashionable schools, and how do I know that? You guessed it, I was indentured in one." (From *High Jinx,* p. 14, Doubleday & Company, 1986)

epistemology (noun) *The study of the method and grounds of knowledge, especially with reference to its limits and validity. [Used in 1991 calendar in a different form, namely,* **epistemological** *(adjective)]*

In an age of relativism one tends to look for flexible devices for measuring this morning's truth. Such a device is democracy; and indeed, democracy becomes **epistemology**: democracy will render reliable political truths just as surely as the marketplace sets negotiable economic values. (From *Up from Liberalism,* p. 149, Stein & Day, 1984)

equanimity (noun) *Evenness of mental disposition; emotional balance, especially under stress.*

Those of us who do not go year after year wondering whether tomorrow will bring yet another war threatening our survival will perhaps find it difficult to understand the relative **equanimity** of the Israeli people. (From "On the Right")

errantry (noun) *A roving in quest of knightly adventure.*

The liberals' mania is their ideology. Deal lightly with any precept of knight-**errantry,** and you might find, as so many innocent Spaniards did, the Terror of La Mancha hurtling toward you. (From *Up from Liberalism,* p. 38, Stein & Day, 1984)

eschatologically (adverb) *Dealing with the ultimate destiny of mankind and the world. [Used in 1991 calendar in a different form, namely,* **eschatological** *(adjective)]*

The Communists' program is capable (at least for a period of time, until the illusion wears off) of being wholly satisfactory, emotionally and intellectually, to large numbers of people. The reason for this is that Communist dogma is **eschatologically** conceived. (From *Up from Liberalism,* p. 145, Stein & Day, 1984)

esoterica (noun) *Items intended for or understood by only a few.*

Fleetwood had been designated to give the first toast. After that, he turned his **esoterica** into a single metaphor that suggested the preeminent concern all civilized persons must have for peace. (From *High Jinx,* p. 123, Doubleday & Company, 1986)

essay (verb) *To make an attempt at.*

The operator evidently knew only a single word of English, which sounded like, "Outzide, outzide." He **essayed** first French and then German, to no better end, and then the cinders of his Russian. (From *High Jinx,* p. 170, Doubleday & Company, 1986)

establishmentarian (adjective) *Allied to the dominant institutional forces.*

The most hotly contested primary of the postwar season was that of New Hampshire, when in 1964 the grass roots forces of challenger Barry Goldwater did a pitched battle with the **establishmentarian** forces of Nelson Rockefeller. (From "On the Right")

ethnocentrism (noun) *The belief that one's own ethnic group, nation, or culture is superior to all others.*

I had in mind journalism and the academy, though perhaps most conspicuous at the time I wrote (1965) was the entrenched **ethnocentrism** of certain unions, in which a job is something you deed to your son or son-in-law, if he is faithful. (From "On the Right")

euphonious (adjective) *Pleasing in sound.*

The forces of fascism were not quite ready to give up, but that would come. Meanwhile, if he had to serve as a lord—Lord Fleetwood? Rather **euphonious**—why, he would simply have to do so. (From *High Jinx,* p. 236, Doubleday & Company, 1986)

Eurocentric (adjective) *The disposition to regard Europe as the central historical, intellectual, and cultural concern for American students.*

Ten lashes is about what some of us had in mind as appropriate for those in Stanford who succeeded in abolishing the theretofore compulsory courses in Western culture, deemed too "**Eurocentric**." It has yielded to a required course called Cultures, Ideas, and Values. (From "On the Right")

evanescent (adjective) *Tending to vanish or pass away like vapor. [Used in 1991 calendar in a different form, namely, evanesce (verb)]*

I and the *Panic* have a way of provoking the unreasoned and impulsive resentment of sailors whose view of ocean racing tends to be a little different from my own. That resentment is wholly spontaneous and, I like to feel, **evanescent.** (From *Rumbles Left and Right,* p. 172, G. P. Putnam's Sons, 1963)

eventuate (verb) *To come out finally or in conclusion; come to pass.*

His fluent French and schoolboy knowledge of English and Japanese suggested a clerical career, which never **eventuated** because a few months after his seventeenth birthday the Japanese surrendered. (From *Tucker's Last Stand,* p. 40, Random House, 1990)

execrable (adjective) *Deserving to be declared evil or detestable.*

Crew A, out of an egregious ignorance and showing **execrable** judgment, elects to go around Block Island north to south. (From *Rumbles Left and Right,* p. 171, G. P. Putnam's Sons, 1963)

exegetical (adjective) *Critical explanation or analysis. [Used in 1992 calendar in a different form, namely, exegete (noun)]*

"I understand Bolshevik theory and do not need your **exegetical** help in this matter." (From *High Jinx,* p. 174, Doubleday & Company, 1986)

exhibitionistic (adjective) *Behaving so as to attract attention to oneself; extravagant or willfully conspicuous behavior.*

In the Gulf, notwithstanding the **exhibitionistic** can-can by Gorbachev during the final hours, it was never conceivable that a nuclear power would stand in the way of our military strategy. (From "On the Right")

exogamous (adjective) *Of or relating to or characterized by marriage outside a specific group, especially as required by custom or law.*

I am allergic to **exogamous** comparative dollar figures, so widely used in workaday polemical chitchat, such as, "For the cost of landing a man on the moon, we might have built one million one hundred and thirty-seven thousand and eight low-middle class dwelling units." (From *Gratitude*, p. 134, Random House, 1990)

expertise (noun) *An operative body of knowledge.*

For those on the radical Left and for so many on the moderate Left, the true meaning of our time is the loss of an operative set of values—what one might call an **expertise** in living. (From *Rumbles Left and Right*, p. 63, G. P. Putnam's Sons, 1963)

expostulation (noun) *Strong demand; remonstrance. [Used in 1991 calendar in a different form, namely, expostulate (verb)]*

With no further attention paid to his **expostulations**, his arms were strapped to his sides with the stretcher's harness and he was lifted into the ambulance and deposited alongside the cab driver. (From *High Jinx*, p. 246, Doubleday & Company, 1986)

extortionate (adjective) *Characterized by, or having the nature of, extortion; excessive; exorbitant.*

This requires negotiating with the Saudis to peg the oil price at a reasonable level for, say, twenty years. Without the cooperation of the Saudis, OPEC can never reassemble its **extortionate** cartel. (From "On the Right")

extravasate (verb) *To force out (as blood) or cause to escape from a proper vessel or channel (blood vessel).*

Can the revolutionary essence be **extravasated** and be made to diffuse harmlessly in the network of capillaries that rushes forward to accommodate its explosive force? (From *Up from Liberalism*, p. 221, Stein & Day, 1984)

exult (verb) *To be extremely joyful, often with an outward display of triumph or exuberant self-satisfaction.*

Most recently the Dartmouth administration's mills ran overtime to **exult** over the appearance, alongside the weekly's logo, of an anti-Semitic remark taken from Hitler's *Mein Kampf.* (From "On the Right")

factionalism (noun) *The process of splitting into parties, combinations, or cliques.*

Boris Andreyvich Bolgin could hardly help hearing—experiencing—vibrations of—a mounting division. There was **factionalism**, spying on one another, the sense that no leader without the strength of Stalin was truly a leader. (From *High Jinx*, p. 43, Doubleday & Company, 1986)

fallow (adjective) *Marked by inactivity.*

It had been more than an entire college generation since he had mingled with the hard left community, either students or faculty. Even the Russian he had learned, he was encouraged to let lie **fallow**. (From *High Jinx*, p. 81, Doubleday & Company, 1986)

fervent (adjective) *Having or showing great emotion or warmth; ardent.*

He greatly missed those **fervent** evenings with the select few, the brainy idealists who recognized that the Soviet revolution was the twentieth century's way of saying no to more world wars, to imperialism, to the class system. (From *High Jinx*, p. 81, Doubleday & Company, 1986)

fiduciary (adjective) *Of, having to do with, or involving a confidence or trust; of the nature of a trust.*

In its administration of the funds, the government does not meet orthodox **fiduciary** standards of the kind stipulated by the laws of most of the states for private insurance companies. (From *Up from Liberalism,* p. 197, Stein & Day, 1984)

fillip (noun) *Something added that tends to arouse or excite; a stimulating or rousing agent.*

When Lord Keynes brushed aside the demurrals of a critic concerned with the long-run effect of his program by saying "In the long run we are all dead," he originated a verbal **fillip** that made its way quickly into the annals of definitive retort. (From *Up from Liberalism,* p. 187, Stein & Day, 1984)

fissiparous (adjective) *Reproducing by fission.*

The tribulations of the **fissiparous** Soviet empire will almost certainly guarantee, at least for the short run, a huge number of refugees. (From "On the Right")

fleeted (adjective) *Felicitious; starry; piquant.*

Blackford wondered whether his path and the Queen's would even cross. He half hoped they would not; half hoped they would, three years having passed since their fleeting, **fleeted** encounter. (From *High Jinx,* p. 208, Doubleday & Company, 1986)

flotsam and jetsam (nouns) *These terms usually appear together to refer to that part of the wreckage of a ship and its cargo found floating on the water or washed ashore. The phrase "flotsam and jetsam" now has an extended meaning of "useless trifles," "odds and ends."*

The **flotsam and jetsam** of Edward Bennett Williams's arguments wash up on the shores of reason in irreconcilable pieces, but on he goes, unperturbed. (From *Rumbles Left and Right,* p. 88, G. P. Putnam's Sons, 1963)

foppish (adjective) *Pertaining to or characteristic of a man who is preoccupied with and often vain about his clothes and manners.*

Mr. Mussolini was in his mid-forties, tall and angular. He was well dressed; the Director thought him even rather **foppish.** (From *High Jinx,* p. 178, Doubleday & Company, 1986)

forswear (verb) *To renounce earnestly, determinedly, or with protestations.*

In other words, the South African government was slipping some money (a relatively modest one hundred thousand dollars, one is told) to that domestic force which **forswore** violence, Communism, and boycotts—over against its opposition. What it did was illegal. But hardly evil. (From "On the Right")

fulmination (noun) *Vehement menace or censure; something that is thundered forth. [Used in 1992 calendar in a different form, namely, fulminator (noun)]*

Rubirosa has come to town. **Fulminations,** of course, are in order, but how pleasant **fulminations** can be at the hands of a master. (From *Rumbles Left and Right,* p. 137, G. P. Putnam's Sons, 1963)

gibbet (noun) *An upright post with a projecting arm for hanging the bodies of executed criminals in chains or irons; gallows.*

Now everybody knows you shouldn't talk about **gibbets** to executioners, especially not when they happen also to be head of state. (From *Up from Liberalism,* p. 129, Stein & Day, 1984)

gird (verb) *To prepare (oneself) for a struggle, test of strength, or other action.*

I cannot complain softly. My blood gets hot, my brow wet, I become unbearably and unconscionably sarcastic and bellicose; I am **girded** for a total showdown. (From *Rumbles Left and Right,* p. 189, G. P. Putnam's Sons, 1963)

granitic (adjective) *Very hard; granite-like.*

Now if you think this is because there is **granitic** resistance within Vassar to students of non-white background, how do we account for it that the presidents-elect of the senior class and the student government are black, and the junior class president-elect is Asian-American, and the president-elect of the sophomore class is Hispanic? (From "On the Right")

gravometer (noun) *A geological instrument designed to detect deposits of oil.*
This morning Murray Kempton speaks of the emergence of Romney as a presidential contender. Like a **gravometer,** he is attracted to the irony of the situation. (From *Rumbles Left and Right,* p. 140, G. P. Putnam's Sons, 1963)

grotesquerie (noun) *Something suggestive or resembling grotesque decorative art or the figures or designs of such art; something grotesque.*
There originated in this Couéism the reckless stampede to inflate the electoral lists, culminating in the **grotesquerie** of the state of Georgia, which voted in 1943 to give the vote to every eighteen-year-old. (From *Up from Liberalism,* p. 148, Stein & Day, 1984)

gull (verb) *To make a dupe of; cheat, deceive.*
Dr. J. B. Matthews painstakingly listed the names of dozens upon dozens of the unfortunate clergymen who had collaborated with the Communist movement, and finally reckoned that, percentagewise, more ministers had been **gulled** into supporting Communist fronts than teachers and lawyers. (From *Up from Liberalism,* p. 52, Stein & Day, 1984)

habituate (verb) *To make familiar through use or experience; to make acceptable or desirable through use or experience.*
They had walked almost eight miles that day, the fifth day of Blackford's exploration, and he was **habituated** now to the redundancy of the Trail's surrounding features. (From *Tucker's Last Stand,* p. 6, Random House, 1990)

hagiography (noun) *The writing or study of lives of the saints. [Used in 1992 calendar in a different form, namely, **hagiographer** (noun)]*
But Lenin, himself as close as any man could be to heartlessness, understood intellectually the need for icons. And as a political matter, he'd have approved the **hagiography** of communism, not because he believed in the elevation of ideological saints, but because he'd have found it useful to accelerate the revolution. (From "On the Right")

hedonism (noun) *An ethical doctrine taught by the ancient Epicureans and Cyrenaics and by the modern utilitarians that asserts that pleasure or happiness is the sole or chief good in life.*
Less conspicuous problems must be thought of as having an economic impact: the instability of family life, listlessness at school, a growing national tendency to corruption, or **hedonism;** and insensitivity to suffering; a callousness that breeds ugliness of behavior. (From *Gratitude,* p. 36, Random House, 1990)

hemidemisemiquaver (noun) *A sixty-fourth note; i.e., thoughts or frustrations lasting for only passing seconds.*
As, wearily, he slid into bed at three in the morning for the second successive night, he blanked out what his musical colleague at Trinity liked to call the **hemidemisemiquavers.**" (From *High Jinx,* p. 196, Doubleday & Company, 1986)

hermetically (adverb) *So as to be impervious to outside interference or influence.*
His brown eyes were either sound asleep (that was when Rufus was given over to analysis, parting company with his surroundings as though **hermetically** insulated from them) or fiercely active. (From *High Jinx,* p. 31, Doubleday & Company, 1986)

hierarchical (adjective) *Of or relating to a classification of people according to artistic, social, economic, or other criteria.*
I note a kind of **hierarchical** polarization going on. When I was at college, it would have been unprecedented to refer to the President of the University other than as "Mr. Seymour." Today, the president is "President Schmidt." Back then, a professor was—"Mr.

Whitehead," which is also what he'd have been called by his students. Today he would be "Dr. Whitehead," and his students would call him Chuck. (From "On the Right")

homophobe (noun) *One who dislikes, disapproves of, or has an irrational hatred of homosexuals or homosexuality.*

If a student these days opposes some of the demands of the Gay Liberation types, he might be branded as a **homophobe,** when all that can verifiably be said about him is that he is opposed to homosexual practices, which is still, though perhaps only just still, a permissible position. (From "On the Right")

hubris (noun) *Overweening pride or self-confidence; arrogance.*

The only autonomy liberalism appears to encourage is moral and intellectual autonomy; solipsism. And that is the autonomy of deracination; the philosophy that has peopled the earth with atomized and presumptuous social careerists diseased with **hubris.** (From *Up from Liberalism,* p. 177, Stein & Day, 1984)

humbuggery (noun) *An attitude or spirit of pretense and deception or self-deception.*

There were those who are free of the superstition of liberalism who joined in denouncing Pérez Jiménez's "election"; for his offense was one of **humbuggery.** (From *Up from Liberalism,* p. 149, Stein & Day, 1984)

hydra-headed (adjective) *Having many centers or branches (from the Hydra, a mythical many-headed serpent).*

The imperative that worldwide attention be given to stop the traffic in **hydra-headed** arms beckons as never before. (From "On the Right")

hypermammiferous (adjective) *Having extremely large breasts.*

The late Congressman Adam Clayton Powell, Jr., once took a highly publicized trip to Greece with a **hypermammiferous** blonde. He was investigating Greek affairs. Congressman Powell, contemplating the bust of Homer. (From "On the Right")

icon (noun) *Object or person attracting worshipful attention.*

Sally was slightly withdrawn, indomitably independent in spirit, dazzling to look at if you began by discarding as irrelevant most of the competition in **icons** of the day—she didn't look like Rita Hayworth or Marilyn Monroe. (From *Tucker's Last Stand,* p. 77, Random House, 1990)

ignominy (noun) *Deep, personal disgrace.*

I am perfectly at home in a small boat, and would, in a small boat race, more often than not come in if not on the side of glory, perhaps this side of **ignominy.** (From *Rumbles Left and Right,* p. 166, G. P. Putnam's Sons, 1963)

impenitent (adjective) *Not repenting of sin; not contrite.*

Norman Mailer and a dozen others signed an advertisement in papers throughout the country under the sponsorship of a group called the Fair Play for Cuba Committee. The episode was less farce than an act of tragedy, though without dire consequence for the players—they are strikingly **impenitent** and insouciant. (From *Rumbles Left and Right,* p. 56, G. P. Putnam's Sons, 1963)

imperturbability (noun) *The quality or state of being extremely calm, impassive, assured, and steady. [Used in 1991 calendar in a different form, namely, **imperturbable** (adjective)]*

I have seen consternation on the faces of more experienced members of my crew at such evidences of inexperience or even ignorance, and I do not myself pretend to **imperturbability** when they occur. (From *Rumbles Left and Right,* p. 170, G. P. Putnam's Sons, 1963)

imposture (noun) *The act or practice of imposing on or deceiving someone by means of an assumed character or name.*

Will Khrushchev respect us more as, by our deeds, we proclaim and proclaim again and again our hallucination, in the grinding teeth of the evidence, that we and the Soviet Union can work together for a better world? It is this **imposture** of irrationality in the guise of rationality that frightens. (From *Rumbles Left and Right*, p. 35, G. P. Putnam's Sons, 1963)

indite (verb) *To write, compose; to set down in writing.*

Fleetwood had been designated to give the first toast, and he had gone out of his way to **indite** a few sentences the meaning of which he knew would be understood by not more than a dozen of the hundred guests there. (From *High Jinx*, p. 123, Doubleday & Company, 1986)

ineradicable (adjective) *Incapable of being gotten rid of completely.*

His scientific intelligence taught him that facts, among them those that had to do with (**ineradicable**? Was this defective loyalty to Marx-Lenin?) human appetites cannot be denied by ideological asseverations. (From *High Jinx*, p. 75, Doubleday & Company, 1986)

ingratiation (noun) *The act of winning favor; the process of insinuating oneself in the good graces of another.*

Mrs. Thatcher's speech was a tribute to her natural eloquence and to her formidable powers of **ingratiation**. Mostly it was a Special Relations speech about the enduring friendship of the two great English-speaking powers. (From "On the Right")

iniquitously (adverb) *Wickedly; sinfully. [Used in 1991 calendar in a different form, namely, iniquitous (adjective)]*

Molotov delivered a speech on the subject of the **iniquitously** close relationship between the U.S. and Japan. (From *High Jinx*, p. 180, Doubleday & Company, 1986)

insularity (noun) *Narrow-mindedness; detachment; isolation; provincialism.*

But Mr. Salinas has gradually eased Mexico away from a protectionism that represented at once socialist **insularity** and yanqui xenophobia. (From "On the Right")

insurrectionary (adjective) *Relating to or constituting an act or instance of revolting against civil authority or against an established government.*

But there was another movement, not properly **insurrectionary** but totally hostile to apartheid. The Inkatha movement is as large as that of the African National Congress, but its leaders were different. (From "On the Right")

intellection (noun) *Exercise of the intellect; reasoning, cognition, apprehension; a specific act of the intellect.*

We believe that millenniums of **intellection** have served an objective purpose. Certain problems have been disposed of. (From *Up from Liberalism*, p. 182, Stein & Day, 1984)

intercredal (adjective) *Conversations or exchanges between members of different faiths.*

The liberals' implicit premise is that **intercredal** dialogues are what one has with Communists, not conservatives, in relationship with whom normal laws of civilized discourse are suspended. (From *Up from Liberalism*, p. 55, Stein & Day, 1984)

intransigence (noun) *Refusal to compromise, to come to an agreement or a reconciliation.*

Mr. Bush having asked Congress for a resolution backing a military response in the Gulf should Saddam Hussein persevere in **intransigence**, a distinction crystallizes. A very important distinction. (From "On the Right")

intrinsic (adjective) *Belonging to the inmost constitution or essential nature of a thing. [Used in 1992 calendar in a different form, namely, intrinsically (adverb)]*

The fact of discrimination in America against the Negro is of no more **intrinsic** concern to the Communists than the fact of discrimination against the Jews in Soviet Russia is of concern to them. (From *Rumbles Left and Right*, p. 114, G. P. Putnam's Sons, 1963)

inure (verb) *To come into operation; flow to; become operative; accrue.*
Those who do not enroll in the program do not make the payments, but neither do the benefits **inure** to them. (From *Up from Liberalism*, p. 205, Stein & Day, 1984)

invective (noun) *Denunciatory or abusive language; vituperation.*
"You, by not using your donkey brain—excuse me donkey," Beria spoke now in a voice of exaggerated deference,—"excuse me, donkey, for insulting your brain by comparing it with Bolgin's!" The **invective** lasted a full ten minutes before Beria sat down. (From *High Jinx*, p. 46, Doubleday & Company, 1986)

irredentism (noun) *A claim by a nation to land that formerly belonged to it. [Used in 1991 calendar in a different form, namely, irredentist (adjective)]*
A few miles to the west, the disorder and the killings go on in Ulster and Ireland, over the dogged question of self-rule: Ulster wants to hold on to its independence as a part of Great Britain, substantial elements within Ireland want **irredentism**. (From "On the Right")

irreducible (adjective) *Impossible to simplify or make easier or clearer; impossible to make less or smaller.*
And one has therefore to pause before proceeding to hold every Iraqi responsible for the crimes of Saddam Hussein and those front-line sadists who disgraced the **irreducible** maxims of human decency. (From "On the Right")

irruption (noun) *A sudden, violent, or forcible entry; a rushing or bursting in; a sudden or violent invasion.*
The question the white community faces, then, is whether the claims of civilization supersede those of universal suffrage. The British clearly believed they did when they acted to suppress the **irruption** in Kenya in 1952. (From *Up from Liberalism*, p. 157, Stein & Day, 1984)

janissary (noun) *A member of a group of loyal or subservient troops, officials, or supporters.*
When it was finally clear that Carmine DeSapio had been thrown out by the ideological **janissaries** and the playboy reformers, there were still the conventional and highly poignant rituals to go through. (From *Rumbles Left and Right*, p. 134, G. P. Putnam's Sons, 1963)

kinetic (adjective) *Supplying motive force; energizing, dynamic.*
The conclusions of Professor Louis Hartz of Harvard are both historical and philosophical. There never was a sure-enough conservatism in America, he maintains, the American experience having been dynamic, revolutionary, pragmatic, **kinetic**. (From *Up from Liberalism*, p. 90, Stein & Day, 1984)

knell (noun) *A death signal or passing bell; a warning of or a sound indicating the passing away of something.*
If we become identified with the point of view that the social security laws toll the **knell** of our departed freedoms, we will lose our credit at the bar of public opinion, or be dismissed as cultists of a terrestrial mystique. (From *Up from Liberalism*, p. 189, Stein & Day, 1984)

lachrymal (adjective) *Marked by tears.*
Mrs. Chamorro, while making all the appropriate **lachrymal** sounds over the death of Enrique, has not overridden her Sandinista authorities to take charge of the investigation. (From "On the Right")

laconic (adjective) *Using or marked by the use of few words; terse, precise. [Used in 1991 calendar in a different form, namely, laconically (adverb)]*
Bertram Heath was a quiet, determined young man with the even-featured straight face and the steady brown eyes that signaled what was coming before the **laconic**

twenty-year-old got out what was on his mind. (From *High Jinx*, p. 86, Doubleday & Company, 1986)

largesse (noun) *Liberality in giving, especially when attended by condescension.*

He felt positively ennobled by the proposed act of generosity, but also tender in the knowledge of whom he stood now to patronize with his **largesse**. (From *High Jinx*, p. 79, Doubleday & Company, 1986)

levity (noun) *Lacking in seriousness; a frivolity.*

"Not even you can talk that way about Comrade Beria. And this business of going to the British Embassy . . . I mean, Alistair, don't ever say such a thing, not even in **levity**." (From *High Jinx*, p. 175, Doubleday & Company, 1986)

licentious (adjective) *Marked by the absence of legal or moral restraints; by lewdness; by neglect. [Used in 1991 calendar in a different form, namely, licentiousness (noun)]*

Such discrepancies as the bigoted churchman, the protectionist free enterpriser, the provincial internationalist, the **licentious** moralist are all well-known anomalies. (From *Up from Liberalism*, p. 35, Stein & Day, 1984)

licit (adjective) *Legally or otherwise allowable; condonable.*

It is easy to imagine (and frightening to do so) the result of a refusal by the minority to abide by the **licit** authority of the majority. (From *Gratitude*, p. 54, Random House, 1990)

locus classicus (noun) (Latin) *A standard passage important for the elucidation of a word or subject.*

It can be argued by orthodox theologians that God prefers the sinner to the saint, always provided it is understood that overnight the sinner can, and in the past often has, become a saint. Augustine is the **locus classicus**. (From *Gratitude*, p. 63, Random House, 1990)

logorrhea (noun) *Pathologically excessive and often incoherent talkativeness.*

That bit of **logorrhea** is a way of saying that the Founding Fathers were incompetent when they gave individual states, instead of just the federal government, the taxing power, because this federalist invitation to centrifugal disruption adds up to people being able to look Mario Cuomo in the face and say, "Raise taxes one more time, and we'll give you a forwarding address in Pennsylvania." (From "On the Right")

lucidity (noun) *The quality or state of being clear to the understanding; readily intelligible; lacking ambiguity.*

"You have, sometimes, a terribly obscure way of expressing yourself, a difficulty you may have noticed that never afflicted my mentor, Jane Austen, who had no problem in expressing thoughts no matter how subtle, with unambiguous **lucidity**." (From *Tucker's Last Stand*, p. 136, Random House, 1990)

lucubrate (verb) *To discourse learnedly in writing.*

Under the Eisenhower program, one could **lucubrate** over constitutional rights and freedoms and forever abandon captured American soldiers. (From *Up from Liberalism*, p. 128, Stein & Day, 1984)

lumpen (adjective) *An amorphous group of dispossessed and uprooted individuals set off by their inferior status from the economic and social class with which they are identified; a geographical area backward and undistinguished.*

Several years ago I wrote in this space that the Soviet Union, were it deprived of its strategic nuclear weapons, would become nothing much more than a vast **lumpen** territorial mass, something on the order of a north India. (From "On the Right")

Machiavellian (adjective) *Crafty, deceitful; of, like, or characterized by the political principles and methods of expediency, craftiness, and duplicity advocated in Niccolò Machiavelli's book* The Prince.

The **Machiavellian** principle that you do not fool with the prince unless you are prepared to kill him was never more clearly vindicated than in the current exercise. (From
"On the Right")

maculation (noun) *Spot, stain, blemish.*

The new conservatives, many of whom go by the name of Modern Republicans, have
not been very helpful. Their sin consists in permitting so many accretions, modifications, emendations, **maculations**, and qualifications that the original thing quite recedes from view. (From *Up from Liberalism*, p. 189, Stein & Day, 1984)

malefactor (noun) *One who does ill toward another; evildoer.*

Whatever good they accomplished it can't be denied that they also did great harm, and
that the principal **malefactor** was Senator Frank Church, who treated the hearings as
a confessional. (From "On the Right")

malfeasance (noun) *The doing by a public officer under cover of authority of his office of
something that is unwarranted, that he has contracted not to do, and that is legally unjustified and positively wrongful or contrary to law.*

Edward Bennett Williams pleads for action to deprive the Congress of the right to
exercise its traditional power to expose crime and **malfeasance**, to forbid the police
from tapping the telephones of putative criminals, to restrain detectives from in-
terrogating suspects. (From *Rumbles Left and Right*, p. 86, G. P. Putnam's Sons,
1963)

malum in se (noun) (Latin) *An act that is evil or wrong from its own nature or by the natural law irrespective of statute.*

What the government of South Africa did is a nice example of the distinction between
a *malum prohibitum* and a **malum in se**. It is legally wrong for a government to subsi-
dize one particular political movement at the expense of another. It is not always
morally wrong to do so. (From "On the Right")

manifesto (noun) *A public demonstration of intentions, motives, or views; a public statement
of policy or opinion.*

Because liberalism has no definitive **manifesto**, one cannot say, prepared to back up
the statement with unimpeachable authority, that such-and-such a man or measure is
"liberal." (From *Up from Liberalism*, p. 36, Stein & Day, 1984)

matrix (noun) *A situation or surrounding substance within which something originates, de-
velops, or is contained.*

She was to keep a sharp eye out for any student who inclined sufficiently toward the
great Communist experiment, of which Russia was the **matrix**, to qualify for possible
recruitment. (From *High Jinx*, p. 70, Doubleday & Company, 1986)

meliorative (adjective) *Resulting in or leading toward betterment.*

There is no guarantee behind the value of the policy taken out with a private insurance
company, which is subject to the depredations of inflation unmitigated by **meliorative**
political pressure. (From *Up from Liberalism*, p. 197, Stein & Day, 1984)

metastasize (verb) *To spread to other parts of the body by metastasis; to change form or matter; to transform.*

And the possibility was also there to be considered that what happened between the
judge and his associate wasn't seductive flirtation but something misinterpreted as
such, growing grotesque in the imagination, sufficient to **metastasize** as an inclination
to bestiality. (From "On the Right")

meticulist (noun) *One who is extremely careful in his use of language, diction; a precise mea-
surer.*

It hurt Governor Sununu, who is a **meticulist** in expression, to use a term inappropri-
ate to his conduct. (From "On the Right")

mille-feuilles (noun) (French: "one thousand leaves") *A light, layered pastry commonly called a Napoleon.*

The braised chicken and petits pois were fine, the claret excellent, the ***mille-feuilles*** sensational. (From *High Jinx*, p. 99, Doubleday & Company, 1986)

mirabile dictu (adverb) (Latin) *"Wonder to relate"; incredible.*

Here is a question for which, ***mirabile dictu,*** I do not have the answer. It is: How much freedom should a college student be given to say or to write what he wishes? (From "On the Right")

miscible (adjective) *Capable of mixing in any ratio without separation of two phases.*

It is a pity that the useless word "equality" ever got into the act, because one cannot in the nature of things make "equal" that which is not the same. You can play around with other words if you wish—fungible? No, the sexes aren't fungible. **Miscible?** Yes: but **miscible** elements retain their identity. (From "On the Right")

miscreant (noun) *One who behaves criminally or viciously.*

That spirit looks upon a nuclear missile not only as a ferule with which to beat the enemy and native **miscreants**, but as a badge of high office. (From "On the Right")

misogynist (noun) *One who hates women.*

Those who believe that a case for differences between the two can be plausibly made might have no trouble suppressing or expelling the student pornographer, but would pause over taking action against the student racist or homophobe or **misogynist** or whatever. (From "On the Right")

monetize (verb) *To coin into money.*

There is a tale (I think it was Ring Lardner's) of an old prospector who shrinks from the attendant complexities and unpleasantness of mining and **monetizing** a rich deposit of gold he has come upon. (From *Up from Liberalism*, p. 181, Stein & Day, 1984)

morphological (adjective) *Of, relating to, or concerned with form or structure. [Used in 1991 calendar in a different form, namely,* **morphology** *(noun)]*

The state can rule, but it cannot command loyalty, let alone effect **morphological** changes in human nature. (From *Gratitude*, p. 48, Random House, 1990)

mortification (noun) *The subjection and denial of bodily passions and appetites by abstinence or self-inflicted pain or discomfort.*

When he decided to enter the monastery, he decided, as a novitiate, to impose upon himself the intellectual **mortification** of learning physics. (From *Tucker's Last Stand*, p. 32, Random House, 1990)

multicentrist (noun) *Those who hold that attachments to many positions, political, social, cultural, are educationally advanced.*

Having dealt with Islamic codes on women, the pilgrims in search of better ideas than those of our own culture can study the attitudes of others toward homosexuality, since homophobia is one of the central targets of the **multicentrists**. (From "On the Right")

munificently (adverb) *Liberally, with lavish generosity. [Used in 1992 calendar in a different form, namely,* **munificent** *(adjective)]*

Big social thinkers assume that any proposal is emasculated that doesn't call for federal funding on a very large scale. What the Bennet school of criticism wishes to see in national service is a full-scale war against poverty. Again; federal programs **munificently** funded. (From *Gratitude*, p. 80, Random House, 1990)

mutatis mutandis (adverb) (Latin) *The necessary changes having been made.*

How many Americans, reflecting on the misuse of a government limousine, have asked themselves whether they should be fired by their employers because every now and again they use a postage stamp from the office supply to mail a personal letter?

Mutatis mutandis, they might say to themselves, that is the equivalent of misusing a government limousine, if you are chief of staff of the White House. (From "On the Right")

mycology (noun) *The properties and life phenomena exhibited by a fungus, fungus type, or fungus group—the study of mushrooms.*

How many things Whittaker Chambers wanted to write about! Mushrooms, for one thing. Some gentleman had recently published a ten-dollar book on **mycology,** heaping scorn on one of Chambers's most beloved species of toadstools. (From *Rumbles Left and Right,* p. 153, G. P. Putnam's Sons, 1963)

naïf (noun) *A naïve person.*

Within ten minutes Tucker knew he was dealing, in the case of the gook, with a total **naïf.** The Russian's background, on the other hand, was considerable. (From *Tucker's Last Stand,* p. 238, Random House, 1990)

necromancy (noun) *Black magic; sorcery; the practice of claiming to foretell the future by alleged communication with the dead.*

When you raise taxes, you raise taxes. When you forecast spending decreases, you are engaged in **necromancy.** (From "On the Right")

nescient (adjective) *From nescience, the doctine that nothing is truly knowable.*

I intended to call my little book "The Revolt Against the Masses," because I thought I saw on the social horizon in America signs of a disposition to reject the **nescient** aimlessness Ortega y Gasset had diagnosed. (From *Gratitude,* p. 15, Random House, 1990)

nether (adjective) *Situated down or below; lying beneath or in the lower part.*

The conservative should shake loose from his disposition to reject out of hand any gesture in the direction of acknowledging different orders of citizenship. That line of demarcation should exist, among other reasons, in order to prompt those on the **nether** side to traverse it. (From *Gratitude,* p. 67, Random House, 1990)

noblesse oblige (noun) (French) *The inferred obligation of people of high rank or social position to behave nobly or kindly toward others.*

But individual employers, acting on an impulse of **noblesse oblige,** aren't to be confused with the government, which must never discriminate in its own hiring practices. (From "On the Right")

nomenklatura (noun) *The elite within the Soviet bureaucracy.*

A. Well there is no doubt they have considerable influence—the **nomenklatura,** the KGB, the military—but I ask you to imagine how much worse off the Soviet Union would be without Gorbachev. (From "On the Right")

nonplussed (adjective) *At a loss as to what to say, think, or do.*

I put the question to the biographer of Mr. Hoover, Dr. George Nash the distinguished historian. He **nonplussed** me by telling me that he was himself **nonplussed.** So much so that he went to the archives and dug up the first one hundred communications sent to President Hoover after he left the White House. (From "On the Right")

nuance (noun) *A subtle or slight degree of difference as in meaning, color, or tone. [Used in 1991 calendar in a different form, namely, **nuanced** (adjective)]*

She discovered that in his subtle way, the slim young man with no trace of beard, a light sprinkle of faded freckles reaching from his nose to his hair, was quick to grasp **nuance** and to expand and improvise on subjects only tangentially touched upon. (From *High Jinx,* p. 72, Doubleday & Company, 1986)

obloquy (noun) *A strongly and often intemperately condemnatory utterance; defamatory or calumnious language; abusive or slanderous reprehension.*

After an elaborate exposition of the problem, he would pronounce sentence. This ranged from disqualification, on the lenient days, to a terrible warning to which, of course, was attached public **obloquy**. (From *Rumbles Left and Right*, p. 165, G. P. Putnam's Sons, 1963)

obsequy (noun) *Gesture of reverence, or piety, or deference, usually toward the dead.*
And poor Senator Gore! He was accused by properly indignant New York Jews of "pandering" to the Jewish vote by his near-sacramental **obsequies** to whatever Tel Aviv's policy was five minutes ago. (From "On the Right")

obstreperous (adjective) *Stubbornly defiant; resisting control or restraint, often with a show of noisy disorder.*
Mike Wallace introduces Randolph Churchill as an "irascible snob." Now for all I know, that is just what Mr. Churchill is; but this is not the way to introduce one's guests, not even **obstreperous** conservative guests. (From *Up from Liberalism*, p. 61, Stein & Day, 1984)

oeuvre (noun) (French: "a work") *Usually, the sum of an artist's lifework.*
Blackford was showing off here, as he wished Sally to know that he knew where Mr. Knightley and Miss Woodhouse had figured in Miss Austen's **oeuvre**. (From *High Jinx*, p. 18, Doubleday & Company, 1986)

oligarchs (noun) *The controlling members of a party or state.*
Being able to vote is no more to have realized freedom than being able to read is to have realized wisdom. Reasonable limitations upon the vote are not recommended exclusively by tyrants or **oligarchs** (was Jefferson either?). (From *Up from Liberalism*, p. 158, Stein & Day, 1984)

ombudsman (noun) *One who investigates complaints, as from consumers, reports findings, and assists in achieving fair settlements.*
Should the federal government pay **ombudsmen** who would stand at the door of the public library, prepared to extract from the mainframe the information desired by the curious citizen? (From "On the Right")

omnicompetent (adjective) *Well qualified in all respects.*
That morning Rufus had arrived at the safe house in London looking old, but not for that reason less than **omnicompetent**. (From *High Jinx*, p. 54, Doubleday & Company, 1986)

ontological (adjective) *Of or relating to being or existence.*
The persistent misuse of the word democracy reflects either an ignorance of its **ontological** emptiness; or (and is this not the logical derivative of the ignorance?), the pathetic attempt to endow it with substantive meaning. (From *Up from Liberalism*, p. 146, Stein & Day, 1984)

opera (noun) *Plural of opus, a set of compositions usually numbered in order of issue.*
Arthur Schlesinger, Jr., for a decade or so was more or less ex officio in charge of disdaining my **opera** and writing the score for others on just how this was to be done. (From *Up from Liberalism*, p. xxi, Stein & Day, 1984)

opprobrium (noun) *Public or known disgrace or ill fame that ordinarily follows from conduct considered grossly wrong or vicious.*
There are circumstances when the minority can lay claim to preeminent political authority, without bringing down upon its head the moral **opprobrium** of just men. (From *Up from Liberalism*, p. 157, Stein & Day, 1984)

organon (noun) *An instrument for acquiring knowledge, specifically a body of methodological doctrine comprising principles for scientific or philosophic procedure or investigations.*
Those liberating perceptions Norman Mailer has been wrestling to formulate for lo these many years are like the purloined letter, lying about loose in the principles and premises, the **organon,** of the movement the Left finds it so fashionable to ridicule. (From *Rumbles Left and Right*, p. 62, G. P. Putnam's Sons, 1963)

paean (noun) *A fervent expression of joy or praise.*
Alice wrote poetry, and her poetry included **paeans** to the Soviet state and its leaders, though she had had on more than one occasion to face the metrical choice either of substituting the name of a new leader in the place of the name that figured in her original lines but was now exposed as having been treasonable, or toss the poem away. (From *High Jinx*, p. 69, Doubleday & Company, 1986)

paralogism (noun) *Reasoning contrary to the rules of logic; a faulty argument. [Used in 1992 calendar in a different form, namely, paralogist (noun)]*
This is the critical **paralogism** in the Choicers' line of argument. What they should be saying is that the woman's right to abort is superior to the right of the fetus to live. (From "On the Right")

parlous (adjective) *Characterized by uncertainty; fraught with danger or risk; attended with peril.*
The situation in South Africa during the past, **parlous** years isn't as vivid seen through the serene eyes of a lecturer at the Kennedy School at Harvard as it has been, and continues to be, for the white South African. (From "On the Right")

parricide (noun) *The act of killing one's father.*
Now, "fraternity" is a word one needs to pause over, inasmuch as the French Revolution, in enshrining that word, in effect committed **parricide**. (From *Gratitude*, p. 55, Random House, 1990)

perdurable (adjective) *Lasting a long time or indefinitely.*
It tends to be true that in England the Establishment prevails. The English Establishment mediates the popular political will through **perdurable** English institutions. (From *Rumbles Left and Right*, p. 17, G. P. Putnam's Sons, 1963)

peremptory (adjective) *(1) Expressive of urgency or command; (2) of an arrogant or imperious nature.*
Mayday moved forward and put her lips on Blackford's—and lingered. Before she was done, Alice felt contrition over her **peremptory** handling of Anthony, and now used lips and hands to express her feeling for him. (From *Tucker's Last Stand*, p. 92, Random House, 1990)

perfidious (adjective) *Characterized by a deliberate breach of faith, a calculated violation of trust, or treachery. [Used in 1991 calendar in a different form, namely, perfidy (noun)]*
"It's your call, Boris. What did bring you out tonight? We have not spoken once in the three years—"
"In the three years in which I have kept pace with your **perfidious** activities, Mr. Chestnut," replied Bolgin. (From *High Jinx*, p. 204, Doubleday & Company, 1986)

philistinism (noun) *The attitudes, beliefs, and conduct characteristic of a crass, prosaic, often priggish individual guided by material rather than intellectual values.*
To paraphrase Mr. Tynan, over here we have the impression that in America everybody thinks alike, that the country is in the grip of an iron **philistinism**. (From *Rumbles Left and Right*, p. 69, G. P. Putnam's Sons, 1963)

plainspoken (adjective) *Frank, straightforward, unadorned.*
Normally, when recruiting someone into the Party, the seniority of the recruiter is utterly **plainspoken**. Her authority rested in her established status as a party member; as a graduate of the University of Moscow; as a linguist; as a longtime resident of the Soviet Union. (From *High Jinx*, p. 77, Doubleday & Company, 1986)

plight (verb) *To put or give in pledge.*
One eulogist said that as a young woman, graduated from Vassar College and the Columbia Law School, she had **plighted** her professional troth to two causes: the first, her

own individual freedom to do as she chose; the second, her absolute commitment to women's "reproductive rights." (From "On the Right")

plutocratic (adjective) *Relating to government by the wealthy; of the rule or dominion of wealth or of the rich.*

I very much wish that the meaning of the word "masses" was not so fixed in the Anglo-Saxon world because the word as we use it has either Marxist or **plutocratic** connotations. (From *Gratitude*, p. 16, Random House, 1990)

polarization (noun) *Division (as of groups, ideologies, systems, or forces) into two opposites.*

The occasion drove home the infinitely sad **polarization** between the Choicers and the Lifers. (From "On the Right")

polemicize (verb) *To engage in controversy; dispute aggressively. [Used in 1991 calendar in a different form, namely, polemical (adjective)]*

Give me the right to spend my dollars as I see fit—to devote them to learning, to taking pleasure, to **polemicizing,** and if I must make the choice, I will surrender you my political franchise in trade. (From *Up from Liberalism*, p. 208, Stein & Day, 1984)

polity (noun) *Political organization.*

Some libertarians will never agree that a responsibility of the **polity** is to encourage virtue directly, through such disciplines as service in the militia, reverence for religious values, and jury service. (From *Gratitude*, p. 50, Random House, 1990)

posit (verb) *To set in place or position; situate; to set down or assume as fact; postulate.*

I **posit** in this case that he is absolutely ignorant of malfeasance. I do this as a matter of character judgment. (From "On the Right")

praepostor (noun) *A monitor at an English public school.*

As **praepostor** at the British public school it had fallen to Anthony Trust to help hold down young Blackford, age fifteen, over one end of a sofa as he received a serious flogging from the headmaster. (From *Tucker's Last Stand*, p. 86, Random House, 1990)

pre-infanticide (noun) *Killing of a child prior to its birth.*

But to defend the reproductive rights, so-called, of women, it is absolutely necessary to celebrate the act of **pre-infanticide,** and this is not easy for fellow Americans to do. (From "On the Right")

preponderant (adjective) *Having superior weight, force, or influence; having greater prevalence.*

This means many things, among them that no economic reform that would get in the way of channeling the **preponderant** economic machinery of the country can be tolerated. (From "On the Right")

preponderate (verb) *To exceed in power, influence, or importance.*

It is well known that in certain quarters in the South where blacks heavily **preponderate,** the marginal black voter (the man whose vote would tip the scales in favor of the Negro block) is, by one evasion or another, deprived of the vote. (From *Up from Liberalism*, p. 156, Stein & Day, 1984)

prepossession (noun) *An attitude, belief, or impression formed beforehand; a preconceived opinion.*

In the hands of a skillful indoctrinator, the average student not only thinks what the indoctrinator wants him to think (assuming no **prepossession** in the way), but is altogether positive that he has arrived at his position by independent intellectual exertion. (From *Up from Liberalism*, p. 83, Stein & Day, 1984)

priapic (adjective) *Preoccupied with or employing the phallus symbolically; featuring or stressing the phallus.*

"At first I thought that his rushing off to see her so often was simply the **priapic** imperative at work." (From *Tucker's Last Stand*, p. 210, Random House, 1990)

primogenitive (adjective) *Of or pertaining to the firstborn.*
The English Establishment is more frozen than our own, primarily because theirs is a society based on class. Their Establishment has rites and honorifics and **primogenitive** continuities. (From *Rumbles Left and Right*, p. 16, G. P. Putnam's Sons, 1963)

pro bono publico (adverb) (Latin) *For the public good.*
Paul Hughes was prepared, *pro bono publico,* to report secretly to the editors of the *Democratic Digest* the secret doings of the Sub-Committee on Investigations. (From *Up from Liberalism*, p. 103, Stein & Day, 1984)

proffer (verb) *To offer; tender.*
"You are the most exciting, and the most handsome, young physicist in the world. Everybody knows that. What they don't know is that you are also the greatest lover in—in—"
"The spy world?" Alistair Fleetwood **proffered**, laughing. (From *High Jinx*, p. 127, Doubleday & Company, 1986)

progenitive (adjective) *Pertaining to those who beget; as in parents, founders, discoverers.*
The proposition that American citizens owe something to the community that formulated and fought to establish their **progenitive** rights was proffered in 1910 by William James, "The Moral Equivalent of War." (From *Gratitude*, p. xvii, Random House, 1990)

propitious (adjective) *Presenting favorable circumstances; auspicious.*
With great solemnity, Alistair had been presented the Order of Lenin. Beria explained, "We left out your name—the space is there for it. Security. When the climate is **propitious**, you may take it to a jeweler and have your name inscribed." (From *High Jinx*, p. 235, Doubleday & Company, 1986)

proprietary (adjective) *Having to do with the owner; befitting an owner.*
My gal Sal, he had referred to her a few letters back, intending to be affectionate. She had replied, "My gal Sal is entirely too **proprietary** for my taste, Blacky my boy (and how do you like 'Blacky my boy'?"). (From *High Jinx*, p. 17, Doubleday & Company, 1986)

proscriptively (adverb) *The adverbial form of "proscriptive"—prohibiting or interdicting; proscribing.*
The persecution in Harvard of Professor Stephan Thernstrom, for the sin of talking about Jim Crow and about slavery in the South descriptively, rather than **proscriptively**. (From "On the Right")

protégé (noun) *A person whose welfare, training, or career is promoted by someone, usually influential or efficient or both.*
By the time Alice Goodyear Corbett had graduated from secondary school she had achieved a minor eminence in the student world of Moscow: the perfectly trained Soviet **protégée**. (From *High Jinx*, p. 68, Doubleday & Company, 1986)

proto- (prefix) *First in time; beginning; giving rise to.*
In "corporatism," the state would have the bureaucracy, and, together with the labor union, would work in harmony, creating something on the order of the syndicalism that later excited the **proto**-fascists. (From *Gratitude*, p. 57, Random House, 1990)

provincial (adjective) *Limited in scope; narrow, sectional.*
Mr. John Crosby writes: "How do you get on a blacklist? Well, some actors have got on by having foreign names." Tacit premise: blacklisters are reckless, **provincial**, xenophobic. (From *Up from Liberalism*, p. 73, Stein & Day, 1984)

pulchritude (noun) *Physical comeliness; beauty.*
"Why Baltimore indeed! First, some of the best beer on the East Coast is made here. Second, much of the best seafood in the East is found here. Third, there is **pulchritude** at hand here." (From *Tucker's Last Stand*, p. 86, Random House, 1990)

pullulate (verb) *To sprout out; germinate; breed quickly; spring up in abundance.*

But only 1.5 percent of black police officers pass the New York sergeants' test: and the result is a failure of effective social integration, and a them-and-us attitude which now and again **pullulates** into such incidents as we saw in Los Angeles. (From "On the Right")

quizzically (adverb) *In a slightly and amusingly eccentric manner; questioningly; curiously.*

Alphonse smiled, and bowed his head. "I feel in a bargaining mood, Mr. Oakes."

Blackford looked up sharply, **quizzically.**

"I will do as you say," said Alphonse, "provided you give me another drink of vodka." (From *Tucker's Last Stand,* p. 160, Random House, 1990)

raillery (noun) *Good-natured ridicule; pleasantry touched with satire; banter, chaffing, mockery.*

I note that the Eighties are held up for scorn and **raillery** by trendy opinion-makers. Everything that came out of the Eighties is held to be somehow contaminated, the grand contaminator being, of course, Ronald Reagan. (From "On the Right")

recision (noun) *The act of rescinding or canceling.*

Former Secretary of Defense Caspar Weinberger was in favor of **recision,** but somehow President Reagan never got around to it, in part because it had become a kind of liberal sanctuary, to which disarmament fetishists took pilgrimages every few days, sowing seeds of alarm that suggested that to amend the ABM Treaty was to say goodbye to disarmament. (From "On the Right")

rectilinear (adjective) *Moving in a straight line; having an undeviating direction; forming a straight line.*

What gets in the way of **rectilinear** moral reasoning is our insistence on dressing up the moral arguments in opportunistic ways. (From "On the Right")

reductio ad absurdum (noun) (Latin) *Reduction of an argument to the absurd.*

But perhaps the example is a ***reductio ad absurdum:*** If the United States had a first-strike force, the Soviet Union would presumably fear that it might be used, never mind that during the twenty-odd years when we did have a first-strike force we did not use it. (From "On the Right")

refractory (adjective) *Resisting control or authority.*

It is easier to deal with **refractory** twelve-year-olds than with eighteen-year-olds. Young children are not consulted on the question of whether they should take instruction. (From *Gratitude,* p. 113, Random House, 1990)

reifiable (adjective) *Convertible into something concrete.*

It is in the nature of natural law that it is not fully comprehensible, let alone **reifiable.** What a belief in the natural law actually amounts to is a propensity to do the right thing. (From "On the Right")

reinstitutionalize (verb) *To incorporate again into a system of organized and often highly formalized belief, practice, or acceptance.*

Gorbachev, who only a year ago declared that the Communist Party's monopoly on political power had to end, is now reaching out for means of **reinstitutionalizing** a Communist hegemony. (From "On the Right")

replete (adjective) *Well filled or plentifully supplied; gorged.*

As is almost always the case, special pleaders will find in a 25,000-word document **replete** with qualifications, favorite phrases or clauses designed to make their point. (From "On the Right")

repristinate (verb) *To restore to an original state or condition.*

Wearily he began to undress, first removing the beard in front of the mirror and staring fondly at his **repristinated** face. (From *High Jinx,* p. 170, Doubleday & Company, 1986)

requital (noun) *Return or repayment for something; something given in return or compensation.*
By asking our eighteen-year-olds to make sacrifices we are reminding them that they owe a debt. And reminding them that **requital** of a debt is the purest form of acknowledging that debt. (From *Gratitude*, p. xiv, Random House, 1990)

resonant (adjective) *Having an effect; being heard; being acted on.*
And, finally, that little boot, quiet but **resonant**, that he finally gave to Mikhail Gorbachev was done adroitly, efficiently, with just the right touch of hauteur: "Gorby, you are getting in the way." Mr. Bush is rightly the man of the hour. (From "On the Right")

restive (adjective) *Inquisitive; tempted to inquiry, defiance.*
The intellectuals of Spain, in hindsight, recognize the inappropriateness of the republic most of them once supported; but they are **restive**, anxious to get on with the job of crafting organic and responsive and durable political mechanisms. (From *Rumbles Left and Right*, p. 39, G. P. Putnam's Sons, 1963)

roistering (noun) *Characterized by or associated with noisy revelry.*
What ensues is an uproar, in part because the tradition of gentility at the University of Virginia is pronounced, and although a certain amount of alcoholic **roistering** is known to go on, the general protocols are that utter discretion is in order. (From "On the Right")

rotarian (adjective) *Of or relating to Rotarian societies; hail-fellow-well-met; concerned with social, civic, and workaday matters.*
People continue to tolerate and to patronize schools and colleges and universities which treat their children like half-rational biological mechanisms, whose highest ambition in life is to develop in such fashion as to render glad the **Rotarian** heart in Anywhere, U.S.A. (From *Rumbles Left and Right*, p. 99, G. P. Putnam's Sons, 1963)

rotund (adjective) *Rounded, plump.*
Dr. Callard, the retired headmaster of Winchester, invited in to tea the pleasant young solicitor. Dr. Callard, silver-haired, **rotund**, and genial, served the tea and reminisced. (From *High Jinx*, p. 115, Doubleday & Company, 1986)

routinization (noun) *Reduction to a prescribed and detailed course of action to be followed regularly.*
She was amusing herself, draining the meeting of the kind of **routinization** which so many of her predecessors had invested it with. (From *High Jinx*, p. 135, Doubleday & Company, 1986)

sacerdotal (adjective) *Of or relating to priests or priesthood.*
A half hour into the walk, Brother Hildred asked "Leo"—the monks called themselves by their **sacerdotal** names—if he would like to visit the school's physics laboratory. (From *Tucker's Last Stand*, p. 31, Random House, 1990)

sass (verb) *To talk impudently or disrespectfully to (an elder or superior).*
Senator McCarthy is dead, but the mania he illuminated lives on, and even now asserts control over sensible men whenever their ideology is threatened, questioned, or **sassed**. (From *Up from Liberalism*, p. 54, Stein & Day, 1984)

satyriasis (noun) *Abnormal or uncontrollable desire by a man for sexual intercourse.*
But Henry VIII enters the history books as an effective monarch, never mind his **satyriasis**, and his inclination to dispose of unsatisfactory wives on the scaffold. (From "On the Right")

sciolist (noun) *One whose knowledge or learning is superficial; a pretender to scholarship.*
[Used in 1992 calendar in a different form, namely, **sciolism** *(noun)]*
"I don't believe you. You are an unaccomplished fake. An academic **sciolist**." (From *Tucker's Last Stand*, p. 48, Random House, 1990)

scrupulosity (noun) *The quality or state of carefully adhering to ethical standards; overstrict in applying the strictest standards to oneself.*

He would work at home. I begged him to desist from what I had denounced as his sin of **scrupulosity**. (From *Rumbles Left and Right*, p. 153, G. P. Putnam's Sons, 1963)

seminal (adjective) *Having the character of an originative power, or source; containing or contributing the seeds of later development.*

In order to penetrate the public mind, it was necessary not only to do such **seminal** thinking as was being done by such as Eric Voegelin, it was necessary also to photograph the ideological father figure in just the right light. (From *Up from Liberalism*, p. xiii, Stein & Day, 1984)

sentimentalization (noun) *The act or process of analyzing a problem with exclusive concern for the sentimental dimension.*

The attempt to answer military questions by asking the question, How much do you love the kid over there who just got married, the youngest son of proud and devoted parents, is a **sentimentalization** of important calculations that are necessarily made, so to speak, in cold blood. (From "On the Right")

skein (noun) *Something suggesting the twistings and contortions of a loosely coiled length of yarn or thread.*

J. William Fulbright is renowned as a leading American liberal, and as the author of a vast **skein** of international scholarships whose aim is to foster world understanding and tolerance. (From *Up from Liberalism*, p. 58, Stein & Day, 1984)

slavish (adjective) *Resembling or characteristic of a slave; spineless, submissive.*

Some companies are moving in that direction, but most of them are **slavish** in meeting the demands of executives they want to stick around. (From "On the Right")

slovenly (adjective) *Lazily slipshod.*

There is indeed a fusion of justice and anti-Communist activity; the redemptions of the tens of millions whom, because of a **slovenly**, cowardly, and unimaginative diplomacy, we turned over to their Communist oppressors. (From *Rumbles Left and Right*, p. 116, G. P. Putnam's Sons, 1963)

sojourn (verb) *To stay as a temporary resident.*

In the spring of 1958, shortly before Mr. Truman was due to **sojourn** at Yale University, I wrote to a professor there whose lot it was to spend hours in close quarters with Mr. Truman. (From *Up from Liberalism*, p. 50, Stein & Day, 1984)

Solomonic (adjective) *Marked by notable wisdom, reasonableness, or discretion, especially under trying circumstances.*

Primakov returned to Moscow and foreign ministry spokesman Vitaly Churkin has given us the **Solomonic** judgment of his superiors. (From "On the Right")

sommelier (noun) *A waiter in a restaurant who has charge of wines and their service; a wine steward.*

At La Tambourine, the recessed little table was reserved and Toi, the grandfatherly **sommelier**, had their champagne waiting. (From *Tucker's Last Stand*, p. 55, Random House, 1990)

sophism (noun) *An argument that is correct in form or appearance but is actually invalid.* *[Used in 1992 calendar in a different form, namely, sophistry (noun)]*

At the moment the nation is very much attracted by the **sophism** of Professor Galbraith, namely that we are not as consumers really free, inasmuch as we are pawns of the advertising agencies. (From *Up from Liberalism*, p. 207, Stein & Day, 1984)

sostenuto (noun) *A movement or passage whose notes are markedly sustained or prolonged.*

They made for a wonderful dialectic, James Burnham's **sostenutos** and Whittaker Chambers's enigmatic descants. (From *Rumbles Left and Right*, p. 157, G. P. Putnam's Sons, 1963)

Stakhanovite (noun) *A worker, especially in the U.S.S.R., whose production is consistently above average and who is therefore awarded recognition and special privileges (after Aleksei Stakhanov, Soviet miner whose efforts inspired it in 1935).*

It is now a solid plank of American history that John F. Kennedy, in respect of American mores, was something of a mess: so to speak, a **Stakhanovite** adulterer. (From "On the Right")

stasis (noun) *A state of static equilibrium among opposing tendencies or forces; quiescence, stagnation.*

No one doubted that he, nineteen-year-old Tucker Montana, had done some heavy rowing against that current of physical **stasis** that kept saying No, you can't get there from here, nature won't permit it. (From *Tucker's Last Stand*, p. 28, Random House, 1990)

stentorian (adjective) *Loud, resonant.*

Alistair said, "Why not your stateroom?"

She hesitated, and said, in a voice now entirely feminine, so different from the lightly **stentorian** voice of Alice Goodyear Corbett, tour leader, "If you like." (From *High Jinx*, p. 78, Doubleday & Company, 1986)

strophe (noun) *Any arrangement of lines together as a unit; stanza.*

Almost every Sunday afternoon I would call him and we would talk, at length, discursively, and laugh together, between the **strophes** of his melancholy. (From *Rumbles Left and Right*, p. 144, G. P. Putnam's Sons, 1963)

stultifying (adjective) *Rendering useless or ineffectual; causing to appear stupid, inconsistent, or ridiculous. [Used in 1991 calendar in a different form, namely, **stultification** (noun)]*

The relative independence of adjacent Yugoslavia and the relative geographical isolation from Bulgaria argued the military plausibility and the geopolitical excitement of a genuine Western salient in the cold war, instead of the tiresome, enervating, **stultifying** countersalients to which the West had become accustomed. (From *High Jinx*, p. 16, Doubleday & Company, New York, 1986)

subsume (verb) *To view, list, or rate as a component in an overall or more comprehensive classification, summation, or synthesis.*

The geopolitical argument in favor of withdrawal is **subsumed** in the moral argument in favor of liberating Iraq from Saddam Hussein. (From "On the Right")

succinct (adjective) *Marked by brief and compact expression or by extreme compression and lack of unnecessary words and details.*

The basic story is uncomplicated, though the account of it by Kenneth Tynan in the current *Harper's* is not. That is too bad, in a man who knows how to be **succinct**. (From *Rumbles Left and Right*, p. 69, G. P. Putnam's Sons, 1963)

summum bonum (noun) (Latin) *The supreme or highest good, usually in which all other goods are included or from which they are derived.*

Self-rule continues to tyrannize over the liberal ideology, secure in its place as the **summum bonum**. (From *Up from Liberalism*, p. 148, Stein & Day, 1984)

sundry (adjective) *Various; miscellaneous; divers.*

We do not know what would be the cost of rebuilding Kuwait City, and it is of course hard to calculate the damages done by torturers, murderers, rapists, and **sundry** sadists. (From "On the Right")

supernumerary (noun) *Exceeding what is necessary, required, or desired; superfluous.*
Did that auxiliary go on to unemployment? Or might it be that he went on to a higher-paying job? An unanswerable question which challenges the dynamic of a free society to decline to hire someone at a lower wage because by doing so someone being paid a higher wage becomes **supernumerary**. (From *Gratitude*, p. 130, Random House, 1990)

syllabus (noun) *A compendium or summary outline of a discourse, treatise, course of study, or examination requirements.*
The final point in Hart's **syllabus** is the most intriguing. He suggests that abusive language can be and often is a form by which general frustrations get expressed by younger people. (From "On the Right")

syllogism (noun) *An argument or form of reasoning in which two statements or premises are made and a logical conclusion drawn from them; reasoning from the general to the particular; deductive logic.*
What is curious about the proposed reform is that its unwritten language is suggesting: Our senators are for sale for speaking fees. Therefore, we shan't have speaking fees. Therefore our senators will no longer be for sale. The **syllogism** is very leaky. (From "On the Right")

synaesthetic (adjective) *Experiencing a subjective sensation or image that appeals to all the senses. [Used in 1991 calendar in a different form, namely, **synaesthetically** (adverb)]*
All I need do to repay everyone from Bach to the piccolo player is to shell out fifteen or twenty dollars for the music that can realize sublimity for the ear and the mind, if the experience, appealing at once to all the senses, is **synaesthetic**. (From *Gratitude*, p. 12, Random House, 1990)

synergistic (adjective) *Having the capacity to act in cooperative action of discrete agencies such that the total effect is greater than the sum of the two or more effects taken independently.*
Moskos believes we are ready to march together under a **synergistic** banner enjoining us to do everything we can for our country, while our country does everything it can for us. (From *Gratitude*, p. 72, Random House, 1990)

syntactical (adjective) *Relating to the rules of syntax, a connected system of order; orderly arrangement; harmonious adjustment of parts or elements.*
It is a highly regarded national secret that Mr. Eisenhower has a way of easing virtually every subject he touches into a **syntactical** jungle in which every ray of light, every breath of air, is choked out. (From *Up from Liberalism*, p. 194, Stein & Day, 1984)

taciturn (adjective) *Temperamentally disinclined or reluctant to talk or converse.*
The reporter talked on and on, but my **taciturn** answers finally discouraged him; we shook hands and he left. (From *Rumbles Left and Right*, p. 145, G. P. Putnam's Sons, 1963)

talismanic (adjective) *Having the properties of something that produces extraordinary or apparently magical or miraculous effects.*
It is a pity that there has developed the **talismanic** view of democracy, as the indispensable and unassailable solvent of the free and virtuous society. (From *Up from Liberalism*, p. 159, Stein & Day, 1984)

taxonomize (verb) *Systematically to distinguish, order, and name type groups within a subject field.*
Now there is of course no set rule by which pork is **taxonomized** as exactly that. (From "On the Right")

temporize (verb) *To act to suit the time; adapt to a situation; bow to practical necessities.*
We are therefore at one and the same time taking, against Saddam Hussein, a principled line with moral appeal; while, with Gorbachev, we **temporize**. (From "On the Right")

thither (adverb) *To or toward that place; in that direction; there.*

Alistair Fleetwood, for the moment confused, pointed vaguely at a corner of the room. **Thither** the porter went. (From *High Jinx*, p. 189, Doubleday & Company, 1986)

toothsome (adjective) *Agreeable, pleasant; abundant.*

He had lived, up until just after his fortieth year, a robust sensual life, in America and in Europe, using up most of the **toothsome** legacy he had been left by his parents. (From *Tucker's Last Stand*, p. 32, Random House, 1990)

torpor (noun) *Mental or spiritual sluggishness; apathy; lethargy.*

If the nation is constantly at war, or subject to plagues and starvation, national **torpor** threatens to set in. (From *Gratitude*, p. 36, Random House, 1990)

totalism (noun) *Exercising total autocratic powers: tending toward monopoly.*

The thoroughly non-Ideological Man is usually designated as steward of the American political community. This is partly a good thing, because everyone knows that ideological **totalism** can bring whole societies down. (From *Up from Liberalism*, p. xxi, Stein & Day, 1984)

totemism (noun) *A system of social organizations based on emblematic affiliations.*

Not a week goes by that we at *National Review* do not need to call a point of order; or fit together the parts to show a current piece of humbuggery; or scrub down someone's shiny new proposal to expose the structure for what it is—usually Liberal **totemism**. (From *Rumbles Left and Right*, p. 66, G. P. Putnam's Sons, 1963)

transcendent (adjective) *Going beyond or exceeding usual limits; surpassing; being above material existence or apart from the universe.*

The dissipation of the moral satisfaction earned by Mr. Bush merits careful examination: because it teaches us that rigid geopolitical formulae have to yield, in special circumstances, to moral considerations, when these achieve **transcendent** importance. (From "On the Right")

transliterate (verb) *To represent or spell (words, letters, or characters of one language) in the letters or characters of another language or alphabet.*

The Japanese use many self-effacing conventions which, **transliterated** into English, are startling to say the least. (From *Up from Liberalism*, p. 119, Stein & Day, 1984)

travesty (noun) *A debased distortion or imitation or representation; sham, mockery.*

In Venezuela, Pérez Jiménez was boss. He decided to hold an "election" at which all the people, of course, would have the option of "approving" the government of Pérez Jiménez or—well, no one was exactly sure, or what. Indeed, here was a palpable **travesty** on democracy. (From *Up from Liberalism*, p. 149, Stein & Day, 1984)

treacle (noun) *Something (as a tone of voice, manner, or compliment) resembling treacle, a blend of molasses, invert sugar, and corn syrup, being heavily sweet and cloying.*

Shall we attempt to mulct some meaning out of that **treacle**? He is suggesting that President Reagan was not "determined." And that he was not a "leader." That will not be very easy to establish about a man who when he ran for reelection, garnered the vote of forty-nine states. (From "On the Right")

tremulous (adjective) *Trembling; quivering; palpitating; timid.*

Never having heard Kirsten Flagstad speak, I can say only that her singing voice was a **tremulous** experience. (From "On the Right")

trenchantly (adverb) *In a keenly articulate or sharply perceptive manner; cogently. [Used in 1991 calendar in a different form, namely, **trenchant** (adjective)]*

The educated man, Russell Kirk has **trenchantly** said, is the man who has come to learn how to apprehend ethical norms by intellectual means. (From *Rumbles Left and Right*, p. 105, G. P. Putnam's Sons, 1963)

tripartite (adjective) *Divided into or being in three parts; composed of three parts or kinds.*
Yes, [the Israeli people] have lined up for gas masks and are practicing civil defense, as who would not at this moment. But the great drama is **tripartite.** (From "On the Right")

tropism (noun) *An innate tendency to react in a definite manner to stimuli; a natural born inclination.*
Because we know that women should be educated and should vote and should exercise their capacity to lead does not dissipate that **tropism** that assigns to the woman primary responsibility for the care of the child, and to the man, primarily responsibility for the care of the woman. (From "On the Right")

truculently (adverb) *Belligerently, pugnaciously. [Used in 1991 calendar in a different form, namely, truculent (adjective)]*
"What's the matter with that?" Baroody's pipe tilted up **truculently.** (From *Tucker's Last Stand,* p. 14, Random House, 1990)

uncongruous (adjective) *Not conforming to the circumstances or requirements of a situation; unreasonable, unsuitable.*
A teacher who devotes himself to undermining the premises of the school at which he teaches, or the society in which he lives, may properly be deemed **uncongruous.** (From *Rumbles Left and Right,* p. 104, G. P. Putnam's Sons, 1963)

urbane (adjective) *Having or showing the refined manners of polite society; elegant, cosmopolitan.*
The aide wrote back to the box number designated. That letter got back an **urbane** letter advising the aide that if the Director was not interested in knowing what the internal fighting within the Kremlin was all about, perhaps the Director should resign his position as head of CIA and become Baseball Commissioner? (From *High Jinx,* p. 177, Doubleday & Company, 1986)

utilitarian (adjective) *Stressing the value of practical over aesthetic qualities; characterized by or aiming at utility as distinguished from beauty or ornament.*
The apartment was appropriately **utilitarian,** as though quickly furnished for a transient client. (From *Tucker's Last Stand,* p. 258, Random House, 1990)

vacuity (noun) *Emptiness of mind; lack of intelligence, interest, or thought; an inane or senseless thing, remark, or quality.*
Six weeks before he was inaugurated, I lunched privately with Senator Quayle, taking the opportunity to search out that highly advertised **vacuity.** I didn't find it. (From "On the Right")

varicose (adjective) *Abnormally swollen or dilated.*
He was habituated now to the redundancy of the Trail's surrounding features—the hanging Spanish moss–like vegetation, the sprouts of sharp underbrush, the **varicose** little ditches engraved by the spring floods. (From *Tucker's Last Stand,* p. 6, Random House, 1990)

variegated (adjective) *Varied; especially marked with different colors or tints in spots, streaks, or stripes.*
At twelve I persuaded my indulgent father to give me a boat. The boat was a sixteen-foot Barracuda (a class since extinct), and I joined the **variegated** seven-boat fleet in Lakeville, Connecticut. (From *Rumbles Left and Right,* p. 165, G. P. Putnam's Sons, 1963)

venial (adjective) *That may be forgiven; pardonable; excused; overlooked.*
It is proper to raise the question whether this is an indication of the dulled morality of the public, or whether the misuse of public transportation is merely a **venial** offense. (From "On the Right")

vexatious (adjective) *Annoying, troublesome.*

On the other hand, to suppose that the latter won't get into **vexatious** troubles is to guess wrong, as witness the matter of Edwin Meese. (From "On the Right")

vinous (adjective) *Caused by or resulting from drinking wine or spirits; showing the effects of the use of wine.*

Bui Tin once said to him, after a long and **vinous** meal, that Le Duc Sy's mutinous inclinations were really undifferentiated; he had not got on with the Reverend Mother, nor with the principal at their primary school; nor had he really got on with his father. (From *Tucker's Last Stand,* p. 118, Random House, 1990)

vitriol (noun) *Virulence of feeling or speech.*

Lyndon Baines Johnson was morose. When that happened, the **vitriol** reigned for the initial period, and then he would focus his powerful mind on the vexation, the irritant, the goddam son of a bitch creating the problem! (From *Tucker's Last Stand,* p. 184, Random House, 1990)

voluptuously (adverb) *Full and appealing in form.*

"Sir Alistair!" He allowed the syllable to pass **voluptuously** through his lips. Until exactly 12:44 that afternoon he had been simply Mr. Alistair Fleetwood. (From *High Jinx,* p. 57, Doubleday & Company, 1986)

vulgar (adjective) *Deficient in taste, delicacy, or refinement. [Used in 1991 calendar in a different form, namely, vulgarian (noun and adjective)]*

The four of them shared the living room for a few minutes, after which they separated. And in due course, in that charmingly **vulgar** room, Minerva was soon giggling as "Charles" expressed his affection for her. (From *High Jinx,* p. 103, Doubleday & Company, 1986)

Wykehamist (noun) *A student or graduate of Winchester College, England.*

Fleetwood had been attracted to the tall, rangy **Wykehamist** who devoted himself equally to physics, soccer, and politics. (From *High Jinx,* p. 86, Doubleday & Company, 1986)

Index